Geology
in the Urban Environment

R. O. Utgard

G. D. McKenzie

D. Foley

The Ohio State University
Columbus, Ohio

Foreword by Robert F. Legget
Formerly (1947-1969) Director,
Division of Building Research,
National Research Council of Canada, Ottawa

Burgess Publishing Company
Minneapolis, Minnesota

Copyright © 1978 by Burgess Publishing Company
Printed in the United States of America
Library of Congress Catalog Card Number 77-77446
ISBN 0-8087-2106-2

0   9   8   7   6   5   4   3   2   1

Contents

PART ONE

INTRODUCTION

Foreword

"It does seem to me strange, to use the mildest word, that people whose destiny it is to live, even for a few short years, on this planet which we call the earth, and who do not at all intend to live on it as hermits, shutting themselves up in cells . . . it seems strange, I say, that such people should in general be so careless about the constitution of his same planet, and of the laws and facts on which depend, not merely their comfort and their wealth, but their health and their very lives, and the health and lives of their children and descendants." These words, to which I fully subscribe today, appear in the preface of a small book published in London, England, in the year 1877, just a century before the publication of this volume.

The author of the book was the Reverend Charles Kingsley, an Episcopalian churchman of note in the England of those days, and so good a writer that some of his books for younger readers are still in print, bringing delight to successive generations of young people. The volume from which the quotation is taken, now long out of print, is entitled *Town Geology*. Its contents were adapted from a series of lectures given by Canon Kingsley to young men in the city of Chester through the Chester Natural History Society. He describes his experience in Chester as "some of the most pleasant passages of my life"—a revealing statement that will be appreciated by all the authors of the papers in this modern volume as they recall the pleasures they have had in demonstrating how the application of geology can so greatly assist in the development of the urban communities today.

Elsewhere, the author of this pioneer volume describes geology as "the science which explains to us the *rind* of the earth" and, after some further explanation, he says, ". . . thus geology is (or ought to be), in popular parlance, the people's science." The people's science—a phrase potent with meaning! Could it be that geology has been so generally neglected in far too much "town and country planning" in North America just because, lamentably, the science has not yet here become the people's science? The papers in this most useful volume testify, all too clearly, to the consequences of this neglect. Publication of all the papers in this convenient form will provide most useful assistance in the future rectifying of this neglect.

The papers that have been assembled by the editors cover a broad field, as is inevitable in view of the various ways in which geology affects the planning, design, construction, and maintenance of urban centres. References will be found to "Urban Geology," "Engineering Geology," and even to "Environmental Geology." These are useful popular terms which assist in the delineation of the problems that have to be faced in all-urban development. It is to be noted, however, that the title of this volume is *Geology in the Urban Environment.*

There is no special type of geology necessary for assisting with urban or environmental problems. Rather must the basic principles of the science, and especially of geological processes as comprehended in geomorphology, be applied in providing the essential background against which sound decisions in all urban engineering, including planning, can be made. This is well illustrated in many of the papers which follow, usefully illustrated (in many cases) by examples from practice. The brief introductions to the several groupings into which the papers have been divided so conveniently also direct attention to this somewhat neglected fact, so easy are the several "handle-terms" to use.

One runs great risks of making invidious distinctions if, in so short a Foreward as this, one singles out a paper for special mention. The risk must be taken, however, and so I invite the attention of all readers to "Lessons Learned from the June 9, 1972, Flood in Rapid City, South Dakota," by Perry H. Rahn. This is a clearly written and well-researched description of an appalling tragedy, the like of which should never happen again in view of the warning that the experience of Rapid City, South Dakota, so sadly provides. Here was a happy, well-settled modern community, the citizens of which probably never dreamed of tragedy so devastating their riverside development. If they had read of other floodplain disasters, their reaction could well have been "But it can't happen here." It did. The lesson has been learned there, the mayor of Rapid City having said publicly that "It is stupid to sleep in the floodplain."

The U.S. Geological Survey had published maps of the floodplain before the flood, yet another of the great contributions that the Survey has made to the solution of urban problems throughout the United States. What of other cities large and small, the communities in which live those who will be reading these pages? It is surely the duty of all who appreciate the relevance of geology to urban living, such as those who will read these pages, to ensure that all useful information about the local geology is well known and not left to gather dust on unused library shelves.

Correspondingly, there is a widespread vital need throughout North America for civic authorities to be alerted to all that geology can contribute to the planning process so that no urban plans, now so widely discussed with public participation, are even considered until the local geology has been fully taken into account. This means, inevitably, that geologists must be prepared to leave their "ivory towers" if their science is to serve the public as it should. Geologists are citizens also; they are informed citizens who have a real part to play in the further growth of their own communities at least. This volume should serve them well.

Ottawa, Canada
December 28, 1976

Robert F. Legget

Preface

Geology in the Urban Environment is a collection of papers and articles on aspects of the interaction of humans and the physical environment in urban areas. It is in the urban environment that this interaction between the human colony and the geological or physical environment is most intense; hence it is fitting to devote more emphasis to this area than traditionally has been done in environmental geology. The urban environment is also the environment where most college courses on environmental geology are taught—indeed some courses are restricted to urban environmental geology as are the field trips which often are a vital part of these courses.

This book is designed as a basic text for courses in geology of the urban environment. It might also be used as a supplementary text in environmental geology courses, or, in conjunction with books such as Legget's *Cities and Geology,* in urban geology courses. Applications for *Geology in the Urban Environment* might also be found in courses on urban geography and city and regional planning.

This book addresses topics that often have been grouped into engineering geology, urban geology, and urban environmental geology. It begins with a review of urban geology and engineering geology to show the importance of these subdisciplines in the geology of the urban environment. The last two articles in the introductory part provide the historical perspective to this subject.

The remaining parts of the book are on geologic hazards, engineering solutions to problems, resource availability, environmental considerations, interpretation and presentation of geologic data, and examples of the use of these data to minimize the loss of resources from poor planning and associated geologic hazards.

Much of this publication is based on work by the U.S. Geological Survey and has appeared in the form of circulars, professional papers, maps, and, in one instance, a news release. We appreciate the assistance provided in preparing these materials for reproduction. Other articles were reprinted from journals of engineering and scientific associations and societies, reports of state, regional, or city governments, and the U.S. Departments of Commerce and Housing and Urban Development. We are also indebted to the National Research Council of Canada and the U.S. National Academy of Science for material used in this compilation.

The editorial revisions were necessarily numerous in the case of long articles that could not be reprinted in their entirety. Illustrations that were repetitive either within or between articles were eliminated and some sections were cut for brevity and to ease the burden of comprehension on the student. For those interested in pursuing the individual topics further, we suggest that the original article and its references be consulted. The references cited in the edited version of the article are retained in this book of readings.

Where possible, difficult material has been eliminated or footnoted. Because this assemblage is primarily for students who have had an introductory course in geology at most, a glossary of geologic and environmental terms is included. It is based in part upon the glossaries that now accompany many of the state and federal publications that are designed to inform interested citizens. The appendices should be consulted when searching for explanations of some geologic and scientific terms and when in need of specific geologic information from state and federal governmental agencies.

Our sincere thanks to our colleagues, students, and staff who have helped in many ways. We also wish to thank our librarians who were always ready to supply materials, and Bob Lakemacher of Burgess who generated the idea for the book. Without the cooperation of the authors and publishers who produced the original material, this compilation could not have become a reality.

Russell O. Utgard
Garry D. McKenzie
Duncan Foley

Columbus, Ohio
November 1, 1977

Introduction

Urban geology is the application of geologic knowledge to the planning and management of metropolitan areas.[1] Involved in this field of geology are the subdisciplines that contribute to water supply and waste disposal, site investigation for hazardous conditions, and delineation of economic rock and mineral deposits. Most aspects of engineering geology are applied in the urban setting, including the analysis and interpretation of rocks, soil, and groundwater for the purposes of planning and design of engineering structures.

Both engineering and urban geology are part of the wider field of environmental geology, which includes the study of resource exploitation, waste disposal, geologic hazards, medical geology, and the environmental impact of humans. Many of these problems are of prime importance in the urban environment, and since the introduction of the term "environmental geology" in the middle 1960s, the terms urban geology, applied geology, and, to a lesser extent, engineering geology, have been less frequently employed. Almost any traditional field of geology can contribute to environmental geology; the determining factor is a commitment to provide information on the geologic environment to serve society's needs.

The four papers in this section provide both an insight into the types and growth of geological practice in the urban environment and an historical perspective on the importance of the physical environment in the development and maintenance of urban societies.

The role of geology in the urban environment is described by John T. McGill in the first article. Rapid urban growth predicates the need for urban planning. Between 1960 and 1980 the land occupied by urban regions will double, and between 1970 and 2000 the metropolitan population will increase from 71 to 85 percent of the total population. The problems that can develop if urban land is not adequately evaluated before development are often expensive to repair and dangerous to humans. Unfortunately, legislative action often comes following a disaster or crisis situation. Urban engineering geology (urban environmental geology) in southern California developed after a dam failure led to a state law requiring geological investigation of all dam sites. Further application of geologic information to the urbanization process followed a series of disastrous landslides.

1. A standard metropolitan statistical area (SMSA) is defined by the U.S. Bureau of Census as a county or group of contiguous counties which contains at least one city of 50,000. In addition to counties containing such cities, contiguous counties are included in an SMSA if, according to certain criteria, they are socially and economically integrated with the central city.

McGill's article provides insight into the problems that can develop without an adequate basis for planning. Although the present rate of urbanization might not continue, associated problems could increase because in many areas the prime urban lands have already been used. The first inhabitants of these urban areas were able to "read the land" and settled in the most suitable areas. With continuing expansion, less suitable land is being used: steeper slopes, floodplains, and unstable coastal zones. Pressure to develop these sensitive or hazardous areas is increasing the potential for human and economic loss. Environmental geologists work toward abating this trend.

One of the basic tools for developing and monitoring a planning program is the map. The need for reconnaissance and detailed mapping has been recognized by the U.S.G.S., and in addition to the programs described in McGill's article, there have been recent studies in Pennsylvania, the Northeast Corridor, the San Francisco Bay area, Tennessee, and Colorado, to name a few. State agencies are also responding to the need for planning information in urban areas. Engineering geologists are producing detailed maps of soils investigations and developing data banks to aid in the selection of sites and design of structures. These problems and solutions are addressed in the second article, written by Robert F. Legget.

How geology has managed to shape both the development of Washington, D.C., and its suburban area is presented in the third article, written by C. F. Withington. Several geological provinces provide different resources in a relatively small region. Human use of the physical environment is quite different from province to province. The selection of town sites, building materials, and type of agriculture has been affected by the geology. In assessing the problems of present-day Washington, Withington provides an outline for the realm of environmental geology in the urban area. Basically, this deals with resource availability (water supplies and building materials) and avoidance of geologic hazards (flooding, erosion, and landslides). The history of Blandensburg, Maryland, over the past 200 years is particularly interesting. This town was transformed from a seaport to an inland town as a result of the natural process of sedimentation that also contributed to flooding which has increased in the last 50 years. This example illustrates the dynamic interaction between the physical environment and the human colony. It also provides a basis for planning as we modify the concept of uniformitarianism to read "the past is the key to the future." These processes will continue to act, and our ability to understand them will determine success or failure in coping with geologic hazards.

The last article in this section provides an even longer-range view of human interaction with the environment. European settlement of North America has produced significant effects on the land in less than five centuries. In the area of the eastern Mediterranean similar land use practices have been carried on for several millenia; here the same problems of coping with geologic processes have contributed to the rise and fall of civilizations. Such problems have been documented by Folk (1975) in the Hellenistic-Byzantine City of Stobi, Yugoslavia, where subsidence, mudflows, earthquakes, and flooding were active. The city was abandoned, mute testimony to the need for an understanding of the geologic environment for planning purposes.

REFERENCE

Folk, R. L. 1975. Geologic urban hindplanning: an example from a Hellenistic-Byzantine city, Stobi, Yugoslavian Macedonia. *Environmental Geology* 1:5–22.

Growing Importance of Urban Geology

John T. McGill

Urban geology is much too broad a subject to cover comprehensively or in any satisfactory detail in a short presentation. It has been with us for many years, yet possesses a timeliness and an urgency that is regrettably little appreciated.

Urban Growth and Its Implications

Urban geology is growing in importance in the United States primarily because urban areas are growing. Urban areas are growing because the population of the nation is increasing and also because proportionally more people are congregating in urban areas. The critical factors are the phenomenal rate, magnitude, and changing pattern of urban population growth that have developed in recent decades. The trends are well documented in the census records.

For more than a hundred years, the urban population has grown more rapidly than the rural, until today approximately 70 percent of our inhabitants live in urban areas. From 1950 to 1960, the total population of the United States grew from nearly 151 million to over 179 million, an increase of well over 28 million, or 19 percent. In the same period, the urban population grew from nearly 96½ million to over 125 million, an increase of nearly 29 million, or 30 percent. All the nation's massive population increase during this 10-year interval occurred in urban areas.

A notable feature of current urban growth is that it is predominantly metropolitan, and furthermore is concentrated in the very largest metropolitan areas. Of the total population increase for the United States from 1950 to 1960, over 84 percent occurred in the 212 Standard Metropolitan Statistical Areas, each of which contains at least one city of 50,000 inhabitants or more. But within these metropolitan areas the growth rate was very uneven. The population of the central cities increased by about 9 percent, while that of the suburban fringes grew by a spectacular 48 percent. Expressed another way, and perhaps more meaningfully, roughly two-thirds of the entire population growth of the United States since 1950 has been taking place in the suburbs. There is no reason to expect any slowing down in the foreseeable future; indeed, acceleration is much more likely.

If the data on population growth and trends seem surprising, the implications are almost overwhelming. The rapidity and the changing pattern of urban growth have given rise to unprecedented

Reprinted with permission of the author from *U.S. Geological Survey Circular 487*, 1964, 4 pp.

problems of city and regional planning in the course of suburban development and urban renewal and redevelopment. The planning problems are noteworthy for their magnitude, diversity, and complexity, but it will suffice here to mention only a few of the areas of greatest difficulty, by way of illustration. Transportation and traffic probably constitute the foremost problem in most growing cities. Also high on the list is the expansion of the various basic city services and utilities, especially water supply, sewerage and sewage disposal, and drainage, including flood control. An immediate concern in the suburbs is the acquisition of appropriate sites for schools and other essential public facilities and for recreational purposes well in advance of local population growth.

Clearly most problems of physical planning are, or soon become, problems of engineering. Therefore the physical planning process necessarily is based to a large degree on engineering principles and practices. Many city planners are, in fact, civil engineers. Since 1923, early in the history of modern city planning, the American Society of Civil Engineers has sponsored a technical division on city planning. Planners, because of their overlap of interests, are coming to realize what civil engineers have been learning slowly and for a much longer time—the value of geologic information.

A major phase of master planning is the evaluation of the advantages and disadvantages of one use of land as compared to another use, so as to make planning and zoning possible for the conservation and maximum beneficial use of land, our most fundamental natural resource. Sooner or later we all pay, directly or indirectly, for unintelligent use of land. So we all have a stake in land-use planning. To a significant degree it is the characteristics of the earth materials underlying its surface that determine how land can be most effectively and safely used. Correlation of the requirements for potential use with pertinent geologic considerations will help assure that land use will not conflict with the limitations imposed by natural conditions. This is especially true when the easily developed sites are depleted and suburban expansion is forced into marginal or hilly areas, where new and more imposing difficulties are encountered. Factors other than geology commonly dictate a given use for land, but this may then make knowledge and consideration of the geology even more important.

Problems of urban land use that are related to geology ultimately involve every aspect of civil engineering through their effect upon the design, construction, and maintenance of specific engineering works. Certain of these problems, such as earthquakes and some landslides, occur as natural geologic hazards inherent in the environment. Other problems, such as instability of cuts and groundwater pollution, pose actual or potential threats because of unwise or poorly planned activities of man. Still others may have more to do with the economics of land use or development than with its safety; problems of difficult excavation or lack of nearby sources of earth material suitable for fill are examples.

The importance of geology to planning and to civil engineering obviously is very great, and is by no means limited to urban areas. On the other hand, it is essential to point out that not all applied urban geology is engineering geology. Sand and gravel and other raw materials of construction are a concern of engineering geologists, but the economic geology of any mineral resource occurring within an urban area may have a critical bearing on local land-use planning and development. Accessibility to valuable mineral lands or their preservation for future use often can be assured through judicious zoning and other regulations.

The Los Angeles Area—An Outstanding Example

Man versus Nature

The Los Angeles area provides an outstanding and instructive example of the growing importance of urban geology. As on the national scene, the importance is the result of the activities of man impinging on the natural environment, but in this megalopolis of southern California both elements are notoriously unpredictable.

Population growth in the Los Angeles area has been truly explosive, and the explosion largely uncontained, as any traveler arriving there by air can easily judge for himself. From 1950 to 1960, the population of the City of Los Angeles grew from nearly 2 million to almost 2½ million, an increase of about 25 percent. Despite the city's vast geographic extent, which is well publicized, the spread of residential subdivisions has been so rapid that now only hilly and mountainous terrain remains as the last large area of relatively undeveloped land. Some 60 percent of the city, or roughly 250 square miles, consists of this hillside area, as it is called in the municipal code. It is perhaps 10 percent built upon, with over 60,000 homes, at least 40,000 of them constructed in the last 10 years. City officials contend there is room in the hills for 2 million people, which also happens to be the population increase anticipated for the city within the next 25 years or so. The story of growth is similar for the entire County of Los Angeles, where about 40 percent of the people of California live. The County's 1960 population of over 6 million was exceeded by that of only 8 states.

The natural setting of the Los Angeles area is characterized by rugged topography, complex and highly variable geology, and a semi-arid climate in which the rainfall is concentrated in a few winter months. This is a combination that resulted in increasingly serious and widespread engineering problems as urban growth accelerated after World War II and thousands of new cuts scarred the hills. Problems of landslides, other slope instabilities, floods, and debris flows have tended to dominate, but the total list is long and the consequences of neglect are extremely costly.

The crisis came with the heavy rains of early 1952, and this crisis turned into a major disaster largely because land developers had generally disregarded things geological. Within months the City of Los Angeles had enacted the nation's first comprehensive grading ordinance and taken other steps to remedy the situation and prevent its recurrence. The County of Los Angeles and other cities and counties within the metropolitan area have since followed suit. Grading and subdivision regulations specify the requirements for rigorous engineering geology and soil engineering investigations, and the regulations are diligently enforced. The relatively minor damage from storms in recent years is proof of how well the controls are paying off.

Urban Engineering Geology

The history of urban engineering geology in southern California has been brief but eventful. It had its real beginnings after the St. Francis dam failure of 1928, which led to a State law making compulsory the geologic investigation of all dam sites. Engineering geology played an important role in the planning and construction of the Metropolitan Water District's famed Colorado River Aqueduct during the 1930s. The local profession grew steadily but very slowly until the late 1940s, when the population increase, and hence new construction, began to assume massive proportions.

Employment of engineering geologists in all types of urban investigations in the Los Angeles area was rather impressive by 1953, even before the full effect of hillside development controls was felt, but there has been a 3-fold increase in the last 10 years, from about 50 to about 150 geologists, including some part-timers. A brief summary of present employment in the Los Angeles area is pertinent because it is the most convincing way of showing the extent to which engineering geology is now being used. Keep in mind that the following figures are all for this one urban area. The summary does not include the many men trained as geologists who are now working essentially as engineers, even though their geologic background commonly was a valuable prerequisite for employment. Nor does it include the numerous engineering geologists headquartered in Los Angeles who are not engaged in local urban investigations to any appreciable degree.

Government geologists total about 70. This is more than double the number 10 years ago, chiefly because of increases in State and county organizations. At the Federal level, the largest group consists of some 11 geologists of the Corps of Engineers district office working mainly on major flood control projects, harbor development, and other civilian applications. The Geological Survey is represented by 5 members of the Engineering Geology Branch, carrying out 3 projects of detailed areal mapping, much of which is being done at the request of and in cooperation with the County of Los Angeles.

The largest of three State agency staffs is that of the Department of Water Resources, with 17 engineering geologists engaged in local studies of ground-water basin geology and development, waste disposal, salt-water encroachment and contamination, and related matters. Nine engineering geologists of the Division of Highways are responsible for all local investigations of bridge foundations for the extensive freeway and State highway systems, as well as for many route surveys and materials investigations. Two geologists of the Division of Mines and Geology, which is the State's geological survey, have been doing detailed areal mapping under a cooperative agreement with the County.

The County of Los Angeles, which has a civil service payroll of more than 40,000 persons, employs engineering geologists in two of its biggest departments. Ten geologists work for the Flood Control District on a wide variety of projects about equally divided between the District's two integrated programs of flood control and water conservation. Their principal effort currently is with salt-water encroachment barrier projects. The Engineering Geology Section of the County Engineer's Department came into existence only 4 years ago, and now has a staff of 5 professionals who are nearly swamped with responsibilities in all geologic aspects of hillside development control and major capital projects. These geologists, in addition, serve as advisers for most other County departments, including the Road Department and the Regional Planning Commission.

Within the City of Los Angeles, several geologists are employed by the Public Works Department, mostly on hillside investigations, and three geologists work for the Dams and Foundations Section of the Water and Power Department, which is the largest municipally owned utility in the United States. Recently a geologist position was established within the Department of Building and Safety in order to provide needed assistance in control over grading on private property.

The Metropolitan Water District of Southern California, a public corporation, employs only 1 or 2 geologists at present, though it has had a larger staff in the past during periods of major construction programs.

The greatest number of geologists is in the field of private geological and engineering firms and consultants, for this field has had a tremendous growth, chiefly because of the necessity or requirement for detailed geologic mapping in connection with hillside residential developments. Today there are about 28 in engineering geology firms plus another 20 or so working for soil and foundation engineering companies.

Lessons to Be Learned

The importance of the Los Angeles experience to geologists, engineers, planners, and indeed to the public, is that it illustrates the sort of thing that can happen and already is beginning to happen elsewhere, though on a lesser scale and with variations because of differing local conditions. Other urban communities would do well to take note and hopefully avoid some of the more violent growing pains in the acquisition and application of geologic information. In particular, the experience suggests an ideal sequence of mapping investigations to best meet the needs for geologic data in an expanding urban area.

First, and an absolute essential, is modern general-purpose mapping of quadrangles or other large areas, such as is undertaken by Federal and State surveys. Where possible, this should precede urban development so that the maps can serve as guides for land planning and zoning, and provide background for more-detailed local studies. The mapping of suburban fringe areas before the central city generally will meet greater needs first and take advantage of better exposures. The 7½-minute, 1:24,000-scale (i.e., 1 inch equals 2,000 feet) topographic maps are becoming the standard base for urban planning activities throughout the country, and thus are also the most appropriate base for general geologic mapping of urban areas. However, in some urban areas geologic complexities may make desirable initial large-scale mapping on an enlarged base.

The most useful general-purpose maps for urban development are those that emphasize geologic processes and characteristics of geologic materials that are significant to land use and civil engineering. But even where such emphasis is lacking, valuable guidance can be derived from interpretations of the basic geologic data.

The second stage in the mapping sequence consists of larger scale and commonly special-purpose mapping of selected areas. Both the County and the City of Los Angeles have recognized the need for maps at a scale of about 1 inch equals 400 feet in areas where landslides are prevalent and where no geologic maps were available at scales larger than 1:24,000. As part of the cooperative program between the County and the State Division of Mines and Geology, the broad coastal peninsula of Palos Verdes Hills recently was mapped at a scale of 1 inch equals 200 feet, with subsequent compilation at 1 inch equals 400 feet. This is an area of approximately 26 square miles. The assembled field maps, properly fitted together, would measure about 8 by 12 feet! Geologists of the City of Los Angeles have embarked on an ambitious program of mapping some 80 square miles of hilly and mountainous terrain on new photogrammetric base maps at a scale of 1 inch equals 400 feet. Such activities are by no means limited to governmental surveys. Private engineering geology firms have done extensive mapping at comparable scales for private developments covering up to tens of thousands of acres.

The third stage in the mapping sequence, and the one involving by far the greatest number of geologists, consists of extremely detailed investigations, chiefly for individual hillside subdivisions or specific engineering projects. A common scale for tentative tract maps is 1 inch equals 100 feet, and for final grading maps 1 inch equals 40 feet. Most such mapping is for private development and is done by geologists in engineering and consulting firms.

Meeting the National Need for Urban Geologic Information

The population figures for the United States show that urban growth, with its Pandora's box of planning and engineering problems, is not peculiar to Los Angeles. It is a nationwide phenomenon. And so also the need for urban geologic information, both basic and specialized, is nationwide. Much can and should be done to take full advantage of such geologic data as are already available in published and unpublished form, but for most urban areas these will afford at best no more than an interim and partial solution.

New York was the first and still is about the only large city in the nation with anywhere near adequate engineering geology information. Most metropolitan areas of the United States desperately need new, detailed mapping, and this can only be achieved through a greatly magnified engineering geology effort involving municipal, county, and State agencies and private firms, as well as our universities and colleges. The master key to real progress belongs to the local governments. They can provide the greatest stimulus for urban geologic investigations, and they are in the best position to insure that the results are applied for the maximum benefit of their citizens. Cities and counties can use the geologic information not only in the formulation of long-range policies and plans, but in the day to day applications that are possible with continuity of local operation.

The recent history of the geological profession in Los Angeles and in a number of other cities fosters optimism about the future job outlook for well-trained engineering geologists interested in urban work. The major emphasis must always be on quality rather than quantity, however, because this is work that deserves and demands the best talents.

The U.S. Geological Survey has been mapping cities for many years as part of its national mapping responsibility. The 1902 folio of the New York metropolitan area was a notable early effort. Most of the older maps, however, are no longer adequate to meet modern requirements for more detailed, specialized, and up-to-date information. In its limited program of urban geology studies, the Geological Survey hopes to encourage by example the greater use of engineering geology in urban areas, and to educate public agencies and private concerns in the needs and applications of this field to the end that they will develop their own capabilities.

Mapping and related research by the Geological Survey in urban areas is intended to provide general background for more detailed site investigations. Individual projects tend to emphasize different aspects of the geology, depending on the local situation. Studies by the Engineering Geology Branch are currently underway in the following metropolitan areas: Boston, Mass.; Washington, D.C.; Great Falls, Mont.; Rapid City, S. D.; Omaha-Council Bluffs, Nebr.-Iowa; Salt Lake City, Utah; Denver and Pueblo, Colo.; Seattle, Wash.; and San Francisco-Oakland, San Mateo-Palo Alto, and Los Angeles, Calif.

Studies have been completed in recent years in Anchorage, Alaska; Knoxville, Tenn.; and Portland, Oreg., and the reports have been published.

The problems of urban growth are a tremendous challenge. Planners and engineers need all the help they can get to meet the challenge most effectively. It is time geologists fully appreciated that a fundamental part of this help must come from their own ranks. The challenge to the geological profession is actually the more urgent because much of the geologists' work should be completed before that of the planners and engineers begins. In short, this is a time of opportunity but also a time for responsibility. We have an obligation as scientists, as educators, and as good citizens to see that the benefits of geologic information are brought to bear as widely and fully as possible in the solution of problems of urban growth.

Engineering—Geological Maps for Urban Development

2

Robert F. Legget

The cities of the world will probably at least double in size before the end of the century, due to world population increases and the apparently irreversible trend from country to city living. The success of the vast building program that this increase will necessitate will depend, ultimately, upon adequate knowledge of the subsurface conditions of all the ground that will be covered by this urban expansion.

Coordination of existing records with the results of new investigations and facts revealed by all new excavation is essential for every urban area. This can be done only in close association with local geology. Engineering-geological maps provide the best means of recording this vital information. Some cities have made a good start at the preparation of such maps; examples are given. All cities must have such maps as basic tools for all future planning if inevitable expansion is to be saved from costly errors. Broad guidelines for this essential public service are presented.

This paper is a summary of my oral presentation at the 1972 Annual Meeting of The Geological Society of America held in Minneapolis, and is based on material in *Cities and Geology* (Legget, 1973), which was in press at the time of the meeting.

The current rate of growth of the cities of North America is little short of phenomenal. This rapid expansion is a reflection of the increase in population growth since the end of the second world war, assisted to a degree by the corresponding increase in the standard of living. It is but a beginning of a growth pattern that will probably see urban development throughout the world doubled by the year 2000.

If this seems to be just alarmist talk, consider this statement from the official press release (No. 19849-69) issued on 29 October 1969 jointly by the Secretaries of the Department of the Interior and of Housing and Urban Development: "by the year 2000, major urban regions will cover about 340,000 square miles as compared to the present 200,000 square miles. Additional areas will be affected by smaller individual centers." The increased urban area, thus officially estimated, of 140,000 sq mi is difficult to visualize; it is roughly equivalent to the combined areas of England, Scotland, Wales, and Czechoslovakia. And this estimated growth of urban areas by the year 2000—little more than 25 years away!

This prospective growth of cities makes the current tag that "The United States of America paves one million acres a year" a lamentable understatement. At that rate, if we assume by the word "paving" the covering up of natural ground for the physical development of cities, it would take a full century to cover 140,000 sq mi; yet we face this prospect in the next 30 years.

The magnitude of the construction job that is involved in this urban expansion is, in itself, monumental, but we are concerned with the necessary and essential planning that must be done before any construction starts. Such planning cannot be properly done unless it is well and firmly founded upon full knowledge and appreciation of the geology underlying the sites to be developed. Engineering geologists and many civil engineers know this, but it is doubtful whether many others who are engaged in the planning process are aware of it.

In some instances, this has had lamentable results; in other instances, the absence of geological studies has not been noticed because fortune has been kind, and planning based purely on topographical information just happened to be satisfactory also in relation to the underlying geology. Chances like this, however, must not be taken in the future, if only because of the magnitude of the task of planning well for future urban development. An added factor is that many sites previously thought to be unsatisfactory will now have to be used for developmental purposes, thus making their geological study imperative before any decisions are made as to the erection of structures.

When things go well, we tend to forget that the essential stability of every man-made structure depends ultimately upon the ground on which it rests, and in this context the word "structure" includes all facilities constructed for the use of man—buildings, bridges, dams, roads, and airport runways. This very familiarity is probably responsible for the neglect of geology in so much of the literature of planning. Even so eminent a guide as the *Urban Planning Manual* of the American Society of Civil Engineers (in all other respects a notable and most useful volume) gives scant attention to geology.

Fortunately, there are some exceptions to this general neglect of geology in our planning literature. Ian McHarg (1969), a distinguished professor of landscape architecture and planning, has given full attention to local geology as a prerequisite for all planning in his fine book *Design with Nature*. The suddenly increasing interest in what is called "environmental geology" is encouraging.

If, then, it can be assumed that the vital need for geology in all urban and regional planning is within sight of general acceptance, how can the necessary information best be made available? A general overview of the local geology for any one region usually can be obtained from existing reports of the local, state, or provincial governments, or even from the national geological survey. This information provides a good starting point, but by itself, it is not enough. The geology must be interpreted in terms that will be useful and meaningful to planners. In most cases, much more detailed information will be necessary for urban planning in particular, and even for many cases of regional planning.

For all cities, there exists a vast amount of such information, but it is usually locked up in the private records of local engineering organizations, including those of the cities themselves. Most tunneling beneath cities, for example, is carried out by some public agency. Invaluable information about the local geology revealed by the bore is thus made available to those on the tunneling operation, but only rarely is this information published. (The major tunnels beneath the city of Boston constitute a notable exception to this statement through the work of Professor Marland Billings and his associates, with the cooperation of the local public agencies.)

During the last few decades, it has become common practice to put down deep borings at the sites of all major buildings in order to determine exactly the subsurface conditions upon which their foundations will rest. This is the work of geotechnical engineers, always fully recorded, generally in the form of detailed reports to the designing engineer or architect. Supplementary reports are made recording the actual materials revealed when excavation is carried out. This information is always (or should be) incorporated in the engineering "As-constructed Drawings." But in almost every case, the foundation is completed, the superstructure is erected, the building or bridge put into use, the foundations forgotten about, and the records of the underlying geology (unique though this information will usually be) put away in filing drawers, never to be looked at again unless needed for future changes to or near the structure.

If, for every city, this collection of invaluable information could be made publicly available and, when so available, expertly assessed against the generally known overall picture of the local geology, it would then be possible to prepare detailed engineering-geological maps for all urban areas. These would be of inestimable use in all planning work. They would provide a sound basis for all proposals for the physical development, or redevelopment, of urban areas. They would have the further great advantage of assisting in the planning of all future geotechnical investigations in urban areas by showing clearly what information was already available around any new site that had to be investigated.

The collecting, assembling, and assessment of all such urban subsurface information is clearly a public responsibility. It may be suggested that it could be, for all cities, part of the responsibility of the city engineer, assisted by requisite geological advice. The service to the public that such urban geological information would provide would far exceed the minor costs involved.

Do any cities have such a service available? They have, in a variety of ways. The city of Warsaw, Poland, had a set of four engineering-geological maps made available to it as early as 1936 through the work of two pioneering professors. The city of Prague in Czechoslovakia, with singularly interesting geology beneath its ancient streets, has an excellent system for recording all local geological information. The city of London, England, has the advantage of having always been the headquarters of the Geological Survey of Great Britain. Voluntarily, subsurface information has been given to this organization in such good measure that even before the second world war an excellent series of Six-Inch Maps for the entire area of the great city was available, showing details of key borings throughout the city from which the underlying geology could be deduced.

The Geological Survey of Northern Ireland has recently produced an excellent map of the geology underlying the city of Belfast, with full explanation of its engineering significance printed on the back. The city of Johannesburg in South Africa has produced a similar map, based on the initial studies of an interested graduate student; a strong committee is now further developing this notable work. Another individual effort started the significant urban geological mapping that is now available for all major Japanese cities, work on the subsurface of Tokyo undertaken individually creating such favorable response that the national government is now assisting financially with a country-wide similar program for the main cities of Japan.

In Canada, The Geological Survey of Canada has recently been engaged on a special winter-works program that has started work of the type described in a number of Canadian cities. An excellent atlas of the *Physical Environment of Saskatoon* (Christiansen, 1970) is already colloquially known as the "Saskatoon Folio." The provincial government of Quebec has recently published a masterly report on the geology of Montreal, prepared by Professor T. H. Clark, in which tribute is paid to the steady accumulation of subsurface information in Canada's metropolis.

For the United States, Boston has already been mentioned appreciatively. Not only has a notable series of papers on the geology of Boston tunnels been published in the *Journal of the Boston Society of Civil Engineers*, but this society has had, since the inception of its journal, a committee responsible for collecting and publishing records of all holes in the city area. It has been humorously observed that the subsurface of Boston has been more probed than that of any other city in the United States, but this remark is really only an indication of the fact that the records of the borings of Boston are better known than those for other cities, since they have been so well assembled and published for general public benefit. Similar work has been done in other cities, although not so extensively; for most United States cities, there are publications of use that do record some useful information about the local subsurface.

The U.S. Geological Survey is now engaged on a number of major programs of studying local urban geology, the results of which will be of wide public benefit. This, however, is only an extension of earlier work. Especially notable were the fine engineering-geological maps published for Oakland and San Francisco in the late fifties. Many of the reports published by the U.S. Geological Survey summarizing long-term studies of the geology of urban regions—such as one on Portland, Oregon—must have proved of great assistance to local engineers, architects, and planners.

If all the examples that could possibly be collected from around the world were to be listed, we would see that only a beginning has been made. If you now consider the "explosion of cities" mentioned at the outset of this paper, then you will recognize the urgency of an immediate and great increase in activity in this field of urban geology if planning for the cities of the immediate future is to be well done. Every geologist would do well to become interested and find out what is being done in his own city about the geology beneath its streets. His support for any local effort in the direction of making local subsurface information publicly available will be, in itself, a minor public service. It will carry with it the distinct possibility that purely scientific information about the local geology will be revealed in this applied work, thus demonstrating yet again the joint engineering and geological benefits to be gained from due attention to urban geology.

REFERENCES CITED

Christiansen, E. A., ed., 1970, Physical environment of Saskatoon, Canada: Saskatchewan Research Council and the Natl. Research Council of Canada, 68 p.

Legget, R. F., 1973, Cities and geology: McGraw-Hill Book Co., N.Y., chap. 3, 624 p.

McHarg, Ian, 1969, Design with nature: Nat. History, 198 p.

Geology—Its Role in the Development and Planning of Metropolitan Washington

3

C. F. Withington

Washington, D.C., is the center of one of the fastest growing communities in the United States. It is also an integral part of a nearly continuous metropolitan complex that extends from Richmond, Virginia, to Portland, Maine. The Washington Standard Metropolitan Statistical Area, as defined by the U.S. Bureau of Census, contains 2,379 square miles, consisting of the District of Columbia, Montgomery and Prince Georges Counties in Maryland, and Arlington, Fairfax, Loudoun, and Prince William Counties in Virginia. The population of this area, which was a little more than 2 million in 1960, is now, 7 years later, estimated at 2.5 million, of which some 800,000 are residents of Washington, 900,000 live in suburban Maryland, and 800,000 in suburban Virginia. By 1980, the population is expected to increase to about 3.7 million, and by the year 2000 to about 5.25 million (Wise, 1965, p. 1). A population that will more than double within the next 33 years presents to the planners and metropolitan officials many problems. The solution to some of these problems will depend to a great extent on a detailed knowledge of the local geology, for the role of geology is as important in planning for the future as it has been in influencing the past.

Geology has been called one of history's most efficient handmaidens (Hulbert, 1930, p. 4). Certainly an understanding of the historical role of geology is important in order to appreciate some of the basic problems facing the metropolitan area, for on the local geology depended such fundamental and diverse decisions as the selection of the site for the early settlements in the city and the architectural form that developed here. Even the economic distribution of population within the metropolitan area is governed to a certain extent by geology.

Of greater importance, however, are the contributions that geology can make toward the plan, design, and development of the metropolitan area. Solutions to such problems as management of water supplies, maintenance of sources of mineral raw materials needed for construction, and decisions on land use, are at least partially dependent on geology. Even in the day-to-day construction, experience has shown that the savings in foundation design and excavation which result from the proper interpretation of geologic information far surpass the costs of obtaining the basic data.

In order to show the significance of geology in the development and planning of the area, it is first necessary to give a brief description of the geologic setting of metropolitan Washington.

Reprinted with permission of the author and publisher from *Journal of the Washington Academy of Sciences* 57:189–99, 1967. Copyright © 1967 by Washington Academy of Sciences and authorized by the Director, U.S. Geological Survey.

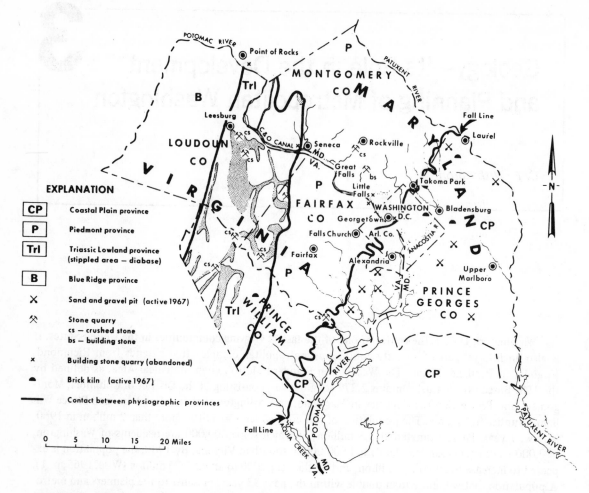

FIGURE 1. Physical provinces of metropolitan Washington, D.C. (after Calver, 1963, Cloos and others, 1964, and Johnston and Otton, 1963).

Geologic Setting of Metropolitan Washington

Metropolitan Washington lies in parts of four physiographic provinces, which are, from east to west, the Coastal Plain, the Piedmont, the Triassic Lowland, and the Blue Ridge (see figure 1).

The Coastal Plain province extends along the coast from northeastern New Jersey to Mexico. It is a gently undulating plain that rises gradually westward from the coast to as high as 400 feet in isolated hills at the western edge of the province where it meets the Piedmont. It is underlain by gravels, sands, clays, and marls of late Mesozoic and Cenozoic age (100 million years old or younger). Broad tidal estuaries such as Chesapeake Bay and the Potomac River, bordered by bluffs as much as 100 feet high, are common.

The western boundary of the Coastal Plain, where it joins the Piedmont, trends northeastward across the metropolitan area, through the eastern parts of Prince William and Fairfax Counties, Virginia, nearly bisects Arlington County, Virginia, crosses the District of Columbia east of Rock Creek, and roughly parallels the Prince Georges-Montgomery County, Maryland line. A few isolated remnants of Coastal Plain rocks occur west of this line on the Piedmont rocks. This physiographic boundary corresponds to the Fall Line, or Fall Zone, shown by a line drawn on figure 1 connecting points on adjacent rivers and streams where the rivers pass from the more resistant rocks of the Piedmont to the more easily eroded sedimentary deposits of the Coastal Plain. It is here that rapids or falls form. The width of the zone in which falls occur ranges from less than a mile to as much as 5 miles, but for the purposes of this report, the Fall Line is drawn joining the lowest falls on each river or stream.

The Piedmont province is west of the Coastal Plain. The rocks of the Piedmont underlie most of Montgomery County, Maryland, and parts of Arlington, Fairfax, and Prince William Counties, Virginia. The Piedmont is a belt of rolling hills that extends from southern New York to Alabama. Elevations range from near sea level along the major drainages at the Fall Line to as much as 1,000 feet in the west. Many large rivers, such as the Potomac and the Patuxent, flow south to southeast across the province in steep-walled valleys as much as 400 feet deep. The Piedmont is 25 to 140 miles wide; near Washington it is 40 miles or less wide.

The Piedmont rocks near Washington are chiefly resistant crystalline metamorphic rocks—schist and gneiss of Precambrian age (600 million years or older) that have been intruded by igneous rocks and by veins of quartz and pegmatite. On the uplands the crystalline rocks are weathered to saprolite, a decomposed, porous, spongy, red-brown material, as much as 200 feet thick. Despite the alteration by weathering, saprolite retains all the structural features of the original rock. The final product of weathering, which is seen on the surface throughout much of the Piedmont, is sticky micaceous sandy and silty clay.

Western Montgomery County, Maryland, and eastern Loudoun and western Fairfax Counties, Virginia, are in the Triassic Lowland province, a gentle rolling plain broken by long low ridges. The province extends southward in an almost continuous belt 10 to 30 miles wide, from the west side of the Hudson River near New York City, to Virginia. The Triassic rocks (deposited about 200 million years ago) are red shales, sandstones, and conglomerates, which were deposited in down-faulted grabens within the crystalline rocks of the Piedmont. These sedimentary rocks are as much as 1,500 feet thick, and were intruded by trap rock (resistant fine-grained diabase and basalt dikes and sills), which on outcrop have been weathered to clay to depths of as much as 10 feet. The Triassic rocks dip 2° to 25° west and are broken by numerous north-trending, steeply dipping faults.

The Blue Ridge province, in the western part of Loudoun County, is a region of valleys and ridges underlain by folded metamorphic and igneous crystalline rocks; in Loudoun County these rocks are predominantly phyllite, granite, greenstone, and quartzite. The province extends southward from southern Pennsylvania to Georgia. The rocks form sharp, north-trending ridges, capped by resistant quartzite beds, that rise more than 1,000 feet above sea level; the ridges are separated by broad valleys.

The Role of Geology in the History of Washington

Geology has played a major, though largely indirect, role in the history of metropolitan Washington. It formed the basis for the original location of early settlements, and to a certain extent it dictated the architecture and the economic distribution of population.

Perhaps most important is the role that geology played in the establishment of many early towns at the Fall Line, the head of navigation on the Potomac and Anacostia Rivers. Here ships tied up to unload their cargo for transportation inland and to load produce from the Piedmont for shipment to distant markets. In addition, the easiest crossing of the rivers, either by bridge or ferry, was in the vicinity of the Fall Line; therefore, the first major overland north-south travel route was along the Fall Line. With the coming of the industrial revolution, manufacturing was attracted to the Fall Line towns because of the readily available transportation and because waterpower provided by the falls could be utilized. It is interesting to note that most of the major cities from Trenton, New Jersey, southward to Macon, Georgia, are on the Fall Line. Of passing interest also is that Atlanta, Georgia, is the only major city in the Piedmont province; it was founded as a railroad junction long after the Fall Line cities were established. In the Washington area, the early Fall Line settlements of Alexandria, Bladensburg, and Georgetown were founded as ports; Laurel was founded at the easiest crossing of the Patuxent River and as a factory town to utilize the power of the falls.

A second example of the influence of geology on history is in architecture. The abundance of brick clay and building stone was a determining factor on the architecture of the city. Some of the earliest houses were built of brick, and today local brick continues to be one of the major building materials in the metropolitan area. The first building stones used were mica schist and gneiss from the Piedmont. The quarries were, of necessity, on the outcrops along the Potomac River near water transportation at the Fall Line because it was difficult to move these stones overland. The foundations of various buildings throughout the area, including the White House, Capitol, and Washington Monument, were built of this stone. Similar stone is still being quarried in Montgomery County.

Another stone that was used in the city is the sandstone of Cretaceous age found near Aquia Creek in Stafford County, Virginia, about 40 miles south of Washington on the Potomac River. This stone is most unusual, for here the Coastal Plain sandstones have been cemented by silica. Only in central Prince Georges County has similar stone been found. The Aquia Creek stone was used in the construction of many public buildings between 1790 and 1840 as it was near water transportation and easy to work. These buildings included the White House, the older parts of the Capitol, and the Treasury. The stone, however, was found to be so inferior in durability and general appearance (Hawes, 1884, p. 358) that by 1840 its use for government buildings was discontinued. Although most of this sandstone in the older public buildings has had to be repaired, painted, or replaced, some of the original stonework can still be seen in interior columns and walls.

Still another sandstone, called "Seneca Stone," was used extensively from about 1840 to 1880. This stone, a red sandstone of Triassic age, was quarried west of the mouth of Seneca Creek, about 20 miles up the Potomac from Washington in Montgomery County on the eastern edge of the Triassic Lowland province. Many of the locks of the "Potowmack" Canal and its successor, the Chesapeake and Ohio Canal, were built of this stone. The canals provided a means of transportation to get the stone to market. The first major government building to be built of "Seneca Stone" was the original Smithsonian Institution, built in the 1840s. Some of this stone was also used as backing for the marble of the Washington Monument. Although these quarries were exhausted by the 1890s, numerous examples of "Seneca Stone" can be seen today in many churches and houses in Georgetown and other older parts of Washington.

One of the more interesting local stones, and one that has received only limited use, is the so-called "Potomac Breccia" or "Potomac marble." This stone was deposited as a series of alluvial fans along the western edge of the Triassic basin, west of Montgomery County. It was first reported in 1817 by B. H. Latrobe, supervising architect of the Capitol. The stone consists of siliceous and calcareous materials of many colors, subangular and subrounded, and ranging in size from sand grains to cobbles as much as a foot in diameter, cemented by calcite. Examples of this stone can be seen in the Capitol, in the pillars in the Old Hall of Representatives (now Statuary Hall), and the former Supreme Court Room. Until the Chesapeake and Ohio Canal was finished, blocks of this material were brought overland from Point of Rocks on the Potomac River near Harpers Ferry, a tremendous task (Mathews 1898, p. 187-190). This stone never became popular because the difference in hardness between the clasts and the matrix made polishing difficult.

After 1840, and with the coming of the railroad, stone from other parts of the country became more readily available, and the use of local stone was largely discontinued.

The third example of geology's role in history is the economic distribution of the population of the metropolitan area. This perhaps can be best examined by comparing the history of the eastern parts of the city and Prince Georges County with that of northwest Washington and Montgomery County.

Prince Georges County and the neighboring parts of the city are on the Coastal Plain. Here the land is relatively flat and easy to farm. The Coastal Plain was, therefore, the first land to be settled. Life in the 17th and 18th century was centered in the plantations, each of which was an isolated and economically self-sufficient unit that had little need for commerce with its neighbors. Towns, therefore, did not fit into the scheme of plantation life, and few developed in the early history of the

Coastal Plain (Hulbert, 1930, p. 111-112). The plantations were along the navigable waterways, the highways by which the plantation owners shipped their crops to market. In Prince Georges County these waterways were the estuaries of the Potomac, Anacostia, and Patuxent Rivers. The crops, mostly tobacco, were worked first by indentured servants, later by slaves. The central part of Prince Georges was the last part of the county to be developed, because of lack of ready transportation and because the gravelly soils of the Pliocene alluvial fan made poor farmland.

Montgomery County and northwest Washington, on the other hand, lie west of the Fall Line on the Piedmont. The land is hilly and more difficult to farm. The area was not settled until the 1750s, about 100 years after the Coastal Plain. A large proportion of the early settlers were tenant farmers and bonded servants who left the plantations when their indenture was up and struck out on their own. The area was, therefore, developed as small farms; towns were established as centers of trade and as outposts against Indian raids (Billington, 1950, p. 44-47). Transportation was mostly overland and by horse. This limited the quantity of products carried to market. Tobacco growing was tried, but as the soil, which is derived from the clayey saprolite, is of "middling or inferior quality" (Bryan, 1914, p. 171), the growing of tobacco was soon abandoned. By 1800, corn and wheat, which were less destructive to the soils, became the main crops.

With the Civil War, depression came to most of Prince Georges County. Almost 200 years of tobacco growing had exhausted the soil; what tobacco was produced could not be readily sold because the established foreign market was reduced. In addition, slaves were no longer available to work the fields. The plantations near Washington gave way to small diversified truck farms, but here as throughout most of the Coastal Plain the soil had been badly eroded, exposing the underlying Cretaceous clays. These clays, which crop out extensively in the eastern part of Washington and nearby Prince Georges County, make poor farmland. On the other hand, Montgomery County prospered. With the soldiers in Washington and a sympathetic population in the county, a brisk trade developed in food, hides for boots, and even corn whiskey. Therefore, a strong market developed for material that could be transported easily overland or by the Chesapeake and Ohio Canal along the Potomac. Montgomery County became an area of prosperous small farms.

A second phase of the development of the two counties started before the Civil War with the advent of the railroads. The first railroad to enter Washington was from Baltimore and was built just east of the Fall Line on the Coastal Plain where the land was flat, construction was easy, and no wide rivers had to be crossed. The railroad attracted small industrial complexes such as coal, brick, and lumber yards. The industry attracted workers. The poorly drained clay soil of the Coastal Plain that predominates in eastern Washington and nearby Prince Georges County made the land less desirable and therefore less expensive than land in northwest Washington. The railroads in Montgomery County were originally built to bring produce and coal to Washington from the west and attracted little industry to the county.

By 1900, the pattern for development of the area was set; residential homes of the middle and upper income groups were spreading northwest from the city into Montgomery County; in Prince Georges County and the eastern parts of the city, on the other hand, the housing was apartment complexes and small row houses. Only a few of the large homes on large acreages away from the city were still occupied by the wealthy. Today in northwest Washington and Montgomery County the individual income is generally higher. In Montgomery County, for instance, the median family income in 1959, the last year for which figures are available, was $9,382, one of the highest in the country. In industrial northeast and southeast Washington and Prince Georges County, on the other hand, the 1959 median family income was about $7,000 (U.S. Bureau of the Census, 1962, p. 364-365).

The Role of Geology in the Solution of Present-Day Problems

Just as knowledge of geology's role in the development of the metropolitan area is important in understanding the background of the physical and social setting of today's urban area, so too can the fundamental principles of geology be useful in anticipating and solving many of the complex problems that arise with the growth of the metropolis. These problems can be divided into two categories: management of natural resources, including water supplies and mineral raw materials used in construction; and reduction of potential geologic hazards, including floods, erosion, and landslides.

Perhaps the most pressing problem is a need for improved water management. Although enough ground water and surface water exist for the future needs of the Washington metropolitan area, the supplies will not be sufficient for the demand unless they are properly managed. In the first 60 years of the city's existence, enough water was available in local streams, springs, and shallow wells to satisfy the needs of the city. After the Civil War, however, it was found necessary to tap the Potomac at Great Falls, and since that time most of the water used in the city and nearby Virginia has come from the Potomac. With the completion of a diversion dam and pumping station at Little Falls in 1959, and the increase in the capacity of the filter system, water supply was expected to be sufficient until the 1990s (Johnston, 1964, p. 42–48). These supplies, however, became critically low in the summer of 1966 during an extended period of drought when ground-water discharge was insufficient to maintain the flow of the Potomac; this forced renewed attention to improvement in water management.

Various government organizations are now making inventories of ground- and surface-water supplies throughout much of the metropolitan area. These data are useful in supplying the basic water facts needed for proper management of the supplies and are a useful guide to such planning problems as the densities of population that can safely be allowed in suburban areas where onsite sewage disposal systems are used and water supplies are derived locally from ground water.

Of lesser importance, but still of concern to the citizens of the expanding metropolis, is the need to have a readily available supply of the basic raw materials used in building: crushed stone, gravel, sand, and clay. The importance of these commodities to the community can be seen in the annual production figure of about $25 million for the metropolitan area. Prince Georges County leads in the production of gravel, sand, and clay, producing about half the total. Fairfax County produces annually about one-fifth of the total in sand and gravel from the Coastal Plain and crushed trap rock from the Triassic Basin. The remaining production is spread among the other counties. Loudoun County produces crushed trap rock; Prince William County produces clay for brick from the Coastal Plain and Triassic sedimentary rocks, crushed granite from the Piedmont, and crushed trap rock from the Triassic Basin; Montgomery County produces crushed rock from the Piedmont.

About three-quarters of the building materials comes from the Coastal Plain in the two largest counties, Prince Georges and Fairfax. In Prince Georges, much of the gravel is produced from the northern and central parts of the county, though deposits in the southern part are now being opened. The sand and gravel in the northern and central parts lie in the path of the rapidly expanding metropolitan area. Reserves here, even if they were to be completely developed at the present rate of production, probably would last no longer than 10 years. The gravel in Fairfax County is similarly situated, and these deposits will probably be exhausted within seven years. Sand and gravel from the Potomac River and crushed stone from Prince William County are brought by barges to the central city. However, plans are being made to redevelop the waterfronts in Washington, and this would effectively eliminate the barge-unloading facilities (Rowe, 1967, p. 149; 184). Within 10 years, under present plans, most of the gravel and sand used for building in the Washington area will have to come from southern Prince Georges County or outside the metropolitan area, thus increasing the cost of transportation and the cost of building.

Planners and zoning officials should be aware of these problems; the reserves should, where possible, be delineated and set aside until they can be worked. Only after the deposits have been exhausted and the land reclaimed should residential or industrial development take place.

A third service that geology can contribute is to define areas of potential geologic hazards in the metropolitan area. Such hazards include floods, erosion, and landslides.

One of the more overlooked aspects of geology, but one of increasing importance in our expanding communities, is the part geology plays in effective use of land. A basic knowledge of the characteristics of the rock and soil is desirable for proper land development, for with the continued growth of communities, land that was once bypassed as being too difficult and too expensive or too dangerous to use, is now being utilized. Development of this submarginal land should be considered with care because indiscriminate use could lead to costly maintenance problems and even disaster.

Flooding is an ever present hazard. The knowledge of the frequency and magnitude of floods can be of help in planning to lessen the damage caused by high water. Investigations are under way to aid in the prediction of floods (Darling, 1959); in addition several government agencies are mapping the extent of flood plains. The metropolitan officials are well aware that they should consider these data in planning, for encroachment on the flood plain by industry and housing is a continuing problem. Unfortunately the flood plain is inviting development, and, as parts of it are inundated infrequently enough to disguise the potential hazards to buildings, real estate developments have often unwittingly been built in the path of floods. In addition, those developments built by filling in parts of the flood plain may restrict the channel of the river during floods and thereby increase flood levels upstream. Protection against flood can best start by recognizing the extent of the flood plains and by planning uses of the land that will limit loss. Pilot projects to make flood-probability maps of drainage are underway in Fairfax County.

Although devastating floods are rare in the Washington area, parts of the city of Alexandria and of Arlington County, Virginia, and Prince Georges County, Maryland, periodically suffer loss from high water. The alternative to costly flood-control measures is some form of urban renewal in which areas subject to flooding can be converted to open spaces where flood damage would be minimal.

A second hazard, excessive erosion, results from an indiscriminate removal of vegetative cover by farming or construction, from poorly conceived grading in highway construction and real estate development, and from improper compaction of artificial fill. All these increase the silt load in streams and rivers by exposing the soil to erosion.

Although erosion is especially serious in the Coastal Plain, other areas are not immune. Runoff that causes erosion is a factor of the slope of the land; the steeper the slope the greater the erosion will be. Proper drainage on slopes is imperative.

The effect of erosion on the economy of a community can be seen in the history of Bladensburg, Prince Georges County. Bladensburg, the first organized settlement in the Washington area, was founded in 1742 as a seaport on a deep and protected harbor at the head of navigation on the Anacostia River. At first, ocean-going vessels reached Bladensburg with little difficulty, and the town became a major center for tobacco export (Bryan, 1941, p. 430). As the land around Bladensburg was cleared for crops, unconsolidated Coastal Plain sediments were exposed to erosion, and the channel of the Anacostia began filling with sediment. By 1800, the maximum depth at low tide had been reduced from the original 24 to 14 feet, and the width of the channel so narrowed that navigation was difficult. By 1830, the river became unnavigable to all except the shallowest draft ships, and Bladensburg was abandoned as a port. Few floods had occurred at Bladensburg before the 1930s, but by then, urbanization upriver from the town had increased the silt load in the river. The silt clogged the channel so that floods occurred with increasing frequency (Williams, 1942, p. 23). By the 1950s, extensive flood-control measures were constructed.

Erosion is a natural geologic process and rivers always will carry some silt. Indeed, a certain amount of sediment load in a stream is necessary to prevent a river from scouring its banks. Controls are necessary, however, to hold erosion to a minimum. Besides those recommended by the Soil Conservation Service, additional controls are needed. These might take the form of grading and subdivision ordinances such as those that have been adopted in Los Angeles County, California, by which the municipal building officials could, in their review of development plans and of construction, be alert to correct such items as poorly designed and poorly drained slopes and uncompacted fills.

Landslides, a third geologic hazard, are present in the Washington area. A landslide is a downslope movement of soil or rock or both. This movement can be rapid, but in the Washington area it is generally slow.

In many slides the failure occurs along a surface that has generally the same shape as the bowl of a spoon. Slides of this type are common throughout the world; they can range in size from only a few feet across to tremendous masses containing millions of cubic yards. Many factors contribute to produce a landslide, and one slide may be the product of many causes. By and large, however, the slides that we see in the Washington area start because a slope has been disturbed, usually by construction. These failures generally are brought about by the removal of the base of a slope, oversteepening of the slope by excavation, or loading the top of a slope with fill. As this type of slide generally moves slowly, the major concern is the property damage that results. Although much can be done to prevent slides of this sort from starting, once a slide starts its control is difficult and costly.

A detailed knowledge of the physical environment can contribute much to the safe and efficient growth of an expanding community because many of the problems that confront the city officials can be at least partially solved by a proper interpretation of the local geology. It is the responsibility of the geologist to gather and present facts from which these interpretations are made. Those responsible for planning and construction of the metropolitan area should be aware of the value of geologic information and avail themselves of this knowledge.

BIBLIOGRAPHY

Billington, R. A., 1950, Westward expansion: New York, Macmillan Co., 873 p.

Bryan, W. B., 1914, A history of the National Capitol: New York, Macmillan Co., v. 1, 669 p.

Calver, J. L., 1963, Geologic map of Virginia: Charlottesville, Virginia Div. Mineral Resources, scale 1:500,000.

Cloos, Ernst, and others, 1964, The geology of Howard and Montgomery Counties: Baltimore, Maryland Geol. Survey, 373 p.

Darling, J. M., 1959, Floods in Maryland: magnitude and frequency: U.S. Geol. Survey open-file rept., 9 p.

Hawes, G. W., 1884, Report on the building stones of the United States and statistics of the quarry industry for 1880: U.S. 10th Census office, v. 10, 410 p.

Hulbert, A. B., 1930, Soil, its influence on the history of the United States: New Haven, Yale Univ. Press, 227 p.

Johnston, P. M., 1964, Geology and ground-water resources of Washington, D.C., and vicinity: U.S. Geol. Survey Water-Supply Paper 1776, 97 p.

Johnston, P. M., and Otton, E. G., 1963, Availability of ground-water for urban and industrial development in upper Montgomery County, Maryland: [Silver Spring, Maryland?] The Maryland-National Capital Park and Planning Comm., 47 p.

Mathews, E. B., 1898, An account of the character and distribution of Maryland building stones: Maryland Geol. Survey Rept., v. 2, p. 125–241.

Rowe, E. H., 1967, The proposed comprehensive plan for the National Capital: Washington, D.C., U.S. Govt. Print. Off., 230 p.

U.S. Bureau of the Census, 1962, Census of population: 1960; Volume 1, Characteristics of the population. Part 22, Maryland: Washington, D.C., 379 p.

Williams, M. T., 1942, A history of erosion in the Anacostia drainage basin: Washington, Catholic Univ. America Press, 59 p.

Wise, H. F., 1965, A program for comprehensive planning and development in the National Capital region—summary: Washington, D.C., Metropolitan Washington Council of Governments, 15 p.

Lessons from the Old World to the Americas in Land Use

4

Walter Clay Lowdermilk

Lands of the Old World bear an indelible record written across landscape after landscape by resident populations. The longer the occupation, the deeper is the record written and the easier it is to read the story of man's stewardship of the earth, whether it be wasteful exploitation or use with conservation of the resource. One finds successful adjustments of populations to the land in remarkable terracing and reclamation works, as well as tragedies of land misuse, in gullied fields and alluvial plains, in rocky hills and mountain slopes washed bare of soils, in shifting soils and sands, in silted-up and abandoned irrigation reservoirs and canals, in ruins of great and prosperous cities and in ruins of olive presses and cisterns in desertlike landscapes. The effects of land use through the centuries are cumulative.

In the United States of America, we have in a comparatively short period written far and wide on the face of our country a story of wasteful exploitation and reckless use of abundant natural resources. We have grown wealthy by an economy of exploitation. The time has come with the occupation of all lands of the earth to change to an economy of conservation. It is of timely interest to the New World to read the story of land use as it has been written in the lands of the Old World, that we may profit by the experience of the past in its failures as well as its successes.

Western civilization had its beginning in the Near East in the alluvial plains of the Nile Valley and of Mesopotamia. Early tillers of soil by irrigation and by selection of food plants produced more food than they themselves required. Surplus food supplies released other members of early societies to engage in useful activities other than food production. Division of labor thus began and increased the command over nature and progress in civilization.

From these far-away lands of the Near East, western civilization has moved westward, until now its vanguard has reached the gleaming billows of the Pacific Ocean that wash the western sands of the Americas. For the first time in the history of the human race there are no more continents to discover, to colonize, and to exploit. The frontiers of new lands are gone forever. The nations of the Americas occupy the last frontier of western civilization.

A survey of land use throughout this westward march of civilization discloses successes and failures in the long use of land. The object of this survey was to profit by failures and achievements of

Extracted from *Proceedings of the Eighth American Scientific Congress,* Washington D.C., May, 1940. Vol. 5, Agriculture and Conservation, pp. 45–59. Published by Department of State, Washington, D.C., 1942.

the Old World in our national movement for the conservation of land. This survey covered 28,000 miles of overland travel by automobile from humid England to the margins of the deserts of Sahara and Arabia. Studies were made in consultation with fully a hundred specialists in 124 areas of special interest within 14 countries and dependencies in a period of 15 months of field work.

No attempt is made in this brief paper to account for the destruction or conservation of lands on economic grounds. To profit by the experience of the past it is important to know what has happened to the land after centuries and thousands of years of use. Complexity of causes cannot hide the menace to national welfare in soil erosion and the necessity for setting up national objectives to conserve basic resources of soils and waters in the land. Means of achieving the objectives of conservation will vary in accordance with the genius of peoples and their institutions. Soil erosion, if not controlled, has demonstrated its ability to undermine nations and civilizations regardless of what may have been the social or economic conditions that set it going or stimulated its destructiveness.

The land of special areas was examined for evidences—in changes of the original soil profiles insofar as they could be reconstructed; in the shifting of soils from slopes by erosion; and in the accumulation of sediments on valley floors and plains; in the shifting of sand dunes; in the cutting out of alluvial plains with deep gullies; in the filling of stream channels with erosional debris producing marshy conditions; and in ruins of agricultural works for the control and conservation of waters for domestic and irrigation use; as well as evidences of changes or stability of climate. Furthermore, the fate of the physical body of the soil resource was given more attention in the survey than problems of fertility maintenance. For if the soil is maintained in place, liberty of action in use is assured to succeeding tillers of the soil, in applying more or less fertilizer, in growing this or that crop; but if the soil itself is destroyed, the present and succeeding generations are deprived of their basic heritage.

Throughout this broad expanse of land it became plain that the fate of land under use has been most influenced by slope. The hazard of soil erosion is low on flat lands, but it is critical on sloping lands. Flat lands have their problems, it is true, in the rise of water tables and in the accumulation of salts, but drainage is usually sufficient. Other problems occur in the formation of sand dunes, for which fixation with vegetation is the solution. But the tiller of soil has met his greatest problem throughout the ages in maintaining cultivation on sloping lands. We found failures and successes throughout this broad expanse of land.

Ancient Phoenicia and Slope Farming

The Near East is believed by archeologists to be the scene of the beginnings of agriculture which made the growth of western civilization possible (10).[1] It is probable that irrigated agriculture preceded rain agriculture. The flat lands of the Nile Valley and Mesopotamia were irrigated before the slopes of ancient Phoenicia were cleared and cultivated. It is probable also that it was on the slopes of the originally forest-clad mountains of ancient Phoenicia that rain agriculture first began, and at the same time the tiller of soil of our western civilization first encountered the hazards of slope cultivation and of soil erosion. It is also probable that the tillers of soil first controlled erosion here with rock walls to terrace sloping lands.

About 5,300 years ago, the Phoenicians migrated from the desert and settled along the eastern shore of the Mediterranean Sea, establishing the harbor towns of Tyre and Sidon, Beyrouth and Byblos. They found their land mountainous, rising to a crest of 10,000 feet and heavily covered with forests, the greatest extent of which were the forests of the famous cedars of Lebanon. These forests became the timber supply for the treeless alluvial plains of the Nile and of Mesopotamia. This conclusion is inferred from inscriptions such as one on the Temple of Karnak, Egypt, placed at 2840 B.C., which announces the arrival in Egypt of 40 ships laden with timber of the cedars of Lebanon (2). Inscriptions found in excavations of Nineveh and of ancient Babylon refer to the use of "huge cedars from Mount Lebanon" in the construction of buildings (8).

1. Numbers in parentheses refer to literature cited.

In this mountainous land rising boldly out of the sea there was little flat land along the coast. The growing population doubtless soon exceeded the carrying capacity of these restricted flat lands and was faced with the alternatives of shipbuilding, trade, founding colonies, and the cultivation of slopes. As these slopes were cleared of forests and cultivated, they were subject to soil erosion under heavy winter rains, then as they would be now. The great area of terrace walls in various states of repair indicate that the ancient Phoenician slope farmer sought to retard or control erosion with rock walls across the slope, 40 or possibly 50 centuries ago.

The famous forests of the cedars of Lebanon, which are associated with the rise of civilization in the alluvial plains of the Near East, retreated before the ax and the hoe until today only a few remnants of the original forest of about 1,000 square miles are left. The best known relic is the Tripoli grove of cedars, consisting of about 400 trees, saved from vandalism by a church and from goat grazing by a stone wall. Restocking of this grove within the protection of a stone wall against grazing signifies that under present climatic conditions the forest would spread and grow where soil enough has escaped the ravages of erosion. The disappearance of these famous forests is symbolic of the decline and deterioration of the resources of the country.

Today one may find on the mountains of ancient Phoenicia bare limestone slopes strewn with remnants of former terrace walls, showing that the battle with soil erosion sometimes was a losing fight (11); elsewhere one may find terraces that have been maintained for several thousand years (figure 1). Such astounding achievements demonstrate that when the physical body of the soil resource is maintained, it may be cultivated and made productive for thousands of years. Its yield in crops then depends upon its treatment.

The cost in human labor to level terrace slopes of 50 to 75 percent as were found in Beit-Eddine, Lebanon, works out at modern wage scales at 2,000 to 4,000 United States dollars per acre. Such costs are not justified when other lands are available; moreover these costs represent what may and sometimes must be paid in an economy of survival. Such remarkable works demonstrate to what lengths a people will go to survive, as well as the necessity of maintaining the soil resources to support a population. Such examples warn us to find ways of saving good lands before necessity drives a people to such extremes in costs of human effort.

FIGURE 1. Not far from Beyrouth is a valley where we found the climax in adjustment of permanent agriculture to steep, sloping lands. September 1939.

A "Hundred Dead Cities"

Syria holds some of the grandest ruins to be found in the ancient world, such as Baalbek and Jerash. But to a soil conservationist the most striking ruins are found in the graveyard of a "hundred dead cities." An area of about a million acres in North Syria lying between Aleppo, Antioch, and Hama exhibits soil erosion at its worst. Here are ruins of villages, market towns resting on the skeleton rock of limestone hills, from which 3 to 6 feet of soil have been swept off. Evidence of the depth of soil eroded from these slopes is found in doorsills of stone houses now 3 to 6 feet above the bare rock.

Here soil erosion has done its worst and spread a ghastly destruction over a formerly prosperous landscape, as judged by the ruins of splendid houses in villages and in cities, such as El Bare, which we examined in the summer of 1939. In reality, these cities are dead, with no hope of resurrection; for the basis of their prosperity is gone. These cities have not been buried, but have been left high and stark by the removal of soil through the irreversible process of erosion. The good earth of terra rossa soils is completely gone from the slopes except in patches where it is held back by walls of ruined buildings or in pockets in the limestone. In these patches a few vines and olive trees stand as sad remnants of a former profitable use of land, which provided exports of olive oil and wine to Rome during the empire. Seminomads now inhabit repaired ruins in a few of the former cities.

Today, after 13 centuries of neglect, of terraces overrun by herds and patch cultivation of grain by seminomadic descendants of the invaders, soil erosion has completed the destruction of the good earth with a thoroughness that has left this formerly productive land a man-made desert, generally void of vegetation, water, and soil. The cities could be made habitable again, but they will remain dead forever, because their soils are gone beyond hope of restoration. Here the "unpardonable sin" of land use has been committed.

The "Promised Land" of Palestine

When Moses stood on Mount Nebo and looked across the Jordan to the "Promised Land" about 3,000 years ago, he described the land to his followers as a "land of brooks of water, of fountains and depths that spring out of valleys and hills; a land of wheat, and barley, and vines, and fig-trees and pomegranates; a land of oil-olive, and honey; a land wherein thou shalt eat bread without scarceness, thou shalt not lack anything in it; a land whose stones are iron, and out of whose hills thou mayest dig brass" (1). The "Promised Land," as it is today, is a sad commentary on man's stewardship of the earth.

The "Promised Land" which 3,000 years ago was "flowing with milk and honey" has been so devastated by soil erosion that the soils have been swept off fully half the area of the hill lands. The soils have been washed off the hills into the valleys, where they are sorted: the finer particles are swept out in flood waters to change the beautiful blue of the Mediterranean to a dirty brown as far as the horizon; the coarser particles are spread out on former alluvium where they are still cultivated but in a progressively reduced area. Acceleration run-off from barren slopes continues to cut gullies through the alluvial valleys and to carry erosional debris out to choke up the channels of streams flowing through the coastal plains.

In times past, such erosional debris together with sand dunes blown in from the coast created marshes in the plains; then malaria came in, practically depopulating the lowlands. The hills also have been greatly depopulated as shown by the studies of Dr. Guy (5). A survey of ancient village sites abandoned and now occupied discloses how the hill lands of Palestine have been depopulated since the seventh century. The watershed of Wadi Musrara of 312 square miles draining the western slope from Jerusalem to Tel-Aviv was divided into three altitudinal zones: (1) the plain, 0–100 meters; (2) the foothills, 100–300 meters; (3) the hills, 300 meters and over. In the plains outside marshy areas, 32 sites are now occupied and 4 abandoned; in the foothills, 31 occupied and 65 abandoned; and in the hills, 37 occupied and 127 abandoned. The break-down of ancient terrace walls and the erosion of soils to bedrock on the upper slopes is sufficient reason to account for the reduction in population. Erosion in the hills as well as marshes with malaria in the coastal plain has been sufficient to reduce the population of the "Promised Land" to one-third of the Roman and Byzantine period.

Palestine can never be restored to its original condition as the "Promised Land"; it can be much improved over its present condition as the splendid works of the Jewish colonies on 5 percent of the total area have demonstrated, but the lands have been so devastated by the irreversible process of soil erosion in the uplands that they can never be restored to their original productivity as the "Promised Land"—it is too late. This case brings home the tremendous lesson that sloping lands may be damaged beyond full restoration; that unless suitable measures are taken in time, land resources are reduced in the face of increasing populations with their augmented demands.

Roman Africa

North Africa bristles with astounding ruins of opulent and populous cities and thousands of villages and works of the Roman epoch (figure 2). A century or more after the destruction of Carthage by Scipio in 146 B.C. Rome began to colonize North Africa and in the course of time established several important and stately cities at the sites now known as Timgad, Sbeitla, Tebessa, Jemila, El Jem, and Lambesis. These cities were established at crossroads and along the southern edge of the great agricultural region, devoted principally to the growing of grain and olives.

FIGURE 2. The market square in the excavated Roman city of Jemila, where once were sold products of the surrounding lands. The denuded erosion-gullied slopes bear mute evidence of this wreckage and soil losses. January 1939.

The Roman city of Thamugadi, at the site called Timgad in Algeria, was one of the more famous centers of Roman power and culture. It was established by Emperor Trajan about A.D. 100 and was laid out in symmetrical pattern, equipped with a magnificent forum embellished with statuary and carved porticoes, with a public library, with 17 Roman baths adorned with beautiful mosaic floors, with a theater to seat some 2,500 and with marble flush latrines. Timgad was a stately city supported by extensive grain fields in the valley plains and olive orchards on the hills.

After the weakening of the Roman power by the Vandal invasion in A.D. 430 the Berbers captured the city, and after the Arab invasion of the seventh century it was lost to knowledge for 1,200 years, buried by dust, the product of wind erosion. Only a few columns and a portion of Trajan's arch stood above undulating mounds as tombstones to indicate that once a great city was here. There is no counterpart today of the magnificence of this ancient city. A wretched village of mud-wall houses sheltering a few hundred inhabitants is the only descendant of this center of Roman power and culture. Water erosion as well as wind erosion has been at work on the landscape. Gullies have cut through portions of the city and have exposed the aqueduct which supplied the city with water from a great spring some 3 miles away.

Ruins of the land are as impressive as the ruins of cities. The hills have been swept bare of soil, a story which may be read throughout the region. The original soil mantle is being washed off the slopes, often showing that the upper edge of the soil mantle is being gradually worked down slope by accelerated run-off from the bared upper slopes. Erosional debris has been deposited on the lower slopes and valley plain. Torrential storm waters cut great gullies into the alluvial plains. Water tables are lowered and rain waters quickly flow off the land leaving it dry and thirsty. The effects of desiccation of the land are brought about even if rainfall has not diminished.

Out toward the Sahara, 70 miles south of Tebessa, were found ruins of remarkable works for conserving and spreading storm run-off. Check dams were constructed to divert storm waters around the slopes and to spread them on a series of terraces, dating back to Roman or pre-Roman times. Why these terraces were constructed is not yet known. At any rate the French Government is rebuilding the works and is spreading storm waters out on these terraces to increase forage growth for the herds of the Arab nomads. These works of water conservation out so near the Sahara Desert might indicate that climate has changed or that all good lands were intensively utilized during the Roman epoch. All North Africa, as indicated by such a vast display of ruins and works in the midst of a sparsely settled and depressing land, must have had an agriculture of remarkable refinement in measures of soil and water conservation.

The striking contrast between the prosperous and populous condition of North Africa in Roman times and present decadence led early students to believe that an adverse change of climate was responsible for the decline of the granary of Rome. But the researches of Gsell (4), Gautier (3) and Leschi (7) discount an adverse change in climate since Roman times (6 and 9). The most telling evidence of unchanged climate in the past 2,000 years is the successful plantation of olive groves on the sites of ruins of Roman stone olive presses. An experimental grove planted at Timgad demonstrates that olive orchards would thrive today where soil still remains on slopes. Moreover, in the vicinity of Sousse, Tunisia, there are a few Roman olive orchards which escaped the destructive invasions of the seventh century and survive to the present day. No pulsations of climate have been sufficiently adverse to kill off this remnant of the agriculture of Roman times.

Such are some instances of the decline in the usefulness of the land due to the wastage of erosion and quickened run-off of storm waters, by the break-down of measures arrived at by long and slow experience of trial and error. The wisdom of the ages was nullified in a brief time, breaking into fragments the glories of the past.

The Insidious Nature of Erosion

Our studies in lands long occupied by man dislcose that soil erosion, i.e., man-induced erosion as distinguished from normal geologic erosion, is an insidious process that has destroyed lands and undermined progress of civilization and cultures. Achievements in the control of soil erosion and in adjustments of a lasting agriculture to sloping lands are steps in the march of civilization as momentous as the discovery of fire and the selection of food plants.

Solutions to problems of population pressure have too often in the past been sought in the conquest and destruction of the works of peoples rather than in conservation and improving the potential productivity of the earth, with provision for exchange of specialty products. The formula of exploitation and destruction has interrupted the orderly solutions to land-use problems in the past and has unleashed the forces of erosion to spread like the tentacles of an octopus through lands of North China, North Africa, Asia Minor, and the Holy Lands, as well as in the United States and other countries of the New World.

One generation of people replaces another, but productive soils destroyed by erosion are seldom restorable and never replaceable. Conservation of the basic soil resource becomes more than a matter of individual interest; it becomes a matter of national interest necessary to the continuing welfare of a people. The day is gone when lands may be worn out with the expectation of finding new lands to the west. The economy of exploitation must give place to an economy of conservation if a people will survive into the unknown future. Peace among nations must rest upon such a policy.

In the face of the limited area now available to the human race, the realization that enormous areas of land are still being destroyed by inconsiderate and wasteful methods must arouse thinking people to action. If man is making deserts out of productive lands, it is a matter not only of national, but of world-wide concern.

If Moses had foreseen how soil erosion induced by inconsiderate use of land would devastate the "Promised Land," as well as vast areas of the earth, resulting in man-made deserts and decadence of civilization; if he had foreseen the impoverishment, revolution, wars, migrations, and social decadence of billions of people throughout thousands of years because of the exploitation and desolation of their lands by erosion, he doubtless would have been inspired to deliver an Eleventh Commandment to complete the trinity of man's responsibilities—to his Creator, to his fellow men, and to Mother Earth. Such a Commandment should read somewhat as follows:

> Thou shalt inherit the holy earth as a faithful steward, conserving its resources and productivity from generation to generation. Thou shalt safeguard thy fields from soil erosion, thy living waters from drying up, thy forests from desolation, and protect thy hills from overgrazing by thy herds, that thy descendants may have abundance forever. If any shall fail in this stewardship of the land thy fruitful fields shall become sterile stony ground or wasting gullies and thy descendants shall decrease and live in poverty or perish from off the face of the earth.

Hitherto, mankind in its conquest of the land, except in very limited areas, has not been governed by such an injunction; on the contrary, mankind has been impelled by an economy of exploitation, looking to the discovery of new lands or new sources of food and materials as needs arise. The lands of the world are occupied and such a policy leads inevitably to conflict.

LITERATURE CITED

1. Bible. Deuteronomy VIII, 7–9.
2. Breasted, James H. 1906. Ancient records of Egypt, vol. 1, p. 146. Chicago.
3. Gautier, E. F. 1935. Sahara, the great desert, pp. 95–99. Translated by D. F. Mayhew. New York.
4. Gsell, Stephane. 1913. Histoire ancienne de l'Afrique du Nord, vol. 1. Paris.
5. Guy, P. L. O. Unpublished notes.
6. Knight, M. M. 1928. Water and the course of empire in North Africa. Quart. Journ. Econ., vol. 43. pp. 44–93, November.
7. Leschi. Unpublished reports.
8. Luckenbill, Daniel D. 1927. Ancient records of Assyria and Babylonia, vol. 1, pp. 98, 194 f. Chicago.
9. Martonne, Emmanuel de. 1930. La degradation de l'hydrographic. Scientia, vol. 47, pp. 9–20, January. (See p. 19.)
10. Peake, Harold J. 1933. Early steps in human progress. Philadelphia.
11. Thoumin, R. L. 1936. Geographic humaine de la Syrie Centrale, p. 125. Paris.

Geologic Hazards in
the Urban Environment

Oakeshott (1970) summarized the interaction of geologic hazards and people by saying "There are no geologic hazards without people; the 'hazards' arise from man's unwise, inept, and careless occupation and use or abuse of the geologic environment." Almost any geologic process, such as floods, landslides, subsidence, earthquakes, volcanic eruptions, tsunamis, sedimentation, and glacier bursts, can become a hazardous situation.

Naturally occurring geologic hazards have destroyed property and caused many deaths. The 1902 eruption of Mt. Pelée, which killed 30,000 and destroyed the city of St. Pierre, is just one example. Earthquakes in China between the 11th and 20th centuries have killed more than 2 million people. Few lives have been lost in earthquakes in North America, but property losses have been high. Few people (114) were killed in the 1964 Alaskan earthquake; 64 were killed in the 1971 San Fernando earthquake. Greater loss of life and property is expected from this natural hazard in the future in spite of precautionary measures that can and are being taken.

Geologic hazards can also be induced by human activity. This type of hazard may include: land subsidence caused by withdrawal of ground water or petroleum, landslides and slumping resulting from highway construction, and earthquakes from ground water injection.

Both naturally occurring and induced geologic hazards are normal geologic processes or events until humans get in the way; it is then that the processes become hazards. Earthquakes are hazards when we live too close to the active fault area, volcanic eruptions are hazards when we live in close proximity to the volcano, and floods become hazards when we inhabit the floodplain.

What can geologists do about geologic hazards? Working with adequate geologic knowledge they can conduct investigations that can be used to prevent a geologic hazard from becoming a disaster. Once actual or potential geologic hazards have been clearly indentified and defined, several approaches to solving the problem, varying with the type of hazard, may be tried. One solution often necessary in the case of naturally occurring hazards is to avoid the problem by changing the proposed location of the reservoir, nuclear power plant, highway, house, or other structure. Another alternative is to eliminate the hazard, by, for example, removing the unstable soil or by diverting the river. Structures may also be engineered to withstand the hazards by careful design to eliminate earthquake effects, by floodproofing, or by placing pilings through unstable soil. Normally, the elimination and design approaches are more costly than avoiding the problem.

The urgency to avoid or prevent geologic hazards is an outgrowth of a society characterized by increasing population and urbanization. Although disasters caused by geologic hazards cannot be eliminated completely, they can be greatly reduced through understanding the geologic aspects of the environment. However, current solutions may not continue to be effective in reducing disasters if present population trends persist. Competition for "choice" space on floodplains or "attractive" building sites in rugged hillside areas above seashore cliffs will place demands on geologists to develop new solutions to problems which we may not presently foresee.

Articles in this section describe several of the more common geologic hazards and contain suggestions for their possible solutions.

REFERENCE

Oakeshott, G. B. 1970. Controlling the geologic environment for human welfare. *Journal of Geologic Education* 18:193.

5

Hydrology for Urban Land Planning

Luna B. Leopold

Of particular concern to the planner are those alternatives that affect the hydrologic functioning of the basins. To be interpreted hydrologically, the details of the land-use pattern must be expressed in terms of hydrologic parameters which are affected by land use. These parameters in turn become hydrologic variables by which the effects of alternative planning patterns can be evaluated in hydrologic terms.

There are four interrelated but separable effects of land-use changes on the hydrology of an area: changes in peak flow characteristics, changes in total runoff, changes in quality of water, and changes in the hydrologic amenities. The hydrologic amenities are what might be called the appearance or the impression which the river, its channel and its valleys, leaves with the observer. Of all land-use changes affecting the hydrology of an area, urbanization is by far the most forceful.

Runoff, which spans the entire regimen of flow, can be measured by number and by characteristics of rise in streamflow. The many rises in flow, along with concomitant sediment loads, controls the stability of the stream channel. The two principal factors governing flow regimen are the percentage of area made impervious and the rate at which water is transmitted across the land to stream channels. The former is governed by the type of land use; the latter is governed by the density, size, and characteristics of tributary channels and thus by the provision of storm sewerage. Stream channels form in response to the regimen of flow of the stream. Changes in the regimen of flow, whether through land use or other changes, cause adjustments in the stream channels to accommodate the flows.

The volume of runoff is governed primarily by infiltration characteristics and is related to land slope and soil type as well as to the type of vegetative cover. It is thus directly related to the percentage of the area covered by roofs, streets, and other impervious surfaces at times of hydrograph rise during storms.

A summary of some data on the percentage of land rendered impervious by different degrees of urbanization is presented by Lull and Sopper (1966). Antoine (1964) presents the following data on the percentage of impervious surface area in residential properties:

Extracted from *U.S. Geological Survey Circular 554*, 1968, 18 pp.

Lot Size of Residential Area (Sq Ft)	Impervious Surface Area (Percent)
6000	80
6000–15,000	40
15,000	25

The percentage decreases markedly as size of lot increases. Felton and Lull (1963) estimate in the Philadelphia area that 32 percent of the surface area is impervious on lots averaging 0.2 acre in size, whereas only 8 percent of the surface area is impervious on lots averaging 1.8 acres.

As volume of runoff from a storm increases, the size of flood peak also increases. Runoff volume also affects low flows because in any series of storms the larger the percentage of direct runoff, the smaller the amount of water available for soil moisture replenishment and for ground-water storage. An increase in total runoff from a given series of storms as a result of imperviousness results in decreased ground-water recharge and decreased low flows. Thus, increased imperviousness has the effect of increasing flood peaks during storm periods and decreasing low flows between storms.

The principal effect of land use on sediment comes from the exposure of the soil to storm runoff. This occurs mainly when bare ground is exposed during construction. It is well known that sediment production is sensitive to land slope. Sediment yield from urban areas tends to be larger than in unurbanized areas even if there are only small and widely scattered units of unprotected soil in the urban area. In aggregate, these scattered bare areas are sufficient to yield considerable sediment.

A major effect of urbanization is the introduction of effluent from sewage disposal plants, and often the introduction of raw sewage, into channels. Raw sewage obviously degrades water quality, but even treated effluent contains dissolved minerals not extracted by sewage treatment. These minerals act as nutrients and promote algae and plankton growth in a stream. This growth in turn alters the balance in the stream biota.

Land use in all forms affects water quality. Agricultural use results in an increase of nutrients in stream water both from the excretion products of farm animals and from commercial fertilizers. A change from agricultural use to residential use, as in urbanization, tends to reduce these types of nutrients, but this tendency is counteracted by the widely scattered pollutants of the city, such as oil and gasoline products, which are carried through the storm sewers to the streams. The net result is generally an adverse effect on water quality. This effect can be measured by the balance and variety of organic life in the stream, by the quantities of dissolved material, and by the bacterial level. Unfortunately data describing quality factors in streams from urban versus unurbanized areas are particularly lacking.

Finally, the amenity value of the hydrologic environment is especially affected by three factors. The first factor is the stability of the stream channel itself. A channel, which is gradually enlarged owing to increased floods caused by urbanization, tends to have unstable and unvegetated banks, scoured or muddy channel beds, and unusual debris accumulations. These all tend to decrease the amenity value of a stream.

The second factor is the accumulation of artifacts of civilization in the channel and on the flood plain: beer cans, oil drums, bits of lumber, concrete, wire—the whole gamut of rubbish of an urban area. Though this may not importantly affect the hydrologic function of the channel, it becomes a detriment of what is here called the hydrologic amenity.

The third factor is the change brought on by the disruption of balance in the stream biota. The addition of nutrients promotes the growth of plankton and algae. A clear stream, then, may change to one in which rocks are covered with slime; turbidity usually increases and odors may develop. As a result of increased turbidity and reduced oxygen content desirable game fish give way to less desirable species. Although lack of quantitative objective data on the balance of stream biota is often a handicap to any meaningful and complete evaluation of the effects of urbanization, qualitative observations tend to confirm these conclusions.

REFERENCES

Antoine, L. H. 1964. Drainage and best use of urban land. *Public Works* (New York) 95:88–90.
Felton, P. N., and Lull, H. W. 1963. Suburban hydrology can improve watershed conditions. *Public Works* 94:93–94.
Lull, H. W., and Sopper, W. E. 1966. *Hydrologic effects from urbanization of forested watersheds in the northeast.* Upper Darby, Pa.: Northeastern Forest Experimental Station.

Extent and Development of Urban Flood Plains

6

William J. Schneider and James E. Goddard

"A flood is when the water gets up to your pocketbook."

Flood plains—the natural overflow channels of rivers, streams, oceans, and other bodies of water —have always attracted man. The rich fertile soils deposited by the floodwaters have sustained an abundant agriculture. The water supplied his needs and carried away his wastes, and the rivers and oceans served as his main artery of transportation long before the railroad or the highway linked the urban centers.

The general and predictable pattern of urban growth has been one of settlement on the flood plain, followed by expansion onto higher ground to the foothills or mountains or less desirable hinterlands. The major cities of the United States, indeed of the world, have followed this pattern. Each also, to one degree or another, has paid the penalty of flooding as complacency or ignorance or sheer gambling has exposed inhabitants to floodwaters. It has been said that "Nature has a preemptive right to the flood plain," but when Nature does not exercise that right for 20 to 50 years, man too often has become complacent, careless, or a holder of short odds.

The fact is that much of our urban areas occupy flood plains. But how much? And how much has been developed? Answers to these questions are being sought to place better perspective on the problems involved in the national goal of effective flood-plain management.

Objectives and Scope

The objective of this study is to evaluate both the amount of flood plain in urban areas and the degree of development of these flood plains.

This report contains data on areal extent and degree of occupancy of flood plains in the urbanized areas of 26 cities (figure 1). Of these, data were supplied for 16 cities by the U.S. Geological Survey, for 1 city by the Tennessee Valley Authority, and for 9 cities by the American Society of Civil Engineers who used basic data provided by the U.S. Army Corps of Engineers. These cities represent a statistical sampling based upon variations in physiography, topography, climate, population, river size, and political entity. They were selected to represent:

Varying populations (50,000 to 7 million)

Varying types of architecture

Extracted with permission of the senior author from *U.S. Geological Survey Circular 601-J*, 1974, 14 pp.

Varying lifestyles
Total population of 20.3 million
10 percent of total U.S. population
Inland, coastal, and estuarine conditions
All major physiographic regions
28 of the 50 states
15 of the 20 major water-resources regions
28 of the 47 U.S. Geological Survey Districts
21 of the 38 U.S. Army Corps of Engineers Districts
TVA in the Tennessee Valley

Approach

For each sample city the general approach for this study was to determine the areal extent of the urban area, to delineate and measure the area of the flood plains within each urban area, and to determine and measure the present extent of usage of the areas of those flood plains.

Defining the Urban Area

The UA (urbanized area) as defined by the U.S. Bureau of Census for the 1970 census was used for this study. An urbanized area consists of a central city or cities and surrounding closely settled territory. The specific criteria for the delineation are as follows:

1. City areas.
   a. A central city of 50,000 inhabitants or more in 1960, in a special census conducted by the Census Bureau since 1960, or in the 1970 census; or

FIGURE 1. Map showing location of cities used in this study. Population given is defined as that of urbanized area.

b. Twin cities, that is, cities with contiguous boundaries and constituting, for general social and economic purposes, a single community with a combined population of at least 50,000, and with the smaller of the twin cities having a population of at least 15,000.
2. Surrounding closely settled territory, including the following (but excluding the rural portions of extended cities):
   a. Incorporated places of 2,500 inhabitants or more.
   b. Incorporated places with fewer than 2,500 inhabitants, provided that each has a closely settled area of 100 housing units or more.
   c. Small parcels of land normally less than 1 square mile in area having a population density of 1,000 inhabitants or more per square mile. The areas of large nonresidential tracts devoted to such urban land uses as railroad yards, airports, factories, parks, golf courses, and cemeteries are excluded in computing the population density.
   d. Other similar areas in unincorporated territory with lower population density provided that they serve:
      to eliminate enclaves, or
      to close indentations in the urbanized areas of 1 mile or less across the open end, or
      to link outlying enumeration districts of qualifying density that are not more than 1½ miles from the main body of the urbanized area.

The urbanized areas based on the above criteria were chosen for several reasons. Primarily, the urbanized area is exactly what its name implies: it is urbanized. It does not include large farmland, open land, or sparsely populated expanses under private or public control that are a major part of political or other "areas" selected for statistical purposes, therefore, its use more accurately reflects the percentage of flood plain in urban areas. Furthermore, the urbanized area is a unit for which the Bureau of Census publishes demographic statistics of widely varying types, thus facilitating comparisons of the flood-plain data with other statistics. Finally, the use of the urbanized area provides homogeneity in occupancy characteristics of the selected urban areas.

Defining the Flood Plain

The flood plain as defined for this study is that area which would be inundated by the natural 100-year flood (the flood level that, on an average, is exceeded once in 100 years).

It should be recognized, however, that there is great variance and freedom in the usage of the term "flood plain" that leads to frequent misunderstandings. The geologic definition of a flood plain is the relatively flat area or low lands adjoining the channel of a river, stream, or watercourse or along an ocean, lake, or other body of standing water, which has been or may be covered by floodwater. However, large parts of geologic flood plains may seldom be flooded or may be insufficiently defined to describe the flood potential. For that reason the current concept of flood-plain management generally recognizes the engineering-type definition of areas subject to specific probabilities of flooding.

Data on the 100-year flood are available from several sources. The Corps of Engineers' flood-plain information reports provide information for their SPF (standard project flood) and for the IRF (intermediate regional flood) which is approximately equivalent to the 100-year flood. The TVA local flood reports provide information for floods generally equivalent to the SPF and the IRF. The U.S. Geological Survey flood-prone area maps show the areas that are subject to flooding by the 100-year flood, and their hydrologic atlas maps show areas inundated by one or more large historic floods with information to generally relate the data to 50-year or 100-year flood. The FIA (Federal Flood Insurance Administration) "Flood Information and Floodway" maps show the areas inundated by the 100-year and 500-year floods plus a basic floodway. FIA flood-insurance studies also include a rate map intended primarily for use by insurance agents to calculate rates. The rate map shows areas inundated by the 100-year and 500-year floods extended to identifible physical features. FIA studies made prior to 1974 often contain only the rate map. The "Flood Hazard Evaluation Guidelines for Federal Executive Agencies," issued by the Federal Water Resources Council in 1972, uses the 100-year flood as one of its major criteria. Hundreds of local communities and cities and counties have adopted flood-plain regulations and some states have established programs designed around the 100-year flood or its equivalent.

Upstream regulating reservoirs, channel improvements, levees, walls, and similar structures have reduced flood hazards at many sites and changed the heights of the 100-year flood. Many of the areas that have been protected in this manner are now developed—some of them prior to the flood-control works and others after their construction.

The purpose of this study was to learn the extent of the flood plain and its relation and (or) effect on urban development; thus, to be consistent with generally accepted practices and programs of other agencies, the term "flood plain" in this study refers to the area, except the channel that will be inundated by a 100-year flood, without consideration of present or future flood-control storage, channel modifications, levees, or other works that may reduce flood levels.

Data for both natural and regulated conditions were obtained for three urban areas. These provide an indication of the relations and effect of flood plains or urban development at those sites.

Defining the Flood Plain Development

The flood plains were classified as "undeveloped" or "developed," and the developed part was measured.

"Developed" flood plains were defined as those flood plains where:

1. More than one-third of the acreage, whether continuous or interspersed, is actively used for residential, commercial, or industrial purposes; or
2. Plans exist for development to a degree outlined in (1) and there is assurance that the development will be accomplished soon; or
3. State or local planning and (or) development agencies have classified the land as being developed; or
4. The Corps of Engineers has classified them as being "built-up" and measured for its Civil Works Information System records.

The Data

The data measured and compiled for this study are given in tables 1 and 2.

Table 1 gives the area and population of the selected urbanized areas. Data are from the U.S. Bureau of Census for 1970 except for Asheville and Texarkana. For Asheville, the Bureau limits were used but new measurements were made of the area. Readily available flood-plain data from the Corps of Engineers for Texarkana included recent expansions of the corporate boundaries.

Table 2 gives the urban flood-plain areas and parts thereof which have been developed. The areas shown are for the 100-year flood under natural or unregulated conditions.

In some areas, local flood-protection works and upstream regulation provide some degree of flood protection, often considerably reducing the areas susceptible to flooding. Measurements were made for both natural and regulated conditions at three urbanized areas. At Omaha-Council Bluffs, for example, structural flood-control measures have reduced the area susceptible to flooding by the 100-year flood from 50.6 square miles to 23.2 square miles with only 8.3 square miles developed. At Monroe, flood-control measures have reduced the flood-plain area from 32.5 to 3.5 square miles with only 0.9 square miles developed; and at St. Louis, from 136.1 to 45.9 square miles with only 7.4 square miles developed.

Analyses of the Data

There is an extremely wide variation in the extent of flood plains in urbanized areas. For the 26 urbanized areas selected for this study, the percent of area in flood plain ranges from 2.4 percent for

TABLE 1. AREA AND POPULATION OF SELECTED URBANIZED AREAS

Urbanized areas	Population (1000's)	Land area (sq.mi.)	Population density (1,000/sq.mi.)
Asheville, NC	72.5	38.2	1.90
Boise, ID	85.2	29.4	2.90
Boston, MA	2,652.6	664.4	3.90
Charleston, SC	228.4	99.2	2.30
Chicago, IL	6,714.6	1,277.2	5.26
Dallas, TX	1,338.7	674.2	1.99
Denver, CO	1,047.3	292.8	3.58
Fargo—Moorhead, ND–MN	85.5	23.5	3.64
Great Falls, MT	70.9	21.8	3.25
Harrisburg, PA	240.8	78.4	3.10
Lansing, MI	229.5	73.4	3.13
Lincoln, NB	153.4	52.1	2.95
Lorain—Elyria, OH	192.3	106.4	1.81
Monroe, LA	90.6	40.1	2.26
Norfolk—Portsmouth, VA	668.3	299.0	2.24
Omaha—Council Bluffs, NB–IA	491.8	151.2	3.25
Phoenix, AZ	863.4	387.5	2.21
Portland, OR	824.9	266.8	3.10
Reno, NV	99.7	37.5	2.66
Richmond, VA	416.6	144.6	2.98
St. Louis, MO–IL	1,882.0	460.6	4.19
Salt Lake City, UT	479.4	184.3	2.60
San Jose, CA	1,025.3	277.2	3.70
Spokane, WA	229.6	77.8	2.95
Tallahassee, FL	77.9	29.8	2.61
Texarkana, TX–AR	58.6	30.8	1.90
Total	20,359.4	5,831.7	

TABLE 2. AREAS OF SELECTED URBAN FLOOD PLAINS

Urbanized area	Flood plain		Developed	
	Area (sq.mi.)	Percent of urbanized area	Area (sq.mi.)	Percent of flood plain total
Asheville, NC	1.6	4.4	1.0	65.0
Boise, ID	2.5	8.5	2.1	84.0
Boston, MA	62.4	9.4	11.9	19.1
Charleston, SC	39.8	40.1	21.2	53.3
Chicago, IL	131.8	10.3	75.1	57.0
Dallas, TX	146.1	21.7	28.0	19.2
Denver, CO	30.6	10.5	19.1	62.2
Fargo—Moorhead, ND–MN	9.4	40.0	5.1	54.3
Great Falls, MT	2.0	9.2	1.9	97.0
Harrisburg, PA	9.7	12.4	8.1	83.5
Lansing, MI	4.8	6.5	.9	18.8
Lincoln, NB	13.8	26.5	6.9	49.6
Lorain—Elyria, OH	5.3	5.0	.6	11.3
Monroe, LA	32.5	81.0	26.8	82.4
Norfolk—Portsmouth, VA	59.2	19.8	15.5	26.2
Omaha—Council Bluffs, NB–IA	50.6	33.5	23.1	45.5
Phoenix, AZ	71.2	18.4	63.5	89.2
Portland, OR	14.5	5.4	8.5	58.7
Reno, NV	2.0	5.3	.9	45.0
Richmond, VA	12.9	8.9	1.7	13.2
St. Louis, MO–IL	136.1	29.6	91.7	67.4
Salt Lake City, UT	12.9	7.0	10.1	78.3
San Jose, CA	80.0	28.8	67.9	84.7
Spokane, WA	1.9	2.4	.9	47.4
Tallahassee, FL	3.1	10.4	2.6	83.9
Texarkana, TX–AR	4.7	13.8	2.1	44.2
Total	941.4		497.2	
Weighted average		16.2		52.8

Spokane, Wash. to 81.0 percent for Monroe, La. It should be noted, however, that the extent of the flood plain in Monroe is exceptional for the areas sampled. The next largest value is less than half of that for Monroe—40.1 percent for Charleston, S.C. The median value is 10.5 percent, and the weighted average is 16.2 percent.

The development of the flood plains in the urbanized areas also varies widely. The least developed of the flood plains of the urbanized areas used in this study is in Lorain-Elyria, Ohio—11.3 percent of the total flood-plain area—and the most highly developed is that of Great Falls, Mont.—97.0 percent developed. The median value is 57.0 percent, and the weighted average is 52.8 percent.

Because of the reconnaissance nature of this study and the original objective of defining solely the extent and occupancy of flood plains in urbanized areas, no attempt was made at collecting detailed supplemental data for analyses. However, readily available data on a few indices related to flooding were developed to provide some preliminary analyses of the data. These attempts are intended more to provoke further study than to provide definitive answers.

Table 3 gives indices of three aspects of flooding (depth of flooding, precipitation, and physiography) for which data were readily available. They have been listed to facilitate some crude analyses. The indices were derived as follows. The index of flooding, to represent possible depth of inundation as a measure of extent of flooding, was computed as the difference (in feet) in elevation of low water and the 100-year flood elevation for the major stream in an urbanized area. Data used for computation were records of the U.S. Geological Survey streamflow-measuring station on the major stream located in or nearest the major downtown area. For regulated streams, the index was computed on the basis of the elevation of the unregulated 100-year flood. The index of precipitation is the average annual precipitation in inches at the principal first-order weather station in the area. The index of elevation is the elevation in feet of the U.S. Weather Service precipitation gage used as the index of precipitation.

Minimal consideration of a few factors or indices indicates there probably is no one factor that explains the inclusion of flood plains in urban areas or the degree of development of those flood plains. However, further studies may develop important relationships for other combinations of factors.

TABLE 3. SELECTED INDICES RELATED TO EXTENT OF FLOOD PLAINS IN SELECTED URBANIZED AREAS

Urbanized area	Index of flooding	Index of precipitation	Index of elevation
Asheville, NC	24	38	2,242
Boise, ID	10	11	2,838
Boston, MA	5	43	15
Charleston, SC	14	37	9
Chicago, IL	19	33	658
Dallas, TX	31	35	481
Denver, CO	12	15	5,332
Fargo—Moorhead, ND–MN	25	18	896
Great Falls, MT	11	14	3,664
Harrisburg, PA	26	38	338
Lansing, MI	16	31	841
Lincoln, NB	25	27	1,150
Lorain—Elyria, OH	21	35	777
Monroe, LA	38	51	78
Norfolk—Portsmouth, VA	8	45	22
Omaha—Council Bluffs, NB–IA	31	28	1,323
Phoenix, AZ	20	7.2	1,117
Portland, OR	30	37	21
Reno, NV	15	7	4,404
Richmond, VA	28	44	164
St. Louis, MO–IL	50	36	555
Salt Lake City, UT	10	14	4,220
San Jose, CA	17	14	95
Spokane, WA	13	17	2,349
Tallahassee, FL	10	57	55
Texarkana, TX–AR	18	48	390

Discussion

The analyses presented in this report must be evaluated in terms of a dichotomic situation. The measurements of the flood plains and their occupancy are precise in terms of the definitions accepted for this study. The flood plains are those of the 100-year flood; the urbanized areas are those defined by the U.S. Bureau of the Census; the occupancy of the flood plains is defined by reasonably precise criteria. These measurements were the primary purpose of this study: to determine through a statistical sampling of the urbanized areas the extent and occupancy of their flood plains. The range of data indicates no consistency in amounts.

At least part of the inconsistency is related to the arbitrary boundaries of the urbanized areas. In many cities, flood-plain areas have been excluded from the urbanized areas because of the particular land-use pattern of the area. Two examples are worth citing.

At St. Louis, considerable flood-plain area lies outside the boundary of the urbanized area but is abutted on one or both sides by the urbanized area. Determining the area of such flood plains is not easy because of the difficulty in associating the plains areas with the urbanized area, but an estimate of 5 square miles of developed flood plain and 60 square miles of undeveloped flood plain is reasonable. Inclusion of this area brings the total flood-plain area to 38 percent instead of 30 percent.

At Portland, major parts of the Columbia River flood plain are not included in the urbanized area. Areas outside the urbanized area include the Portland Air Force Base, the Portland International Airport, and other commercial developments. Although these areas were not determined accurately because of the difficulty in defining limits, as much as 30 square miles of flood plain could be considered in this category. This would triple the proportion of flood plain, increasing the flood plain from 5.4 to 16.7 percent.

It should again be pointed out that the flood plains designated for this study are those for the natural 100-year flood. Flood-protection measures in many areas have reduced the areas susceptible to flooding.

Only limited attempts were made to relate the extent and occupancy of the measured flood plains to associated factors. Again, it must be emphasized that the original scope of the effort—to delineate the flood plains—precluded any major research effort in describing causative factors. The reconnaissance relationships explored here are not intended as definitive attempts, but rather as stimuli to further detailed efforts to understand the natural physiographic setting and the economic social stimuli that control occupancy of flood plains.

REFERENCE

Goddard, J. E. 1974. An evaluation of urban flood plains: Am. Soc. Civil Engineers, Tech. Memo 19, 40 p. (Also available from the Natl. Tech. Inf. Service, U.S. Dept. of Commerce, Springfield, Va. 22151, NTIS PB–227337.)

7

Lessons Learned from the June 9, 1972, Flood in Rapid City, South Dakota

Perry H. Rahn

Introduction

On the evening of June 9, 1972, a strong easterly flow of moist low-level warm air collided with a cold front over the Black Hills. The warm moist air was forced upward, aided by the orographic effect of the Black Hills (Thompson, 1972). A stationary group of thunderstorms developed and as much as 15 inches of rain fell at some locations in less than 6 hours (NOAA, 1972).

The rains caused record-breaking floods on streams draining the eastern slopes of the Black Hills. Some small streams had discharges several times the expected 50 year peak discharge (Orr, 1973). At least 238 people died and 5 bodies have never been recovered. The Corps of Engineers (1972) estimated direct flood damage was $128 million. Most of the death and destruction occurred in Rapid City, South Dakota, where Rapid Creek reached a peak discharge of 50,000 cfs at USGS station #06414000 (Larimer, 1973).

The purpose of this paper is to show the relationship of the flood loss to the location of flood plains in Rapid City, and to document the post-flood changes that have occurred in the flooded areas.

Rapid City

Rapid City takes its name from Rapid Creek, which drains a large part of the Black Hills. The name "Rapid" itself is indicative of the stream's nature. The white water produced in Rapid Creek as it flows across its boulder-cobble channel appears quite different than the meandering sluggish streams of the prairie. When the founding fathers first camped along the banks of Rapid Creek in June, 1876, they were apprehensive that heavy rains could cause it to flood their campsite that night. The early settlers did not build their homes close to the stream.

The population of Rapid City had grown to 43,000 by 1972. After World War II, extensive residential development occurred in the western part of Rapid City. Some of Rapid City's finest homes were built or were being constructed in the wide flood plain in west Rapid City, and in the narrow "Dark Canyon" where Rapid Creek leaves the Black Hills.

Presumably, many people felt that building along the edges of Rapid Creek was safe because of the construction of Pactola Dam and Reservoir, located about 14 miles upstream from Rapid City.

Reprinted with permission of the author and publisher from *Bulletin of the Association of Engineering Geologists* 12(2):83–97, 1975. Copyright © 1975 by Association of Engineering Geologists.

Built by the U.S. Bureau of Reclamation in 1956, Pactola Reservoir provides 43,000 acre-feet of storage space allocated to flood control. The total drainage area of Rapid City above U.S. Geological Survey stream gaging station #06412500 just west of the Cleghorn Springs Fish Hatchery in west Rapid City is 371 square miles, of which 52 square miles are below Pactola Reservoir. Unfortunately, it was precisely on this 52 square miles that the most extensive precipitation fell on June 9, 1972. In this respect, Pactola Dam gave the people of Rapid City a false feeling of security in that Pactola eliminated most small floods, and people were not alerted to the potentially serious flood hazard.

Rapid City Flood

At 9:30 p.m. on June 9 heavy rains prompted the cancellation of the Band Concert in Stevens High School. Television and radio alerts were broadcast, urging people with property adjoining Rapid Creek to leave their homes. A peak discharge of 31,200 cfs was recorded at about 11:00 p.m. at U.S. Geological Survey gaging station #06412500 above Canyon Lake. The dam at the 40 acre Canyon Lake, located in west Rapid City, gave way at about the same time. Survivors report that the nightmare of death and destruction was compounded by fires set off by broken electric wires, broken propane tanks, etc. First hand accounts of the tragedy have been recorded in a historical document by Newlin (1972):

"... We could hear people down off of the street back in the trees screaming for help, and when it would lightning, the lightning was terrible, we could see people hanging in the trees and we could see trailers and automobiles and all kinds of debris floating behind us. ..."

FIGURE 1. Intense destruction at "Braeburn Addition," along Rapid Creek, just west of Rapid City limits. Arrow shows location of house foundation. Rapid Creek is at base of forested slope.

On Saturday morning, June 10, the scene was of utter destruction. I spent the day searching through the mud and debris for dead bodies, along with most of the rest of the dazed citizenry. Figure 1 shows the type of destruction that occurred near gaging station #6412500 where Rapid Creek empties from Dark Canyon. Here, only three weeks previously, I had lectured to my engineering geology class about the folly of construction along Rapid Creek. The flood plain is only about 500 feet wide at this point, but widens to about 3,000 feet in west Rapid City. This location is similar to the apex of an alluvial fan.

In west Rapid City, the destruction was almost as severe. Eyewitnesses reported local surges of water ("walls of water") up to 20 feet high. These were presumably created by alternating formation and breaking of local debris dams (cars, crushed homes, trees, logging slash, etc.). Many people lost their lives in this area as homes collapsed under the force of the water and the impact of a collision with floating debris. Some houses (figure 2), built on concrete slabs, were not bolted to their foundations and simply floated away!

The damage to trailer courts in eastern Rapid City and in adjacent downstream portions of Pennington County was particularly severe. Mobile homes are especially vulnerable to floods, because they easily float away on the rising waters, and pile up and smash to pieces on some downstream obstruction.

The limits of the flooded area were mapped by the South Dakota Remote Sensing Institute (Myers, et al., 1972) and by the U.S. Geological Survey (Larimer, 1973). Figure 3 shows the area inundated on June 9, 1972. This is almost exactly the same area inundated by the 1907 flood according

FIGURE 2. This house floated 5 blocks to this position at intersection of Jane Street and Janet Drive, western Rapid City.

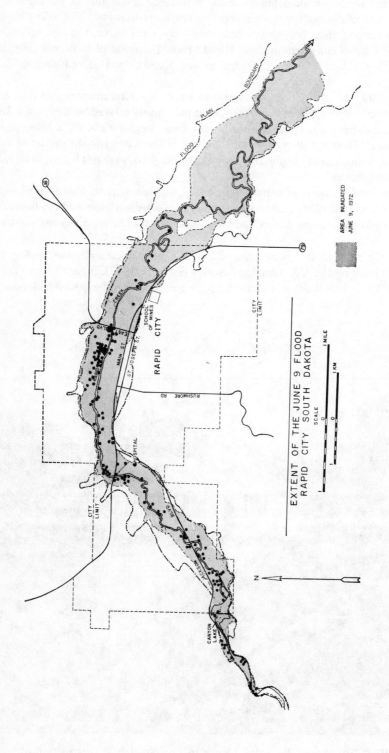

FIGURE 3. Map of Rapid City showing the area inundated by the June 9, 1972, flood (Larimer, 1973) and the area mapped as Quaternary alluvium on U.S. Geological Survey 7½ minute quadrangle maps (Cattermole, 1969, 1972). Black dots show location of bodies recovered after flood.

to unpublished maps in the city engineering office. Figure 3 also shows the location of recovered bodies. Some of the bodies were found in cars, others in houses, many floated downstream. No bodies are known to have floated more than ¼ mile from the point where individuals were last seen or presumably located prior to the flood. Floating bodies seemed to be pushed laterally, out of the main current, and soon became lodged in trees or stationary objects along with other debris.

Rapid Creek Flood Plain

Of particular interest to engineering geologists are 1 : 24,000 scale geologic maps of the Rapid City area. These maps were published before the flood by the U.S. Geologic Survey (Cattermole, 1969, 1972). Figure 3 shows the area mapped as Quaternary alluvium [flood plain] in the Rapid City area. The coincidence between the area inundated and the alluvium (figure 3) is remarkable. The small differences can be accounted for by: (1) man-made features such as railroad fills and houses which diverted flood waters, and (2) Quaternary alluvium along some small tributary streams were not flooded on June 9. Those who understand fluvial processes were not surprised by the area inundated. Floods are natural events, predictable in terms of space (area inundated) and time (statistical probability). The problem was that Rapid City allowed residential development upon the flood plain.

Post-Flood Recovery and Planning

Recovery efforts in Rapid City got underway immediately. Interim and long-range programs were set up and millions of federal dollars are still being spent in Rapid City and the surrounding flood-stricken communities. The Small Business Administration made over $65 million in disaster loans. Public facilities were restored with funds from the Federal Disaster Assistance Administration. Perhaps the major factor has been the disaster recovery-urban renewal program made possible by a $48 million grant from the Department of Housing and Urban Development. After the Corps of Engineers decided that it would be economically infeasible to build a large flood-control dam in Dark Canyon the City Council approved a "floodway" or "greenway" concept, and HUD funds are currently being used to convert most of the flood plain into a large park. The city is purchasing the heavily flooded residential areas, and the flood-damaged homes are being sold at public auction to be demolished or moved to new locations.

As a result of federal moneys and post-flood planning, the flood plain in Rapid City is now zoned mainly non-residential where only commercial establishments are allowed to remain. The next time Rapid Creek floods, businesses and merchandise may be swept away, but few homes will be destroyed and hopefully no deaths will occur.

The sale of commercial real estate property on the flood plain is proceeding on a "business as usual" basis. Figure 4a shows an intersection near the Baken Park shopping center on Saturday morning, June 10, 1972, the morning after the flood. Note the flood water still draining from the flood plain. High water was almost to the "Piggly Wiggly" sign on the shopping center in the background. Figure 4b also shows the same intersection in December, 1974. Note the sign "OUT OF FLOOD PLAIN." This property is right along Rapid Creek and is obviously *in* the flood plain. In fact, high water on June 9 would be at the top of the sign itself! What the sign means is that the area is zoned commercial, and *caveat emptor*[1] prevails.

Areas Outside of Rapid City

Landowners in flood-stricken areas outside the city limits of Rapid City have not been as judicious as those in Rapid City in planning for future floods. On June 9, Keystone was almost demolished by the flooding Grizzly Bear and Battle Creeks. Eight people were killed in this small mountain com-

1. Let the buyer beware.

munity. Yet a new two story motel that was destroyed by the flood was replaced one year later by a three story motel that was constructed at exactly the same place. It remains to be seen how long this motel will last.

The worst example of post-flood urbanization is on the flood plain of Rapid Creek from the eastern edge of Rapid City several miles downstream. Here dozens of new mobile homes are being erected on the flood plain right in the middle of area inundated on June 9, 1972. The Pennington County

FIGURE 4. Looking west towards "Baken Park" from intersection of west Main Street and Mountain View Road. (a) On June 10, 1972, water is still flowing across the street and parking lots. (Photograph courtesy of Rapid City Journal). (b) Same location as above, photograph taken in December, 1974. Note "OUT OF FLOOD PLAIN" sign.

Planning Commission has allowed this development to occur on the excuse that they don't know exactly where the flood plain is.

In 1974, the new Custer County Courthouse was constructed on the flood plain adjacent to French Creek in Custer, South Dakota. French Creek did not flood as severely as other streams in the Black Hills on June 9, 1972. Nevertheless, the location of the courthouse is so obviously hazardous that even average laypeople in Custer were outraged at the decision to build there.

Railroad bridges have been periodically washed out by Black Hills floods, as evidenced by the numerous, old, abandoned railroad grades along streams. Figure 5 shows some of the damage to the Burlington-Northern spur line into Keystone caused by the June 9 flood of Battle Creek. Most of this line was rebuilt but the last mile into Keystone was permanently abandoned.

Dams

The June 9, 1972, floods caused many dam failures in the Black Hills, Dalton, Victoria, Fort Meade, and Canyon Lake Dams were completely destroyed. Horsethief, Lakota, and Sheridan Dams were damaged. In each case the main contributing factor in the dam's failure was an inadequate spillway.

Fort Meade Dam, in the Northern Black Hills, was built in 1909 by the Corps of Engineers. The original dam was raised to 56 feet in 1924. The spillway had only 54 square feet of freeboard area, and the dam was easily overtopped by the flood. The downstream portion of the rock and mortar dam eroded away, leaving only a thin concrete slab supporting the weight of the water in the reservoir. Fortunately for the citizens of Sturgis three miles downstream, this wall held until the Corps of Engineers pumped the water out of the reservoir. The remaining dam was then demolished. The dam was of dubious value even before the flood, since it was designed as a surface water catchment source for

FIGURE 5. Washed-out Burlington-Northern Railroad tracks one-half mile west of Keystone, South Dakota. Battle Creek washed out the Keystone-Hill City road and the railroad at many places in this vicinity.

the Fort Meade army hospital, but never held water longer than a few weeks. It lost the water to the underlying cavernous Pahasapa Limestone (Corps of Engineers, 1972).

Canyon Lake Dam, built in 1933 as a WPA project, was located in west Rapid City. The spillway was 101 feet long but had a foot bridge across it with four supporting piers. On the night of June 9, floating cars and debris began collecting in the spillway and, despite attempts by city engineers to free debris, the dam was overtopped and quickly eroded away, adding about 20,000 cfs of water to the flood which was already near peak discharge.

Cedar Canyon Dam was built by the Corps of Engineers in 1959 in Red Dale Gulch ¼ mile west of Rapid City. The drainage area above the dam is less than ½ square mile. The reservoir has a storage area of 136 acre-feet. Despite the fact that the adjacent areas in Cleghorn Canyon had peak discharges of 61 times the greatest expected every 50 years (Orr, 1973), Cedar Canyon Dam only collected 12 acre-feet of water behind it. Clearly this dam is over-designed, and had little value in alleviating flood damage anywhere.

Conclusion

The floods of Rapid City may not have caused as much damage as Hurricane Agnes where, on June 23, 1972, $3 billion was estimated lost in Pennsylvania alone (Parizek, 1972). The Mississippi River floods of spring of 1973 will long be remembered as record-breaking in terms of flood stages and area inundated (Deutsch, et al., 1973), but the Rapid City flood ranks close to the May 31, 1889, Johnstown, Pa., flood in terms of number of lives lost in a very limited area.

In the case of Rapid City, the area of death and destruction was completely limited to the flood plain of Rapid Creek, an area that had been mapped in detail years before the flood. The problem was that no one paid attention to the maps; people thought that because Pactola Reservoir had reduced the annual or 20 year flood, that the flood plain was safe from any flood. Now Rapid City residents know differently. The creation of a 5-mile long "floodway" park through the city should serve as a model for other cities.

REFERENCES

Cattermole, J. M., 1969, Geologic map of the Rapid City West quadrangle, Pennington County, South Dakota: U.S. Geological Survey Map GQ–828.
Cattermole, J. M., 1972, Geologic map of the Rapid City East quadrangle, Pennington County, South Dakota: U.S. Geological Survey Map GQ–986.
Corps of Engineers, 1972, Flood report, Cheyenne River Basin, South Dakota. Black Hills area, flood of 9–10 June 1972: U.S. Army Corps of Engineers, Omaha District, 108 p.
Deutsch, M., Ruggles, F. H., Guss, P., and Yost, E., 1973, Mapping of the 1973 Mississippi River floods from the Earth Resources Technology Satellite (ERTS): Remote Sensing and Water Resources Management, Air Water Resources Association, Proceedings N. 17, p. 39–55.
Larimer, O. T., 1973, Flood of June 9–10, 1972, at Rapid City, South Dakota: U.S. Geological Survey Atlas HA–511.
Myers, V. I., Waltz, F. A., and Smith, J. R., 1972, Remote sensing for evaluating flood damage conditions—the Rapid City, South Dakota flood, June 9, 1972: South Dakota State Univ., Remote Sensing Institute, Rept. 72–11, 28 p.
Newlin, D. M., 1972, The Black Hills flood of June 9, 1972: Midwest Research Publishers, Box 1526, Rapid City, South Dakota, 643 p.
NOAA, 1972, Black Hills flood of June 9, 1972: USDC-NOAA, Natural Disaster Survey Report 72–1, 20 p.
Orr, H. K., 1973, The Black Hills (South Dakota) flood of June 1972: impacts and implications: U.S. Forest Service General Technical Report RM–2, 12 p.
Parizek, R. R., 1972, Agnes, aftermath and the future (Abs): Geological Society of America, Annual Meeting, Minneapolis, p. 621.
Thompson, H. J., 1972, The Black Hills flood: Weatherwise, V. 24, N. 4, p. 162–167.

8

Sediment Problems in Urban Areas

Harold P. Guy

Introduction

A recognition of and solution to sediment problems in urban areas is necessary if society is to have an acceptable living environment. Soil erosion and sediment deposition in urban areas are as much an environmental blight as badly paved and littered streets, dilapidated buildings, billboard clutter, inept land use, and air, water, and noise pollution. In addition, sediment has many direct and indirect effects on streams that may be either part of or very remote from the urban environment. Sediment, for example, is widely recognized as a pollutant of streams and other water bodies.

One obstacle to a scientific recognition and an engineering solution to sediment-related environmental problems is that such problems are bound in conflicting and generally undefinable political and institutional restraints. Also, some of the difficulty may involve the fact that the scientist or engineer, because of his relatively narrow field of investigation, cannot always completely envision the less desirable effects of his work and communicate alternative solutions to the public. For example, the highway and motor-vehicle engineers have learned how to provide the means by which one can transport himself from one point to another with such great efficiency that a person's employment in this country is now commonly more than 5 miles from his residence. However, providing such efficient personal transport has created numerous serious environmental problems. Obstacles to recognition of and action to control sediment problems in and around urban areas are akin to other environmental problems with respect to the many scientific, engineering, economic, and social aspects.

Problem Extent

In a study of sediment problems in urban areas, it is necessary to remember that sediment movement and deposition was a part of the natural environment before the intervention of civilization. Like flooding, the sediment problems become important only when man is affected. Sometimes the problems result from natural conditions, but usually they result when the natural circumstances are altered to effect such a different kind of environment that previous small unnoticed problems are greatly magnified. Severe sediment problems occur, for example, when covering vegetation is removed in construction areas, when the flow regime in channels is altered by realinement or by increased or decreased flow, or when fill, buildings, or bridges obstruct the natural flowway.

Reprinted with permission of the author from *U.S. Geological Survey Circular 601-E,* 1970, 8 pp.

TABLE 1. EFFECT OF LAND-USE SEQUENCE ON RELATIVE
SEDIMENT YIELD AND CHANNEL STABILITY
[Modified from Wolman (1967)]

Land Use	Sediment Yield	Channel Stability
A. Natural forest or grassland.	Low	Relatively stable with some bank erosion.
B. Heavily grazed areas.	Low to moderate	Somewhat less stable than A.
C. Cropping.	Moderate to heavy	Some aggradation and increased bank erosion.
D. Retirement of land from cropping.	Low to moderate	Increasing stability.
E. Urban construction.	Very heavy	Rapid aggradation and some bank erosion.
F. Stabilization.	Moderate	Degradation and severe bank erosion.
G. Stable urban.	Low to moderate	Relatively stable.

The average sediment yield from the landscape and the condition of the stream channels tend to change with the advancing forms of man's land-use activity, as indicated by table 1. As in many other situations involving intensive use of resources and rapid growth, one can expect that sediment problems will be most serious during the urban construction period (E). This is not to say that problems are not likely to occur during the stable period (G) because physical and esthetic values or quality standards with respect to both water and property are expected to increase with time. For example, a stream carrying an average suspended-sediment concentration of 200 mg/l (milligrams per liter) after 2 years into the stable period may be more acceptable than 100 mg/l after 20 years into the stable period.

It is impossible to isolate sediment problems completely from the many interrelated problems associated with urban development, especially with respect to water (Anderson, 1968; Leopold, 1968). However, the sediment problems can usually be classed into groups related to land and channel erosion, stream transport, and deposition processes (Guy, 1967), regardless of the land-use phases mentioned in table 1. Land erosion, including the sheet, rill, and gully forms, is likely to be most severe during the urban construction period (E), though it may be present to some degree regardless of land use. Channel erosion is most severe during the stabilization period (F), especially when channels have been realined, waterways have been constricted, and (or) the amount and intensity of runoff have been increased because of imperviousness and "improved" drainage. Sediment transport problems are usually associated with the pollution of water by sediment from either or both the esthetic or physical utilization viewpoints. Transport problems also occur in regard to coarse sediment when the transport capacity in a stream section does not match the input supply of the coarse sediment—hence, aggradation or degradation. The sorting and differential transport of sediment result in deposition problems ranging from the fan deposits at the base of graded banks to deposits in reservoirs and estuaries.

The following is a list of some of the urban sediment erosion, transport, and deposition problems:
1. Public health may be affected in a number of ways. Efforts to control mosquito breeding have been ineffective because sediment has filled drainage channels. Also harmful bacteria, toxic chemicals, and radionuclides tend to be absorbed onto sediment particles. The absorbed substances may not be harmful in their original residence but become hazardous when transported into a water supply or deposited and perhaps concentrated at a new location.

2. Sheet, rill, and gully erosion and associated deposition may cause undesirable changes in graded areas typical of urban construction sites. Figure 1, from Wolman and Schick (1967, p. 455), shows the effect of the intensity of construction and drainage-basin size on sediment yield. In figure 2 it will be rather expensive to remove the deposit in the yard, to repair the erosion damage on the graded bank, and to repair the drainage channel on the terrace. Erosion and subsequent deposition in cut-and-fill areas can easily exceed 1 cubic yard for each 100 square feet.

3. Dispersion of soil particles by raindrop impact seals the land surface and thereby reduces infiltration, increases stream runoff, and decreases groundwater recharge.

4. Deposition of coarse sediments may reduce the flow capacity or completely plug natural and manmade channels (figure 3) as well as close drains.

5. Floodwater damage is increased manyfold in homes, stores, and factories because of sediment. Evaporation can erase many of the effects of a "pure water" flood, but it cannot do so when the flow contains suspended sediment.

6. Streams and other bodies of water are damaged esthetically by unsightly deposits as well as by fine sediment in suspension. Though stream esthetics are considered much more inclusive than recreation alone, Brown (1948, p. 79) has estimated that recreation losses in the Meramec River basin near St. Louis, Mo., in 1940 amounted to 49,090 person-days as a result of above-normal flows (but less than floodflows) of high turbidity.

7. Water-treatment costs for domestic and industrial uses are increased. Reduction of Potomac River sediment turbidity to optimum could produce an annual savings of $25,000 per year (1963 values) for Washington D.C. (Wolman, 1964, p. 68).

8. Erosion and (or) deposition in channels, estuaries, and other water bodies may cause bridge or culvert failure as well as serious ecological changes by alteration of species composition and population density (Peters, 1967).

9. Impoundments for municipal water storage are often built upstream from cities. The release of clear water from such impoundments can create serious degradation and bank erosion in downstream areas where picnic and other recreational facilities are planned.

10. Reservoir storage and channel conveyance for water supply are lost. Wolman (1964, p. 63) indicated that the alternative cost per acre-foot of storage lost to sediment in water storage and recreation reservoirs in Maryland ranges from less than $100 to over $78,000.

11. Maintenance costs are increased for streets, highways, and other public-use areas. (See figure 4.)

12. As implied in the introduction, perhaps the most serious urban sediment problem is the general deterioration of the total environment—a condition usually not recognized by the public.

As with many hydrologic problems, most urban sediment problems have visual impact for relatively short periods of time because they are rainstorm related (Guy, 1964). Also, because these problems are usually rooted within the urban or urbanizing area, they are limited to relatively small areas of the country. However, because of the intense capital investment in and human use of urban areas, the recognition of and solution to sediment problems become socially and economically very important.

Sediment damage is apparent when a storm-drain inlet becomes clogged, rill erosion cuts a graded area, a traffic accident occurs because of a wet fine-sediment deposit on a street, a swimming area must be closed because of turbid water, a water-treatment plant cannot clarify water, or a recreation lake is filled with sediment (Guy and Ferguson, 1962). Because sediment is often part of a complex environmental problem (Ferguson and Guy, 1970), many other sediment problems go unnoticed even though they cannot be economically significant. A study of air pollution in Chicago showed that dustfall amounts ranged from 21 to 61 tons per square mile per month at 20 stations during 1966 (American Public Works Association, 1969, p. 25). The Chicago study also showed that street-litter sweepings consisted of more than 70 percent dirt and rock by weight—the remaining was classified as metal, paper, vegetation, wood, and glass. Higher percentages of dirt occurred in the litter after rainstorms, even in a business area that was 100 percent built up.

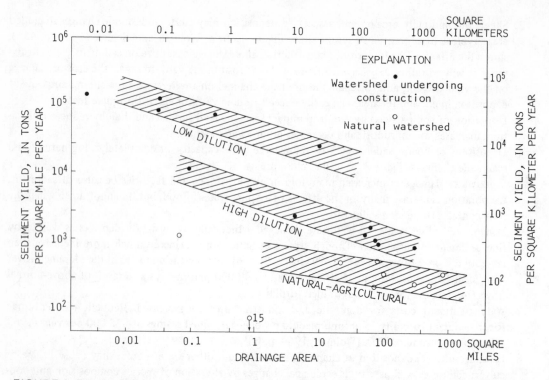

FIGURE 1. Effect of construction intensity and drainage area on sediment yield (from Wolman and Schick, 1967, p. 455). Most of the data are from the Baltimore and Washington, D.C., metropolitan areas. The term "dilution" refers to drainage from relatively stable nonconstruction areas.

FIGURE 2. Severe rill and gully erosion from the January 1969 storms in a new residential area near San Bernardino, Calif.

FIGURE 3. Effect of coarse-sediment deposition on flow capacity in urban channels. *A*, Flow of sediment in floodwater from the January 1969 storms plugged a Glendora, Calif., concrete-lined channel and caused overflow and deposition on nearby property. The channel had been partly cleaned after the flood and before the picture was taken. *B*, Three feet of deposition in the lower part of this boulevard channel in Boulder, Colo., caused flooding by a flow of less than one-fifth the design capacity of the channel.

FIGURE 4. More than 1,000 cubic yards of debris deposited on a short section of Ledora Avenue, Glendora, Calif., during the January 1969 storms by sediment flow and floodflow from nearby recently burned foothill area.

A sound sediment-measurement program in and adjacent to urban areas will help people to recognize what the problems are, where they occur, and when to expect them. Such a sediment-measurement program should document erosion sources and amounts, concentration in runoff, stream-channel changes, and the location and amounts of deposition. The measurement program, though mostly a documentaion of the nature of conditions, will provide the basis upon which research needs (Guy, 1967) can be evaluated.

Some Aspects of Problem Solution

Of the many facets of sediment problems in urban areas, the foremost are recognition and evaluation. Recognition would be easier if specific data on the cost of the many kinds of sediment problems in urban areas were available. The costs of sediment problems are rarely computed, and then they are generally estimated, even under the relatively less dynamic and more familiar rural conditions. Moore and Smith (1968) showed that "rural erosion and sediment" problems in the United States cause more than a $1-billion loss each year, $800 million of which occurs from erosion of cropland. Brown (1948) reported that annual damage from sediment deposition alone in rural areas amounts to $175 million. This in itself is 1.7 times the average annual flood damages for the 20-year period 1925–44. In the accounting of flood damages, sediment deposition was apparently not considered a flood cost.

As already mentioned, heavy loads of sediment are moved into channels below construction areas; the fine particles move through rapidly and the coarser particles tend to fill the channel system. In regard to the period of returning stability after development, Dawdy (1967, p. 242) stated,

> the slug of coarse sediment produced during construction may well travel through a channel system as a discrete mass or wave, causing geomorphic changes. These, in turn, change the hydraulics of the channel, cause bank erosion, and may alter the ecology of the stream. No data nor studies of the impact of urban sediment on downstream ecology are available, however. If a channel system is steep enough and discharge is sufficiently great to transport the contributed sediment, the geomorphic and hydraulic effects may be short lived, and the impact of the sediment and of its associated problems is transferred downstream to a major river, a lake or reservoir, an estuary, or the ocean.

With our advanced state of technology, solutions to the physical urban sediment problem are usually available even though the problem may occur under a dynamic and complicated environment. Such solutions may seem economically and socially expensive, but in the light of our high standard of living the expense will prove to be relatively low. Because of the importance of sediment control, it is to be hoped that implementation will not be fraught with institutional difficulty.

In many situations, a program to obtain sediment knowledge is justified in order to wisely choose a suitable solution among many alternatives. A complete sediment-evaluation program may, in reality, be a complete system study of input-storage-output components. For example, where the problem involves a stream channel, it is essential to know the sources of the inflowing sediment, the degree and extent of transport in the stream, and the nature of the deposit, in terms of time and space, at the estuary or other body of water.

Several steps needed to achieve control of urban sediment have been outlined by Guy and others (1963). These are:

1. Public-program adjustments, including a specific policy toward potential problems, planning and zoning, local ordinances, and assistance to insure proper judicial interpretation.

2. Erosion-control measures, including the proper use of vegetation for both temporary and permanent control, diversions and bench terraces, stabilization structures, storm drainage systems, storage of excess rainfall on lots, floodwater retarding structures, and the provision of "blue-green areas," usually parks, along streams and in headwater areas having critical runoff.

3. Adequate education of both the general public and urban officials is essential. Such education in turn requires adequate sediment information, without which neither 1 or 2 can be effectively accomplished.

A good example of an institution attempting to control sediment in urban development, and thus to eliminate or reduce many sediment problems, is Montgomery County, Md. It was the first county (July 1965) to adopt a "Sediment Control Program" that requires approval of subdivision development plans by the Department of Public Works, which in turn is in consultation with the Soil Conservation Service. If the developers' plan for erosion and sediment control seems inadequate, then the Soil Conservation Service is asked to recommend suitable measures. Sometimes the measures may include only revision in timing and location of construction activity. In October, 1966, the Fairfax (Va.) Board of Supervisors adopted a set of subdivision land-erosion-control measures similar to those of Montgomery County.

Sediment control is also being effected as a result of Executive Order 11258 issued in 1966 through the authority of the Water Quality Act of 1965. This order requires a review of all Federal and federally aided operations where there is a significant potential for reduction of water pollution by sediment. The reviewers may prescribe suitable remedial practices as necessary. This should prove particularly significant in view of sediment problems in connection with urban and suburban highway construction (Vice, Guy, and Ferguson, 1969).

Conclusions

Much of the disturbed soil in urban construction areas erodes and becomes sediment in streams; the sediment damages water-control works and aquatic habitat, degrades water quality, increases flood damages, and lowers the environmental attractiveness. During the process of stabilization of an area after construction, streams tend to erode their beds and banks as a result of increased runoff. All such sediment, whether from construction erosion or from channel erosion, is transported by streams and often deposited somewhere downstream at a location previously assigned to the movement or storage of water.

Documentation of erosion sources and amounts, of sediment concentration in runoff, of stream-channel changes, and of the location and amounts of deposition together with an economic analysis of sediment damages and a pertinent research program will provide the knowledge needed to find the best solutions to a wide variety of existing and future urban sediment problems. Aside from the knowledge needed for better design of systems, documentation of sediment conditions will provide baseline information from which damages, both on site and downstream, can be evaluated. Defense against damage claims often rests upon attempts to demonstrate that the claimant had no knowledge of preexisting conditions, that the source of damages was not discernable, or that conditions had always been so.

Increasing numbers of communities will likely attempt to alleviate their many sediment problems because of the adverse effects of such problems on the local environment. The public sentiment needed to support such programs to control sediment is built from a series of events that restrict, offend, or otherwise concern people.

REFERENCES CITED

American Public Works Association, 1969, Water pollution aspects of urban runoff: Federal Water Pollution Control Adm., Pub. WP–20–15, 272 p.

Anderson, D. G., 1968, Effects of urban development on floods in northern Virginia: U.S. Geol. Survey open-file report, 26 p.

Brown, C. B., 1948, Perspective on sedimentation—purpose of conference: Federal Inter-Agency Sediment Conf., Denver, Colo., 1947, Proc., U.S. Bur. Reclamation, p. 307.

Dawdy, D. R., 1967, Knowledge of sedimentation in urban environments: Am. Soc. Civil Engineers Proc., v. 93, no. HY6, p. 235–45.

Ferguson, G. E., and Guy, H. P., 1970, Sedimentation as an environmental problem: Jour. Soil and Water Conserv. (In press.)

Guy, H. P., 1964, An analysis of some storm-period variables affecting stream sediment transport: U.S. Geol. Survey Prof. Paper 462–E, 46 p.

——1967, Research needs regarding sediment and urbanization: Am. Soc. Civil Engineers Proc., v. 93, no. HY6, p. 247–254.

Guy, H. P., and Ferguson, G. E., 1962, Sediment in small reservoirs due to urbanization: Am. Soc. Civil Engineers, Proc., v. 88, no. HY2, p. 27–37.

Guy, H. P., and others, 1963, A program for sediment control in the Washington Metropolitan Region: Washington, D.C., Interstate Comm. Potomac River Basin, May, 48 p.

Leopold, L. B., 1968, Hydrology for urban land planning—a guidebook on the hydrologic effects of urban land use; U.S. Geol. Survey Circ. 554, 18 p.

Moore, W. R., and Smith, C. E., 1968, Erosion control in relation to watershed management: Am. Soc. Civil Engineers Proc., v. 94, no. IR3, p. 321–331.

Peters, J. C., 1967, Effects on a trout stream of sediment from agricultural practices: Jour. Wildlife Management, v. 31, no. 4, p. 805–812.

Vice, R. B., Guy, H. P., and Ferguson, G. E., 1969, Sediment movement in an area of suburban highway construction, Scott Run Basin, Fairfax County, 1961–64: U.S. Geol. Survey Water-Supply Paper 1591–E, 41 p.

Wolman, M. G., 1964, Problems posed by sediment derived from construction activities in Maryland: Annapolis, Md., Report to the Maryland Water Pollution Control Commission, p. 1–125.

——1967, A cycle of sedimentation and erosion in urban river channels: Geografiska Annaler, v. 49, ser. A, p. 385–395.

Wolman, M. G., and Schick, A. P., 1967, Effects of construction on fluvial sediment, urban and suburban areas of Maryland: Water Resources Research, v. 3, no. 2, p. 451–464.

Soil Slips, Debris Flows, and Rainstorms in the Santa Monica Mountains and Vicinity, Southern California

9

Russell H. Campbell

Introduction

The exceptionally heavy rainstorm of January 18 to 26, 1969, covered a large part of coastal southern California. The area affected includes the Santa Monica Mountains, the southernmost of the east-west-trending Transverse Ranges. The central Santa Monica Mountains has been the subject of a continuing program (since 1961) of general-purpose geologic mapping by the U.S. Geological Survey in cooperation with the Department of the County Engineer, Los Angeles County (figure 1). A post-storm reconnaissance of the project area was made in early February 1969 to assess the effects of the storm on slope stability. Although many different kinds of landslide activity were in evidence, from rockfalls to deep rotational slumps, it was immediately obvious that hundreds of shallow scars had resulted from the mass failure of colluvial soil cover of steep hillsides and colluvial fill in steep ravines (Campbell, 1969). Most scars were on natural slopes, though some also occurred on manmade slopes.

Investigation of the downslope effects of these shallow failures indicates that, in many instances, the initial movement of slabs of soil and wedges of ravine fill caused reconstitution of the sliding wet masses into flowing, viscous, debris-laden mud, which then flowed down available drainage courses (accelerating to avalanche speed in some) until reaching a gradient gentle enough for deposition to occur. Structures in the paths of these flows were either inundated or subjected to high-velocity impact, and sometimes both. On Saturday morning, January 25, 1969, 8 debris flows ("mudslides" in the press vernacular) of this probable origin caused 12 fatalities among residents of the Santa Monica Mountains and nearby hill areas. One month later, on the morning of February 25th, two more debris flows, probably of the same origin, resulted in eight more fatalities—five in the Santa Ana Mountains and three in the San Gabriel Mountains. Further study added three more fatalities to the list of the past decade—two during a storm in February 1962 and another during a storm in December 1965. On this record, these shallow, relatively small landslides present a greater risk of bodily injury to southern California residents than the more slowly moving deep rotational and block-glide landslides. Furthermore, this hazard is not unique to coastal southern California. Debris flows that have apparently resulted from storm-related soil slips have also caused extensive damage in Brazil (Vargas and Pichler, 1957), Japan (Oka and Katsurajima, 1971), coastal Alaska (Bishop and Stevens, 1964; Swanston, 1969), and other parts of the world.

Extracted with permission of the author from *U.S. Geological Survey Professional Paper 851*, 1975, 51 pp.

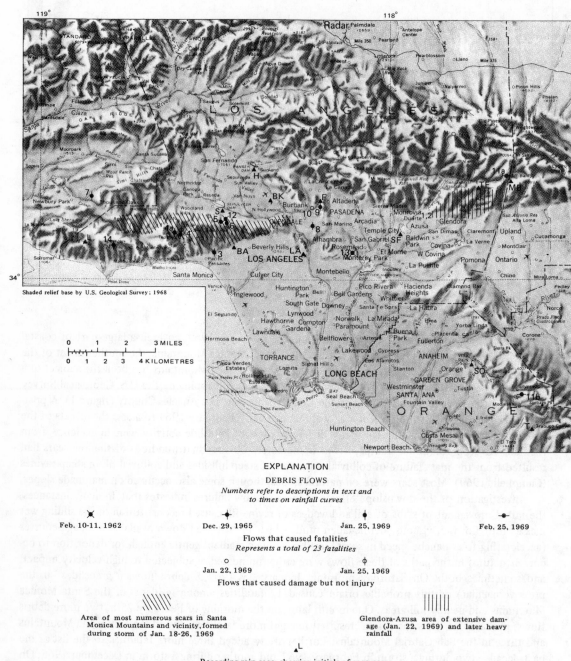

119°　　　　　　　　　　　　　　　　　　118°

Shaded relief base by U.S. Geological Survey; 1968

34°

0　1　2　3 MILES

0　1　2　3　4 KILOMETRES

EXPLANATION

DEBRIS FLOWS

*Numbers refer to descriptions in text and
to times on rainfall curves*

✖　　　　　　　＋　　　　　　　●　　　　　　　●

Feb. 10-11, 1962　　Dec. 29, 1965　　Jan. 25, 1969　　Feb. 25, 1969

Flows that caused fatalities
Represents a total of 23 fatalities

○　　　　　　　　ϕ

Jan. 22, 1969　　　　Jan. 25, 1969

Flows that caused damage but not injury

\\\\\\　　　　　　　　　　　　　　　|||||||

Area of most numerous scars in Santa　　　　Glendora-Azusa area of extensive dam-
Monica Mountains and vicinity, formed　　　age (Jan. 22, 1969) and later heavy
during storm of Jan. 18-26, 1969　　　　　　rainfall

▲L

Recording rain gage, showing initials of gage name

L, *Lechuza Pt FC;* S, *Sepulveda dam;* BA, *Bel Air FC;* BK, *Burbank;* LA, *Los Angeles
Civic Center;* F, *Flintridge FC;* TF, *San Dimas Tanbark flat;* MB, *Mount Baldy;* SF, *Santa
Fe dam;* SO, *Santiago dam;* T, *Trabuco;* H, *Hansen*

FIGURE 1. Location of debris flows discussed in this report and of recording rain gages used to relate
rainfall and soil slips, central Santa Monica Mountains, southern California.

The initial failures are slab or wedge shaped, with length per thickness ratios generally in excess of 10:1. In the scheme of Skempton and Hutchinson (1969, see especially p. 295), they are probably best characterized as "slab slides"; in coastal California they are more commonly called "soil slips" (Kesseli, 1943; Bailey and Rice, 1969). The masses that continue downslope as flows are probably best termed "debris flows"—a relatively broad class that may be interpreted to include subclasses such as "mudflows" and "silt flows" of more specific grain size. "Semiarid mudflow" and "debris-avalanche" are terms proposed by Sharpe (1938, p. 57–63) that would include the flowing masses; however, Sharpe's emphasis was clearly on events of larger volume and, although he inferred an origin by "slip-page" (1938, p. 61) for debris-avalanches, mudflows and debris-avalanches can occur in semiarid regions in some circumstances that do not require concurrent heavy rainfall nor restrict the originating slippage to the surficial mantle. For the purposes of this report it seems preferable to use the compound term "soil slip-debris flow" to specify debris flows that are known or reliably inferred to have originated from soil slips. Many soil slip-debris flow events have been referred to as "mudslides" in press reports and other nontechnical accounts; however, "mudslide" has been applied to other events of such diverse character that its connotations are too broad to be appropriate here.

The exceptional storm of January 18–26, 1969, provided a unique opportunity to examine the relations between rainfall and the debris-flow hazard in the Los Angeles area because: The wide areal distribution of heavy rainfall ensured that representatives of the full range of slope angles, soil types, bedrock type, and vegetation were subjected to rainfall intensities, durations, and totals that were closely monitored by a net of continuously recording rain gages; and the affected region included several populated areas where the severe damage and injuries drew attention to the times of failure causing many events to be reliably reported by the press or by other investigating agencies (figure 1). The comparisons permit some approximations of limiting slope angles, and some rough qualitative observations of the effects of geologic soil type, soil thickness, parent material (bedrock or other), and vegetation. In addition, an empirical correlation between rainfall total and intensity and the times of observed slope failures leads to interpretations of the probable frequency of recurrence during lesser storms and to suggestions for minimizing the hazard to residents.

Soil Slips and Other Landslides

Shallow failures of colluvial soil and ravine fill have a number of characteristics and storm associations in common that set them apart from other classes of landslides, such as rotational slumps and block glides. The latter, for example, depend upon deep percolation of ground water and may not begin to move until many days or weeks after a storm. In contrast, soil slips occur only during heavy rainfall, and new ones do not appear after the rain ceases. (At higher altitudes, such as the higher parts of the San Gabriel Mountains, the water input into the soil may be provided by rapidly melting snow, instead of rain.) Because soil slips are generally limited to steep slopes, the kinds of landslides more commonly seen on gentle slopes are rotational slump, block glide, failure by lateral spreading, or liquefaction of sand and sensitive clay. The damage that may result is also different; differential movement of foundations is the major cause of structural damage by the more deeply rooted landslides, whereas inundation and lateral impact by flowing debris are the chief causes of damage that result from soil slips.

Soil Slips: Antecedent Slope Conditions

The association of soil slips with rainstorms is clear evidence that slope-mantle materials that are stable under "normal" conditions become unstable during rainfall of sufficient duration and intensity. The antecedent conditions on the slopes that fail are probably best seen by examining the slopes adjacent to soil-slip scars. Although the parts that fail and slide off must be less stable than those remaining, movement generally alters the soil structures so thoroughly that its nearest representative is the material that remains behind.

Slope Angles and Channel Gradients

Although the total relief of the Santa Monica Mountains is not much more than 2,900 feet, many slopes exceed 30°, and slopes of 40° and more are common. Precipitous cliffs are present but are generally limited to the risers of flat-lying ledges of thick individual beds of resistant sandstone or volcanic rocks or to steeply dipping surfaces of resistant sandstone beds or volcanic rocks. Generally, slopes steeper than about 56° (ranging from about 45° to 60°, depending on the character of the bedrock and the type of vegetation) are bare bedrock, too steep to retain a continuous mantle of colluvium. Generally, though by no means invariably, profiles of slopes of less than about 27° (50 percent) tend to be rounded, and profiles of steeper slopes tend to have relatively long straight segments. Depositional slopes of about 11° (20 percent) are common in the heads of many fans; consequently, the upper edges of depositional slopes are commonly marked by sharp breaks with steeper erosional slopes above. The more distal parts of fans have more gentle slopes. Alluviated valleys are more common on the north and south flanks of the mountains than in the mountain core where most of the canyons are V-shaped, and deposits in the bottoms are periodically flushed out by floods.

Parent Material, Colluvial Soil, and Ravine Fill

The storm of January 18–26, 1969, was accompanied by soil slips in terrain underlain by every bedrock unit in the Santa Monica Mountains. Scars of similar shape and size were formed in the colluvial soils overlying granitic slaty basement rocks, as well as the sandstone, shale, and volcanic rocks of the entire superjacent sequence. (For summary descriptions of the "basement" and "superjacent" rocks see Yerkes and others, 1965, p. 20–46.) The only evident controls by parent materials are indirect: (a) Generally, but not invariably, units containing more resistant rocks support steeper and longer slopes, and (b) colluvial soils developed over the volcanic rocks tend to be thinner and less continuous, perhaps because they do not generally support so dense a vegetal cover as the other bedrock types.

Almost all the soils on slopes steeper than about 11° are colluvial. They are derived from the parent material that underlies the slope (whether bedrock or surficial deposit, including artificial fill) by weathering and gravitational creep. Root wedging by vegetation, burrowing and walking by animals, and alternate swelling and shrinking of clays with changes in moisture contribute much to the break-up of the parent material and the downslope creep of the detritus. Rilling and other evidence of sheet-wash by surface runoff are not common on the well-vegetated slopes, and raindrop impact is generally cushioned by the canopy of grass or chaparral. It seems probable that in years when rainfall intensities are low to moderate, soil creep on vegetated slopes during the dry season exceeds movement during the wet season, as reported by Anderson, Coleman, and Zinke (1959) and Krammes (1965) for slopes in the San Gabriel Mountains.

The thickness to which colluvium accumulates on the slopes generally ranges from 1 to 4 feet, and the full range is from a few inches to an unknown upper limit that may be as much as several tens of feet. The ravines at the foot of the slopes serve as repositories for detritus from both adjacent slopes, and 2–10 feet is the most common range of thickness of the ravine fill. The retention of a colluvial soil mantle on slopes steeper than 34° (the common angle of repose for loose, dry colluvial materials) is probably best attributed to the cohesive effects of vegetation roots and soil moisture.

Vegetation, Fire, and Soil Moisture

Although vegetation has long been regarded as effectively retarding hillside erosion, grass and chaparral seem much less effective in preventing slabs of soil from sliding than in retarding grain-by-grain erosion. The vegetal canopy and litter reduce susceptibility to grain-by-grain erosion by raindrop impact and sheetwash, but the ratio of infiltration to runoff is thereby increased, leading to a more rapid and thorough saturation of the soil mantle. The consequence may be an increased susceptibility to soil-slip erosion, depending on specific site conditions. Vegetal cover has not prevented large numbers of soil-slip events on steep slopes covered by all kinds of grass and chaparral; however, the rooting character of the plants probably has a significant effect on susceptibility to failure by soil slip. Spreading, inlocking roots tend to bind relatively shallow parts of the soil together, and roots that penetrate deeply into the subsoil (including cracks in bed-rock) tend to bind the soil and subsoil zones together and wedge bedrock blocks apart. Detailed studies in the San Dimas Experimental Forest near Glendora (Corbett and Rice, 1966; Rice and others, 1969; and Rice and Foggin, 1971) have demonstrated that the frequencies and areas of soil slips are three to five times greater for grass-covered slopes than for brush-covered ones. A significant correlation between vegetation and the minimum angles at which soil slips occurred was also noted by Corbett and Rice (1966, p. 4-6) and Rice and Foggin (1971, p. 1488 Table 1, p. 1493, 1496) who found that the minimum angles for failure were less for grassy cover than for most chaparral vegetation. No comparable quantitative data are available for the Santa Monica Mountain area, where similar correlations would be in accord with general impressions but might be biased by the greater visibility of scars on grassy slopes. The rooting characteristics of the various kinds of vegetation also probably affect the degree to which the soil structure in different zones is remolded by movement.

The density and variety of vegetation may also affect the width and shape of slab failures. Where the slopes were covered with grass, mustard, and sage, the scars from the January 1969 storm were as much as several tens of feet wide, but where the stronger chaparral plants prevailed, the scars were generally only a few tens of feet wide and relatively longer, tending to resemble the failure of ravine fill. Where the chaparral plants were widely spaced and not mixed with grass, as in many areas underlain by the volcanic rocks, soil slips were less abundant. So many interrelated factors are involved, however, that these associations are not satisfactorily documented. The distribution of the grassy vegetation, for example, is controlled partly by slope (many low slopes have been cleared and pasture grasses encouraged), by the recency of destruction of the larger bushes by fire, and by the chemistry of the soils developed over the various parent materials. Grassy vegetation is particularly common over shaly bedrock units, and the steep slopes developed over shaly bedrock tend to be shorter than those developed over sandstone strata where chaparral predominates. The relatively long, narrow aspect of the slides in chaparral, therefore, may be as much (or more) dependent on slope length as on the variety of vegetation.

From the historical record, it seems clear that during heavy rainstorms, watersheds that have been recently burned over yield greater amounts of debris than those that have not been burned (for example, see Simpson, 1969, p. 21). Fire destroys the vegetal canopy and some of the shallower roots, thereby exposing the surface to greater erosion by rain impact and sheetwash. Dry-season sliding is intensified (Krammes, 1965), probably resulting in much faster accumulation of channel-bed material (ravine fill). These conditions should not be expected to increase the probability of slab failures on the slopes but could increase the likelihood of ravine-fill failure and mobilization of bed materials in lower channel reaches. Soil slips do occur on burned-over slopes, for Scott (1971) found that the 1969 debris flows generated in the burned watersheds above Glendora resulted from mobilization of channel-bed material, triggered, at least in part, by surficial slope failures. There were no large burned-over areas in the Santa Monica Mountains at the time of the January 1969 storms, so no comparative studies could be made there.

Loss of soil moisture during fire and, perhaps, drought conditions also may promote dry sliding because air-water surface tension in the soil interstices contributes to the cohesiveness of the colluvial soil. (At the other end of the scale, air-water surface tension is also reduced when excess water displaces the air in the interstices.)

As Krammes and DeBano (1965) report, many soils in chaparral watersheds have hydrophobic properties that appear to be associated with an organic coating on soil particles. The "nonwettability" may be intensified by the effects of brush fires. Hydrophobic properties are locally restricted to depth zones within the soil mantle where they can cause variations in moisture content and rate of infiltration in layers that are recognized without specific testing.

Soil Slips: Failure Conditions and Mechanism

Failure and Rainfall

Even though most of the soil slips occurred in uninhabited areas where they were not observed, the poststorm reconnaissance established that a vast multitude of scars had appeared during the general 8-day period of storm activity. Of the many slides that occurred in inhabited areas, the best documented as to time are those that resulted in injuries and property damage. (See figure 1.) These times are markedly clustered into two periods, a 9-hour period between midnight and 9:00 a.m., January 22, and an 8½-hour period between 12:30 a.m. and 9:00 a.m., January 25, and undoubtedly represent two climaxes of soil-slip activity in the area shown (figure 2). The relationships suggest that few, if any, soil slips occurred at other times during the 8-day storm. Consequently, for the purpose of comparison with the time and distribution of rainfall of varying intensity, the times of the documented debris flows have been taken as representative of the time span of the great majority of the soil slips. Indeed, there seems little room for doubt that these failures occurred while rain was falling, and that failure was caused by dynamic conditions—conditions that were created by the storm; continued to build toward failure during periods of rainfall, and ceased when rainfall ceased.

The correlation in time between failure and heavy rainfall is strongly supported by comparisons of the documented slides with the hourly rainfall distribution maps made by the ESSA Weather Bureau Office (Radar), Palmdale, Calif., using FAA (Federal Aviation Administration) Air Traffic Control Radar. The time of a debris flow in the Old Topanga Canyon area could be determined only as between 1:00 a.m. and 9:00 a.m., January 25, 1969; however, neighbors reported that many debris flows occurred, beginning about 1:00 a.m., and were particularly frequent for the next 4 to 5 hours. Figure 3 shows the damage to the residence.

The radar maps document that rain was falling at the sites of failure when failure occurred, and they indicate that the rainfall at the sites of failure was "moderate to heavy" (about 0.2 in/hr or greater) at the times of failure.

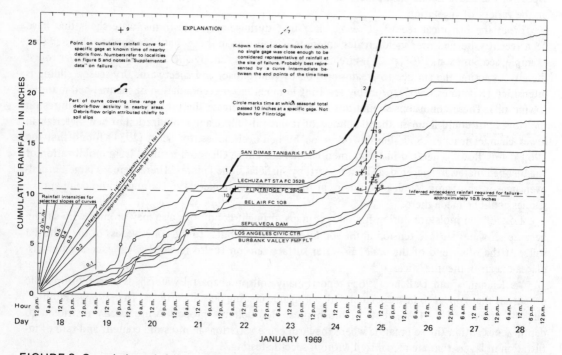

FIGURE 2. Cumulative rainfall at selected continuously recording gages in and near the Santa Monica and San Gabriel Mountains, southern California.

FIGURE 3. Residence in Old Topanga Canyon damaged by soil slip-debris flow between 1:00 a.m. and 9:00 a.m., January 25, 1969; one fatality. A. Flow broke though rear wall of lower story of two-story house after "ski-jumping" from top of vertical cut about 8 feet high. Upper story splattered (note broken window) but not entered by main flow. B. View through house from the front. Refrigerator and other heavy appliances, carried from kitchen in rear and through partition into living room in front, trapped and killed one occupant. All coarse debris remained inside, only muddy water flowed out the front.

All the time-documented debris flows are believed to have originated from soil slips. I examined all but two of the sites (Glendale and Highland Park) and found distinctive scars in the source areas of each. Photographs of the Highland Park site by the City of Los Angeles, Department of Building and Safety, clearly show a slide scar in the source area (figure 4). Only newspaper accounts of the debris flow at the Glendale site have been examined, and although they do not explicitly indicate the presence of slide scars in the source area, a soil-slip origin may be inferred from the reports of many "mudslides" that occurred in this neighborhood at about the same time as the fatal one.

Mechanism

The strong correlations between debris-flow activity and rainfall of moderate to high intensity (figure 2) support the hypothesis of Kesseli (1943, p. 347) attributing the disintegrating soil slips of the California Coast Ranges to the buildup of water in the regolith when infiltration at the surface takes place at a greater rate than deep percolation—a dynamic imbalance that can occur only when rainfall intensity exceeds the rate of deep percolation.

FIGURE 4. Scar above site of residence destroyed by debris flow indicates origin by soil slip; Highland Park, two fatalities at about 9:00 a.m. January 25, 1969. Photograph by City of Los Angeles, Department of Building and Safety.

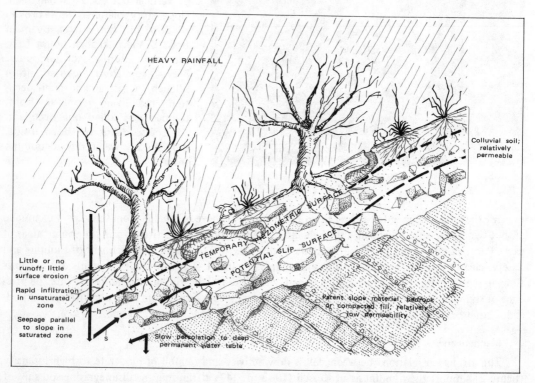

HEAVY RAINFALL

Colluvial soil; relatively permeable

TEMPORARY PIEZOMETRIC SURFACE

POTENTIAL SLIP SURFACE

Little or no runoff; little surface erosion

Rapid infiltration in unsaturated zone

Seepage parallel to slope in saturated zone

Parent slope material; bedrock or compacted fill; relatively low permeability

Slow percolation to deep permanent water table

FIGURE 5. Diagram showing buildup of perched water table in colluvial soil during heavy rainfall. Bedrock subsoil is shown here; however, soil slips also occurred over compacted fill slopes where the transition from parent material to colluvial soil is more obviously gradational.

The mechanism is illustrated by figure 5, which shows shallow-rooted vegetation with a thin mulch of dead leaves and grass growing in a regolith of colluvial soil, the upper part of which contains abundant living and dead roots as well as animal burrows. When the rate of infiltration into and through the upper layers is equal to or less than the capacity of the bedrock to remove it by deep percolation, the water moves toward the permanent water table far below, and the stability of the surficial material on the slope is not affected. When infiltration through the regolith exceeds the transmissive capacity of the rocks below, a temporary perched water table is formed. Its head will continue to increase as long as infiltration continues at the high rate until the whole surficial zone is saturated, at which time all the rainfall in excess of the transmissive capacity of the bedrock is distributed as surface runoff and downslope seepage within the saturated surficial zone. In this manner, the slope approaches the special condition described by Haefeli (1948, p. 59-60) of seepage flow parallel to the slope surface.

Rainfall Intensity and Duration

From the foregoing mechanism, the minimum conditions for failure would seem to be: an initial period of enough rainfall to bring the full thickness of the soil mantle to field capacity (the moisture content at which, under gravity, water will flow out as fast as it flows in), followed by rainfall intense enough to exceed the infiltration rate of the parent material underlying the soil mantle, and lasting long enough to establish a perched ground-water table of sufficient proportional thickness to cause failure. (Note that rainfall intensity need not exceed, nor even equal, the maximum infiltration rate for the soil; therefore, surface runoff may not be in evidence on a slope about to fail.) Evaluation of the data from the storm of January 18-26, 1969, suggests that, in the greater Los Angeles area, these minimum conditions were reached when the sites of failure had received a total of about 10 inches of rain, after which they were subjected to rainfall intensities of about 0.25 inch per hour or more. (See figure 2.) The numerical values are, of course, preliminary and subject to revision as more data are examined.

Certainly, the threshold total rainfall should be expected to be less for thin soils than for thick soils, and the 10-inch antecedent total suggested here must reflect conditions for colluvial soil mantles of average thickness. Any loss of soil moisture by evaporation or transpiration during dry interstorm intervals should tend to increase the minimum threshold for a following storm; however, comparisons of the records for the storm seasons of 1961-62, 1965-66, and 1968-69 suggest that the threshold may be more closely associated with antecedent rainfall for the season than the immediately preceding hours of storm.

The curves for the storm of January 18-26, 1969 (figure 2) show varying areal, orographic, and episodic characteristics of the storm. The high totals for the gages at San Dimas Tanbark Flat and Lechuza Pt. Station represent the orographic effects of their relatively high altitudes in the San Gabriel and Santa Monica Mountains, respectively. Most of the episodes of moderate- to high-intensity rainfall during the storm period were recorded by all the gages. However, during the high-intensity rainfall along the front of the San Gabriel Mountains on January 22 (as represented by the San Dimas and Flintridge gages), only light rain was falling in the Santa Monica Mountains and vicinity. As the curves indicate, there were early episodes of high-intensity rainfall during which soil slips did not occur. Rainfall of similar, in part greater, intensity than that associated with the failures of January 22 and 25 occurred during earlier episodes on January 19 and 21 when no significant number of debris flows were observed. This lack of sliding during the earlier storm episodes seems to indicate that at those times the total antecedent rainfall had not been sufficient to bring the regolith up to field capacity.

The 10.5-inch "threshold total" indicated in figure 2 is probably an empirical representation of the range of minimum field capacities for the slope mantle materials of the general Los Angeles area. The numerical value of the "threshold total" may be different for different storms, depending upon the soil moisture content at the beginning of the storm. Soil moisture at the time the storm of January 18-26, 1969, began was probably relatively low for that time of year because the total rainfall through January 17 was only a little over half of the seasonal normal to that date (Simpson, 1969, p. 12). This condition contrasts markedly with the antecedent conditions at the beginning of the storm series of February, 1962, which began after seasonal totals of 6-11 inches, approximately the "normal to date," had already been attained.

Recurrence Intervals

The recurrence interval for storms of the magnitude of that of January 18-26, 1969, has been reported at 75 to 150 years by Simpson (1969, p. 14). Some residents have interpreted news reports that this was an 80-year storm to mean that they need not expect another such storm and its associated hazards for the next 80 years—a dangerously misleading belief. Perhaps only an "80-year storm" could cause such widespread and numerous soil slips, but it may be more important to note that during the storm period of January 18-26, 1969, a great many of the soil slips occurred well before the end of the storm, before the rainfall had reached its record and near-record totals. Debris flows probably caused by soil slips have resulted in fatal injuries during at least four storms in the decade 1960-70—February 1962, December 1965, January 1969, and February 1969—and have occurred, with less disastrous results, during some of the storms of the 1960's.

The recurrence interval for rainfall intensities of over 0.25 inch per hour in the greater Los Angeles area may be inferred to be less than 1 year. The "Rainfall frequency atlas of the United States" (Hershfield, 1961) indicated (p. 23) that 1-hour periods of rainfall ranging from 0.40-0.80 inch normally recur each year. Therefore, the inferred minimum intensity to trigger soil slips (0.25 inch per hour) may be expected at least once each year, and some years twice. The observed recurrence is less frequent, perhaps because the soil moisture content derived from antecedent rainfall must exceed the field capacity when high-intensity rainfall occurs.

The normal annual rainfall at the Los Angeles Civic Center is 12.63 inches (U.S. Environmental Science Services Administration, 1969 p. 44), nearly all of which falls during the October through March rainy season. Most nearby hillside areas probably have higher "normals" than the Los Angeles station because of the pronounced orographic effect so common in storms in the area, therefore, in most "normal" years most hillsides will have received the inferred threshold "seasonal to date" total of about 10.0 inches by the latter part of the season. Combinations of minimum antecedent rainfall and rainfall intensity that may cause a few scattered soil slips, particularly at higher altitudes, probably recur nearly every year.

Some inferences may also be made about the recurrence intervals of more severe storms. The data for the storm of January 18-26, 1969 (see figure 2) show that a significantly large number of soil slips had taken place by the time the storm total had reached about 13 inches. Miller (1964, p. 20-21) indicates that the return interval for a 7-day period of rainfall totaling 10 inches is 10 years, and that for a return interval of 25 years as much as 15 inches may be expected during a similar period (7 days). It would seem, therefore, that storms capable of causing numerous soil slips in the Santa Monica Mountains and vicinity may be expected to recur at intervals of between 10 and 25 years.

Change of State

When a relatively rigid slab changes to a viscous fluid (a characteristic also observed by Bishop and Stevens, 1964, p. 11), the conditions of resistance to downslope movement change from sliding friction to viscous flow. This change helps to explain how, on a given slope, a mass that has just become unstable (under conditions of sliding friction) can accelerate to avalanche speed rather than move at a steady slow velocity. Although the exact manner in which the change of state begins has not been observed or reported, some reasonable speculations may be made on the basis of the postulated mechanism for the slab failures together with the phenomenon of "spontaneous liquefaction" (Terzaghi and Peck, 1967, p. 108). For instance, the change should begin in the saturated zone adjacent to the slip surface of the slab failure and quickly encompass all the saturated zone. If an upper zone of the soil remains unsaturated (but at field capacity), it, too, may become fluid if field capacity provides enough moisture to surpass the liquid limit and if the soil structure is reworked thoroughly enough to effect remolding. That many such zones did not become completely fluid is shown by clumps and blocks of sod found well downstream from their scars of origin.

Debris Flows

Once a slab of soil becomes detached at an underlying slip surface and at the margins and begins moving, part or all of the mass is effectively remolded by its own motion, and it changes from a rigid slab to a viscous fluid. As it moves downslope, the material flows together into a relatively narrow stream, moving down established drainages—ravines, gullies, swales, and so on—as a discrete slug. The speed of the flow depends on its fluidity and on the length and gradient of the channel.

A comprehensive discussion of the mechanics of downslope flow of debris slurries is beyond the scope of this report. In general, the tendency of the flows to accelerate on steep slopes seems to indicate that the dominant conditions are those of viscous flow. Because visible effects of viscous or plastic creep of the soil mantle are not commonly associated with the storm-related slab failures in the Santa Monica Mountains, it seems necessary to consider elements of plastic or quasiplastic deformation (Leopold and others, 1964, p. 31) only on gentle slopes where flows decelerated to slow speeds just before depositing. Bagnold (1968, 48–51) and Johnson (1970, p. 456–534) have recently discussed the mechanics of viscous slurry flow (mudflows).

Downslope Transport

Many flows clearly moved at avalanche speeds; damage caused by high-velocity impact attests to this. Other flows reportedly oozed slowly down relatively gentle slopes, building up against the upslope walls of structures until a window or some other weak point gave way under the lateral pressure, permitting fluid mud to inundate the interior. Judging from the appearance of the deposits, the character of the damage, and newspaper accounts of witnesses, most of the slower flows probably moved at not much less than 1 ft/s (foot per second), and the extremely rapid flows probably moved at not much more than 40 ft/s. Slower and faster flows are, of course, not excluded by the mechanism, and the estimated range of rates cannot be expected to apply where other conditons of slope angle, slope length, soil character, and climate prevail.

The flows were generally laminar in appearance; however, considerable turbulence must have occurred in at least two general circumstances: (1) Where relatively wide slabs were funneled into relatively narrow ravines downstream; and (2) where the roughness of a channel bottom imposed a cascading, plunge-and-pond character to the flows.

Remedial Measures and Warning Systems

The hillside sites where soil slips may generate future debris flows are so small, numerous, and widely scattered that the safety of all downslope residents cannot be ensured merely by the construction of defensive works such as check dams, debris basins, and levees. Preventive measures, particularly the careful control of all surface and subsoil drainage, are generally practicable only where an entire slope is carefully engineered. Many hazardous sites, however, lie downslope from natural, undeveloped areas, where access is difficult; moreover, the slopes on which the debris flows originate may be divided among several owners. Both of these factors may complicate the installation, operation, and maintenance of preventive and protective works. In some locations, where the anticipated flows would be of sufficiently low volume and velocity, and where the probable paths of debris flows can be predicted, relatively simple protective structures might be erected. However, these would have to be carefully located after hillsides above vulnerable dwellings had been thoroughly studied. The extensive literature on snow-avalanche defenses may suggest some kinds of structures of possible practical value (for example, U.S. Dept. Agriculture, 1961; Buchner, 1956; Flaig, 1955; Fuchs, 1955; and Roch, 1956). Of particular interest might be the design, bracing, and reinforcement of unslope walls of dwellings so as to deflect or resist lateral pressures and impacts from material moving downslope. In general, however, it does not seem economically feasible to prevent debris flows from forming, nor to protect all dwellings within the immediate future. On the other hand, the injuries caused when those dwellings are damaged or destroyed by debris flows must be classed as preventable because with warning people can avoid the relatively small flowing masses.

The Value of Warning

During the early morning hours of January 25, 1969, there were 12 fatalities from 8 debris flows in the Santa Monica Mountains and adjacent areas. All the victims were inside residential structures that were damaged by impact or inundation by flowing debris. Eight—six adults and two children—were in their own bedrooms when crushed beneath collapsing walls or buried by muddy debris. The mother of the two children had reportedly awakened and was on her way to their bedroom when the house was crushed and part of it was pushed into the flooding stream below, resulting in the death of all three. Two of the victims who were awake were also small children, playing in one room of their home while their mother worked in another. Only one fatally injured adult was awake and fully clad. He had evacuated his family and had just returned to his house when it was struck by a high-velocity flow, which trapped and killed him (figure 3).

The stories of many who escaped injury when their homes were damaged or destroyed are also enlightening. If an adult of the household was alert to the problems outside the house (chief concerns were storm-runoff drainage, including small mudflows), almost invariably the approaching hazard was recognized in time to evacuate the remaining occupants—though very hastily in several instances.

The value of advance warning, therefore, seems clear. Residents who are notified that storm conditions have reached a point where debris flows may be generated by soil slips if high-intensity rainfall continues should be alert, should be prepared to recognize approaching danger, and should move quickly out of harm's way. Small children, invalids, and elderly people might be evacuated at such a time, but general evacuation of whole neighborhoods should not be necessary. The records show that even without advance planning, many people were able to react in ways that saved them from injury. Obviously, advance planning would provide for quicker and better protective response.

Contingency Plans

Because each hillside dwelling is in a unique position and orientation with respect to the slopes above, each household needs an individual set of contingency plans. When residents are warned that critical rainfall conditions have been reached in their area and are likely to be exceeded, some may elect to leave immediately, others to evacuate only small children and invalids; still others to remain at home, trusting in their ability to keep a sharp lookout, recognize approaching danger, and evacuate only when and if the hazard becomes an immediate threat. Those who remain after being alerted should be prepared for a round-the-clock vigil until the end of the storm. Their preparations should provide for a nighttime illumination of the slopes above them.

The preparations for each adult and older child should also include a careful look at the slopes above and below their homes during clear weather. They should take careful note of slope angles and of the locations of small guillies (and even gentle swales) which may become the channels for flowing mud. Note should also be taken of prestorm soil moisture conditions that might advance the time of the threat to their property from upslope locations. Such conditions might be recognized in irrigated gardens or in natural springs and seeps. Downslope areas should also be examined for similar conditions, and care should be taken in design of landscaping and drainage so as not to increase the hazard to residents below. Evacuation routes and destinations should be planned, and alternatives studied.

Evacuation centers should be carefully selected to avoid the sort of tragedy that occurred in Silverado Canyon on February 25, 1969, where a fire station being used to shelter about 60 storm refugees was struck by a debris flow, killing 5 persons and injuring 20.

Satisfactory contingency planning by individuals clearly requires effective and timely public education. Given a timely warning and a well-planned response, alert adults can expect to avoid injury, even though they may not be able to prevent damage to their homes.

A Warning System

The many variables that influence the origin of each individual debris flow make the prediction of small soil slips in specific places extremely difficult. Prediction might be possible if the geologic properties of entire slope areas were studied in detail and a network of instruments capable of continuously monitoring soil moisture were installed. Such extensive studies and instrumentation may be feasible during construction of a large subdivision but are not generally economic for one or two small residences at the foot of a steep slope area covering several acres.

A means by which the general time of greatest debris-flow hazard may be recognized is suggested by the empirical association of soil slips with a threshold total of about 10 inches of rainfall and a minimum intensity of 0.25 inch per hour. Although these specific empirical numbers should be tested further and may need considerable revision, the basic association appears established. Moreover, it should be possible to use slope maps or topographic maps, in conjunction with hourly radar weather maps showing areas of moderate- to high-intensity rainfall, to determine areas subject to the greatest hazard at particular times during a storm. A warning system, therefore, could be constructed of three major elements, each of which is partly or wholly operative at the present time: (1) A system of rain gages, recording total rainfall on an hourly basis; (2) a weather-mapping system capable of recognizing centers of high-intensity rainfall in the storm area and, at frequent intervals, plotting the locations of these centers with respect to locations of gages with adequate registry for accurate transfer to slope maps or topographic maps; and (3) an administrative and communications network to collate the data, recognize when critical factors have been exceeded in a particular area, and inform the residents there. Such a system is probably well within the capability of existing technology.

REFERENCES CITED

Anderson, H. W., Coleman, G. B., and Zinke, P. J., 1959, Summer slides and winter scour—dry-wet erosion in southern California mountains: U.S. Dept. Agriculture, Forest Service, Pacific Southwest Forest and Range Expt. Sta. Tech. Paper 36, 12 p.

Bagnold, R. A., 1968, Deposition in the process of hydraulic transport: Sedimentology, v. 10, 45–56.

Bailey, R. G., and Rice, R. M., 1969, Soil slippage: an indicator of slope instability on chaparral watersheds of southern California: Prof. Geographer, v. 21, p. 172–77.

Bishop, D. M., and Stevens, M. E., 1964, Landslides on logged areas in southeast Alaska: U.S. Forest Service Research Paper NOR-1 1964, 18 p.

Bucher, Edwin, 1956, Contribution to the theoretical foundations of avalanche defense construction: U.S. Army Corps Engineers Snow, Ice, and Permafrost Research Establishment, Translation 18, 109 p.

Campbell, R. H., 1969, Rapid debris flows in the central Santa Monica Mountains, California [abs.]: Assoc. Eng. Geologists, Program, 1969 ann. mtg., p. 20–21.

Corbett, E. S., and Rice, R. M., 1966, Soil slippage increased by brush conversion: U.S. Forest Service Research Note PSW-128, 8 p.

Flaig, Walther, 1955, Lawinen: Abenteuer und Erfahrung, Erlebnis und Lehre: Wiesbaden, F. A. Brockhaus, 251 p.

Fuchs, Alfred, 1955, Avalanche conditions and avalanche research in the United States: U.S. Army Corps Engineers Snow, Ice, and Permafrost Establishment, Tech. Rept. 29, 29 p.

Haefeli, R., 1948, The stability of slopes acted upon by parallel seepage: Internat. Conf. on Soil Mechanics and Foundation Eng. 2d, Rotterdam 1948, Proc., v. 1, p. 57–62.

Hershfield, D. M., 1961, Rainfall frequency atlas of the United States, for durations from 30 minutes to 24 hours and return periods from 1 to 100 years: U.S. Weather Bureau Tech. Paper 40, 115 p.

Johnson, A. M., 1970, Physical processes in geology: San Francisco, Freeman, Cooper and Co., 577 p.

Kesseli, J. E., 1943, Disintegrating soil slips of the Coast Ranges of Central California: Jour. Geology, v. 51, no. 5 p. 342–352.

Krammes, J. S., 1965, Seasonal debris movement from steep mountainside slopes in southern California: U.S. Dept. of Agriculture Misc. Pub. 970, p. 85–88.

Krammes, J. S., and DeBano, L. F., 1965, Soil wettability: a neglected factor in watershed management: Water Resources Research, v. 1, no. 2, p. 283–286.

Leopold, L. B., Wolman, M. G., and Miller, J. P., 1964, Fluvial processes in geomorphology: San Francisco, W. H. Freeman and Co., 522 p.

Miller, J. F., 1964, Two- to ten-day precipitation for return periods of 2 to 100 years in the contiguous United States: U.S. Weather Bureau Tech. Paper 49, 29 p.

Oka, S., and Katsurajima, S., 1971, Topographic investigations for debris flows occurred by the heavy rain in Ashiwada-mura District: Japan Geol. Survey Bull., v. 22, no. 4, p. 19(179)–60(220).

Rice, R. M., Corbett, E. S., and Bailey, R. G., 1969, Soil slips related to vegetation, topography, and soil in southern California: Water Resources Research, v. 5, p. 647–659.

Rice, R. M., and Foggin, G. T., 1971, Effect of high intensity storms on soil slippage on mountainous watersheds in southern California: Water Resources Research, v. 7, p. 1485–1496.

Roch, André, 1956, Mechanism of avalanche release: U.S. Army Corps Engineers Snow, Ice, and Permafrost Research Establishment, Translation 52, 11 p.

Scott, K. M., 1971, Origin and sedimentology of 1969 debris flows near Glendora, California, *in* Geological Survey research 1971: U.S. Geol. Survey Prof. Paper 750-C, p. C242–C247.

Sharpe, C. F. S., 1938, Landslides and related phenomena: New York, Columbia University Press, 136 p.

Simpson, L. D., 1969, Hydrologic report on storms of 1969: Los Angeles County Flood Control District, 286 p.

Skempton, A. W., and Hutchinson, J. N., 1969, Stability of natural slopes and embankment foundations: Internat. Conf. on Soil Mechanics and Foundation Eng., 7th, Mexico City 1969, State of the Art Volume, p. 291–340.

Swanston, D. N., 1969, Mass wasting in coastal Alaska: U.S. Dept. Agriculture Forest Service Research Paper PNW-83, 15 p.

Terzaghi, Karl, and Peck, R. B., 1967, Soil mechanics in engineering practice: New York, John Wiley and Sons, Inc., 729 p.

U.S. Dept. Agriculture, 1961, Snow avalanches: A handbook of forecasting and control measures: U.S. Dept. Agriculture, Agriculture Handb. 194, FSH2 2332.81, 84 p.

U.S. Environmental Sciences Services Administration, 1969, National summary, annual 1968: Climatological Data, v. 19, no. 13, 97 p.

Vargas, M., and Pichler, E., 1957, Residual soil and rock slides in Santos (Brazil): Internat. Conf. on Soil Mechanics and Foundation Eng., 4th, London 1957, Proc., v. 2, p. 394–398.

Yerkes, R. F., McCulloh, T. H., Schoellhamer, J. E., and Vedder, J. G., 1965, Geology of the Los Angeles basin, California—an introduction: U.S. Geol. Survey Prof. Paper 420-A, 57 p.

Landsliding in
Allegheny County, Pennsylvania

10

Reginald P. Briggs, John S. Pomeroy, and William E. Davies

Most scientific and technical workers familiar with slope-stability problems in the Allegheny County (figure 1) agree that man's modification of sensitive slopes causes more than 90 percent of the landsliding in the area. If man causes landslides, he also can control or prevent them, actively by engineering or passively by judicious land use.

A recent study of the county was made to define areas where a significant degree of susceptibility to landsliding can be expected and thus where special engineering attention of land-use control are most needed.

The report has two chief parts: (1) A discussion of landsliding causes and evidences of landsliding and (2) a discussion of geologic factors affecting landslides. The geographic focus is Allegheny County, but advice and discussion also have applications to adjacent parts of the Appalachian Plateaus.

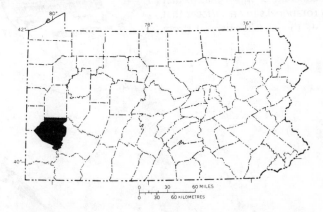

FIGURE 1. County outline map of Pennsylvania showing location of Allegheny County (shaded).

Extracted with permission of the authors from *U.S. Geological Survey Circular 728*, 1975, 18 pp. The report and a companion map (Pomeroy and Davies, 1975) were prepared as part of a larger program sponsored by the Appalachian Regional Commission, a program chiefly aimed at improved management of land resources in Allegheny County. The report and map are contributions to a U.S. Geological Survey environmental analysis of the Greater Pittsburgh region.

Recommendations and Advice for the Nontechnical Reader

Landslides affect many Allegheny County residents, in some places sporadically, and in others more or less constantly. Sometimes they pose a severe financial threat or they may be a minor but almost constant nuisance.

Figure 2 shows the general form of many landslides and gives nomenclature commonly used. Slump (figure 3) is the prevalent type of landslide in Allegheny County. All prehistoric and many recent landslide deposits are largely the result of slumping. Earthflows (figure 4) are common, and rockfalls (figure 5) and debris slides (figure 6) are rather frequent, particularly from highway and railroad cuts.

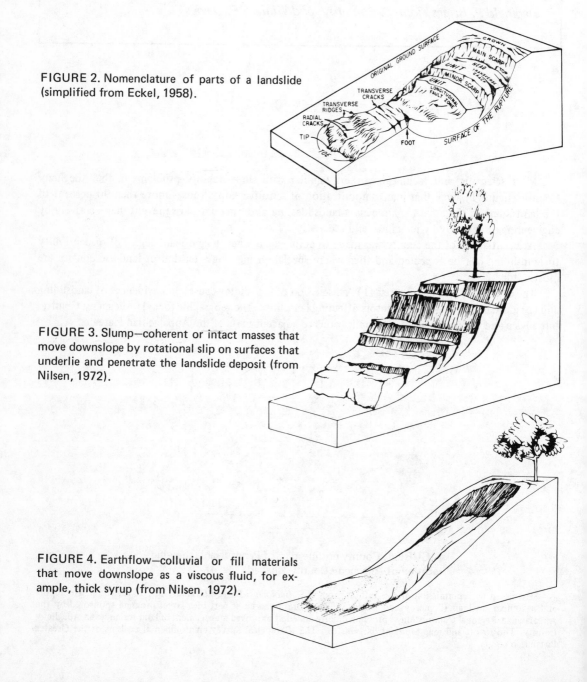

FIGURE 2. Nomenclature of parts of a landslide (simplified from Eckel, 1958).

FIGURE 3. Slump—coherent or intact masses that move downslope by rotational slip on surfaces that underlie and penetrate the landslide deposit (from Nilsen, 1972).

FIGURE 4. Earthflow—colluvial or fill materials that move downslope as a viscous fluid, for example, thick syrup (from Nilsen, 1972).

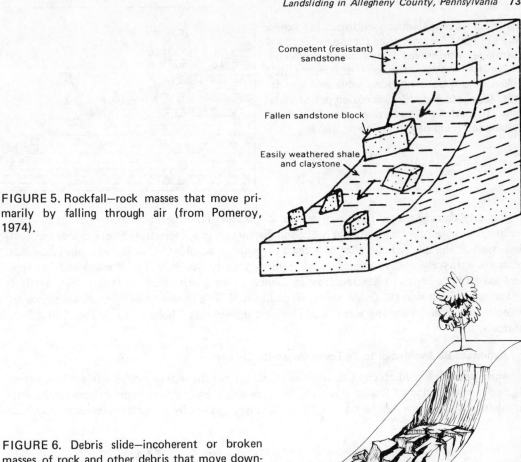

FIGURE 5. Rockfall—rock masses that move primarily by falling through air (from Pomeroy, 1974).

Competent (resistant) sandstone

Fallen sandstone block

Easily weathered shale and claystone

FIGURE 6. Debris slide—incoherent or broken masses of rock and other debris that move downslope by sliding on a surface that underlies the deposit (from Nilsen, 1972).

Most landslides actually are composites of two or more of these types, but usually a given landslide is labelled for the dominant type present. For example, a large slump may have rockfalls and debris slides at its head, and earthflows may occur at its base.

Rockfalls are the most rapid landslides, ranging in duration from a split second to a few seconds at most. Debris slides normally last from seconds to minutes, but if the source of debris is large, for example, a huge mine-refuse bank, a debris slide can move more or less continuously for hours. Duration of an earthflow depends largely on its size. Smaller earthflows can be finished in minutes, but most probably last for an hour or more. Slumps commonly move relatively slowly, forming in hours or even months; some slumps, however, can take place in minutes.

Soil creep is a gradual, more or less continuous downslope movement of soil (figure 7), and usually is not considered a landslide process, but it can be accelerated into landsliding. The basic distinction is that an area of creep does not show significant ground breakage—no scarps or cracks.

Generally landslides in the county are slow-moving so there is ample time to avoid personal hazard; deaths and injuries are rare. Rockfalls are the chief exception. In one place in adjacent Beaver County in 1942, 150 cubic yards of rock fell and crushed a bus, killing 22 passengers and injuring four (Ackenheil, 1954).

FIGURE 7. Creep—Common evidence: (*A*) moved blocks of rock; (*B*) trees tilted at appreciable angles downslope with curved trunks concave upslope; (*C*) displaced posts, poles, and monuments; (*D*) broken or displaced retaining walls and foundations; (*E*) roads and railroads moved out of alinement; (*F*) turf rolls occurring downslope from creeping soil (modified from Sharpe, 1938).

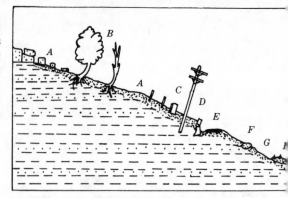

Property damage ranges from very serious in relatively rare cases, such as the destruction of a dwelling, blockage of a transportation route, and destruction of a reservoir, to minor in very frequent cases, such as slumping at the edge of a lawn or highway shoulder. Thus few individual landslide events are extremely costly, although the Allegheny County Department of Planning and Development has estimated costs of damages from landsliding in the county from 1970 to 1974 at nearly 2 million dollars each year (W. C. Morrison, oral commun., 1974). Doubtless unreported, and so not included in this figure, are many events that may cost the individual homeowner perhaps 100 dollars for repair.

Actions to Be Avoided or to Be Taken Only with Caution

Most landslides in Allegheny County result from loading the tops or cutting into sensitive slopes (figure 8), construction of fills on slopes (figure 9), or altering water conditions of slopes (figure 10). No significant actions should be taken without site investigations by competent technical personnel.

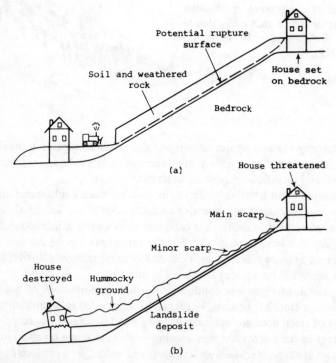

FIGURE 8. (a) Sensitive slope excavated at bottom; (b) potential consequences (from Pomeroy and Davies, 1975).

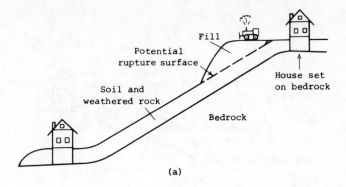

(a)

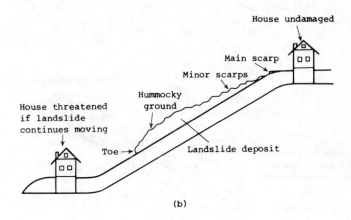

(b)

FIGURE 9. (a) Backyard fill placed on slope improperly; (b) potential consequences (from Pomeroy and Davies, 1975).

Loading.—The most common loading (actually overloading) of a slope is by emplacing earth materials or slag as a fill, usually to extend the backyard of a house on the slope or on a ridgetop. Loading can cause the formation of surfaces of rupture in underlying soil and rock, resulting in failure. Structures also are loading factors. In most places they are set on bedrock, but when they are not, destruction may result—as occurred on Lawnwood Avenue (figure 11).

Cutting into a slope.—Because valleys of the region are rather narrow, excavation of the foot of a slope to make more flat ground is very common. This can be disastrous, particularly if the cut is in the toe of an unidentified prehistoric landslide deposit.

Placing fills on slopes.—Proper construction of a fill on a slope involves engineering practice, and should be designed for the particular slope on which it is to be placed; it includes removal of natural vegetation before emplacement and lift-by-lift compaction. If vegetation is not removed, surfaces of rupture or slip planes can form on decaying vegetation between the new fill and the former natural slope; if fill is not compacted, failure can take place within it. The Lawnwood Avenue (figure 11) locality is an example of fill failure, as are many other residential and backyard fills in Allegheny County.

Altering water conditions.—Natural slopes largely are protected from excessive infiltration of water by their vegetation; removal of vegetation can increase filtration and thus increase susceptibility to landsliding. Faulty drainage systems, such as inadequate disposal of downspout water also can affect slopes.

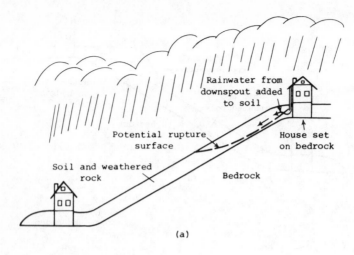

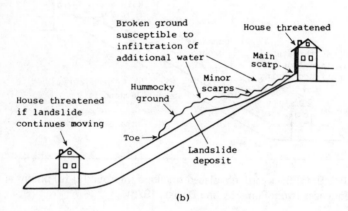

FIGURE 10. (a) Water added to soil on sensitive slope by poor drainage system, here a downspout; (b) potential consequences (from Pomeroy and Davies, 1975).

What the Buyer, Builder, or Homeowner Should Look For

The buyer, builder, or homeowner must always bear in mind that areas susceptible to landslides commonly are larger than most individual properties. Thus, it pays to look not only at the property in question but also at adjacent areas, particularly those upslope and downslope. If the property slopes more steeply than about 15 percent (15 feet of drop or rise vertically in 100 feet of horizontal distance), or if adjacent uphill or downhill slopes (or both) are significantly steeper than the slope of the property, site examinations should be made. In addition, if the property is on relatively flat ground on a ridge top or in a valley, but close to a fairly steep slope, an examination of the slope is recommended.

The following features are indications that a property may have a potential or real landslide problem. All the features listed have been associated with landsliding in Allegheny County. If any of these are observed, the buyer, builder, or owner should seek advice from competent technical personnel.

(1) *Cracks in buildings.*—Most older buildings have minor cracks, but these probably result largely from normal settlement. In general, the fact that a building is old and shows no significant damage is an indication that the building probably will remain undamaged by landsliding. Many or large cracks in newer structures are reasons for concern, although the cause of cracking may well be something

FIGURE 11. Landslide largely in fill, Lawnwood Avenue, Brentwood and Baldwin Boroughs. Warped wall of partially dismantled house in right foreground results from movement of footings that were not set in bedrock. House in right background is set on bedrock and apparently is not distressed structurally even though side and backyards have slipped away. Note large trees inclined strongly downslope behind car and house, evidence of a history of movement in the area. Photographed in April 1975.

other than landsliding. Major cracks commonly are repaired by owners, but evidence of repair usually is visible on close examination. Wet basements may be evidence of cracks in foundation.

(2) *Cracks in brick walls around yards and other outside brick and concrete features.*—Unlike buildings, which generally are set in bedrock, most yard walls and other ancillary features rest on soil. They thus are sensitive to creep which can cause cracking or can pull such features away from structures.

(3) *Doors and windows that jam.*—A door that sticks or otherwise does not seem to fit well or a sash window that jams may be evidence that the frame of a house has been warped.

(4) *Retaining walls, fences, curbs, gas meters, posts supporting porches, and other features out of plumb or not alined in a normal way.*—Fences and similar features usually are vertical and straight when built, curbs normally are straight, and gas-meter piping generally is horizontal when installed. Leaning fence posts, bowed fence or curb lines, and other departures from the expected thus require explanation.

(5) *Breakage of underground pipes and other utilities.*—Downslope movement can upset the alinement of buried utilities. For example, a pipeline parallel to a slope can be bowed by compression or strained by tension and ultimate breakage can result. Evidence of breakage includes otherwise unexplained wet ground, lowered water or gas pressure, and failure of service.

(6) *Leaky swimming and decorative pools.*—Concrete pools are rigid and tight when constructed. Soil movement can cause cracking, which creates an additional hazard in that water leaking from cracked pools can enter the ground and perhaps accelerate movement.

(7) *Tilted trees, grapevines, reeds.*—Trees are probably somewhat less reliable indicators of slope movement than are manmade objects, for trees on slopes tend to bend outward somewhat as they seek sunlight. However, trees leaning at appreciable angles (figure 11) or numbers of trees leaning in different directions strongly suggest areas of landsliding or strong creep. Many grapevines and reeds have been observed on many prehistoric landslide deposits, perhaps as a result of water conditions within the deposits. They thus are general indicators of possible instability.

(8) *Tilted utility poles and taut or sagging wires.*—Most utility poles are more or less vertical and alined when new, and wires between poles usually sag uniformly, so appreciable tilting of poles and variations in amount of sag of wires between adjacent poles are abnormal and noteworthy.

(9) *Cracks in the ground.*—Cracks more or less parallel (across) to a slope usually are indications that the slope is moving.

(10) *Steplike ground features.*—Slumping of ground usually results in steplike scarps (figure 2) that may range from very low to many feet high. When relatively new, the "risers" of the scarps usually expose fresh earth (figure 12). Older scarps may have subdued angles because of erosion and may be vegetated, making them more difficult to identify. Whether old or new, these features are evidence of unstable conditions.

(11) *Hummocky ground.*—Hummocks, low mounds, are common irregularly spaced features of the toes and lower ground surfaces of both prehistoric and recent landslides (figure 12). They do not occur naturally on any other surfaces in Allegheny County.

(12) *Water seeps.*—Seeps and springs are very common at the toes of landslide deposits. Water from seeps on upper slopes may saturate the ground and so contribute to the mobility of downslope materials. Swampy ground and small and perhaps short-lived areas of ponded water are common evidences of ground-water seepage on slopes.

FIGURE 12. Slumped area above northwest-facing roadcut for northbound lane of Interstate 79, Glenfield area. Scarps define slump blocks on which tilted trees are in contrast to upright trees on undisturbed slopes above. Note small scarps and hummocky ground below trees and above bench. Photographed in April 1975.

Geologic Factors Affecting Susceptibility to Landsliding in Allegheny County

Bedrock in Allegheny County is entirely composed of coal-bearing rocks of Pennsylvanian and Permian age (between 320 and 225 million years ago). Formation names, from oldest to youngest, are the Freeport in the Allegheny Group, the Glenshaw and the Casselman in the Conemaugh Group, the Pittsburgh and the Uniontown in the Monongahela Group, and the Waynesburg and the Washington in the Dunkard Group.

Significant factors bearing on landslide susceptibility include:

(1) *Rock types.*—Rocks appearing at the surface are mostly sandstone, siltstone, shale, claystone, and limestone. Coal constitutes less than 2 percent of the rocks exposed in the area. Of particular significance to slope stability are widespread red beds, dusky red layers of claystone and shale. Landslides clearly are most common on deeply weathered red-bed slopes, but thick beds of gray to brown claystones also weather rapidly and underlie extensive areas where slopes are unstable. Sandstone and limestone commonly are harder and more resistant to weathering than are siltstone, claystone, and shale. This explains why sandstone and limestone form ledges and cliffs on many slopes, whereas other rock types rarely are well exposed except in cut banks of streams, in other very steep natural slopes, and in manmade exposures such as highway cuts.

(2) *Rock layering.*—Rock types alternate and form layers that are commonly 1 inch to 10 feet thick, but in places, layers are thicker than 30 feet. Some rock layers are traceable for miles, but most sandstone layers, for example, grade laterally into another rock type in short distances, and some conspicuous lateral changes in rock types can be seen in a single exposure. If, for example, a red-bed layer beneath a sandstone layer is decomposed by weathering, then the overlying hard rock is less firmly supported and may move downslope in response to gravity.

(3) *Rock fractures.*—Two types of rock fracture occur: faults—fractures along which rocks on one side are offset from rocks on the other side; and joints—tight to open fractures, along which no evidence of movement can be seen. Open joints are those in which rocks on either side are sufficiently far apart to allow relatively free passage of air or water. Along tight joints, rocks on either side are in close contact with each other. Faults are relatively rare in Allegheny County. The harder rock layers, composed of sandstone and limestone, are well jointed in outcrop, joints commonly being open and spaced one to several feet apart. Closely spaced joints occur in many siltstone, claystone, and shale layers, but most of these joints are tight. Most joints are nearly perpendicular to the plane of layering. Joints contribute to landslide susceptibility, for if rock layers were not jointed, their tendency to break off when underlying rock is removed would be less. Open joints are also an important factor in rock permeability.

(4) *Attitude of rock layering.*—Most rock layers in Allegheny County are tilted at such small angles from the horizontal that their attitude can best be measured in feet per mile rather in degrees or in percent of grade. Rock attitude is most critical to landsliding on slopes where rock layers dip in the same general directions as the slopes but at lesser angles than the slopes, for on such overdip slopes, ground-water discharge is enhanced, and water is an important factor in most landslides (Briggs, 1974).

(5) *Soil cover.*—Soils are composed chiefly of fine-grained mineral constituents derived from rock decomposition during weathering. However, the term "soil" means different things to different people. To a soil scientist, soil means the material that supports plant life and that has undergone near-surface zonation resulting from the interaction of climate and living matter, conditioned by slope and relief. An agricultural soil rarely is more than 6 feet deep and may rest on and be developed from a parent material that is itself decomposed rock. To an engineer, soil includes all unconsolidated material above hard bedrock, and so includes the parent material of many agricultural soils. Only where depth to hard bedrock is relatively shallow will there be virtual agreement between a soil scientist and an engineer as to thickness and composition of a soil. "Soil" is used in this report in the engineering sense; it thus applies not only to material resulting from rock weathering in place, but also to masses of fragmented and decomposed rock particles that have been transported and redeposited elsewhere.

Examples of transported soils are colluvium (soil accumulated at the base of slopes) and alluvial terrace deposits (deposited from running water). Both of these types can be subject to landsliding.

In Allegheny County, soils of the hilltops are relatively thin, less than 6 feet thick in many areas. Soils of hill slopes are absent where bedrock crops out, are relatively thin on many upper slopes, and are made up of more than 20 feet of colluvium on many lower slopes. Valley-bottom soils generally have nearly level surfaces and so are not a significant factor in most landsliding; they may exceed 100 feet in thickness.

The composition of a soil reflects the composition of the rock from which the soil was derived, for sandstone will weather to a sandy soil, shale to a clayey soil, and hard blocky rocks may weather to a rocky soil. Most soils are loose to moderately cohesive and are finer grained near the surface than they are at depth. They will not stand long on steep slopes, and, in Allegheny County, soils weathered from red beds and, to a somewhat lesser extent, limestone are particularly sensitive to undercutting, overloading, or other processses. Clayey soils when dry commonly are crumbly and relatively low in weight per unit volume. When wetted, clay soils retain water and so become heavier, become plastic, and, depending on their mineral composition, may become very slippery. Many wet clayey soils resemble modeling clay in feel, relative weight, and plasticity.

(6) *Permeability of rocks and soils.*—Permeability as used here means the capacity of bedrock and soil to transmit water. Sandstone in the county commonly is moderately permeable; water may pass around grains of sand and through voids between the grains. In addition, sandstone layers may have open joints that facilitate passage of water. Limestone is fine grained, and solid unfractured limestone is more or less impermeable. However, most layers of limestone are permeable because they are closely jointed, and these joints commonly are open because of dissolution and removal of minerals by moving ground water. In contrast, siltstone and shale are fine grained and tightly jointed; they commonly are less permeable than most coarser grained rocks. Similarly, most sandy and rocky soils are more permeable than are soils composed largely or entirely of clay. Rocks and soils are most likely to be saturated by water zones where permeable materials overlie relatively impermeable materials. Complete saturation commonly results in increased pore pressures that decrease cohesiveness between particles and increase buoyancy in the saturated material. The effect is similar to lubrication and enhances susceptibility to landsliding.

Permeability of rocks and soils and other facets of the shallow ground-water regime relevant to the landsliding process have been described in greater detail by Subitzky (1974a, b, c).

(7) *Steepness of slopes.*—Allegheny County is a land of hills and ridges separated by valleys through which streams and rivers flow at levels commonly 300 feet, and locally more than 600 feet, below adjacent ridge crests. The valley walls are relatively steep; slopes of 25 percent (25 feet of drop in 100 feet of horizontal distance; about 14°) or greater occupy about one-fourth of the area. These steep natural slopes are leading factors in the occurrence of landslides, for if the area was largely one of relatively flat or gently sloping land surfaces, it is unlikely that even red beds would become involved in significant landsliding on natural slopes.

Relative importance of factors.—All the above stated factors are interrelated. At a given place, one factor may be the chief control of susceptibility to landsliding, whereas at another place, the same factor may be less important than others. For example, where a major stream is undercutting its bank by flowing against it, oversteepening will occur and slope failure ultimately will ensue regardless of whether the bank material is rock or soil; where a thick soil cover becomes saturated with water, failure may occur even on relatively gentle slopes. Some slopes can be consistent landslide hazards because of natural or manmade steepness or excessive rock fracturing; some overdip slopes, on the other hand, may be less susceptible to landsliding because only one type of rock is present.

REFERENCES CITED

Ackenheil, A. C., 1954, A soil mechanics and engineering geology analysis of landslides in the area of Pittsburgh, Pennsylvania: Pittsburgh, Pa., Univ. Pittsburgh, Ph.D. dissert., 121 p. (Ann Arbor, Michigan, Univ. Microfilms, Pub. no. 9957, 1962.)

Briggs, R. P., 1974, Map of overdip slopes that can affect landsliding in Allegheny County, Pennsylvania: U.S. Geol. Survey Misc. Field Studies Map MF-543.

Eckel, E. B., ed., 1958, Landslides and engineering practice: Natl. Research Council, Highway Research Board Spec. Rept. 29 (Natl. Acad. Sci.-Natl. Research Council Pub. 544), 232 p.

Nilsen, T. H., 1972, Preliminary photointerpretation map of landslide and other surficial deposits of parts of the Los Gatos, Morgan Hill, Gilroy Hot Springs, Pacheo Pass, Quien Sabe, and Hollister 15-minute quadrangles, Santa Clara County, California: U.S. Geol. Survey Misc. Field Studies Map MF-416, 2 sheets, scale 1:62,500.

Pomeroy, J. S., 1974, Landslide susceptibility map of the Pittsburgh West 7½-minute quadrangle, Allegheny County, Pennsylvania: U.S. Geol. Survey open-file report 74–228, 16 p., 1 pl., 7 figs.

Pomeroy, J. S. and Davies, W. E., 1975, Map of susceptibility to landsliding, Allegheny County, Pennsylvania: U.S. Geol. Survey Misc. Field Studies Map MF-685B.

Sharpe, C. F. S., 1938, Landslides and related phenomena; a study of mass-movements of soil and rock: New York, Columbia Univ. Press, 136 p. [reprinted 1960, Paterson, N.J., Pageant Books].

Subitzky, Seymour, 1975a, A summary of behavior of the hydrologic regime as related to land-use characteristics, Allegheny County, Pennsylvania: U.S. Geol. Survey Misc. Field Studies Map MF-641A [in press].

——, 1975b, Hydrogeologic framework and generalized shallow ground-water circulation system, Allegheny County, Pennsylvania: U.S. Geol. Survey Misc. Field Studies Map MF-641B [in press].

——, 1975c, Heavy storm precipitation and related mass movement, Allegheny County, Pennsylvania: U.S. Geol. Survey Misc. Field Studies Map MF-641D [in press].

11

Land Subsidence

Frank Forrester

Although several hundred square miles of land have experienced subsidence (sinking) in the Santa Clara Valley south of San Francisco, California, the rate has decreased markedly in the past few years. Between 1934 and 1967, part of the area sank more than eight feet as a result of excessive pumping of ground water (figure 1). Since 1966, however, because of a rise of ground water levels, the rate of subsidence has slowed down dramatically.

Results of continuous measurements of subsidence made by the U.S. Geological Survey at San Jose and Sunnyvale since 1960 show that the rate of subsidence has decreased by about 95 percent. At San Jose, the rate decreased from about 1 foot per year in 1961 to about 0.07 foot per year in 1970 (figure 2). At Sunnyvale, it decreased from about half a foot per year in 1961 to 0.02 foot per year in 1970.

Subsidence is likely to develop when a large amount of water is removed from unconsolidated artesian aquifers (subsurface water-bearing rocks). As ground water is pumped from the aquifer the artesian pressure decreases, and more of the weight of the overburden must be carried by the granular structure of the sediment. The additional weight compacts the unconsolidated sediments and squeezes water out of the pore spaces in the fine-grained clays and silts into the coarse-grained aquifer. The resulting reduction in porosity of the fine-grained sediments causes a reduction in volume which causes subsidence of the land surface.

In Santa Clara Valley the pumping of ground water for a variety of uses increased from about 13 billion gallons (40,000 acre feet) in 1916 to about 58 billion gallons (180,000 acre feet) a year during the early 1960s. As a result, the artesian pressure "head" fell as much as 250 feet. With the loss of this artesian support, sediments in the aquifer compacted and the land settled. Between 1934 and 1967, this compaction amounted to a volume loss of about 20 billion cubic feet (500,000 acre feet). Compaction takes place slowly over a period of years so there is no violent movement of land such as occurs during an earthquake. However, land subsidence remains an important and costly problem.

The Santa Clara County Flood Control and Water District estimates that about $9 million of public funds has been spent on levee construction and other remedial work on stream channels to prevent flooding as a result of land subsidence, especially along the southern shore of San Francisco Bay.

Reprinted from *California Geology* 24(8):148–49, 1971. Originally from U.S. Geological Survey News Release.

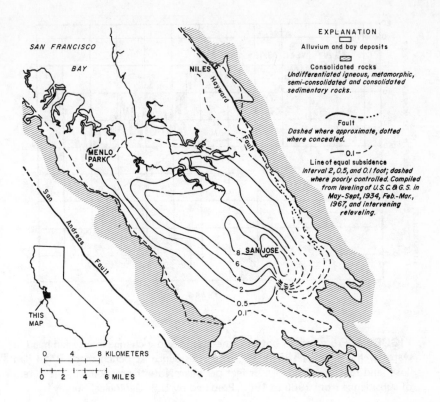

FIGURE 1. Land subsidence from 1934 to 1967, Santa Clara Valley, California. Modified from an open-file map of the U.S. Geological Survey.

Other valley officials have estimated that the cost of repairing or redrilling several hundred damaged wells amounts to at least $4 million.

Although subsidence can't be fully reversed, it can be stopped. The most dramatic decrease in the rate of subsidence has occurred since 1966 as a result of imports of larger quantities of surface water. These large surface-water imports have permitted a decrease in the amount of ground water that has been withdrawn. As a result, the artesian water level, sometimes called the piezometric surface, has risen about 60 feet. This rise in the artesian water level has reversed the trend of increasing grain-to-grain stress on the sediments and thus has slowed the rate of subsidence. If the artesian head could be raised and maintained at least 200 feet above present levels, then subsidence would be stopped.

The Santa Clara Valley was the first area in the United States where land subsidence caused solely by excessive ground water removal was recognized. The extent and amount of subsidence was first realized in 1933 when bench marks established in 1912 were resurveyed by the Coast and Geodetic Survey, and were found to have subsided as much as 4 feet. Between 1934 and 1967, the year of the most recent survey of bench-mark altitudes, the amount of subsidence increased southeast from Menlo Park and Niles to San Jose, where it exceeded 8 feet.

Local agencies have been working since the 1930s toward the goal of obtaining water supplies adequate to stop the overdraft of ground water and raise the artesian head. From 1964–65 to 1969–70, the amount of water imported from outside the valley increased fourfold—from 30,000 to 125,000 acre-feet a year. To pay for these efforts and to encourage use of imported water, Santa Clara County levies a county-wide ad valorem tax and a charge for water extracted from the ground-water basin. The rise in water level that has nearly eliminated the subsidence is due to this great increase in the use of imported water.

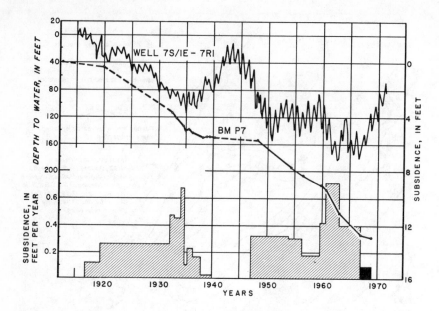

FIGURE 2. From top to bottom, the graphs show change in artesian head in water well near bench mark P7, land subsidence at bench mark P7 in San Jose, and rate of subsidence in feet per year. Note the marked change in rate of subsidence from 1966 to 1969. Prepared by U.S. Geological Survey.

Land-subsidence problems are not limited to the Santa Clara Valley area of California. Similar problems have either developed or exist potentially in such areas as the San Joaquin Valley; the Houston, Texas area; in Mexico City, Mexico; and in Venice, Italy.

The most serious problems are in Japan where more than ten areas have subsided as a result of ground-water overdraft. In Tokyo, two million people live in an area that has sunk below high tide level, and in Osaka, over 600,000 people live under similar conditions.

The U.S. Geological Survey is working in close cooperation with the California Department of Water Resources and various federal, state, and local agencies in studying land-subsidence problems, and in evaluating methods and techniques that might be applied to avoid or alleviate subsidence damage. Subsidence can be reduced or even partially reversed through water management. A reduction or reversal can be achieved only by increasing the artesian pressure either by reduced ground-water withdrawal, or by increased ground-water recharge.

Seismic Hazards and Land-Use Planning

12

D. R. Nichols and J. M. Buchanan-Banks

Introduction

Urban planners and public officials in California and in many other parts of the United States have become increasingly concerned about the possible effects of future earthquakes and how to minimize damage and reduce loss of life. Interest in seismic hazards has increased further after the adoption in 1971 by the California legislature of an amendment to the State Planning Law that includes a "Seismic Safety Element" as a mandatory element of the General Plan (Chapter 150, Section 65302 of the Government Code). This requirement, along with concerns for other geologic hazards and for conservation of natural resources, has focused the attention of planners on the contributions that geology and other earth sciences can make to the planning process.

This report outlines those earthquake-induced geologic conditions that could be hazardous, the type of problems they may pose, how information can be obtained to assess the degree of hazard, and some possible implications to land use. The availability of earth-science information, of itself, does not insure that it will be used (Mader, 1972, p. 78). However, where it exists and the citizenry is aware and concerned, significant steps can and have been taken to amend land-use policies to reflect seismic and geologic conditions even without legislative encouragement (City of Hayward, Planning Commission Subcommittee on Land Use and Development Regulations, 1972).

Seismic Hazards and Implications for Land Use

Earthquakes commonly give rise to various geologic processes that may cause severe damage to structures and death to people in them. These processes include surface faulting, ground shaking, associated ground failure, generation of large waves in bodies of water, and regional subsidence or downwarping.

These seismic hazards vary widely from area to area, and the level of hazard depends on both geologic conditions and the extent and type of land use. This section describes geologic conditions that may contribute to seismic hazard, how to determine their significance in a given area, the level of data desirable for land use decisions, and some possible implications for land use.

Extracted from *U.S. Geological Survey Circular 690,* 1974, 33 pp.

Surface Faulting

The earth is laced with faults—planes or surfaces in earth materials along which failure has occurred and materials on opposite sides have moved relative to one another in response to the accumulation of stress. Most of these faults have not moved for hundreds of thousands or even millions of years and thus can be considered inactive. Others, however, show evidence of current activity or have moved recently enough to be considered active, that is, capable of displacement in the near future. Any fault movement beneath a building in excess of an inch or two could have catastrophic effects on the structure, depending upon design and construction and the shaking stresses the structure undergoes at the same time (figure 1). Therefore, it is important to know not only which faults may move but how they may move.

The definition of what constitutes an "active fault" may vary greatly according to the type of land use contemplated or to the importance of the structure. For example, the Atomic Energy Commission regards a fault as active or "capable" with respect to nuclear reactor sites if it has moved "at or near the ground surface at least once in the past 35,000 years," or "more than once in the past 500,000 years" (Atomic Energy Commission, 1971). A definition for purposes of town planning in New Zealand defines as active, any fault on which movement has taken place at least once in the last 20,000 years (Town and Country Planning Branch, Ministry of Works, 1965; originally published as 1,000 years by typographical error). Commonly, faults are regarded as active and of concern to land-

FIGURE 1. House damaged by displacement along a reverse fault during the San Fernando earthquake, February 1971.

use planning when there is evidence that they have moved during historic time or, through geologic evidence, there is a significant likelihood that they will move during the projected use of a particular structure or piece of land. Because geologic evidence may be lacking, obscure, or ambiguous as to specific times of past movement, geologists may be able to estimate relative degree of activity only after a regional analysis that may extend far beyond the locality under consideration. Such analysis may be based on historic evidence of fault movements, seismic activity (occurrence of small to moderate earthquakes along the fault trace even though not accompanied by obvious fault movement), displacement of recent earth layers (those deposited during the past 10,000 years), and presence of geomorphically young, fault-produced features (scarps, sag ponds, offset stream courses, and disruption of manmade features such as fences and curbs) (figures 2, 3).

Knowing that a particular fault is active, however, is only part of the problem. The other part is predicting the likely location of fault ruptures during the next significant earthquake. Geologists generally accept the premise that the next rupture will probably occur along the fault trace that ruptured last, especially if there is evidence of repeated earlier movements on the same fault trace (figure 2 and Wallace, 1968a, p. 17). However, movement seldom is limited to a single fault surface throughout the lifetime of a fault system such as the San Andreas. In many places tens or even hundreds or thousands of individual fault surfaces make up the San Andreas in a zone varying in width from a few hundred to many thousands of feet. Any individual fault surface may have ruptured at any time during the last 40 million years or so that the fault has been active. It is speculated, however, that most of these surfaces

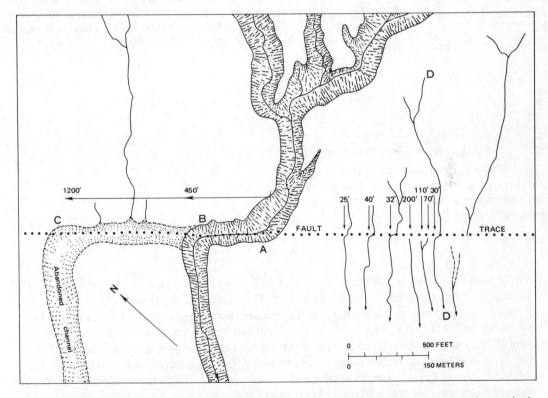

FIGURE 2. Progressive lateral shifting in stream alinement due to repeated displacement along a single trace of the San Andreas fault. The major stream channel has been deflected 450 feet from A to B; earlier displacements are suggested by the beheaded stream segment C, 1,200 feet from A. The small stream channel at D displays a series of offsets—represented by one deflection and three abandoned downstream segments—measuring 30, 70, 110, and 200 feet. (From Wallace, 1968a, figure 8.)

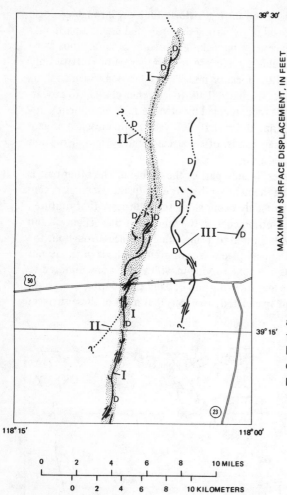

FIGURE 3. Map showing main fault traces (I), branch faults (II), and secondary faults (III). Dashed lines indicate uncertainty of specific fault locations. (From Bonilla, 1970, figure 3.4).

FIGURE 4. Logarithmic plot relating maximum amount of surface displacement to the length of surface rupture on the main fault trace. Points record known historic surface faulting accompanying earthquakes in the continental United States and adjacent parts of Mexico. (From Bonilla, 1970, figure 3.17).

probably have not moved in millions of years, and only infrequently may a new rupture surface develop or is fault movement transferred from one part of the fault zone to another.

Faults that commonly produce significant displacement (more than several inches at a time) often have related branches that diverge from the main fault but usually have less movement along them (figure 3). They may also have secondary faults that are not directly or obviously connected physically to the main fault trace. Secondary faults are usually nearby (within hundreds of feet of the main rupture), but they may extend as much as several miles away. As with branch faults, displacement along secondary faults is usually only a fraction of that along a main fault.

The amount of displacement that can occur during a single earthquake can be related in a general way to the total length of a fault. The longer the fault, the greater the potential for a great earthquake and the greater amount of displacement likely (figure 4 and Albee and Smith, 1967, p. 432; Bonilla, 1970, figure 3.16). The maximum displacement ever recorded during a single earthquake is

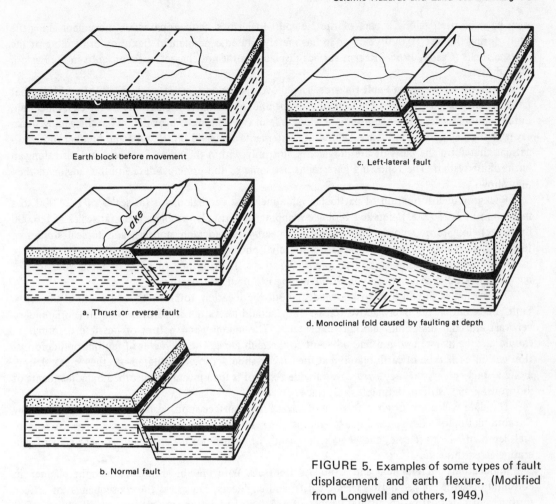

Earth block before movement

c. Left-lateral fault

a. Thrust or reverse fault

d. Monoclinal fold caused by faulting at depth

b. Normal fault

FIGURE 5. Examples of some types of fault displacement and earth flexure. (Modified from Longwell and others, 1949.)

about 42 feet of vertical displacement (Bonilla, 1970). Horizontal movement of as much as 20 feet occurred along the San Andreas fault in 1906 (Bonilla and Buchanan, 1970).

In addition to the location and amount of displacement, the sense of movement is extremely important in estimating the amount and type of damage that might be produced. This was evidenced by the great damage over faults during the moderate (magnitude 6.6) San Fernando earthquake which produced a *reverse or thrust fault* movement (figure 5a); movement occurs along a similar plane, but in an opposite direction on the *normal* (figure 5b) Wasatch *fault* in Utah. *Left-lateral movement* (figure 5c) and *right-lateral movement,* which is common to the San Andreas fault, probably are less potentially damaging to most structures than normal or thrust faulting.

Not all surface faulting need be rapid nor need it occur during major earthquakes. Imperceptibly slow movement, called "fault creep," occurs along the Hayward, Calaveras, and some other faults and may be accompanied by microearthquakes. Similarly, not all deformation of the earth's surface produces fault displacements. Strains in the earth deform the rocks until their strength is exceeded and they rupture, producing the earthquake. Accompanying this bending, however, is a certain amount of *plastic deformation*. Both rupture and plastic deformation commonly occur along active fault zones and may be sufficient to damage or destroy structures over particularly strongly deformed rocks. Earthquakes deep within the earth may result from rupture of deeply buried rocks but without fault displacement at the ground surface, although the surface rocks may be deformed (figure 5). This may have occurred along a part of the Newport-Inglewood fault zone where movement along the fault during the last 10,000 years or so has merely caused a permanent flexuring or bending of the surface rocks (Castle, 1966). Recent surface displacement is not characteristic of faults in the Eastern United States.

Methods for Assessing Fault Hazards. The above discussion focuses on the kinds of problems that need to be assessed and gives a clue as to why specific, quantitative predictions on the exact location, nature, amount, and time of movement along a fault can seldom be provided. What the geologist can say and the degree of confidence behind the statements are based on the type and number of investigations that form the basis of the judgments, not only within the area of concern but also along an entire fault system. The following paragraphs list some of the principal data and the judgments they may allow.

Background information of particular value includes: geologic maps (at scales of 1:24,000 to a maximum of 1:250,000), detailed geologic mapping of particular problem areas (at scales of 1:6,000 or larger), long-term records from numerous, nearby seismograph stations, and topical studies of faulting, which may include interpretation of aerial photographs, examinations of trenches and bore holes, age dating of samples, and geophysical surveys. Lacking one or more of these categories of background studies may seriously limit the geologist's predictive capability.

These studies should lead to knowledge about the location, total length, and width of the active fault zones and all the likely active traces. They should assess the sense of movement (horizontal or vertical) and the maximum amount expectable. The amount and nature of possible deformation should also be assessed within and adjacent to the fault zone. The character of faulting and deformation within each type of earth material at the surface should also be evaluated—do they break sharply along a single plane, do they *shear* over a wide zone, or is the movement absorbed by adjustments of individual grains with no definable fault trace?

The data collected for an evaluation of hazard from surface rupture should be sufficient to allow the formulation of a design earthquake—that is, the maximum expectable earthquake *magnitude*, general depth of energy release, and general frequency of occurrence for each fault zone capable of generating an earthquake.

Implications for Planning and Land-Use Controls. With the above information, the planner, in consultation with the geologists, seismologists, and engineers, can assess the consequences of surface rupture and deformation to different types of existing planned, or possible land use (if uncontrolled or under existing regulations) in the areas subject to ground displacement. Where these consequences suggest unacceptable levels of damage to property or loss of life, alternative land uses that would be compatible with fault rupture, and with adjacent and regional land uses, should be recommended. One alternative that might be considered would be to allow the planned use but to impose controls on the method of construction and its location so that an undue hazard would not occur. Implementation regulations might call for establishing a fault hazards easement (Mader and others, 1972) that would require a setback distance from the active fault traces (figure 6). The amount of setback might differ with the type of faulting and deformation expected. It might also vary with respect to the character of individual faults and even segments of a single fault as well as with the knowledge or lack thereof of the fault zone and the structure or development being considered. Thus the more critical the structure, the greater the likely setback limit.

In addition to adoption of a fault hazards easement, similar to a scenic easement, jurisdictions might consider adoption of "fault hazard zoning" or the broader "geologic hazard zoning," which would include such hazards as landslides and floods as well as faults. Such zoning might override conventional zoning, prohibit human occupancy, require a land use compatible with both the hazard and adjacent uses, or stipulate minimum site investigative and safety standards. Certainly, any development to be considered within, or immediately adjacent to, an active fault zone should require geologic studies to demonstrate that the proposed construction would conform to standards of community safety and that an undue hazard to life and property would not ensue.

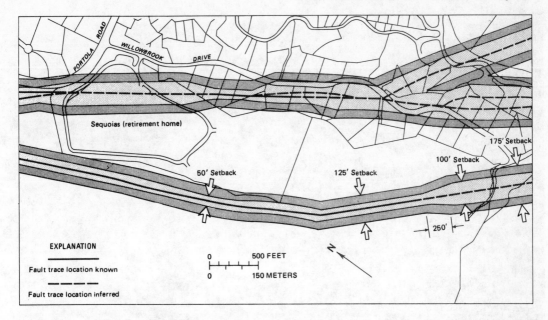

FIGURE 6. Example of minimum easements required for building setbacks from active fault traces by town ordinance in Portola Valley, Calif. All new building construction is prohibited within the 100-foot wide, lightly shaded zone (50 feet on each side of the well-located portion of the San Andreas fault); structures with occupancies greater than single family dwellings are required to be 125 feet from the fault trace (dark shading). Where location of the fault trace is less well known, the more conservative setbacks of 100 feet for single family residences and 175 feet for higher occupancies are required. (Modified from Mader and others, 1972, figure 5.).

Alternatively, prohibition of all uses other than those essential to the public welfare (utility and transportation facilities) could be considered in areas of extreme high hazard. Certain types of land use are completely compatible with the high level of hazard attendant to areas such as the San Andreas fault zone. Some of these include open space, recreation areas (including golf courses, nurseries, horseback riding, bike trails, and so on), cemeteries, freeways (but not interchanges), parking lots and solid-waste disposal sites (under some conditions) (figure 7).

Where development already occurs within active fault zones, jurisdictions can adopt policies leading to the removal of critical engineering structures on the most accurately located active fault traces. Nonconforming building ordinances should be considered that could require eventual removal of structures in the greatest danger, starting with those that endanger the greatest number of lives—schools, hospitals, auditoriums, office buildings and apartment houses, followed by commercial buildings, and perhaps eventually by single-family residences. The nonconforming building ordinances might be based on either an arbitrary time schedule or the expected lifetime of the structures involved. Other innovative options for control of development include tax incentives and adoption of urban renewal policies that would encourage removal of hazardous structures and that would prohibit reconstruction in hazardous areas after earthquakes or other natural disasters (Diplock and Nichols, 1972).

Ground Shaking

Earthquake-generated ground shaking, in many instances, causes the most widespread earthquake damage. However, ground shaking—what most people and structures react to during an earthquake—is one of the most difficult seismic hazards to predict and quantify. Data from past earthquakes have

FIGURE 7. View showing approximate location of fault traces within a part of the Hayward fault zone, some of which ruptured during the October 21, 1868, earthquake (Radbruch, 1967). The plant nursery, undeveloped open space, freeway, and cemetery are land uses most compatible with the hazards posed by this active fault. Other such uses might include drive-in theatre, golf course, riding stable, and other recreational activities.

shown that the intensity of ground shaking can be several times larger on sites underlain by thick deposits of saturated sediments than on bedrock. Consequently, the greatest losses, resulting solely from shaking, may occur where tall structures are built on thick, relatively soft, saturated sediments and the least where they are built on firm bedrock (Wallace, 1968b, p. 67).

In addition to the amplification effects of local geologic deposits, the amount of ground shaking at a particular site depends on (1) characterisitcs of the earthquake source (for example, magnitude, location, and area of causative fault surface) and (2) distance from the fault. To anticipate the severity of ground shaking likely to occur at a site, each of these factors must be taken into account. The extent of shaking damage is also dependent partly on the structural integrity of buildings before the earthquake. (See Page and others, 1972, for a discussion of ground motion values used in the seismic design of structures.)

Characteristics of the earthquake source and distance can be crudely estimated from the seismic history of the area and detailed geologic mapping studies. The amount of data available for such estimates varies widely for different parts of the country, but in some areas (for example, the San Francisco Bay area) detailed research programs are providing data expressly for this purpose. With such estimates, it then becomes possible to examine potential variations in shaking due to variations in local geologic conditions.

Methods for Assessing Shaking Hazards. Earth-science data bearing on possible effects of ground shaking are varied and often incomplete. Starting with a prediction of a design earthquake, an evaluation of shaking intensity can be made at the ground surface that reflects the effect of the local geology (rock, firm soil, and thick wet soil) on modifying the earthquake motion. One useful tool to assess potential building damage from knowledge of ground conditions is to relate the fundamental period of a building to the ground on which it rests. A damaging resonance commonly develops where the fundamental building period coincides with the natural period of the ground. In a very general way,

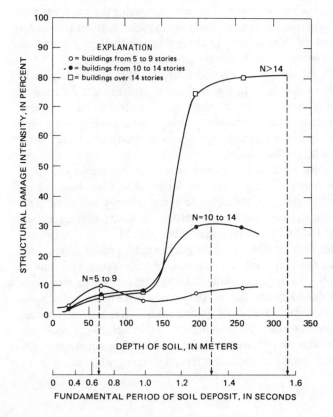

FIGURE 8. Structural damage intensity for different height buildings related to soil deposit. N = number of stories. Where the fundamental period of soil deposit is short (between 0.6 and 0.8 sec), the greatest damage will occur to buildings from five to nine stories tall. With longer soil periods, damage intensity to higher structures increases. (From Seed and others, 1972, figure 12).

the fundamental building period is related to its height or number of stories and that of the ground to its firmness, thickness, and degree of saturation. Taller buildings have a longer fundamental period (2 sec or more) and are subject to greater damage where they stand on ground with a long fundamental period (figure 8). Conversely, 1- or 2-story buildings with a short fundamental period may be more vulnerable on firmer ground.

Ideally, therefore, one means of expressing ground shaking is in terms of the likely response of specific building types—wood frame residences, single-story masonry structures, low-rise (3- to 5-story), moderate-rise (6- to 15-story), and high-rise (more than 15-story) buildings. Each of these building classes, in turn, can be translated into occupancy factors and generalized into land-use types.

Although we cannot presently predict when, where, or how great the next earthquake will be[1] several qualitative approaches can be used for planning purposes to anticipate where ground shaking will be most severe. Selection of any one approach depends upon the use to which it may be put, the money available, and recent improvements and sophistication in methodology.

(1) Correlation of earthquake effects with the general firmness of rock and soil is an empirical technique based on examination of damage from numerous historic earthquakes. Because few earthquakes have occurred in areas where stringent building codes and modern construction standards are in effect, this correlation requires careful interpretation. Some examples of high shaking damage include areas of thick, soft sediments in downtown San Francisco, Santa Rosa, and San Jose during the 1906 San Francisco earthquake and parts of Caracas, Venezuela, during a 1967 earthquake. Areas of firmer soil and rock much nearer the epicenter during both earthquakes suffered considerably less damage.

Areas with relatively different shaking characteristics commonly can be determined from most good geologic maps that distinguish between different kinds of bedrock and unconsolidated deposits. Although such maps may not explicitly rank units by degree of firmness, give total sediment thickness, or assess degree of saturation, most geologists may be able to make such interpretations on the basis of knowledge of the age of the geologic units and some additional engineering field and test data (Nichols and others, 1972). Any determination of the fundamental ground period requires knowledge of sediment thickness and measurements of the shear velocity of the geologic units. Maps prepared on this basis should only purport to serve as a general guide to relative ground shaking effects.

(2) *Intensity* maps, based on the *Modified Mercalli* or a similar intensity scale, have been made in many areas from damage studies of past earthquakes. In a general sense, intensity is a function of ground conditions and distance from the *epicenter*. Lower numbers on the scale indicate less severe shaking and are based on what people feel; intermediate numbers are assigned according to the type and amount of building damage sustained (without regard to age of construction), and higher numbers principally to secondary geologic effects (ground failure).

Where intensity maps, based on previous earthquakes, do not exist or do not reflect the maximum expectable earthquake, they can be prepared using a recently developed method. Intensity increments, commensurate with local ground conditions, are added to a base intensity computed for a specified design earthquake. This technique has been used extensively in the Soviet Union (Barosh, 1969) and has been applied to the State of California (Evernden and others, 1972).

Analyses based on (1) and (2) provide only general qualitative guidelines for ground shaking and earthquake-resistant design. They do not provide quantitative estimates of ground shaking for use in estimating engineering design parameters. Nor do they necessarily distinguish the effects on structures due solely to ground shaking from those due to ground failure. They can be made more useful, however, by applying empirical relations from parallel studies of ground motion characteristics determined from distant natural or manmade microseismic events (Borcherdt and others, 1972). Such studies provide a measure of amplification effects on different kinds of ground at low strain levels. Because the amplification effects from small ground motions are generally linear, while those from

1. See article 13.

strong motion may be nonlinear, such measurements cannot be extrapolated directly to large earthquakes. Most soils and rocks have elastic properties up to certain levels of strain; beyond these levels, they deform plastically or rupture. Consequently, as the strain increases, the ground motion increases up to a point that varies from one ground condition to another. Strain increases that result from very large amounts of energy release, as in a great earthquake, probably are not matched by comparable increases in ground motion. Instead, the strain exceeds the strength of the earth materials that yield, damping the motion.

Theoretical models to predict surface ground motion have existed for many years. Not until relatively recently, however, have enough observations been available from earthquakes and from in situ ground measurements to provide reliable data to use in the models and on which to base an evaluation of the validity of the models (Seed and Schnabel, 1972). Because theoretical modeling techniques require detailed knowledge of geologic and soil conditions and assumptions as to the character of the bedrock motion, their use has been fairly expensive and limited as a predictive tool to anticipate the effects at a single site—usually one to be occupied by a critical structure. These techniques are still in the developmental stage and have not yet won complete acceptance among the experts (Hudson, 1972, p. 41 and Newmark and others, 1972, p. 115–117). Increasing sophistication in analysis, along with expanding knowledge of earthquakes and their mechanism, may soon generate more widespread acceptance and perhaps eventually allow their application to general land-use problems.

In the meantime, the very broad generalized approach in characterizing the firmness of the ground appears to be adequate to assess the gross effects of ground shaking for general planning purposes. Where intensity maps representative of expectable earthquakes exist or can be prepared by modern techniques, they would be valuable for general plan purposes and for specific plans such as an urban renewal program or a large-scale redevelopment proposal. On the other hand, builders of proposed structures that are critical or that will have high occupancies might be required to have a dynamic analysis prepared of the structure and site as a means of assessing their safety and design.

Implications for Planning and Land Use. Seldom can a structure, without regard to its height, be declared inappropriate if it is carefully designed specifically for a given site. Nevertheless, as a broad planning tool, knowledge of expectable ground shaking effects, in combination with other considerations, could lead to low-density land uses in some areas. Elsewhere, such knowledge can lead to the adoption of building code provisions appropriate to areas with different ground shaking characteristics. For example, "geologic hazard zoning" might be applied to areas of very thick saturated sediments with high (long) fundamental ground periods equivalent to that of buildings likely to be in that zone, for example, high-rise structures. Ordinances might require that increasingly detailed geologic, soil engineering, and structural engineering analyses be performed for buildings with the highest projected occupancies in areas of greatest expected shaking motion. Because, as discussed earlier, it is difficult to predict strong ground motion (strong motion) characteristics and their effects quantitatively, it is desirable to establish a legal and procedural framework that remains flexible enough to accomodate increasingly sophisticated methods of prediction.

Other measures that are critical to a lessening of potential loss of life include the adoption and strict enforcement of a hazardous building abatement ordinance and an ordinance to require removal of dangerous parapets. Because of the potential economic impact, hazardous building abatement regulations might best be imposed gradually on a priority basis, selecting first those structures that are the most dangerous and with the highest occupancies, followed by buildings that constitute a lesser hazard and that have lower occupancies. Parapet ordinances, if enforced in urbanized areas, particularly where older high-rise structures may have poorly secured appendages, have the potential of sharply reducing casualties and property damage during major earthquakes.

Ground Failure

Earth materials in a natural condition tend to reach equilibrium over a long period of time. In geologically young and active areas such as California and Alaska, there are many regions where earth materials have not yet reached a natural state of stability. For example, most of the valleys and bay margins are underlain by recent loose materials that have not been compacted and hardened by long-term natural processes. Landslides are common on most of the hills and mountains as loose material moves downslope. In addition, many activities of man tend to make the earth materials less stable and hence to increase the chance of ground failure. Some of the natural causes of instability are earthquakes, weak materials, stream and coastal erosion, and heavy rainfall. Human activities that contribute to instability include oversteepening of slopes by undercutting them or overloading them with artifical fill, extensive irrigation, poor drainage or even ground-water withdrawal, and removal of stabilizing vegetation. These causes of failure, which normally produce landslides and differential settlement, are augmented during earthquakes by strong ground motions that result in rapid changes in the state of earth materials. It is these changes, by means of liquefaction and loss of strength in fine-grained materials, that result in so many landslides during earthquakes as well as differential settlement, subsidence, ground cracking, ground lurching, and a variety of transient and permanent changes in the ground surface.

Mechanisms of Failure. Liquefaction is a common mechanism causing many types of ground failure. It occurs when the strength of saturated, loose, granular materials (silt, sand, or gravel) is dramatically reduced, such as may occur during an earthquake. The earthquake-induced deformation transforms a stable granular material into a fluidlike state in which the solid particles are virtually in suspension, similar to quicksand. The result, where the liquefied materials are in a broad buried layer, may be likened to the action of ball bearings in reducing friction in the movement of one material past another. The Juvenile Hall landslide during the 1971 San Fernando earthquake resulted from liquefaction of a shallow sand layer and involved an area almost a mile long and a failure surface that had a slope of only 2½ percent (Youd, 1971, p. 107, 108). Where the liquefied granular layer is thick and occurs at the surface, structures may gradually sink downward. The tilting and sinking of buildings during the Niigata earthquake illustrate this phenomenon (figure 9A, B).

Loss of strength in fine-grained cohesive materials is another mechanism of ground or foundation failure and might manifest itself in squeezing or "lateral spreading" of soft, saturated clays such as San Francisco Bay mud. It can result in rapid or gradual loss of strength in the foundation materials so that structures built upon them gradually settle or break up as foundation soils move laterally by flowage.

Other causes for loss of resistance include raising the ground water to reduce frictional resistance along a potential failure surface and removal of water or earth masses that may be serving as a buttress to prevent downslope movement.

Results of Ground Failures. Although the basic causes of ground instability are simple in concept, the consequences are often complex and highly variable. They include numerous varieties of landslides, ground cracking, lurching, subsidence, and differential settlement. Moreover, these types of ground failure occur on a wide variety of ground conditions. Landslides, for example, do not require a steep slope on which to form, particularly during earthquakes. Many occur on slopes that are virtually flat, and the surface on which they fail may be very shallow (1 to 2 feet deep) or as much as hundreds of feet below the ground surface. The type of ground failure that develops in a given area is determined partly by the nature of the natural or manmade disturbance that occurs and partly by the topographic, geologic, hydrologic, and geotechnical characteristics of the ground.

Ground cracking usually occurs in still surface materials and is associated with changes in surface topography or materials. For example, during the 1964 Alaskan earthquake, much of the ground cracking that occurred along river flood plains adjacent and parallel to stream channels and along road and railroad embankments resulted from differential movement owing either to liquefaction or to lateral spreading of a relatively soft, deeper layer under a stiff surface layer. Cracks may be only hairline or several feet wide and from a few feet to hundreds of feet long.

Ground lurching may be both a transitory and permanent phenomenon. During earthquakes, soft saturated ground may be thrown into undulating waves that may or may not remain when the ground

FIGURE 9. Niigata earthquake phenomena. *A,* Tilting and sinking of buildings caused by reduction of foundation support due to liquefaction of near-surface sand deposits during the 1964 Niigata, Japan, earthquake. (From Kawasumi, 1968, pl. 7.) *B,* Residents salvaging furniture and personal possesions by carrying them down the exterior walls of apartment building tilted by liquefaction. (From Kawasumi, 1968, pl. 7.)

motion ceases. The same or similar ground surface appearance may also result from permanent differential settlement of the ground, which can be caused by loss of soil strength or by liquefaction. Commonly, the water freed by liquefaction of buried and confined granular layers is forced to the ground surface, moving laterally toward steep slopes or vertically along the planes of weakness in the overlying layers. As the water moves toward the surface or *free face,* it often carries with it some of the sand. Thus, *sand boils, sand volcanoes, sand ridges,* and similar anomalous features attest to the occurrence of liquefaction. As sand and water are removed from the subsurface, the ground settles, often differentially because the sand and water are seldom removed evenly over broad areas. The resulting effects on buildings can be catastrophic.

Subsidence of as much as several feet may occur over a broad area underlain by a thick sequence of sedimentary deposits. For example, after the 1906 earthquake, a well casing was reported to have "risen" 2 feet out of the ground, when, in fact, the ground around it probably liquefied or compacted as a result of the shaking. Subsidence is likely to be greatest in areas where there has been withdrawal of fluids (ground water or oil) over a long period of time. Lesser amounts of subsidence can occur even where fluid withdrawal has not taken place, as in the Homer area of Alaska in 1964. Compaction effects may be predicted with some degree of assurance over fairly broad areas (up to 1 or 2 miles) and even on a site basis, especially when the cause may be liquefaction.

Methods for Assessing Ground Failure Hazards. Basic data on ground failure should include maps and data on areas most subject to landslides, liquefaction, and ground lurching or cracking. These are areas that, because of steep slopes, saturated granular subsurface deposits, or weak or unstable ground conditions, might fail during major earthquakes. One or more maps showing the areal distribution of slopes and each of these ground conditions is desirable, although not always possible. An absolute predictive capability is virtually impossible except for specific sites after careful exploration and analysis.

Implications for Planning and Land-Use Controls. General land-use policy might be guided partly by knowledge of broad areas where instability is believed to be so pervasive that, along with other considerations, its preservation as open space or other nonoccupancy, may be indicated. On the other hand, except during earthquakes, such failures generally occur fairly slowly, may be preceded by indicators, and usually do not result in loss of life, even though extensive or complete destruction of property is common. Therefore, the problem might be ignored. Alternatively, since ground failures can be life hazards during earthquakes, areas of known or likely low stability might be designated as geologic hazard zones. In such zones background studies (geologic and soil engineering reports) should be required to demonstrate that both static and dynamic hazardous conditions either do not exist or can be overcome by site preparation work or engineering design prior to approval of subdivision and site development applications. Although individual structures may be sited safely in such areas, roads, gas, water, and sewer lines can seldom be built without crossing unstable areas. Long-term costs in the form of public services may be great and generally must be borne by the entire community (table 1).

Other solutions to instability problems that are being pursued include adoption of a program to allow tax deductions for property owners whose land is particularly susceptible to ground failure. Such a program might be designed to alleviate tax burdens on property where existing structures are being damaged and on unimproved land as long as it remains unimproved or until the owner can demonstrate that he has eliminated the hazardous conditons. For those relatively few developed areas where severe instability problems are known to exist and disaster merely awaits the triggering action of an earthquake or an exceptionally wet winter, consideration should be given to the implementation of a hazardous building abatement ordinance or the initiation of nonconforming use procedures.

Earth-Science Data Needed to Assess Seismic Hazards

A rational formulation of land-use policies and of implementing regulations to minimize seismic hazards must rely on a broad base of earth-science information. Pertinent existing information, however, varies considerably from one locality to another. It should be recognized that the type, scope, and detail of geologic information needed will vary considerably in different areas depending on the complexity of the geology, the seismic history, type and distribution of existing and anticipated development, and the level of the planning effort. In a county where simple geologic relations and low seismic activity prevail, existing geologic mapping at a scale of 1:250,000 may be an adequate minimum informational level if the data are relatively recent and of high quality. In such instances compilation of existing information for analysis by planners in developing a comprehensive plan and its translation into model ordinances and land-use controls should require little additional data collection and should be relatively inexpensive. In areas of high seismicity and where complex geologic relations have not been resolved, however, an adequate comprehensive plan probably cannot be prepared without additional highly detailed (1:24,000 or larger scale) geologic, seismic, and engineering studies. Costs of these studies can vary considerably according to the amount of additional data needed, the number and type of disciplines involved, and the sophistication of interpretation provided. Consulting groups in the San Francisco Bay region in 1972–73 estimated costs for preparing seismic analyses as ranging between $2,000 and $20,000 for fairly simple geologic areas, where many data were available, or where the scope of interpretations was limited. In areas requiring much new detailed information, where the geology was complex, or where extensive, detailed analysis of the data was undertaken, these costs were estimated to range from $20,000 to $100,000 or more. These cost figures are offered as representative, and they may be exceeded under some circumstances.

Because detailed studies or complex analyses may take 2 years or more, interim policies based on a rapid geologic reconnaissance should guide development planning. These interim policies, since they would reflect unknown levels of risk, probably should be conservatively framed in areas of potential seismic hazard.

Small jurisdictions with few sesimic hazards and without direct access to a staff of planners, geologists, and soil and structural engineers may find it necessary to contract for an evaluation of seismic risk. But, whatever the size of the jurisdiction, agency, or developer, such an evaluation, if comprehensive and thoughtful, will probably be the product of a multidisciplinary team effort, whether prepared solely by consultants, by jurisdiction staff, or by a combination of both.

TABLE 1. SOME ECONOMIC COSTS RESULTING FROM DEVELOPMENT ON UNSTABLE AREAS[1]

The economic loss as a consequence of development on these landslide deposits is already large, will continue to grow, and will probably become significantly greater if additional development is permitted without thorough engineering geology investigations of the area. The estimated 1969-70 loss in market value for all houses in San Jose Highlands, for example, was $228,000, the loss for lots was $195,000, and the loss in valuation for specific landslide damage to certain houses was $61,520— a total loss of $484,520 (Santa Clara Assessor's Office, written commun., Sept. 22, 1971). The cost data below, provided by the San Jose Department of Public Works (written commun., Sept. 28, 1971), reveal the variety and magnitude of expenses to a municipality when landslide activity takes place within a subdivision area.

Actions taken by and financed by the City of San Jose
in the San Jose Highlands area, 1968-71

Soils study and consultant fees	1968	$ 10,000
Soils study and consultant fees	1969	10,000
Consultant for new road	1970	30,000
Construct 1,400 foot gravel-fill interception ditch	1969	15,000
(no water was apparently removed).		
Clean Hydraughers several times		3,000
Construct dewatering wells	1969	25,000
(deactivated after 1 year, no apparent help).		
Above-ground flexible aluminum sanitary sewer	1968	4,500
Sewer photograph survey	1971	3,000
Replace sanitary sewer	1971	7,000
Aerial photography		2,000
Abandon 600 feet of only access road and build 4,000 feet of new access around landslide area		550,000
	1967	0
Winter and spring road maintenance to	1968	9,000
remove ground swells and increasing	1969	30,000
grade due to downward creep	1970	32,000
	5 months of 1971	30,000
Total		$760,500

Estimated value of city streets in San Jose Highlands
(exclusive of new access road) $750,000
Estimated value of city utilities (street lights and sewers)
in San Jose Highlands $300,000

Landslide damage to gas lines in San Jose Highlands totaled $20,000 by late 1970 (Pacific Gas and Electric Co., written commun., Nov. 18, 1970). Landslide damage to water lines has become progressively worse according to the following figures provided by the San Jose Highlands Water Company (written commun., Nov. 3, 1971):

1967-68 (1 repair)	$ 215
1968-69 (5 repairs)	$1,570
1969-70 (7 repairs)	$1,660
1970-71 (20 repairs)	$5,816

No information was obtained on the cost of landslide damage in the map area outside of the San Jose Highlands, but landslides were a substantial and presumably costly problem during and after construction of terminal facilities for the South Bay aqueduct (California Department of Water Resources, 1966).

[1] Taken from Nilsen and Brabb, 1972.

REFERENCES CITED

Albee, A. L., and Smith, J. L., 1967, Geologic criteria for nuclear power plant location: Soc. Mining Engineers Trans., v. 238, no. 4, p. 430–434.

Atomic Energy Commission, 1971, Nuclear power plants, seismic and geologic siting criteria: Federal Register, v. 36, no. 228, p. 22601–22605.

Barosh, P. J., 1969, Use of seismic intensity data to predict the effects of earthquakes and underground nuclear explosions in various geologic settings: U.S. Geol. Survey Bull. 1279, 93 p.

Bonilla, M. G., 1970, Surface faulting and related effects, chap. 3 *in* Wiegel, R. L., ed., Earthquake engineering: Englewood Cliffs, N. J., Prentice-Hall, p. 47–74.

Bonilla, M. G., and Buchanan, J. M., 1970, Interim report on world-wide historic surface faulting: U.S. Geol. Survey open-file report, 32 p.

Borcherdt, R. D., Joyner, W. B., Nichols, D. R., Chen, A. T., Warrick, R. E., and Gibbs, James, 1972, Ground motion predictions, *in* Microzonation Conference: Internat. Conf. on Microzonation for Safer Construction Research and Application, Seattle, Wash., Oct. 30-Nov. 3, 1972, Proc., v. II, p. 862.

Castle, R. O., 1966, Preliminary study of the geology at two proposed sites for a nuclear-powered desalting plant near Sunset Beach and Pelican Point, Orange County, California: U.S. Geol. Survey report, prepared on behalf of the U.S. Atomic Energy Comm., January 1966, 73 p.

City of Hayward, Planning Commisson Subcommittee on Land Use and Development Regulations, 1972, Hayward earthquake study: Hayward City Planning Commission, Calif., 50 p.

Diplock, L. R., and Nichols, D. R., 1972, Governmental responses to development hazards in California, *in* Microzonation Conference: Internat. Conf. on Microzonation for Safer Construction Research and Application, Seattle, Wash., Oct. 30-Nov. 3, 1972. Proc., v. II, p. 837–843.

Evernden, J. F., Hibbard, R. R., and Schneider, J. F., 1972, Interpretation of seismic intensity data, *in* Microzonation Conference: Internat. Conf. on Microzonation for Safer Construction Research and Application, Seattle, Wash., Oct. 30-Nov. 3, 1972, Proc., v. I, p. 363–378.

Hudson, D. E., 1972, Strong motion seismology, *in* Microzonation Conference: Internat. Conf. on Microzonation for Safer Construction Research and Application, Seattle, Wash., Oct. 30-Nov. 3, 1972, Proc., v. I, p. 29–60.

Kawasumi, Hirosi, ed., 1968, General report on the Niigata earthquake of 1964: Tokyo, Japan, Tokyo Electrical Engineering College Press, pl. 7.

Longwell, C. R., Knopf, Adolph, and Flint, R. F., 1949, Physical geology: New York, John Wiley & Sons, 602 p.

Mader, G. G., 1972, Land use planning, *in* Gates, G. O., ed., The San Fernando earthquake of February 9, 1971 and public policy: Spec. Subcommittee of the Joint Committee on Seismic Safety, California Legislature, p. 73–89.

Mader, G. G., Danehy, E. A., Cummings, J. C., and Dickinson, W. R., 1972, Land use restrictions along the San Andreas fault in Portola Valley, California, *in* Microzonation Conference: Internat. Conf. on Microzonation for Safer Construction Research and Application, Seattle, Wash., Oct. 30-Nov. 3, 1972, Proc., v. II, p. 845–857.

Newmark, N. M., Robinson, A. R., Ang, A. H.-S., Lopez, L. A., and Hall, W. J., 1972, Methods of determining site characteristics, *in* Microzonation Conference: Internat. Conf. on Microzonation for Safer Construction Research and Application, Seattle, Wash., Oct. 30-Nov. 3, Proc., v. I, p. 113–129.

Nichols, D. R., Lajoie, K. R., and Helley, E. J., 1972, Geologic parameters for ground response maps, *in* Microzonation Conference: Internat. Conf. on Microzonation for Safer Construction Research and Application, Seattle, Wash., Oct. 30-Nov. 3, 1972, Proc., v. II, p. 860–861.

Nilsen, T. H., and Brabb, E. E., 1972, Preliminary photointerpretation and damage maps of landslide and other surficial deposits in northeastern San Jose, Santa Clara County, California: U.S. Geol. Survey Misc. Field Studies Map MF-361.

Page, R. A., Boore, D. M., Joyner, W. B., and Coulter, H. W., 1972, Ground motion values for use in the seismic design of the trans-Alaska pipeline system: U.S. Geol. Survey Circ. 672, 23 p.

Radbruch, D. H., 1967, Approximate location of fault traces and historic surface ruptures within the Hayward fault zone between San Pablo and Warm Springs, California: U.S. Geol. Survey Misc. Geol. Inv. Map I-522, scale 1:62,500.

Seed, H. B., and Schnabel, P. B., 1972, Soil and geologic effects on site response during earthquakes, *in* Microzonation Conference: Internat. Conf. on Microzonation for Safer Construction Research and Application, Seattle, Wash., Oct. 30-Nov. 3, 1972, Proc., v. I, p. 61–85.

Seed, H. B., Whitman, R. V., Dezfulian, Houshang, Dobry, Ricardo, and Idriss, I. M., 1972, Soil conditions and building damage in 1967 Caracas earthquake: Am. Soc. Civil Engineers Proc., Jour. Soil Mechanics and Found. Div., v. 98, no. 8, p. 787–806.

Town and Country Planning Branch, Ministry of Works, 1965, Town planning and earthquake faults: Ministry of Works, Bull. no. 7, p. 1–6, Wellington, New Zealand.

Wallace, R. E., 1968a, Notes on stream channels offset by the San Andreas fault, southern Coast Ranges, California, *in* Dickinson, W. R., and Grantz, Arthur, eds., Proceedings of conference on geologic problems of San Andreas fault system: Stanford Univ. Pubs. Geol. Sci., v. 11, p. 6–21.

——, 1968b, Minimizing earthquake hazards: Am. Inst. of Architects Jour., v. 19, no. 1, p. 65–69.

Youd, T. L., 1971, Landsliding in the vicinity of the Van Norman Lakes, *in* The San Fernando, California, earthquake of February 9, 1971: U.S. Geol. Survey Prof. Paper 733, p. 105–109.

13

The Status of Earthquake Prediction

Robert M. Hamilton

The September 1, 1975, issue of "Time" magazine focused national attention on the rapid progress that has been made in recent years toward earthquake prediction. The "Time" cover story accurately reflects the mood of optimism that currently pervades the scientific community. It also highlights the many scientific problems that remain to be solved before, and the many socioeconomic problems that must be dealt with after, earthquake prediction becomes a reality.

One of the reasons for the current optimism about prediction is that some very startling news has been received in recent months from the People's Republic of China. A strong earthquake, measuring about 7.3 on the Richter scale, took place there in February 1975. Apparently the shock was predicted, and actions were taken that saved many lives—perhaps tens of thousands.

The prediction was made by a gradual refining, or homing in, on the place, time, and magnitude of the upcoming shock by using a variety of techniques. As early as 1970, the area of Liaoning Province in northeast China, where the shock took place, was identified as an area of possible risk, apparently on the basis of long-term variations in seismicity. This concern was reaffirmed in June 1974 when the State Seismological Bureau called for increased vigilance in the area. This warning was based on a combination of observations, including migrations of seismic activity, tilting of the ground surface, changes in the water level in wells, changes in electric currents in the ground, and strange animal behavior. These observations prompted the Chinese to move more seismographs and tiltmeters into the area. On December 20, 1974, the local government was warned to expect a large earthquake. Apparently this warning resulted in a false alarm on the part of local officials, and people slept outside in the snow for 2 days. In mid-January 1975, the State Seismological Bureau met again, concluded that an earthquake was imminent, and on January 28, the villages were warned to be prepared. Extra seismographs were set up. On February 1, anomalous earthquake activity began, which was interpreted as foreshocks, and it increased markedly on February 3. At 2 pm on February 4, people were told to expect a major quake within 2 days. Shops were shut in the town of Yingkow, and general evacuation of buildings was ordered in Yingkow and Haicheng Counties. The quake came at 7:36 pm that evening.

This all sounds like the fantasy of a science-fiction writer. If the reports we have received accurately describe the events that transpired, then the Chinese achievement represents a milestone in the quest for earthquake prediction.

Reprinted from Earthquake prediction—opportunity to avert disaster. *U.S. Geological Survey Circular 729*, 1976, pp. 6–9.

Earthquake prediction has long been a lively topic of after-dinner conversation, a proclaimed capability of mystics and soothsayers, and an elusive goal of scientists. The fascination with earthquakes derives mainly from their mysterious nature and their awesome power—the ability to level cities within seconds.

Historical accounts are rich with reports of strange events before earthquakes: dogs howling, strange lights in the night sky, weird sounds, withdrawal of the sea from a harbor, and so on. The significance of these reports has been discounted in many cases, but many of the observations have been sufficiently good to keep alive the hope that earthquakes can be predicted.

Many of the reports of earthquake precursors have come from Japan. A particularly impressive anomaly was observed for the magnitude-7.5 earthquake that caused heavy damage in the city of Niigata in 1964. Level surveys and a tide-gage station revealed anomalous land uplift starting 10 years before the shock. Reports such as this one led Japan in 1965 to establish a formal program to predict earthquakes.

A serious attempt to predict earthquakes is also underway in the Soviet Union. Near the village of Garm, in the seismically active Republic of Tadzhikistan, scientists have been working on prediction for more than 25 years. The fruit of these labors was revealed in the late 1960s; some results were truly electrifying. The Soviet scientists reported that prior to some earthquakes, the speed with which vibrations or waves travel through rocks deep in the Earth showed a distinctive variation. Until then, seismic-wave velocity was thought to be constant. This startling finding opened a new realm of scientific investigation. Incidentally, American scientists are now working at Garm with the Soviet scientists under a long-term program of scientific exchange. The activities of this exchange program were reported to President Ford October 31, 1975, by Russell Train, head of the Environmental Protection Agency, and Academician Israel of the Soviet Union.

Variation in seismic-wave velocity was but one of a variety of phenomena reported from the Soviet Union as earthquake precursors. Radon gas in well water increased anomalously before an earthquake at Tashkent in 1966. Electrical resistivity of the Earth behaved unusually before earthquakes near Garm and in Kamchatka. Migration of centers of seismic acitivity and reorientation of earthquake-causing rock stress were also observed. Taken together, these findings presented an impressive case that earthquakes indeed have precursors.

These observations have an explanation. It is widely believed that earthquakes are caused by a gradual buildup of stress in rock to the point at which the rock can no longer withstand the forces, and it fails suddenly along a preexisting plane of weakness, or a fault. This, of course, takes place on a large scale in the Earth, the larger earthquakes involving areas of hundreds of square miles. The stresses are created by large plates of the Earth's crust scraping past each other or colliding in a process called by a variety of names: continental drift, sea-floor spreading, or plate tectonics.

The failure process can be simulated in the laboratory by squeezing a rock specimen only inches across. As the stress builds up and the rock nears failure, tiny cracks form that actually cause the rock to expand in volume. Laboratory measurements show variations in seismic-wave velocity, electrical resistivity, and other properties of a rock undergoing such expansion that are similar to the anomalies observed before earthquakes.

American results have by and large confirmed the Soviet findings. In hindsight, it appears that the magnitude-6.5 earthquake near San Fernando, Calif., in 1971 was preceded by a velocity anomaly, as was a smaller shock of magnitude 5.0 in central California in 1972. In the Adirondack Mountains region of New York State, a small earthquake was successfully forecast on this basis in 1973. A resistivity anomaly preceded a magnitude-3.9 earthquake in central California in 1973.

The most encouraging new results in the United States came in November 1974 for a magnitude-5.2 earthquake that struck on Thanksgiving Day near Hollister, Calif. Just south of Hollister, the Geological Survey operates a dense network of instrumentation in an experimental earthquake-prediction system. Strong precursors to the shock were observed in the Earth's magnetic field—the first such anomaly recorded—and in the tilting of the land surface. At a lower level of certainty, anomalies were also observed in the length of survey lines. Such a variety of precursory phenomena had not been previously observed for a single earthquake.

Thus, by 1974, the Soviet Union, Japan, and the United States had taken on earthquake prediction as a national goal and had convincingly established that earthquakes have precursors. At that time, the Chinese effort was virtually unknown to us, but word reached the West that a major prediction program was underway. The opportunity to find out about it came when former President Nixon's visit there led to an exchange of earthquake specialists. The Chinese came to the United States in spring 1974. They gave little information on their program, saying that they were here to learn of our activities, but they dropped enough hints about their own program to alert American scientists that they had some surprises in store when the U.S. delegation, of which I was a member, visited China in October 1974.

What we found was a well-organized, large-scale effort of research specifically aimed at earthquake prediction. The program began soon after two very destructive earthquakes hit Hopeh Province of China in 1966. China's leaders, including Premier Chou En-lai, visited the stricken area and proclaimed that a serious effort would be undertaken to reduce the dreadful impact that earthquakes have had on the Chinese people. More than 800,000 people were killed in 1556 from a shock near Sian, in central China, and about 180,000 were killed in 1920 near Kansu.

The biggest surprise we found in China was that roughly 10,000 people, including several hundred scientists, were working very hard to predict earthquakes, using a wide variety of instrumentation that includes some of the best in use anywhere in the world today. Virtually every technique that has ever been suggested as a basis for prediction is being studied to some degree. Many precursors have been observed, ranging from reports of unusual animal behavior to well-documented anomalies recorded on the finest instruments. About 10 earthquakes have been successfully predicted, and warnings have been issued, but the Chinese readily acknowledge that many predictions have not been successful.

The Chinese success in predicting the Liaoning earthquake signals that the age of earthquake prediction may be upon us. The laboratory studies show that earthquake precursors should exist, and the many field observations seem to confirm that they are observable. The big questions now are whether all earthquakes have precursors—and whether these precursors are sufficiently regular or uniform in nature to be reliable as predictors. These questions can be answered only through continued studies.

The one area in the United States that has a comprehensive prediction system, mentioned before with regard to the Thanksgiving Day earthquake, is in central California astride the San Andreas fault south of the town of Hollister. This area was chosen for intensive study by the Geological Survey because of its high seismicity. The instrumentation system used there is very much in the experimental phase of development, but at the same time it is a prototype of what could be installed elsewhere in the future.

As is the case with most new technological developments, progress can be a mixed blessing. Earthquake predictions undoubtedly can save lives, as has already been demonstrated in China, but in the finely balanced socioeconomic structure of the United States, a prediction can also cause serious problems. One can imagine, among other things, that prediction of a shock near a major city could lead to a drop in tourism, nonrenewal of earthquake insurance policies, fleeing of the area by the panic striken, and convergence on the area by the thrill seekers. Failure of the earthquake to occur could result in recriminations, lawsuits, and loss of confidence in the scientists who made the prediction. Unlike a hurricane that veered off course, there would be no way to convince people that they had had a near miss. The fallout of legal, political, social, and economic problems could be serious.

Predictions, however, have the potential to provide enormous benefits. Tens of thousands of lives were saved in 1971 because the lower Van Norman Reservoir was lowered before the earthquake struck at San Fernando, Calif., and caused near-collapse of the dam. Although the action was based on general concern for the dam, rather than on an earthquake prediction, the lesson is clear. Many critical facilities are of necessity sited in regions that will experience strong earthquakes. A warning could avert serious consequences from damage to pipelines, storage tanks, and nuclear reactors.

   Much remains to be accomplished before earthquake prediction becomes as useful as weather forecasting. Nevertheless, hopes are high that progress will be rapid. The greatest need is for additional observations of earthquake precursors. Observations are needed from a variety of geologic settings to assure that each area will not be a special case. The current level of effort will permit progress toward meeting these needs; however, it does not provide for establishment of any prototype earthquake-prediction system. As a result, the transition to a reliable prediction capability will not be very rapid. Even in the areas that are now under study, the development phase for prediction may stretch over the next decade. In the meantime, we can expect to see many scientific predictions based on fragmentary data, and we must develop a system for reporting these predictions and for responding to them effectively.

PART THREE

Engineering Aspects
of Land Use

Geologic hazards caused by attempts to use the geologic environment for construction purposes are often amenable to engineering solutions. There are a variety of philosophic approaches to the problem; one extreme is that all such problems can be solved by proper engineering techniques, although costs may be unreasonable. Another approach is that these high-cost solutions can be avoided through proper planning based on adequate geologic information. However, it should be acknowledged that in many cases the option to place the structure elsewhere does not exist and areas that require expensive design features to reduce possible damage from geologic hazards must be used.

In this section we investigate some of the engineering solutions to problems of foundation stability, flooding, landslides, and construction in permafrost regions. In the article by Stephen S. Hart, the serious problems of structural failure as a result of swelling soils are discussed. Incorporation of water into the clay in the soil increases the volume of the clay, and if the foundation is not properly designed, damage to the entire structure might occur. Avoidance of this problem begins with some simple engineering soil tests followed by appropriate design modifications which include proper drainage systems as well as foundation adjustments. Areas where such problems are serious can be delineated by reconnaissance mapping and less intense development can be planned for these areas.

Groundwater levels often drop as a result of urbanization in humid climates. This drop occurs because permeability of the land surface is decreased by covering it with roads, parking lots, and buildings as described earlier by Luna B. Leopold (article 5). In dry climates the situation may be reversed, as the water table is raised by watering of lawns and in some cases the operation of septic tank systems. This may result in flooded basements, as Judith L. Hamilton and Willard G. Owens discuss in article 15.

Highways that traverse unstable bedrock and colluvial materials frequently do not have better alternate routes available. Landsliding that affects such routes may be alleviated by engineering techniques; however, care must be taken not to over-engineer such solutions which might result in higher cost. The article (16) by David L. Royster on problems of highway failure in Tennessee includes solutions such as excavation, stable fill, rock buttresses, gabions, and drains and wells to intercept the groundwater flow, which is one of the main factors causing landslides.

As an urban area develops the complexity of handling the city's vital functions of water supply and waste disposal changes. The first stage is the individual well and outhouse; next comes a centralized reservoir with an urban distribution system for water, and sewers for conveyance of waste to rivers or lakes. When contaminants added to streams outweigh the stream's capabilities of natural purification and cleansing, sewage treatment plants are added to reduce pollution. During periods of high runoff raw sewage combined with storm water often has to be dumped directly into the river, bypassing the inadequate treatment facilities. Article 17 describes how Chicago is using engineering techniques to solve this problem. The project, known as the Chicago Underflow Plan, is one of many plans originally considered. Although concern has been expressed over possible negative environmental impact and increased costs, many people expect it to be an outstanding engineering solution to the problem of inadequate treatment of waste water.

The last paper in this section discusses site selection, foundation design, and drainage in permafrost regions. A large knowledge base is developing concerning construction in polar regions because of renewed interest in natural resources of these areas. Such problems do not respect national boundaries and it is appropriate that the authors are from different nations.

14

Potentially Swelling Soil and Rock in the Front Range Urban Corridor

Stephen S. Hart

Introduction

Swelling soils are a nationwide problem, as shown by Jones and Holtz (1973):

> Each year, shrinking or swelling soils inflict at least $2.3 billion in damages to houses, buildings, roads, and pipelines—more than twice the damage from floods, hurricanes, tornadoes, and earthquakes! . . . Within the average American's lifetime, 14% of our land will be lashed by earthquakes, tornadoes and floods—but over 20% will be affected by expansive soil movements. . . Over 250,000 new homes are built on expansive soils each year. 60% will experience only minor damage during their useful lives, but 10% will experience significant damage—some beyond repair. . . One person in 10 is affected by floods; but one in five by expansive soils.

Swelling is generally caused by expansion due to wetting of certain clay minerals in dry soils. Therefore, arid or semiarid areas such as Colorado with seasonal changes in soil moisture, experience a much higher frequency of swelling problems than eastern states which have higher rainfall.

Rocks containing swelling clay are generally softer and less resistant to weathering and erosion than other rocks and, therefore, more often occur on the plains and along the sides of mountain valleys than in the high mountain areas. Because the population of Colorado is also concentrated on the plains and in mountain valleys, most of the homes, schools, public and commercial buildings, and roads in the state are located in areas of potentially swelling clay. In fact, most of Colorado's hard crystalline rock, which presents no swelling hazard, is located on public land—wilderness areas, national parks, and national forests.

The Front Range Urban Corridor includes the foothills and piedmont area of Colorado from Fort Collins and Greeley on the north to Pueblo and Canon City on the south (figure 1). This area includes more than 80 percent of Colorado's population in less than 6 percent of the state's area. Although only half of the 30 sedimentary bedrock formations that are exposed in the Urban Corridor contain swelling clay, these swelling formations underlie all of the major cities. Swelling clays are, therefore, one of the most significant, widespread, and costly, but least publicized, geologic hazards in Colorado.

Extracted with permission of the author from *Environmental Geology No. 7,* 1974, 19 pp. Published by Colorado Geological Survey, Denver. Project funded in part by U.S. Geological Survey, Front Range Urban Corridor Program.

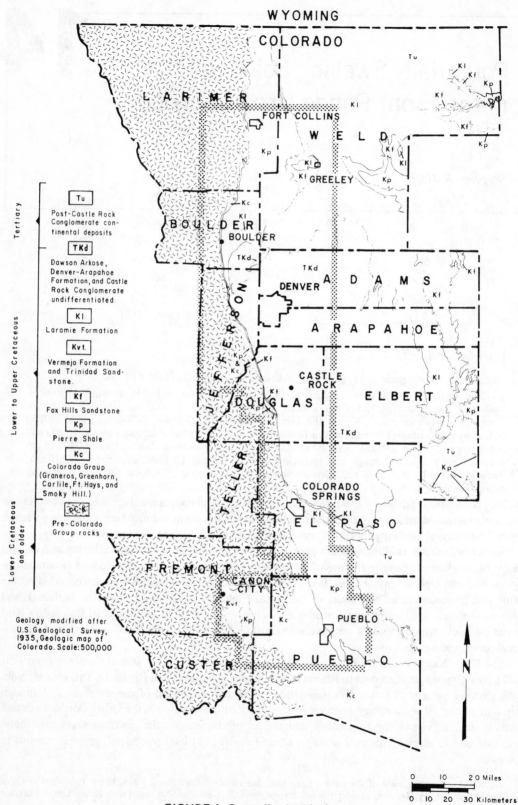

FIGURE 1. Generalized geologic map.

What Is Swelling Clay?

Sedimentary rocks and surficial soils*[1] are composed of gravel, sand, silt, and clay* particles. In order to visualize the relative grain sizes of these particles, an example using familiar objects can be given. Although the average diameter of a gravel particle is approximately ¾ in., suppose that an average gravel particle were the size of a basketball. An average sand particle then would be the size of a baseball, and a silt particle the size of a pea. The average clay particle, however, would be almost invisible, with a pencil dot representing a large clay particle. These clay particles may consist of a variety of minerals—quartz, feldspar, gypsum, or clay minerals. Common clay minerals in Colorado are montmorillonite, illite, and kaolinite. To return to the previous analogy, gravel, sand, silt, and some clay particles are often round, three-dimensional objects. Clay minerals, however, are generally flat, nearly two-dimensional plates just as the above-mentioned pencil dot is flat and two-dimensional.

The clay minerals in rocks and soils are responsible for their expansion, or "swell," as it is generally called. This swelling is caused by the chemical attraction of water to certain clay minerals. Layers of water molecules are incorporated between the flat, submicroscopic clay plates. As more water is made available to the clay, more layers of water are added between the plates, and adjacent clay plates are pushed farther apart, as shown below:

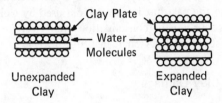

FIGURE 2. Diagrammatic sketch of a montmorillonite clay particle as it incorporates water within the clay structure.

This pushing apart, or swelling, occurs throughout the mass of soil that is being wetted, and causes increased volume and high swell pressures within the mass. The opposite effect, called shrinkage, may occur if a previously wet swelling clay is dried. Although no large pressures are exerted, shrinkage will cause a volume decrease of the soil mass. These processes of swelling and shrinkage may occur any number of times for a single soil mass. Either swell or shrinkage may cause damage to streets and buildings, but swell accounts for most of this damage in Colorado.

Montmorillonite Clay (Bentonite). The clay mineral responsible for most swelling is montmorillonite, often called "bentonite*." A sample of pure montmorillonite may swell up to 15 times its original volume. However, most natural soils contain considerably less than 100 percent montmorillonite, and few swell to more than 1½ times their original volume (a 50 percent volume increase) (Jones and Holtz, 1973). A small load may decrease the actual swell to less than 1¼ times the original volume (25 percent volume increase). However, a 25 percent volume increase can be extremely destructive because volume increases of 3 percent or more are generally considered by engineers to be potentially damaging and require specially designed foundations.

Gypsum and Alkali Salts. Swelling minerals, other than clay, also occur widely in the Front Range Urban Corridor. Hydrated calcium sulfate, or gypsum, and sodium sulfate, or white alkali, may have moderate "swell potential" if they constitute more than 15 to 20 percent of a soil. This "swell potential" is not, however, caused by expansion of clay plates due to increased moisture content, but by the pressures developed during crystal growth.

Although there have been suspected cases of damage due to swelling sulfates, these minerals are more generally considered a hazard due to their corrosive properties. Corrosion of concrete and metal by high sulfate concentrations is responsible for several million dollars in damage annually to side-

1. * denotes words in glossary.

walks, driveways, roads, storm sewers, metal pipes, and buried utility cables. Such damage can be greatly minimized by recognition of the presence of sulfate. When recognized, proper engineering design procedures can be specified to minimize corrosion damage, e.g., Type II, air-entrained cement and cathodically protected metal pipes.

How Can One Recognize Swelling Soil or Rock?

Although several visual methods for identification of potentially swelling clays exist, only a *competent, professional soil engineer and engineering geologist should be relied upon to identify this potential hazard.* Some warning signs for swell might include: a) soft, puffy, "popcorn" appearance of the soil when dry; b) surface soil that is very sticky when wet; c) open cracks (desiccation polygons) in dry heavy clay soils; e) soils that are very plastic and weak when wet but are "rock-hard" when dry.

Engineering soil tests include index tests and design tests. Rapid, simple index tests are used to determine whether more complex design tests are necessary. Some index properties that may aid in the identification of probable areas of swelling clay include Atterberg limits*, plasticity index*, grain size determination, activity ratio*, dry unit weight*, and moisture content (Asphalt Institute, 1969). The Potential Volume Change (PVC) test developed for the Federal Housing Administration (Lambe, 1960) has been widely used in the past but is now seldom used by Colorado soil engineers. The primary design tests for swelling soils are the consolidation-swell* test for buildings, and the California Bearing Ratio* (CBR) swell test for roads (Asphalt Institute, 1969).

Examples of Swelling Clay Damage

Damage from swelling soils can affect, to some extent, virtually every type of structure in the Front Range Urban Corridor. Some structures, such as downtown Denver's skyscrapers, generally have well engineered foundations that are too heavily loaded for swelling damage to occur. At the opposite extreme are public schools and single-family homes, which are generally constructed on a minimal budget and which may have under-designed, lightly-loaded foundations that are particularly subject to damage from soil movements. Homeowners and public agencies who assume they cannot afford more costly foundations and floor systems often incur the highest percentage of damage and costly repairs from swelling clay. This has led many homeowners to make cheap, "cover-up" repairs and quickly place their homes on the resale market. This attitude of "cover-up and sell-out" has precluded extensive publicity in the media of swelling clay damage to homes. Schools and other public buildings, have, however, received both extensive swelling clay damage and extensive publicity by the media.

Pueblo. On May 27, 1974, local media announced that the Life Science Building at Southern Colorado State College (S.C.S.C.) in Pueblo would be closed pending repairs of swelling clay damage. Structural beams supporting the roof and floors of the 6-year-old building were being pulled off of their supporting columns due to the uplift pressure on the foundation caused by wet "bentonite" soils. More than $100,000 in repairs will be necessary before the building can be reopened. Another building on the campus experienced 3 in. of heave in 5 months during the spring and summer of 1974. Only a year earlier, $170,000 in repairs to swelling clay damage were required at the 7-year-old library at the same school.

Denver. In 1970 repairs to damage from swelling clay were undertaken at Ridge Home, the state school for mentally retarded children, in Wheat Ridge. The $490,000 spent for repairs to cracked walls, floors, ceilings, doors, and windows represented nearly one third of the original cost of the 6-year-old buildings. Another Denver metropolitan area school that has received damage was reported in *Cervi's Rocky Mountain Journal* on June 5, 1974. Issac Newton Junior High School in Littleton has received ". . . cracks where floors and walls had pulled away from support columns, bowed prestress concrete panels, floor cracks, and fallen ceiling tiles." Repairs to this swelling clay-related damage have cost taxpayers nearly half of the initial construction cost of $1.5 million in a building only 12 years old.

Boulder. Another school district that has had a continual struggle with swelling clay damage is the Boulder Valley School District in Boulder (figure 3). When the present director of planning and engineering began his job, the school district employed one full-time carpenter whose only job was to cut off the bottoms of doors. This was necessary because floor slabs, pushed upward by swelling clays, interfered with the closing of the doors. Damage from swelling clay has been so costly in Boulder schools that an average additional cost of $42,000 for structural floors is being spent on each new school in the eastern half of the school district.

Urban Corridor Streets and Highways. Highways in some parts of the Front Range Urban Corridor have required frequent and expensive maintenance resulting from swelling damage. Part of the Boulder Turnpike (U.S. 36) near Louisville required extensive maintenance in the early 1950s. Pavement along the Turnpike heaved as much as 7 in. (Holtz, 1959) shortly after construction. Interstate Highway 25 has several sections of swelling damaged pavement both north and south of Denver. Heaved and cracked city streets, sidewalks, curbs, driveways, and patio slabs (figure 4) are very common indicators of swelling soil and rock throughout the Urban Corridor.

Potential Hazard Areas in the Urban Corridor

Pierre Shale. Of the approximately 15 sedimentary bedrock formations that contain swelling clay, 4 underlie most of the Front Range Urban Corridor (figure 1 and figure 5). One of these, the Pierre Shale, contains some montmorillonitic shale and numerous white or yellow "bentonite" beds ranging in thickness from ¼ in. to 6 in. This formation underlies the area from central Colorado Springs south through eastern Pueblo and from Canon City to Florence and Wetmore. North of Denver it extends from Roxborough Park to just west of Green Mountain, from Golden to Boulder west of Colorado 93, and from Boulder northeast to Longmont, Loveland, Fort Collins, and Windsor. In the Pierre, swell potential may range from low to very high, but the swell potential within specific parts of the formation is generally predictable.

Laramie Formation. A less predictable bedrock unit that underlies a large part of the Urban Corridor is the Laramie Formation. This formation is composed of thick, white to yellowish-gray sandstone beds alternating with greenish-gray claystone beds. Some of these claystone beds are

FIGURE 3. Cracked ceiling in Boulder school district building caused by 2 in. of uplift on left wall.

FIGURE 4. Patio slab broken by 3 in. of heave.

montmorillonitic, particularly in the middle one-third of the unit. Other claystones in the Laramie, however, contain a high percentage of kaolinite, a clay mineral that does not swell significantly and is used locally in the manufacture of brick and tile (Gude, 1950). One of the best exposures of this formation is in the claypits immediately east of U.S. Highway 6 in Golden. Because the Laramie is also the principal coal-producing formation along the Front Range, areas underlain by outcropping or shallow Laramie beds are generally associated with coal mines and mining districts. One such district is the Boulder-Weld Coal Field, which runs from Leyden and Marshall on the southwest, through Lafayette, Louisville, Erie, Frederick, and Dacono, to Platteville and Hudson on the east. Another old Laramie coal-producing area lies in a narrow southeast-trending band located southwest of the Austin Bluffs and Palmer Park in Colorado Springs. The Laramie Formation forms the bedrock in the Eaton-Ault area north of Greeley but is generally covered by surficial deposits including wind-blown sand and stream-deposited gravel and sand in the area.

Dawson and Denver-Arapahoe Formations. The Dawson Arkose and Denver-Arapahoe Formation underlie most of the area from northern Colorado Springs on the south to Golden, Broomfield, and Brighton on the north. These formations consist of extremely variable beds of sandstone, conglomerate, siltstone, and claystone. In Colorado Springs the Dawson Arkose includes a potentially highly swelling zone that trends southeasterly from the Air Force Academy to Peterson Field, along the northeast side of Austin Bluffs. Other major areas underlain by swelling clays in the Dawson include the Parker and Cherry Creek Reservoir areas. The Denver-Arapahoe Formation is the principal bedrock unit underlying metropolitan Denver. Some parts of this unit contain very highly swelling clays that have caused millions of dollars in damage. The areas that have suffered the most costly damage include southeast Denver, Littleton, Aurora, Green Mountain, Applewood, Westminster, and Northglenn. However, no part of the Denver metropolitan area is completely free of potentially swelling soils. Other sedimentary bedrock units in the Urban Corridor, such as the Graneros, Carlile, and Smoky Hill Shales, Greenhorn Limestone, and Fox Hills Sandstone, normally contain some swelling clay. However, as these units generally underlie only small parts of the Urban Corridor, no specific areas of potential hazard are described.

Surficial Geology. Surficial geologic units, such as stream gravel and wind-blown sand, often cover the sedimentary bedrock units mentioned earlier. Most of these units have little or no swell potential. However, some such units are overlain by potentially-swelling, clayey "subsoil" that is generally found only in the upper one to five feet of the unit. This clay-rich layer is formed by weathering of transported rock and is known as the "B horizon" by geologists. Wind-blown silt, termed loess by geologists, will sometimes present a dual hazard when wetted due to the possible swell of this B horizon "subsoil" and possible collapse, or hydrocompaction, of the underlying silt. Other surficial units that may locally contain swelling clay are colluvium and residuum. Both units are generally found where bedrock is near the surface, with colluvium found on slopes and residuum on flatter areas. They are formed from a mixture of weathered bedrock and debris from other surficial units. If the weathered bedrock is a swelling claystone or shale, the colluvium or residuum will also have some potential for swell. A third surficial unit that may be influenced by the character of the local bedrock is the Piney Creek Alluvium. This unit is a black, organic, micaceous silt or sand that is found along most small streams in the Urban Corridor. Where the local bedrock consists of Pierre Shale, Laramie Formation, or other potentially swelling bedrock formations, the Piney Creek Alluvium may contain swelling, montmorillonitic clay derived from erosion of the claystone bedrock.

No general statements, or even maps, can determine the exact conditions that will be found on a specific building site. Therefore, *all potential building sites in the Front Range Urban Corridor should be evaluated by a professional soil engineer and/or engineering geologist before construction.*

What Can Be Done To Minimize Damage?

Many methods of preventing or minimizing damage from swelling clays have been used in the Front Range Urban Corridor. Some of these methods should be included at the design stage of con-

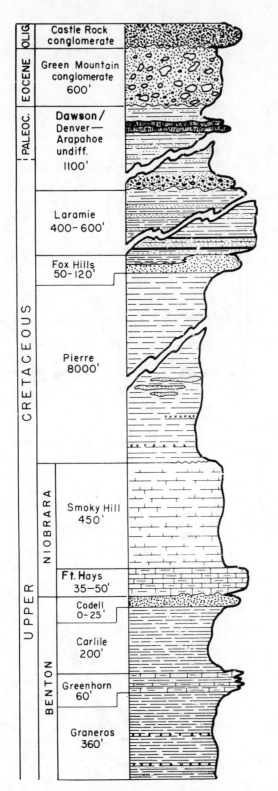

CONGLOMERATE AND GRAVEL: pebbles up to 2 feet; occasional lenses of tan to maroon siltstone; commonly forms escarpments; best developed near town of Castle Rock; generally low swell potential.

CONGLOMERATE: igneous and metamorphic boulders up to 3 feet, unconsolidated; lenses of tan, silty claystone containing leaf imprints; caps Green Mountain south of Golden; generally low swell potential; moderate to very high swell potential in some claystone.

SANDSTONE AND SILTSTONE: tan to light brown feldspathic, fine- to medium-grained sandstone, siltstone, and claystone; conglomerate at base; Table Mountain "basalt" flows in upper part; well exposed on west side of Green Mountain, below flows east of Golden, and in the Austin Bluffs near Colorado Springs; low to moderate swell potential in conglomerate and sandstone; moderate to very high swell potential in siltstone and claystone.

SANDSTONE AND CLAYSTONE: sandstones fine-grained, feldspathic to quartzose, white to light tan, compact; claystones dark gray, carbonaceous; thin lignitic coal beds in lower part; exposed in pits west of School of Mines campus; low swell potential in sandstone; moderate to very high swell potential in claystone.

SANDSTONE: light tan, very fine-grained, arkosic, friable; upper part grades laterally into silty shales; boundaries gradational and interfingering; aquifer; low swell potential in sandstone; moderate to high swell potential in silty shale.

SHALE: dark gray, silty, carbonaceous, claystone, shale, and siltstone; frequent thin layers of bentonite; fine-grained sandstones in middle part; lower boundary gradational to unconformable; well exposed along I-25 from Colorado Springs to Pueblo; generally moderate to very high swell potential; low swell potential in sandstone and some siltstone.

CHALK AND SHALE: dark gray, weathers light tan, highly calcareous; lower boundary gradational; well exposed along Arkansas River between Florence and Pueblo; generally low swell potential; moderate swell potential in some upper shales.

LIMESTONE: light gray thin-bedded, argillaceous; numerous 1-inch layers of calcareous shale; commonly forms minor ridge east of Dakota hogback; well exposed along Arkansas River near Florence; low swell potential.
SANDSTONE: light gray, fine- to medium-grained, slightly calcareous, low swell potential.
SHALE: dark gray, sometimes silty; occasional calcareous concretions and thin layers of bentonite; well exposed in Canon City area; generally moderate to very high swell potential.
LIMESTONE AND SHALE: limestone light gray, argillaceous, dense, shale dark gray; well developed bentonite beds near base; lower boundary generally sharper than upper; well exposed in Canon City area; low swell potential in limestone; moderate to high swell potential in shale; very high swell potential in bentonite.

SHALE: dark gray, thin-bedded, occasional cone-in-cone concretions in lower part; bentonite beds (up to 6") throughout; occasional thin sandstones in lower part; well exposed in Canon City and Perry Park areas; moderate to very high swell potential.

FIGURE 5. Stratigraphic section of bedrock geologic units studied for swelling potential. (Modified from Colorado School of Mines, Generalized composite stratigraphic section, Front Range of Colorado.)

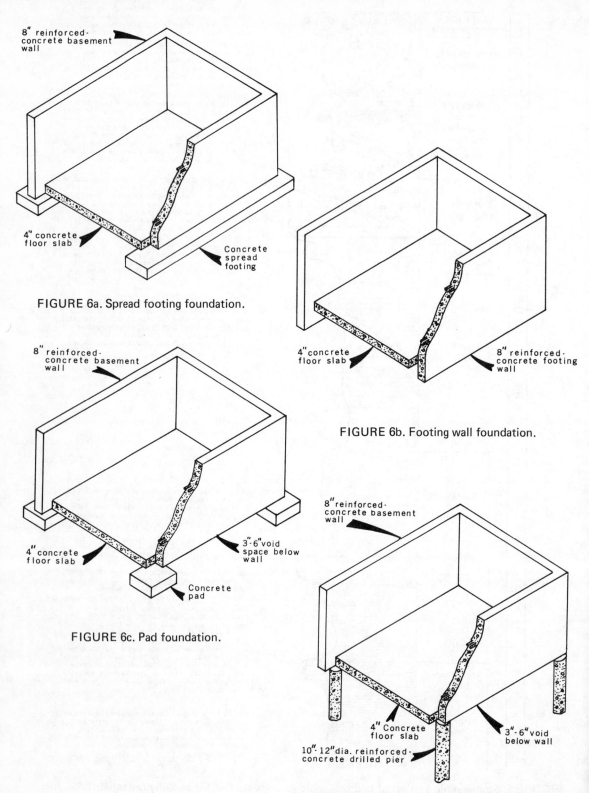

8" reinforced-concrete basement wall

4" concrete floor slab

Concrete spread footing

FIGURE 6a. Spread footing foundation.

4" concrete floor slab

8" reinforced-concrete footing wall

FIGURE 6b. Footing wall foundation.

8" reinforced-concrete basement wall

4" concrete floor slab

3"-6" void space below wall

Concrete pad

FIGURE 6c. Pad foundation.

8" reinforced-concrete basement wall

4" Concrete floor slab

10"-12" dia. reinforced-concrete drilled pier

3"-6" void below wall

FIGURE 6d. Drilled pier and grade beam foundation.

struction of any structure on potentially swelling soils. Other damage-reducing techniques should be utilized by the owner of the structure after the completion of the construction. A technique that includes properly engineered and constructed formations and proper lot drainage has become the most widely used and most successful method for coping with swelling soil conditions (table 1).

TABLE 1. *GEO-LOGIC*—THE SENSIBLE WAY TO BUILD IN SWELLING CLAY

Do	*Don't*
1. Hire a registered professional soil engineer for foundation investigation.	1. Build without a foundation investigation and recommendation.
2. Utilize properly designed foundation (low swell potential—spread footing; moderate swell potential—bearing wall or pad; high swell potential—drilled pier and grade beam) with specific design by the soil engineer.	2. Use a foundation type based on the types used in other parts of the country.
3. Insist on careful inspection of all foundation construction.	3. Allow careless cleaning of foundation excavations or sloppy concrete work on piers, footings, grade beams, or floors.
4. Utilize procedures to provide maximum drainage around building and provide for positive drainage of entire lot.	4. Allow uncompacted backfill around foundations which may settle and pond water.
5. Surround building with 4-ft-wide or wider impermeable membrane (asphalt, concrete, or plastic sheeting).	5. Allow the surrounding impermeable membrane to slope toward the building.
6. Allow minimum separation of 5 ft between building and all grass, shrubs, and sprinkler systems.	6. Use so-called "foundation plantings" to hide the foundation.
7. Utilize floating floor slabs for all on-grade floors, and consider alternative of structural floor with crawl space.	7. Neglect to provide for freedom of movement.

Foundation Design. To be considered properly engineered and constructed, *a foundation must be designed and inspected by a registered professional soil and foundation engineer.* The necessity for professional foundation design in areas of swelling clay was not widely accepted in the early 1950s. However, costly damage from swelling clay to the concrete slab foundations of many post-war homes in Denver rapidly changed this acceptance. Slab foundation* design was replaced with spread footing, bearing (footing) wall, and drilled pier and grade beam designs. Each of these foundations was designed to concentrate the weight of the structure on a much smaller area than was possible with the concrete slab. This concentration of weight was necessary to resist pressures developed when swelling clay was wetted.

In areas of relatively low swell potential, spread footings are commonly used. In this design, the weight of the building is transmitted to the soil through walls supported on concrete strips, or footings, that are wider than the walls (see figure 6a). For slightly higher swell pressures, extended bearing walls (footing walls) (figure 6b) or pads may be used. Pads are generally used on large buildings rather than homes (figure 6c) in the Urban Corridor. In areas containing moderately to highly swelling clay, drilled pier and grade beam foundations are used (figure 6d). With this foundation design, the weight of the building is transmitted through bearing walls to horizontal grade beams. The grade beam consists of specially-designed additional reinforcement of the lower part of the concrete bearing wall to allow bridging of building weight between individual piers. These beams rest on cylindrical, reinforced-concrete piers that concentrate the weight on a very small area below the zone of seasonal moisture change. The foundation is thereby founded upon soil that, because its moisture content remains constant throughout the year, should not experience a volume change.

With each of these special foundation designs, floating slabs are commonly used for all on-grade floors (figure 7). These interior concrete floor slabs are completely isolated by joints or void spaces from all structural components. Complete isolation from bearing walls, columns, nonbearing interior partitions, stairs, and utilities allows the slab to move freely without damaging the structural integrity of the building. Structural floors have been used extensively in large commercial buildings but have found only limited use in residential and school buildings owing to their high cost relative to slab floors. This type of floor system consists of flooring supported several feet above the ground by beams attached to bearing walls. The "crawl space" below the structural floor provides a large void between the floor and the swelling soil, preventing floor slab heave.

In the Denver area, swelling soil below the level of the proposed floor slab is sometimes excavated to a depth of several feet. The original swelling soil, placed slightly above optimum moisture content and 5 to 10 percent below maximum density, or imported, nonswelling soil is then backfilled into the excavation and compacted. This "over-excavation" method generally has been successful where slabs are poured immediately after compaction to prevent drying of the fill (Sealy, 1972).

In designing foundations for roads, the Colorado Divison of Highways has tried various methods to offset the effects of swelling clay. The most commonly used method is excavation and recompaction of the subgrade soil. The depth of excavation is determined from the plasticity index*, e.g., 2 ft of soil is excavated if the plasticity index is between 10 and 20. The backfill is then recompacted at approximately the same moisture-density conditions mentioned above for floating floor slabs (Leo O'Conner, 1973, personal communication). Although not a preventive measure, the substitution of flexible pavements (asphalt) for rigid pavement (concrete) has reduced the costs of repairs to pavement heaved by moderately swelling clay. In recent years asphalt has also been used for membranes to seal water out of swelling subgrade soils. Because much of the water that causes swelling beneath pavements is formed in the porous subbase gravels below the asphalt pavement, nonporous asphalt subbases have been successfully used to prevent swell. Due to the expense of these methods and the continual excavation of city streets for utility lines, more economical and less easily-damaged solutions must be found to prevent swell of streets in urban and suburban areas.

Pre-construction chemical soil stabilization utilizing lime or organic compounds may reduce the potential of swelling soil damage more economically than the utilization of structural floors and special foundations. The chemical stabilization technique has a short history and limited use in Colorado. Where it has been used, it appears to have been successful for the period of time since application.

Drainage. The Federal Housing Administration recommends slopes of no less than 6 in. of vertical fall in 10 ft (12 in. in 10 ft is safer) around all buildings for drainage (Federal Housing Administration, 1966). These slopes must drain water into drainage swales, streets, or storm sewers. *Water must not be allowed to stand near foundations* in areas of swelling clay due to the potential for wetting foundation soils. All downspouts and splash blocks should be placed so that roof runoff will be carried at least 4 ft from the building. Interior drains for roof runoff are not recommended because an interior drain, cracked or broken by differential vertical movement, will immediately saturate the foundation. Peripheral drains of clay tile or perforated plastic pipe are often used around the foundations of buildings to carry away extraneous subsurface water (figure 7). In areas of heavy lawn irrigation, these drains have proven effective in helping to prevent the formation of perched water tables and the resulting downward seepage of surface water (Sealy, 1972).

Landscaping. Proper design and construction will not solve all swelling-clay problems. The owner of a structure is responsible for maintaining proper drainage by careful landscaping and maintenance. Backfill around foundations is often not properly compacted. Therefore, additional soil may be required on the slope around the structure in order to compensate for settlement of the backfill. This prevents "ponding" and percolation of water around the foundation. Although not esthetically pleasing to many persons, asphalt, concrete, or gravel-covered plastic sheeting should be placed around the entire foundation (figure 7). These 4-ft or wider strips prevent surface moisture penetra-

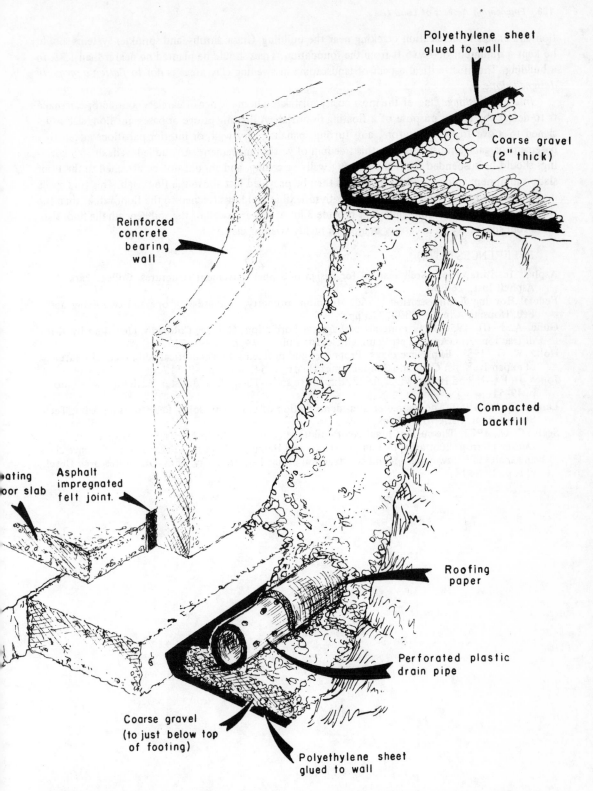

FIGURE 7. Details of a typical floating floor slab, peripheral drain, and surface moisture barrier, showing specific components but not intended as a model for a specific foundation design (modified from Federal Housing Administration, 1966, p. 91).

tion and excessive dessication cracking near the building. Grass, shrubs, and sprinkler systems should be kept a minimum of 4 to 5 ft from the foundation. Trees should be planted no nearer than 15 ft to a building. The most critical aspect of landscaping in swelling clay areas is *not to flatten a properly designed slope.*

Interior finishing. One of the most costly mistakes a homeowner or careless contractor can make is to defeat the design purpose of a floating floor slab. A floating garage or basement floor slab is designed to move freely. Therefore, any furring, paneling, dry wall, or interior partitions added to a basement or garage must maintain this freedom of vertical movement. Any added walls or wall coverings should be suspended from the existing walls or ceiling, and should not be attached to the floor slab. A minimum void space of 3 in. should then be provided just above the floor slab. This void space may be covered with flexible molding or with inflexible molding attached to the floor rather than the wall. Although these recommendations provide 3 in. of upward swell of the soil beneath the floor slab, more void space may be necessary in areas of highly swelling clay.

REFERENCES CITED

Asphalt Institute, 1969, Soils manual for design of asphalt pavement structures: College Park, Md., Asphalt Inst., 267 pp.

Federal Housing Administration, 1966, Minimum property standards for one and two living units: Fed. Housing Adm. No. 300, 315 pp.

Gude, A. J. III, 1950, Clay minerals of Laramie Formation, Golden, Colorado, identified by X-ray diffraction: Am. Assoc. Petroleum Geologists Bull., v. 34, p. 1699–1717.

Holtz, W. G., 1959, Expansive clays—Properties and problems, *in* Theoretical and practical treatment of expansive soils: Colorado School Mines Quart., v. 54, no. 4, p. 89–117.

Jones, D. E., Jr., and Holtz, W. G., 1973, Expansive soils—The hidden disaster: Civil Eng., v. 43, no. 8, p. 49–51.

Lambe, T. W., 1960, The character and identification of expansive soils: Fed. Housing Adm. Tech. Studies Rept. FHA-701, 51 pp., 4 pls.

Sealy, C. O., 1972, The current practice of building lightly loaded structures on expansive soils in the Denver metropolitan area, *in* Lambe, D. R., and Hanna, S. J., eds., Workshop on expansive clays and shales in highway design and construction proc.: Fed. Highway Adm. Office Research Devel., v. 1, p. 295–314.

Effects of Urbanization on Ground-Water Levels

15

Judith L. Hamilton and Willard G. Owens

Introduction

Urbanization in the East and Midwest has had its effect on ground water, but changes in ground-water conditions due to urbanization are most pronounced in semi-arid Rocky Mountain and Western States.

Most of the major cities in the U.S. have rainy climates. The area from eastern Texas through central Illinois east to southern Maine receives over 40 inches of rain per year. There is little prolonged lawn irrigation in these areas except in times of drought. Large expanses of pavement increase runoff from storms. Thus, the total amount of water recharging underground supplies is likely to be less under urban conditions than under undeveloped conditions.

In the semi-arid West, however, urbanization often results in pronounced changes in the ground-water environment. Denver, Colorado, averages about 16 inches of precipitation per year. Because of low humidity, much of this water evaporates, so it is less effective than even a similar amount in humid climates. The water necessary to provide green lawns comes primarily from irrigation. The amount of water applied to lawns is close to 24 inches per year, and in areas of sandy soils or overzealous gardeners it can run higher.

Since most of the water used for lawn irrigation is applied at slow steady rates during cooler periods of the day, the recharge to ground water from irrigation is considerably greater than that from precipitation. We believe it is on the order of 40 percent rather than the 10 to 15 percent that occurs from natural precipitation. Thus under urban conditions the recharge to ground water is 6 to 7 times that occurring under natural conditions.

In many areas the water table is sufficiently low that this extra amount of water is advantageous. In areas of preexisting high water, however, the rise may be sufficient to cause basement flooding problems. Aurora, Colorado, an eastern suburb of Denver, is one such case.

Aurora city officials had been plagued by repeated and numerous complaints from property owners having flooding basements. Willard Owens Associates was retained by the city to determine specific causes of the problem and to offer constructive solutions which individual property owners and the city could apply.

Reprinted with permission of the authors, both of Willard Owens Associates, Inc., Wheat Ridge, Colorado, and the publisher from *Bulletin of the Association of Engineering Geologists* 9(4):327–34, 1972. Copyright © 1972 by Association of Engineering Geologists.

Drainage Conditions in Aurora, Colorado

The overall topography and drainage in Aurora are shown in figure 1. The topography generally is almost flat, sloping an average of 1 foot per hundred feet. The Highline irrigation canal traverses the area perpendicular to the slope of the land, and truncates the natural drainageways. Seepage from the canal, which is unlined, causes a ground-water "mound" along its route. This "mound" decreases the gradient of the water table upstream of the canal, thus decreasing water flow rate. In effect, this creates a hydrologic barrier, inhibiting the natural drainage to the northwest.

Our preliminary investigations showed that flooded basements were sometimes caused by poor subdivision design or poor construction and landscaping techniques. For example, a street which parallels the slope of the land acts as a drainage channel. If the street makes a sharp bend, the water tends to follow the slope of the terrain and water flowing down the slope may overtop the curb and flow onto yard areas. The possibility of this occurring is increased by the design of a rolled rather than a right-angled curb.

In some areas, improperly compacted backfill immediately adjacent to houses has settled, allowing irrigation water for lawns or gardens to pond and flow toward the houses. Houses that have no splash blocks at all or very short splash blocks leading from their downspouts permit large quantities of rain water to discharge immediately adjacent to their foundations. Faulty landscaping also may affect basement flooding problems. Where large shrubs and other plants are too close to a residence, irrigation water may soak into the soil along the foundation and seep into the basement.

In some parts of Aurora, however, even good drainage and planning have not prevented basement flooding. At one house where numerous precautions have been taken, plastic tubing extends from the base of the downspout, rolls out as the water comes down, and discharges the water completely away from the house. The slope of the land away from this house is good also, and the whole yard is gravelled, yet basement flooding still exists. A pipe leading from the basement to the street regularly discharges water accumulated in a sump. The problem, then, is not just individual or local. The rise in ground water levels has a more widespread cause.

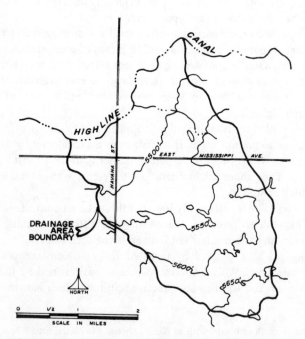

FIGURE 1. Topography and drainage, Aurora, Colorado.

Subsurface Conditions

Our preliminary study of subdivision soils reports and our review of city sewer boring logs and logs of domestic wells disclosed a buried bedrock channel in one of the major problem areas. To define this channel and obtain information on the subsoils and water levels, we installed 18 observation wells equipped with plastic tubing for water-level observations. Our investigations indicated that very clean, fine to medium sands in the channel area were the main reason for many of the problems. Clean sands absorb and transmit water very readily. Flow of water out of the area is relatively slow, however, owing to the flat slope of the land and of the water table and also to the hydrologic barrier created by seepage from the Highline canal. A combination of factors has thus caused a gradual rise in water levels to a few feet below the surface. Figure 2 shows the depth to the water table. In some areas ground water is as shallow as four or five feet below the surface. Figure 2 also shows that the water table generally slopes northwest, directly toward the Highline canal.

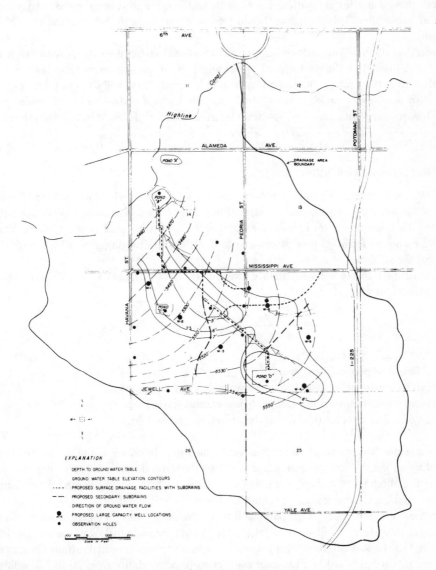

FIGURE 2. Depth to water table, water table elevation contours, and proposed sub-drainage facilities.

Surface Drainage System

The city of Aurora is undertaking alleviation of the ground-water problem by installing a storm-drainage system to carry off the heavy precipitation flows. In Aurora much of the precipitation is in very brief, but intense, storms. The storm-drainage system will help prevent surface water from ponding and seeping down to recharge the ground water. However, to prevent excessive uplift pressure, an unlined sewer or a lined sewer with seep holes is recommended.

The storm-sewer route passes through very sandy soils which will readily absorb seepage from the storm-sewer channel. A storm sewer by itself, thus, will not very effectively prevent high ground-water problems. In addition, a major future problem will be the gradual rise of ground water owing to increased lawn irrigation.

The city will also install holding ponds to temporarily hold storm drainage from very intense floods. Two of these ponds are to be located in the channel area where the subsoil is very clean sand. Seepage from these ponds will raise the already high ground water level. We recommend that the silty surface soil be stockpiled after excavation, mixed with a little more clay, and then used to reline the sand areas after excavation. This procedure should prevent excessive seepage during the 8- to 24-hour holding periods.

Implementation of these suggestions will prevent additional recharge to the ground water from storm-drainage facilities. But the problem of preventing a rise in ground water from lawn watering and the problem of getting rid of the ground water that is already there will still exist. Our proposed solution to the ground-water problem is to integrate a sub-drainage system with a storm-sewer system, to install a secondary sub-drainage system under utility lines, and also to install wells in selected locations.

Subsurface Drainage System

Calculations for drain spacing based on formulas and information which we obtained from the U.S. Bureau of Reclamation and the Soil Conservation Service (oral communications) indicate that a subdrain under the main storm sewer will not be effective over the entire channel width. Various theoretical and empirical formulas gave estimates of effective width ranging from 50 feet to 500 feet on either side of the subdrain.

To compute flow into the main subdrain we adapted Butler's formula (Butler, 1957, p. 141–42) for flow into a trench or gallery:

$$q = k \frac{(y_2 - y_1)}{x} \frac{(y_2 + y_1)}{2}$$

where q = inflow to gallery, gpd/ft/side,
    k = coefficient of permeabiltiy, gpd/ft.^{2}
    y_1 = depth to impermeable layer below the water level of the gallery.
    y_2 = existing depth to impermeable layer below normal water level.
and   x = the horizontal distance over which the drop in water level occurs.

Drawing the water table down by five to ten feet at the subdrain center would prevent uplift pressures from acting on the storm sewer and would still keep the subdrain at a reasonable depth of 10 to 15 feet. While the subdrain would be increasingly effective with increasing depth, the expense of extra excavation and backfill necessitates a somewhat less-than-optimum depth.

The estimates of k (the coefficient permeability of the soils) were obtained from percolation tests in the upper three feet of soil, from computations of inflow and outflow in the area, and from tests run by the U.S. Geological Survey on material of a similar grain-size distribution. These various methods of computation resulted in a range in coefficient of permeability from 20 to 220 gallons of water per day per square foot, but generally 100 or less. To provide a factor of safety we used 200 gallons per day per square foot.

Our estimate of x (the width over which the drop in water table occurs) was obtained from an equation suggested by U.S. Bureau of Reclamation personnel. The Bureau of Reclamation (Dumm, 1968) has determined from numerous water level observations that the curve for drawdown versus distance from a subdrain approximates a fourth degree parabola. Most of the drawdown occurs within a distance of .15L, where L is the distance over which drawdown occurs. Based on a 1,000 foot distance for L the length of x (= 15L) is 150 feet. Using these assumptions, we obtained an inflow of .0005 cfs per foot of trench.

Because the main subdrain itself will not be effective over a great width we proposed a secondary subdrain system under utility lines which run perpendicular to the main subdrains in the storm sewer. Suggested locations are shown in figure 2. These drains will act as interceptors since they are perpendicular to the direction of ground water flow. The inflow to these subdrains was computed by determining the quantity of water to be removed to lower the water table from existing conditions to the desirable depth, and also the amount of water that will be added by future development upstream. In theory, an interceptor drain will permanently lower the water table downstream (Donnan, 1959), and only one drain would be required. Because of lawn watering downstream, however, we recommended an additional subdrain location downstream of drain No. 1.

Local areas will still be unaffected by the subdrains, and some areas will require temporary and rapid lowering of the water table. To dewater these areas we proposed to install five or six wells that we estimate will provide about 100 to 200 gallons per minute. The effect of these wells will be monitored by observation holes that we already have installed. These wells would be constructed with well screen and with liquid-level controls so as to maintain relatively constant water levels.

The entire dewatering system is designed to lower the water level about five feet so that water will remain eight to ten feet below the ground surface. This depth will be sufficient to eliminate basement flooding. In addition, we are recommending that the city of Aurora consider lining the Highline canal throughout the area to prevent seepage. The lining of the canal would be in conjunction with a larger excavation to dispose of water removed from the area.

REFERENCES

Butler, Stanley F., 1957, Engineering Hydrology: Prentice-Hall, Inc., New Jersey 365 pp.

Donnan, William W., 1959, Drainage of Agricultural Lands Using Interceptor Lines: Journal Irrigation and Drainage Division, Proceedings American Society of Civil Engineers, v. 85 part 1, p. 13–23.

Dumm, Lee D., 1968, Subsurface Drainage by Transient Flow Theory: paper 6315, Journal Irrigation and Drainage Division, Proceedings American Society of Civil Engineers, v. 94, N. IR4, p. 505–19.

United States Department of Agriculture, Soil Conservation Service, 1959, Subsurface Drainage of Irrigated Land in Arid and Semiarid Areas: Section 16, Chapter 3, National Engineering Handbook.

Van Schilfgaarde, Jan, Kirkham, Don, and Frevert, R. K., 1956, Physical and Mathematical Theories of Tile and Ditch Drainage and their Usefulness in Design: Iowa State College Agricultural Experiment Station, Research Bulletin 436.

Highland Landslide Problems along the Cumberland Plateau in Tennessee

16

David L. Royster

Introduction

Throughout the years, many of the greatest problems associated with the construction and maintenance of highways in Tennessee have occurred along the Cumberland Plateau, one of the six major physiographic provinces of the state (figure 1). The Cumberland Plateau is the southern section of the greater Appalachian Plateau that extends across Tennessee from New York to Alabama. The northern section is referred to as the Allegheny Plateau, and most geologists accept the Kentucky River in Middle Eastern Kentucky as the dividing line.

In Tennessee, the plateau encompasses an area of approximately 5,400 square miles. The average elevation is about 2,000 feet, but elevations of 3,500 feet are reached in the Cumberland Mountains area in the northeastern portion (figure 1).

Most of the problems involving highway construction and maintenance have occurred not on the plateau itself but rather on the slopes of the escarpments that border the Ridge and Valley of East Tennessee, the Sequatchie Valley of Middle Eastern Tennessee and the Eastern Highland Rim of Middle Tennessee (figure 2). This paper describes some of these problems and the means that were used to correct them. It also discusses some of the things that might be done to minimize such problems in the future.

Geologic Setting: Materials and Conditions

The surface rocks of the Cumberland Plateau are largely sandstones, siltstones, and shales with occasional interbedded coal layers. Most of these rock types, being moderately to highly resistant to the processes of weathering, produce relatively shallow soils. Except for the faulted eastern escarpment and the geologic structures associated with the Sequatchie Valley, Crab Orchard Cove, Grassy Cove, and the Elk Valley-Pine Mountain area, the formations are essentially horizontal. Thus, major roadway and slope failures resulting from adverse soil and geologic conditions are somewhat rare for the plateau itself.

Extracted with permission of the author and publisher from *Bulletin of the Association of Engineering Geologists* 10(4):255–87, 1973. Copyright © 1973 by Association of Engineering Geologists.

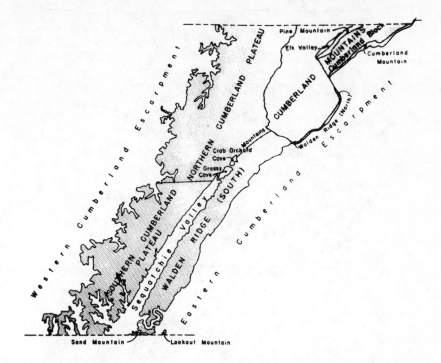

FIGURE 1. Physiographic subdivisions of the Cumberland Plateau (Wilson, Jewell, and Luther, 1956).

Along the slopes of the escarpments, however, the conditions are quite different. In traversing these areas, whether along one of the Sequatchie Valley-Cumberland Plateau escarpments, the Highland Rim-Plateau escarpment, or the Ridge and Valley-Plateau escarpment, one encounters a rather distinct and identifiable yet highly complex assemblage of soil and geologic materials and conditions. In broad terms, the materials that most affect roadway and slope stability in these areas are clay shales, colluvium, and water. The conditions are a rugged surface configuration with 600 to 1,200 feet of total relief in the project areas, unpredictable subsurface drainage patterns, and highly irregular zones of weathering. In more precise terms, the clay shale that is involved in most of the major landslides is the Pennington Shale (figure 3), named for Pennington Gap, Virginia, where it was first described by geologist M. R. Campbell in 1893. John Rodgers further described the Pennington in 1953 as follows:

> The Pennington formation is heterogenous and varicolored, including red, purple and green clay shale, pink, red, green and brown (normally calcareous) sandstone, and yellow shaly or silty fossiliferous limestone. The limestone is everywhere minor in amount; the proportions of shale and sandstone vary widely. Shale predominates from the Georgia line to Rockwood, but thin sandstone beds are present, and these become thicker and more numerous farther northeast, though shale continues to form more than half the formation.
>
> The Pennington varies in thickness from 200 feet to more than 500 feet.

The most significant engineering property of the Pennington is that it weathers and breaks down very rapidly to a relatively weak, highly plastic impervious clay. This is especially significant where the formation occurs in a slope that is overlain by colluvium—the second of the three major materials involved in stability problems along the plateau escarpments. Colluvium is a heterogeneous mixture of clay, silt, sand, rock, and boulder-sized particles that are up to 100 feet in thickness. It is material that has moved downslope, primarily under the force of gravity, over a rather long span of geologic time. The silt and clay are products of the weathering of the shales and siltstones that underlie the

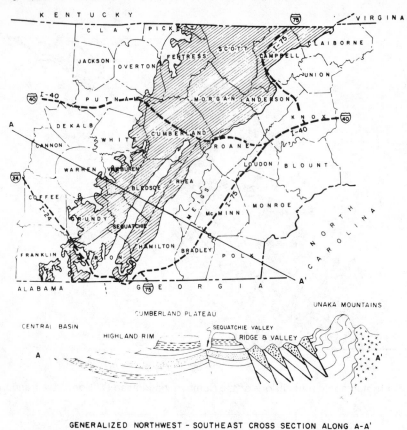

GENERALIZED NORTHWEST – SOUTHEAST CROSS SECTION ALONG A-A'
(Vertical scale highly exaggerated in relation to horizontal scale)

FIGURE 2. Alignments of Interstate Routes -24, -40, and -75 across the Cumberland Plateau (shaded area), and generalized cross section.

sandstone which caps the top of the escarpment. The sand, rock fragments, and boulders are derived chiefly from the cap rock itself. Some of the boulders are "room size" in dimension. The colluvium veneers or drapes over the escarpment (figure 3). It may vary considerably in thickness over a relatively small area; for example, from 5 to 50 feet in thickness over a distance of 100 to 200 feet. This variance is due more to the troughs and lows filled with colluvium in the highly undulating and irregular sub-topography of the area than to build-ups of colluvium over a uniform under-surface. This condition is one of the primary reasons why it is so difficult to measure and predict and thus quantify the forces and resistances for engineering analyses.

The third major material involved in slope stability along the escarpment is water. The soils engineer and geologist recognize three types of water or moisture: gravitational water, capillary water, and hygroscopic water. Gravitational or free water moves downward through a material under the force of gravity and, quite simply, is the water that will drain from a soil. Capillary water is held in the pores in a soil. Like gravitational water, it is free water, but it can be removed from soil only when the water table is lowered or when evaporation is faster than capillary flow. Hygroscopic water is retained by soil after the capillary and gravitational water are removed. It forms a thin film around each soil grain. Moisture is always expressed as a percentage of the weight of dry particles in the soil (Spangler, 1953).

Moisture content and drainage in general vary greatly from one material to another and from one locale to another throughout the escarpment slope. The sources of water are highly variable and

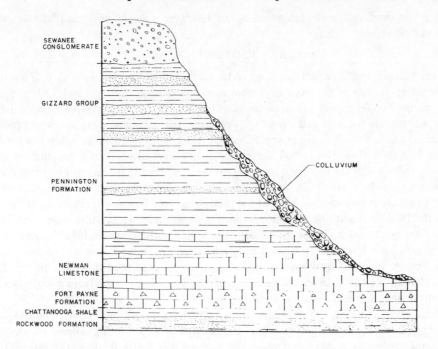

FIGURE 3. General sequence of geologic formations and materials encountered along the Plateau Escarpment near Rockwood.

unpredictable; especially where spring and seep outlets are covered by colluvium. The primary source is very difficult to trace under these conditions. Furthermore, the colluvium is highly permeable, permitting ready access to both surface and subsurface water. By contrast, the clay shales and residual clays are virtually impermeable. This significant difference in permeability allows groundwater to collect and sometimes become trapped along the interface between the two materials so that the resistance to sliding along the contact and within the soil mass itself is overcome, and failure occurs.

All the problems along the Cumberland escarpment cannot be attributed to Pennington Shale, colluvium, and water, and their associated conditions, for other geologic formations, materials, and conditions are sometimes involved. However, it is not the purpose of this paper to describe all the detailed ramifications of the escarpment-slope problems so only the major materials and conditions involved will be discussed. For convenience, and to avoid repetition, the entire material-condition grouping or assemblage along the escarpments will be referred to simply as the PC complex. This term takes in the three principle materials: the Pennington Shale, colluvium, and water, as well as the usual group of associated conditions, such as rugged topography, high relief, unpredictable subsurface drainage patterns, and all the factors involved in the processes of weathering in this particular environment.

The Failure Mechanism: Cause and Effect Relationships

From the previous discussion, it should be fairly obvious that most of the Cumberland Plateau escarpment is in a very delicate state of equilibrium. In some areas the safety factor against failure in the natural slope probably is not much in excess of 1.00. The safety factor is defined as the ratio between the ultimate bearing capacity or strength of a material and the stress, load, or force applied to that material. Hence, a safety factor of 1.00 is at the point of failure, 1.20 is marginally stable, and anything less than 1.00 is failing. Let's assume that a material in the upper portion of a slope is applying a stress (designated S_a) of 1,000 psf (pounds per square foot) to a material at the base of the slope with a measured resistance (designated S_r) of 1,500 psf. Our safety factor (S_f), then, would be calculated as follows:

$$S_f = S_r/S_a = 1{,}500 \text{ psf}/1{,}000 \text{ psf} = 1.5,$$

which means that we would expect the slope to have a fairly high degree of stability. If, on the other hand, the load at the top of the slope (S_a) were increased to, say, 1,600 psf and the toe support not increased, we then could expect the slope to fail. Similarly, if the toe support (S_r) were reduced by removal to 900 psf and the load at the top (S_a) were to remain constant, we could expect failure.

In brief, the above conditions are approximately what takes place in the failures of the PC complex. Along Interstate 40 at Rockwood, for example, fills were placed across marginally stable areas which simply failed under the increased load. In cut areas, where the toe support was removed by excavation, the upper slope failed. Of course, the same is more or less true of landslides everywhere; they result primarily from increased loads at the head or reduced support or resistance at the toe. The failures in the PC complex do not fall into a specific classification (rotational, planar, or flow) but, rather, they are combinations of all three. They begin more or less as rotational failures at the toe, becoming more planar toward the middle and crown. After the initial failure within the sliding mass, drainage is further impeded, and the slide develops into a viscous mud flow. The failure then continues as a flow in the toe area, and as support is reduced or removed, the scarp retrogresses upslope where the movement becomes, once again, more planar.

The basic cause and effect relationships in these slides are not difficult to comprehend; however, rather formidable problems are encountered in quantifying, with any high degree of accuracy, the amounts of material in motion, or that additional material which may be subject to failure, as well as the hydrostatic pressures and other forces involved. One may be somewhat misled, also, by the engineering properties of the materials. Shearing resistances, which are measured in terms of cohesion and angle friction, are usually much higher in the individual materials than one might expect. Therefore, if these values were the sole criteria by which the problem was analyzed, the safety factor that is derived may be much too high, and the design that is developed from this information may be inadequate. This is where the importance of the geologic history of the area becomes significant. One simply must be aware of, and be able to delineate, the subsurface troughs that occur throughout the project area for, by and large, the angle of slope along the contact between the colluvium and shale or clay within these troughs determines or controls stability, rather than the cohesion and angle of friction of the individual materials. As we shall see, failure may also result when subsurface drainage along this interface is impeded by the consolidation of these materials from the weight of an overlying fill. This may effect a slow build-up of pore pressure which ultimately results in failure. But the delineation of these materials and conditions is not a simple matter, for the subsurface conditions within the PC complex, as has been emphasized throughout this paper, are just that—extremely complex. Subsurface investigations are difficult because of the roughness and relative inaccessibility of the terrain, and because during periods of wet weather the slide areas become virtual quagmires. And even after access is gained, drilling is slow and laborious because of the tendency of bore holes to collapse and the presence of sandstone boulders. But without numerous borings, delineation of the zone of failure through material identification and correlation is virtually impossible. Where the colluvium-clay shale interface is clear-cut, delineation is fairly simple. However, delineation is more difficult when gouge from old failure surfaces or zones is penetrated by the drill and brought to the surface.

Though the problem is complex, it is not insurmountable. It is merely a matter of accepting the fact that such investigations take a great deal of time and that appropriate corrective measures cannot be arrived at without such investigations.

Recent Problems

Most problems since 1960 have involved three of Tennessee's main Interstate routes—I-40, I-24 and I-75 (figure 2). These routes must traverse the escarpments that front the Valley and Ridge, the

Sequatchie Valley and the Eastern Highland Rim at seven locations. Five of these crossings have resulted in cut slides and roadway failures that have cost hundreds of thousands to several millions of dollars to correct. Only Interstate-40 between Monterey and Cookeville and Interstate-24 between Monteagle and Jasper have thus far escaped serious landslide problems.

I-40 at Rockwood

By far the most exasperating landslide problems in the history of highway construction in the state have occurred along a 4-mile section of Interstate-40 near Rockwood in Roane County. Construction on this segment began in late 1967 and, beginning with the failure of a massive fill in January 1968 along the east-bound lanes between stations 2001 + 00 and 2018 + 00, more than 20 major slides have developed. Each of these is a story in itself, each has involved the PC complex, and each has resulted from the conditions outlined in the section entitled "The Failure Mechanism."

Once the failure mechanism for each individual slide is understood and all the forces and resistances have been analyzed and evaluated, the appropriate remedial measure is selected. Obviously, accurate data must be gathered in order to arrive at the appropriate remedial measure. All the materials and conditions must be thoroughly analyzed and properly interpreted. A treatment for one slide may not be adequate for another or, worse, may violate the mechanics involved and actually accelerate movement. In other words, one so-called "cure" might produce side effects that are worse than the original failure.

Since, for the most part, the original alignment and gradient of the roadway are being held, the remedial measures being utilized at Rockwood consist of various forms of drainage, partial to complete removal, partial removal and restraint, or "total" restraint. Two methods of restraint are being utilized: rock buttresses and gabions.

Rock buttresses (figures 4 and 5) are free-draining gravity structures consisting primarily of large blocks of nondegradable sandstone or limestone. The specification being utilized at Rockwood calls for 50 percent of the material to be greater than one cubic foot, with no more than 10 percent passing the No. 2 mesh sieve. It must be free of coal, shale, and soil materials. Because of its free-draining

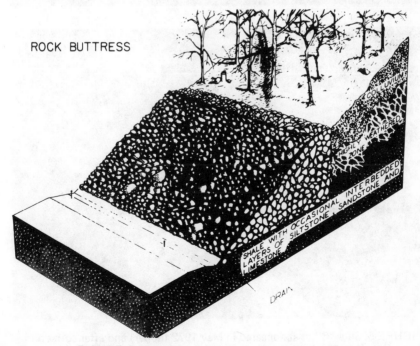

ROCK BUTTRESS

FIGURE 4. Three-dimensional sketch of a rock buttress.

characteristics, the rock buttress works well in restraining colluvial slides. Movement is prevented by restraint, while, at the same time, the large quantities of water associated with these slides drain virtually unrestricted, thus greatly reducing the likelihood of "ponding" and pore pressure build-up. It is essential that any large buttress be founded on in-place (residual) soils or sound material below the colluvial contact. Placing such a massive structure directly on the colluvium would only promote failure through shear or subsidence. The greatest disadvantage to rock buttresses is that they require a much greater area than other types of restraint structures because of their relatively wide bases. Hence, they must always be founded at the toe or foot of the slide rather than at the middle or crown.

FIGURE 5. Slide"C" as it appeared in May 1972 (upper) and after correction with rock buttress in August 1972.

The second type of restraint structure being utilized is the gabion wall (figure 6), a free-draining, heavy, monolithic gravity structure consisting of wire mesh baskets (gabions) filled with coarse non-degradable rock. The gabions are made of zinc-coated Number 11 steel wire and range in size from 3′ X 3′ X 3′ to 3′ X 3′ X 9′. In the construction of the wall, each basket is secured to an adjacent basket with a tie-wire and then loaded in place. Gabion walls were chosen for this project in lieu of concrete retaining walls partly on the basis of cost, but primarily because they provide the flexibility needed to cope with the differential settlement so typical of the site conditions. They also provide excellent permeability, which is needed to facilitate drainage of the restrained material. And finally, they generally require less lateral space than rock buttresses and, therefore, are used where space is somewhat limited.

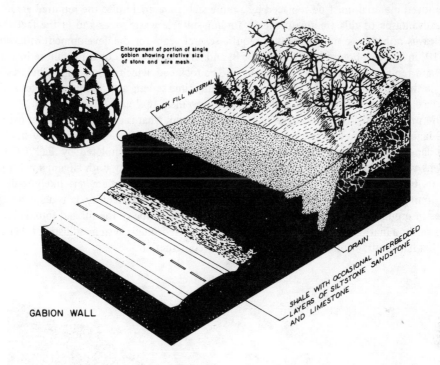

FIGURE 6. Three-dimensional sketch of gabion wall.

The cost of the gabion walls at Rockwood compares favorably with rock buttresses, although cost alone cannot be the prime consideration in determining which type of structure to use. Furthermore, such a comparison is much like comparing apples and oranges. In any event, the following data concern the west gabion wall on slide 4 and the slide "A" buttress along the west-bound-lane:

Slide 4 (West Gabion Wall)

Length: 268′
Height: 29′
Base Width: 16′
Excavation: 41,750 cubic yards
Excavation Costs: $82,247.50
Backfill (#57 stone): 12,488 cubic yards
Gabion Quantities ("baskets" and stone): 3,451 cu/yds.
Gabion Costs: $151,844.00 ($44.00 cu/yd.)
Total Cost: $321,507.50

Slide "A" (Buttress along West Bound Lane)

Length (approximate): 700'
Excavation: 404,302 cu/yds.
Excavation Costs: $687,313.40
Buttress Rock (2 contracts involved):
$3.00 × 10,321 cu/yds. = $30,963.00
$6.00 × 11,288 cu/yds. = $67,728.00
Total Cost: $786,004.40

At Rockwood partial or total removal may involve as little as a few hundred cubic yards or as much as 500,000 or nearly 1,000,000 yards for one slide. Where embankments (fills) are concerned, the removed material must be replaced by a more stable material up to the required grade. The greatest disadvantages of this treatment are in finding suitable waste areas and in the fact that removal often leaves rather large ugly scars that require several years for the development of new vegetation. Slide 10, in the east-bound lane (figures 7, 8, and 9) is an example of a fill failure in which the removal and replacement method has been used. The rock pad, which is made up of buttress-type rock, serves as the foundation for the fill while at the same time serving as a drainage blanket and outlet for subsurface drainage and a buttress against further movement upslope.

The problems at Rockwood have been frustrating and, what is more, they are not over. The west-bound lanes were opened in December 1972, but the conditions there are not totally stable. The east-bound lanes, discounting further major difficulties, should be completed by Fall 1973. However, problems will no doubt continue to crop up at various points along both alignments for many years to come. For example, a number of fills apparently stable at present are very likely to deteriorate to some point of instability within the next several years. Such instability is usually brought on by changes in ground-water levels followed by further deterioration of the fill and foundation materials. This is really a matter of a particular soil, geologic, and hydrologic system adjusting to a new environment that has resulted from changes brought on by construction.

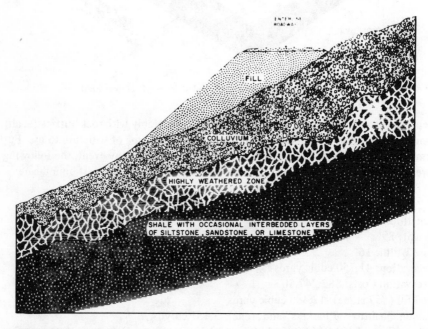

FIGURE 7. Schematic of materials and conditions in Slide 10 area before failure.

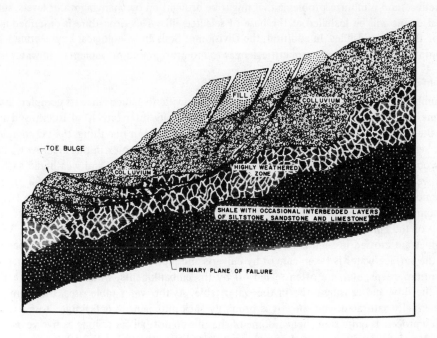

FIGURE 8. Slide 10 after failure.

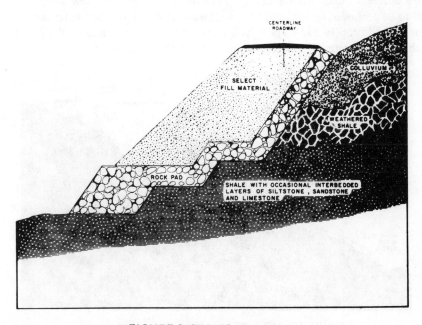

FIGURE 9. Slide 10 after repair.

To reduce and minimize problems that might be brought on by changing water levels, subsurface horizontal drains will be installed at the base of selected fills. This procedure is described in the discussion of the I-75 landslides. In addition, the Division of Soils and Geological Engineering will install instrumentation in some of the more critical areas to monitor ground movements and water levels.

I-75 in Campbell County

A number of slides have occurred on I-75 from Caryville to Jellico since its completion in 1967. While some parallels may be drawn between the failures along Interstate-40 at Rockwood and those on I-75, the I-75 failures, for the most part, are quite different. For one thing, the PC complex is not involved, because the roadway is well above the elevation of the complex in this area. As we have seen at Rockwood, water moving along the interface between the colluvium and weathered shale or clay creates a weak zone. Failure occurs once a load is applied, as in the construction of a fill, or once support is removed, as in the excavation of a cut. Water also plays a significant role in the I-75 failures but in a somewhat different way.

Many of the embankments along I-75 are constructed across relatively deep ravines. Very often these ravines are crossed in such a way that natural drainage may be impeded or even blocked. While most of the surface water is taken care of by culverts and pipes, etc., the subsurface drainage outlets, such as springs, seeps, etc., are often sealed off by the embankments, which then act as earth dams, blocking the flow and causing a rise in the water table. As the water table rises, the fill material becomes essentially saturated, and since it is primarily shale, it begins to deteriorate, lose strength, and fail. Such a process is quite slow, hence, some of the fills do not fail for as long as five years after construction. Most of the failures along I-75 are so attributed (figures 10, 11, and 12).

Both the landslide problems along I-75 and the overall situation are different from those at Rockwood. It is one thing to repair landslides where no traffic is involved but quite another when high volumes of traffic must be kept moving virtually through the construction. It is doubly difficult when the lanes are very close and the success of repair of one is dependent on the stability of the other.

Since alignment changes, by and large, were not feasible, and since complete removal and replacement were not altogether possible (although preferable in some cases), a concept had to be devised utilizing three different treatments for the four most recent failures. First, essentially all of the failed material had to be removed; second, since the high water table and perched water zones were contributing to the instability, they had to be lowered; and third, those portions of the fills that had not failed, plus the replaced material, had to be supported or buttressed.

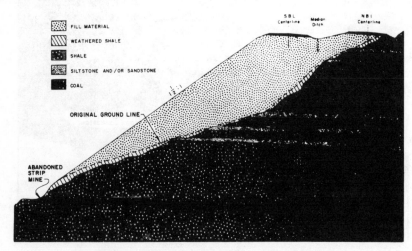

FIGURE 10. 840 + 00 embankment as constructed.

To lower the water table, the department borrowed a method used quite frequently in California and Oregon. This method involves horizontal holes drilled with a special boring machine that permits the insertion of a 1½″ I.D. perforated plastic pipe as the drill stem is removed. The plastic pipe serves as a casing to keep the holes from squeezing closed and allows water to drain through the perforations to the outside fill slope.

The three slides presently under contract called for approximately 50,000 feet of horizontal drains at a cost of $6.00 per foot. Several of the holes drilled were 600 feet in length, and the initial flow of some was up to 400 gallons per hour. Subsequent measurements two and four weeks later showed flows up to 200 gallons per hour. This is the first time this technique has been used in the Southeast on this scale.

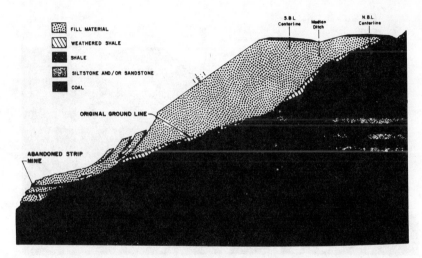

FIGURE 11. 840 + 00 embankment—first stage of failure.

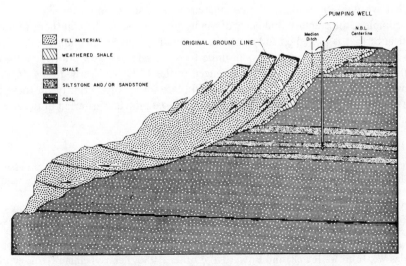

FIGURE 12. 840 + 00 embankment—final stages of failure.

To lower the water table at the 840 + 00 south-bound lane slide, the department employed a still different method (figure 13). Here, twelve 100 foot vertical wells were drilled on 25-foot centers along the median above the slide, and equipped with submersible automatically actuating pumps. Horizontal drains could not be used because of the height, steepness, and deteriorated condition of the outside slope. Since the 840 + 00 slide was to be repaired by the removal and replacement method, and since the removal of this material was expected to jeopardize the stability of the north-bound lane, it was determined that the median area had to be dewatered. Hopefully, dewatering would increase the shear strength of the material that was to be exposed in the median. Although this repair has not been completed, the results to date have been quite satisfactory. All the wells have been very active, pumping up to twelve hundred gallons an hour each for durations of one-half minute to ten or fifteen minutes or more. Recharge or recovery for the twelve wells varies generally from five minutes to twelve hours, depending on ground water levels, which fluctuate considerably with each rainfall.

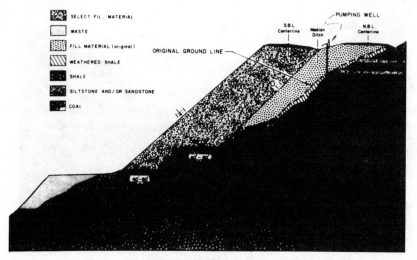

FIGURE 13. 840 + 00 embankment—after repair.

Future Outlook

From what we now know about the escarpment area of the Cumberland Plateau, especially in terms of PC complex, the stability and costs of roadways constructed there in the future will depend on the significance that is placed on soil and geologic conditions in the planning, location, and design stages. If, as in the past, these conditions continue to be of relatively low priority, we can expect to have the same sort of problems we have experienced in the 1960s and early 1970s. If, on the other hand, we have learned from our experiences, we will place a very high priority on these conditions. We might be well advised to establish these conditions as *the* principal criterion in the selection of all future routes in these areas.

REFERENCES

Royster, David L., January 1965, Highway Landslide and Stability Problems in Tennessee: Proceedings of the 46th Annual Tennessee Highway Conference, Bulletin Number 30, Engineering Experiment Station, The University of Tennessee at Knoxville, p. 72–87.
——, January 1970, The Trend Toward a Greater Utilization of Specialists in the Highway Engineering Field: Proceedings of the 51st Annual Tennessee Highway Conference, Bulletin Number 36, Engineering Experiment Station, The University of Tennessee at Knoxville, p. 22–40.
Spangler, M. G., 1953, Soil Engineering, (2nd Prtg.): International Textbook Co., Scranton, Pa., p. 84–91.
Wilson, Charles W., John W. Jewell, and Edward T. Luther, 1956, Pennsylvanian Geology of the Cumberland Plateau: State Division of Geology, Nashville.

17

The Chicago Underflow Plan

Chicago Flood Control Coordinating Committee

Nineteenth Century Problems

The history of the development of drainage and sewerage of the Chicago Metropolitan Area dates back to the early decades of the nineteenth century. From the beginning, the type of drainage was that of "combined" sewers, conveying in the same conduit systems, the combined flow of stormwater runoff and household and industrial wastes, which was generally considered, by most cities at that time, to be the most logical and practical scheme of urban drainage. These initial systems of "combined" sewers have now spread their lines to serve 375 square miles of the Metropolitan Area, having a total length of more than 5,000 miles.

For many decades from 1833 to 1900, all or most of the pollution originating within the growing City and some adjacent areas spilled, untreated, from the combined sewer outlets into the Chicago River and Lake Michigan.

Although the deepening of the small Illinois and Michigan Canal in the year 1871 allowed partial diversion of some of this pollution into the Mississippi River Watershed, it was not until after the formation of the Sanitary District of Chicago in 1889 now named The Metropolitan Sanitary District of Greater Chicago, that a major and successful effort was made toward pollution and flood control.

The Canal System

The original program of the Sanitary District of Chicago produced the Sanitary and Ship Canal, completed on January 16, 1900, and its two tributary canals, the North Shore Channel in 1910 and the Calumet-Sag Canal in 1922 (figure 1). Intercepting conduits and pumping stations completed in 1907 intercepted all open discharge of polluted waters into Lake Michigan, and delivered this pollution to the Chicago River System at Lawrence Avenue and at 39th Street and to the Calumet-Sag Channel at 127th Street. Clean water withdrawn from Lake Michigan diluted the pollution and conveyed the mixture southwestward through the new canal system into the drainage basin of the Illinois River, and thence to the Mississippi River. This reversal of the direction of flow in the Chicago and Calumet Rivers was widely publicized . . . first as a great achievement but later as lake diversion, con-

Extracted with permission of the Metropolitan Sanitary District of Greater Chicago from *The Chicago Underflow plan,* 1972, 29 pp. Metropolitan Sanitary District, Chicago, Illinois.

sidered unfair by other states bordering on the Great Lakes. Dilution ratios for the untreated sewage equal to $3\frac{1}{3}$ cfs per 1,000 population were recommended to maintain what was then considered a sufficient level of sanitation, pending the development of sewage treatment facilities, which began in the twenties with the completion of the initial stages of the Calumet Sewage Treatment Works in 1922 and North Side Sewage Treatment Works in 1927. Construction was, however, limited by the economic capabilities of the growing city.

World's Largest Facilities for Pollution Control

The Metropolitan Sanitary District of Greater Chicago now serves more than 5,500,000 persons living in an 860 square mile area which includes the City of Chicago and 117 adjacent communities within Cook County. The industrial load which must also be collected and treated is equivalent in pollution content to approximately 4,500,000 additional persons, making a total population equivalent of approximately 10,000,000 persons.

The Expanding Problem

The burgeoning population and industrial growth, coupled with the restricted dilution imposed by the edicts of the Supreme Court,[1] have created an imbalance in the oxygen conditions of the waterways so that the so-called "complete" treatment of sewage must now be upgraded, and all or most of the combined-sewer spillage must be captured and routed through the upgraded treatment plants.

Also, the increased proportion of impervious surfaces, in the form of roofs and pavements and the more rapid conveyance of runoff by auxiliary outlet sewers have so greatly increased the peak runoff rates from the combined-sewer drainage areas as to greatly overload the flow capacity of the open watercourses (including the Sanitary and Ship Canal) and make necessary the reversal of flow in the main waterways during periods of high stormwater runoff. Figure 1 shows the points where the surcharge of polluted backflow is released into Lake Michigan from the North Shore Channel, the Chicago River, and the Calumet River. These backflows are now occurring at increasing frequencies, thus reinstating the basic problem of lake pollution which plagued the city government a century ago.

Under the financial sponsorship of the Metropolitan Sanitary District of Greater Chicago, The State Institute for Environmental Quality, and the Department of Public Works, City of Chicago, a systems study was undertaken to develop a plan for that part of the Chicagoland Area served by combined sewers.

After a thorough search of records and extensive investigation, twenty-three separate alternatives were identified for study.

After extensive review of the evaluation report, the Flood Control Coordinating Committee unanimously agreed that the "Chicago Underflow Plan" was less costly and would be more environmentally acceptable to the community than any of the other plans presented. Detailed studies and layouts along the lines of these plans were then continued to develop the final plan.

Recommended Plan

The system recommended herein, a composite of the several Underflow Plan Alternatives, is outstanding in its relative storage economy and simplicity. It will capture the total runoff from all of the record meteorological sequences of history, if they were to recur on future ultimate developed drainage basins, except for the peak few hours of three of the most severe storm events. The system will

1. The United States Supreme Court in 1967 limited the total withdrawal to 3,200 cfs average flow including domestic water supply and runoff from the Chicago and Calumet River Drainage Area, originally tributary to Lake Michigan.

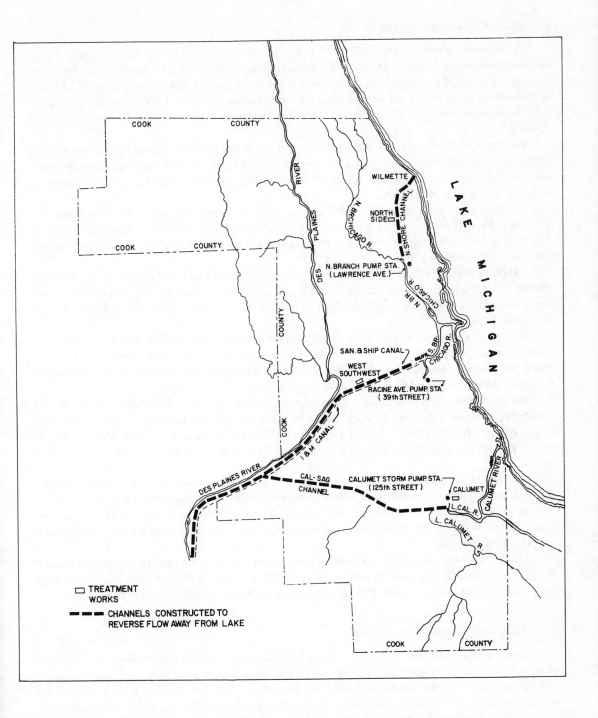

FIGURE 1. Canal system.

convey these captured combined sewer flows through high velocity, out-of-sight underflow tunnels below the routes of the existing surface water-courses to large pit-type detention reservoirs. Figure 2 shows the general location of the conveyance tunnel system and storage reservoirs.

Storage Reservoir Facilities

The primary storage reservoir is located in the area now occupied by the sludge lagoons of the Metropolitan Sanitary District in the McCook-Summit area (figure 2). This reservoir will be in the form of a 300 to 330 feet deep rock quarry, with a maximum water depth of approximately 200 feet, in the heaviest storm event, and water surface dimensions averaging about 1,000 feet wide by 2½ miles long. Total storage capacity of the reservoir with the water surface at its maximum level will be 57,000 acre-feet.

The lower 100 feet of depth of the reservoir will be divided into three basins by transverse dikes, providing two small basins, each with a volume of 5,000 acre-feet for the more frequent small runoff periods. The larger runoff volumes will flood the remaining basin and the water surface will rise in elevation over the entire reservoir.

The dewatering pumping station will discharge from the storage reservoir to the West-Southwest Treatment Plant (figure 2) at an average rate of about 700 cfs. The station's total capacity will be 2,400 cfs in order to dewater the conveyance tunnels and Stearns Quarry into the reservoir within three days following a storm.

Computer studies indicate that the storage utilized in Basins 1 and 2 will exceed their combined volume (10,000 acre-feet) at an average frequency of six or seven times per year and that these two basins alone will entrap more than 70% of the annual combined sewer spillage containing over 95% of the annual Suspended Solids.

The use of a deep pit storage basin of such magnitude and depth requires that aeration be provided to insure positive odor control by floating equipment. This is necessary because the range of liquid levels varies over 200 feet. It is proposed to use submerged turbine aerators provided with a downflow draft tube with air injection below the propeller.

The submerged turbine aerators will be provided with a bar screen to prevent large ice chunks from being drawn into the draft tube and damaging the blades. The aerators will be provided with legs to protect the draft tube and will need a minimum of 20 feet of water to operate. When floating at greater depths, it is considered that active aeration will be limited to the upper 50 feet of the water in storage.

Aerators, in the heaviest rainfall year will be in near continuous operation in or above Basins 1 and 2. A lesser amount of aeration on an intermittent schedule will be required for Basin 3.

An aerated reservoir of lesser depth and volume of 1,800 acre-feet will be provided near the proposed O'Hare Water Reclamation Plant to serve the combined sewered area of the suburban communities to the northwest.

Another reservoir will utilize the existing Stearns rock quarry in the vicinity of 28th and Halsted Streets. This reservoir will provide approximately 4,000 acre-feet of storage space and will be used only during record storm events to flatten out the peak discharge through the conveyance tunnels.

Underflow Conveyance Tunnels

There are approximately 120 miles of underflow conveyance tunnels intercepting 640 sewer overflow points in the 375 square mile area served by combined sewers. Most of the conveyance tunnels will be constructed in the Silurian Dolomite rock formation 150 to 300 feet below the surface of the waterways (figure 3). In some areas, the smaller tunnels will be constructed in the clay overburden.

The tunnels will in general be drilled by mining machine (moles), except for the largest sizes which will probably be constructed by the conventional drill and blast method.

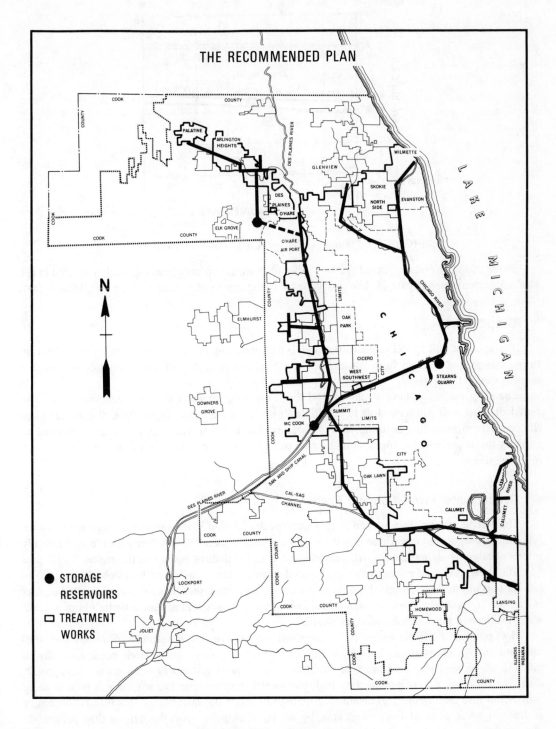

THE RECOMMENDED PLAN

N

● STORAGE
  RESERVOIRS
□ TREATMENT
  WORKS

FIGURE 2. Recommended plan.

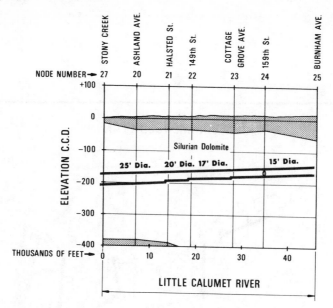

FIGURE 3. Tunnel profile of Little Calumet River.

Three main conveyance tunnel systems fork out from the primary reservoir facility located in the McCook-Summit area (figure 2). The storage space in the conveyance tunnel system is 9,100 acre-feet.

Drop Shafts

The spillages will be delivered to the underflow tunnels by hundreds of vertical drop shafts, capturing the present spillage from the existing riverbank sewer outlets of 5,000 miles of near-surface sewer systems (figure 4).

The drop shafts will have a split vertical shaft, one side for water and the other side for air. The center dividing wall will have slots to insufflate air in the falling water. This reduces the impact when the air-water mixture hits bottom. An air separation chamber is provided to reduce the amount of air entering the tunnel. At the top, a vent chamber will allow air to escape during filling and to be drawn in during dewatering.

Groundwater Protection and Recharge

The Recommended Plan is sited in rock units of the Silurian System of the geologic strata underlying the Chicagoland area. These limestone and dolomite rock units, together with the hydraulically interconnected overlying glacial drift, comprise the so-called shallow aquifer of the region.

The preservation of groundwater quality and quantity can be achieved by establishing or maintaining two physical conditions throughout the project area: high piezometric level within the aquifer in relation to hydraulic grade levels in subsurface project features, and adequate limitation of groundwater infiltration into the subsurface excavations.

High piezometric levels within the aquifer will provide protection against exfiltration from tunnels and storage excavations, thus preserving groundwater quality. These levels occur naturally in much of the project area, and must be established by recharge systems in other parts of the project area. The differential head provided by high piezometric levels within the aquifer will tend to cause infiltration into underground excavations. The limitations of the quantity of this infiltration can be realized in some parts of the project area, by relying principally upon the natural flow permeabilities which are known to exist within the lower dolomitic rock formations. A low leakage rate can be

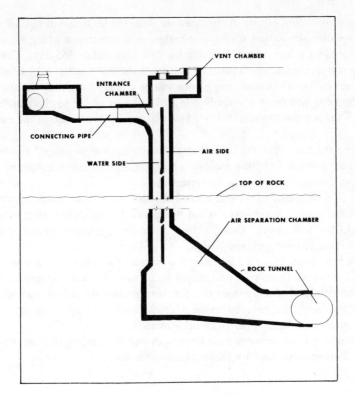

FIGURE 4. Vertical drop shaft.

achieved by grouting of only major fractures and fissures in the rock. In other areas, extensive grouting and/or lining of the tunnels will be required to prevent high infiltration rates.

Additional data on protection of groundwater and limitation of infiltration into tunnels and storage areas is available in the Technical Reports.

Operation

The general operation of the Underflow System is as follows: Rainfall runoff and/or snow-melt enters the sewer system mixing with household and industrial wastes. This combined flow travels through the sewers to a control or diversion chamber located near the waterways. In dry weather or very minor rainfall periods all of the flow is diverted to the existing interceptor for conveyance to the sewage treatment plants.

In storm runoff periods exceeding the interceptor or treatment plant capacity, storm overflow passes through the drop shafts to the large conveyance tunnels under the waterways. Flow is conveyed to the storage reservoirs. At McCook, it will first enter the primary basins Nos. 1 and 2. If flow exceeds 10,000 acre-feet, the capacity of the two primary basins, spillage will occur to basin No. 3. Immediately after the flows in the conveyance tunnels have subsided, the dewatering pumps are turned on at the principal reservoir site to pump the water in the tunnels to the reservoir. The pumps have capacity to perform this operation in two days. If the Stearns Quarry is filled, it will require a total of three days. Flushing water may then be taken in from the waterway at selected drop shafts to cleanse the conveyance tunnels.

The combined sewer overflows will be detained in the storage basins from the maximum single storm for up to 50 days. The most frequent occurrence for a single storm, however, will range between

2 and 10 days. Overflow water will be in the reservoir from the sequence of rainfall events for much longer periods. Computer simulation studies show that in a recurrence of the heaviest water year, 1954, the basins would have live detention water for 288 days out of 365 days. This is based on the average dewatering rate to the treatment plant of 700 cfs in the dry weather post rainfall periods.

In the post storm period, the dewatering pumps will be operated to pump the stored water to the treatment plant. Pumping will be at a variable rate which, when added to the plant's raw sewage influent, will equal 1.5 times the dry weather flow. This will require expansion of the existing treatment plant facilities.

In the very large storms, when the stored water has undergone prolonged aeration, pumping at rates in excess of those acceptable by the secondary and tertiary treatment units can be routed directly to the chlorination facilities and then to the waterways.

If the storm is of a magnitude that will exceed the storage or conveyance capacity, gates at the drop shafts on selected gravity sewer systems can be operated to force the water to overflow at such selected locations to the waterways. Thus, in these rare events, priority protection can be given to small streams and the low elevation pumped areas.

The solids that have been deposited in the aerated storage basin have to be removed periodically. It is estimated that a two to three year period will be allowed for solids storage. The solids in this period of time will be stabilized to the extent that further digestion should not be necessary. The aeration equipment in the basin can be used to aerobically digest recently deposited solids that might occur immediately prior to a planned quarry cleaning operation.

The settled material will be removed by a floating dredge discharging through a pipe system with other sludge to the Metropolitan Sanitary District land reclamation.

Benefits

A brief listing of anticipated benefits to be derived from completion of the system of flood and pollution control proposed herein, includes the following:

1. Protection of the valuable water resources of Lake Michigan from flood release of river water as now required through the existing Chicago River, the North Shore Channel, and the Calumet River into Lake Michigan.
2. Achieving and maintaining acceptable water quality (in accordance with regulations of the Illinois Pollution Control Board and the Metropolitan Sanitary District) in the open waterways known as the Chicago River and its branches, the Sanitary and Ship Canal, the North Shore Channel, the Calumet-Sag Channel, and those portions of the Calumet River, Des Plaines River, Salt Creek, and other open waterways under the jurisdiction and control of the Metropolitan Sanitary District of Greater Chicago.
3. Reduction of surface and basement flooding by underground backwaters or overbank flooding.
4. Improvement of recreational values of all surface waterways.
5. Increase in property values due to general improvement of environment.

Post Construction Environmental Impact

The surface environmental disturbances of project features after construction will be minimal. Most elements of the project are located underground. Features on the surface are generally to be located in areas that are already in industrial use. Quarry and surface reservoirs are already surrounded by lands that would provide an effective barrier to urban encroachment.

Since odor nuisances must be avoided, all reservoirs expected to detain water for over 3 days will be designed with sufficient mechanical aeration equipment to oxidize matter contained in the combined sewer overflow from the maximum storm.

Conveyance tunnels will be located in the Niagaran Group about 300 feet below the ground surface. Groundwater levels in the Niagaran aquifer should be above the proposed tunnels in most places. These high ground water levels will cause water flow into the tunnels and consequently there will be no danger of aquifer pollution. The quantities of water infiltrating into the tunnels would be small in relation to the aquifer potential and there would be no adverse effects on the long term water supply. In areas such as McCook where the upper aquifer is overdeveloped and water levels are low, the aquifer would be recharged with potable water to prevent exfiltration of polluted water from tunnels and reservoirs.

It is expected that little or no fish kills would occur during overflow periods. In the first place, the prevalent dry weather Dissolved Oxygen (DO), temperature during the summer, and ammonia-nitrogen levels in the Mainstream Waterway and Calumet-Sag Channel would not be conducive to game fish life. In other watercourses, warm water biota and native game fish would not be greatly affected by the short dips in DO during the infrequent overflow events.

18

Engineering Design and Construction in Permafrost Regions: A Review

Kenneth A. Linell and G. H. Johnston

Introduction

In North America, development of the permafrost regions is advancing at a rapidly accelerating rate. This creates increasingly intense pressure on the technical community to formulate engineering design and construction principles that will accurately ensure predictable behavior and minimum costs. In North America, research to develop such criteria was started in the 1940s. This has provided an invaluable base and fund of fundamental knowledge to meet this construction need. In the past decade, entirely new construction situations, new and more stringent requirements for structural and environmental stability, and the continuing increase in knowledge of the nature of permafrost have contributed new intensity and scope to the challenge and have provoked especially intense research and investigation efforts.

Because of the large volume of information currently available on construction in permafrost regions, it is impossible to reference all significant literature in this paper. Therefore, references herein have been selected only to be indicative of the current state of the art.

Site Selection and Investigation for Engineering Purposes

The importance of proper selection and investigation of a site or route for construction in permafrost areas, by reconnaissance and detailed site, environmental and material availability studies, cannot be overemphasized. Unfortunately, the fact that rational design requires an adequate base of factual knowledge and that this is doubly important in permafrost regions has sometimes in the past been overlooked or ignored. The record of the past shows many failures of construction on permafrost from lack of this information base. Consequences of encountering unexpected conditions during construction include lost construction time schedules, improvised foundation redesign, carrying of work unexpectedly into severe fall and winter weather, very large cost increases, delay in beneficial occu-

Extracted with permission of the authors, the National Research Council of Canada, and the U.S. National Academy of Sciences from *North American Contribution, Permafrost, Second International Conference,* 1973, pp. 553–75. Organizing Committee of Canada and U.S. Planning Committee. Published by National Academy of Sciences, Washington, D.C., 1973. K. A. Linell was with the U.S. Army Cold Regions Research and Engineering Laboratory at the time of publication of this paper; G. H. Johnston is with the Division of Building Research, National Research Council of Canada, Ottawa, Canada.

pancy, heavy repair and maintenance expenses, and disruption of operations. During the last several years, however, recognition of the fundamental need for adequate area, route, and site studies prior to engineering design and construction decisions has increased. Existing and new techniques for obtaining the required surface and subsurface information have been increasingly employed on new construction.

Investigational techniques may be divided into two categories: indirect, including aerial photographic and geophysical methods, and direct, including drilling and sampling and allied techniques.

Use of conventional aerial photographic techniques for terrain and site evaluation in permafrost areas was extensively investigated beginning more than two decades ago and results were reported by Frost.[24] The U.S. Army Corps of Engineers has included summaries of these techniques in two engineering manuals.[83,84] The discovery of vast oil and gas and other mineral resources in northern North America in the last few years has greatly spurred the widespread practical use of these aerial photographic techniques. Very extensive application of aerial photographic methods is now being made for both route selection and detailed route and site examination in combination with surface and subsurface investigations on the proposed Alaska pipeline, on several proposed pipelines in northern Canada,[64] and on associated transportation systems and on other projects. In current practice, airphoto analysis is used not only for reconnaissance evaluation of geological, soils, vegetation, drainage, accessibility, and similar factors but also to assist in detailed layout of roads, buildings and other facilities and in detailed engineering evaluation of permafrost conditions in relation to these projects. Engineering design and construction problems may often be enormously simplified by placing the facility in the most favorable location.

An interesting special case is the use of aerial photographs taken during the thaw-melt period to determine topographic positions of maximum snow accumulation, especially from snow drifting. This approach was used by the Arctic Construction and Frost Effects Laboratory in Greenland in the 1950s for selecting route locations for roads and more recently within the continental United States to minimize facility snow removal problems. Granberg describes a technique for indirect mapping of snow-cover to aid in predicting localized occurrences of permafrost.[33]

As outlined by Haugen *et al.*,[37] the current Earth Resources Terrain Survey (ERTS) program promises to give a wealth of information on terrain and permafrost conditions in Alaska and Canada that will be useful for engineering purposes. Information will be obtained on any given location every 18 days on such surface details as vegetation, snow and ice covers, ground temperatures, and geomorphic and other evidences of permafrost, as well as stream levels and sedimentation patterns, forest fires, etc.

Urgent need exists for new geophysical exploration equipment and techniques that will permit large areas or distances (such as for pipelines and roads) to be covered quickly, conveniently, and economically on a continuous basis, with positive capability to detect problem ice-rich locations and isolated permafrost and ice bodies under specific sites, especially in areas of sporadic permafrost. Electromagnetic sensing systems, both airborne and surface-operated and capable of yielding subsurface information to depths of 15 m or more in frozen soil, have been used on an experimental basis. Hoekstra,[39] Frischknecht and Stanley,[23] and Bertram *et al.*[6] have discussed technical approaches in this area. Such equipment is capable of distinguishing, with depth, materials such as soils, ice, and rock having different electrical properties. Although not yet routinely used on major projects, such equipment can be used operationally for some purposes and is in a state of rapid and continuing development. As reported by Garg[28] and Hunter[40] in Session VI, both resistivity and refraction types of conventional seismic systems have utility in permafrost areas. Roethlisberger[68] has recently summarized the state of the art of seismic exploration in cold regions. Experiments have been performed with acoustic reflection-type sounding equipment with inconclusive results thus far; however, additional research is in progress.

Special equipment and techniques for subsurface exploration and sampling of frozen soil (including clean gravels well bonded by ice), ice, and bedrock by core drilling are available, although improvements over the last decade seem to have been less rapid than in the previous decade. Sellmann and Mellor are summarizing the current state of the art in a monograph.[75] The frozen condition may actually offer a distinct advantage in gravels or in fractured or weathered rock provided the material is well ice-bonded. Lange has described for this conference techniques by which these materials can be sampled effectively.[49] Frozen bedrock should never be assumed free of ice if thawing of the rock is possible and if the consequences of undetected ice in the rock would be significant. McAnerney has described a case in which thaw sink holes and subsurface drainage channels developed in bedrock thought free of ice on the basis of nonrefrigerated core drilling.[60]

Though northern development has greatly spurred employment of special equipment and techniques, refrigerated core drilling should be used much more than it is, as undisturbed frozen cores permit visual examination and accurate measurement and tests of almost completely undisturbed materials. As shown by Smith *et al.,* however, a small degree of disturbance may be present even in frozen cores which has to be taken into account in precise analyses.[78]

In fine-grained frozen soils above $-4°$ C drive sampling is feasible, as has been described by Kitze,[45] and is often considerably cheaper, simpler, and more rapid. Samples are structurally disturbed, but still permit accurate detection of ground ice and measurement of moisture content of specimens. Test pits and power-driven augers of various sizes are also widely used to obtain both disturbed and undisturbed samples and for *in situ* examination of the frozen soil profile.

Restrictions against surface movement and operations on the tundra in summer in order to avoid damage to the arctic environment have resulted in the use of helicopters to move exploration rigs from location to location. The rigs have even been mounted on the undercarriage of the helicopter itself.

Both thermistors and thermocouples are used for ground temperature measurements, the choice depending on the degree of precision required.[79] Diodes have also been used occasionally as sensors to measure ground temperatures. Groundwater table measurements are often difficult to obtain on a routine basis, except in summer. Some experiments have been made with systems that use air displacement (Gilman[30]) or kerosine in the groundwater well to prevent freezeup. Methodology of groundwater measurements in permafrost regions is discussed in greater detail by Williams and van Everdingen.[96] Under the stresses encountered on construction projects, soil moisture cells may not always perform reliably.[2]

In both the United States and Canada an extension of the Unified Soil Classification System is in use in detailed or simplified form for engineering classification of frozen material.[52, 65, 90] During the last decade, significant effort has been applied to development of methods of field and laboratory testing of foundations materials for engineering analysis. For example, Crory,[18] Luscher and Afifi,[56] and Smith *et al.*[78] have reported studies to evaluate thaw-consolidation behavior of foundations. Again, Sayles,[73] Stevens,[80] Ladanyi and Johnston,[48] and Garg[28] have carried out studies to measure the mechanical properties of frozen foundation materials useful for engineering analyses, such as strength, creep, and dynamic response characteristics.

For special structures and facilities and where permafrost conditions are particularly complex, full-scale field tests are necessary and should be carried out in advance of construction to provide information for evaluations of the interaction between the atmosphere, the structure, and the ground.

Principles of Environmental Engineering and Protection for Permafrost Terrain

In North America, great public pressure now exists for preservation of the natural environment as well as for correction of pollution and environmental degradation effects where these have been allowed to develop. In the United States, this pressure is backed by laws at the federal level and increasingly at lower governmental levels that require a detailed evaluation and statement of the environmental impact of the construction or facility be submitted to show its acceptability before any new construction is started. In Alaska, these restrictions are further supplemented by a prohibition against operations on the natural tundra surface in summer because experience has shown that even a single vehicle pass may result in uncontrolled permafrost degradation and erosion where conditions are especially fragile. In Canada, similar legislation with regard to pollution and environmental impact is in effect or is being promulgated; Land Use Regulations must be complied with by anyone going anywhere on the lands north of 60° and a specific land use permit is required for every activity that involves going on the surface of the land at any time of the year.

The severe cost and operational penalties that may be encountered if a facility is not environmentally stable serve as further constraints on the engineer. The impact analysis cannot be limited to the structure itself; the total impact of all activities and environmental changes relating to the project must be considered. At a special symposium of the Royal Society of Canada[36] on "The Tundra Environment" some of the factors to be considered were discussed. The fragile nature of the ground thermal regime and the effects that natural and man-made changes can have on the environmental conditions under which permafrost exists have been described by Watmore,[92] Mackay,[58] and Gold *et al.*[31] among others. Wein and Bliss[95] have presented a summary of the effects and of methods of coping with them. Changes in vegetation, drainage, and water quality or temperature will affect animal aquatic life. Erosion may not only destroy utility of land for future generations but may add siltation in streams, which affects aquatic life. Spills of oil or other substances may destroy many types of vegetation. Wildlife migration patterns may be changed.

In the United States, the need to incorporate environmental protective measures into construction on permafrost was recognized by the U.S. Army Corps of Engineers as early as World War II, and positive control requirements began to be incorporated into construction specifications in Alaska many years before the current public pressures and legal restrictions existed. Construction on difficult permafrost terrain at Kotzebue, Alaska, in 1957 as described by Jensen[41] is a case example. In Canada the Division of Building Research of the National Research Council, as the primary research agency for the Canadian construction industry, translated the results of research and field experience into technical guidance.

These efforts have led to the current situation as described by J. Brown[8] of greatly accelerated effort by scientists and engineers under sponsorship of both industry and government to develop both better fundamental understanding and better technology for utilization of permafrost terrain.

Much research to develop practical methods for predicting thermal effects in construction has been carried out by many investigators and many of the useful results have been summarized in manual form by the U.S. Army.[86] Sanger[71] has been very active in developing computation methods useful for engineering purposes. Research in use and maintenance of vegetative cover to control degradation of permafrost areas is in its infancy, but some relationships are known, as given in papers by Linell,[50] Heginbottom,[38] Brown *et al.*,[9, 10] and others. Of particular interest is the indication that in borderline permafrost areas, such as Fairbanks, Alaska, a living cover of low vegetation cannot by itself be relied upon to control permafrost degradation, but in a colder area such as Inuvik, N.W.T., it can be sufficient.

The practical effectiveness of modifying heat exchange at the ground surface on a long-range basis by control of surface color has been demonstrated in pavement applications as reported in papers by Aitken,[1] Fulwider and Aitken,[26] Berg and Aitken,[5] Wechsler and Glaser,[94] and Kritz and Wechsler[46]. In-ground insulation has been found in several Corps of Engineers studies[3, 4, 27, 77, 89] to be effective in slowing or delaying permafrost degradation in marginal permafrost areas, but not in preventing it. Esch,[22] in carrying out similar studies, has thus far found similar short-term effectiveness of insulation in degradation control; however, the test duration has not yet been long enough to show long-term behavior.

Numerous research studies have been carried out and/or are currently in progress on environmental engineering for construction of hot and cold pipelines and on effects of, and remedial measures for, oil and gasoline spills in permafrost areas.

Foundation Design and Construction

Current concepts of foundation design on permafrost are outlined in a manual prepared by the U.S. Army,[85] and Sanger has published a monograph on foundations of structures.[72] On materials identified as thaw-stable under the extension of the Unified Soil Classification System developed for frozen soils,[52, 65, 90] foundation design is commonly identical with temperate zone practice, even though foundation soils are frozen below the foundation level. Difficulty sometimes is encountered, however, in determining whether or not clean granular soils containing ice will consolidate after thaw, and elaborate sampling, testing, and compaction experiments have sometimes been conducted in an effort to resolve this question. Terzaghi reported more than 20 years ago that shrinkage or settlement per unit depth of thaw of coarse-grained frozen soils at a site in the vicinity of Fairbanks, Alaska, not containing buried bodies of ice, decreased from an upper limiting value close to the ground surface to almost zero at a depth of about 9 m.[81] He concluded that settlement of the surface under these conditions is by no means necessarily negligible. However, it can also be concluded that settlement of foundations supported at depth in such materials may be entirely tolerable; this is confirmed by observations of thaw settlement of actual construction in the Fairbanks area.[88]

On thaw-unstable foundation materials, unlimited challenge and opportunity for design ingenuity are presented. Here design to ensure preservation of the permafrost is by far the most commonly used foundation approach for permanent construction. Normally, acceptance of permafrost degradation, and design therefore, is used only when the foundation materials are thaw stable or where only expedient or short-term construction is involved. Notable exceptions to this approach have been the designs used for the sand fill dikes at the Kelsey and Kettle Generating Stations[12, 44, 57, 59] and the foundations for several buildings at Thompson in marginal permafrost in northern Manitoba. Removal and replacement of unacceptable materials has been used extensively by the Alaska District of the Corps of Engineers at Fairbanks, Alaska, where silts up to about 6 m thick overlay thaw-stable sands and gravels. Similar procedures have been used occasionally in northern Canada to obtain suitable bearing for building foundations.[35, 74] Excavation of ice-rich materials to limit settlements to an acceptable amount was carried out for the Kettle dikes.[59] Except for steam or cold water thawing of overburden for gold placer mining operations in Alaska and the Yukon Territory, Canada, no documented case is known to the authors where prethawing to completely eliminate permafrost has been used in North America. However, based on water and stream thaw tests and recommendations by Terzaghi,[81] prethawing of sandy gravels to a depth of 9 m below the original ground surface has been used by the Corps of Engineers in the Fairbanks region with and without blasting as described by Waterhouse and Sills[91] to ensure consolidation of the looser upper strata in advance of foundation construction.

It is widely accepted that structures that cannot tolerate differential movements or seasonal vertical displacements must be supported on permafrost rather than on or in the annual zone of freeze and thaw. However, for structures that have very low movement tolerances, designers should be aware that some seasonal movements may occur in permafrost to at least as deep as 10 m and placement to as deep as 20 m may be required.

The time- and temperature-dependent properties of frozen soils that are subjected to loading are important considerations in foundation design. Creep displacement and decrease in strength with increase in ground temperature may be particularly significant. Long-term strengths may be as much as an order of magnitude less than the strength of a soil subjected to a short-term or instantaneously applied load. From a study of building foundations in Canada's permafrost region, R. J. E. Brown has concluded that "anything can be built in any soil and permafrost conditions, provided the conditions are investigated thoroughly and proper design precautions are taken."

Footings

Spread footings, continuous footings, raft or mat foundations, or post and pad construction have been successfully used on thaw-unstable as well as thaw-stable permafrost at such diverse locations as

Churchill, Manitoba, Canada[21]; Fairbanks, Alaska[19, 66, 88]; Fort Yukon, Alaska; Pangnirtung, N.W.T., Canada; and Thule, Greenland, with careful planning for structural and thermal stability as appropriate for the foundation conditions. Principles and techniques for design of footings on permafrost have been expressed in manual form by the Corps of Engineers, including such aspects as creep and dynamic response analysis.[85]

Thermal control provided for footing-type foundations to maintain permafrost usually consists of either a simple ventilation space between the structure and the ground surface or one of various types of duct systems. Costs of providing ducted foundations easily become excessive unless care is exercised, however. Duct-ventilated gravel fills placed on the ground surface are receiving increasing use in Canada to support slab-on-grade construction, e.g., for aircraft hangars, maintenance garages, and heated oil storage tanks. These vary from simple systems where small diameter pipes are placed in the fill and depend on natural air flow during the winter to remove ground heat, to more complex systems incorporating ventilating fans to ensure adequate air flow. One such system utilizing 1.1-m-diameter pipes on 2.6-m centers has been proposed for a huge railroad maintenance building on Baffin Island.[34] In the United States, the U.S. Army Corps of Engineers began to investigate and use this type of construction in the later 1940s[53] and has since made numerous installations of many types and magnitudes in areas of both warm and cold permafrost. Experience has shown that duct systems placed below the ground level tend to collect ice and sediment, which block air flow, causing serious maintenance problems.[82] Steam thawing is required to open frozen ducts, which, in turn, may cause serious ground thermal disturbance. Instead, it is desirable that ducted foundations be sufficiently elevated above, or positioned relative to, the surrounding terrain so as to be self-draining in summer of any accumulation of ice and snow from the preceding winter. It is also essential that ducts be carefully designed to provide proper duct diameter and spacing. Stacks are used when necessary to increase natural airflow or to raise intakes and outlets above snow accumulation levels. Mechanical blower systems to increase volume of air circulation in ducts are generally avoided because of costs, increased mechanical complexity, and the dependence on alertness and care in operation that they introduce. Mechanical refrigeration systems are employed for maintenance of permafrost only in special problem situations or for remedial purposes.

Pile Foundations

Pile foundations incorporating an air space between the structure and ground surface are the most common type of design for permanent construction on thaw-unstable permafrost. Creosoted wood and steel pipe or H-section piles are the most commonly used types. Precast concrete piles are used much less frequently in permafrost in North America and cast-in-place concrete piles only occasionally. Cast-in-place concrete piles have been used at Thompson, Manitoba, where small islands of permafrost were encountered[32]; the designs assumed no support to a depth equal to twice the thickness of permafrost and allowance was made for negative skin friction when the permafrost thawed and the soil consolidated. Cast-in-place concrete piles were also used at the Birch Hill Ski Lodge, Fort Wainwright, Fairbanks, Alaska. Where substantial frost heave forces are experienced, concrete piles with conventional amounts of reinforcement are easily cracked in tension, exposing the steel to corrosion. Cast-in-place piles, of course, have to cope with the problems of setting and strength gain of the concrete and of thaw and freeze of surrounding materials in the permafrost zone.

Piles are placed either by slurrying in an auger-drilled hole or by driving. Steam thawing is used only occasionally. Slurry may be the same soil as removed by the auger or concrete sand mixed with water. Use of carefully controlled high-quality backfill around the pile is one approach to increasing effective pile diameter under poor ground conditons. By avoiding excessively wet slurries, freezeback is hastened and made more positive in areas of warm permafrost. When piles exposed to below freezing temperatures are placed by slurrying, an ice layer may form on the surface of the pile that may control the allowable tangential shear strength that may be developed. In marginal permafrost areas, circulation of refrigerant through tubing attached to the pile is commonly used to assure ex-peditious and positive freezeback of slurried piles unless the piles are installed in the spring months (March through early June) when the ground is sufficiently cold to assure natural freezeback. Artifi-cial refrigeration is not considered necessary where the mean annual ground temperature is −4° C or colder. In fine-grained frozen soils at temperatures down to about −4° C, both steel pipe and H piles have been installed by driving with diesel, vibratory, or other heavy hammers. Very extensive pile loading test programs have been carried out in Alaska by the U.S. Army Corps of Engineers, only part of which have been reported to date.[2, 16, 17, 20] Newcombe and Rowley *et al.*[68] have performed pile tests at Prudhoe Bay, Alaska, and Inuvik, N.W.T., Canada, respectively, which extend available data into new soil and/or ground temperature conditions. The studies reported by Rowley *et al.* include the first results published in North America on lateral load tests of piles imbedded in permafrost.

Since effective adfreeze bond is the major variable affecting the realizable pile bearing capacity of non-end-bearing piles, many methods for increasing the effective skin friction or surface area or for maintaining values at high levels in the critical period of the year have been examined, including use of thermal piles. Thermal piles of various designs are in use, finding their greatest applicability in marginal permafrost areas where extra assurance of freezeback and/or maintenance of design adfreeze bond strength is needed. The most commonly used types have been the two-phase Long thermopile[54] (patented) and the single-phase Balch liquid-filled pile[43] (patented). Long recommends ring and helix types of thermal piles in combination with ground insulation as methods of maximizing pile capacity at competitive costs.[55] Johnson[43] has studied thermal convection loops, which are thermal pile ele-ments interconnected to provide loop circulation. Babb, Garlid, and Shannon have suggested a "tube-in-tube" concept in which a single phase liquid device is placed within a "cold storage" tube contain-ing ethylene glycol solution in order to increase effectiveness. Reed has demonstrated the potential of forced air circulation piles.[67] U.S. Army Corps of Engineers practice is to neglect end bearing for piles of about 15 cm tip diameter or less; in larger diameter piles or caissons, end bearing is taken into ac-count.[85]

Without question, a stable pile foundation can be constructed on any type of frozen soil regard-less of the ice content, no matter how borderline the conditions, but each situation must be carefully investigated to ensure that all pertinent factors have been taken into account in order to obtain the most economical designs and satisfactory performance.

Drainage

Poor drainage is a typical condition of permafrost terrain because of the presence of impervious frozen ground at shallow depth, even in the summer. Saturated ground conditions in the summer and the frozen surface in the winter cause infiltration rates from precipitation to drop to as low as zero. When air temperatures drop below 0° C, icings form where water emerges on the surface, in turn, tending to block drainage facilities and cause operational obstacles. Even where precipitation is slight, drainage facilities must be provided to accommodate the large and quickly occurring flow of snow and ice meltwater, possibly combined with precipitation, over the frozen ground surface during a few days of breakup. Subsurface drains are effective only for limited portions of the year or under special conditions, as when a talik (unfrozen zone) exists. Nevertheless, subsurface flow of water within the annual thaw zone may be a very significant factor in the design of engineering structures; even in rela-tively arid climates of the Far North extensive subsurface flow may occur. Difficulties have been ex-perienced both summer and winter from subsurface flow of water in frost-shattered rock at a seismo-meter vault placed partially underground at Resolute Bay, N.W.T., Canada. At Thule Air Force Base, studies in 1957–1960 verified the fact that large quantities of water move in summer through the coarse granular materials in the upper soil layers.[61-63] Such water movement is capable of producing greater depth of thaw than would be otherwise experienced. During thaw, ordinary gravity flow is the principal mechanism acting. New supplies of water may be added into the subsurface flow section both from surface infiltration and from thaw of ground ice. However, when seasonal freezing begins in the fall, strong moisture movements in the soil may also occur toward the planes of freezing. In fine-grained soils, seepage flow in the annual thaw zone is slow and may amount to only a few centimetres per year under gravity effects, but in very coarse cobble or broken rock materials, flow rates as high as 750 m/h[62] have been measured. It appears to be within the technological state of the art to control the direction and paths of gravity-induced subsurface flow in the annual thaw zone by controlling depth of subsurface thaw penetration. For example, at Thule, Greenland, painting the airfield pavements white as described by Fulwider and Aitken[26] raised the permafrost table under the pavements and created barriers to cross-pavement seepage flow.[63]

A case is reported by Linell in which uncontrolled artesian flow from a subpermafrost source caused serious thaw of permafrost together with icing, a frost blister, and surface subsidence.[51] This occurred in a borderline permafrost area, and artificial refreezing of the ground was required to restore stability. In very cold permafrost areas such an upset of the thermal balance is normally rapidly self-correcting after removal of the cause. However, when the thermal disturbance is long range, as under a hot oil pipeline, thawing of permafrost and flow of resulting groundwater may continue indefinitely on a year-round basis. Lachenbruch has presented an analysis of resulting thermal, environmental and structural stability effects.[47] In their reports on pipeline performance and requirements, Watson *et al.*[93] and Rowley *et al.*[70] have presented some information on groundwater as a factor.

An excellent example of the potential adverse effects of groundwater flow on permafrost stability is the case described by Tobiasson of serious settlement of hangar floors caused by warm groundwater derived from snow infiltrated into cooling ducts, from runoff of snowmelt and rain from pavements, roofs, and natural surfaces flowing toward wells installed to keep the groundwater below the foundation cooling system.[82]

As pointed out by Johnson in 1950, Alaskan mineral soils, which usually are medium textured and single-grain structure, are highly susceptible to erosion when thawed.[42] It is presumed that this may apply in many other parts of the Arctic and Subarctic. Experience shows that merely damaging the natural surface vegetation may be sufficient to lead to catastrophic erosion under adverse conditions.[38, 58, 92] The damage may be not only to the terrain itself but also to waterways and to fish and wildlife. Where massive terrain adjustments such as described by Smith and Berg are induced by construction,[76] care must be taken to prevent damage to streams by silt-bearing icemelt runoff.

Icings are an engineering and operational problem throughout the cold regions. A bibliography on river, ground, and spring icings has been prepared by Carey,[13] as well as a monograph on icings developed from surface water and groundwater.[14] The latter summarizes current approaches to control icings. Culverts present a special icing problem because of their tendency to become partially or completely blocked with ice during the winter, with the result that flow cannot be handled during thaw runoff. As reported by Carey, Huck, and Gaskin, a cooperative field and laboratory research program to develop methods to improve the control or prevention of icings in culverts has been in progress for several years by CRREL, the Alaska Department of Highways and the U.S. Department of Transportation.[15] Gaskin and Stanley report that carefully controlled applications of electrical heat have been found promising.[29] Criteria for design of culvert foundations for stability against thawing of underlying foundation materials are discussed in a U.S. Army structure foundation manual.[85] During route selection it is desirable to minimize the number of points where drainage must cross roads or other construction. However, little or no research appears to be in progress to improve techniques for recognizing and predicting icing susceptible locations and conditions during planning, design, and construction.

Experience indicates that in areas of relatively warm permafrost such as Fairbanks, Alaska, road fills can be built of very coarse materials to allow surface water to seep through them in lieu of using culverts, provided the amounts of water involved are relatively small. However, experience in very cold permafrost areas near Thule, Greenland, where the mean annual temperature is about −11 to −12° C, shows that in such a climate even the coarsest fills become ice-choked within about 3 years;

thereafter, the embankments act as impervious dams rather than drainage fills. As shown by Fulwider, this effect can be exploited to advantage in the design and construction of water supply dams and reservoirs in very cold climates.[25]

Johnson concluded in 1950 that methods for design of storm water drains developed for temperate regions are applicable in arctic and subarctic regions if certain specific limitations are observed.[42] These limitations pertain to such factors as design storm indexes, infiltration rates, and retardance coefficients. The 1950 recommendations were used as the original basis for U.S. Army surface drainage criteria for airfields. These have been supplemented and updated with more recently available information in an Army technical manual.[87]

REFERENCES

1. Aitken, G. W. Highway test section for passive control of thermal regime in the Subarctic. Tech. Rep., U.S. Army Cold Regions Research and Engineering Laboratory, Hanover, New Hampshire. (In preparation)
2. Arctic Construction and Frost Effects Laboratory. 1957. Freezeback control and pile testing. Kotzebue Air Force Station, Alaska, Tech. Rep. 66, ACFEL, Boston, Massachusetts.
3. Banfield, A. F., Jr., and H. Csergei. 1966. Results of sampling insulating layers in runway test sections—Alaska field station. Tech. Note. CRREL, Hanover, New Hampshire.
4. Berg, R. L. 1970. Insulation in roads and runways—a bibliography, Tech. Note TN 29. U.S. Army Cold Regions Research and Engineering Laboratory, Hanover, New Hampshire.
5. Berg, R. L., and G. W. Aitken. Passive methods of controlling geocryological conditions in roadway construction. This volume.*
6. Bertram, C. L., K. J. Campbell, and S. S. Sandler. 1972. Locating large masses of ground ice with an impulse radar system. *In* Proceedings 8th International Symposium on Remote Sensing of Environment. University of Michigan, Ann Arbor.
7. Black, R. F. 1957. Some problems in engineering geology caused by permafrost in the Arctic Coastal Plain, northern Alaska. J. Arctic Inst. N. Am. 10:230–40.
8. Brown, J. Environmental strategies for the utilization of permafrost terrain. This volume.
9. Brown, J., W. Richard, and D. Vietor. 1968. Effect of disturbance on permafrost terrain. Spec. Rep. SR 138. CRREL, Hanover, New Hampshire.
10. Brown, J., and G. C. West. 1970. Tundra biome research in Alaska. The structure and function of cold-dominated ecosystems. Misc. Publ. 87. CRREL, Hanover, New Hampshire.
11. Brown, R. J. E. 1970. Permafrost in Canada: Its influence on northern development. University of Toronto Press, Toronto. 234 pp.
12. Brown, W. G., and G. H. Johnston. 1970. Dykes on permafrost: Predicting thaw and settlement. Can. Geotech. J. 7(4):365–71.
13. Carey, K. L. 1970. Icing occurrence, control and prevention, an annotated bibliography. Spec. Rep. SR-151, U.S. Army Cold Regions Research and Engineering Laboratory, Hanover, New Hampshire.
14. Carey, K. L. 1973. Icings developed from surface water and ground water. Monograph III-D3. U.S. Army Cold Regions Research and Engineering Laboratory, Hanover, New Hampshire.
15. Carey, K. L., R. L. Huck, and D. A. Gaskin. Prevention and control of culvert icing. Summary report on studies, FY 1966–70. Prepared in cooperation with State of Alaska Department of Highways and U.S. Department of Transportation, Federal Highway Administration, by U.S. Army Cold Regions Research and Engineering Laboratory, Hanover, New Hampshire. (In press)
16. Crory, F. E. 1966. Pile foundations in permafrost, p. 467–76. *In* Permafrost: Proceedings of an international conference. National Academy of Sciences, Washington, D.C.
17. Crory, F. E. 1968. Pile foundations in permafrost areas, Goldstream Creek, Fairbanks, Alaska. Tech. Rep. TR-180. U.S. Army Cold Regions Research and Engineering Laboratory, Hanover, New Hampshire.
18. Crory, F. E. Settlement associated with thawing of permafrost. This volume.
19. Crory, F. E. Design of ventilated floor system, Bldg. No. 16, Alaska Field Station, Tech. Rep. U.S. Army Cold Regions Research and Engineering Laboratory, Hanover, New Hampshire. (In press)
20. Crory, F. E., and R. E. Reed. 1965. Measurement of frost heaving forces on piles. Tech. Rep. 145. U.S. Army Cold Regions Research and Engineering Laboratory, Hanover, New Hampshire.

*Refers to: *North American Contribution, Permafrost, Second International Conference,* 1973, National Academy of Sciences, Washington, D. C. 783 pp.

21. Dickens, H. B., and D. M. Gray. 1960. Experience with a pier-supported building over permafrost. J. Soil Mech. Found. Div., (Proc. ASCE) v. 86(SM5):1–14.
22. Esch, D. C. Prevention of thaw degradation of underlying permafrost with roadway subgrade insulation. This volume.
23. Frischknecht, F. C., and W. D. Stanley. 1971. Airborne and ground electrical resistivity studies along proposed TAPS route. *In* Second international symposium on arctic geology, San Francisco, California. American Association of Petroleum Geologists, Tulsa, Oklahoma.
24. Frost, R. E. 1950. Evaluation of soils and permafrost conditions in the territory of Alaska by means of aerial photographs. Prepared at Purdue University for St. Paul District U.S. Army Corps of Engineers. Tech. Rep. 34. Arctic Construction and Frost Effects Laboratory, Boston, Massachusetts.
25. Fulwider, C. W. Thermal regime in an arctic earth-fill dam. This volume.
26. Fulwider, C. W., and G. W. Aitken. 1962. Effects of surface color on thaw penetration beneath an asphalt surface in the Arctic, p. 605–10. *In* Proceedings, International conference on the structural design of asphalt pavements, Aug. 20–24, University of Michigan, Ann Arbor.
27. Fulwider, C. W., and R. L. Berg. Effect of insulating layers on permafrost degradation. Tech. Rep. U.S. Army Cold Regions Research and Engineering Laboratory, Hanover, New Hampshire. (In preparation)
28. Garg, O. In situ physicomechanical properties of permafrost using geophysical techniques. This volume.
29. Gaskin, D. A., and L. E. Stanley. Control of culvert icing. This volume.
30. Gilman, G. D. 1967. Displacement method for ground water observations during freezing periods. Intern. Rep. 39. CRREL, Hanover, New Hampshire.
31. Gold, L. W., G. H. Johnston, W. A. Slusarchuk, and L. E. Goodrich. 1972. Thermal effects in permafrost, p. 25–46. *In* Proceedings Canadian northern pipeline research conference. Assoc. Com. Geotech. Res. Tech. Memo. 104. National Research Council of Canada, Ottawa.
32. Goodman, K. S., and R. M. Hardy. 1962. Permafrost occurrence and associated problems at Thompson, Manitoba, p. 140–48. *In* Proceedings 1st Canadian conference on permafrost. Assoc. Com. Geotech. Res. Tech. Memo. 76. National Research Council of Canada, Ottawa.
33. Granberg, H. B. Indirect mapping of snowcover for permafrost prediction at Schefferville, Quebec, Canada. This volume.
34. Hahn, J., and B. Sauer. 1968. Engineering for the Arctic. J. Eng. Inst. Can. April:23–28.
35. Harding, R. G. 1962. Foundation problems at Ft. McPherson, N.W.T., p. 159–66. *In* Proceedings 1st Canadian conference on permafrost. Assoc. Com. Geotech. Res. Tech. Memo. 76. National Research Council of Canada, Ottawa.
36. Hare, F. K. [ed.]. 1970. The tundra environment. Trans. Roy. Soc. Can. Sect. III Fourth Ser., Vol. VII. Winnipeg.
37. Haugen, R. K., H. L. McKim, L. W. Gatto, and D. M. Anderson. 1972. Cold regions environmental analysis based on ERTS-1 imagery. Proceedings, 8th international symposium on remote sensing of environment, University of Michigan, Ann Arbor, 12 pp.
38. Heginbottom, J. A. Some effects of surface disturbance on the permafrost active layer at Inuvik, Northwest Territories, Canada. This volume.
39. Hoekstra, P. Electromagnetic probing on permafrost. This volume.
40. Hunter, J. A. The application of shallow seismic methods to mapping of frozen surficial materials. This volume.
41. Jensen, W. C. 1961. Timber piles in permafrost at Alaskan radar station. Soil Mech. Found. Div. (Proc. ASCE) 87(SM1):15–27; discussions by K. Linell *et al.* 1962. 88(SM4):141–53.
42. Johnson, L. A. 1950. Investigation of airfield drainage, arctic and subarctic regions, in three volumes: Part I, Supplement to Part I, and Part II. Prepared by St. Anthony Falls Laboratory for St. Paul District, U.S. Army, Corps of Engineers. Tech. Rep. 19. Arctic Construction and Frost Effects Laboratory, Boston, Massachusetts.
43. Johnson, P. R. 1971. Empirical heat transfer rates of small Long and Balch thermal piles and thermal convection loops. Rep. 7102. Institute of Arctic Environmental Engineering, University of Alaska, Fairbanks.
44. Johnston, G. H. 1969. Dykes on permafrost, Kelsey Generating Station, Manitoba, Can. Geotech. J. 6(2):193–57.
45. Kitze, F. F. 1967. Soil sampling and drilling near Fairbanks, Alaska. Equipment and procedures. Tech. Rep. 191. U.S. Army Cold Regions Research and Engineering Laboratory, Hanover, New Hampshire.

46. Kritz, M. A., and A. E. Wechsler. 1967. Surface characteristics, effect on thermal regime, phase II. Tech. Rep. TR-189. U.S. Army Cold Regions Research and Engineering Laboratory, Hanover, New Hampshire.

47. Lachenbruch, A. H. 1970. Some estimates of the thermal effects of a heated pipeline in permafrost. Geol. Surv. Circ. 632.

48. Ladanyi, B., and G. H. Johnston. Evaluation of *in situ* creep properties of frozen soils with the pressuremeter. This volume.

49. Lange, G. R. Precision sampling of frozen ground and fractured rock by core drilling. This volume.

50. Linell, K. A. Long-term effects of vegetative cover on permafrost stability in an area of discontinuous permafrost. This volume.

51. Linell, K. A. Risks of uncontrolled flow from wells through permafrost. This volume.

52. Linell, K. A., and C. W. Kaplar. 1966. Description and classification of frozen soils. Tech. Rep. 150. U.S. Army Cold Regions Research and Engineering Laboratory, Hanover, New Hampshire.

53. Lobacz, E. F., and W. F. Quinn. 1966. Thermal regime beneath buildings constructed on permafrost, p. 247–52. *In* Permafrost: Proceedings of an international conference. National Academy of Sciences, Washington, D.C.

54. Long, E. L. 1966. The long thermopile, p. 487–91. *In* Permafrost: Proceedings of an international conference. National Academy of Sciences, Washington, D.C.

55. Long, E. L. Designing friction piles for increased stability at lower cost. This volume.

56. Luscher, U., and S. S. Afifi. Thaw consolidation of Alaskan silts and granular soils. This volume.

57. MacDonald, D. H. 1966. Design of Kelsey dikes, p. 492–496. *In* Permafrost: Proceedings of an international conference. National Academy of Sciences, Washington, D.C.

58. Mackay, J. R. 1970. Disturbances to the tundra and forest tundra environment of the western Arctic. Can. Geotech. J. 7(4):420–32.

59. MacPherson, J. G., G. H. Watson, and A. Koropatnick. 1970. Dykes on permafrost foundations in northern Manitoba, Can. Geotech J. 7(4):356–64.

60. McAnerney, J. M. 1968. Investigation of subsurface drainage at BMEWS facility, Thule, Greenland. Spec. Rep. SR-111. U.S. Army Cold Regions Research and Engineering Laboratory, Hanover, New Hampshire.

61. Metcalf and Eddy. 1957. Pavement condition report 1957 supplement. Tech. Rep. ENG-445. U.S. Army Corps of Engineers, Eastern Ocean District, North Atlantic Division, New York.

62. Metcalf and Eddy. 1958. Airfield drainage investigations. Tech. Rep. ENG-455. U.S. Army Corps of Engineers, Eastern Ocean District, North Atlantic Divison, New York.

63. Metcalf and Eddy. 1960. Airfield drainage investigation. Tech. Rep. ENG-465. U.S. Army Corps of Engineers, Eastern Ocean District, North Atlantic Division, New York.

64. Mollard, J. D. 1972, Airphoto terrain classification and mapping for northern feasibility studies, p. 105–127. *In* Proceedings Canadian northern pipeline research conference. Assoc. Com. Geotech. Res. Tech. Memo. 104. National Research Council of Canada, Ottawa.

65. Pihlainen, J. A., and G. H. Johnston. 1963. Guide to a field description of permafrost for engineering purposes. Associate Committee on Soil and Snow Mechanics. Tech. Memo. 79. National Research Council, Ottawa.

66. Quinn, W. F. 1965. Design analysis for thickness of ground pad, Bldg. 16, Fairbanks, Alaska. Intern. Rep. U.S. Army Cold Regions Research and Engineering Laboratory, Hanover, New Hampshire.

67. Reed, R. E. 1966. Refrigeration of a pipe pile by air circulation. Tech. Rep. TR-156. U.S. Army Cold Regions Research and Engineering Laboratory, Hanover, New Hampshire.

68. Roethlisberger, H. 1972. Seismic exploration in cold regions. Monograph II-A2a. CRREL, Hanover, New Hampshire.

69. Rowley, R. K., G. H. Watson, and B. Ladany. Vertical and lateral pile load tests in permafrost. This volume.

70. Rowley, R. K., G. H. Watson, T. M. Wilson, and R. G. Auld. Performance of a 48-inch warm-oil pipeline supported on permafrost. Presented at 25th Can. Geotech. Conf. Ottawa, Dec. 1972.

71. Sanger, F. J. 1966. Degree-days and heat conduction in soils, p. 253–62. *In* Permafrost: Proceedings of an international conference. Publ. 1287. National Academy of Sciences, Washington, D.C.

72. Sanger, F. J. 1969. Foundations of structures in cold regions. Monograph III-C4. CRREL, Hanover, New Hampshire.

73. Sayles, F. H. Triaxial and creep tests on frozen Ottawa sand. This volume.

74. Sebastyan, G. Y. 1962. Department of Transport procedures for the design of pavement facilities and foundation structures in permafrost subgrade soil areas. p. 167–206. *In* Proceedings 1st Cana-

dian conference on permafrost. Assoc. Com. Geotech. Res. Tech. Memo. 76. National Research Council of Canada, Ottawa.

75. Sellmann, P., and M. Mellor. Drilling in frozen ground. Monograph III C. U.S. Army Cold Regions Research and Engineering Laboratory, Hanover, New Hampshire. (In press)

76. Smith, N., and R. Berg. Massive ground ice formation in road construction in central Alaska. This volume.

77. Smith, N., R. Berg, and L. Muller. The use of polyurethane insulation in expedient roads on permafrost in central Alaska. This volume.

78. Smith, W. S., R. E. Smith, J. A. Schuster, and K. Nair. Sample disturbance and thaw consolidation of a deep permafrost. This volume.

79. Sohlberg, E. T. Subsurface temperature measurements. Tech. Rep. 192. U.S. Army Cold Regions Research and Engineering Laboratory, Hanover, New Hampshire. (In press)

80. Stevens, H. W. Viscoelastic properties of frozen soils under vibratory loads. This volume.

81. Terzaghi, K. 1952. Permafrost. J. Boston Soc. Civ. Eng. 39(1):1–50.

82. Tobiasson, W. Performance of the Thule hangar soil cooling systems. This volume.

83. U.S. Army. 1966. Terrain evaluation in arctic and subarctic regions. Tech. Man. TM5-852-8.

84. U.S. Army/Air Force. 1954. Arctic and subarctic construction, site selection and development. Tech. Man. TM5-852-2/AFM 88-19. Chap. 2.

85. U.S. Army/Air Force. 1967. Arctic and subarctic construction structure foundations. Tech. Man. TM5-852-4/AFM 88-19. Chap. 4.

86. U.S. Army/Air Force. 1966. Arctic and subarctic construction calculation methods for determination of depths of freeze and thaw in soils. Tech. Man. TM5-852-6/AFM 88-19. Chap. 6.

87. U.S. Army/Air Force. 1965. Arctic and subarctic construction, surface drainage design for airfields and heliports in arctic and subarctic regions. Tech. Man. TM5-852-7/AFM 88-19. Chap. 7.

88. U.S. Army Cold Regions Research and Engineering Laboratory. 1966. Thaw penetration and subsidence. 500-Man Barracks, Ladd AFB, Alaska. Inter. Rep. 12.

89. U.S. Army, St. Paul District, Corps of Engineers. 1950. Investigation of military construction in arctic and subarctic regions, comprehensive report 1945–48; Main report, and appendix III–Design and construction studies at Fairbanks research area. ACFEL Tech. Rep. TR-28.

90. U.S. Department of Defense. 1969. Unified soil classification system for roads, airfields, embankments and foundations. Military Standard MIL-STD-619B (includes system for frozen soils).

91. Waterhouse, R. W., and A. N. Sills. 1952. Thaw-blast method prepares permafrost foundation for Alaskan power plant. Civ. Eng. 22(2):126–29.

92. Watmore, T. G. 1969. Thermal erosion problems in pipelining, p. 142–62. *In* Proceedings of the 3rd Canadian conference on permafrost. Assoc. Com. Geotech. Res. Tech. Memo. 96. National Research Council of Canada, Ottawa.

93. Watson, G. H., R. K. Rowley, and W. A. Slusarchuk. Perfomance of a warm oil pipeline in permafrost. This volume.

94. Wechsler, A. E., and P. E. Glaser. 1966. Surface characteristics, effect on thermal regime, phase I. Spec. Rep. SR-88. U.S. Army Cold Regions Research and Engineering Laboratory, Hanover, New Hampshire.

95. Wein, R., and L. C. Bliss. Biological considerations for construction in the Canadian permafrost regions. This volume.

96. Williams, J. R., and R. O. van Everdingen. Groundwater investigations in permafrost regions of North America: a review. This volume.

PART FOUR

Resource Availability
in the Urban Environment

Development and growth of urban areas are limited to a great extent by the availability of certain earth resources. These include water, industrial rocks such as stone and gravel, basic metals such as iron and aluminum, and energy resources. With few exceptions, resources need not originate locally. Resources that should be present in the vicinity of an area undergoing urbanization include water and industrial rocks.

Availability of water must be considered in planning for development of urban areas. Historically, many early settlements were located specifically because of the availability of water. Although water was considered as a geologic hazard in Part Two, it is also an essential resource, as discussed in the first article of this section. Water is used in urban areas not only for residential and industrial purposes, but also for recreation, aesthetic values, and dilution of wastes.

Water, in contrast to mineral resources, is renewable and requires proper management. Urbanization often results in decreased quality and quantity of water. The buildings and pavement of urban areas prevent natural recharge of ground water, thus lowering the water table. Construction of cities disrupts natural drainage patterns and results in increased siltation and sedimentation of surface waters. As cities grow they may reach beyond the urban area for water, necessitating better planning for utilization of this vital resource.

Mineral resources are essential for the development of urban areas since they are required for construction and for the materials consumed by many industries; these include industrial rocks, such as stone, sand, and gravel, and metals and fossil fuels. Of all the mineral resources used, the one that must be produced locally because of high transportation costs is aggregate (Bates, article 20). Conflicts of interest for land use exist in growing urban areas because development may eliminate the potential for mineral extraction. Surface installations built without regard for the presence of rock and mineral deposits may render unavailable resources urgently needed for future development. Assessment of the potential earth resources must be an integral part of urban planning, as outlined for the San Francisco Bay area in article 22.

A necessary ingredient for urban development, which we typically do not think of as a geologic resource, is space. With increasing demands for office, industrial, and storage areas, we may be forced to look below, as well as above, the surface for additional space. Article 21 deals with the use of mined-out space for underground urban expansion. Underground areas may also be used for disposal of nuclear wastes, storage of petroleum and natural gas, and, as in Chicago, for temporary storage of sewage (see article 17).

Water as an Urban Resource and Nuisance

Harold E. Thomas and William J. Schneider

Introduction

Generally, when people speak of water as a resource, they are considering its good aspects and recognizing that it is essential for life and living. Sometimes or at some places or to some people, the same water may be annoying or unpleasant and thus a nuisance—for example, rain at a picnic, snow at any time except Christmas Eve, ground water in a basement, floodwater inundating personal property, and any water after it has been polluted by somebody else.

For purposes of this circular, water as a resource will be defined more broadly and as a nuisance more narrowly. Water is part of the natural resource base including all aspects of the land, the air, and the water that must be considered in planning if an environment suitable for the well-being of all life is to be maintained. A nuisance, private or public, is a cause of annoyance, inconvenience, or injury that is an invasion or disturbance of the rights of some particular person or of members of a community, and it is punishable under the laws or customs accepted by the community. An activity harmful to mankind but widely practiced by the general public may be condoned by human laws and thus not be defined legally as a nuisance; the punishment for this activity is deterioration of the natural environment until it becomes unsuitable for living.

The Water Resource

Water is a replenishing resource. The fresh water on or in the land masses of the earth is replenished by precipitation. The vapor lost from the atmosphere by precipitation is replenished by evaporation of water, partly from the land masses but chiefly from the oceans. The net water loss from the oceans —evaporation from the water surface less precipitation over the oceans—is replenished by runoff from the land masses. This is the hydrologic cycle, simple in principle but complex in process.

The average annual precipitation over the conterminous United States is equivalent to a layer of water 760 millimeters (30 inches) thick. About 28 percent of this water, equivalent to a layer 220 mm thick, eventually runs off to the oceans, but in the meantime it constitutes the fresh water potentially available for man's continuing uses and enjoyment. The rest of the gross supply returns to the atmosphere as water vapor by evaporation from water surfaces and moist land and by transpiration from vegetation, both native and cultivated.

Reprinted from *U.S. Geological Survey Circular 601-D,* 1970, 9 pp.

Geographically there is a wide range in average annual precipitation, in evapotranspiration, and in the difference between the two. A water-balance map (Piper, 1965), based on average annual precipitation and potential evapotranspiration, indicates the areas and amounts of surplus and deficiency throughout the conterminous United States. The principal areas of perennial surplus are the eastern 31 states, the Pacific Northwest, and several high mountain ranges in the west. Perennial water deficiency is characteristic of most of the western half of the country. In areas of perennial deficiency the natural water economy and human activities respond to the water-scarce environment and rely wherever possible on inflows from areas of perennial surplus, regulation and use of seasonal or occasional local surpluses, and depletion of stock resources of ground water for temporary benefit. In areas of perennial surplus human activities are adapted to the environment of water abundance. The surpluses are needed for various uses and for carrying away wastes and are managed to overcome occasional deficiencies and to protect against damaging floods.

Human Modifications of the Natural Flow Systems

Thanks to the renewability afforded by the hydrologic cycle, water as a resource serves the continuing needs of mankind and other forms of life. Beneficial use of water, essential for urban life, is recognized as a social good. Many types of uses of water either reduce the quantity or impair the quality of the natural resource; such uses may be detrimental to other individuals or to the public. The right to use water, however, is recognized and protected as a property right, so that proving a nuisance involves weighing the merits of the respective rights of all parties involved.

The use of water may require substantial structures or other developments such as dams to provide storage and regulation of the natural flow, canals and pipelines to divert and distribute water to places of use, collecting systems, treatment plants for impure water, wells to yield ground water, pumps to lift water, and channels and dredging to provide navigability. All these are intended to modify the natural flow systems for the benefit of mankind. The degree of benefit may vary among individual water users who are dependent upon the development. In some places or to some people the effects of water development may be detrimental and qualify as nuisances.

The natural flow systems may be modified by human activities concerned primarily with elements of the natural-resource base other than water. The development and use of the land—or, more broadly, of the solid earth or lithosphere—are not primarily concerned with water, but rather are concerned with fossil fuels, the soils for agriculture, metallic and other minerals for manufacturing, rocks and sediments for construction, and the land surface for occupancy. In such development water, not sought as a resource, may be incidental or accidental and even a hazard at some times and places. The use of the land may require drainage of unwanted water or protection from excesses of water during storm and floods. Water may constitute a nuisance if it harms the development and use of the solid-earth resources or otherwise invades recognized property rights. Conversely, the development and use of the land resources may have effects on water that interfere with the water rights of others; such interference may also be a nuisance.

Urbanization

"Of all land-use changes affecting the hydrology of an area, urbanization is by far the most forceful" (Leopold, 1968). More than two-thirds of the nation's population is currently in urbanized areas occupying about 7 percent of the land. This clear majority could, under unifying leadership, control the destiny of the urban area and also the 93 percent of the land that is relatively vacant. The total population is increasing; however, the urban population is increasing at a more rapid rate. These trends suggest that the urban population in A.D. 2000 will be three-fourths of the total population and more than the total population today. The urbanized area will also increase to perhaps 10 percent of the land area.

The great majority of urban dwellers are not concerned with individual rights and responsibilities in water as a resource. These rights have necessarily been delegated to the community because individual plots of land are generally too small to provide adequate supply, storage, or disposal of water for its occupants. On the other hand, each individual is concerned about water as a nuisance. Water may disrupt his well-ordered urban life by accumulating in low spots (such as lands, basements, and underpasses), by making mud in unpaved areas, by eroding ground laid bare by construction, by carrying debris and filth, and by damaging property during floods. Sometimes individual responsibility for such nuisances can be clearly identified. However, the natural environment has been modified so thoroughly in many urban areas that the responsibility for specific nuisances may be widely dispersed. For that reason, the community, or the public, has assumed increasing responsibility for the correction of and protection against the detrimental effects of water.

The Demand for Water

Municipal water supply, including domestic, commercial, and industrial supplies, is at an average daily rate of 600 liters (157 U.S. gallons) per capita throughout the United States. A population of 500,000 requires about 100 million cubic meters annually, equivalent to about 70 mgd (million U.S. gallons a day), and there are 35 municipal systems of this size or larger. The demand of the largest municipal systems, in New York City and Chicago, is 15 to 20 times this rate (Durfor and Becker, 1964).

Of the 35 largest cities, five have abundant supplies from the Great Lakes and 10 from major rivers. The others originally depended on wells, springs, or small streams in the vicinity, but with progressively increasing and concentrated demand they have had to reach out beyond the urban area for their supplies. Today only three of these cities—Miami, San Antonio, and Memphis—obtain their entire municipal supply locally from ground water. Houston relied upon wells until its population exceeded half a million and then had to add a supplemental surface supply from Lake Houston. Local sources now provide less than 5 percent of New York City's supply, which comes chiefly from the Croton, Catskill, and Delaware systems of reservoirs as much as 200 kilometers (about 125 miles) from the city. In California the cities of San Francisco, Oakland, and Los Angeles have long pipelines to the Sierra Nevada for municipal water supply. Los Angeles and San Diego also import water from the distant Colorado River. Other large cities rely on streams and impoundments that are less distant but nevertheless beyond their incorporated areas.

Municipal systems meet the water requirements of most commercial and industrial establishments and of the great majority of the people in urban regions. The aggregate withdrawal of these systems, however, is less than one-fifth of the amount withdrawn nationally by "self-supplied" industries. Most of these large industrial users are also in urban areas and may be in competition with municipal systems for the available water resources.

Municipal and industrial uses of water are chiefly nonconsumptive. Thus large quantities of water can be withdrawn from a river and quickly returned, with little loss in volume and therefore negligible depletion of the flow. However, the used water brings to the river dissolved chemicals, organisms, floating debris, sediment, gases, or heat, which are all pollutants that may be detrimental to other water users downstream.

Effects of Land Occupancy

Buildings, streets, sidewalks, parking lots, and other structures provide an impervious cover on the land surface and thus prevent infiltration into the soil and recharge of ground water. The water from storms is diverted instead into storm sewers. Years ago, when Brooklyn was troubled by seawater encroachment into some of its wells, part of the cause was the reduction of recharge caused by the buildings and pavements that covered about half of the total land surface of the borough (Lusczynski, 1952).

This urban sprawl, with its quota of impervious cover, commonly extends across natural valleys which, although not occupied by a perennial stream, would carry storm runoff into stream channels. The natural drainage may be replaced by storm sewers. For example, the suburbanized drainage basin of Rock Creek, tributary to the Potomac River in the Washington metropolitan area, had 102 km of natural flowing stream channels in 1913, but only 43 km can be found above ground today (U.S. Department of Interior, 1968).

Storm runoff is substantially modified by the impervious cover and the storm sewers that are introduced by urbanization. Lag time, the time from the peak of rainfall to the peak of runoff, is decreased by the impermeable surfaces and by storm sewers. Leopold (1968) used data from studies of the effects of urbanization in various parts of the United States and stated that for unsewered areas the differences between 0- and 100-percent impervious cover will increase peak discharge on the average 2.5 times. For areas that are 100-percent sewered, peak discharge will be about 70 percent greater than the mean annual flood for unsewered areas under conditions of no impervious cover and about eight times greater under conditions of 100-percent impervious cover.

By modifying infiltration rates and storm runoff, urbanization reduces the ground-water recharge and also causes adjustment in the stream channels to accommodate the flows. As channels are enlarged by the increased number and volume of floods, they frequently develop unstable and unvegetated banks and scoured or muddy beds. The low flows may be less than under natural conditions because of reductions in ground-water recharge.

A significant percentage of the nation's population and tangible property is concentrated on flood-prone areas. A recent survey shows that in New York State 260, or 79 percent, of the 330 communities having populations greater than 2,500 have problems of local flooding or drainage. Much urban growth in the United States is by encroachment upon the flood plains, which are the river's natural freeways for discharge of exceptional floodwaters. Flood damages are a direct consequence of flood-plain infringement, both public and private.

In the United States flood damage in 1967 totaled $1.7 billion; practically all this damage was in urban and suburban areas. Perhaps more significant than the dollar value is the fact that, according to the [U.S.] Water Resources Council (1968), flood damage will continue to increase even while we continue our flood-control programs and protective measures. Despite past history and future projects, there is continuing pressure to develop flood plains and other lands subject to water and flood hazards.

Evidence that natural catastrophes can be aggravated by land development has recently been provided by southern California. Damage from the catastrophic floods of January and February 1969 was intensified by the urban sprawl (Rantz, 1970). Although record-breaking rainfall was the prime cause of flooding, peak discharges were increased and mudflows were accelerated by the excess water in areas where natural plant cover was destroyed and where slopes were undercut by erosion or grading; such areas include many of the more desirable and expensive real estate developments.

Effects of Surface Revisions

Preparation of land for use commonly involves clearing, grading or leveling, digging for foundations, and perhaps landscaping. During these activities, as Wolman (1964) points out,

> Because construction denudes the natural cover and exposes the soil beneath, the tonnage of sediment derived by erosion from an acre of ground under construction in developments and highways may exceed 20,000 to 40,000 times the amount eroded from farms and woodlands in an equivalent period of time.

In Fairfax County, Virginia, 197 acres undergoing highway construction over a 3-year period contributed 37,000 tons of sediment to the local stream (Vice and others, 1969). The highway construction was limited to 11 percent of the Scott Run basin, but the sediment contributed by this area was 94 percent of the total sediment yield during the 3-year period. In Montgomery County, Maryland, more than 4,500 tons of soil was eroded during construction of 89 houses on a 20-acre site during a 5-year period.

Construction activities commonly cover very small portions of most urban areas at any one time, and as a rule the rate of sediment yield decreases with increasing drainage area. Nevertheless, Anderson and McCall (1968) report a positive correlation between urban development and sediment throughout New Jersey. In the urbanized northeastern part of the state, sediment yield is three to five times greater than in the rural and forested northwestern part. Sediment yield in the vicinity of Trenton and in the urban area adjacent to New York City is many times greater than in rural areas. Also, the increasing average turbidity of the Passaic River, in 1965 more than twice as great as in 1954, reflects increasing urbanization.

During excavations some materials can maintain stable walls until the contruction is completed. Others remain stable as long as they remain dry, but water from rain, overland flow, or shallow ground water may lubricate clayey elements enough to cause sliding or caving. The instability of walls or steep slopes composed in part of materials that can be lubricated by water has its natural counterpart in areas of landslides or potential landslides. In several places natural landslide areas have been subjected to urban development. Indeed, some of the earliest records concerning landslides are of those which occurred within the city of Bath, England, in 1790 and again in the extremely wet year 1799. William "Strata" Smith, called the father of geology in England, achieved considerable fame for his remedial work, which included tunneling into the hillside to intercept ground water. Thorough drainage of the landslide area and development of public gardens has prevented further sliding. Although the land slopes are generally in the range of 12 to 15 degrees, they remain stable as long as they are adequately drained and not overloaded (Kellaway and Taylor, 1968).

Some materials, though unstable when wet, may nevertheless be included in urban development and do not reveal their hazardous character until some triggering geologic event, such as the earthquake at Anchorage on March 27, 1964, where the principal damage was from landslides, ground fracturing, lurching, and shaking. In its recovery from the effects of that earthquake and in future land development for human needs, the Borough of Anchorage is insuring that the planning is based on understanding of the geologic and hydrologic environment (Dobrovolny and Schmoll, 1968).

Many excavations penetrate below the water table, and water is pumped out to permit continuation of activities. As has been seen in many areas of intensive pumping and ground-water depletion, the dewatering of some sediments is accompanied by compaction, resulting in subsidence of the land surface. In the Santa Clara Valley in California, the land since 1934 has subsided more than 3 feet in an area of more than 100 square miles and up to 8 feet in places because of ground-water withdrawal. Damage to wells has exceeded $2 million; the cost of levees to prevent flooding from San Francisco Bay has been about $6 million.

A common type of excavation near urban areas is for the purpose of obtaining construction materials, whether rock, gravel, sand, or clay. If these excavations penetrate below the water table, water will accumulate to form a pool or pond after the extraction has ceased, and the landowner may be accused by neighbors of maintaining a nuisance—an "attractive nuisance" that lures children to play, wade, and swim dangerously.

Abandoned quarries, pits, strip mines, and spoil banks are among the less desirable land areas for urban development, along with such natural features as steep hills, narrow ravines, and undrained depressions. Adjacency to an urban area may induce the owners to make wholesale rearrangement of these surfaces because of the higher land value that may be anticipated. This rearrangement involves cutting into natural materials at various places and filling at others, with problems of stabilization comparable to and perhaps more difficult than those in highway construction. Some of the problems will be caused by water because of interruptions or modifications of the natural flow system—changes in rates of infiltration and overland runoff and changes from the natural drainage and ground-water movement.

Some revisions of the land surface involve development of artificial lakes to enhance the quality of the urban environment and the value of land in the vicinty. These lakes may range from a water-hole on a golf course to a lagoon in a city park to a lake for boating, fishing, and other recreation in a suburban area. As many people have learned after they construct swimming pools on their property, these water bodies are a resource if they are properly managed; otherwise, they become nuisances. Artificial lakes become part of the hydrologic flow system and as such are vulnerable to flooding, sedimentation, accumulation of floating debris, fertilizers and other chemicals washed from adjacent lands, septic wastes or other dissolved solids contributed by ground water, and growth of algae or other undesirable organisms.

The Problem of Wastes

Each individual must dispose of some wastes, whether by individual or community effort. The average per capita daily waste load of organic materials from food sources is about 100 grams (a quarter of a pound) in sewage and 400 grams in garbage. To this basic load must be added the waste products of minerals, wood, fiber, and other natural resources after use. This load varies widely from one individual to another because it increases with increasing affluence and capability to depreciate the "old" and purchase the "new." A further load is the by-products of the materials and energy used in developing, processing, and maintaining the desired products of our natural resources. Inexorably, the total volume of waste products increases with increasing population and economic growth. These wastes are portions of our natural resources that are considered to have no current value. Nevertheless they are among the products, perhaps the grossest products, of our gross national product.

For disposal of his wastes primitive man had the alternatives of burning them, resulting in smoke to be dissipated by the atmosphere and ashes to remain on the ground; placing them underground or on land and perhaps covering them, where they might decompose, remain unchanged, or be added to soil or ground water; or discharging them into stream, lake, or ocean, where liquid and dissolved materials would be mixed with other water and solids would float or sink to the bottom. Modern man has developed only one other alternative; currently he has more than 1,100 individual items circling the globe as satellites. With increasing population, land for disposal of wastes of air and water for dilution are becoming progressively less; moreover, we have more wastes per capita to dispose of. Because of the concentrations of people, economic production, and wastes for disposal, the problem is most critical in urban areas.

Here we are concerned with water as a resource in which wastes, whether dissolved, floating, or suspended, have nuisance value and often are of sufficient concentration that the water itself is deemed a nuisance. However, water pollution is only one aspect of the overall problem of disposal of urban wastes. As the campaigns for clean water, clean air, and better environmental quality coalesce, the common objective must be to develop technologies for conversion of unwanted materials to wanted materials wherever possible and to dispose of the rest in a form and place in which they will be least detrimental to mankind.

In the early stages of change from rural to urban conditions, septic tanks are usually the principal means of disposal of domestic wastes and continue to operate and increase in number until the suburbanites are numerous enough to finance sewerage systems or until the density of septic tanks is so great that serious pollution problems develop. Sparse data indicate that effluent from septic tanks is cleansed of pathogenic bacteria in unsaturated soil at a rate and effectiveness that depend upon the type of soil. However, even proper spacing to minimize bacterial pollution does not prevent pollution by dissolved inorganic materials, which may become nutrients to algae and other organisms. A prime example of widespread pollution of shallow ground water is provided by Long Island, New York. Septic tank effluents from more than half a million homes have contaminated the shallow aquifer over much of the island. Concentrations as high as 32 mg/l (milligrams per liter) of synthetic detergents (alkylbenzenesulfonate, or ABS) have been detected (Perlmutter and others, 1964) along with increased concentrations of chloride, nitrates, sulfates, and phosphates.

The disposal of solid wastes, whether by sanitary landfill or unsanitary dump, may also cause pollution of ground water by infiltration of rain, snowmelt, or overland flow and leaching of soluble organic or inorganic materials. This is true particularly if the dump is in an abandoned pit or other depression where some of the waste may be saturated by ground water. Landfills in valley floors may contribute pollutants to streams in time of floods. Few studies have been made of this problem. Obviously, the kind of pollution will depend upon the composition of the refuse and the conditions of disposal. Organic matter such as garbage, decomposing under anaerobic conditions, produces methane, carbon dioxide, ammonia, and hydrogen sulfide. The carbon dioxide combines readily with the water to form carbonic acid, which in turn increases the power of the water to dissolve mineral matter from the refuse and from soil or rock minerals. Objectionable amounts of iron, excessive hardness, and other undesirable constituents may be present in the leaching water. In leachant water high biochemical oxygen demand has also been measured, indicating high bacterial concentrations in the landfills.

Industrial wastes have contaminated ground-water reservoirs seriously enough in some places to reduce their suitability for use. An example is the Baltimore Harbor area in Maryland, which a century ago had many flowing artesian wells. A shallow aquifer has become contaminated by sulfuric acid and copper sulfate from acid and metal-refining plants. The acid water has corroded the casings of many wells, leaked through them into a deeper aquifer, and also contaminated it locally. Heavy pumping encouraged contamination also from brackish water in the harbor. Because of the high cost of maintaining wells in the corrosive shallow zone and the deteriorated quality of some of the water, the pumpage from wells was reduced by half between 1940 and 1955 (Otton and others, 1964). Fortunately, the Baltimore municipal supply was adequate and available as a replacement.

Many urban areas are served by sanitary-sewer systems and sewage treatment plants which were adequate at the time they were built for the needs of the service areas and a reasonable expansion of population. Commonly this system was combined with the storm-sewer system. The combined system theoretically works out well to the extent that flushing the streets carries the wastes through the treatment plant, although there must be facilities for bypassing the treatment plant during periods of excessive storm runoff. Unfortunately, some of the sanitary sewage then also bypasses treatment. It became evident to many people that adequate pollution control would require separation of the sanitary-sewer system from the storm-sewer system. Further study has brought second thoughts: first, recognition that such separation in many cities at this time would be exceedingly disruptive and costly; second, realization that the storms sewers would not carry pristine waters, but rather all the crud that had been washed from the atmosphere, roofs, pavements, and streets of the area served. Many analyses of runoff from storm sewers in Seattle, Washington (Sylvester, 1960), showed that the water sometimes contained excessive numbers of coliform bacteria and had other characteristics of pollution.

A proposed solution to the problem of storm runoff is impoundment of excess water during flood runoff, with subsequent release according to the capacity of treatment facilities. Because urban land is at premium prices, cities are beginning to look for space underground. Currently there are two proposals for the Chicago area: one, by the sanitary district, would provide a network of tunnels in the Galena and Platteville Formations, about 200 meters below the surface; another, by the city, would place tunnels in the Niagara Dolomite, less than 100 meters below the surface, and line the tunnels adequately to seal them from usable ground-water reservoirs. The water and wastes temporarily stored in these tunnels would be pumped out and treated and then discharged into streams.

Subsurface disposal of industrial wastes by means of deep wells is undertaken in several places, especially in Texas, Louisiana, and Michigan, but also in some other states. If these wastes are toxic, radioactive, or otherwise noxious, safe disposal requires permanent isolation from all usable water resources. Without adequate studies of all the geologic, engineering, and chemical parameters at each project, and constant monitoring of the effects of the disposal, underground disposal can cause serious problems. What is considered to be a safe disposal site today may be a scene of exploitive activity in the future.

REFERENCES

Anderson, P. W., and McCall, J. E., 1968, Urbanization's effect on sediment yield in New Jersey: Jour. Soil and Water Conserv., v. 23, pp. 142–44.

Dobrovolny, Ernest, and Schmoll, H. R., 1968, Geology as applied to urban planning: Internat. Geol. Cong., 23d, Prague, 1968, Proc., v. 12, pp. 39–56.

Durfor, C. N., and Becker, Edith, 1964, Public water supplies of the 100 largest cities in the United States: U.S. Geol. Survey Water-Supply Paper 1812, 364 pp.

Kellaway, G. A., and Taylor, J. H., 1968. The influence of landslipping on the development of the city of Bath, England: Internat. Geol. Cong., 23d, Prague, 1968, Proc., v. 12, pp. 65–76.

Leopold, L. B., 1968, Hydrology for urban land planning—a guidebook on the hydrologic effects of urban land use: U.S. Geol. Survey Circular 554, 18 pp.

Lusczynski, N. J., 1952. The recovery of ground water levels in Brooklyn, N.Y., from 1947 to 1950: U.S. Geol. Survey Circular 167, 29 pp.

Otton, E. G., Martin, R. O. R., and Durum, W. H., 1964, Water resources of the Baltimore area, Maryland: U.S. Geol. Survey Water-Supply Paper 1499-F, 105 pp.

Perlmutter, N. M., Lieber, Maxim, and Frauenthal, H. L., 1964, Contamination of ground water by detergent in a suburban environment—South Farmingdale area, Long Island, New York *in* Geological Survey research 1964. U.S. Geol. Survey. Prof. Paper 501-C, pp. C170–75.

Piper, A. M., 1965, Has the United States enough water?: U.S. Geol. Survey Water-Supply paper 1797, 27 pp. [1966].

Rantz, S. E., 1970, Urban sprawl and flooding in southern California: U.S. Geol. Survey Circular 601-B, 12 pp.

Sylvester, R. O., 1960, An engineering and ecological study for the rehabilitation of Green Lake: Washington University, Seattle.

U.S. Department of Interior, 1968, The Nation's river: A report on the Potomac: Washington, D.C., 128 pp.

[U.S.] Water Resources Council, 1968, The Nation's water resources; the first national assessment: Washington, D.C., U.S. Govt. Printing Office.

Vice, R. B., Guy, H. P., and Ferguson, G. E., 1969, Sediment movement in an area of suburban highway construction, Scott Run basin, Fairfax County, Virginia, 1961–64: U.S. Geol. Survey Water-Supply Paper 1591-E, 41 pp.

Wolman, M. G., 1964, Problems posed by construction activities in Maryland: Report to the Maryland Pollution Control Commission, Annapolis, Maryland.

20

Mineral Resources for a New Town

Robert L. Bates

Earth Materials to Order

The physical entity of a new town will consist predominantly of materials taken out of the earth. Aristocrats among these earth-derived materials are the metals: structural steel, of course, together with copper for pipes and wires, aluminum for frames and trim, and the many special-purpose alloys for the motors, bearings, filaments, and switches by which the community's complex machinery will operate. Added to these are the essential nonmetals, such as glass, brick, tile, and insulation. Once built, the town will run on earth-produced energy, derived from uranium, coal, or petroleum.

All these diverse materials have another aspect in common besides their origin in the earth's crust. This is that the town's planners won't need to be concerned with their production. It will not be necessary to plan for a steel mill, glass factory, or an oil refinery. Assuming reasonable availability, the required materials will be delivered to the site when needed, from points of origin scattered far and wide across the land or even overseas. In short, there need be no concern for community self-sufficiency in mineral resources.

With one major exception: concrete.

This crucially important material will constitute the foundation, and much of the fabric, of the industrial and office buildings, motels and supermarkets, airports and terminals, homes and apartment houses of which the new town is to be constructed—to say nothing of its streets, bridges, and overpasses. Steel skeletons may grow, but they will be clothed in concrete. This indispensable substance must be in abundant supply from the first day of construction.

The Stone Age

Cement, the ingredient of concrete that makes it "set" to rock hardness, is a manufactured product that is readily available at reasonable cost wherever called for. But at least 80% of concrete consists of inert rock fragments, collectively termed *aggregate,* which take up space and strengthen the mixture. Aggregate generally includes a fine fraction of sand, and a coarse fraction of gravel or crushed

Reprinted with permission of the author and publisher from *Geoform* 6:169–76, 1975. Copyright © 1975 by Pergamon Press, Oxford, England.

stone. The enormity of the demand for these materials is indicated by a remark of Morgan (1973, p. 30): "In terms of tonnages in use and annual new tonnages required, we are still in the Stone Age, because about half of United States annual demand for new mineral supplies involves sand, gravel, and stone." It is clear that very large amounts of fine and coarse aggregate will be required in building a new town. And since these substances are far too heavy, bulky, and cheap for cross-country transport, they cannot be shipped in from a distance. *They are the only construction materials needed in quantity that must be obtained locally.* As a good supply is vital to all construction, plans must be made early to assure their continuing availability.

Sand, gravel, and stone are common earth materials, and one might conclude that they are available in adequate amounts wherever needed. Such a conclusion, however, is quite unwarranted; these materials, like mineral deposits generally, are sporadic in distribution. Workable deposits, if present at all, are situated in accordance with the geologic rules that govern their formation: sand and gravel generally along present or former stream courses, and sound stone in hills, escarpments, or ridges. For these reasons, an aggregate industry cannot be fitted into the urban picture after other needs for land space have been satisfied. It must be planned for from the very beginning.

Aggregate is a notably low-cost commodity. In 1972, gravel was quoted at an average of about $1.40 per metric ton at the pit, and good-quality crushed stone at about $2.20 at the quarry. Inasmuch as it costs some 3.4 cents per metric ton per kilometer to move aggregate to the construction site, the original cost is doubled at 40 km for gravel and at 65 km for stone. Obviously, the nearer the source of aggregate to point of use, the lower is the cost of basic construction in the community.

And here we have a built-in conflict which may be illustrated by the following imaginary account. In 1945, when the Agmix Sand and Gravel Company went into business, their pit was 15 km from the center of town and 8 km from the outer fringes. In the intervening decades, the suburbs gradually approached and eventually bypassed the Agmix property, and now they completely surround it. Since the extraction and processing of the company's products are dusty, noisy processes, which must be carried on right out in the open, the pit is scarcely an esthetic addition to a newly incorporated suburb. Indeed, it can only be described as a bad scene. The site appears to be a chaos of holes in the ground, immense piles of rock material, and heavy machinery, all presided over by rough-looking men in hard hats. Big trucks roar in and out, and are encountered on suburban roads and streets. Regularly the town fathers are served with demands from nearby residents that this intolerable nuisance be forced to move away.

Turning to an actual example, we cite a study by French *et al.* (1970) of urbanization and surface mining in the Atlanta area. Here gravel is lacking and the major aggregate utilized is crushed granite. French and his coworkers found that the trend in this rapidly growing metropolitan center is toward larger quarries—which generate porportionately more drilling and blasting, dust, truck traffic, and waste-disposal problems. At the same time, competition for land on the fringes of the city is keen. As the authors put it, "The rapid diminution of open land has at least two serious implications for the minerals industry. First, a substantial part of the half which still will be rural/vacant [in 1988] will be in the speculative urban real estate market. . . . Second, rural land may be converted to urban use without regard for its value as a source of crushed stone, sand, or clay. Urban growth will prohibit retention of land for potential quarry or pit sites." Yet the same authors foresee a need for 10–15 new quarries by 1988!

Thus it happens that, in the urban expansion that has become normal for our time, an essential industry finds itself in conflict with the very community that it serves. It is no wonder that on this subject one encounters expressions like the 'social incompatibility of producer and consumer,' and 'an alienation gap.' Or, as put by Dennis O'Harrow of the American Society of Planning Officials (quoted in Bell, 1962), 'In some ways, the sand, gravel and concrete industry has the characteristics of a public utility. The industry is indispensable and it is local.'

Toward Planning

When an aggregates concern returns its neighbors' hostility with arrogance or belligerence, its days are numbered, because in the long run the community has the upper hand. But even where a company has a long record of civic responsibility and good citizenship, it may find itself effectively zoned out of business, as happened to a stone company in a suburb of Boston (Stearn, 1966). At present, no town in eastern Massachusetts will permit a new quarry to be opened. Hudec (1970) writes, 'No new sand and gravel operation has been allowed in Nassau County (Long Island, New York) in the last 10 years, although theoretically the local laws permit it.' One large producer of sand, formerly located at Port Washington, Nassau County, now operates a pit in central New Jersey, from where the sand must be shipped to market by train and barge (Trauffer, 1975). In Connecticut, Siebert (1970) says, 'All towns within the urban core restrict the excavation of construction aggregates.' While production of aggregate resources is barred, the suburbs spread apace.

Most of these depressing situations do not result from poor planning. Although Flawn (1970, pp. 112–13) cites a county-wide zoning plan for Indianapolis in which the planners cheerfully assumed that sand and gravel were distributed equally throughout the area, this was more than 20 years ago. Few planning agencies today would be so innocent of geological knowledge. Rather, what militates against the rational development of aggregate resources is impassioned opposition by a generally uninformed but highly vocal public.

Yet in many urban areas there have been successful attempts to meet the problem. Perhaps most commonly, these have taken the form of promoting sequential land use (figure 1). This is a concept that the public can understand, and with which it can—sometimes—be made to agree. In Montclair, New Jersey, a stone company was allowed to quarry more than 2,700,000 metric tons of high-quality traprock from state land, right beside the campus of a state college (figure 2). In return, it left some 80,000 m^2 of level ground to the college, which used the space for greatly needed expansion. The procedure was unique and created much public interest. In Azusa, California, on the fringes of the Los Angeles megalopolis, a sand and gravel company was finally—after repeated rebuffs and more than two years of negotiation—permitted access to a large gravel deposit. Thirty-seven restrictions were written into the final agreement; what "sweetened the package" to the point of community ap-

FIGURE 1. Picture on left, taken in 1946, shows gravel pits along Scarlett Road in Toronto, Ontario. Picture on right, taken in 1962, shows subdivisions that now occupy the former gravel pits, which are outlined in white.

proval was a promise by the company to construct an 18-hole municipal golf course. At various localities in the Midwest, producers of aggregate have carried on landscaping concurrently with extraction, with the result that worked-out areas have become attractive residential tracts and park sites (figure 3).

The examples just cited are *ad-hoc* solutions of the problem when it involves only one company or a single instance of conflict. A few political entities, as pointed out by Hudec (1970), have moved or are moving toward an over-all policy position on conserving resources of sand, gravel and stone. Hudec cites Fairfax County, Virginia, which has introduced zoning plans outlining and setting aside mineral-resource areas, and the province of Ontario which—at the producers' behest—has passed legislation toward the same end. The San Fernando Valley of southern California has had such a policy since 1959.

The Fully Planned Situation

For those planning a community from scratch, the lesson is obvious: appropriate areas where aggregate materials occur must be set aside for extractive industry. The plan should require that the site or sites be rehabilitated as extraction proceeds, so that the land may remain in utilization.

FIGURE 2. Removing traprock (diabase) adjacent to state college at Montclair, New Jersey. The stone company removed more than 2,700,000 metric tons of aggregate and the college obtained some 80,000 m² of flat land for expansion.

FIGURE 3. Lake and residential properties formed by planned excavation of aggregate.

Of course it is the geologist's responsibility to provide the basic information. Presumably the planning agency will have at hand a general geologic map and report, with sections on water supply, waste disposal, foundation stability, and mineral resources. In the last-named part of this report, the planners should be supplied with the following information.

(1) A statement as to occurrence of materials for aggregate in the subject area, with a recommendation as to whether gravel, crushed stone, or both should be utilized. If neither is present, recommendation should be made as to best outside sources.

(2) Assuming that sand and gravel are present and preferred—large-scale maps of those areas containing sufficient supplies to be of economic interest, preferably with air photos, so as to show topography and relation to surrounding areas.

(3) An estimate of tonnage, with projections of length of commercial life at various rates of consumption.

(4) Information on local geologic factors, such as effect of extraction on water table; water supply needed for washing the gravel; and excess of sand in deposit, or presence of thick overburden, that might lead to accumulation of excessive waste.

(5) Suggestions as to the best way to exploit the deposit with minimum damage to the environment and disturbance to neighbors.

(6) Suggestions as to use of the area after it has been worked out, e.g., sanitary landfill with later industrial use, or park area with lakes serving not only for recreation but also for recharge of groundwater supplies. This item, as well as several of the others, will require close cooperation between geologists working on mineral resources and those whose concern is groundwater.

Should it turn out that crushed stone, rather than gravel, is the desired material, more or less analogous information will be needed. Large-scale maps, with air photos if possible, will show the areas in which desirable rock formations are at or near the surface, and will indicate the rock's topographic expression. Because stone is more expensive to extract than sand and gravel, is of many types, and occurs in a variety of ways, information will be included on such matters as composition and lateral variation; structural position, or attitude, of the rocks; thickness of the weathered zone; presence of fractures and solution patterns; and relation to the water table.

Estimates of available tonnage and length of commercial life of the deposits will of course be included, as will suggestions on screening from surrounding areas while in operation, minimization of adverse effects on the environment, and use of the site after depletion.

During its active life, a rock quarry is a source of vibration from blasting, and of noise and dust from crushing. After abandonment, it is an irresistible attraction for car junkers, small boys, and other irresponsibles. An alternative method of extraction of stone, which should be considered by planners and geologists, is underground mining. Though somewhat more costly, this has distinct advantages. The operation can be carried on out of sight and sound. Work can proceed in all weathers. The land surface is only negligibly disturbed in comparison with large surface quarries. If the mine can be situated in or near the urban center, costs may be kept comparable with those of quarrying, because transportation costs will be lower. Finally, underground mining has significant sequential-use potential. Worked-out aggregate mines are being used for mushroom-growing in New York, storage of bank records in Pennsylvania, and warehousing and manufacturing near Kansas City (figure 4).

Hence the geologic report on stone resources should include a statement of feasibility of subsurface mining, should indicate where it might be possible, and should give at least preliminary estimates of costs per ton as compared with quarrying.

It is possible that, after planners have evaluated all geological and other studies of the projected townsite, it will be found that no allowance for extraction of aggregate within the town need be made. For example, extraction of minerals is prohibited within the new city of Columbia, Maryland. Weaver and Cleaves (1969) explain that this is no problem because 'large quantities of sand, gravel, and crushed stone are available locally.' Certainly there is no point in setting up an aggregates industry in a community if the community can obtain adequate supplies nearby at prices no higher than it would

FIGURE 4. Rail and truck facilities in worked-out part of a limestone mine, Kansas City, Kansas. Sections of this facility are used as a refrigerated warehouse, for manufacturing, for storage of valuable records, and as a Foreign Trade Zone.

pay for identical material produced on the spot. At Columbia this can apparently be done. But Columbia is expected to grow to a population of 100,000 by 1980, and perhaps it will keep on growing. If this happens, its outer fringes will sooner or later come into contact with the pits and quarries that are producing the aggregate being used today. Then it will only be justice if the planners—or perhaps their descendants—are called in to settle this newest skirmish in the seemingly endless conflict between community and mineral producer.

REFERENCES

Bell, J. N. (1962): Where do the rock industries fit in urban planning? *Rock Products,* **65**, 51–53.

Flawn, P. T. (1970): *Environmental Geology,* Harper and Row, New York.

French, R. R., A. W. Stuart and D. H. White (1970): Socioeconomic aspects of mining in selected cities: urbanization and surface mining, Atlanta, Ga. *Inf. Circ. U.S. Bur. Mines* 8477.

Hudec, P. P. (1970): Long range planning for aggregate materials in metropolitan New York. *Penn. Geol. Survey, Mineral Resour. Rep.* M64, pp. 165–77.

Morgan, J. D., Jr. (1973): Future use of minerals: the question of "demand," in: *The Mineral Position of the United States* (E. N. Cameron, ed.) Univ. Wisconsin Press, Madison.

Siebert, H. L. (1970): Connecticut's declining sand and gravel resources. *Penn. Geol. Survey, Mineral Resour. Rep.* M64, pp. 43–54.

Stearn, E. W. (1966): Wake up to a travesty of zoning. *Rock Products,* **69**, 88–93.

Trauffer, W. E. (1975): McCormack Sand Division uses unit train and barges to supply New York metropolitan area from New Jersey sand-gravel plant. *Pit & Quarry,* **67**, 64–68.

Weaver, K. N., and E. T. Cleaves (1970): Geology and the "new city" concept—Columbia, Maryland (abstract); *Geol. Soc. Am. Abstracts with Programs for 1969,* Part 1, p. 63.

Kansas City: A Center for Secondary Use of Mined-out Space

21

Truman P. Stauffer, Sr.

Introduction

Secondary use of mined-out space in underground limestone quarries is emerging in the Kansas City area where abandoned quarry sites are being renovated into warehouses, factories, and offices. Mining techniques, ceiling heights, and pillar distribution are being altered as planning for the secondary use of mined-out space is combined with the quarrying process. Even the historic urban-quarry land use conflict invites a reappraisal in that this development provides a potential resolution of the problem. Mutual subsidization by dual rock and space interest is changing the economics of rock production.

A city is much more than a surficial adjunct superimposed upon the topography of an area. Its development and growth are deeply rooted in the resources, benefits, and problems of its underlying geology. The environmental geologist must address himself to more than the quality of a particular resource. He must comprehensively relate resource extraction and processing with the urban emphasis of optimal use which favors long-term usage of land over one-time economic ventures. Limestone quarrying, closely allied with the growth of many cities, has commonly left a series of scarred landscapes in the path of the burgeoning metropolis. These abandoned quarry sites are barriers to orderly city growth and fail to serve the people as useful and taxable land. Where quarries are functional, supplying the city with needed growth minerals, problems of blasting damage, noise, and dust exist. Technology faces the challenge of making mineral production and processing good neighbors to the urban market they serve. Continued growth of cities may require some efficient use of space below as well as above the surface, optimizing land usage so that long-term economic benefits may be reflected in improved mining methods.

The Kansas City area exemplifies the secondary usage of mined space in that over 1,500 employees earn $13,000,000 annually in rooms mined out of limestone. Warehousing, light and heavy industry, and offices make up part of the uses to which this otherwise wasteland has been put. Land use problems of an urban-quarry nature are being resolved as quarry operators sit with developers and plan the future of their mining site as a permanent industrial park with storage facilities, factories,

Reprinted with permission of the author and publisher from Proceedings of the Engineering Foundation Conference, Berwick Academy, South Berwick, Maine, June 25–29, 1973. *National Policy for the Use of Underground Space,* pp. 50–79. Copyright © 1973 by Engineering Foundation.

and offices below ground, and regular use of the surface for stores, parks, and common urban development. Long range plans are laid for the use of the mined-out space which is more valuable than the once-over exploitation of the rock. The neighborhood accepts the planned secondary use of a mine with far greater approval than the specter of fenced wasteland often left by mining and later engulfed in the path of urban growth.

A national survey conducted by the author early in 1971 revealed that Missouri led the contiguous United States in the secondary use of space mined out of limestone matrix with the greatest concentration occurring in the Kansas City area. Kansas City has been cited as the capital of underground space use by many sources (*Business Week,* 1961, 166–70; *Fortune,* 1966, 175–76; *New York Times,* 1971, 13).

Currently there are 28 subsurface sites in varying stages of development in the Kansas City area, encompassing nearly 120 million square feet of space, 30–200 feet below the surface (figure 1).

The first classification of "Underground Space Sites in Greater Kansas City, 1971" includes those sites where both the surface and the subsurface have been developed. An example is the Downtown Industrial Park, Site No. 1, where 44 acres of surface area is developed for such uses as Gateway Sporting Goods, Burstein-Applebee, and Dean Machinery. Some 100 feet below this there are 23 tenants of the underground development. These include Standard Oil, Aero Draperies, Hooper Printing, and Hallmark Card Company.

In the second class (Sites 2–10) are those who are equally well developed below the surface, as far as secondary use is concerned, but the surface has not yet been developed beyond worker and customer parking facilities. These include factories and warehouses.

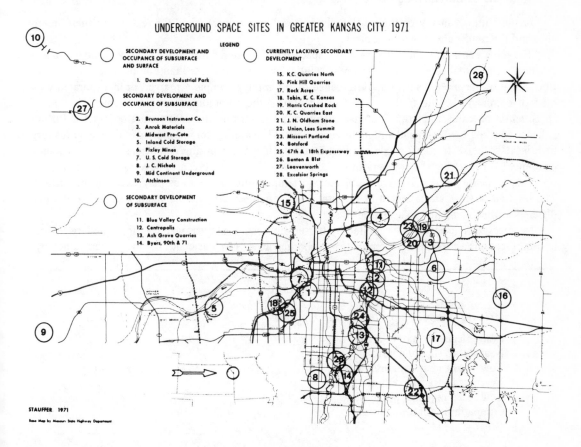

UNDERGROUND SPACE SITES IN GREATER KANSAS CITY 1971

FIGURE 1.

To the third group (Sites 11-14) belong those who are developing their subsurface area but are not yet ready for tenancy. The last group (Sites 15-28) is lacking any effort to develop at the time of this research. Some sites in this latter group may be quite impossible to convert to secondary usage due to the hazardous condition of the overburden which was encumbered through mining methods not compatible to later use of the mined space.

The total area of underground space in all 28 sites approximates 120,000,000 square feet, of which some 25% may be deducted for pillar space netting some 90,000,000 square feet. Of this total there is currently 15,000,000 in secondary usage and an additional 27 million being developed. This study found an increase of 5.03 million annually as a result of current rock removal.

Major secondary uses are warehousing, factories, and offices in that order. One-seventh of Kansas City's warehousing is now underground. The Department of Agriculture reports that Kansas City has 34,473,000 cubic feet capacity for frozen food storage—about one-tenth of the total such capacity of the entire nation, most of which is underground. A lawnmower-parts factory makes use of the unlimited carrying capacity of the floors for its heavy industrial tooling and milling, while a sailboat factory utilizes the easily controlled humidity for setting its lacquers and glues. Printing shops take advantage of the controlled humidity for maintaining quality control.

These findings inspired further research to define those factors which are ubiquitous to subsurface development, evaluate the social and economic impact of this phenomenon, and project its relevance by suggesting generalizations applicable to similar situations.

Analysis of Subsurface Preference

In the author's survey of the underground sites the users were asked the reasons for their preference and the results are shown in Table 1.

The most consistent choices were "low space rental or purchase" and "low overhead and maintenance." The rental rate for underground facilities averages 40% less than comparable surface location. Since ownership is usually a continuance of the mining company merged or incorporated with men of commercial, industrial, and realtor adeptness, the common tenure arrangement is that of space rental or lease rather than purchase. This initial savings on the base tenure contract is further enhanced by the low overhead and maintenance cost. The average temperature of 56° F requires very little heat to make it comfortable for human occupancy and working conditions. Air conditioning equipment for lowering the temperature to that desired for storage can be less costly in outlay and operating expense since it is never subjected to temperature extremes as may exist on the surface. The resultant savings are reflected in the user's lease arrangements and can make a sizeable economic difference when compared to a surface site.

Nearness to transportation was cited by those whose major use was warehousing. The larger warehousing locations were supplied by spurs from major rail lines as well as major highways located nearby.

TABLE 1

Main Advantages of an Underground Location	Number	Percent
Convenience to market area	14	12
Nearness to supply source	3	3
Low overhead and maintenance	35	30
Nearness to transportation	6	5
Low space rental or purchase	32	27
Compatibility of underground	25	21
Other	2	2
TOTAL	117	100

Convenience to market area was cited by those whose uses were local in nature of supply sources and markets.

Compatibility of underground environmental conditions, usually interpreted as absolute humidity control, was cited by all users which dealt in paper storage and printing. These users were able to maintain quality control for their storage stock and for printing efficiency. A sailboat factory cited the same quality for drying of glue and lacquer. Candies, cookies, and cereals are stored with greater assurance of taste control as they are unaffected by climatic changes in the underground location.

Other reasons cited were security and fire protection. Roofs and sides are inaccessible, leaving a small entrance area which can be easily protected and guarded. Fire insurance is reduced to its lowest rate.

These caverns are far different from the dark and musty caves of our club-wielding ancestors. With fluorescent lighting, air conditioning, tile and wood paneling, and other amenities, their interiors are transformed into comfortable, modern work areas.

Analysis of the types of uses made of underground space shows warehousing and storage as the principal usage, making up 89% of the total; manufacturing accounts for an additional 7%, and the rest is composed of offices. Space, as we have seen, is the marketable by-product of the mined-out quarry and space is the cardinal necessity for storage.

The ability to create freezer space from part of the storage total at a low cost due to natural insulation of the surrounding rock is reflected in the location of the world's largest refrigerated storage in Kansas City with some 3,000,000 square feet available.

Major reasons for the location of public warehouses in Kansas City are its geographical position and excellent transportation facilities. Ninety-five percent of the underground space users reported dependence on regional and national sources of supplies and markets. This involves extensive use of space in receiving, stocking, and preparing for delivery.

Low cost of underground space has enabled the warehousing economy of Kansas City to expand into its role of national leadership. Blasting the rock loose and piling it underground costs from 28 cents to 58 cents a ton. The rock may often be sold for 40 cents a ton which about equates the cost of blasting it loose and piling it to one side. The rock, crushed and hauled a radius of 15 miles, may bring $4.00 a ton. The approximate cost of creating space, without utilities, is close to $1.25 per square foot of which the sale of the rock may offset one-third. No lights, heat, nor cooling are included in this figure. Where the rock is crushed and retailed or processed into asphalt paving, the profit from the rock is rewarding and the space is an added bonus.

Uses for the limestone in the Kansas City area normally run as follows:

Crushed stone 20%
Concrete 40%
Asphalt 30%
Agriculture 5%
Cement 5%
Mineral filler negligible

In 1952, Leonard Strauss, president of a mining company, realized that the worked-out areas of the limestone mines constituted a highly negotiable and valuable asset. As a major railroad hub, Kansas City was an ideal place to store food and other items being shipped across the U.S. Intervals of storage in the underground warehouses soon became a part of the Kansas City economy as crops became capital resources.

The geographic location of Kansas City in the great "food basket" of the U.S. and midway between the western area of the U.S., which produces some 50% of the nation's processed and frozen foods, and the eastern region, which buys two-thirds of the production, is ideally suited for a storage-in-transit point. The first underground freezer storage room was developed in 1953 and Inland Cold Storage (Site No. 5) took the lead as the world's largest refrigerated warehouse, handling 8 million pounds daily. Over a pound of food for each person in the U.S. can be stored in this facility at a given time.

Eighty freight cars, each capable of holding 100,000 pounds of food, can be accommodated at one time at Inland's two underground rail spurs (figure 2). Many jobs are created by the handling and redistribution of goods.

The continuing process of mining provides Inland with about 12 acres of new space every year and Inland converts as much of it into storage facilities as demand will support. When the limestone reserves are depleted in 30 years, the company has reported plans for still another coup: *the land on top of its bountiful hill may be used for a housing development* (*Fortune*, Jan. 1966, p. 175).

Tunneled into one of the numerous limestone bluffs that characterize the terrain around Kansas City is the Brunson Instrument Co. (figure 3), which manufactured the surveying instruments used on the moon. Personnel in its 140,000 square feet factory 77 feet below ground ranges as high as 435, among whom are technicians in optical tooling. Precision settings are made at any hour in this vibration-free environment whereas only the low traffic hours of 2–4 a.m. could be used in a former surface location (Harbinger, 1970, pp. 3–9).

Amber Brunson was the first to quarry rock as a secondary process with the thought of obtaining the underground space for a factory being his primary objective. Occupation of the underground factory began in 1960 and his facilities have since been an object of interest, both nationally and internationally. He is recognized as the "father" of planned secondary use since the previous uses of underground space were an afterthought. Brunson led in preplanned mining and pillar arrangement which served the purpose of secondary occupance.

The number of employees in stone production totaled an approximate 345, with an annual payroll of $3,000,000 for the primary rock production, whereas over 1,500 earned $13,000,000 in secondary use of mined-out space. This impact of secondary usage is of greater magnitude when one considers that each year some 115 acres of land is consumed in primary usage by stone production whereas the secondary usage of the underground space is continuous year after year. Secondary usage has now exceeded stone production as an economic factor in the Kansas City area by some 4.7 times in numbers employed and 4.3 times in annual wages.

Locational analysis has clearly demonstrated several distinct advantages in use of the underground environment, for example:

1. mined-out space can be purchased or leased at a fraction of the cost for comparable surface facilities.
2. roof and foundation problems are reduced or eliminated.
3. floors are capable of supporting unlimited installations or storage weight.

FIGURE 2. Underground storage of both dry and refrigerated products tends to even surpluses of southwestern United States with demands of northeastern market areas.

4. complete noise and vibration control is possible.
5. the areas are fireproof and command the lowest insurance rates in the area
6. greatly reduced costs in heating, air conditioning, or freezing as the consequences of insulation from the rock, 15% to 20% of surface cost.
7. vastly improved security for equipment, records, and personal protection.

The main reason for locating underground is the savings in rental cost. Rental costs are found to average 40% below surface facilities of the same quality. Rental space may range from 75 cents to $2.00 a square foot annually, depending on what is wanted. Maintenance, utilities, and insurance may run as low as 15% to 20% of comparable surface cost.

Physical Factors Limiting Underground Development

There are a number of questions come to mind regarding the feasibility of extending underground space development to other regions. It is reasonable to suspect that more than mere coincidence produced the use of secondary space in mined-out areas. The analysis of those factors which limit or control such development are vital to understanding the potential for extension of space use (Dean *et al.*, 1969, pp. 35-55).

A combination of six major physical factors have provided the opportunity for this development. They are:

(1) *A massively bedded limestone.* The unit must be massively bedded in order to support its own weight when undermined. Thin to medium bedding, persistent jointing and interlayering of clay or shale are prohibitive factors.

FIGURE 3. Brunson Instrument Company showing smooth ceiling left by blasting along a bedding plane.

(2) *Sufficient thickness.* Economically viable room height and an adequate roof are the two factors determining the thickness of the potential rock unit. According to this study, 12–13 feet room height suffices for economic rock production as well as most secondary uses, and sufficient roof thickness seems to require a minimum of 8 feet in order to include at least two massive beds of rock. It appears, therefore, that rock units with potential for secondary use should be at least 20 feet thick. Modifications from this limitation may possibly be accomplished by a different room height or by lowering the floor into the underlying strata.

(3) *Overlying impermeable shale.* The fact that karst topography does not occur in the Kansas City area can be partially attributed to the sealing effect of the overlying shales. Where the shales have been dissected or removed by erosion, seepage, roof fall, and surface caving can result. The existence of an intact overlying impermeable shale member is necessary to avoid the danger of mine subsidence.

(4) *Nearly level stratigraphy.* Tilted strata obviously defy secondary development within competitive economic range. Slight inclination also introduces problems. A 4% grade presents difficulty in efficient railroad car switching, and benching of the floor creates steps and ramps which add to the problems of handling of goods by trucks, carts, and forklifts. Leveling the floor by filling robs the ceiling height and leveling by added excavation involves diversified matrix materials. Drainage can be an expensive maintenance problem where any slope occurs opposite to the underground extension. Whereas problems begin with even a small bedding inclination, a 4% grade appears to be the point beyond which development is not feasible. The average dip of the Bethany Falls limestone in the Kansas City area is 10–20 feet per mile, a dip of approximately one-fifth of a degree.

(5) *Competent overburden.* For minimum roof stability and surface preservation above underground space, a sufficient thickness of overburden should be present which includes impermeable shales and a buffer against erosion and mass wasting. In the Kansas City area, this requires a minimum of 40 feet of overburden, thus indicating the need for the superjacent Winterset member. In this area, such a thickness of overburden generally provides sealant shales which protect the underground openings from vadose water and insure the strength of overlying rock by virtue of its mass. Exceptions occur where aeolian deposits constitute the overburden. These areas must be considered independently.

(6) *Natural accessibility.* Vertical shaft mining of limestone necessitates the use of elevators for secondary use of the resulting space. Where rent values are sufficiently high, this may be economically feasible, but it is highly unlikely that underground space use on a grand scale is apt to develop except with a more economical means of accessibiltiy. A dendritic drainage pattern which dissects the strata and exposes the potential rock matrix to accessibility by horizontal means appears to be a more reasonable prerequisite to extensive development of both the mine and the mined-out space. Valley walls provide natural accessibility and valley floors are the natural locus for rail and highway routes.

An artist's drawing brings together these six salient features into a composite sketch which typifies the physiographic setting wherein both primary stone production and secondary development of mined space is apt to occur (figure 4).

Modification of Mining Methods

Earlier mining methods were focused on recovery of the limestone rock and the method was "mine and abandon." The robbing of pillars and ceiling was a common practice and the aftermath of wasted land was accepted as inevitable. Tracts, containing many acres of land, were abandoned and their mine-scarred surface, punctuated by subsidence pits, became a common sight in the rural-urban fringe of our cities. These abandoned waste lands often stood in the path of orderly urban growth, forcing streets to terminate and traffic to be permanently detoured. Residential and industrial development was forced to leap-frog these areas, which are nonproductive in usage or tax support due to their unstable surfaces.

The secondary use of mined-out space brought a reorientation of purpose in limestone mining. Suddenly, a new economic resource, the value of the mined-out area, began to compete with the

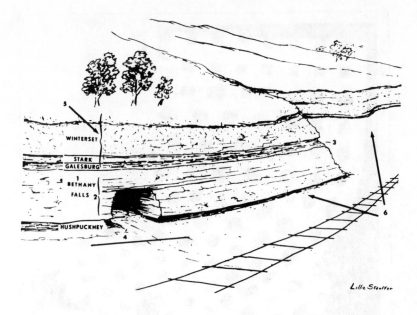

FIGURE 4. An artist's sketch showing 6 features salient to the development of underground space.

value of the rock and attention was directed toward the dual objective of mining for the rock and for the later use of the created space. This development placed increased emphasis on the stability of the overburden as a surface for the development above ground and as a ceiling to the development below ground.

Current mining practice is to remove 12 to 13 feet of the limestone and leave 8 to 10 feet overhead coinciding with a prominent bedding plane. This supports the roof of the mine, reduces scale to a minimum and leaves a level ceiling amenable to many secondary uses. Roof bolting is unnecessary though used in renovating abandoned mines which were not planned for secondary use.

A change in blasting techniques referred to as smooth blasting is the widely accepted method for controlling overbreak. By shooting with minimum delay between the holes, a shearing action is obtained which gives smooth walls with minimum overbreak.

This modification of mining practice in the Kansas City area has reduced income from rock extraction only slightly while it has stabilized the surface area by virtually freeing it from danger of collapse. It has at the same time made a stable ceiling to the mined-out rooms, leaving them available for secondary usage.

The second major area of change in mining methods has been in the distribution of pillars. The irregular spaced pillars, relics of the day when no thought was given to use of the mined space, were often untenable to secondary use layout. Companies that require long assembly lines were handicapped by lack of linear patterns. Storage facilities requiring lengthy rail and truck lines found difficulty in bending their routes through and around an irregular pillar system. Offices were highly irregular in size and shape as they were fitted into existing pillar arrangement.

Quarry operators have altered their methods of pillar spacing with the advent of secondary use. The frontier of this effect is visible in every mine which has been in operation through both the old and new periods and a composite sketch shows the planned and unplanned pillar arrangements with the frontier of planned pillar spacing reflecting the effect of secondary development (figure 5). This grid pattern facilitates incorporation of pillars into partitioning walls, descriptive location of subdivided areas, designation of subdivision for recovery of stored items, arrangement of assembly lines,

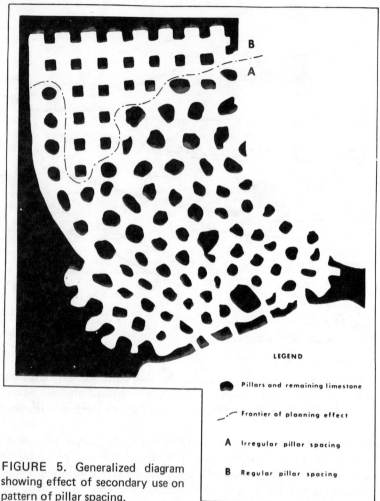

LEGEND

⬤ Pillars and remaining limestone

–·–⌐ Frontier of planning effect

A   Irregular pillar spacing

B   Regular pillar spacing

FIGURE 5. Generalized diagram showing effect of secondary use on pattern of pillar spacing.

and linear office patterns. Pillars of the older mines, though irregularly spaced, have been incorporated into partitioning walls, business entrances, and office decor in some rather ingenious ways (figure 6). However, regularly spaced pillars in a grid pattern make more optimal use of the mined space.

Pillars currently used average 20 to 30 feet, are usually square and spaced 50 to 60 feet on center. Where 20-foot pillars are used, the center to center spacing is normally held to 50 feet. This leaves a 30-foot corridor and an area of approximately 2,100 square feet per module (figure 7).

It is very important that the shales overlying the Bethany Falls member are not broken since they serve as a sealant against vadose ground water. Surface water moves downward to this shale and is deflected laterally by its impervious quality which protects the underlying Bethany Falls from seepage. This has kept solution channels from developing in the limestone of the Kansas City area. When secondary usage requires the penetration of these shales for vents, they are resealed with bentonite, a high swelling colloidal clay.

The air of an underground development is flushed by static pressure. Air is pumped into the underground space, forcing itself through all open air space and finally exhausting itself to the surface through prepared vents or open tunnels. The air is usually treated by heating or cooling to accommodate the particular need of the underground facility. This treatment occurs immediately after the air enters the intake vent and it is the treated air which is then forced through the facility.

FIGURE 6. Office area of the Overland Distribution Center. Note how the pillar has been incorporated into the total office decor. These carpeted offices are as modern as any surface arrangement.

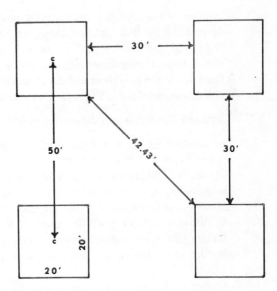

FIGURE 7. Typical pillar and tunnel arrangement.

Conclusions

1. Certain physiographic and geologic features are salient to the development of underground space, namely:

   —A massively bedded limestone
   —Sufficient thickness of matrix member
   —Overlying impermeable shale
   —Nearly level stratigraphy
   —Competent overburden
   —Natural accessibility

2. Certain geographic features relate to the secondary development of underground space, namely:

   —Urban market for rock products which created an abundance of mined space
   —Valleys dissecting and exposing limestone for horizontal mining

  —Transportation routes generally located in valleys having proximity to both industrial areas and mined areas
  —Mid-continent location of Kansas City area
  —Comparative economic advantage of underground location over a surface site
  —Warehousing or storage demand making up some 89% of current usage
  —Rock removal is currently creating an additional 5.03 million square feet annually

3. The secondary use of mined space has altered mining techniques so as to be more adaptable for later use of the mined space, namely:

  —A competent overburden
  —Leaving 8–10 feet of limestone ceiling in place
  —Arrangement of pillars in a grid pattern
  —Change from single venture of rock removal to a multiple land-use economic enterprise

4. Areas of greatest impact made by the secondary occupance and use of underground space in the Kansas City area are:

  —Creation of employment which greatly exceeds that of the stone industry
  —An annual wage that greatly exceeds that of the stone industry
  —The use of land which would otherwise be abandoned
  —The creation of permanent rather than one-shot usage of mining areas
  —The effecting of neighborhood compatability between mine site and residence
  —The extension of the urban regime by a vertical dimension in the use of the underground area

5. Continued development if done efficiently indicates a need for research suggesting:

  —An institute for the development of underground space
  —A repository for materials relative to the occupancy of underground space
  —Laboratories to test the effect of human occupancy
  —Interdisciplinary studies combining law, psychology, sociology, geology, and geography
  —Studies of split fee title for dual surface ownership
  —Studies of taxation on two-tier basis
  —Studies pertaining to development of new uses
  —Reduction of surface land use conflict such as excessive noise by locating such uses underground
  —Studies in the extension of public buildings, streets, and university campuses by underground usage
  —Studies of areas comparable to Kansas City where similar development may occur

REFERENCES

Business Week, 1961, "Industry Tries Living in Caves," Vol. 1655, pp. 166–70.
Dean, Thomas J., Jenkins, Gomer, and Williams, James H., 1969, "Underground Mining in the Kansas City Area," "Mining in Kansas City, Missouri," *Mineral-Industry News*, Vol 9, No. 4.
Fortune, 1966, "Double Duty from Hidden Assets," Vol. 73, pp. 175–76.
Harbinger, 1970, Brunson . . . "The Man and His Company," Vol. II, No. 9, pp. 3–9.
New York Times, 1971, "Business Underground," Aug. 1, p. 13.

22

Mineral Resources of the San Francisco Bay Region, California— Present Availability and Planning for the Future[1]

Edgar H. Bailey and Deborah R. Harden

Introduction

In a little more than a century, the predominantly rural, agricultural area around San Francisco Bay has become a great metropolis that includes several major cities and hundreds of square miles of ever-expanding peripheral residential suburbs. The population has increased from less than 100,000 people in the 1850s to more than 5 million in the early 1970s. The quantity of mineral resources needed to support the expanded population has gone up at an even greater rate because with an increase in the standard of living, each individual requires more. Fortunately, within the bay region the mineral commodities needed in large amounts for construction and industrial use could be found and extracted locally, hydrocarbon and geothermal energy resources were available, and some mineral products, such as salines and mercury, were even abundant enough to be exported. However, mineral resources, being nonrenewable, can be mined to exhaustion, or urban expansion can make them unavailable by covering them with streets and buildings or rendering their use undesirable because of environmental considerations. Will there be enough of the mineral resources still available to maintain growth, or just to support the necessary renewal, of the bay region metropolis 10 years from now—or what about 100 years from now?

A favorable response to the questions of future availability of resources lies in long-range planning leading to the optimum use of the mineral-bearing land, and this report was prepared especially to provide background data for planners and land-use decisionmakers on whom this future availability depends. On the basis of this, the report and accompanying map[2] (1) indicate what and where the mineral resources in the bay area are, (2) examine future bay area requirements in light of present uses and projected growth, and (3) suggest steps that might be taken to assure that the identified resources will be available when needed.

A consideration beyond availability is that of the desirability of utilizing a resource in spite of environmental disruption that may accompany its extraction. The removal of many mineral resources

1. Jointly supported by the U.S. Geological Survey and the Department of Housing and Urban Development as part of a program to develop earth-science information in a form applicable to land-use planning and decisionmaking.
2. Not included here.

Extracted with permission of the authors from Mineral Resources of the San Francisco Bay Region, California —Present Availability and Planning for the Future, Explanation Accompanying *U.S. Geological Survey Map I-909,* 1975, 12 pp.

may be accompanied by dirt, noise, earth vibrations, unsightly pits or dumps, or contamination of water or air. Much of this can be either totally avoided or minimized by proper planning and regulation. It is not the purpose of this report to recommend for or against the utilization of local resources, but we do feel an obligation to point out potential deleterious environmental effects and possible actions that can be taken to minimize or eliminate them.

Mineral Resource Utilization

Past and Present

The nine counties of the San Francisco Bay Region have an area of almost 7,000 square miles, and in a general way they form a semicircular area centered on San Francisco and extending outward for a distance of 75 miles. Within this area live about 5 million people (1970), most of whom dwell on less than 5 percent of the land that comprises the relatively flat alluvial plains bordering the bay. Much of the rest of the land is mountainous, reaching altitudes of 3,845 feet at Mount Diablo and 4,344 feet at Mount St. Helena, but between the ranges are intermountain valleys that are intensively used for both agriculture and residences. The mineral sources are chiefly in the populated plains or valleys rather than in the mountains, but despite this, few inhabitants of the bay area are more than vaguely aware that there has been any production of mineral resources in the area. Yet, the total value of mineral products extracted in the bay area by 1970 exceeds $2,000,000,000 and in the past few years has annually exceeded $100,000,000. Although a few commodities account for most of the value, at least 26 individual mineral commodities have been recovered in sufficient amounts to be considered in this report. Most mineral products have been used locally, fulfilling a need for low-cost construction materials and a supply of energy, as well as providing the basis for employment for thousands of people.

Trends in mineral production in response to the huge increase in population in the bay area are shown graphically in figure 1. This chart is based on the dollar value of the mineral products at 20-year intervals, utilizing years selected as representative of normal peacetime periods. The figure shows clearly that the major mineral resources recovered in the bay area are (1) construction materials, such as limestone and oyster shells (used in manufacture of cement), sand and gravel, and crushed stone; (2) energy sources such as gas, oil, and geothermal power; and (3) salines. Together these mineral commodities account for more than 90 percent of the value of the bay area mineral products, and it is also significant that virtually all were used within the bay area. In contrast, most of the mercury recovered from bay area ores has been exported.

Figure 1 also indicates that with the urbanization of the bay area, which received its greatest impetus in the early 1940s, the dollar value of local production has doubled every decade. Although a part of this can be attributed to rising unit value, owing to inflation, more than half the increase is a result of greater local requirements for the growing population. Also, as indicated by the figures at the base of the diagram, per capita mineral requirements, in terms of dollar value, have doubled every 20 years.

Through the past 60 years the change in relative amounts of different mineral commodities produced in the bay area is remarkably small, though a few commodities provide notable exceptions (figure 1). The overall production pattern for 1970 is much like that of 1950, but geothermal power, first produced in 1960, has become significant. Similarly, sulfur, recovered in large amounts as a valuable by-product of oil refining in 1970, was formerly (until about 1950) dissipated into the atmosphere, constituting an undesirable pollutant. On the other hand, magnesite, though once important, has not been mined since 1961 and has been of little importance since World War II. Mineral water, another relatively minor commodity, also appears now to be proportionally in much less demand than 50 years ago, but reliable data for the more recent decades are not available. The commodities with major production, accounting for 90 percent of the total, although being used in rapidly increasing amounts, are all tied to the urban economy and population growth so that the production of each

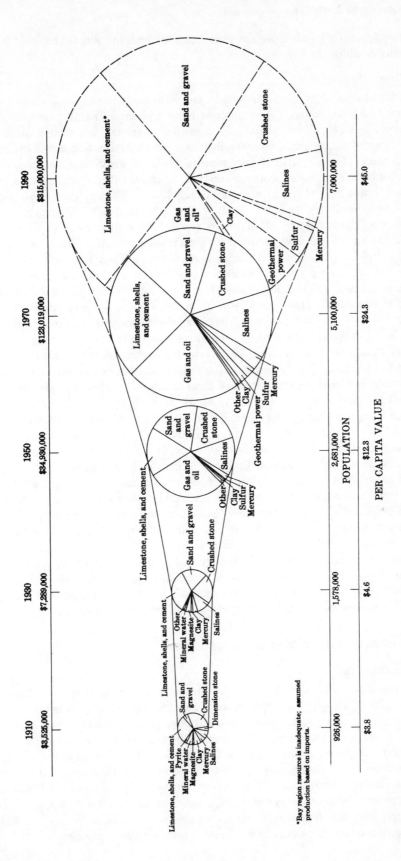

FIGURE 1. Past and projected mineral production, San Francisco Bay Region.

*Bay region resource is inadequate; assumed production based on imports.

increases uniformly with the others. We can expect similar trends to continue, but only as long as resources are available within the bay area.

Future Mineral Utilization

The quantity of mineral products that will be recovered in the bay area in the next two decades depends upon: (1) the population, (2) per capita mineral and energy needs, (3) availability of the mineral resources, and (4) policies adopted by regulatory agencies. This section discusses future production in terms of future needs, assuming that currently available resources will still be available and used when needed. Consideration of environmental impact, desirability of continued production, and steps that can be taken to assure proper mineral utilization are deferred until a later section.

Estimates of future mineral requirements are closely linked with population projections, and for the bay area there currently is considerable variation in projections made by different groups. It seems certain that there will be as many people in the bay area in 1990 as there are now (1974), and projections of population growth indicating an increase of less than 50 percent to about 7 million seem reasonable. If we accept the projection, and if mineral needs for buildings, roads, energy, and so on are locally supplied at the same per capita rate as now, the 1990 mineral industry will have an annual production value of about $200 million. However, as the per capita mineral production has historically increased at a rate that doubled every 20 years, one may project an annual production for 1990 closer to $350 million. Owing to the expected depletion of some mineral commodities, this high level of production is not likely to be reached, but the magnitude of the figures indicates the importance of a local mineral industry to the economy of the area. It also emphasizes the need to plan for development of the San Francisco Bay Region in such a fashion that the mineral resources needed in the future will be available in amounts that are several times as large as are presently being used.

The mineral products to be recovered in the future will probably come chiefly from the sources now known and being used, though the possibility of new discoveries always exists. Figure 2 shows, for each of the bay area counties, the location, magnitude, and prospect for utilization for each of 26 mineral commodities that have been recovered locally. In addition, figure 3 shows an areawide summation of past production and outlook for future production by commodity.

Continued or renewed production of many of the bay area mineral resources, especially in the large amounts to be required in the future, offers potential environmental problems. These differ according to the commodity involved, the site of extraction, the method of extraction, and the processing necessary to yield a usable product. For each commodity listed in figure 3, we have indicated the possible environmental disturbances of the land, water, or air that might accompany its utilization. The requirements for mineral products and the effects of obtaining them locally are summarized in the following section by groups of related mineral commodities, and for more details of environmental considerations for individual commodities the reader is referred to the separate chapters on each mineral product contained in the supplementary report that has been released in open file.

Characteristics of Related Mineral Commodities

Construction Materials

Mineral commodities quarried in the bay region for use in the construction of buildings and roads have an annual value of more than $70 million and account for considerably more than half the total value of mineral products produced. They are indispensable to modern society and, because of their bulk and low unit value, are generally mined as close to the point of use as possible. Included are vast quantities of sand and gravel, crushed stone, and limestone and shells used in the manufacture of cement. Also included are dimension stone and expansible shale, but these are quarried in such small amounts as to be relatively inconsequential and are not further discussed under this heading. Because the major construction products are needed in huge amounts, are mined at the surface in large quarries, and have unit value that is small as compared to transportation costs, they present similar environmental and economic problems and require the most consideration in planning.

Commodity	Alameda	Contra Costa	Marin	Napa	San Francisco	San Mateo	Santa Clara	Solano	Sonoma
Asbestos	+	O		+					
Chromite	+	O	O	+	O	O	+	O	+
Clay	+	■	■	+	O	O	+	■	+
Coal	O	O							
Copper	O	O	O	O			O		O
Diatomite		■		■					□
Expansible shale	■	■	■	■	O	O	O	O	O
Gemstones	O	O	+	+	+	+	+	O	+
Geothermal resources				+					■
Limestone and shells	⊠	□	O	O		⊠	⊠	O	O
Magnesite	O			O			O		O
Manganese	+	O	O	O			+		O
Mercury	O	+	□	□	O	O	■	+	□
Mineral water		+	+	■		■	■		■
Oil and gas	O	⊠	O	O		+	O	⊠	O
Peat		■					O	□	
Pumice		+		■	O			+	+
Pyrite	O								
Salines	■		+	■		■	■	■	
Sand and gravel	■	O	O	■	■	O	■	■	■
Sands, specialty	O	■			O	O			
Silver				+					
Stone, crushed and broken	■	■	■	■	O	■	■	■	■
Stone, dimension	O	O	■	■	O	O	O	■	■
Stone, ornamental			+					■	
Sulfur, by-product		■							

EXPLANATION

O   Occurrence, not likely to be used

+   Small resource, or usable only at high price

□   Significant resource not being used but likely to be used within next 20 years

■   Significant resource being used

⊠   Significant resource being used but likely to be exhausted, seriously depleted, or uneconomic in 20 years

FIGURE 2. Mineral resources of the San Francisco Bay Region by county.

Commodity	Approximate total value to 1973, in dollars	Approximate value recent year, in dollars	Bay region importance[1]	Statewide or national importance[2]	Availability[3]	Outlook[4]	Kind of operation[5]	Potential environmental effects[6]
Asbestos	600,000	0	−	−	+	−	Q	S, N
Chromite	520,000	0	−	−	±	−	Q	S, N, W
Clay	19,000,000	1,000,000	+	−	+	+	Q	S, W
Coal	16,000,000	0	−	−	±	−	Q	S, W
Copper	60,000	0	−	−	−	−	UM, BP	W
Diatomite	1,000,000	200,000	+	−	+	+	Q	S, N, A
Expansible shale	40,000,000	400,000	+	−	+	+	Q	S, N, A
Gemstones	11,000	(0?)	±	−	+	+	C	None
Geothermal resources	5,000,000	1,500,000	+	+	+	+	W	W, A, N
Limestone and shells	500,000,000 (includes cement)	30,000,000 (includes cement)	+	−	+	+	Q, SM	A, S, N
Magnesite	10,000,000	0	−	−	+	−	UM, Q	S, N
Manganese	620,000	0	−	−	+	−	UM, Q	S, A, N
Mercury	110,000,000	3,200,000	+	+	±	±	UM, Q	S, A, N, W
Mineral water	5,000,000(?)	?	−	−	+	±	W	None
Peat	1,000,000(?)	100,000	−	−	+	+	Q, SM	S
Pumice	1,200,000	4,000	−	−	+	−	Q	S, A
Pyrite	2,000,000	0	−	−	±	−	UM	S, A, W
Salines	290,000,000	16,000,000	+	+	+	+	W	S
Sand and gravel	370,000,000	22,500,000	+	−	±	+	Q, SM	S, A, N
Sand, specialty	200,000	53,000	±	−	+	+	Q, SM	S
Silver and gold	1,600,000	0	±	−	±	±	UM	S, N, W
Stone, crushed and broken	273,000,000	18,700,000	+	−	+	+	Q	S, N, A
Stone, dimension	4,600,000	45,000	−	−	+	±	Q	S, N
Stone, ornamental	150,000	?	±	−	±	±	Q	S
Oil and gas	420,000,000	26,500,000	+	+	±	+	W	S, W, A
Sulfur, by-product	25,000,000	2,500,000	+	−	+	+	BP	None

[1] +   Should mine if possible.
    ±   Could import or get along without.
    −   Unnecessary or unavailable.

[2] +   Supply other parts of United States.
    −   None.

[3] +   Widespread or readily available.
    ±   Limited supply, or available only at high price.
    −   Unavailable.

[4] +   Expect continued or greater exploitation.
    ±   Declining or doubtful production.
    −   Will terminate, or has terminated.

[5] UM   Underground mine.
    Q   Quarry.
    SM   Submarine mining.
    W   Well, spring, or pond.
    C   Collected.
    BP   By-product.

[6] S   Surface disturbance, such as quarry or dump.
    A   Air pollution.
    W   Water pollution.
    N   Noise.

FIGURE 3. Summary of availability and projected availability of mineral resources, San Francisco Bay Region.

A steady, and doubtless increasing, supply of mineral products for construction is a necessity for the continuing development and renewal of the bay region. Fortunately, suitable sand, gravel, and rock are available locally in adequate amounts, if the known sources remain accessible. By proper land-use planning they can be kept accessible, or in rare instances be made available after some other temporary utilization of the land. Whether or not they should be kept available for use will depend chiefly upon the results of balancing the increased costs that would result from obtaining these mineral products elsewhere against at least temporary on-site environmental damage. However, the large increase in cost that would result from importing these commodities makes it very likely that the residents will continue to be supplied from local sources, and it seems prudent to keep these sources available.

Some representative figures illustrate the increase in costs that would result from importing. The value of bulk construction materials, though variable, can be generalized as a little more than a dollar a ton. The cost of hauling by truck also varies depending on quantity hauled, distance, whether through city or countryside, and similar factors, but a general figure of 10 cents per ton-mile is reasonable. It thus becomes apparent that transporting sand, gravel, or rock 10–15 miles might double their cost, and bringing them from even just beyond the periphery of the bay region into San Francisco could increase their cost three times or more. Importing by ship should also be considered, but here unloading followed by truck transport also raises the cost significantly.

Sources of mineral commodities are generally limited and fixed by both geology and local conditions. If multiple sources are available, planners have some freedom in selecting areas to be set aside for mineral extraction or to be used for other purpose, but if sources are few the choice may be only whether to use them or not. For each of the bulk commodities, sand and gravel, crushed rock, and limestone, the conditions are a little different, so each in turn is discussed briefly in the following paragraphs.

Sand and Gravel. Sand and gravel usable for aggregate most commonly occur in flat valley floors where former streams have dropped their load of worn rock fragments as they emerged from the bedrock uplands. Not every sand and gravel accumulation, however, is usable, because the rock fragments in it must be physically sound, chemically nonreactive varieties. Within the bay region, every county has some suitable deposits, but sources large enough to be quarried profitably occur in only half the counties. In major deposits, large equipment can be used for quarrying and for the necessary washing and sizing, resulting in low-unit-cost production. Nevertheless, owing to haulage costs, as previously mentioned, a small operation may supply a local need more cheaply than can a remote major producer. Both large and small quarries must generally be sited on flat land that is also suitable for agriculture or even residences, and owing to their size and the character of their operation, the quarries are likely to produce environmental problems unless careful planning is done before dense urbanization of their surroundings.

In places beneath the waters of San Francisco Bay and offshore from the Golden Gate Channel are sand deposits now exploited on a limited scale but perhaps having greater potential. In most areas the sand is too muddy or too fine to be usable, but some areas readily reached by modern dredges contain coarser material. The Point Knox-Alcatraz-Presidio shoals and parts of the Golden Gate bar seem most amenable to utilization. This material is publicly owned, and its utilization has not yet caused significant environmental disruption, but large-scale extraction might result in undesirable effects.

Crushed Rock. Crushed rock suitable for commercial use must be durable and strong. Such material generally is found on hillsides, commonly those with steep slopes. Quarries for crushed rock therefore are dug literally into the sides of hills and are likely to leave visible scars, in contrast to gravel pits, which are normally dug down into flat areas and may be largely out of view. Suitable rock sources are found in all the bay area counties, and all have produced millions of dollars worth of crushed rock. Sources of riprap blocks larger than about 3 feet, however, are sparse, and special consideration should be give to preservation of their availability. Because of the abundance of possible sources of crushed rock, and the relatively high costs of hauling, many small local quarries have been operated to fill nearby demands. Doubtless others will be needed if costs of crushed rock are to be kept low. There is really no way to hide a rock quarry, but with many potential locations available it should be possible to site rock quarries either behind small hills or in areas unsuited for residential or recreational use where the environmental impact would be minimal.

Limestone. Limestone suitable for the manufacture of cement is now quarried in only one place, in the Santa Cruz Mountains west of Cupertino, and although many other deposits are known, they all appear to be too small to warrant building a new cement plant to make use of them. This is unfortunate, as the present plant capacity of the bay area is too small to meet even the near-future needs. In addition to limestone deposits, the southern part of San Francisco Bay contains a reserve of oyster shells suitable for cement manufacture, but a cement plant at Redwood City Harbor that formerly utilized this resource ceased production in 1970. As the needs of the area increase, it will be necessary to import either cement or the raw material for cement, which can be brought in most economically by ship. Requests to build portside plants or to reactivate those now in existence can be expected. The utilization of the submerged shell beds, perhaps in conjunction with imports of limestone, is an alternative that may be desirable from the viewpoint of minimal environmental impact, but this needs further investigation. In addition, the potential use of limestone deposits for purposes other than cement may be considerable; for example, crushed limestone is as suitable for concrete and bituminous aggregate as some other types of rock now being used, and its calcium carbonate content makes it useful for such processes as sugar refining and neutralization of acid waste water.

Environmental Considerations. Quarries from which natural materials for construction purposes are removed are generally large, some being over half a mile long, and without careful development and reconstruction they will normally form unsightly scars on the landscape. Proper planning, however, can encourage screening them from view during their operation, and more significantly in the long run, planning can often turn the resulting pits into economic or social assets after the mineral product has been removed. For example, in the Livermore area a park has been established on a former quarry site, and in Los Gatos excavations have been converted to ground-water percolation ponds that are used as recreational lakes. In other areas, excavations have been used for sanitary solid-waste disposal. If properly planned, quarrying can be an ephemeral land use leading to the development of a permanent asset, and in some instances tax payments from the quarrying might finance such development.

During the operational phase, sand and gravel quarries can be made least noticeable by initially locating them away from the public eye if there is a choice in site selection, or they can be hidden by appropriate screening with low peripheral mounds or trees. New quarries located in undeveloped areas can be kept isolated by greenbelt or protective zoning. For rock quarries on hillsides, however, probably only natural barriers such as a shielding hill can be effective, so the initial siting of these is critical if they are to be as unobtrusive as possible.

Other environmental damage relates to the processing of these bulk commodities, but much of it can be avoided or corrected by proper planning and applied engineering. Sand and gravel must be cleaned and sized, and settling ponds, designed to avoid clogging ground-water intake areas, are necessary to remove the extracted clays or fines from the discharge water. Cement plants create much dust from fine grinding, and their exhaust stacks require advanced-design precipitators to avoid spreading a mantle of white dust over the surrounding areas. Special technology is also required to avoid air pollution from kiln exhaust gases. Rock crushers are a source of dust, but this too can be largely controlled. Considerable noise also generally accompanies bulk commodity mining and processing operations, and the transport of their products to the site of use requires heavy-truck haulage. Thus, it is evident that the use of bulk mineral commodities for construction produces environmental damage of various kinds—some of which can be eliminated, some minimized, and some of such a character that it apparently cannot be avoided.

Energy Sources

Mineral commodities used as energy sources in the bay region have an annual value of about $30 million, or about a fourth of the value of all the area's mineral products. Most of the value is in natural gas, but some oil is recovered, and steam for geothermal production of electricity is becoming increasingly important. Coal and peat are not generally used for fuel in the bay region because they are not economically competitive with other products, but they are present in limited amounts.

Reserves of oil and gas are small and far from adequate to meet either the present or long-term energy requirements of the area. Known geothermal resources are believed to be large, and the prospects for new discoveries are good, but it seems unlikely that the energy needs of the bay region can be met without either large import of fuel and electrical energy or use of nuclear reactors. Fortunately, neither the search for these natural energy commodities nor their utilization produces environmental problems that cannot be solved.

Oil and Gas. Oil and gas are both sought and produced through deep wells located more or less directly above oil or gas reservoirs. In the bay region most of the reservoirs have been found in broadly folded, relatively young rocks underlying plains, valleys, or low hills. Hence, most wells are in land suitable for other uses, including homesites, and future exploratory drill holes will be located in similar areas, with the possible exception of some drilled offshore. Drilling a well causes some environmental problems, but once a well has been completed and the rig removed, the permanent wellhead installation is small and readily concealed. Both the drilling and subsequent exploitation are controlled by existing antipollution regulations of the State of California and the Federal Government. Some consideration must be given to the possiblity of the adverse effects on urban development of surface subsidence and faulting caused by the extraction of oil and gas.

Geothermal Steam. Geothermal steam, which is a most attractive cheap source of energy, is also sought and recovered through deep wells. The only productive steam field in the United States is at The Geysers in the northern part of the bay region. This is in a remote section of the Mayacmas Mountains, as are all the other areas in the bay region offering the greatest promise for future discoveries. This resource was not utilized until 1960, and the large energy potential of the area adjacent to The Geysers was not fully appreciated until even more recently. As this report was prepared, exploratory drilling to extend the known steam field or to find new fields was still in progress. Doubtless geothermal steam will be sought in less promising areas in the immediate future, but the chances of finding new exploitable fields elsewhere in the area appear to be quite small from a geological viewpoint.

Environmental Considerations. The drilling of any kind of deep well creates a potential for disruption or contamination of aquifers, but drilling practices are regulated and closely supervised by the California Division of Oil and Gas. Generally drilling also temporarily disrupts the surface at the site. Roads must be provided for access, a drill rig must be erected, ponds for retention of drilling fluids must be dug, and storage tanks and other temporary structures are generally required. Upon completion of the well, however, the site can be restored to its original condition, or the surface may be made even more attractive and productive than formerly. If the well is successful, a pipe must be installed to lead off the gas, oil, or steam, and for oil a simple pump is also generally necessary. If unsuccessful, the well pipe can be capped and easily hidden, in some places by burial.

Oil and gas are transmitted through buried pipes, or by boat or truck, to refineries for processing. Formerly, refineries discharged considerable sulfur and other undesirable gases into the air, but now in the bay region the sulfur is profitably recovered, flammable waste gas is burned, and emissions are closely monitored by the Air Pollution Control District. Geothermal steam is transmitted by pipe to low-pressure turbine-generators, and subsequently a condensate containing most of the undesirable boron, ammonia, and hydrogen sulfide initially contained in the steam is returned to the ground through special reinjection wells. Escaping steam creates a noise problem that can be only partly controlled, but existing wells are in remote areas and few people are affected.

Salines

About $16 million worth of saline products are extracted annually from the seawater of San Francisco Bay through solar evaporation. Most of the value comes from the production of more than 1 million tons of ordinary salt; magnesium salts, gypsum, and bromine are also recovered. Some of the salt and most of the other products are used within the bay region, and the bulk of the excess salt is shipped to consumers in the Northwestern United States. Present capacity is great enough to meet the local needs in the immediate future, and for reasons noted below it is not unlikely that the productive capacity will be expanded.

The salt is recovered by evaporation of the bay water in large shallow ponds created from the marshlands bordering shallow parts of the bay. These salt ponds now cover about 35,000 acres, chiefly rimming the southern part of the bay but including some in the extreme northern part. A complete pond system consists of concentrating ponds, crystallizing ponds, bittern ponds, and salt-washing ponds.

Present production is limited by the amount of marshland available for ponds, and less than 10,000 additional acres that might be suitable remain in the San Francisco Bay borderland. However, less land is likely to be used for ponds in the future, owing to pressure of urban expansion and increasing value of the lands for real estate development, waste disposal, wildlife habitat, and recreation. The local production of salines is a source of income and fills a bay region need, but the lands may be needed more for other purposes. Salt can be imported at a price nearly competitive with local manufacture.

Environmental Considerations. The conversion of marshland to salt ponds puts into mineral production land that in large part is otherwise useful as a duck hunting area or bird refuge, or important as a spawning area for fish and as an environmental modifier in the unique fashion of all marshlands. In 1972, part of the south bay area was converted into the San Francisco Bay National Wildlife Refuge and included were several thousand acres of salt ponds. This did not, however, result in termination of the salt-evaporation operations as they were considered to be compatible with the aims of the refuge. A potential environmental problem connected with the evaporation process results from the quantity of highly concentrated bittern that remains after the extraction of the salt. In part the bittern can be used as a source of other saline products, but at present much of it is not being used, and some of the pond area must be devoted to its storage. Disposal of the bittern is a serious, as yet unsolved, problem that could ultimately limit the use of the area for salt production.

Strategy for Future Mineral Utilization

From a purely monetary viewpoint, entirely omitting environmental or esthetic considerations, it is desirable to utilize any mineral resource in the bay region that can be profitably recovered because use creates wealth within the area in contrast to capital outflow that results from importing. In terms of dollar return on land use, mineral extraction gives a yield that is exceeded only under unusual circumstances in limited areas. The value of the production from all the lands exploited for mineral products in California in 1965 averaged $10,000 per acre. For more restricted areas high yields have been obtained over a period of many years; for example, in the New Almaden mercury district, less than 1,000 acres of mineralized ground has yielded nearly $100,000,000, or roughly $100,000 per acre. As is well known, land underlain by oil or gas can give large dollar yields from wells, and at the same time the surface can be used for farming or other productive purposes. The high yield from mineral extraction, however, is a one-time result, as mineral resources are nonrenewable, in contrast to water, timber, or agricultural resources, which with proper management can give continuing yields.

The utilization of local mineral resources, in contrast to importing, has other economic advantages. The capital it generates goes partly to provide jobs and partly to support satellite service industries, and a substantial part generally goes for tax revenue to meet other local needs. In addition, the lower cost of the locally derived product is a significant factor in promoting other industries that use this product.

Thus, purely economic considerations favor maximum use of whatever mineral resources are available and especially those closest to the need, which means closest to population centers. But, the extraction of most mineral products is accompanied by at least some undesirable environmental impact, which leads to the need for consideration of the balance between economic and environmental factors. An inviting way to escape the impact of environmental damage is to site all points of mineral exploitation back in the mountains beyond most human notice, but even this will not eliminate disturbance by heavy truck haulage of bulk commodities. Unfortunately, in the bay region this choice of quarrying in remote mountains generally is not available, as the positions of the deposits, particularly those of the most needed bulk commodities, are fixed, and most lie in the valley area, which is also prime land for residences and agriculture. Consequently, plans for mineral use must begin with "do" versus "don't" decisions, which generally will be tentative and hinge on a study of need, economics, methods of exploitation, environmental effects, regulation required, and possible use of land after the resource is exhausted. It seems probable, however, that economics will require use of locally available resources, and well in advance of their utilization, or even the development of their sites, three aspects of land use unique to mineral production might be considered by planning and regulatory agencies. These aspects are: (1) the protection and conservation of known deposits, (2) regulation of the extractive and processing operation, and (3) reclamation and use of the site upon completion of the operation.

Planning for Protection and Conservation of Mineral Resources

To preserve the availability of mineral deposits, especially those of construction materials, in the bay region requires a series of actions in advance of extraction. First, future needs must be forecast and analyzed, and second, potential resource sites of adequate size must be identified, inventoried, classified, and ranked, unless it is readily apparent that every deposit regardless of size will be needed. Then, to assure future availability of resource sites, measures must be taken to protect them from other preemptive uses, although if there is no need for immediate extraction, interim temporary uses might be permitted. Consideration should be given to reserving adequate space for processing plants, access roads, and buffer zones. As mineral processing normally uses energy, high-load electrical lines also may be required. Companies holding mineral resource land will normally pursue these considerations and request appropriate governmental action, but effective protection of resources remote from urbanization may depend upon the preparation of land-use plans before requests are received from developers.

Measures to assure the protection of mineral resources are provided for by existing land-use regulations. Regional and local planning and regulatory agencies can include plan elements that provide for mineral resource preservation and use in the regional land-use plan or the General Plan required by the California Government Code 65302. Properly prepared, these plans would include forecasts and analyses of future mineral needs, development of objectives and standards, comparison and evaluation of alternative plans, selection and detailing of one of the alternative plans, and specific implementation recommendations.

In California, one useful plan element is the Open Space Element required by the California Government Code Section 65560 et seq. This element could provide for the protection of specified recreational mineral resources such as gemstones, beach sands, and mineral waters. Another plan element is the Conservation Element required by the California Government Code Section 65302(d), under which areas are preserved specifically for mineral resources that can be economically extracted with minimum damage to the environment and existing development. This plan element should show the location, depth, areal extent, and estimated quantity of the mineral deposits. It should also consider accessibility, electric power, processing plants, market proximity, and the existing, interim, and ultimate land uses of the mineral sites.

For the implementation of such plan elements several methods are available, any of which if properly designed and enforced would protect and conserve the mineral resource until needed. These methods include zoning ordinances, special land-use regulations, or public acquisition depending upon state enabling legislation.

To permit interim use of a mineral deposit site until needed for mineral extraction, a Mineral Conservation District can be designed to permit nondevelopment-type uses such as crops, floriculture, plant nurseries, vineyards, hay, livestock, orchards, paddocks, recreation, and parklands, all of which involve little or no construction.

Proposals for extraction of the mineral resource would require an application for, and rezoning to, a Mineral Extraction District. Any extraction or separating of mineral resources would be conditioned use in such a district and require a special permit to which conditions of operation, reclamation, and sureties would be legally binding. Manufacture and processing not attendant upon, or related to, the extractive and separation operations would not be permitted in the Mineral Extraction District but would require an application for, and rezoning to, a Heavy Industrial District.

Planning for Regulation of the Extractive Operation

Regulations to ensure minimum environmental damage during mineral extraction should be considered in advance of the operation. Environmental problems vary with the type and location of the deposit, but some to be considered are: destruction of flora and fauna, erosion, flooding, siltation of streams and lakes, disruption of drainage patterns, clogging of ground-water intake areas, other ground-water contamination, surface-water pollution, damage to roads, and other property, stimulation of landslides, subsidence or faulting due to removal of fluids, noise, unsightliness, storage of toxic wastes, disposal of bittern, fires, traffic congestion, overloading of access roads, adverse effects on neighboring land values, and other losses or hazards.

Many of these problems can be prevented or mitigated by careful design and strict enforcement of performance standards, conditions, and financial sureties attached to a conditional use permit, or for publicly owned land, a public lease agreement. Performance standards for mineral extractive operations may be adopted as part of a city or county zoning ordinance or incorporated into a public lease agreement. Such performance standards may include specific controls on emissions, fire and explosive hazards, glare and heat, liquid and solid wastes, sound levels, odors, radioactivity, dust, electric disturbances, and vibrations.

In addition, the extraction can be controlled by the specific requirements of a conditional use permit or public lease agreement. For effective review the application for such a permit should include a description of the proposed operation, detailed list of equipment, machinery, and structures to be used, and source, quantity, and disposition of water. It should also include a photograph and survey of the site showing existing topography by contours, and vegetation, access roads, other proposed roads, and excavation depths. And, if complete, it contains a statement regarding the proposed reclamation program. Some of the conditions that may be attached to a conditional use permit, depending upon the type and location of extractive operation, include hours of operation, lighting control, fencing, traffic routes, parking requirements, spoil storage, landscaping, settling ponds, buffer zones, commencement and completion dates, deed restrictions, increased setbacks, filing of engineering maps, energy conversion, type of construction, special pollution-control equipment, and the stripping and stockpiling of topsoil, nutrient-rich rocks, or marginal ore.

Reclamation of the site and financial sureties to assure such reclamation can also be conditions attached to the conditional use permit or a public lease agreement. Although this subject is discussed below, it must be considered before an operation commences and be included as a part of the conditional use permit.

Planning for Reclamation of the Site

After land has been exploited for its mineral resources, its mineral potential has normally been completely removed. In the absence of any program for rehabilitation, after mineral extraction is completed, land containing either a mine or quarry will have become unsightly with open holes, piles of waste, and abandoned processing plants, and it may also include safety hazards such as open tunnels or unstable ground. With sufficient funds, an exploited area can be returned to a condition approximating its original appearance, but generally this is too costly to be practical and alternate better uses are available, especially if they have been anticipated and planned for.

Quarries made during the removal of sand and gravel need not be just holes to be filled in, as they can provide the basis for other desirable land use. With planned restructuring, a quarry area might be converted to a park, golf course, stadium, or safe target practice range. Multiple uses also are possible; for example, in Los Gatos lakes that are primarily ground-water percolation areas are used as duck and boating ponds, forming the focal area for a much-used civic park. Even sequential uses are available; for example, quarries have been used as solid-waste disposal areas until filled and then converted to park or agricultural land. It is thus obvious that quarries resulting from extraction of sand and gravel can be regarded as useful excavations rather than as eyesores, if imagination is used in the original planning. Rock quarries that are generally sited on hillsides are more of a problem, but a few might be given over to those who wish practice areas for their hobby of rock climbing.

Underground mine areas, which contain dangerous holes and piles of waste rock, are not readily converted to any other use, but fortunately most will be in mountainous areas containing land of minimal value. Locally, a few tunnels are now being used for bombproof storage of valuable records, for raising mushrooms, for aging wine, or as low-yield water tunnels to supply a ranch or two. Nevertheless, the need for abandoned mines for these purposes is limited. For safety most open mines can be sealed at the portal or shaft collar when no longer in use.

The most readily available means for ensuring the design and enforcement of a site reclamation program is to provide for this in a conditional use permit or public land agreement. This can specify the method and degree of land restoration or modification required, and it should lead to converting the land to continuing usefulness after the exhaustion of the mineral resource.

For successful reclamation, not only are a plan and regulatory conditions needed, but also strict enforcement is required. One method to ensure compliance with the conditions of the use permit is that of requiring of the applicant to file, before the permit is granted, financial sureties adequate for the regulatory agency or unit of government to repair any damage and to complete the restoration if the applicant faults. Fees adequate to provide for inspection, engineering, legal, and administration costs may also be required of the applicant.

Depending upon the type, size, and duration of the extractive operation, staged operations and reclamation may be required. Staging reduces the sureties required, allows modification of the conditions and reclamation program as experience is gained, and ensures that the first stage is restored before the second stage is permitted to begin. Staging the reclamation can also result in major savings, as it is much less expensive to perform earthmoving work concurrently with the extraction while heavy equipment is on the site.

SELECTED REFERENCES

Selected published materials that discuss environmental problems and suggested solutions related to mineral extractive operations are listed below for interested citizens and local officials.

Ahearn, V. P., Jr., 1964, Land use planning and the sand and gravel producer: Washington, D.C., Natl. Sand and Gravel Assoc., 30 pp.

American Society of Planning Officials, 1961, Land use control in the surface extraction of minerals: Inf. Rept. 153, pt. 1, 18 pp.

Bauer, A. M., 1965, Simultaneous excavation and rehabilitation of sand and gravel sites: Washington, D.C., Natl. Sand and Gravel Assoc., 60 pp.

California Council on Intergovernmental Relations, 1973, Guidelines for local general plans, State of California: California Council Intergovt. Relations, 91 pp.

California Division of Mines and Geology, 1972, Hazardous excavations: California Geol., pp. 247–57.

——, 1973, Urban geology, master plan for California: Phase 1: California Div. Mines and Geology, pp. 1-1–A-26.

Coates, D. R., ed., 1972, Environmental science workbook: New York State Univ. Pubs. in Geomorphology, 412 pp.

Council on Environmental Quality, 1973, The President's 1973 environmental program: Washington, U.S. Govt. Printing Office, 585 pp.

Evans, J. R., and Davis, F. F., 1973, Mining, waste discharge requirements, and water quality: California Geol. pp. 231–239.

Garvey, J. R., Chn., 1973, Research and applied technology symposium on mine-land reclamation, 1st, Pittsburgh, Pa.: Natl. Coal Assoc., 355 pp.

Rickert, D. A., and Spieker, A. M., 1971, Real-estate lakes: U.S. Geol. Survey Circ, 601-G, 19 pp.

U.S. Dept. of the Interior, 1967, Surface mining and our environment: Washington, U.S. Govt. Printing Office, 124 pp.

PART FIVE

Environmental Considerations of Urban Resource Development

Although many different types of pollution may be created through the use of a resource, the role of geology in pollution generation is greatest during either the extraction or post-use disposal of that resource. The preceding part of this book dealt mainly with resource availability and extraction in urban areas; in this part we are concerned with some of the processes and problems associated with waste disposal.

Acceptability of disposal systems is partially a function of social pressures. In many rural societies, it is not unusual to have uncontrolled dumping of solid wastes. As population density increases and more consumer goods are transferred into waste, open dumps become unacceptable and are replaced by sanitary landfills. Alternatives to traditional landfills are now being investigated. These include source reduction of waste, source classification for recycling, composting, and energy generation, all of which would reduce the volume of waste that needs to be buried.

The first article in this part looks at one of the important problems facing urban areas today— solid waste management. About 100 years ago, the average household obtained a 4-page newspaper each week, but now a 40-page daily newspaper is common. As recently as three decades ago, the family car was kept for many years, but now it is not expected to last beyond five. Convenience foods and excess packaging, together with the fascination for gadgets and the equating of "newer" with "better" have helped to precipitate the problem of waste generation. The magnitude of the problem and the constraints on landfill operation and availability have prompted a look at new technologies. City governments often do not have the expertise to evaluate the many recycling techniques that have been developed or proposed and to select the one most suitable for their needs. Thus our need for sanitary landfill sites is growing as landfill-siting regulations become more stringent. Site evaluation is becoming a more complex process, with a need to evaluate both the geology and hydrology of the site and the types of wastes to be buried. Sites suited to one type of waste may not be suited to another; a cattle feedlot creates different problems than an industrial complex. Potential for pollution is increased if geological site analysis or engineering is inadequate.

The second article in this part discusses a resource that urban areas may inherit from their topography—lakes. Although this article is primarily concerned with natural lakes, many of the processes and problems are also found in reservoirs and lakes created for real-estate developments. The geologists, planners, and engineers who must deal with urban lakes frequently do not understand the processes that occur in lakes. The natural life cycle of a lake, from oligotrophic to eutrophic, can be accelerated by human interference, thus lowering the lake's aesthetic and recreational values. Water quality in a lake is a result of physical, chemical, and biological factors. Increased sediment and fertilizer reaching the lake can shorten its life and reduce its value as an urban resource.

Pollution can be defined as a resource out of place. The third article in this part describes an example of an undesirable waste product, sewage sludge, being turned into a resource, fertilizer. The Metropolitan Sanitary District of Greater Chicago has acquired strip-mined land, and has found that by adding the nutrient-rich sludge, the land can be reclaimed quite successfully.

Application of both old and new technology to the problems of waste management is needed if we are to solve the problems of urban resource development in a quality environment.

23

Evaluating Pollution Potential of Land-based Waste Disposal, Santa Clara County, California

W. G. Hines

Introduction

As a result of recently initiated programs such as the San Francisco Bay Region Environment and Resources Planning Study, planners in the San Francisco Bay region are becoming increasingly aware of the types and possible uses of earth-science data. These data encompass a wide spectrum of disciplines including hydrology, topography, geology, geomorphology, and seismology. If properly integrated with the planner's competence in demography, sociology, economics, and other fields, earth-science data can be invaluable for evaluating and controlling many critical environmental problems in urban areas.

In a rapidly developing area such as the San Francisco Bay region, vital land and water resources can be seriously endangered if planners make land-use decisions that fail to adequately account for the existence of certain pollution hazards. These pollution hazards are basically a function of several interacting factors: (1) The type, location, and emission characteristics of pollution sources, (2) the proximity and sensitivity of land and water resources to these pollution sources, and (3) the existence of one or several critical physical conditions that may affect the generation, transport, and distribution of pollutants in the environment. An understanding of these factors and their interactions is a prerequisite for evaluating and controlling many of the pollution and waste-disposal problems encountered in the San Francisco Bay region.

Purpose and Scope

The purpose of this report is to acquaint planners with the utility of earth-science information for analyzing pollution and waste-disposal problems in relation to land-use planning and the protection of land and water resources. The following topics are emphasized:

(1) An identification and description of factors that interact to form pollution hazards.
(2) A presentation of selected examples of, and possible control measures for, pollution hazards typically encountered in the bay-region environment.
(3) Criteria and methodology needed for the preliminary evaluation of the suitability of land areas intended for waste-disposal sites.

Reprinted with permission of the author from *U.S. Geological Survey Water-Resources Investigations 31–73*, 1973, 21 pp.

Much of the discussion is keyed to Santa Clara County, a typical rapidly developing county in the San Francisco Bay region, for which selected physical information has been compiled.

Interacting Factors That Form Pollution Hazards

Major Sources of Pollution

Many sources of pollution have the potential for detrimental impact on the bay-region environment. Table 1 lists the major sources and types of pollutants that are most common in the bay region. The significance of each of the sources and types of pollutants varies considerably within specific locales. For example, a planner in San Jose might be most concerned with the effects of a new solid-waste landfill on a shallow ground-water reservoir whereas a planner in Marin County might be more concerned about how drainage from a dairy feedlot may affect the quality or usability of water from an adjacent stream. Thus, planners in different geographical areas may find it necessary to rank sources and types of pollutants in order of local importance.

After preparation of a list of the most important local pollution sources, the location of these sources can be mapped separately or identified on an existing map. Such a map can be helpful for evaluating potential pollution hazards, particularly if utilized in conjunction with resource information such as depicted on the accompanying Santa Clara County map. Regionwide information necessary for preparation of pollution-source maps has been compiled by Limerionos and Van Dine (1970), California Water Resources Control Board (1971), and Goss (1972). These publications include information on the location of municipal and industrial wastewater outfalls, descriptions of wastewater characteristics, and summaries of data on solid-waste disposal sites. Specific information on types and sources of pollutants within county or municipal jurisdictions usually can be obtained from sources identified in table 1.

Critical Land and Water Resources

In order to evaluate the overall significance of sources of pollution in an area, planners need to assess the sensitivity of major land and water resources to various types of pollution. Major land and water resources that are sensitive to pollution can be classified as critical resources that require special consideration with regard to land-use planning.

In a general sense, *critical land resources*[1] could be described as (1) land that is primarily used for man's living, working, and recreational habitat; and (2) biologically-productive land essential for the well-being of important plant and animal life and for a pleasing habitat for man's enjoyment. *Critical water resources* could be described as (1) those that supply man with water for drinking, hygienic, industrial, recreational, and agricultural purposes; and (2) those that support important aquatic and wildlife habitats.

Table 2 includes a list of critical land and water resources commonly found in the bay region. An example of each critical land or water resource listed in the first column of table 2 is given in the second column and each example can be identified on the large map[2] showing physical information or on the small maps[2] showing precipitation and estimated depth to the water table. Table 2 also includes a list of information sources that should be useful to planners wishing to gather data or prepare a map of critical land and water resources.

1. The description of critical land resources implies the importance of existing or proposed land use in assessing the critical nature of a particular land resource. Land use has often been classified in the context of sociopolitical considerations, but for convenience in this report certain land uses shown in table 2 have been classified with natural physical considerations.

2. Maps not included in this reprint.

TABLE 1. MAJOR SOURCES AND TYPES OF POLLUTANTS

Major types of pollutant emissions:

a. Noxious or toxic chemicals, acids, caustics, pesticides
b. Toxic metallic substances
c. Soluble and particulate organic substances
d. Nutrients, particularly compounds of nitrogen and phosphorus
e. Pathogenic microbes
f. Mineralized water
g. Airborne noxious or toxic gases, and particulate matter
h. Suspended sediment and turbidity
i. Debris (paper, rags, cans, trash)
j. Grease and oil

Source of pollutants	Type of pollutant	Possible additional sources of information
1. Agricultural wastes and irrigation return flows[1]	a,c,d,f	U.S. Department of Agriculture; California Department of Agriculture.
2. Animal wastes	c-e	U.S. Department of Agriculture; California Department of Agriculture.
3. Dredge spoils	a-d,h	U.S. Army Corps of Engineers, Bay Conservation and Development Commission.
4. Heavy construction or landscape alteration[1]	h,i	County planning and public works departments
5. Incinerators; open burning	b,g	Bay Area Air Pollution Control District
6. Industrial stack gases	b,g	Bay Area Air Pollution Control District
7. Junkyards	b,i,j	County planning departments
8. Mining and mine wastes	a,b,f,h	California Division of Mines and Geology
9. Motor vehicles	b,g,j	California Division of Highways; Bay Area Air Pollution Control District.
10. Pesticide spraying	a	U.S. Department of Agriculture; California Department of Agriculture.
11. Septic tanks[1]	a,c-e,j	County public health or environmental engineering departments.
12. Solid-waste disposal sites[1]	a-j	California Department of Public Health
13. Storm-water runoff[1]	a-e,h-j	County public works departments
14. Toxic-chemical storage areas	a,b	California Department of Industrial Relations; California Regional Water Quality Control Board, San Francisco Bay Region.
15. Municipal and industrial wastewater-treatment plants and outfalls[1]	a-j	California Regional Water Quality Control Board, San Francisco Bay Region.
16. Wastewater-injection wells	a,b,f	California Regional Water Quality Control Board, San Francisco Bay Region.
17. Watercraft	e,i,j	U.S. Coast Guard

[1] Most important source of pollutants.

TABLE 2. CRITICAL LAND AND WATER RESOURCES

Critical resources	Example on map[1] showing physical information	Information sources
Land resources		
1. Urban land	San Jose area	U.S. Geological Survey, Washington, D.C.; state and county planning departments.
2. Parks, campgrounds, game preserves, and large recreational areas.	Henry W. Coe State Park.	California Department of Parks and Recreation; county parks departments.
3. Marshlands	Areas identified by "marshlands pattern."	Bay Conservation and Development Commission
Water resources		
1. Shallow tidal reaches of the San Francisco Bay estuary.	Tidal sloughs near top of sheet 1.	Bay Conservation and Development Commission; U.S. Army Corps of Engineers; California Regional Water Quality Control Board, San Francisco Bay Region.
2. Major water-storage reservoirs,[2] lakes, and their immediate peripheral watershed areas.	Lake Elsman	California Water Resources Control Board; California Regional Water Quality Control Board, San Francisco Bay Region; county water departments.
3. Major recreational reservoirs, lakes, and their immediate peripheral watershed areas.	Anderson Reservoir	Do.
4. Major streams, rivers, and their immediate peripheral watershed areas.	Guadalupe River	Do.
5. Major ground-water reservoirs	See map showing estimated depth to water table for extent of principal aquifer system.	Webster (1972a,b,; 1973); county water departments
6. Major ground-water-recharge areas	Percolation ponds near Vasona Reservoir.	California Department of Water Resources; U.S. Geological Survey, Menlo Park, Calif; county water departments.

[1] Map not included.
[2] Many water-storage reservoirs are of multipurpose design. Planners should consider the most sensitive beneficial uses (drinking-water supply and fish propagation) when evaluating land-use plans.

Critical Physical Conditions

Certain naturally occurring physical conditions can accentuate pollution problems by facilitating the excessive generation, transport, or distribution of pollutants in the environment. These critical conditions are particularly important in the dynamic and physically diverse environment of the bay region. Table 3 lists eight critical conditions commonly encountered in the bay region, gives example pollution problems that may be caused by the various conditions, and shows possible sources of information for each critical condition.

Several of the physical phenomena described in table 3 have been recognized by planners and have, in fact, had a limited effect on land-use practices in the bay region. For example, local and county governments have ordinances requiring that septic-tank systems meet criteria relative to depth to ground water and soil permeability. In some places, flood-prone areas have been zoned to preclude intensive development. Road construction is restricted in certain areas where land slopes are steep and erosion problems are prevalent. In most places, however, such physical conditions have not been sufficiently recognized or evaluated with regard to their interactions with various types of land-use practices.

Evaluation and Control of Pollution Hazards

In previous discussion it was shown that the existence of a major pollution hazard is dependent upon the presence of at least two conditions: (1) A pollutable land or water resource within the sphere of influence of (2) a source of pollution. The pollution hazard is significantly increased when geologic and hydrologic conditions are such that they allow excessive generation, rapid transport, or distribution of pollutants. By utilizing information given in tables 1–3 and on a map showing appropriate physical information, planners have the initial tools needed for the identification and preliminary evaluation and control of many of the pollution hazards encountered in the bay region.

From information contained in tables 1–3, one could identify hundreds of unique pollution hazards. A description of a selected number of types of these pollution hazards and possible control measures is compiled in table 4 as a guide to planners for relating various land-use practices and planning activities to pollution hazards.

Preliminary Evaluation of Sites for Waste Disposal on Land

The information and methodology for the evaluation and control of pollution hazards are directly applicable to the preliminary evaluation of the suitability of land for several types of onland waste-disposal systems, hereafter referred to as land-based waste-disposal systems. The following four general types probably are of most interest to planners in the bay region:

1. Septic tanks
2. Solid-waste landfills
3. Wastewater-spray irrigation
4. Waste-containment ponds

Preliminary evaluation of potential land-based waste-disposal sites is perhaps best accomplished by placing potential sites on a map and identifying obvious constraints related to proximate land or water resources and the presence of critical earth-related conditions. For example, urban land is, with rare exception, preempted for use as a solid-waste landfill site. Similarly, it is not advisable to locate an evaporation pond for toxic industrial wastewater on land that is subject to flooding. An area with land slopes greater than 15 percent will not, without drastic alteration, be suited for septic tanks. By identifying these types of obvious constraints at an early stage of evaluation, large areas of land can be eliminated from unnecessary consideration. Areas not eliminated by obvious constraints then can be evaluated in more detail from the standpoint of hydrologic and geologic suitability in conjunction with the planner's concurrent evaluation of social, economic, and esthetic considerations.

TABLE 3. CRITICAL CONDITIONS, EXAMPLE POLLUTION PROBLEMS, AND INFORMATION SOURCES

Critical condition	Example pollution problems caused by the critical condition	Example on map[1] showing physical information	Information source
Flood-prone areas	Inundation of pollution sources; rapid transport and distribution of pollutants; damage to waste-treatment and waste-disposal facilities.	Area bordering Guadalupe River	Limerinos, Lee, and Lugo (1973), U.S. Geological Survey, Menlo Park, Calif., U.S. Army Corps of Engineers, San Francisco, Calif.
Severe land slopes	Rapid transport and distribution of discharged pollutants.	Area identified as having land slopes greater than 15 percent.	U.S. Geological Survey, Menlo Park, Calif.
Heavy precipitation	Dissolution and leaching of stored chemicals and other potentially polluting materials; increased production of polluted leachate and drainage at solid-waste landfills.	Areas on precipitation map where rainfall exceeds 50 in/yr.	Rantz (1971)
Shallow ground-water reservoir.	Pollution of ground-water system from septic tanks, solid-waste landfills, and other pollution sources.	Areas on map where depth-to-water is less than 10 feet.	Webster (1973), U.S. Geological Survey Menlo Park, Calif.
Highly permeable soil	Easy movement of pollutants to the ground-water system.	Areas where soil permeability is greater than 2.0 in/hr.	U.S. Soil Conservation Service (1968).
Susceptibility to erosion, gullying, or landsliding.	Excessive production of debris, sediment, and turbid water; damage to waste-treatment and waste-disposal facilities.	None. See information source	Brown and Jackson (1973)
Susceptibility to severe movement during earthquakes.	Damage to waste-treatment and waste-disposal facilities.	None. See information source	Brown (1970); Brown and Lee (1971) and U.S. Geological Survey, Menlo Park, Calif.
Bedrock or impermeable deposit near land surface.	Rapid transport and distribution of discharged pollutants in sloped areas; ponding of discharged pollutants in flat areas.	None. See information source	U.S. Geological Survey, Menlo Park, Calif. U.S. Soil Conservation Service.

[1]Map not included.

Criteria for Evaluating Land-Based Waste-Disposal Sites

The following publications were reviewed during the compilation of this report and aided in the formulation of land-based waste-disposal site criteria: Franks (1972); Schneider (1970); California Water Pollution Control Board (1961); Hughes, Landon, and Farvolden (1971); Geological Survey of Alabama (1971); U.S. Soil Conservation Service (1968); American Society of Civil Engineers (1959); Born and Stephenson (1969); Hughes and Cartwright (1972); Williams and Wallace (1970); California Department of Public Health (1968); and McGauhey, Krone, and Winneberger (1966).

Table 5 contains suggested criteria to assess the suitability of land for four types of land-based waste-disposal systems. The table includes criteria on land and water resources (criteria 1, 4, and 5); geologic and hydrologic phenomena (criteria 2, 3, and 6 through 10); numerical suitability ratings (on a scale of 0–3) for evaluating each of four types of land-based waste-disposal systems. Table 5 is intended as a guide for making site selections and assessments of areas under consideration for use in land-based waste-disposal systems. The criteria are not intended to preempt or replace local, state, or federal standards or regulations for land-based waste-disposal practices. Those wishing to obtain specific standards or regulations should contact county or state public health agencies, the California Regional Water Quality Control Board, San Francisco Bay Region, or the Environmental Protection Agency.

To use table 5 most effectively the following steps are suggested:

1. Compile and examine available data and information relative to the 10 criteria listed in the table.

2. Prepare a map, or maps, to summarize as much of this information as possible. (For example, maps showing information on land resources and land uses, land slopes, floods, surface-water resources, and soil permeabilities. Supplemental maps at a less detailed scale show information on precipitation and ground-water resources.)

3. Locate the proposed site of the land-based waste-disposal system on the map.

4. Evaluate the suitability of the proposed site on the basis of criteria and numerical ratings given in table 5. Sites receiving several "0's" or a mix of "0's" and "1's" usually can be eliminated from consideration. Sites receiving "3's" and "2's" and no "0's" or "1's" should be noted and reserved for further evaluation relative to remaining criteria not adequately defined by available information.

Criteria not evaluated in steps 1–4 above usually can be evaluated by aerial-photograph interpretation, site visitations, and field measurements. Criteria for erosion, geology, soil permeability, and ground-water resources commonly will have to be evaluated in this manner. For information on earthquakes and floods (in places where flood-prone areas have not been mapped), consultation with geologists and hydrologists may be necessary.

If the preliminary evaluation indicates that the site may be suitable, comprehensive field investigations can be undertaken to insure that no critical considerations were overlooked. Final design of a particular land-based waste-disposal facility should be made on the basis of data obtained from the field investigation. The nature and detail of the field investigation will depend upon several factors including size and type of facility, the quality of the preliminary evaluation, and the requirement for engineering modifications where potential pollution hazards are present. Generally, solid-waste landfills and wastewater-spray irrigation systems will require the most comprehensive field investigation.

TABLE 4. EXAMPLES OF POLLUTION HAZARDS WITH POSSIBLE IMPACTS AND CONTROL MEASURES

	Description of possible pollution hazard	Possible impact of hazard	Possible control measures for minimizing the existing hazard or for avoiding a similar hazard in the future
1.	Irrigation return flows from an agricultural area enter a stream which is utilized for a drinking water supply farther downstream.	The concentration of salts and pesticides in the stream is increased making it unsuitable for a drinking water supply.	a. Change to spray irrigation technique to preclude irrigation return flows. b. Divert return flows to a collection drain for discharge below the point of drinking water-supply usage. c. Zone upper watersheds of water-supply streams to preclude intensive irrigated agricultural development.
2.	A dairy-cattle feedlot is located on permeable land above a shallow ground-water reservoir.	The ground-water reservoir becomes contaminated with fecal bacteria and nitrate.	a. Move the feedlot to less permeable land that does not overlie a shallow ground-water reservoir. b. Construct an impermeable liner under the feedlot and install a wastewater collection and treatment system. c. Require future feedlot sites to meet waste containment pond criteria (table 5) or to be carefully engineered to control pollutant emissions.
3.	Navigation dredge spoils are placed on a tidal mudflat in the marshlands.	A waterfowl feeding area is ruined	a. Prohibit the disposition of dredge spoils in the marshlands. b. Allow future disposition of dredge spoils only in areas specified by the U.S. Army Corps of Engineers.
4.	Massive earthmoving, road work, and vegetation removal begin during September as the preliminary phase of subdivision construction.	Heavy erosion, gullying, and sediment transport commence with the first rains in November. A downstream watershed is choked with debris.	a. Install temporary drainage facilities and sediment entrapment basins around construction areas. b. Schedule heavy construction projects to avoid landscape disturbance during the rainy season. c. Limit vegetation removal to a minimum in all projects. d. Prohibit heavy construction, particularly extensive road networks, in highly erodable areas. Zone these areas for limited development whenever possible.
5.	A large incinerator is operated near a ground-water recharge basin.	Soot and noxious particulate matter are deposited in the recharge basin. Water quality is degraded and the bottom of the recharge basin is clogged.	a. Increase incineration efficiency and treatment of emissions. b. Close or move the incinerator. c. Locate future incinerator sites in remote areas, downwind of critical land and water resources.
6.	Noxious sulfur and nitrous oxides are emitted in the stack gases of an industrial plant located adjacent to an urban residential area.	Air pollution endangers public health and damages residential structures.	a. Provide increased treatment for stack gases. b. Zone land so as to prohibit conflicts between industrial and residential land use. Allow only light, nonpolluting industries to locate in areas adjacent to residential developments.
7.	A large automobile salvage yard is located on the marshlands.	Drainage (water, oil, and grease) from the salvage yard enters a tidal slough and endangers shellfish.	a. Incorporate grease traps in drainage facilities. b. Divert drainage to the municipal storm-sewer system. c. Zone marshlands to prohibit the location of automobile salvage yards.
8.	A remote county park becomes crowded with motor vehicles during summer weekends.	Obnoxious fumes, dust, and noise threaten the esthetic appeal and enjoyment of the park.	a. Discourage vehicular traffic in the park by using shuttle buses and by encouraging more pedestrian and bicycle traffic. b. Plan future remote parks to accomodate large crowds without reliance on motor vehicles for transportation.
9.	Herbicides are heavily applied in a flood-control channel to eradicate dense growths of weeds. The channel leads to a tidal slough.	Herbicides concentrate in the bottom sediment of the slough and endanger aquatic life.	a. Replace herbicide applications with mechanical weed-control methods. b. Reduce the quantity of herbicide application and use short-lived biodegradable types. c. Design flood-control channels and zone surrounding flood plains to accommodate a reasonable amount of seasonal weed growth (that is, expect weeds and other debris to cause somewhat increased water levels during floods).

10. A village septic tank drainage field located on steeply sloped, impermeable land erodes and overflows during a rainstorm.	A downstream watershed is polluted with nutrients and fecal bacteria.	a. Move the drainage field to flatter, more permeable land less susceptible to erosion. b. Install a wastewater-collection system and a simple, efficient treatment facility such as a multistage oxidation pond. c. Plan future septic-tank systems to meet site criteria similar to those shown in table 5 or to be engineered to preclude pollution problems.
11. A solid-waste landfill is located on permeable land overlying a shallow ground-water reservoir. A heavy rain produces a large quantity of leachate.	The ground-water reservoir is polluted with organic compounds, hydrogen sulfide, toxic trace metals, and other noxious material.	a. Seal the landfill with an impermeable layer of clay and close. b. Move the landfill to a new site located on less permeable land where ground water is at greater depth. c. Plan future landfills to meet site criteria similar to that shown in table 5 or to be engineered to control pollution problems.
12. Storm-water runoff from a parking lot at an urban shopping center enters a pond at a nearby recreational park.	Floatable debris, greases and oils, and toxic materials such as lead are deposited in the pond.	a. Clean the parking lot thoroughly and often—especially just before and during the seasonal runoff period. b. Construct grease and debris traps in the parking-lot-drainage system. c. Divert drainage to the municipal storm-sewer system. d. Design future recreational ponds and lakes to include provision for periodic dredging and flushing with high quality water. e. Plan future recreational ponds to exclude runoff from areas contaminated by motor vehicles.
13. Liquid chlorine is stored in containers adjacent to an industrial plant in an area prone to flooding.	A large flood inundates the area, damages the storage containers, and causes the release of toxic chlorine gas.	a. Build flood protection levees and spillage-containment structures around toxic chemical-storage facilities. b. Move the storage facilities to an area not prone to flood damage. c. Zone flood-prone areas to prohibit the storage of toxic chemical materials.
14. A municipal sewage-treatment plant is located on poorly-consolidated land on the periphery of San Francisco Bay.	An earthquake damages the plant and causes raw sewage to be discharged to the bay.	a. Install emergency wastewater-holding and treatment facilities to preclude discharge of raw sewage. b. Incorporate earthquake protection considerations into all future plant and pipeline designs.
15. Brine wastes from an industrial process are injected into a well for underground disposal.	The quality of water in the ground-water reservoir is degraded by salt-water encroachment.	a. Close the injection well and construct another facility, such as an evaporation pond, for disposal of the brine waste. b. Prohibit the future use of wastewater-injection wells unless a comprehensive geologic investigation is undertaken to insure that brines can be injected safely.
16. Powerboats are allowed to operate on a small reservoir used for a drinking water supply.	Gas and oil spillage from boats pollute the reservoir.	a. Prohibit the use of powerboats
17. A large pile of waste ore from an abandoned mercury mine is located near a major stream.	A flood transports the waste ore into a downstream recreation reservoir. High mercury concentrations are detected in fish which inhabit the reservoir.	a. Require that waste ore from mining operations not be placed in areas prone to flooding. b. Contact State or Federal environmental regulatory agencies to investigate the contamination problem and make recommendations for control measures.

TABLE 5. PRELIMINARY SUITABILITY EVALUATION OF PROPOSED LAND-BASED WASTE-DISPOSAL SITES

[0, unsuitable; 1, poor suitability; 2, moderate to good suitability; 3, most suitable]

Criteria for consideration	Septic tanks	Solid-waste landfills	Wastewater-spray irrigation	Waste-containment ponds	Comment
1. Land resources and land use[1]					
a. Urban	0-1	0	0	0	Septic tanks may be the only possible method of domestic wastewater treatment in isolated recreational areas. In some locations parks and recreational areas can be reclaimed from land previously used as a land-fill. Small-scale spray irrigation systems may be feasible under controlled conditions for parks, golf courses, and other vegetated areas.
b. Parks, campgrounds, game preserves, and large recreational areas.	*1	*0	*1	0	
c. Marshlands	0	0	0	0	
d. Agricultural	1-3	1	3	1-2	
e. Open space	3	3	3	3	
2. Land slope[1]					
a. 0 to 5 percent	3	3	3	3	Slopes greater than 15 percent can be built upon only with great precaution.
b. 5 to 15 percent	1-2	1-2	1-2	1-2	
c. Greater than 15 percent	0	0	0	0	
3. Floods[1]					
Within flood-prone areas (100-year flood).	0	0	0	0	Normally, flood-prone-area mapping for the bay region is based upon a flood with a theoretical recurrence interval of 100 years corrected for present-day flood-control facilities.
4. Surface-water resources[1]					
a. Within 1,000 ft of major domestic water-supply reservoir, lake, or stream.	0	0	0	0	Land-based waste-disposal systems should be located as far away from and as far downstream of surface-water resources as possible. It may be possible in many cases to locate land-based waste-disposal sites closer to surface-water resources provided that engineering safeguards are included in the design of facilities.
b. Within 500 ft of major tidal water or reservoir, lake, or stream utilized for recreation or non-domestic water supply.	0	0	0	0	
c. Within immediate peripheral watershed of major water-supply or recreational reservoir, lake, or stream.	0-1	0-1	0-1	0-1	
5. Precipitation[1] (mean annual)					
a. Greater than 50 inches	0	0	0	0	Precipitation criteria presented here applies to the San Francisco Bay region. For detailed evaluation, a proposed site should be studied to determine expected monthly or weekly rainfall and evaporation rates. The difference between rainfall and evaporation can be used to estimate possible quantities of leachate production in landfills or overloading of septic tank fields.
b. 30 to 50 inches	1	1	1	1	
c. 20 to 30 inches	2	2	2	2	
d. 0 to 20 inches	3	3	3	3	

				Comment
6. Ground-water resources[2]				Depth-to-ground-water criteria should be based upon the depth-to-the-seasonal high level of the saturated zone (water table). In much of the bay region, the water table is <u>not</u> accurately defined by the level at which water stands in wells. In many cases, the water level in wells is either above or below the water table because of upward or downward components of ground-water flow. Planners involved in site evaluations should consult with ground-water geologists or hydrologists who have knowledge of the area in question.
a. Within 1,000 ft of major ground-water recharge basin.*	0	0	0	
Depth to ground water from land surface.*				
b. 0 to 10 ft	0	0	0	
c. 10 to 50 ft	1	1	1	
d. 50 to 100 ft	2	2	2	
e. Greater than 100 feet	3	3	3	
7. Soil permeability[2,3]				Desired permeability range for wastewater spray irrigation depends upon whether the system is designed for infiltration or overland runoff. Permeability data always should be examined in conjunction with depth-to-water data to preclude ground-water pollution in areas where wastes are applied to high permeability soils.
a. 0 to 0.2 in/hr	0	*	3	
b. 0.2 to 0.63 in/hr	1-2	*	1-2	
c. 0.63 to 2.0 in/hr	2-3	*	0-1	
d. Greater than 2.0 in/hr	3	*	0	
8. Erosion[2] Within area of active landsliding, gullying or obvious surface instability	0	0	0	Planners should be aware that even limited vegetation removal or construction in the bay region can initiate erosion problems.
9. Geology[2] Bedrock or impermeable deposits exposed or near land surface.	0	*0	*0	Solid-waste landfills and waste-containment ponds can be located on level impermeable bedrock if diked and properly designed for collection and treatment of leachate.
10. Earthquakes[2] Areas peripheral to active faults and areas underlain by unconsolidated deposits susceptible to severe shaking.	0	0	0	Any part of a land-based waste-disposal facility requiring pipelines, holding ponds, or treatment works should be examined with regard to earthquake susceptibility.

[1] Criteria for land resources and land use, land slope, floods, surface-water resources, and precipitation usually can be evaluated first because data normally are available.

[2] Criteria for ground-water resources, soil permeability, erosion, geology, and earthquakes usually are not adequately described by available data. These criteria usually need be evaluated only for sites not eliminated on the basis of criteria in footnote 1.

[3] Soils are often not homogeneous in character with respect to depth or horizontal extent. Therefore, soil permeability rates obtained from existing soils maps should be verified with field data before final site selection.

*See comment column.

Discussion and Conclusions

The evaluation and control of pollution hazards and preliminary evaluation of sites for land-based waste-disposal systems are but two of the many potential uses of earth-sciences information. Planners in most urban areas are increasingly being called upon to provide more sophisticated means of predicting and controlling environmental impacts associated with urbanization, resource development, and land-use practice. This need can be best met if planners are able to formulate land-use plans that are compatible with the types of constraints described in this report. These constraints and the nature of hydrologic and geologic information needed to evaluate them vary depending upon the particular type of land use intended. However, the compilation of available earth-science information on a map is often sufficient to form a basis for a preliminary impact assessment of alternative land-use plans.

As planners gain knowledge about an area's unique physical conditions and other factors such as pollution sources, land-use planning can be conducted on the basis of a rational environmental analysis. Hazards can be identified in advance of development and avoided or effectively controlled. Economic, social, and esthetic benefits will accrue as land-use practices are tailored to conform with the land's developmental capacities.

REFERENCES CITED

Alabama Geological Survey, 1971, Environmental geology and hydrology, Madison County, Alabama, Meridianville quadrangle: Atlas Series 1, 71 pp.

American Society of Civil Engineers, 1959, Sanitary land fill: Am. Soc. Civil Engineers, Manuals of Engineering Practice No. 39, 61 pp.

Born, S. M., and Stephenson, D. A., 1969, Hydrogeologic considerations in liquid waste disposal: Jour. Soil and Water Conserv., v. 24, no. 2, pp. 52–55.

Brown, R. D., Jr., 1970, Faults that are historically active or that show evidence of geologically young surface displacement, San Francisco Bay region, A progress report: U.S. Geol. Misc. Field Studies Map MF-331.

Brown, R. D., Jr., and Lee, W. H. K., 1971, Active faults and preliminary earthquake epicenters (1969–70) in the southern part of the San Francisco Bay region: U.S. Geol. Survey Misc. Field Studies Map MF-307.

Brown, W. M., 3d, and Jackson, L. E., Jr., 1973, Erosional and depositional provinces and sediment transport in the south and central part of the San Francisco Bay region, California: U.S. Geol. Survey Misc. Field Studies Map MF-515.

California Department of Public Health, 1968, Solid wastes and water quality—a study of solid wastes disposal and their effect on water quality in the San Francisco Bay-delta area: Prepared for the California Water Resources Control Board, 6 chap. and app.

California Water Pollution Control Board, 1961, Effects of refuse dumps on ground water quality: Pub. no. 24, 107 pp.

California Water Resources Control Board, 1971, Interim water quality control plan for the San Francisco Bay basin (basin 2): 72 pp.

Franks, A. L., 1972, Geology for individual sewage disposal systems: California Geology, v. 25, no. 9, pp. 195–203.

Goss, Joseph, 1972, Solid-waste disposal in the San Francisco Bay region: U.S. Geol. Survey Misc. Field Studies Map MF-430.

Hughes, G. M., and Cartwright, Keros, 1972, Scientific and administrative criteria for shallow waste disposal: Civil Eng., v. 42, no. 3, pp. 70–3.

Hughes, G. M., Landon, R. A., and Farvolden, R. N., 1971, Hydrogeology of solid waste disposal sites in northeastern Illinois: Prepared for the U.S. Environmental Protection Agency, EPA pub. SW-12d, 154 pp.

Limerinos, J. T., and Van Dine, Karen, 1970, Map showing areas serviced by municipal and private sewerage agencies, San Francisco Bay region, California, 1970 (revised and reprinted, 1971): U.S. Geol. Survey Misc. Field Studies Map MF-330.

Limerinos, J. T., Lee, K. W., and Lugo, P. E., 1973, Flood-prone areas in the San Francisco Bay region, California: U.S. Geol. Survey Water-Resources Investigations 37–73, 3 maps.

McGauhey, P. H., Krone, R. B., and Winneberger, J. H., 1966, Soil mantle as a wastewater treatment system—review of literature: Sanitary Eng. Research Lab., rept. no. 66–7, California Univ., Berkeley, 120 pp.

Rantz, S. E., 1971, Mean annual precipitation and precipitation depth-duration-frequency data for the San Francisco Bay region, California: U.S. Geol. Survey open-file report, 23 pp.

Schneider, W. J., 1970, Hydrologic implications of solid waste disposal: U.S. Geol. Survey Circ. 601-F, 10 pp.

U.S. Soil Conservation Service, 1968, Soils of Santa Clara County: 227 pp. with accompanying soils map.

Webster, D. A., 1972a, Map showing ranges in probable maximum well yield from water-bearing rocks in the San Francisco Bay region, California: U.S. Geol. Survey Misc. Field Studies Map-431.

———, 1972b, Map showing areas in the San Francisco Bay region where nitrate, boron, and dissolved solids in ground water may influence local or regional development: U.S. Geol. Survey Misc. Field Studies Map MF-432.

———, 1973, Map showing areas bordering the southern part of San Francisco Bay where a high water table may adversely affect land use: U.S. Geol. Survey Misc. Field Studies Map MF-530.

Williams, R. E., and Wallace, A. T., 1970, Hydrogeological aspects of the selection of refuse disposal sites in Idaho: Idaho Bur. Mines and Geology Pamph. 145, 31 pp.

An Introduction to the Processes, Problems, and Management of Urban Lakes

L. J. Britton, R. C. Averett, and R. F. Ferreira

Lakes and reservoirs are significant and ever-changing features of the landscape. Because they form in depressions on the earth's surface, they are depositories for material moved by both air and water. Their ultimate fate is to become filled with sediment and support terrestrial life.

Man's attraction to lakes is well marked in his history. Yet, in spite of his long use of lakes and reservoirs for water supplies, waste disposal, power generation, navigation, and recreation, he understands very little of their characteristics. The study of inland waters (limnology) is less than 100 years old (Welch, 1952, p. 4) and only in the past several decades has a significant literature developed.

Much recent literature on limnology has been concerned with eutrophication, the enrichment and filling of lakes with plants and sediment. Today, accelerated eutrophication, resulting from man's activities, is a serious problem in many lakes. As a result, new approaches to lake and reservoir management are being sought, and public awareness of the need for lake management is increasing.

Many lakes and reservoirs, which were once far removed from significant human impact, are now found near the edges and sometimes well within urban areas. Thus urban planners are now faced with the task of managing lakes for maximum public benefit.

Urban lakes and reservoirs have a multitude of uses, and lake management must take these uses into consideration. In many areas, natural lakes are scarce, and reservoirs have been formed to provide water for agricultural and domestic consumption, as well as for recreation.

While reservoirs differ somewhat from natural lakes, both have a number of characteristics and problems in common. Unless otherwise specified, the term "lake" will be used in this report to denote both natural and manmade standing bodies of water.

The framework for this circular is based upon experience in studying lakes of the San Francisco Bay area. While urban lakes in other parts of the country may have somewhat different physical, chemical, and biological characteristics than those near San Francisco, all such lakes have one thing in common—intensive use of their water and watersheds by the public. The result is a need for greater understanding of lake processes, and how lakes can be managed to insure the highest possible quality of water compatible with optimum use.

Ownership and management of urban lakes are under the jurisdiction of various agencies. Too often each agency collects limnological data independently of the other agencies, and a comparison of

Extracted from *U.S. Geological Survey Circular 601-K*, 1975, 22 pp.

results between lakes is difficult to make. Consequently, there is a need for consistency and accuracy of sampling and sampling techniques if a meaningful comparison is to be made.

What This Report Is All About

This circular was written as a part of a comprehensive reconnaissance of the physical resources of the San Francisco Bay area begun in 1969 by the U.S. Geological Survey, in cooperation with the Department of Housing and Urban Development.

Specifically the circular has three major objectives:

1. To provide the urban planner with a brief introduction to the properties and processes of lakes and how these properties and processes affect water quality.
2. To inform the urban planner of common lake problems and possible management solutions to these problems.
3. To provide the urban planner with guidelines for making lake reconnaissance surveys.[1]

Pertinent literature on the various subjects discussed is referenced, and the reader is urged to consult the literature for a more thorough discourse. Problems and management of real-estate lakes, lakes created for particular housing or commercial areas or developments, have been thoroughly covered in a report by Rickert and Spieker (1971).

Physics, Chemistry and Biology of Lakes

The physical, chemical and biological systems of lakes are complex and interrelated. Any one influences and is influenced by the others. For example, sunlight penetrating the water triggers the growth of phytoplankton (floating one-celled plants). If conditions are favorable, the phytoplankton become so numerous that they reduce light penetration. Reduced light penetration may not only result in the arrest of continued phytoplankton production, but it may also influence the rate of warming of the lake water by the sun (Welch, 1952, p. 176). Thus a biological process (phytoplankton production) is influenced by and influences light penetration, which in turn influences the heat balance of the lake.

Physical Characteristics

Light Penetration. Limnologists have defined distinct zones in lakes, based upon the extent of light penetration in the water (figure 1). The *littoral zone* is the shallow-water area where light reaches the bottom. At times, wave action may cause shoreline erosion and bring materials into suspension in the water. These suspended materials may cause a "turbid" condition and reduce the penetration of light and thus the depth of the littoral zone. Emersed (above water) and submersed (below water) rooted green plants grow in the littoral zone.

The *limnetic zone* is the open-water area of a lake that extends from the surface to the depth where light intensity is reduced to about one percent of the surface light (Odum, 1971, p. 301). In theory, the lower boundary of this zone is the *compensation level,* which is the depth at which oxygen uptake by bacteria, plant, and animal respiration equals photosynthetic oxygen release by green plants. The depth of the compensation level depends upon the light-scattering and absorbing material in the water. The limnetic zone is inhabited by free-floating and swimming organisms, such as plankton and fish. The combined littoral and limnetic zones are referred to as the *euphotic zone,* the area where there is sufficient light for photosynthesis.

The *profundal zone* is the deepwater area where only respiration and decomposition occur. Light intensity is too low in the profundal zone for photosynthesis to occur. Therefore, organisms that live in the profundal zone depend upon food produced in the euphotic zone. Major profundal-zone organisms are zooplankton, benthic invertebrates, fungi, and bacteria.

1. In original report, USGS Circular 601-K.

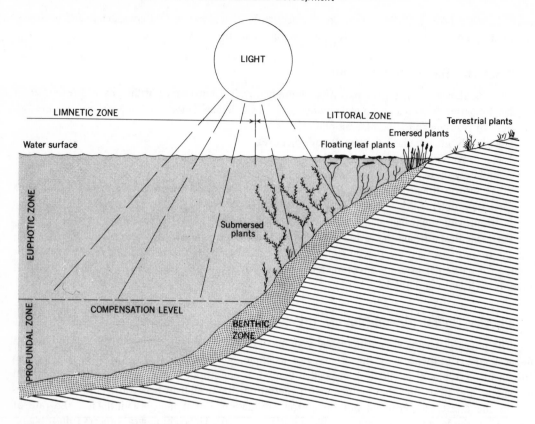

FIGURE 1. The major life zones of a lake.

The *benthic zone* is the lake bottom, where falling material accumulates and decomposes. It is inhabited by numerous types of burrowing animals.

Temperature. The thermal properties of a lake are controlled by the length of exposure and intensity of the sun on the lake, by materials in the water which scatter and absorb light, and by wind mixing. Thermal stratification is most pronounced during the summer in lakes of the warmer latitudes, and water-quality conditions often become critical in the deep water because the water is stagnant.

Water is unique in that it reaches its greatest density at $4°$ C (actually $3.98°$ C). At temperatures above or below $4°$ C, the density of water decreases. This property of water results in a regular pattern of seasonal mixing and stratification in many lakes.

Figure 2 shows the thermal profiles for warm monomictic lakes (Hutchinson, 1957, p. 438), such as those in the San Francisco Bay area. In autumn, the surface water of the lake begins to cool and becomes more dense. The cool, dense surface water sinks or is circulated by the wind, and mixes with the warmer, less dense water below. Wind action aids the mixing process until the entire water mass becomes *homothermous* (same temperature) and has the same density throughout. The lake is then in its most unstable condition, and wind action can mix the entire water mass. At this time the lake is in the autumn overturn period, and the deeper water becomes oxygenated.

With the onset of winter, cool air continues to lower the temperature of the lake water. During the winter the lake remains homothermous and well mixed, resulting in a uniform distribution of the chemical constituents in the lake.

In the early spring, increasing exposure to the sun warms the surface water, which becomes less dense than the cooler underlying water. Continued heating during late spring and summer results in thermal and density stratification, which limits wind mixing to the upper water layer. The result is

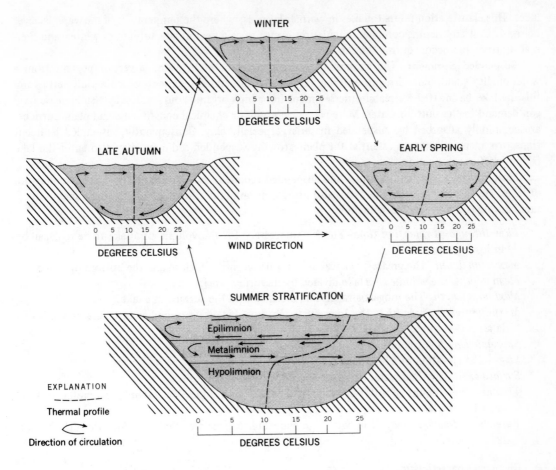

FIGURE 2. Seasonal thermal profiles of a warm monomictic lake.

the formation of three water layers. The upper water layer, the *epilimnion,* is thermally uniform and contains the warmest water in the lake. The lower water layer, the *hypolimnion,* is usually thermally uniform and contains the coldest and most dense water in the lake. Between these two layers is the *metalimnion,* a water mass with a temperature that rapidly decreases with depth. When these three water layers are distinct, the lake is thermally stratified and is referred to as being in the summer stagnation period (Welch, 1952, p. 59). With the cooler air of autumn, the surface water of the lake begins to cool, and the annual thermal cycle repeats itself.

There are many variations in the thermal cycle. In colder areas, the surface water freezes in the winter. Once the lake surface is frozen, circulation by wind action is prevented, and further loss of heat to the atmosphere is reduced. The water just below the ice is near freezing, but the water at greater depths may only cool to the temperature of maximum density ($4°$ C). Thus, inverse thermal stratification may occur in these lakes during the winter.

Many shallow lakes become stratified during periods of calm, but may be completely mixed by moderate winds. Moreover, shallow lakes of small surface area are more quickly heated or cooled by atmospheric or other external influences than deep lakes of relatively larger surface area. Other lakes are continuously mixed and thermal stratification never occurs.

There are several schemes for the classification of lakes, but that proposed by Hutchinson (1957, p. 438) is perhaps the most useful. His classification is based upon the thermal and circulation patterns of lakes. For example, the San Francisco Bay area lakes would be classified as *warm monomictic* lakes. This classification refers to lakes in warmer latitudes where the temperature of the water is never below 4° C at any depth, complete circulation occurs once a year in late autumn or winter, and thermal stratification occurs during the summer.

Suspended Sediment. The amount of suspended sediment in water is very important from a water-quality standpoint. Streams entering lakes carry suspended sediment, which rapidly settles and fills the lake basin. If the streamborne sediment has a high organic content, it may also increase oxygen demand in the bottom water. Moreover, several minor chemical constituents and plant nutrients are commonly adsorbed by suspended material, especially clay. Consequently, suspended sediment transports many substances essential for plant growth. Suspended sediment may also enter the lake from runoff or wave action.

Morphology. Light, temperature, and suspended sediment are important physical characteristics of lakes. However, other characteristics also provide meaningful information, and are frequently measured during lake surveys. These include:

Flow-through or *retention time*—The time necessary for the volume of a lake to be replaced by inflowing water.

Maximum depth—The greatest vertical distance between the surface and the bottom of a lake.

Mean depth—The volume of a lake divided by its surface area.

Maximum length—The longest straight-line distance over the surface of a lake.

Maximum width (breadth)—The longest straight-line distance perpendicular to the long axis of a lake.

Shoreline length—Circumference of a lake.

Stage—The elevation of a lake surface.

Surface area—The total water surface enclosed within a lakeshore.

Volume—The amount of water in a lake basin at any given time. *Maximum volume* refers to total capacity of a lake.

Watershed (drainage area)—The total land and water surface area that is drained through the outlet of a lake.

Chemical Characteristics

Chemical constituents in water consist of dissolved solids, such as calcium and magnesium, gases, such as oxygen and carbon dioxide, and organic compounds. The chemical characteristics of lakes are very important from the standpoint of water quality. Useful categories for discussing the chemical properties of water are (1) major chemical constituents, (2) minor chemical constituents, (3) major plant nutrients, and (4) dissolved gases. A complete discussion of the individual constituents in these categories is given in Hem (1970).

In the analyses of water for chemical constituents and major plant nutrients, the constituents may be in solution or sorbed (taken up) by particulate matter. The separation of dissolved and particulate materials is accomplished by filtration. Usually a filter having a pore size of 0.45 micrometre is used. However, some of the materials that pass through a filter of this pore size may be colloidal and not truly in solution (Hem, 1970, pp. 87-8). But from a practical standpoint, dissolved materials are those not removed when the water is filtered.

Major Chemical Constituents. The major chemical constituents of dissolved solids in freshwater are listed below. The concentration of major chemical constituents is usually expressed in mg/l (milligrams per litre). Simple and accurate methods are available for their analysis, and for this reason, they are commonly determined in most lake studies. Under natural conditions, the concentrations of these constituents are related primarily to the minerals in the surrounding rocks. However, man's waste materials may add significant amounts of these constituents to water. An analysis of major chemical constituents is of value in assessing pollution and eutrophication problems in lakes. Most, if not all, of the major chemical constituents are essential for the growth of plants.

Major chemical constituents

Silica (SiO$_2$)	Carbonate (CO$_3$)
Calcium (Ca)	Sulfate (SO$_4$)
Magnesium (Mg)	Chloride (Cl)
Sodium (Na)	Fluoride (F)
Potassium (K)	Nitrate (NO$_3$)
Bicarbonate (HCO$_3$)	

Minor Chemical Constituents. The minor chemical constituents occur in low concentrations in water (generally less than 1 mg/l). Their concentrations are usually expressed in μg/l (micrograms per litre), which is one thousandth of 1 mg/l. Minor chemical constituents are important in water, as most of them are essential plant nutrients. Moreover, when found in even modest concentrations, some may be toxic to plants and animals. Some of the minor chemical constituents found in freshwater are listed below.

Minor chemical constituents

Aluminum (Al)	Copper (Cu)
Iron (Fe)	Lead (Pb)
Manganese (Mn)	Mercury (Hg)
Boron (B)	Molybdenum (Mo)
Arsenic (As)	Nickel (Ni)
Bismuth (Bi)	Titanium (Ti)
Cadmium (Cd)	Vanadium (V)
Chromium (Cr)	Zinc (Zn)
Cobalt (Co)	

Major Plant Nutrients. A nutrient is any substance necessary for the promotion of growth, repair of tissue, or energy needs of an organism (Fruh, 1967). Nitrogen, phosphorus, and carbon (in their several forms) are considered to be the major plant nutrients because their concentrations in water are most likely to be exhausted by phytoplankton and limit further growth (Talling, 1962). However, a literature review by Greeson (1971, p. 75) revealed that there are at least 21 elements, in some chemical combination, essential for the growth of phytoplankton (table 1). Most of these elements do not become limiting in water.

Dissolved Gases. The dissolved gases that are commonly measured in water are oxygen and carbon dioxide. While carbon dioxide is the end product of respiration, it is also a form of carbon that green plants can use in photosynthesis to form organic compounds used for cell structure and metabolism. During the photosynthetic process plants consume carbon dioxide and produce oxygen. This oxygen may be reused by plants and animals in respiration.

Usually the carbon dioxide concentration in water is not measured directly because of analytical difficulties. Dissolved oxygen, however, can be accurately determined using field techniques. As a result, oxygen is the gas commonly measured during lake surveys.

Biological Characteristics

Lakes support a great variety of bacteria, plankton, higher plants, insect and fish species (figure 3). These organisms can be placed into three broad categories: plankton (drifters and some swimmers), benthos (bottom-dwellers), and nekton (swimmers). The relationships and interactions among these various groups of organisms must be considered if a lake is to be successfully managed for aquatic crop production or for the control of biological nuisances.

Plant and animal life are affected by changes in water quality. Lakes are relatively closed systems, and interacting organisms remain in balance only in suitable water-quality conditions. The introduction

TABLE 1. COMMON FORMS, MINIMUM REQUIREMENTS, AND SOME SOURCES OF ELEMENTS ESSENTIAL FOR THE GROWTH OF ALGAE

[The minimum nutrient requirements of algae in the aquatic environment are difficult to determine, and this uncertainty is shown by the wide range of concentrations in the table. "Trace" quantities generally refer to concentrations less than 1 mg/l, and more exact concentration requirements for these elements have not been determined. "Quantities always sufficient in surrounding medium" refers to those elements that are never below minimum concentrations so as to limit algal growth]

Element[1]	Symbol	Some common forms in water[1] [2]	Minimum requirements[3]	Examples of natural sources[1] [4]	Examples of manmade sources[5] [6] [7]
Aluminum	Al	Al^{+3}, $AlSO_4$, AlO_2, (salts of aluminum)	Probably trace quantities	Clay minerals, silicate rock minerals	Domestic sewage, industrial wastes, mine drainage.
Boron	B	B, H_3BO_3	100 $\mu g/l$	Evaporite deposits, igneous rock minerals, springs, volcanic gases	Cleaning aids, detergents, industrial wastes, irrigation, sewage.
Calcium	Ca	Ca^{+2}, $CaCO_3$, $CaSO_4$	20 mg/l	Igneous rock minerals, rainwater, sedimentary rocks, soil	Industrial wastes (metallurgy, steelmaking), treatment plant wastes.
Carbon	C	CO_2, CO_3, HCO_3, H_2CO_3, $CaCO_3$	Quantities always sufficient in surrounding medium	Atmosphere, organic compounds and decay products, rainwater, soil	Industrial wastes (carbonation, metallurgy, pulp and paper, soda, and steelmaking), domestic sewage.
Chlorine	Cl	Cl^{-1}, (oxides of chlorine)	Trace quantities	Evaporite deposits, igneous rock minerals, ocean water, rainwater, sedimentary rocks, volcanic gases	Chlorinated hydrocarbon process, cleaning aids, industrial wastes (petroleum and refining), irrigation, salt mining.
Cobalt	Co	Co	500 $\mu g/l$	Coal ash, soil, ultramafic rocks	Manufacturing wastes (tools and instruments), metallurgy.
Copper	Cu	Cu^{+2}, Cu, $CuSO_4$	6.0 $\mu g/l$	Crustal rocks, ground water, marine animals	Industrial wastes (fabrication of pipes, refining, smelting), manufacturing wastes (electrical, foods), mill tailings, mine wastes, ore dumps, treatment plant wastes.
Hydrogen	H	H^+, H_2S, H_2O, HCO_3, H_2CO_3, OH	Quantities always sufficient in surrounding medium	Atmosphere, oxidation processes, rainwater, volcanic activity	Industrial wastes (hydrocarbon process), oils.
Iron	Fe	Fe^{+2}, Fe^{+3}, $FeSO_4$, $Fe(OH)_2$	0.65–6,000 $\mu g/l$	Ground water, igneous rock minerals, iron minerals, organic decomposition, soil	Acid drainage from mines, industrial wastes (steelmaking), iron ore mining, manufacturing wastes, oxides of iron metals (car bodies, refrigerators).
Magnesium . . .	Mg	Mg^{+2}, $MgSO_4$	Trace quantities	Igneous rock minerals, ground water, rainwater, sedimentary rocks	Irrigation, manufacturing wastes (transportation vehicles).
Manganese . . .	Mn	Mn^{+2}, MnO_2	5.0 $\mu g/l$	Ground water, plants, rocks, soil, tree leaves	Acid drainage from coal mines, industrial wastes

TABLE 1. COMMON FORMS, MINIMUM REQUIRMENTS, AND SOME SOURCES OF ELEMENTS ESSENTIAL FOR THE GROWTH OF ALGAE—CONTINUED

Element[1]	Symbol	Some common forms in water[1][2]	Minimum requirements[3]	Examples of natural sources[1][4]	Examples of manmade sources[5][6][7]
Molybdenum	Mo	Mo, MoO_4	Trace quantities	Ground water, rocks, soil	Industrial wastes (electrical devices, metallurgy, steelmaking), manufacturing wastes (alloys).
Nitrogen	N	N, NO_2, NO_3, organic nitrogen, NH_3	Trace quantities to 5.3 mg/l	Atmosphere, bacterial and plant fixation, limestone, rainwater, soil	Agricultural wastes (feedlots, fertilizers), domestic sewage, industrial wastes, storm drainage.
Oxygen	O	O_2, H_2O, oxides	Quantities always sufficient in surrounding medium	Atmosphere, oxidation processes, photosynthesis, rainwater	Industry (metallurgy).
Phosphorus	P	P^{+5}, PO_4, HPO_3, organic phosphorus	0.002–0.09 mg/l	Ground water, igneous and marine sediments, rainwater, soil, waterfowl	Agricultural wastes (feedlots, fertilizers), domestic sewage (detergents), industrial wastes.
Potassium	K	K^+ (salts of potassium)	Trace quantities	Evaporite deposits, igneous rock minerals, plant ash, sedimentary rocks	Agricultural wastes (feedlots, fertilizers), industrial wastes (preservatives, pulp ash).
Silicon	Si	Si^{+4}, SiO_2	0.5–0.8 mg/l	Diatom shells, igneous rock minerals, metamorphic rocks	Domestic sewage, industrial wastes.
Sodium	Na	Na^+, Na salts ($NaCl$, $NaCO_3$	5.0 mg/l	Ground water, igneous rock minerals, ocean water, soil	Industrial wastes (paper and pulp, rubber, soda, water softeners), manufacturing wastes (dyes and drugs).
Sulfur	S	SO_2, HS, H_2S, SO_4	5.0 mg/l	Animal and plant decomposition, igneous rocks, rainwater, sedimentary rocks, springs, volcanic activity	Agricultural wastes (fertilizers), industrial wastes (fuels, paper and pulp).
Vanadium	V	V^{+2}, V^{+3}, V^{+4}, V^{+5} (salts and oxides of vanadium)	Trace quantities	Ground water, plant ash	Industrial wastes.
Zinc	Zn	Zn^{+2} (salts of zinc), ZnO_2	10–100 μg/l	Igneous and carbonate rock minerals	Industrial wastes (piping, refining), mine wastes.

1. Hem (1970).
2. McKee and Wolf (1971).
3. Greeson (1971).
4. Reid (1961).
5. Gurnham (1965).
6. Nebergall, Schmidt, and Holtzclaw (1963).
7. Sawyer and McCarty (1967).

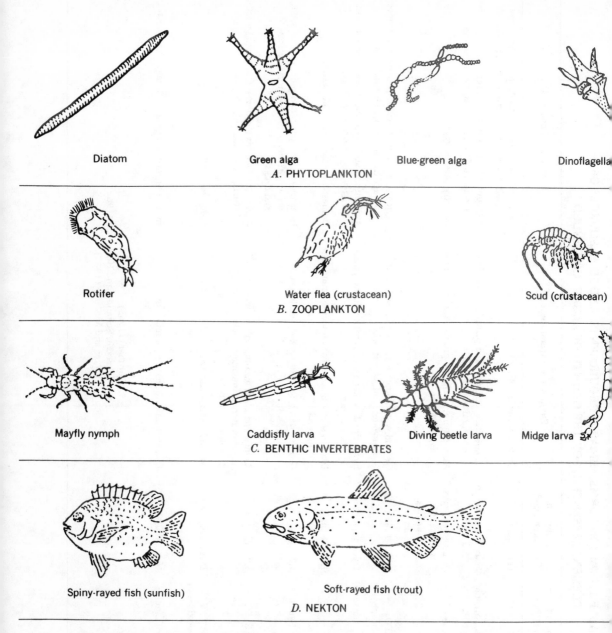

Diatom	Green alga	Blue-green alga	Dinoflagella

A. PHYTOPLANKTON

Rotifer	Water flea (crustacean)	Scud (crustacean)

B. ZOOPLANKTON

Mayfly nymph	Caddisfly larva	Diving beetle larva	Midge larva

C. BENTHIC INVERTEBRATES

Spiny-rayed fish (sunfish)	Soft-rayed fish (trout)

D. NEKTON

FIGURE 3. Representative lake organisms.

of excessive amounts or inorganic and organic materials in the water disrupts the organism balance. This may lead to an unstable ecosystem, often resulting in conditions adverse to man's use of the water.

Plankton. The planktonic community is composed of organisms that inhabit all the water zones of a lake. Two major categories of plankton are recognized—phytoplankton (plants) and zooplankton (animals). Phytoplankton are mostly microscopic, whereas zooplankton can frequently be seen with the unaided eye. Phytoplankton usually drift with the currents, while some zooplankton are strong swimmers. Phytoplankton growth depends upon solar radiation and nutrient elements, while zooplankton feed on phytoplankton, bacteria, or dead organisms.

The phytoplankton community (primary food producers) includes several major groups of plants collectively known as algae. The most common groups of free-floating algae are the diatoms, green algae, and blue-green algae. Usually it is the blue-green algae that become overabundant and cause esthetic, taste, and odor problems in lakes.

Other types of plants which may inhabit lakes are the algae attached to solid surfaces (periphyton) and rooted submersed and emersed higher plants. Rooted plants are found in the littoral zone of lakes, where sufficient sunlight for photosynthesis reaches the bottom.

The zooplankton community (primary consumers) is dominated by small crustaceans and rotifers. Typically the zooplankton spend the daylight hours in the deeper water and rise toward the surface in late afternoon and early evening. The kinds and numbers of zooplankton in a lake are closely controlled by the available food supply and by grazing of predators such as fish.

Benthos. The benthic community (consumers and decomposers) includes a number of different types of organisms, such as bacteria, insect larvae and nymphs, snails, clams, and crayfish. These organisms are an integral part of the food chain of an aquatic environment. Benthic organisms feed on both plants and animals, and they in turn are fed upon by higher organisms. The bacteria and fungi are especially abundant on the lake bottom and decompose the organic materials that settle there.

Nekton. The nektonic community (consumers) consists of relatively large free-swimming organisms. This community consists primarily of fish and certain insects. Nektonic organisms feed on benthos and plankton in the lake. In most lakes, fish are at the end of the food chain and are often the most economically important organism to man.

Processes in Lakes

Most of the properties and materials of lakes are easy to measure and describe. In contrast, their interactions as they relate to plants and animals are somewhat more difficult to describe, and measurements of these processes often more difficult to make. As a result, some of the processes in lakes are not well understood. Energy and material transport between plants and animals, and between animals themselves, is among several of the poorly understood biological processes in lakes. Other processes, such as photosynthesis, respiration, eutrophication, and basic geochemical cycles are somewhat better known, and can be described in general terms.

Photosynthesis and Respiration

Photosynthesis is carried out only by green (chlorophyll-containing) plants and some bacteria. Respiration is carried out by both plants and animals. Both processes are essential to life and have a profound effect upon water quality in lakes.

As mentioned earlier, photosynthesis is the process whereby green plants take up carbon and synthesize carbon compounds, while producing oxygen. When plants take up carbon, generally as carbon dioxide, they combine hydrogen, sulfur, nitrogen, or phosphorus with the carbon, to form cellular materials such as carbohydrates, proteins, and fats. The oxygen produced during this process goes into solution.

Respiration is the process whereby organisms obtain their energy by oxidizing food (organic material) to carbon dioxide and water. Because their energy need is continuous, all organisms respire throughout their lives. Plants emit oxygen as a result of photosynthesis, but they must also use oxygen for respiration.

Photosynthesis and respiration result in daily and seasonal fluctuations of dissolved oxygen and carbon dioxide levels in lakes. As a result, the carbon dioxide and dissolved oxygen concentrations are not always in balance. These imbalances have a significant effect upon the quality of water. For example, all lakes contain some algae, but in the presence of sufficient sunlight and plant nutrients, photosynthesis by phytoplankton may result in an excessive production of oxygen. At this time, the phytoplankton may increase to concentrations of a million cells per litre, a condition known as an algal bloom (Lee, 1970, p. 19).

Respiration removes dissolved oxygen from the water. For example, in a thermally stratified lake during the summer, respiration by bacteria may oxidize organic materials at such a rapid rate in the bottom water that the dissolved oxygen becomes drastically depleted. Thus, when large quantities of decomposable organic wastes are introduced into natural water, severe oxygen depletion can occur.

Decreases in oxygen concentration also affect the solubilities of compounds contained in sediment. For example, iron in natural water is found in either the ferrous (Fe^{+2}) or the ferric (Fe^{+3}) state. Under aerobic (oxygenated) conditions, iron is in the ferric (or highly oxidized) form as a complex with other inorganic constituents, and as simple decomposition products (Reid, 1961, p. 193). Under anaerobic conditions, the insoluble ferric complex in the lake sediment loses oxygen and is reduced to the more soluble ferrous state. This not only puts more iron in solution, but also releases other combined constituents, such as silicate, phosphate, and bicarbonate. The ions that go into solution all act as plant nutrients.

Eutrophication

Eutrophication is the enrichment of lakes by nutrients and filling by sediment. Although eutrophication is a natural phenomenon, recent concern has been with the acceleration of this process by man's activities. Presently, it is a major problem of many lakes and reservoirs.

The aging process of a lake begins with its formation in a basin. As the lake accumulates plant nutrients and sediment deposits, plant production increases and shoreline vegetation invades the lake. As the depth of the lake decreases and emergent vegetation increases, the lake becomes a bog and is referred to as a *dystrophic* system. Eventually the original lake becomes land.

Unenriched lakes are classified as *oligotrophic*. Oligotrophic lakes have high concentrations of dissolved oxygen at all depths, low concentrations of dissolved substances, and usually clear waters. Although sufficient oxygen is available to support life throughout the water mass of oligotrophic lakes, the low quantity of dissolved materials and plant nutrients limits plant production and thereby restricts the abundance of animal life. Many newly created real-estate lakes and reservoirs are oligotrophic. However, many older reservoirs and natural lakes, such as Lake Tahoe, may still be considered oligotrophic because they contain minimal plant nutrient concentrations (Goldman and Carter, 1965; Crippen and Pavelka, 1970).

The second enrichment stage of a lake is *mesotrophy*. This stage is characterized by increased concentrations of dissolved materials and plant nutrients, and thus increased plant production. A mesotrophic lake may support a large plant population but generally plant production is not so excessive as to be undesirable, in terms of human use of the water, nor to seriously deplete the dissolved oxygen concentration.

The third stage of the enrichment process is called *eutrophy* (hence eutrophication). This is the final stage of the lake before filling and extinction are complete. The symptoms of a eutrophic lake are high concentrations of dissolved materials, excessive numbers of phytoplankton represented by only a few tolerant species, and oxygen depletion in the deeper water. The reduction of oxygen is caused by bacterial decomposition of organic matter (Redfield and others, 1963, p. 27) and may result in fish kills. Other characteristics of eutrophic lakes may be discolored water from excessive algae production and unpleasant odors attributable to decay.

The effect of man on the eutrophication process is shown in figure 4. The diagram shows the effect of nutrient enrichment upon the natural eutrophication of lakes. Regardless of the enrichment status of lakes, nutrient inputs by man can hasten lake extinction. However, the rate of eutrophication, and thus the extinction of lakes, can be retarded by nutrient removal.

The Biogeochemical Cycle

Materials that enter a lake from tributaries or from the atmosphere may settle in the lake basin, be removed through the outlet, or remain in solution. Those that remain in solution, and that are required for plant production, may be incorporated into living tissue.

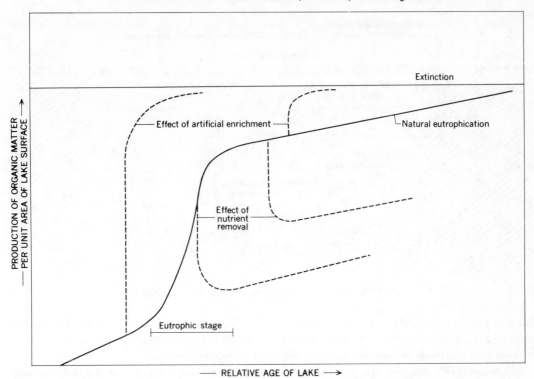

FIGURE 4. Effect of man upon the eutrophication of lakes. After Greeson, 1971; modified from Hasler, 1947.

Sedimentation. The major pathway for the flow of plant nutrients and other elements into a lake is sedimentation. Sedimentation is the process whereby fragmental material originates from the disintegration of rocks and from other sources, is transported, and is deposited in layers or remains suspended in the water (Colby, 1963, p. A3). Lakes receive sediment from both inflowing water and from the wind. The sediment accumulates permanently in areas little affected by wave action. Because most lake-bottom sediments are relatively permanent deposits, sediment deposition is a major cause of the aging and extinction of lakes.

Many lakes retard inflow sufficiently to trap all incoming coarse sediment, as well as part of the fine sediment. The trap efficiency of a lake depends in part upon the fall velocities of the sediment particles, the density of the water, and how much the water is slowed as it passes through the reservoir (Brune, 1953). As a lake fills with sediment, its trap efficiency usually decreases (Colby, 1963, p. A35).

Besides being a mechanism for lake filling, sedimentation introduces plant nutrients and dissolved materials into lakes. The quantity of plant nutrients sorbed by sediment particles may be high, and the nutrients can become more soluble upon entering the different chemical environment of a lake. Once in the lake, plant nutrients are subjected to cycling.

Nutrient Cycling. A generalized scheme of element sources, losses, and cycling in lakes is shown in figure 5. Some elements, such as phosphorus, nitrogen, silicon, and perhaps soluble carbon, may undergo such extensive use by plants that these nutrients are virtually depleted in the water. Thus, they may become limiting nutrient elements to plants and restrict plant production until the elements are recycled or new supplies enter the lake.

Many elements are cycled through a number of chemical forms. For example, nitrogen may be taken up by plants as the stable nitrate ion (NO_3^-). In the plant cell it is reduced and makes up an important part of plant and animal protein. Upon death of the organism, the nitrogen may be released

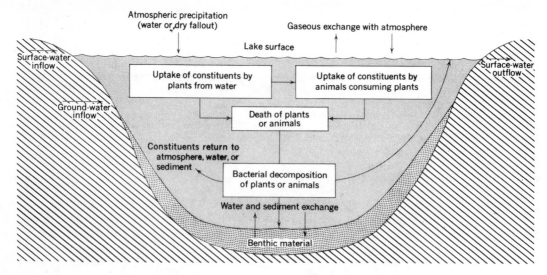

FIGURE 5. Sources and cycling of elements in a lake.

either as ammonia gas (NH_3), or the ammonium ion (NH_4^+). Further oxidation of these forms by specific bacteria results in the unstable oxidized form, nitrite (NO_2^-). Further oxidation of the nitrite by other bacteria results in the stable nitrate form, thus completing the cycle.

Phosphorus (P), inorganic phosphate (PO_4^{-3}), and organic phosphorus (OP—the fraction bound in plant and animal cells) follow a cycle similar to nitrogen. Carbon also occurs in several forms. In water it is found as carbon dioxide gas (CO_2), as the organic ions bicarbonate (HCO_3^-) and carbonate (CO_3^{-2}), or as the solid compound calcium carbonate ($CaCO_3$). Organic carbon is that fraction of total carbon within plants and animals.

The sorption (absorption and adsorption) of chemical elements and compounds by sediment is well known. Lake bottom sediment is often a rich source of plant nutrients. The release of these nutrients from the sediment is regulated by various factors, such as temperature, pH, and dissolved oxygen. For example, a lack of oxygen in the bottom water of lakes (hypolimnion) may trigger the release of phosphorus compounds from the sediment. When the bottom water becomes oxygenated again, the phosphorus compounds precipitate and reenter the sediment. There they are unavailable as plant nutrients until oxygen depletion again occurs in the hypolimnion.

Planning and Management of Watersheds and Lakes for Water-Quality Control

The foremost goals in lake management are to prevent or reduce the undesirable effects of eutrophication and to provide water of high quality. Factors associated with eutrophication of lakes are excessive algal production, dissolved oxygen depletion in the hypolimnion, objectionable taste and odor, and general esthetic depreciation of the environment. In the past, management of lakes was commonly limited to volume manipulation and water releases. In recent years, intensified demands for water of high quality have caused more attention to be focused on lake-basin planning, watershed and lake management, and water-quality control (Keup and Mackenthun, 1970).

Lake Basin Planning

Good lake-basin planning can minimize water-quality problems. The selection of an appropriate site for a reservoir is of paramount importance. A preimpoundment survey of the physical, chemical, and biological characteristics of the proposed lake basin is most beneficial when done before construction begins. In addition, basin planning and dam construction should take seismic safety into consideration. This becomes especially important in fault regions like the San Francisco Bay area.

A primary characteristic of a good reservoir is a high ratio of volume to surface area, which is desirable for land conservation and water-quality control (Linsley and Franzini, 1964, p. 168). For example, a deep reservoir is preferable to a shallow one because of lower land costs per unit of capacity, less evaporation loss, and less area for weed growth. The watershed, of course, must have a suitable damsite, and the reservoir site must have enough capacity for its intended use. If a reservoir site has tributaries which produce much sediment and plant nutrients, rapid eutrophication may result after construction of the reservoir. Therefore, a preimpoundment survey that includes a nutrient-loading estimate of at least nitrogen and phosphorus for all waters entering the planned impoundment will enable the planner to assess the eutrophication potential. Open mines in the basin may cause toxic water conditions. Reconnaissance surveys of reservoir sites can reveal such potential problems, so plans can be formulated to avoid or deal with them.

An important step, after selection of an appropriate reservoir site, is to remove trees and vegetation from that part of the basin that will be inundated, because the decomposition of this organic material may cause oxygen depletion and undesirable taste and odor in the reservoir water. The ideal practice is to remove the topsoil and contained plant nutrients also, but the cost of such an operation may be prohibitive in large reservoir basins (Houghton, 1966, p. 180). If the topsoil is not removed when the reservoir is cleared, removal of vegetation from the site with as little disturbance of the soil as possible will reduce the amount of plant nutrients released from the soil and decrease the incidence of algal blooms (Houghton, 1966, p. 180).

Watershed Management

Effective watershed management can prevent or reduce the rate of eutrophication; thus attention must be given to the quality of inflowing water.

The disturbance of soil in the watershed from natural events and human activities increases the transport of sediment and combined plant nutrients into the lake. Maintaining a good vegetative cover around the lake will help prevent excessive erosion of the watershed. However, if the soil in the watershed must be disturbed, construction of sediment traps (temporary debris basins) below the disturbance will minimize the amount of sediment entering the lake (Rickert and Spieker, 1971). Because fertilizer is a rich source of plant nutrients, its use should be limited within the lake basin.

Control or diversion of all waste inflows (wastes high in biochemical oxygen demand or rich in nutrients) is probably the best way to control lake enrichment. This can be accomplished by rerouting the effluent to the outlet of the lake. Advanced methods of sewage treatment, rather than the use of septic tanks, reduce the seepage of nutrients into the lake. If sewage discharges into the lake cannot be avoided, then sewage that has had secondary treatment, but preferably tertiary treatment, will keep nutrients entering the lake to a minimum. Secondary and tertiary treatment of wastewater reduces the oxygen demand, disease potential, and nutrient levels of wastes.

Inflowing streams, or lakes themselves, may receive heated effluent from industrial plants. Heat can greatly alter the chemistry and biology of the water. Thus, heated water should be cooled before its introduction into lakes and reservoirs. There are several cooling devices used in thermal industrial plants. The most effective is the dry-cooling tower. Cooling and spray ponds, although not as effective, are more economical and are used more frequently (Linsley and Franzini, 1964).

Lake Management

Although lake water-quality problems are best controlled by effective management of the watershed area, some within-the-lake management tools are often necessary. Multipenstock release systems on a reservoir allow for greater flexibility in releasing water from various depths, and hence reducing potential water-quality problems. For example, domestic wastewater containing undesirable chemical constituents, such as manganese and iron, can be passed through the lake by regulating the release of water at the dam. Mechanical aeration can be used to increase the oxygen in the water, to prevent the buildup of hydrogen sulfide concentrations, and to depress high levels of manganese or iron before the water enters the distribution system. Regulating recreation on the lake may help prevent accelerated eutrophication. Many recreational lake areas do not have adequate sanitary facilities, and drainage of human wastes into the lake may cause bacterial contamination.

Water-Quality Control

Although preventive measures for water-quality control are always preferable, it is often necessary to manage a lake system to control after-the-fact water-quality problems. These problems generally arise as part of the eutrophication process, and are often accelerated by man.

Algal Blooms. Algal blooms are a troublesome problem in lakes. An algal bloom is an excessive amount of phytoplankton production which usually occurs during the spring and summer in nutrient-enriched lakes. Minimum conditions for an algal bloom are a sufficient concentration of plant nutrients in the water, adequate sunlight, and a water temperature suitable for growth. The concentration of algae that constitutes a bloom is not precise, and it depends upon the type of algae. Lee (1970) proposed that a concentration of ½ million to 1 million cells per litre indicates a bloom condition.

When minimum conditions for algal growth are met, the growth of algae takes place at a more or less constant rate (figure 6). If no property is limiting, the algae grows rapidly, causing a bloom. At some point, an essential condition becomes limiting and restricts further algal growth. The cell density may remain stable for a few days, but because of limiting materials for growth and tissue repair, the cells begin to die. As the algal cells die, they sink and are decomposed by bacteria, which results in the uptake of dissolved oxygen and release of cellular materials back to the water or lake sediment.

Although algae are essential for other organisms to live, algal bloom may cause coloration or fouling of the lake water. Algae may clog sand filters at water treatment plants. Recreational activities, such as boating and fishing, may be hindered by mats of floating algae, and water sports may prove harmful because of the presence of toxic algae (Mackenthun and Ingram, 1967, pp. 157–66).

Effective treatment and control of algae requires some knowledge of the number, kind, and distribution of algae in the water. The application of an algicide is the most frequent method of control. Copper sulfate is the most common and effective algicide used today, because it is toxic to many algae at comparatively low concentrations, has a relatively low toxicity to man and other animals, and is inexpensive (Gratteau, 1970, p. 25). The concentration of copper sulfate which is toxic to a particular type of algae varies with the abundance of the algae, the temperature, pH, alkalinity, and amount of organic matter in the water. Mackenthun and Ingram (1967, pp. 258–60) present application rates for copper sulfate based on these variables. The most effective time for the application of an algicide is at the junction of the initial growth phase and the rapid growth phase. To determine the growth-phase junction, several algal-growth curves are needed. These can be prepared by frequently collecting water samples and counting the algal cells. Once several growth curves are established for the algal species of the lake, it will be possible to predict with some reliability the growth-phase junction, and hence the best time to apply an algicide. Mechanical removal of algae may be an alternative control, especially in water where localized blooms occur (Thomas, 1965). The harvested material is usually hauled to shore and burned, or removed to a disposal site (Gratteau, 1970, p. 25).

Higher aquatic plants may be killed with herbicides or removed by mechanical means. Livermore and Wunderlich (1969, pp. 498–512) and Mackenthun and Ingram (1967, pp. 264–73) discuss the removal of both submersed and emersed aquatic plants. If the plants are removed mechanically, they are usually hauled out of the watershed area so that their contained nutrients will not reenter the lake upon decomposition.

Anaerobic Conditions. The quantity of available dissolved oxygen in a lake is often a limiting factor to productivity. When thermal stratification occurs in a lake, the lighter water at the surface forms a density barrier which prevents reaeration by atmospheric oxygen in the bottom waters. The sinking and decomposition of algae following a bloom may add to the depletion of dissolved oxygen in the lower water. The introduction of large amounts of other oxygen-demanding materials, such as organic wastes, raises the BOD (biochemical oxygen demand) of the water, and thus depletes the oxygen supply.

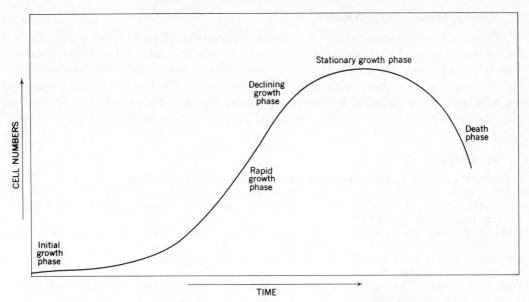

FIGURE 6. Typical growth pattern of blooming unicellular algae.

Under anaerobic conditions, water quality often depreciates. For example, concentrations of hydrogen sulfide, soluble manganese, and iron may increase in the bottom water. Anaerobic conditions also can result in undesirable taste and odor from hydrogen sulfide buildup. Obviously, aquatic life will be adversely affected.

Mechanical aeration of lakes has become a useful management tool in reducing anaerobic conditions. Pumping or drawing off the deoxygenated water, combined with recirculation of oxygenated water from the surface, will help to relieve hypolimnetic oxygen depletion (Thomas, 1962, p. 303; Irwin and others, 1969).

Fish Kills. Fish kills may become an important problem in some lakes. Fish are killed by exposure to toxins in waste discharges and by some algicides. Anaerobic conditions may suffocate fish. Rapidly changing or excessively high water temperatures may kill fish, or cause an increase in fish respiration. This means that more water passes through their gills, and hence introduces more toxins into their bloodstream.

Fish kills can be prevented only by treating the cause, which involves proper planning and management of the lake. Obviously there are no after-the-fact control measures for fish kills. However, immediate cleanup of dead fish along the shores of lakes will reduce odors and improve recreation and the esthetic value of beaches. Chemical tests for the investigation of fish kills can be used on distressed or dead fish. Any conditions at the site of the kill that might help identify the cause of death should be investigated, such as oxygen depletion or evidence of toxicity (Burdick, 1965; Slack and others, 1973, pp. 158–59).

Sediment Deposition. Sediment deposition is one of the most prevalent problems with real-estate lakes (Rickert and Spieker, 1971), and it has become increasingly evident in all lakes. Reservoirs in particular are depositories for sediment. Accelerated sediment deposition usually results from soil disturbances in the watershed. Common causes of soil disturbances are logging, road construction, farming, and overgrazing. Sediment deposits may fill the lake, introduce nutrients, or reduce the esthetic value of the lake. Organic sediment may place an oxygen demand upon the lake water.

Once deposition has occurred, the life of the lake may be extended by dredging, or if the reservoir can be drained, the sediment can be removed with earthmoving equipment. Both sediment-removal techniques are expensive, and unless watershed-protection measures are undertaken, the success of these techniques may be shortlived.

Summary of Management Options

There are few management options available for reducing eutrophication once it occurs. The best management is prevention—choosing the reservoir site carefully, understanding the potential nutrient loads of the tributaries, and clearing the reservoir site completely and carefully. Most important, however, is the wise management of the watershed. The maintenance of a plant cover with a minimum of soil disturbance in the watershed is of prime importance. The removal or prevention of domestic and industrial waste is of course a desirable feature and a prerequisite for the reduction or prevention of eutrophication.

REFERENCES CITED

Brune, G. M., 1953, Trap efficiency of reservoirs: Am. Geophys. Union Trans., v. 34, pp. 407–18.

Burdick, G. E., 1965, Some problems in the determination of the cause of fish kills, *in* Biological problems in water pollution: U.S. Public Health Service, Cincinnati, Ohio, Robert A. Taft Sanitary Eng. Center, pp. 289–92.

Colby, B. R., 1963, Fluvial sediments—A summary of source, transportation, deposition, and measurement of sediment discharge: U.S. Geol. Survey Bull., 1181-A, 47 pp.

Crippen, J. R., and Pavelka, B. R., 1970, The Lake Tahoe basin, California-Nevada: U.S. Geol. Survey Water-Supply Paper 1972, 56 pp.

Fruh, G. E., 1967, The overall picture of eutrophication: Water Pollution Control Federation Jour., v. 39, no. 9, pp. 1449–63.

Goldman, C. R., and Carter, R. C., 1965, An investigation by rapid carbon-14 bioassay of factors affecting the cultural eutrophication of Lake Tahoe, California-Nevada: Water Pollution Control Federation Jour., v. 37, no. 7, pp. 1044–59.

Gratteau, J. C., 1970, Potential algicides for the control of algae: Water and Sewage Works, v. 117, pp. R-24–R61.

Greeson, P. E., 1971, The limnology of Oneida Lake with emphasis on factors contributing to algal blooms: U.S. Geol. Survey open-file report, 185 pp.

Gurnham, F. C., 1965, Industrial wastewater control: New York, Academic Press, 476 pp.

Hasler, A. D., 1947, Eutrophication of lakes by domestic drainage: Ecology, v. 28, pp. 383–95.

Hem, J. D., 1970, Study and interpretation of the chemical characteristics of natural water (2d ed.): U.S. Geol. Survey Water-Supply Paper 1473, 363 pp.

Houghton, G. U., 1966, Maintaining the safety and quality of water supplies, *in* Lowe-McConnell, R. H., ed., Man-made lakes: New York, Academic Press, pp. 173–82.

Hutchinson, G. E., 1957, A treatise on limnology—Volume 1, Geography, physics and chemistry: New York, John Wiley and Sons, Inc., 1015 pp.

Irwin, W. H., Symons, J. M., and Robeck, G. G., 1969, Impoundment destratification by mechanical pumping, *in* Symons, J. M., ed., Water quality behavior in reservoirs: U.S. Public Health Service, Cincinnati, Ohio, pp. 251–74.

Keup, L. E., and Mackenthun, K. M., 1970, Lakes—restoration and preservation: Water and Sewage Works, v. 117, reference no. 1970, pp. R16–R21.

Lee, F. G., 1970, Eutrophication: Wisconsin Univ., Water Resources Center, Occasional Paper no. 2, 39 pp.

Linsley, R. K., and Franzini, J. B., 1964, Water resources engineering: New York, McGraw-Hill Book Co., 654 pp.

Livermore, D. F., and Wunderlich, W. E., 1969, Mechanical removal of organic production from waterways, *in* Eutrophication: Causes, consequences, correctives: Washington, D.C., Natl. Acad. Sci., pp. 494–519.

McKee, J. E., and Wolf, H. W., 1971, Water quality criteria (2nd ed.): California Water Resources Control Board, Pub. no. 3-A, 548 pp.

Mackenthun, K. M., and Ingram, W. M., 1967, Biological associated problems in freshwater environments—Their identification, investigation and control: U.S. Federal Water Pollution Control Adm., 287 pp.

Nebergall, W. J., Schmidt, F. C., and Holtzclaw, H. F., Jr., 1963, General chemistry (2d ed.): Boston, D. C. Heath and Co., 791 pp.

Redfield, A. C., Ketchum, B. H., and Richards, F. A., 1963, The sea—Volume 2, The influence of organisms on the composition of sea water, *in* Hill, M. N., ed., Comparative and descriptive oceanography (2d ed.): New York, John Wiley and Sons, Inc., pp. 26–77.

Reid, G. K., 1961, Ecology of inland waters and estuaries: New York, Reinhold Pub. Corp., 375 pp.

Rickert, D. A., and Spieker, A. M., 1971, Real-estate lakes: U.S. Geol. Survey Circ. 601-G, 19 pp.

Sawyer, C. N., and McCarty, P. L., 1967, Chemistry for sanitary engineers (2d ed.): New York, McGraw-Hill Book Co., 518 pp.

Slack, K. V., Averett, R. C., Greeson, P. E., and Lipscomb, R. G., 1973, Methods for collection and analysis of aquatic biological and microbiological samples: U.S. Geol. Survey Techniques Water-Resources Inv., book 5, chap. A4, 165 pp.

Talling, J. F., 1962, Freshwater algae: New York, Academic Press, 757 pp.

Thomas, E. A., 1965, The artifical eutrophication of our waters, *in* Biological problems in water pollution: U.S. Public Health Service, Cincinnati, Ohio, Robert A. Taft Sanitary Eng. Center, pp. 299–305.

Welch, P. S., 1952, Limnology: New York, McGraw-Hill Book Co., 538 pp.

25

Chicago Reclaiming
Strip Mines with Sludge

Gene Dallaire

In the middle of the 1960s the Metropolitan Sanitary District of Greater Chicago (MSD) recognized the need for a better method of sludge disposal. At that time about half the sludge produced from the primary and secondary treatment of 1.5 billion gallons/day of sewage was heat dried to 95% solids and the resultant fertilizer-base sold to a broker. The rest of the sludge was first digested, then stored in 11 sludge lagoons near an MSD treatment plant in suburban Chicago.

But these sludge disposal methods left much to be desired. The sludge drying process created air pollution, consumed large quantities of natural gas, and was costly. Space for new lagooning in the urban area was rapidly running out; and existing lagoons, with an accumulation of 30 years of sludge, were taking up valuable urban land. So, though lagooning was once a good solution, in that the lagoon complex was once an undeveloped area, urban growth brought dense, fully developed suburban communities all around them.

Incineration, dewatering, drying, improving existing sludge-disposal operations—these alternatives were studied by Chicago engineers. Then, several years ago MSD decided that the best solution for sludge disposal was *land reclamation.*

The plan was to digest sludge and transport it to rural Fulton County, about 200 miles (320 km) southwest of Chicago. Spraying digestive sludge on abandoned strip-mined land and on other areas with poor soils (e.g. low-grade pastures) would have several advantages: it would eliminate land, air, and water pollution from sludge processing in the urban area; it would cost less than other sludge disposal methods; it would solve the problem once and for all—no more hunting for lagoon space in urban areas; and it would make beneficial use of the organic materials, nutrients, and water making up sludge.

Innovative

It was a bold move on the part of MSD and the Fulton County Board of Supervisors. In the past, many sewage authorities had simply assumed that sludge was a waste to be disposed of. But MSD took the view that sludge is not a waste to be discarded, but a resource to be used. Today, MSD officials see the return of sludge to the soil as the most practical and cheapest method of sludge disposal.

Reprinted with permission of the author and publisher from *Civil Engineering* 44(6):43–47, 1974. Copyright © 1974 by American Society of Civil Engineers. This project received the Award for Outstanding Civil Engineering of 1974.

To date, MSD has made a good start in its land reclamation project. Because of the boldness of the concept, and the promise it holds, the American Society of Civil Engineers recently awarded it the Outstanding Civil Engineering Achievement of 1974. Presently MSD owns 10,200 acres (41 km²) in Fulton County. By July MSD expects to have 2,000 acres (8 km²) of this land ready for sludge application. Of this 1,100 acres (4.5 km²) was formerly strip-mined land; and 900 acres (3.6 km²) row cropland.

To get the formerly strip-mined land ready for sludge application, MSD has spent $2,000 to $3,000 per acre to grade the rugged strip-mined terrain to near levelness suitable for farming; and create berms around farm fields to contain runoff, recycling it if still polluted. In the past, then, much of this land was no better than poor-grade pasture land; but today much of it has been transformed into farmland and more will shortly be so. To date, MSD has spent about $20 million in Fulton County for sludge handling facilities, land regrading, and other site preparation.

Significance

The Fulton County land reclamation project symbolizes a new partnership between cities and rural areas. Some believe such partnerships could become increasingly prevalent across the country as more stringent water-quality standards force hundreds of crowded municipalities to treat their sewage more thoroughly, thus producing more sludge. Believed to be the largest land reclamation project now under way in the world, the MSD project is being closely watched by engineers and public officials. Though land reclamation in Fulton County is still in its initial phases, in the next few years MSD, if all goes according to plan, should have enough formerly strip-mined land restored to productive farmland to make it a very persuasive showcase.

The most difficult part of implementing a land reclamation project is not the specific technology used to process, transport and apply sludge to land. Rather, it is the difficulty of winning citizen support for such projects. If the Fulton County reclamation project lives up to its promise of reclaiming thousands of acres of formerly strip-mined land, then it could ease the way for many other cities across the U.S. and it could dramatically lessen the opposition that cities will face in trying to get rural counties to accept the urban areas' sewage sludge. For then it will be clear that there are benefits for both city and rural area; the city will be able to dispose of its sludge in an economical way; and the rural areas will have strip-mines and other low grade lands restored to good condition.

MSD civil engineers played a key role in getting this innovative project off the ground. In addition to having to cope with problems of public acceptance, civil engineers had to pull together many different disciplines to make the project go—mechanical engineers, electrical engineers, soils scientists, agronomists, environmentalists.

Project Starts

In the summer of 1972 the Metropolitan Sanitary District of Greater Chicago began spraying digested sludge on a former strip-mined site in Fulton County, Illinois, about 200 miles (320 km) southwest of Chicago.

After leaving digesters at a treatment plant in Chicago, sludge is pipelined to storage tanks at a nearby loading dock. There, it is soon pumped aboard barges, which travel down a water channel to the Illinois River, and then down the Illinois River 180 miles (290 km) to Fulton County. The barges tie up at Liverpool, Illinois, and the sludge is pumped through a 20-in. (510 mm) diameter pipeline to holding basins in Fulton County, 10.8 miles (17 km) away.

Currently about 7,500 wet tons (6,800 metric tons) per day—the equivalent of 410 dry tons/day (372 metric tons/day)—is being shipped. This is about 50% of the daily sludge production in the Metropolitan Sanitary District. In Fulton County the sludge is being stored in large holding basins. About 10% of the sludge being barged to Fulton County is now being applied to about 1,200 acres (4.9 m²). By July, this figure is expected to be up to about 2,000 acres (8.1 km²) and by the summer of 1975, to 3,000 acres (12.2 km²).

For decades, many small cities around the world have spread sludge on croplands—with beneficial results. The only thing new about the Fulton County land reclamation project is its size: whereas other cities have done it on a small scale, Chicago is reclaiming strip-mined land on a large scale.

Presently, there is a big shortage of nitrogen and phosphorus fertilizers. The price of ammonia in the past few years, says University of Illinois agronomist, John Hinesly, has soared from $90 to $350 per ton and phosphorus has gone from $100 to $350 per ton. This has produced a turn-around in the farmer's attitude toward sludge. Many farmers are now much more willing to accept sludge—especially for its phosphorus nutrients.

Digested sludge, which is roughly 95% water, 5% solids, contains nitrogen, phosphorus, and some potassium—three basic elements needed for plant growth. The liquid portion contains about half of the nitrogen and a small amount of phosphorus. The solids contain the remaining half of the nitrogen and most of the phosphorus. In contrast to inorganic commerical fertilizers, digested sludge is high in organic materials, high in humus content. This improves soil fertility and soil structure, helping soil to hold moisture and plants to establish roots.

Benefits of Land Reclamation

By the summer of 1974, MSD hopes to be irrigating 2,000 acres of farmland. Some 55% of this was once strip-mined land. The rugged strip-mined land, with high spoil banks, was first leveled with earthmoving equipment. To contain runoff, earth berms have been constructed around 37 farm fields created on the site. Corn is now growing on 900 acres.

MSD also pays Fulton County quite a bit in real estate taxes. Its current property holdings are assessed for between $2.5 and $3.0 million. Last year, MSD paid the county about $200,000.

Another benefit of the project is the stimulus it is giving to the local economy. For example, contracts for grading, piping, farming, have gone to local people. And supplies and equipment such as tractors, seed, tractor parts, and farm implements have been purchased locally. Presently, about 163 residents of Fulton County are employed on the reclamation project, either as farmers or workers making capital improvements, such as regrading strip-mined lands.

MSD has set up a 750-acre (3 km^2) site on its land for the benefit of Fulton County citizens. Administered by the Fulton County Board of Supervisors, this acreage contains many lakes and ponds with excellent fishing. A large picnic site has been set up for public use. Persons are admitted for $1 a day per car. Many residents have been taking advantage of this facility. Since it opened in 1971, it has taken in $44,000 for the county.

Search for a Land Reclamation Site

By far the biggest problem Chicago had in implementing their land reclamation project was finding suitable acreage for sludge application. Starting about 1970, MSD began looking for suitable sites within 50 miles (80 km) of Chicago. Their encounter in Kankakee County is revealing. When the district offered to purchase private marginal land, county citizens resisted. The reaction of some citizens was: "Chicago's not going to dump its waste out here." MSD had to look elesewhere.

How, then, did MSD finally get approval in Fulton County? A low-density area, consisting mainly of farm and small towns, Fulton County had much disturbed strip-mined land, where soft coal had been removed without significant land restoration for over 20 years. Fulton County officials wanted to restore these scarred lands to good condition, so they could be used for farming or recreation—and at the same time, generate tax revenues for the county. Aware that MSD was looking for a sludge-application site, Fulton County officials approached MSD people about the prospects of getting strip-mined lands reclaimed. Thus, there was a mutual interest. MSD would have a place to get rid of its sludge at a reasonable cost. Fulton County would get its strip mines reclaimed—and be paid taxes by the party doing it! An agreement was struck and MSD purchased 7,000 acres (28.4 km^2) from private landowners in the county. Though farther from Chicago than originally hoped—about 200 miles (320 km)—the site was near both rail and water transportation and had good balance between agricultural and strip-mined lands.

Eventually, Fulton County hopes to restore 40,000 acres (162 km²) of strip-mined lands to productivity. One problem, though, is that much of these stripped areas are scattered, making reclamation more costly. According to MSD's Frank Dalton, land parcels of 2,000 acres or more are needed for economical sludge distribution and reclamation.

Coal companies are strip-mining land in Fulton County at the rate of about 2,000 acres/year (8 km²/year). But a new Illinois law requires these companies to do considerable site reclamation once finished with mining operations. According to Dalton, MSD is now talking with coal companies about the prospects of providing sludge to assist in land restoration efforts.

In the future, MSD will need more than 30,000 acres (120 km²) to dispose of all its sludge. Where will this land come from? MSD is currently: looking to buy more land both in Fulton County and other areas of Illinois; talking with farmers about direct sludge shipments from holding basins to farmfields; and negotiating with coal companies, as mentioned, about their reclamation efforts.

Ideally, says Dalton, the best disposal site would be pasture or farmland closer to Chicago. This would cut both transportation and reclamation costs.

Fulton County Holding Basins

In August 1971, MSD started filling the first of three big holding basins in Fulton County. The three basins, each separate from one another, have a combined capacity of 8 million cubic yards (6 million m³).

Why these basins? Their main function is to hold sludge until ready for land application. Sludge is applied only eight months of the year; distribution lines would freeze up in winter. Another purpose is to allow more time for the sludge to age, which helps to guard against objectionable odors.

A typical holding basin in Fulton County is about 40 feet (12 m) deep. Many of the solids in the sludge settle to the bottom of the basin. The top layer supernatant has about 1% solids; the bottom layer, 10 to 12% solids. Since the dredging equipment is unable to pick up sludge deeper than about 20 feet (6 m), MSD has been applying only the *supernatant* fraction to the land. Failure to use the remaining solids fraction means much nitrogen and phosphorus are not being put on the soil. The soil is also not getting the benefit of the organic matter in the sludge solids, valuable in improving the physical properties of the strip-mined soil—needed so it can better hold water and roots can take hold. (Where land has been strip mined, generally the good topsoil has been buried, exposing humus-poor earth layers.)

To overcome this difficulty, MSD started transporting some of this supernatant back to Chicago during the return trips of the barges. (This step is lowering the levels in the holding basins, so that eventually the dredges will be able to reach the higher-solids-content sludge near the bottom of the basins and apply that to the land.) Once back at Chicago, the supernatant is run through an activated sludge treatment plant, then discharged to surface waters.

Within the new few years, MSD plans to begin barging a higher-solids-content sludge (about 10% solids, rather than the present 5%) to Fulton County. How will this be accomplished? After leaving digesters, the sludge will first be stored in lagoons in Chicago. After settling for about six months, there will be two layers in the lagoon: a bottom layer of about 10% solids, and a 1% solids supernatant. Just the thicker bottom layer will be barged to Fulton County; the supernatant will be run through a Chicago treatment plant and discharged to a stream. With the thicker sludge being sent to Fulton County, it should no longer be necessary to barge supernatant back from the holding basins. This whole scheme would be implemented now, except that there are not yet any empty lagoons in Chicago for letting the digested sludge settle out.

Sludge Distribution and Application

The sludge distribution system consists of pipes (supplied by Naylor Pipe Co.), an above-ground header system, and a "big gun" spray vehicle. The spray gun is mounted on a carriage. In a typical field, the carriage may take all day to travel 132 feet (40.2 m). Sweeping out an arc, the gun sprays up to 300 feet (91 m). Gun and carriage are then moved to another field. Three or four passes like this each year can apply the permitted maximum voltage of sludge.

Among crops grown are corn, soybeans and winter wheat. One reason for growing different crops, rather than, for example, all corn, is a need to stagger the sludge application times. The different crops have a need for fertilizer at different times.

Application rates in the first several years are higher than in later years—to build up the barren strip-mined soil. During the first year, at least 75 dry tons/acre (16.8 kg/m^2) can be safely applied—without causing pollution. This will be tapered to 20 dry tons (18,100 kg) per year within five years.

MSD continues to spray sludge on land. But because of fears of some residents about possible viruses in the spray, a fear that MSD says is unfounded, the District is experimenting with other ways to apply sludge to soil. Sludge injection beneath the surface was considered but rejected because the many rocks near the surface tend to break the injection mechanism. MSD is now applying some sludge to soil by means of a plow towed behind a tractor. The plow opens up the ground, sludge is placed, and soil is folded back into the furrow, but this technique can't be used when crops are growing.

Strip Mine Reclamation Project Faces Some Citizen Opposition

In the past year, opposition to the MSD reclamation project has been building among some citizens in Fulton County. According to Mrs. Barbara Luthy, co-chairman of the Fulton County Citizens for Better Health and Environment (FCCBH), that group circulated a petition among county residents asking if agencies outside the county should be stopped from spreading sludge on lands there. To date, 7,610 people have signed the petition—about 25% of the registered voters in the county. As a result, there will be an *advisory* referendum in November asking whether the county should try to halt the project.

FCCBH is suing Fulton County and the Metropolitan Sanitary District. The suit, seeking $1 million in damages, says "residents have been made ill by vile odors and their premises have been rendered unfit for habitation and use."

Opinions of citizens opposing the project range from "Let's get MSD to close down the project" to "Let's make sure that our county has firm control over MSD."

According to Mrs. Luthy, part of the issue is odor. About 500 homes within a 5-mile radius of the sludge holding basins are affected by odor, she says, adding that last summer there were many complaints and at least one family near the lagoons said they became sick as a result. During this past winter, though, says Luthy, there have been no further complaints about odor. But they'll have to wait and see what happens during the warm months of July and August.

Though odors have been a problem, said Luthy, the main concern is uncertainty about the impact of heavy metals on soil and crops and concern that viruses may be present in the sludge spray. "Will the land be rendered sterile," asks Mrs. Luthy, "by the application of sludges containing metals? No one knows for sure and many citizens in the county have the feeling that we're being experimented on."

Another gripe, according to Luthy, is that MSD has not followed through, for the most part, on its promise to reclaim strip-mined areas. "With the exception of about 100 acres (0.4 km^2) of strip-mined land that has now been reclaimed," she says, "there hasn't been much in the way of leveling existing strip mines and restoring soil." According to Mrs. Luthy, MSD has been buying up farmland and applying sludge primarily to that. It's a lot easier and less costly to apply sludge to farmland, rather than regrading strip-mined land.

Sympathizing with the need for large metropolitan areas like Chicago to dispose of their sludge, Mrs. Luthy feels that such sludge should be applied to arid areas, as in Texas—not to farmlands in Fulton County. Applying the sludge to *strip-mined lands,* though, she says, would be acceptable to Fulton County Citizens for Better Health and Environment—*provided* experts can prove there is no harmful long-term effects to the soil.

What does the Fulton County Citizens for Better Health and Environment want? First, they would like MSD to halt all land purchases until more information is available as to impact of heavy metals on soil and crops. Two, to prove that sludge spray does not carry viruses. Three, to keep heavy metals out of the sewage sludge that's applied to land. According to Mrs. Luthy, the sludge MSD is applying "is 49.7% heavy metals."

Rebuttal

Because of the pending lawsuit, no one at MSD is admitting that there is or has been an odor problem. But several witnesses say there was a strong odor last year. According to John Trax, sanitary engineer with EPA, Washington, D.C., the odor problem was caused by a batch of old, septic sludge that was barged out to the county from Chicago. With proper management and proper sludge digestion, says Trax, sludge odors can be eliminated.

On the heavy metals issue, counters Fulton County planning administrator Charles Sandberg, the county and MSD have no intention of sterilizing the soil with metals. The state EPA limits them to applying a maximum of 150 tons (136 metric tons) of sludge per acre over a long period of time. Yet this is only 1/10 the loading rate used in different areas around the world without any harmful soil effects. Harmful soil effects, he says, could not possibly set in until loading rates are very high.

What about possible viruses in the sludge spray? According to much current research, says Sandberg, it's likely that most viruses are killed during the sludge digestion process. If any survive, they would probably be killed as soon as sprayed into the air. The experience of applying sludge on land in many parts of the world has resulted in no adverse health problems. As Jim Frank, of the Illinois EPA points out, sewage plant operators have been working around raw sewage and sludges for 30 years there, and no one has ever died as a result. And there has been much digested sludge applied to land in Illinois, still without any illnesses. The trouble, says Frank is that citizens want an *absolute* guarantee that there will never be any harm as a result of sprayings. "We can't give an *absolute* guarantee."

The experts MSD consulted said that the *digested, chlorinated* sludge the district sends to Fulton County was very unlikely to have any residual viruses. As a sort of "fail-safe" extra step, though, MSD stores the digested sludge in holding basins in Fulton County for at least 6 months. This is thought to make it virtually impossible for viruses to survive.

Both the Fulton County Health Dept. and Illinois EPA have reviewed MSD plans and granted permits for construction and operation on the 2,000 acres (8.1 million m^2) that will be available for irrigation this summer. These agencies are charged by law with protecting the public health.

Putting things in perspective, one MD, speaking at a hearing in Fulton County, said there was a greater chance of catching a virus from the proximity to other people in the room than from any possible virus in the spray.

Finally, ground water and surface water pollution levels are extensively monitored. MSD presently monitors ground water through 21 wells, checking 32 parameters. Local creeks are also monitored.

Patience Needed

MSD flatly denies that it has been buying up mainly farmland. According to MSD and Fulton County sources, MSD has purchased a total of 10,200 acres in Fulton County, 71% of this land, they say, was formerly strip mined. According to Fulton County's Charles Sandberg, MSD has done quite a bit of earthwork to regrade strip-mined areas to date. Responding to Mrs. Luthy's charge that "there is no prairie plan," he says it took 40 years to create all the strip-mine damage; it won't all be restored overnight.

Progress in reclaiming strip-mined lands, believes Illinois EPA's Jim Frank, has moved much more slowly, than MSD originally expected. But he says that considerable reclamation has been done, the vast majority of the land MSD purchased has been badly scarred with strip mines. And MSD has done a lot of work to restore the strip-mined areas.

How does Sandberg account for the more than 7,600 petition signatures? Certainly, he says, 7,600 people are not affected by adverse odors. The main point is that many citizens of Fulton County don't like to think of their community as being the dumping ground for big cities. Much of the citizen criticism, though, is poorly informed.

According to Dan Holman, managing editor for the *Canton Daily Ledger,* the leading newspaper in the reclamation area, the majority of Fulton County citizens could live with the MSD project *provided* there is no odor and no danger of virus in the sludge spray. As for the upcoming referendum in November, this is an *advisory* vote only. About the only thing that could come out of it, believes Holman, is more stringent county environmental standards on MSD. A majority of the Fulton County governing board is in favor of the project. Holman feels strongly that the project will stay.

Summing up the situation, editor Holman believes that "the MSD project is a good idea for the county as a whole. Fulton County is not the richest county in the world. It has many strip mines that decrease the county's tax base and increase the tax burden on citizens. Getting MSD to buy and upgrade strip mines is a sound, progressive step for the county."

PART SIX

Interpretation and Presentation
of Geologic Data
on the Urban Environment

Lack of availability of data on the environment has been only one of the problems facing planners searching for a stronger basis for preparing alternate plans for land and resource use. Planners who realized the need for geologic information often found it difficult to obtain pertinent data, since many reports were not directed toward their needs. Even if reports were available, some planners were not trained to interpret geological information. As a result, many plans were developed without the aid of basic data on the geology of the region and, as is now known, hazardous situations sometimes resulted.

Public awareness of geologic hazards and legislation to control planning errors resulted in some geologists responding to the need for geologic reports that were more useable. State geological surveys also responded to the need for environmental information in a form suitable for planning in the rapidly expanding urban areas of the 1960s. The Illinois State Geological Survey was one of the first with its *Environmental Geology Notes* series beginning in 1965. The U.S. Geological Survey also began many studies of urban geology; one of the best known is the cooperative study with the Department of Housing and Urban Development in the San Francisco Bay area.

Soon more geologists began to develop ways to present their research results to the public—not just to other geologists. Report styles changed and new techniques were developed for illustrating inventories of the physical environment that were being compiled (Nichols and Campbell, 1971; Wermund, 1974). Some of these reports for planning purposes were well illustrated and detailed, covering not only the traditional aspects of geology (Moser, 1971) but also describing climate, engineering properties of soils, and present land use (Christiansen, 1970).

The basic geologic factors for most planning purposes continued to be geologic hazards and the availability of resources, as described by C. F. Withington in Part One of this book. In these studies, *basic data* such as those describing bedrock type, surficial material, and groundwater quality, were usually reported on maps for each category. From basic data maps, interpretive maps showing the most favorable to least favorable sites for a specific resource use, such as sanitary landfill, could be derived. These maps are known as *resource capability* maps. A traffic-light color coding system, developed for illustrating soils data for planning purposes (Quay, 1966), was adapted for easy reading of these interpretive maps. In this system, green indicates the most capable areas for a specific resource use, red indicates the least capable areas, and yellow indicates areas of intermediate capability. The concept could be used with lettered (R, Y, G) maps (Gross, 1970) instead of expensive colored maps.

The step from basic data maps to a specific resource capability map was originally made with a series of transparent basic data overlays which could indicate the capability of regions for the resource use. Later, with the basic data stored on magnetic tape, the important factors of the basic data could be evaluated for a specific resource and the resulting resource capability map could be generated by computer. This technique provided a savings in time and money compared to making overlay and colored maps and also provided flexibility in the selection of factors that might be important in making a specific resource capability map. Although the basic data would not change very much with time, some factors of the basic data that are used to define capability might change. Such changes could result from improved technology or through changes in social, cultural, or economic attitudes toward land use.

Production of maps completes the geologist's role in the planning process; however, the planner must assemble data on the biological, social, and cultural aspects in a similar fashion. When these data are complete, a land-use *suitability map* is prepared which shows areas that are not only capable environmentally for a particular use, but which also are suited economically, socially, and politically for that particular use.

In this part of the book, the geologic input for planning purposes is presented in different ways for three geologically distinct regions; San Francisco Bay area, Denver area, and the State College area in Pennsylvania. These reports have been selected to show the diversity of planning problems in geologically different regions. The last paper in this section describes and illustrates the use of computer-based systems for handling geologic data for planning purposes. This approach has solved many of the problems of interpreting and distributing information on the physical environment at a rapid rate, but the problem of gathering data remains. To some extent data collection has been facilitated by remote sensing techniques, but for detailed studies surface mapping and investigation are required.

Even if the planning is well executed and the best of several alternate plans is adopted, extensive variation for political reasons can nullify not only the planning process, but also the expected resource savings. Fortunately, some states have recognized the need to protect sensitive areas such as coastal and mountain zones and have implemented necessary legislation for this purpose.

The importance of planning for long-range use of the land is understandable when we consider that children born in 1977 might retire in 2037 and could live to see the tricentennial celebrated in the United States. With an increasing population coupled with increasing resource use, the seriousness of a myopic view in planning is readily apparent.

REFERENCES

Christiansen, E. A., ed. 1970. *Physical environment of Saskatoon, Canada.* Ottawa, Canada: National Research Council of Canada, NRC-11378.

Gross, D. L. 1970. *Geology for planning in DeKalb County, Illinois.* Environmental Geology Notes 33.

Moser, P. H. 1971. *Environmental geology and hydrology, Madison County, Alabama, Meridianville, Quadrangle.* Geological Survey of Alabama, Atlas Series 1.

Nichols, D. R., and Campbell, C. C., eds. 1971. *Environmental geology and planning.* Washington, D.C.: U. S. G. P. O. No. 2300–1195.

Quay, J. R. 1966. Use of soil surveys in subdivision design. In *Soil surveys and land-use planning,* pp. 76–87. Soil Science Society of America and American Society of Agronomy.

Wermund, E. G., ed. 1974. *Approaches to environmental geology.* Texas Bureau of Economic Geology. R. I. 81.

The Geology of the San Francisco Bay Area and Its Significance in Land-Use Planning

26

Julius Schlocker

Introduction

The Bay Region planning area has a wide range of topographic features and contains many types of natural earth materials (figure 1). Information on the geologic condition, and on the geologic processes operating in the area, is an essential part of the basic data needed for land-use planning. If the geologic conditions and processes are disregarded, the consequences may be needless wasting of natural resources, inefficient and costly engineering works, and even loss of property and life. The purpose of this report is to describe the materials that make up the land, to discuss briefly some of the important geologic processes that affect the land, and to indicate the significance of the geology in land-use planning.

The influence of geology upon urban development is shown by the following examples: (1) the severity of building damage in San Francisco from the earthquake of April 18, 1906, was clearly related to the geology of the ground on which the structures were built. Damage was much greater to buildings founded on soft water-saturated sediments and man-made fill near the shore of San Francisco Bay than on the firm material of the hills. (2) Landslides are common in shear zones, in some interbedded clay and gravel beds of Pliocene age, and in cuts in thick shale sections that dip downward into the cut. The steady rise in property losses from landsliding is a consequence of the increasing use of hilly land for urban development. (3) Badly cracked homes, roads, sidewalks, etc., in some localities in the Bay Area, have resulted from construction on clayey material that expands greatly and becomes plastic when wet and shrinks and cracks when dried. (4) Buildings have subsided, some nearly 10 feet, in several land areas created by improper filling on soft sediments on the margins of San Francisco Bay. (5) Parts of the urban areas of Fremont, Alviso, and other places are intermittently covered by flood water.

Property damage and loss of life from these and other active geologic processes can be substantially reduced by early consideration of the geologic environment in planning urban developments.

Reprinted with permission of the author from *Regional Geology,* Supplemental Report IS-3, 1968, 47 pp. Association of Bay Area Governments, Berkeley, California. Also reprinted in *Urban Environmental Geology of the San Francisco Bay Region,* 1969, pp. 7–24, Danehy, E. A., ed. Association of Engineering Geologists, San Francisco Section.

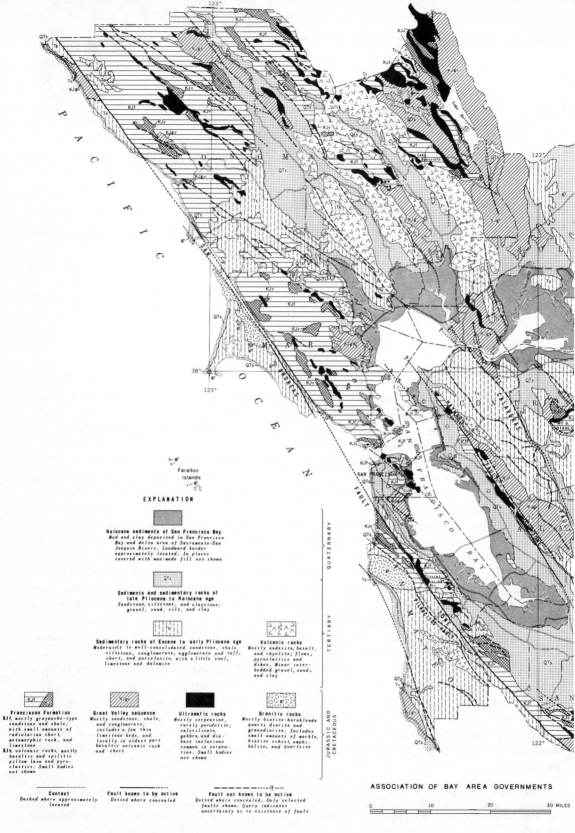

GENERALIZED GEOLOGIC MAP OF THE SAN FRANCISCO BAY AREA COUNTIES

FIGURE 1.

The success of major engineering works such as the bridges across San Francisco Bay and the Golden Gate, tall buildings in San Francisco and Oakland, housing subdivisions, and the freeway depends upon an evaluation of the nature and relationship of the rocks and soils on which they rest and on the geologic processes that may affect them. The performance of even a small structure such as a home or sidewalk also depends on how well it fits the geologic environment.

Production of mineral and rock commodities in the Bay Region must be coordinated with use of the land for industrial and residential sites and other purposes. Because large quantities of portland cement and construction materials such as sand and gravel for concrete and bituminous aggregate and crushed and broken rock for riprap and fill are used in urban development, producing sites should be located close to urban construction activity so as to reduce transportation costs; former quarries and gravel pits may be used for residential and industrial or even recreational purposes.

Valuable mineral resources may have to be protected by zoning in order to avoid their loss through residential development. In 1966, the value of mineral production in the area was approximately $117 million and included natural gas, petroleum, sand and gravel, stone, salt, magnesium compounds, bromine, clays, cement, mercury, diatomite, perlite, volcanic cinders, lime, peat, and natural steam. The Permanente Cement Co. plant in Santa Clara County is the largest producer of portland cement in California.

Mercury is an unusual and important mineral resource in the study area. Mercury production in 1966 was approximately one-tenth that of the total U.S. production. Cumulative production in Santa Clara County is the largest in the United States. Napa and Sonoma counties are also important producers. Mercury mines in the New Almaden area in Santa Clara County have produced mercury valued, at present prices, at approximately $500 million. These mines are threatened with extinction because of the encroachment of urban development. Mercury mines in Sonoma and Napa counties are generally in mountainous areas remote from present urban development.

The geologic information needed for land-use planning, for the design of an engineering work at a specific site, and for efficient exploitation of mineral resources is obtained mostly through field investigations and published reports.

The geologic map, figure 1, which shows the general distribution of the principal rock units and major faults was compiled largely from maps published at a scale of 1:250,000 by the California Division of Mines and Geology. The map sheets that cover the ABAG area are: Santa Rosa, Sacramento, San Francisco, San Jose, and Santa Cruz. Each map sheet includes a comprehensive list of published and unpublished references used in its compilation. Many details of the map sheets used to compile figure 1, such as small exposures of some rock types and many small faults, had to be omitted; some changes were based on the author's knowledge of geology of some localities. The position of the landward border of San Francisco Bay underlain by Holocene sediments is only approximate. It was compiled largely from the location of shorelines and marshlands shown on nautical charts and work sheets of the U.S. Coast and Geodetic Survey made in 1850 and later.

The units shown on the geologic map classify rocks with respect to age, origin, and composition. Such a classification gives only an approximate indication of the specific engineering behavior of the units. In general, older sedimentary rocks are better consolidated and better cemented than younger ones and, for practical engineering purposes, are harder and more competent. However, younger volcanic rocks in this area are generally less fractured, fresher, and harder than the older volcanic rocks.

A map unit consisting of a single rock type may show considerable variation from place to place in engineering behavior because of local variation in cementation, fracturing and shearing, ground-water conditions, etc. Thus variations of engineering behavior within a single map unit, which generally consists of more than one rock type, may be as great or greater than those between two different map units. On the other hand, rocks differing greatly in age, origin, and composition may have somewhat similar engineering properties.

Despite these variations in a single unit and similarities in different units, a generalized geologic map, such as figure 1, is useful for some broad early-stage planning purposes; larger scale maps are desirable for more detailed planning and detailed geologic exploration is a necessity at specific sites. The site exploration can be much more effective if the geology of the surrounding region is known.

Major Rock Units

The following description of the geologic rock units in the San Francisco Bay Area is intended only to provide a general idea of the relationship between the rock units, their engineering properties, and their economic potential. Locations of the rock units are shown in figure 1. The stability of earth materials in a foundation or on a natural slope or a man-made cut slope depends not only on the age, origin, and composition of the rock at the site but also on such other local conditions as the degree of jointing and fracturing of the rock, the orientation of fractures and of bedding in sedimentary rocks, the steepness of slope, and the ground-water regime. Furthermore, the value of a rock unit as a construction material, such as for concrete or bituminous aggregate, road base, riprap, or core and shell of earthfill dams, depends on its composition, state of chemical alteration, texture, fabric, fracture and shear characteristics, geometry, etc., at a particular locality. The suitability of the rock for construction purposes generally cannot be determined except from a detailed geologic investigation at the site.

Granitic Rocks

Granitic and associated metamorphic rocks are the oldest unit west of the San Andreas fault zone in Marin and Sonoma counties and west of the Pilarcitos fault in San Mateo County. They are not found east of these faults in the San Francisco Bay Area.

The rocks are mostly coarse-grained biotite-hornblende quartz diorite and granodiorite. They have intruded older metamorphic rocks, mostly marble and schist. Remnants of the metamorphic rocks are present in a few places as small masses, usually less than 100 feet across, on Point Reyes Peninsula and in small isolated bodies on Bodega Head and Montara Mountain. The granitic and metamorphic rocks are pervasively altered, but to only a minor or moderate degree. Weathering, generally to a coarse, clayey sand, is common to depths of 10 feet, and in places to as much as 70 feet.

Much of the granitic rock is crudely foliated, as shown by a more or less parallel arrangement of biotite and dark granitic inclusions, mostly inclined at a steep angle to the horizontal, but striking from due west to northwest and northeast. Well-developed sets of joints and shear planes, spaced a few inches to 2 feet apart, cut the rock, some parallel to the foliation and some in other directions. Broken rock and clay gouge are common along faults. In some places faults are 10 to 30 feet apart, and the fault is an inch to 5 feet in width.

Engineering Properties. The granitic and associated metamorphic rocks are suitable for heavy loads except where they are locally severely fractured, sheared, weathered, or otherwise chemically altered to weak material. They are generally excellent sources of general-purpose fill and small-size riprap, but they do not meet specifications for concrete aggregate or breakwater stone because of the pervasive alteration and because of the many joints and shear planes.

Franciscan Formation

The Franciscan Formation is a heterogeneous assemblage of rock types, mostly sedimentary and volcanic, that accumulated on the deep sea floor in Late Jurassic to Late Cretaceous time. Sandstone and shale make up 80 to 90 percent of the formation. The remainder is predominantly volcanic rocks and minor amounts of ferruginous chert and shale, conglomerate, limestone, and metamorphic rocks. These have been intruded by ultramafic rocks, chiefly serpentine. In some places the less abundant rock types crop out in areas as much as 5 square miles in extent.

Rock Types and Engineering Properties

Sandstone and Shale

Franciscan sandstone generally consists of fine- to medium-grained, angular feldspar, quartz, and rock particles embedded in a clay and silt matrix, so that the rock has very little permeability or porosity. The shale consists of silt- and clay-sized grains and contains substantial amounts of feldspar, quartz, and rock debris. Sandstone occurs in massive beds, in places more than 30 feet thick, separated by thin beds of shale; or in beds 2 to 12 inches thick alternating with shale beds 3 to 4 inches thick. In places shale sections may be more than 20 feet thick.

Engineering Properties. Fracturing is so pervasive that pieces of sandstone and shale are generally less than 3 or 4 inches in diameter. In scattered areas the fracture spacing is greater and coherent pieces of sandstone as much as 4 feet in diameter are found. The sandstone and shale, where fresh or only moderately weathered, generally form satisfactory foundations for most types of construction in urban developments where slopes are moderate. However, if there are shear zones or pervasive and randomly oriented fractures, careful design is required for cut slopes, dams and tunnels. Thick shale members, in particular, may require support when excavated. The sandstone and shale may be weathered to depths of as much as 60 feet, and this weathered mantle is subject to landsliding on steep slopes, especially where it is water-saturated. The weathering process has increased the amount of clay and disintegrated the once-whole rock to small particles.

Volcanic Rocks

Volcanic rocks are generally widespread in the Franciscan Formation. The larger bodies are shown on the generalized geologic map. Small, widely scattered bodies also occur in the vast Franciscan terrain of the Diablo Range of eastern Santa Clara and Alameda counties. The rocks are basaltic in composition, and exhibit the typical pillow structure of lavas erupted on the sea floor. The pillows are roughly spherical or ellipsoidal in shape, 6 inches to 4 feet in maximum dimension, and are separated by 1 to 12 inches of fragmental volcanic material. Where the pillow lava is chemically unaltered, the pillows are hard rock but the surrounding matrix is generally softer. Where it is weathered or altered, the pillows and enclosing material both are soft and friable. Locally the enclosing material has been altered to a weak expansive clay, allowing pillows to fall out of steep cuts. Fragmental volcanic rocks, in beds as much as 100 feet thick, are interbedded with pillow lavas. Generally the fragmental volcanic rocks are not as coherent as pillow lava, although this is not true in the Pacific area, where more than 4 square miles of fairly coherent fragmental volcanic rock is exposed. The weathered mantle on Franciscan volcanic rocks may reach a thickness of 60 feet, and commonly is the locale of landslides.

Chert

Chert is widespread in the Franciscan Formation, but it is not shown separately in figure 1. Chert is especially abundant on the Marin Peninsula, on the hills of central San Francisco, and in the hills of San Mateo, Belmont, and San Carlos. This rock also occurs in northeastern Santa Clara County and adjoining parts of Alameda County. It is usually less than 100 feet thick and is commonly associated with volcanic rocks. Chert beds, generally 1 to 4 inches thick, alternate with shale beds up to ¼ inch thick. Franciscan chert generally forms bold outcrops with no soil, because it is resistant to weathering and erosion.

Engineering Properties. Chert is generally excellent for foundation purposes. However, problems arise (1) where the rock is thoroughly altered to clay along some faults, (2) on steep slopes where chert is badly fractured or overlies volcanic rocks altered to clay, or (3) where the interlayered shale is altered to clay and the beds dip parallel to the slope.

Metamorphic Rocks

Metamorphic rocks known as blueschist, from the blue mineral glaucophane, and eclogite, a rock that contains garnet and pyroxene, are widely scattered in the Franciscan but make up only about

1 percent of the formation. They occur in isolated patches that grade into unmetamorphosed rock, in isolated rounded masses a few feet to a few hundred feet in diameter, and in belts several miles wide and tens of miles long. In many places the metamorphic rocks are exceedingly tough and fractures in them are widely spaced. Weathering is generally less than 10 feet deep and is usually less intense than in the Franciscan sandstone or volcanic rocks. Many of the isolated rounded masses are unweathered, possibly because their exposed position above the general surface allows wind and rain to remove the weathered rind, or possibly because it has been removed by shearing and scraping in landsliding.

Shear Zones

Fracturing and shearing has occurred repeatedly in Franciscan rocks and has been so thorough that coherent, unfractured pieces more than a few inches in diameter are scarce. In shear zones, which are common in the Franciscan Formation, fracturing and shearing has been more intense. These zones range in width from an inch to more than a mile and in length from a few feet to several miles. Within these zones the rocks consist of hard spheroidal masses, rounded and streamlined by shearing, set in a soft clayey smeared-out matrix. The matrix generally consists of large amounts of swelling clay minerals, such as montmorillonite, that expand into soft plastic material when wet. The hard competent pieces are of all sizes up to hundreds of feet, but are generally less than 20 feet in diameter. Chemical alteration of rocks in the shear zones is common and contributes to the low strength of the sheared rock. The distribution of the shear zones and of the less severely fractured or relatively unbroken rock is erratic; consequently the extent of the zones is difficult to estimate. In general, shear zones remain unmapped except on a few modern geologic maps of small parts of the Bay Region. It is inevitable that landslides will occur on slopes underlain by sheared and chemically altered rock. The erratic distribution of hard coherent rock masses within shear zones gives rise to considerable local variations in physical characteristics, and may lead to erroneous appraisal of foundation conditions unless the nature of the shear zones is understood.

Economic Value

Rocks of the Franciscan Formation are the major source of riprap, crushed stone, and sand and gravel in the Coast Ranges. Sandstone is the principal rock used. Because of the close spacing of the fractures in the Franciscan Formation, riprap blocks as much as 4 feet in maximum dimension can be obtained only at a few localities. Larger pieces of riprap for breakwater construction are available from Franciscan volcanic rocks, from gabbro inclusions in serpentine, or from Franciscan metamorphic rocks. Crushed standstone is used for fill, bituminous aggregate, and base for roads and airfield runways. Volcanics and ferruginous chert and shale, generally referred to as redrock, are used also for road base as well as for general-purpose fill. Crushed Franciscan sandstone and volcanic rocks are generally unsatisfactory for concrete aggregate except from sources in which the amount of poor quality material such as shale and altered rock is low. Nevertheless sand and gravel in stream-bed, floodplain, alluvial-fan, and terrace deposits derived from Franciscan rocks (principally sandstone) are generally of good quality and are the main source of concrete aggregate in the San Francisco Bay Area. The principal stream-laid deposits exploited today are in the Livermore Valley. Fresh sandstone, chert, and metamorphic rocks are used for masonry walls and building veneer. Franciscan limestone is used as aggregate in bituminous road surfacing and for general fill purposes. It is used also as a cement raw material and as a chemical in sugar refining. Limestone deposits are generally small and scattered, but a deposit west of Cupertino is large enough to supply one of the largest cement plants in the world.

Expansible shale, used as lightweight concrete aggregate, is made by heating Franciscan shale in several plants in the San Francisco Bay Area.

Mercury, mentioned in the introduction, is associated with serpentine and Franciscan rocks.

Copper, amounting to 40,000 pounds of recorded production, was obtained from the Clayton Mining district in Franciscan volcanic rocks on the northwest slope of Mount Diablo, mostly in the 1860s. The district is unlikely to become productive again.

Small deposits of manganese minerals occur in chert of the Franciscan Formation. Manganese ore has been mined in northeastern Santa Clara County, southeastern Alameda County, and in Sonoma and Napa counties.

Conglomerate is widespread in small lenses in the Franciscan Formation. In places it consists of hard well-rounded pebbles of chert and volcanic rock of obscure origin and is excellent for road base and general fill purposes.

Great Valley Sequence

Great Valley sequence is a name applied to a thick succession of sandstone, shale, and conglomerate, well exposed along the west border of the Sacramento Valley. The sequence differs generally from the sedimentary rocks of the Franciscan Formation in the greater persistence of individual beds, abundance of fossils, the occurrence of folds that are broad and open, and the absence of small-scale, pervasive crumpling, fracturing, and shearing. Volcanic rocks and chert are generally absent, except in the basal part which contains pillow lavas, pyroclastics (volcanic rock fragments ejected from a vent), and chert. The Great Valley sequence is exposed over widely scattered parts of the Bay Region.

Engineering Properties. Most of the rocks of the Great Valley sequence are compact dense sandstone and shale similar in composition and texture to the sandstone and shale of the Franciscan Formation and, where moderately fresh, are generally capable of supporting heavy loads. Jointing along several sets of fractures is common, but the rocks are not as severely and randomly shattered and sheared as the Franciscan Formation though shear zones do occur in these rocks. On slopes the shales tend to ravel and thus reduce the stability of the sandstone with which they are interbedded. As in the Franciscan Formation, the fresh shales contain small to moderate amounts of clay minerals that swell and become plastic when wet; the weathered shales contain large amounts of swelling clay. The weathered sandstone also contains significant amounts of swelling clays that contribute to low strength. Depth of weathering may be as much as 70 feet.

In the Berkeley Hills, Cretaceous sedimentary rocks are generally good for foundation purposes, especially where sandstone predominates. In many places they are stable in 1 to 1 cuts (a cut slope that in a horizontal distance of 1 foot rises vertically 1 foot) with only minor sloughing. However, they are involved in several large landslides and, where sheared, may squeeze plastically into tunnels during excavations.

Conglomerate of the Great Valley sequence also is a compact competent rock where fresh, but it generally weathers to a clayey sandy gravel.

Economic Value. Rocks of the Great Valley sequence make good construction material such as fill. Shales can be used for the impervious zone and sandstone and conglomerate for pervious zones of earth dams. Riprap is obtained where the sandstone beds are thick and relatively unfractured. Partly weathered conglomerate makes an excellent fill consisting of gravel with a cohesive matrix. Shales are a potential source for the preparation of expansible lightweight aggregate by heating. Natural gas is produced from Cretaceous sandstone in Solano and Contra Costa counties.

Ultramafic Rock

Ultramafic rocks intrude rocks of the Franciscan Formation and Great Valley sequence. Most of the ultramafic rocks occur as sheetlike bodies generally along the thrust faults on which the Great Valley sequence moved westward over the Franciscan Formation. Later compressions of the earth's crust have squeezed the faults and ultramafic rocks into large folds. In northeastern Napa County ultramafic rocks are exposed in a single contiguous sheet over more than 50 square miles. Some occur as pluglike bodies. Large areas southeast of San Jose, in San Francisco and Hayward, and in Alameda, Marin and Sonoma counties are underlain by ultramafic rocks.

The sheetlike bodies are mostly serpentine but contain inclusions of gabbro, diabase, and calcsilicate rocks. Serpentine in the Bay Region is generally green, blue, brown, gray, or yellow and consists of moderately hard rounded pieces encased in a soft waxy matrix of thoroughly sheared serpentine.

The proportion of hard pieces to soft matrix varies from place to place, but averages about 3:1. The size of the hard pieces also varies considerably, ranging from an inch to more than 6 feet in maximum dimension. In places the serpentine is almost entirely sheared for distances of more than 100 feet; in rare occurrences the serpentine is fairly competent, and the soft material makes up less than 10 percent of the mass. Some of the small serpentine bodies are lenticular and their borders are severely sheared. Both the serpentine and the adjoining rock, in zones that may be more than 100 feet wide, may be completely altered to a clay that becomes plastic and swells when wet.

The pluglike ultramafic bodies, such as the Cedars ridge, about 4 miles north of Cazadero, Sonoma County, are largely unserpentized olivine rock and are usually more competent and less sheared than serpentine.

Serpentine does not generally weather to form soil, but the surface material of some areas underlain by serpentine, probably highly sheared and chemically altered, is a dark gray clay that swells and becomes highly plastic when wet and shrinks and cracks when dry.

Engineering Properties. Because ultramafic rocks vary from hard rock to swelling clay, careful exploration and testing is required to determine their suitability for foundation purposes.

Economic Value. A variety of commercial mineral commodities occur within or at the borders of the serpentine bodies. These include mercury, magnesite, chromite, short-fiber asbestos, and jade.

Sedimentary Rocks of Tertiary Age

Tertiary rocks include sandstone, shale, siltstone, claystone, mudstone, conglomerate, agglomerate and tuff, silica-rich sediments such as diatomite, chert, and porcelanite, and small amounts of coal, limestone, and dolomite. Most of them were deposited in the sea, but some were deposited on land. Tertiary sedimentary rocks are widely disseminated in the Bay Region.

Engineering Properties. The wide variety of rock types in this unit gives rise to a great range in physical characteristics and uses. Most of the rocks older than Pliocene, however, are well compacted and have a high bearing capacity; consequently they make fair to good fill. Nevertheless, some of these older rocks, especially the fine-grained shale and claystone and some poorly cemented clayey sandstone, may slump badly on slopes steeper than 2 to 1. For example, the Markley Sandstone Member of the Kreyenhagen Formation, an Eocene sedimentary rock near Martinez, contains many beds of swelling clay; numerous landslides occur on slopes steeper than 2 to 1. Zones of shearing and chemical alteration are also found in the Tertiary sedimentary rocks, but they are not as common as in the Franciscan Formation. In the Siesta Formation, which is predominantly a claystone, and in the Orinda Formation, which consists mostly of poorly cemented conglomerate, sandstone, siltstone, and claystone that swells and becomes plastic when wet, slope stability is poor and landslides are common both in the formations themselves and in soil developed on them. Swelling and shrinking of the expansive clay can cause serious damage to structures unless due consideration is given to the design of the foundation. All of the Tertiary sedimentary rocks may be chemically altered to soft clay or locally sheared to a weak material. In tunnels near Stanford University Eocene bentonitic shale caused squeezing, swelling and slaking. Swelling of this rock is also responsible for considerable damage to homes and roads. Collapse of Miocene chert and shale and associated altered diabase dikes created difficulties in the excavation of the Caldecott Tunnel in the Berkeley Hills.

Economic Value. Sedimentary rocks of Tertiary age provide a variety of commercial products. Eocene sedimentary rocks in Contra Costa and Alameda counties contain coal; foundry, refractory, and glass sand; and ceramic and fire clay. The mines on the northeast slopes of Mount Diablo in Contra Costa County were the principal coal producers in the state until mining ceased in 1902. The mines on Corral-Hollow Creek in northeastern Alameda County were the main coal producers in the state in 1904, but operations ceased a few years later. About 1913 the largest production of porcelain ware in California came from Contra Costa County where clay from the coal mines of the Mount Diablo area was used.

Sufficient travertine or algal-reef limestone was taken from the west flank of Mount Diablo to supply the beet sugar industry, the Selby smelter, and the Cowell cement plant for more than 20 years. The deposits were worked until 1946.

Diatomite beds occur in sedimentary rocks of Eocene, Miocene, and Pliocene age. As of 1957 the only production of diatomite in the area was from a small deposit in Napa County.

Bentonitic clays are common in Tertiary sedimentary rocks, but no commercial production is known. Pozzolans, which can substitute for as much as one-third of the portland cement used in concrete, can be produced from a variety of clay- and opal-rich rocks; probably the best sources in this area are the opaline chert, porcelanite, and shale of Miocene age. Tertiary sedimentary rocks also contain enormous tonnages of shale potentially suitable for making expansible shale for lightweight concrete aggregate. Small quantities of phosphate pellets and nodules, thus far not produced commercially, have been found in shales of Miocene age in Marin County, of Eocene age in Solano County, and of Paleocene to Oligocene age adjacent to the Bay Region.

Natural gas is produced from Eocene sandstone in Solano and Contra Costa counties. The Rio Vista gas field, 20 miles northeast of Mount Diablo, has been the leading field in gas production in the state since 1943.

Total oil production from Eocene and Miocene beds in southern San Mateo County is approximately 1,000,000 barrels. Pliocene beds near Half Moon Bay have produced 40,000 barrels of oil. In 1967 oil was produced commercially from sedimentary rocks of probably Tertiary age near Livermore in Alameda County.

Volcanic Rocks of Tertiary Age

Volcanic rocks of Tertiary age include lava flows, associated dikes, and pyroclastics. In composition they are mostly basalts, andesites, and rhyolites, but they are interbedded with river and lake deposits of gravels, sands, and clays. They range in age from Oligocene to Pliocene.

Engineering Properties and Economic Value. Basalt, andesite, and some rhyolite flows of the Sonoma Volcanics are massive fresh rocks of high strength and hardness. Enormous quantities of basalt and andesite were shaped by hand and used as paving stone for streets in San Francisco many years ago. Today these rocks are important sources of concrete aggregate, fill, and flagstone. Pyroclastic rocks, mostly rhyolite in composition, contain fresh pumice that is used to make concrete blocks. In general, the pyroclastic rocks are not as durable as flow rock, and some are altered to swelling clays. The fragmental character of some of the basaltic pyroclastics favors economical production of crushed rock. More than $1.3 million in silver and gold was produced from quartz veins in the Sonoma Volcanics in northwestern Napa County from 1874 to 1940.

The Pliocene Moraga Formation in the Berkeley Hills consists chiefly of basalt and andesite flows and interbedded sediments. The lava flows generally make good foundations, in contrast to the associated sediments that are involved in numerous landslides. Crushed volcanic rock of the Moraga Formation is a major source of fill and coarse material for road base; some is also suitable for riprap.

The Pliocene (?) Leona Rhyolite, exposed in a narrow belt within and near the Hayward fault zone from Berkeley southward to Union City, is also a major source of fill and base rock. From 1891 to 1934 two mines in massive sulfide bodies in the Leona Rhyolite yielded more than 250,000 tons of pyrite that was used to make sulfuric acid. Small amounts of copper and silver were also recovered from the sintered pyrite. The now abandoned mines are located in Oakland, one about one mile north, the other about one-half mile northeast of Mills College. Acid waters from the abandoned mines draining into nearby residential areas corrode concrete sewer pipes.

The Tertiary volcanic rocks of San Mateo County vary from fresh hard rock to soft clay. Below the surface zone of weathering, which may be as much as 35 to 40 feet, the basalt flow rock is exceedingly hard and dense: however, it is highly fractured, sheared, and jointed into pieces less than 5 inches in maximum dimension. The agglomerate pyroclastic rock consists of fragments of volcanic rock as much as 5 inches in size in a fine-grained matrix that was formerly volcanic ash and mud. This rock and the fine-grained pyroclastic tuffaceous rock are generally much softer and weaker and more altered than the flow rock. The Tertiary volcanic rocks of San Mateo County are used for general-purpose fill and road base, but the rock is too sheared and fractured to use for riprap and concrete aggregate.

Sediments of Late Pliocene to Holocene Age

Unconsolidated sediments form the floor of broad valleys and other flatlands of the area and are therefore of great importance for urban and agricultural use. They would constitute more than one quarter of the Bay Region, if San Francisco Bay were excluded as well as the slopes covered with Quaternary debris derived by gravity and rainwash from weathered older rocks upslope. The largest areas covered by unconsolidated sediments are the Santa Clara Valley south of San Francisco Bay, the Great Valley portion of Solano County, and the contiguous Sacramento-San Joaquin River delta area. More than half of San Francisco is covered by Holocene dune sands and Quaternary marine deposits. Much of the urban development of the San Francisco Peninsula and the area east of the Bay is located on alluvial plains that slope gently towards San Francisco Bay. Urban areas are rapidly expanding over the alluvium-floored valleys of Livermore, San Ramon, Ignacio, Napa, Sonoma, and Petaluma-Cotati-Santa Rosa.

Sediments in the flatlands are gravel, sand, silt, and clay of alluvial plains, terraces, fans, river floodplains, channels, levees, mudflows, and lake bottoms. Marine deposits, mostly of silt and clay, but also of deltaic sand and gravel, are interbedded with the nonmarine deposits in the flatland adjoining the Bay. In the valleys north of the Bay, the deposits include a few beds of volcanic ash and thin lava flows. Thickness of the sediment varies from place to place, the broader valleys generally containing the thickest deposits. Sediments in the middle of the Santa Clara Valley near San Jose, in Livermore Valley, and in the Great Valley are more than 1,000 feet thick and may be as much as 3,000 feet thick in places. Near Santa Rosa, the thickness is 650 to 900 feet; near Cotati 800 feet; near Petaluma 500 feet; near Napa more than 1,000 feet; near Schellville in Sonoma Valley more than 750 feet. The uppermost deposit in parts of the Sacramento-San Joaquin River delta area of Contra Costa County is a bed of peat 40 to 60 feet thick.

Engineering Properties. Engineering properties of the sediments vary with their composition, origin, texture, fabric, etc.; and their use for foundation purposes is strongly influenced by the topography, ground-water conditions, and detailed geology of the site. Sand and gravel with or without small amounts of clay and silt are generally satisfactory as foundation materials. Structures on silt and clay may subside, or settle differentially, or the foundation may fail by shearing, or become damaged by expansion of the foundation materials during the winter wet season and shrinkage during the summer dry season. Sand and gravel are generally good for foundation purposes.

Economic Value. Sand and gravel are sources of good-quality fill, road metal, and concrete and bituminous aggregate. A good source of sand and gravel for fill and concrete aggregate is Livermore Valley where the deposits are several hundred feet thick.

Peat from the delta area east of Suisun Bay is mined and ground up for soil conditioning.

Sediments of San Francisco Bay

General Features of the Bay. San Francisco Bay, exclusive of Carquinez Strait and Suisun Bay, is about 50 miles long and 1 to 12 miles wide. It is a "drowned valley" aligned mostly northwest. Despite the general northwest-southeast alignment, its connection with the ocean is through a comparatively narrow east-west channel—the Golden Gate. Near the northeast end of the Bay (San Pablo Bay) it is connected with the Suisun Bay through a narrow east-west channel (Carquinez Strait) ½ to 1½ miles wide and 8 miles long. Suisun Bay is approximately 12 miles east to west and 6 miles north to south. A large volume of fresh water, amounting to millions of acre-feet, per year, from the combined Sacramento-San Joaquin River enters the Bay on the north; much smaller amounts enter the Bay from local streams draining adjoining parts of the Coast Ranges and the Santa Clara Valley.

Most of the Bay is shallow. About 70 percent is less than 18 feet deep; 80 percent is less than 30 feet deep. The tidal flow maintains a system of channels that branch out north and south of the main channel at the Golden Gate. These channels have the swiftest currents and the greatest depths.

Character of Sediments. The borings and the limited geophysical investigations in the Bay south of San Pablo Bay indicate that the Franciscan Formation and serpentine form most of the rock of the trough in which the Bay sediments were deposited. The rough topography of this trough probably resulted from erosion by ancestral streams in the Santa Clara Valley that were tributary to the stream system of the combined Sacramento-San Joaquin River to the northeast. The ancestral river system flowed out of the trough through a canyon—now the Golden Gate channel. Largely because of the repeated submergence and emergence of the trough during the Pleistocene, it is covered by an alternating succession of freshwater sediments, that accumulated in river channels, floodplains, lakes, etc., and marine and estuarine deposits.

The youngest deposits are mostly soft clay and silt (mud) and minor amounts of sand and gravel. In the north-central part of the Bay, sediments are generally coarser in the tidal channels than near the shore, probably because the finer particles are carried out of the Bay by swift tidal currents or are deposited in shallow tidal marshes. Bedrock or sand and gravel are found in the main trunk channel of the Golden Gate and as far north as San Pablo Strait; soft mud or clay are common along and near the shoreline. Local exceptions are the shores of rocky headlands where boulders, gravel, and sand are mixed with mud. Scattered sand deposits are also found near locations where ebb tides are concentrated into narrow powerful currents by shoreline projections. North-south sand ridges as much as 6 to 8 feet high, are common between San Francisco and Angel Island, and may be related to the interaction of ebb and flood tidal currents.

Engineering Properties. Recent bay muds generally contain more than 50 percent by weight of water. Many if not most of the foundation problems, such as shear failure and differential settlement in and around the Bay, and in much of the area considered to be reclaimable, are related directly to the presence of the uppermost soft bay mud. The problems arise because of its low shearing strength and high compressibility. Such properties as water content, shearing strength, swelling and shrinking, as well as its thickness, vary from place to place. The top 2 to 4 feet of bay mud loses water and becomes stronger in areas that have been diked off and drained. In some places in the Bay a marked increase in strength of the mud, believed by Treasher (1963) to be the result of desiccation during a glacial period of low sea level, has been found 40 to 70 feet below the top of the mud.

Sand and silt layers in the bay mud and clay may pose hazards to structures built upon them. During earthquake shocks these layers have a tendency to lurch, subside, and slide. Earthquake vibrations in thick soft bay mud are believed to be larger in amplitude and tend to have longer periods of vibration than those in firm soil or rock. Because these longer periods might be in the same range as the natural periods of vibration of some highrise structures, it is necessary to pay special attention to their design. Peat layers in the marshlands around San Francisco Bay, especially in the Suisun Bay area and the adjoining delta area, are highly compressible as foundation material. The stability of the fill overlying San Francisco bay mud is discussed by engineers in the three reports published in May 1967 by the San Francisco Bay Conservation and Development Commission.

Economic Value. Shell deposits, which supply the raw material for cement manufacture and poultry grit, occur as small lenses at various horizons in the upper 30 to 50 feet of bay mud. The deposits are erratically distributed in the bay mud between the latitude of Bay Farm Island and Dumbarton Bridge. The lenses consist mostly of individual shells embedded in silty clay or in sand. Approximately 30 million tons have been dredged since 1924. One recent estimate indicates that at least 75 million tons still remain. The shells are mostly the small thin native oyster, *Ostrea lurida*, about 2 inches long. Radiocarbon analysis show that most of the shells are more than 2,300 years old.

Mud, clay, and sand from the Bay are used for fill. Mud is used as a raw material for making cement in the same plant that uses shells as a source of calcium for the cement. Bay mud and clay have been used as binder for foundry sand and as pozzolan in the concrete of the San Francisco-Oakland Bay Bridge.

Landslides

Landslides are common in the San Francisco Bay Area, and are one of the chief agents of erosion. Most landslides involve failure of slope material under shear stress; thus the major factors to guard against are those contributing to high shear stress and to low shear strength. The most common causes of high shear stress are the removal of lateral and underlying support and loading at the head of slopes. Low shear strength may be inherent in the material of the slope or may develop by weathering and other physical and chemical changes in the material. Water is a very important factor in landsliding, because it contributes both to high shear stress and to low shear strength.

The great amount of landsliding in the area is due mostly to (1) hilly terrain with slopes underlain, in many areas, by unconsolidated surficial deposits and (or) sheared and shattered bedrock readily susceptible to sliding; (2) the common occurrence in surficial deposits and bedrock of clays that swell and become highly plastic when wet; (3) occasional periods of prolonged rainfall; (4) occasional strong earthquakes; and (5) activities of man that disturb relatively stable slopes by cutting and removing support; by loading the slope with excavated material, engineering structures, and irrigation water; or by disturbing the surface and ground-water regime.

Landslides will occur both in the surface mantle of weathered rock debris and soil in any geologic rock unit whenever the shear strength of the material in the slope is exceeded by the shear stress. For some rock units, such as the volcanic rocks and sandstone and shale of the Franciscan Formation, landslides are common in the weathered mantle but not as common in the rock itself. Landslides are very common on slopes made of the Orinda, Siesta, and Moraga Formations all of Pliocene age; in sheared rock of the Franciscan Formation; and in sheared serpentine (shown as "Ultramafic rocks" on figure 1). Landslides may also develop on low slopes in bay mud, especially during the construction stage when muds are excavated or covered with fill.

The use of geologic investigations and slope stability analyses in the planning and design of engineering structures may help to avoid landslide areas or to reduce the damage caused by sliding.

Earthquakes

The major active fault zones recognized in the San Francisco area are the San Andreas, Hayward, and Calaveras, all of which have a northwest trend (figure 1). The San Andreas fault zone is near the western border of the Bay Region. In the vicinity of San Francisco Bay the Hayward fault zone is approximately 20 miles east of and nearly parallel to the San Andreas fault zone. It extends southeastward from San Pablo Bay to Warm Springs. Its location northwest of San Pablo and southeast of Warm Springs is not definitely known. The Calaveras fault, a wide and complex zone, generally lies to the east of the Hayward fault zone, but may merge with it in the vicinity of, or south of, Calaveras Reservoir and may join the San Andreas fault zone 10 to 15 miles southeast of Hollister.

Slight nearly continuous movements, usually not accompanied by felt earthquakes, are known as tectonic creep. Such movements have been detected in the Hayward fault zone; in the San Andreas fault zone about 8 miles south of Hollister, San Benito County; and on the Calaveras fault zone in the city of Hollister; and elsewhere. A building on a line of movement in the San Andreas fault zone 8 miles south of Hollister is being sheared at the rate of about half-an-inch per year. Study of a damaged building in the Irvington District of Fremont indicates that at least 6 inches of differential horizontal movement has occurred since about 1920. Thus, in designing structures on active fault zones, the possibility of tectonic creep as well as sudden rupturing should be considered.

The earthquake record of the Bay Region is fairly well known from about 1850. Since that time more than 1,000 shocks, mostly of small magnitude, have been recorded. The major earthquakes, all accompanied by strong shaking and severe damage to man-made structures, were in 1865, 1868, and 1906. Two other less well documented shocks were in 1836 and 1838. The 1838, 1865, and 1906 shocks originated on the San Andreas fault zone; the 1836 and 1868 shocks on the Hayward fault zone. From this history and from seismic instrument records, which show continuous seismic activity originating within the area, it is clear why the Uniform Building Code has incorporated earthquake design and must continue to do so. The degree of hazard may be crudely assessed by the seismologist, geologist, and engineer. They consider the site in terms of the historic earthquake record; the regional and local geology, such as proximity and orientation to active faults; local foundation and slope stability conditions; prediction of the duration and intensity of shaking and acceleration; and possibility of displacement of the engineering work. For sites within or adjacent to an active fault zone, design must include the possibility or probability of violent movement and displacement accompanied by surface rupturing.

Despite the freedom from strong earthquakes since 1906, it is prudent and sensible to anticipate strong earthquakes and surface rupturing in and near the active fault zones. Such a possibility must be considered in making risk calculations for engineering works in the area.

REFERENCES CITED

San Francisco Bay Conservation and Development Commission, 1967, Fill—three reports on aspects of fill in San Francisco Bay: Bay mud developments and related structural foundations, by Lee and Praszker, 38 pp.; Seismic problems in the use of fills in San Francisco Bay, by H. Bolton Seed, 43 pp.; Seismic risk to buildings and structures on filled lands in San Francisco Bay, by Karl V. Steinbrugge, 44 pp.

Treasher, R. C., 1963, Geology of the sedimentary deposits in San Francisco Bay, California: California Div. Mines and Geology Spec. Rept. 82, pp. 11–24.

Engineering Geologic Maps for Regional Planning

27

Maxwell E. Gardner and Charles G. Johnson

The Project

Early in 1967, a controversy arose over the proposed subdivision of a small hillside tract near Boulder, Colorado. Opponents of the development pointed to the haphazard growth of residential subdivisions and to the hazardous soil and geologic conditions on some hillsides along the eastern margin of the adjacent Front Range. Awakened to the pressing need for geologic information, local government officials searched for information which would give their planners and engineers a basis for evaluating the geologic environment and potential problems of its development. In response to their inquiry, the U.S. Geological Survey arranged for a manuscript copy of a geologic map of the Boulder quadrangle (Wrucke and Wilson, 1967), to be placed promptly in open, or public, files. Although much useful information could be derived from this map, the regional, county, and city planners and engineers were reluctant to interpret the geologic information it contained in terms of engineering and land-use application.

Almost coincident with the request from Boulder, the Denver Regional Council of Governments (formerly the Inter-County Regional Planning Commission) sought the cooperation of the Geological Survey in conducting a regional planning study of geologic conditions as they might affect land-use development along the eastern margin of the mountains near Denver. A cooperative engineering geologic research project was started in August 1967, the first such project between the Geological Survey and a regional planning body. Initially the project was financed cooperatively by the regional planning commission, several city and county governments in the project area, and the Geological Survey. Since July 1968, it has been financed cooperatively by the Denver Regional Council of Governments and the Geological Survey.

The purpose of the project is threefold. First, to interpret the geology of the mountain area, foothills belt, and adjacent plains area in such a manner that the geologic information is of maximum value to planners, engineers, developers, builders, architects, financiers, and others concerned with land use and construction. Second, to develop ways in which that goal can be achieved and to obtain from map users opinions, ideas, and evaluations based on actual experience, which will serve as

Reprinted from *Environmental Planning and Geology*, 1971, pp. 154–69, Nichols, D. R., and Campbell, C. C., eds. Published cooperatively by Geological Survey, U.S. Department of the Interior, and the Office of Research and Technology, U.S. Department of Housing and Urban Development.

guides in the development of future engineering geologic maps and reports. Third, to develop and stimulate awareness among local government agencies and officials of the need for geologic information and professional engineering geologic services.

Part of the eastern front of the Rocky Mountains lies about 15 miles west of downtown Denver (figure 1). Against or near this mountain front lie the rapidly growing cities and towns of Boulder, Golden, Morrison, Littleton, and Lakewood, and suburban Boulder, Jefferson, and Arapahoe Counties. Within this area, eight 7½-minute quadrangles were chosen for study. All had been mapped topographically at a scale of 1:24,000 and were chosen chiefly for two reasons: (1) terrain and geologic conditions are more adverse to high-density development than elsewhere in the Denver region, and (2) geologic maps of the quadrangles are available, or basic geologic mapping is in progress.

As engineering geologic study is completed for each quadrangle, the resulting map and report are released to the public in open files to expedite availability of the information to local users. Two such engineering geologic reports—on the Boulder and Eldorado Springs quadrangles—have been released to date and are being used by local planners, engineers, and others.

The Geologic Setting

The geologic environment of the area west of Denver can be divided on the basis of topography and geology into three principal divisions: the plains area, the foothills belt, and the mountain area, as shown in figure 1.

The plains area consists of shallow valleys and wide flood plains of streams, separated by broad gravel- and loess-mantled divides. Locally, modern streams have cut down into clay shale that dips gently eastward to form steep valley sides scarred by landslide deposits.

The foothills form a narrow belt about 2 miles wide between the plains and the mountains. The foothills consist of a series of gravel- and lava-capped hills and sandstone- or conglomerate-crested hogbacks, commonly separated by strike valleys eroded in mudstone. Claystone lies at the base of the eastern dip-slope flank of the hogbacks and at the sides of the gravel- and lava-capped hills.

The mountain area west of the belt of eastward-dipping sedimentary rocks is composed of resistant metamorphic and igneous rocks. Along deep valleys and precipitous canyons the rock is slightly weathered and thoroughly jointed; locally, the steep slopes of valleys are covered with rock debris. Upland areas between streams are rugged and constitute remnants of an ancient erosional surface underlain by thoroughly weathered rock of uneven thickness.

Certain engineering geologic problems occur in all three landform divisions, but some are restricted to a single division. The severity of the problems varies chiefly with the kinds of bedrock and types of surficial material, surface slope, and ground-water conditions.

Land-development problems in the plains area include: widespread poor foundation conditions related to expansive clay and compressible loess; local, potentially unstable slopes, particularly on landslide deposits and along oversteepened valley sides; permeability that is too low in claystone and too high in alluvial gravel for sewage disposal systems; seepage along valley sides; and high water tables in valley alluvium, both locally associated with high concentrations of dissolved salts that are corrosive to steel pipe and deleterious to some concrete.

The foothills belt poses the most severe problems to urban development because of steep slopes, wide variation in strength of rock strata, and moderately steep dip of beds. As many as 14 geologic units, each with differing topographic expression, strength, slope stability, permeability, and erosional characteristics, crop out within the belt. Steep slopes, clay shale, and existing landslide deposits, together with the extensive hillside grading necessary, limit severely the safe economic development of hillside land in this area.

Hard crystalline rocks of the mountainous area cause problems different from those of the sedimentary rocks of the plains and foothills areas. The crystalline rock, though contorted, tilted, fractured, and faulted, is coherent and resistant, and therefore generally is expensive to excavate.

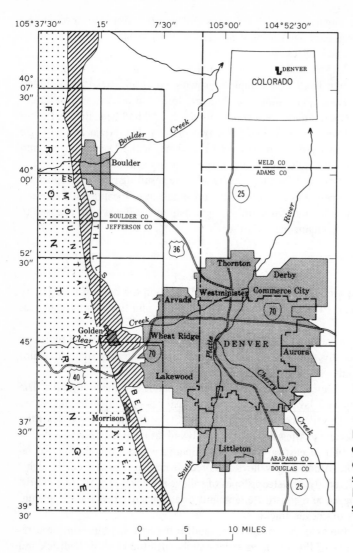

FIGURE 1. Map showing the area, quadrangles, and location of the co-operative engineering geologic research project in the Denver region. ES, Eldorado Springs quadrangle southwest of Boulder.

Thoroughly weathered rock is easily excavated, and thus such areas are better suited for relatively dense suburban development. Major problems encountered in mountain development include limited domestic water supplies available from wells and a growing number of polluted wells and streams caused by the many private underground sewage disposal systems. Potentially, the most hazardous and troublesome situation is in the deep mountain valleys and canyons, where slides and falls of debris and rock periodically threaten life, property, and roadway access.

The Engineering Geologic Maps

Engineering geologic maps and texts prepared for this project required a geologic map as a basic reference. The units of the geologic maps are in part subdivided and regrouped according to dominant compositions and textures. Additional information on special characteristics of the engineering geologic map units, and laboratory testing of selected samples, are required. As such information generally is not recorded during geologic field mapping, some additional field work may be required. Laboratory analyses include Atterburg limits, potential volume change, and X-ray analysis of clay.

Of the geologic maps available for this project, all are at a scale of 1:24,000. Some maps show bedrock only; others show exposures of undifferentiated bedrock among carefully differentiated units of surficial deposits. Some areas are covered by two maps—one showing surficial deposits, the other bedrock. However, the entire area eventually will have geologic maps showing both surficial and bedrock information.

An engineering geologic map should show, as precisely as map scale and technique allow, such information as the distribution of geologic materials; their structural characteristics, such as faults, joints, and foliation; hydrologic features, such as springs or the quality of water; and depth of weathering. Ideally, subsurface—or vertical—distribution, and areal—or horizontal—distribution of the map units are both depicted. Areal distribution is readily shown, but wholly satisfactory methods of illustrating vertical distribution are lacking. Conventional- and exaggerated-scale cross sections, plus abbreviated logs of soil borings and wells, are used to show representative subsurface relations.

A geologic map of the Eldorado Springs quadrangle by John D. Wells was published in 1967. Some of the formations shown on the geologic map were subdivided and regrouped on the basis of similar texture and composition to obtain units on the engineering geologic map of the same quadrangle (Gardner, 1969). To retain stratigraphic information and provide ready reference to basic geologic data, the geologic map units, or such parts as appropriate, are shown as equivalents of each engineering geologic map unit in the tabular text.

For example: Slocum Alluvium shown on the geologic map has a sandy, silty, and clayey matrix. Colluvium, also shown on the geologic map, has a sandy, silty, and clayey matrix only locally. On the engineering geologic map the entire sandy, silty, clayey Slocum Alluvium is combined with only the sandy, silty, clayey part of colluvium to yield the single engineering geologic map unit "Bouldery sand, silt, and clay." The remainder of colluvium on the geologic map is sand free, but is clayey and contains pebbles and boulders. On the engineering geologic map it alone constitutes the map unit "Pebbly, bouldery clay."

Similarly: on the geologic map the Fort Hays Limestone Member of the Niobrara Formation is mapped separately from the Smoky Hill Shale Member of the same formation. However, the Glennon Limestone Member (LeRoy, 1946) within the Lykins Formation is not mapped separately from the rest of that formation, which is calcareous siltstone and fine-grained sandstone. In the engineering geologic map, because of their similar composition, texture, and behavior, the Fort Hays Limestone Member of the Niobrara Formation and the Glennon Limestone Member within the Lykins Formation are mapped as a single engineering geologic map unit: "Limestone."

Symbols for bedrock units on the engineering geologic maps consist of lowercase letters that abbreviate the names of the geologic rock types such as conglomerate. Symbols for surficial deposits consist of combinations of uppercase letters, which denote the dominant texture, and lowercase letters, which denote qualifying compositional or textural adjectives.

Characteristics of engineering geologic map units having special engineering significance are emphasized by special notations. For example, clay shales are subdivided into three units on the basis of their shrink-swell potential, and thereby, on their potential for damaging structures on inadequately designed foundations. The symbol for the highly swelling clay shale unit is underscored three times; the symbol for the moderately swelling unit is underscored twice; the symbol for the slightly swelling unit is underscored once; and the symbol for the nonswelling unit is shown with no underscore. Bedrock units, which are hard and generally require blasting before excavation, are overscored.

The engineering geologic maps contain specialized information on four topics of significant local concern: expansive clay, landslide deposits, hydrologic conditions, and mined areas. Each topic poses a potential problem to land development.

Expansive clay derived from bedrock formations is widespread and poses the greatest problem to construction. The clay developed—in part by weathering—from shale formations of marine origin and may be residual, colluvial, or alluvial in character. Variations in expansive properties of the clay-bearing map units appear to be the result of differences in the kinds and amounts of clay minerals present, and the grain size and degree of cementation of the surficial deposit in which they occur. Both clayey surficial units and clay shale in the Denver region thus can be subdivided on the basis of expansive properties, and once the amount of expansion of a map unit is established, the mapping is not difficult.

Near Boulder, the Pierre Shale has been subdivided into four mappable engineering geologic units (Gardner, 1968). Boundaries of these units correspond in part to lithologic boundaries shown on the geologic map, and in part to boundaries between different clay-mineral suites. The engineering geologic map units coincide, moreover, with fossil zones described by Scott and Cobban (1965). Thus boundaries of the biostratigraphic zones are used in turn for boundaries of the engineering geologic units. In the Boulder area, residual clay derived from the upper part of the Pierre Shale was found the most likely to cause damage to concrete slabs and foundations of small buildings. The upper part of the shale forms a belt that parallels the foothills, and ranges in width from about 5 miles near Boulder, to several hundred feet near Golden (Scott and Cobban, 1965).

Expansive clay developed within surficial deposits is nearly as widespread as expansive clay derived from bedrock formations, but generally poses a less severe problem. Soil-forming process produced clay minerals and deposited them in thin layers or "clay-pans," in ancient soil profiles in the upper parts of surficial deposits of Quaternary age. These ancient soils are not mapped, because such mapping is very time consuming at the scale 1:24,000, but their general character and occurrence are described in the tabular text.

Landslide deposits are derived from bedrock formations and surficial deposits, including man-made fill. They are locally numerous and present a significant problem to development. Active landslide deposits are easily identified, but stable deposits may not be. Landslide deposits that have been stable for a long time are difficult to recognize because their most distinguishing features are modified, concealed, or obliterated with time, and exposures are generally poor or absent. Thus there may be a few landslide deposits that have not been identified and mapped.

Where landsliding is observed in the field, or where landslide origin can be demonstrated by geologic and topographic evidence, perhaps with the aid of aerial photographs, maps, or written records and reports, the deposits are mapped as *known* landslide deposits. Where displacement cannot be demonstrated without trenching, but where geologic and topographic evidence indicates movement probably occurred, the feature is mapped as an *inferred* landslide deposit. Finally, where geologic or topographic information only suggests that displacement has occurred, the feature may be mapped as a *possible* landslide deposit. The classification of landslide deposits and the explanation of map symbols used for the deposits are shown in figure 2.

The kind of information about individual landslides that is *not* given in a regional study is competent evaluation of the present or future stability of landslide deposits. The map is not a landslide hazard map, but is a record of the existence and history of the landslide deposits. Evaluation of the hazard must come as the result of detailed studies, including a subsurface investigation, at the site of each landslide deposit.

Hydrologic information that is valuable and easily obtained also appears on the engineering geologic maps. Springs, in addition to those already on the topographic base, are indicated by conventional symbols. Wet areas, including areas of high water table, ground-water seepage, and leakage from reservoirs and canals, are shown by pattern overprints; discharge areas of ground water high in concentrations of alkali and sulfates are indicated by appropriate chemical symbols. These hydrologic data increase the information available to the user for evaluation of the effect of water on foundation stability, slope stability, waste disposal, and corrosion.

Mined areas are represented in two ways. Abandoned coal mines, clay pits, quarries, and prospect pits in the plains area and foothills belt are shown by conventional symbols. In addition, patterned overprints show known areas of underground mining, and special contour lines or annotations give elevations of underground workings above sea level.

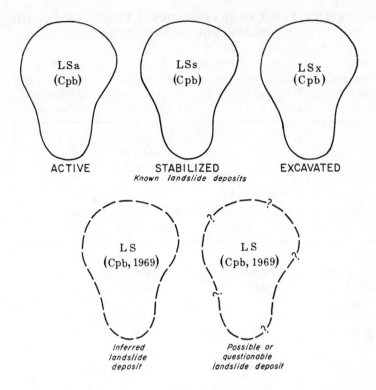

FIGURE 2. Classification of landslide deposits, and the engineering geologic map symbols used for them. LS, landslide deposit; LSa, active landslide deposit; LSs, stabilized landslide deposit; LSx, excavated landslide deposit. (Cpb), unit, or units, that constitute a landslide deposit. (Letter symbols enclosed in parentheses indicate soil texture of the landslide deposit, in this case Pebbly bouldery clay.) (1969), year landslide moved, or year landslide deposit was excavated, as appropriate.

The Tabular Text

Each engineering geologic map is accompanied by a tabular text for easy reference to and from the map. The first column of the table contains the name of each engineering geologic map unit, together with its map symbol. Other headings across the top of the tabular text, shown in table 1, categorize engineering geologic information supplied within the table for each unit. The information contained in a table is partly descriptive and partly interpretive. The information is phrased in qualitative terms, but is based on the quantitative data available.

Most of the purely descriptive information contained in columns 3 through 5 of the tabular text is obtained from existing geologic maps, reports, and additional field observations. The information placed in column 3 is outlined in table 2.

The interpretive information consists primarily of the inferred engineering behavior of each map unit. The inference is based largely on field observations of physical characteristics of each unit. It is based partly on the interpretation of results obtained by standard engineering tests made on selected samples in laboratories of the U.S. Geological Survey at the Denver Federal Center and partly on engineering reports and performance records obtained from numerous private and local government sources.

TABLE 1. TABULAR TEXT HEADINGS, TO ACCOMPANY THE ENGINEERING GEOLOGIC MAPS

DESCRIPTIVE INFORMATION

(1) Engineering geologic map unit, with map symbol	(2) Equivalent geologic map unit(s)	(3) Description structure and thickness	(4) Topographic expression, and surface relief	(5) Weathering, and ancient soil profiles
		(see Table 2 for outline of contents)		

INTERPRETIVE INFORMATION (with topics included)

(6) Workability	(7) Surface drainage, and erosion	(8) Ground water	(9) Suitability for waste disposal

Excavation:
  Equipment type, or method
Compaction:
  Characteristics
  Equipment type
Drilling
	Runoff rate
	Erosion susceptibility
		Permeability
		Water table:
		  Depth
		  Character
		  Yield to wells
		  Quality
		  Use
			Soil absorption, Septic tanks Sanitary-landfill sites

(10) Foundation stability	(11) Slope stability	(12) Probable earthquake stability	(13) Use
Expansive clay Collapsible (loessial) silt Subsidence	Possible failure types Hazardous situations Trench-wall stability	Most hazardous potential	Building or construction material Common land use

TABLE 2. OUTLINE OF TOPICS INCLUDED IN COLUMN 3 OF THE TABULAR TEXT: "DESCRIPTION, STRUCTURE, AND THICKNESS," TABLE 1.

Dominant lithology and texture
Minor lithologies and textures
Grain size
Grading or sorting
Significant mineral composition
Consolidation of overburden
Relative density
Consistence
Stratification
  Character
  Continuity
  Problem strata

Color
Potential volume change (for clayey materials)

Structure
  Attitude
  Bedding
  Foliation
  Joints
Thickness

Uses for Engineering Geologic Maps

Engineering geologic maps prepared for this cooperative research project have two principal uses. One is as a source of information from which special-purpose engineering geologic maps may be pre-

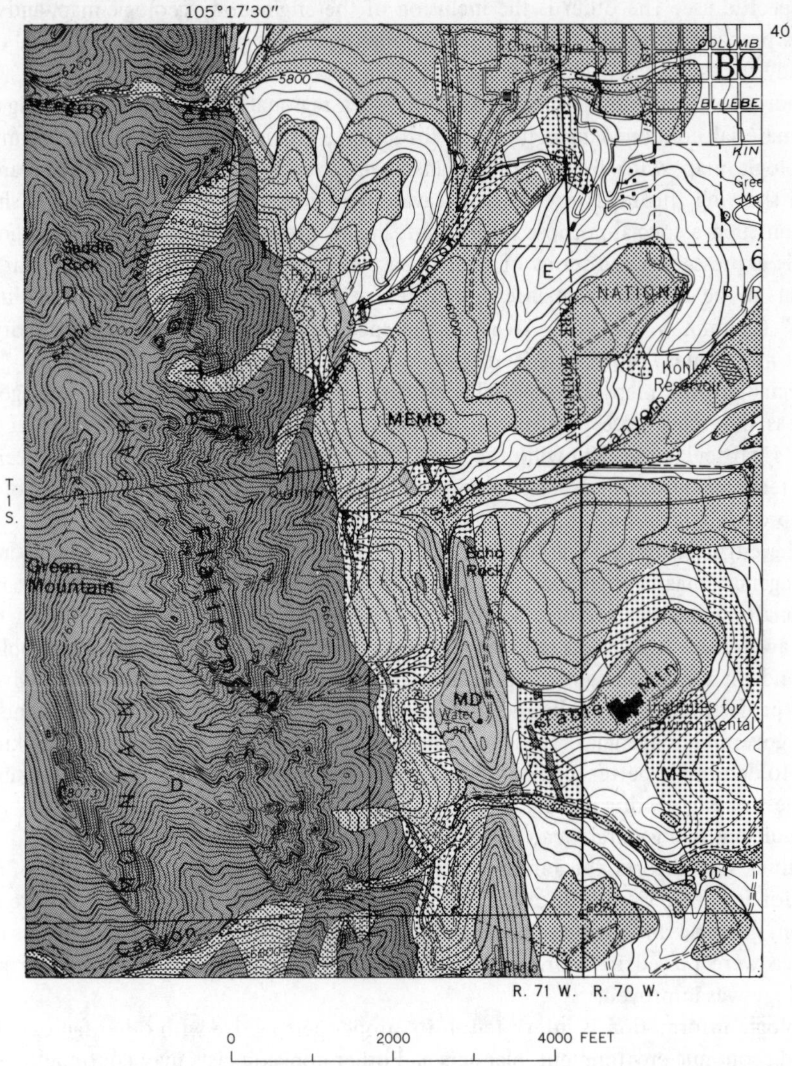

FIGURE 3. Special-purpose engineering geologic map: Ease of excavation
Explanation:
E, Easy with most power equipment
ME, Moderately easy with small rippers and scrapers
MEMD, Moderately easy with small rippers and scrapers, but moderate-
ly difficult with backhoes and trenchers because of numerous large
boulders
MD, Moderately difficult with large rippers and scrapers: locally requires
blasting
D, Difficult—requires blasting

pared for a specific use. The other is the inclusion of the engineering geologic map, and any special-purpose maps prepared from it, in a set of comprehensive plans prepared by a regional or local governmental body for the orderly development of a given area.

Special-purpose maps may be prepared readily by a regional planner or others using appropriate interpretive material contained in columns 6 through 13 of the tabular text. For example, the engineering geologic map, with the use of a transparent overlay, may be used to prepare a special-purpose map showing the relative ease of excavation of materials in various areas as shown in figure 3. Units on such a special-purpose map might, in this instance, consist of five categories of geologic materials expressed in the terms of relative ease of excavation shown in the tabular text. These categories can all be derived from interpretive textual materials contained in the column headed "Workability" (column 6, table 1). Areas on the special-purpose map for each category are taken from the appropriate areas of the engineering geologic map.

Such special-purpose maps are especially valuable in alerting both individuals and governmental bodies to areas that may pose problems to development and, conversely, to areas that may be appropriate for a particular use. Knowing the general potential of a given area, those concerned should seek detailed technical advice in order to determine the exact nature and degree of the potential problem or the appropriateness of a site, and thus to facilitate further planning and design.

Use of the engineering geologic maps in Colorado by the general public and by local and State officials and agencies has been increased by a growing awareness of the need for geologic information and professional engineering geologic services. One purpose of this cooperative project has been to heighten the awareness. Illustrated talks on the engineering geologic maps, on local problems related to geology, and on possible engineering geologic contributions to their solution are given to civic, business, and professional groups. In addition, close contacts are maintained with planners and engineers in local government agencies. These meetings and discussions are necessary to gain knowledge of user's needs, to determine better map and text format, and to encourage awareness by public officials of the usefulness of engineering geologic maps in approximating the existence of adverse—or favorable —geologic conditions in a general area.

As a result of such efforts, the Jefferson County Planning Department revised part of its Comprehensive Plan for Jefferson County. For the first time in the area, geologic conditions were considered. In the revision, geologic and planning concepts were integrated, local geologic conditions of engineering importance were placed in appropriate perspective, and technical phraseology pertinent to engineering geology was improved.

Until geologic information is integrated in its proper perspective with other factors of the physical, social, and economic environment, planners and other nongeologists may continue to use geologic information and professional services of the engineering geologist only occasionally, and then only in a "panic" response *after* a geologic problem has caused loss of property or even life. Undue emphasis on so-called "geologic hazards" may cause engineering geology to be used only as a salve to an irritant. Instead, engineering geology should be applied as an integral part of total environmental planning for engineering and land development.

REFERENCES CITED

Gardner, M. E., 1968, Preliminary report on the engineering geology of the Boulder quadrangle, Boulder County, Colorado: U.S. Geol. Survey open-file report.
——, 1969, Preliminary report on the engineering geology of the Eldorado Springs quadrangle, Boulder and Jefferson Counties, Colorado: U.S. Geol. Survey open-file report.
LeRoy, L. W., 1946, Stratigraphy of the Golden-Morrison area, Jefferson County, Colorado: Colorado School of Mines Quart., v. 41, no. 2, 115 pp., [April].
Scott, G. R., and Cobban, W. A., 1965, Geologic and bio-stratigraphic map of the Pierre Shale between Jarre Creek and Loveland, Colorado: U.S. Geol. Survey Misc. Geol. Inv. Map I-439.
Wells, J. D., 1967, Geology of the Eldorado Springs quadrangle, Boulder and Jefferson Counties, Colorado: U.S. Geol. Survey Bull. 1221-D, 85 pp.
Wrucke, C. T., and Wilson, R. F., 1967, Geologic map of the Boulder quadrangle, Boulder County, Colorado: U.S. Geol. Survey open-file report.

28

An Environmental Approach to Land Use in a Folded and Faulted Carbonate Terrane

Richard R. Parizek

Most engineers and engineering geologists have focused their activities on local projects and for individuals, rather than on regions and for groups of people. Clients and technical personnel have not, in general, been concerned with the influence of their projects on others or on man's environment except as required by codes, laws, or economic competition. Increasingly in recent years, local constraints imposed by the geologic setting have influenced site selection, exploration procedures, design, and construction in both rural and urban regions. Experiences with failures, costly delays in construction, costly corrective actions, and related difficulties have shown legislative and natural constraints to be worthy of greater consideration. Moreover, the expansion of geotechnical sciences—knowledge gained from years of successful engineering and geologic practice—has made it possible to predict in advance the problems likely to be encountered under certain field conditions.

Little attention has been paid, by contrast, to the composite influences of man's diverse activities on his environment—influences which have regional impact. From the earth scientist's point of view, it is becoming clear that all factors bearing on the environment must be evaluated, even when considering the suitability of a site for a single activity. The earth scientist, to meet his responsibilities in this more encompassing environmental approach, must expand his outlook beyond that of the traditional engineering geologist or even the broadly based urban geologist. The responsibilities of the environmental geologist are not only to individual clients but also to the population at large. He must be concerned with man-related activities in rural as well as urbanized areas, to determine the suitability of a region for a particular activity and the region's response to that activity.

The details of the hydrologic, geologic, topographic, biologic, and climatic setting vary from place to place to such an extent as to produce a labyrinth of complexity. It is desirable to reduce this complexity through analysis and classification in order to understand how an environmental system will respond to a particular set of stresses, either natural or man made. In general it is easier to catalog the stresses that are acting, or are likely to act, within a region than it is to predict the resultant strains. Such prediction requires a detailed understanding of all the interacting natural laws governing stress-strain relationships in nature—the relating function shown in figure 1. The strains frequently result from chain reactions or complex interactions of conditions and processes which often are obscured

Reprinted from *Environmental Planning and Geology,* 1971, pp. 122–43, Nichols, D. R., and Campbell, C.C., eds. Published cooperatively by Geological Survey, U.S. Department of Interior, and the Office of Research and Technology, U.S. Department of Housing and Urban Development.

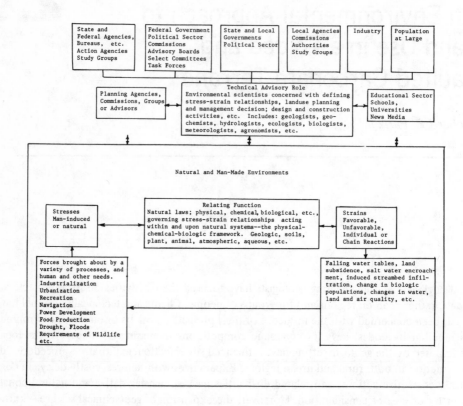

FIGURE 1. A conceptual framework in which to view environmental science.

by the nature and magnitude of the strains. Furthermore, there are a great variety of natural settings within which stress-strain relationships must be distinguished.

Figure 1 shows a conceptual framework within which the environmental scientist must operate. Although the environmental geologist is directly responsible for only a fraction of the entire system, his role is critical. For simplicity, a single geologic terrane has been selected to illustrate this role. Stresses operating in this terrane are common to many others, although the particular strains and the magnitude of the effects encountered may be in part unique.

Folded and Faulted Carbonate Terrane of the Ridge and Valley Province

General Geologic Setting. A brief review of the general geologic setting in folded and faulted carbonate rock terranes will provide a framework for review of land-use problems. The following discussion of folded and faulted carbonate rocks pertains particularly to the Nittany and Penns Valleys —the westernmost carbonate valleys of the Ridge and Valley Province (figure 2). However, the discussion also applies to other provinces of Pennsylvania underlain by carbonate rocks and to similar carbonate valleys to the south within the Ridge and Valley Province.

Carbonate rocks, which constitute this particular terrane, consist of up to 7,200 feet of interbedded limestones and dolomites with lesser amounts of sandstones, sandy dolomites, and shales. Also present are 3,200 feet of noncarbonate shale, sandstone, and quartzite which were deposited on

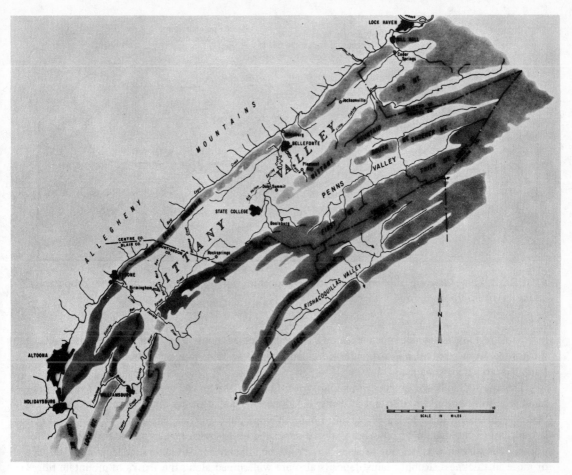

FIGURE 2. Geographic features of Nittany and Penns Valleys, central Pennsylvania. Mountain ranges are shaded gray.

the carbonate rocks. The hardest of these rocks are more resistant to erosion and form ridge crests which surround canoe-shaped lowlands underlain by less-resistant carbonate rocks and shale.

Bedrock units have been folded to produce overturned folds and broad to tight folds, and commonly are complexly faulted (figure 3). It may be seen from figure 3 that individual rock units vary abruptly in their distribution, both horizontally and vertically. Voids or conduits have developed where flowing water enlarged partings between layers, dissolved rock on either side of joints or cracks in the rock, or dissolved layers in which ground-water flow was concentrated.

Relief between adjacent ridge crests and carbonate lowlands may be from 500 to 2,000 feet. Within carbonate lowlands, relief may vary from a few tens of feet to more than 300 feet, particularly in the westernmost carbonate valleys of Pennsylvania.

Residual soils vary from 0 to more than 200 feet in thickness over the carbonate rocks. Bedrock may be exposed at the surface over broad areas or in some localities not at all, depending upon such things as topographic setting, rock type, and degree of erosion. Soils may be of sand, sandy clay, silt, or clay. Typically they are layered and reflect relict bedding in the parent rock material. Sags and depressions, developed locally on the surface of carbonate bedrock, have produced contortions in the bedding. Residual soils in many areas have been under cultivation for 100 to 200 years. Individual layers of these soils cause permanent to intermittent perched ground-water lenses and surface ponds

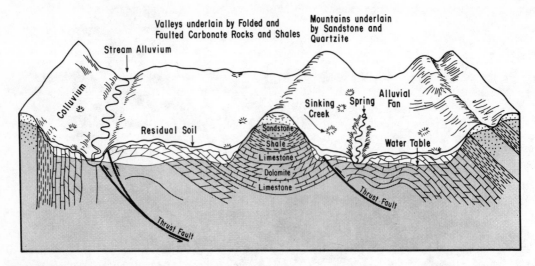

FIGURE 3. Block diagram showing common relationships among rock type, structure, topography, and soils within the Ridge and Valley Province.

in upland regions. Elsewhere, open solution cavities in rock or sink holes exposed at the surface occur downslope from resistant noncarbonate ridges and in valleys underlain by carbonate rocks but containing intermittent streams.

Transported soils are of three principal types: (1) alluvial deposits in flood plains of valleys containing permanent and intermittent streams; (2) alluvial terrace deposits built on residual soils or on bedrock surfaces leading to water gaps in mountain ridges, and alluvial fans at the base of mountain slopes; and (3) colluvium or unsorted material deposited at the base of steep mountain slopes. Transported soils vary in texture, but in general they are rich in clay and silt and range from 5 to 100 feet or more in thickness. Rubbly talus deposits also are widespread along the flanks of mountain ridges formed by sandstone and quartzite. Because of the relative impermeability of transported soils on mountain flanks, the soils are commonly poorly drained, contain shallow water tables, springs, and seeps, and are located within former or present ground-water discharge areas.

The water table in carbonate rocks adjacent to mountain ridges varies in depth, depending upon the depth of incisement of the local tributary and master drainages. A few to nearly 100 feet to the water table is common for low-relief areas, and 100 to 400 feet may be typical for more deeply dissected carbonate areas. Water in most tributary drainages moves wholly or in part beneath the surface. Solution conduit systems are well developed. These may transmit ground water for hundreds of feet or even for miles from recharge areas to discharge areas. Ground-water flow rates within deep conduits average 50 feet per hour or more, and flow volumes may exceed 10 million gallons a day along individual conduits. Two to five percent of the rocks, by volume, may be voids which store ground water. Individual well yields may range from 1 to 10 gallons per minute at unfavorable locations and 1 to 3 million gallons per day for wells where rock fractures intersect in valley bottoms or other favorable settings (Lattman and Parizek, 1964; Siddiqui and Parizek, 1969).

Regional Growth. Early growth corridors in the carbonate valleys of Pennsylvania were along canal, road, and railroad routes. Today these corridors are experiencing rapid urban and industrial growth within a natural framework which is particularly vulnerable. Lands underlain by carbonate rocks are close to the major growth corridor that spreads from Washington, D.C., through Baltimore, Philadelphia, and New York to Albany.

The sensitivity of the folded and faulted carbonate terrane to man's activities can be readily appreciated even in rural to semirural areas such as the Nittany Valley where man-induced stresses are still relatively simple. In urban regions where these stresses are highly concentrated, strains are still more pronounced, and the responses of the natural system to individual stresses are often more difficult to determine. For purposes of illustration, the semirural area of Spring Creek Basin, near State College, will be considered (figure 2).

Spring Creek Drainage Basin within Nittany Valley has an area of about 140 square miles. Nearly 65,000 people live in Bellefonte and State College, the principal towns, and in 7 to 10 smaller communities and subdivisions. The population density is approximately 465 people per square mile. Roughly 30 percent of the basin area is forested, 50 percent under cultivation, and about 20 percent in light urban developments. High-quality limestone is mined both from open pits and from 400 to 900 feet below ground.

Specific stresses include crop fertilization, disposal of farm wastes, urban solid wastes, sewage and chemical effluents, ground-water development, highway and pavement construction facilitating rapid runoff and limiting ground-water recharge, limestone mining, and storm-water disposal.

Examples of Stresses and Strains

Agricultural Activity. Natural and chemical fertilizers are extensively used on cultivated and pasture lands. Barnyards are numerous, with exercise yards and manure storage representing concentrated chemical and organic stresses on the soil-rock-water biologic system. Locally, where soils are only a few feet to less than 20 feet thick, leachates derived from agricultural wastes and chemicals have exceeded the soil's adsorption capacity and the biologic system's renovation capacity, and the result has been contamination of ground water. Runoff from and through pastures, barnyards, and cultivated lands moves into surface and subsurface water sources with little or no alteration. This comparatively light loading of pollutants over a prolonged period means that the chloride, nitrate, phosphate, and bacteria concentrations in local ground water—which may serve as a water source for nearby users—are in excess of recommended drinking-water standards.

Domestic sewage disposal in rural and small community areas is by the septic tank and tile-field method, direct disposal to dry wells open to bedrock, and open surface drains. There is little if any treatment, and additional pollution results. Nitrate and phosphate concentrations are sufficient to stimulate excessive aquatic plant growth in local streams even in the absence of sewage effluent discharged from modern treatment plants. Dissolved oxygen levels in such creeks may be low enough at night to produce fish kills, particularly during low flows when water temperatures are highest. A combination of cavernous bedrock, thin soils, gaping sink holes receiving surface runoff, and poor management practices have combined to produce the problems noted.

Vegetable processing and freezing plants also produce vast volumes of process water which must be disposed of. In the past, these plant effluents were pumped directly into streams or stored in leaky lagoons located above cavernous carbonate rocks. In more recent years, spray irrigation procedures have been used to provide treatment, relying upon physical-chemical and biological processes operating in the soil for water purification. At times, loads have been applied to irrigation plots that exceed the renovation capacity of the system. Elsewhere soils may be thin or absent, hence no treatment was achieved, or heavy irrigation promoted runoff of untreated waste waters to open sink holes where direct contamination of ground water resulted.

Little can be done in some rural areas to minimize ground-water pollution resulting from agricultural wastes. Practices are deeply rooted in tradition and barns remain where they were built years ago. However, uses of potentially harmful pesticides and herbicides can be outlawed and farmers can be educated to the risks of overapplication of such chemicals.

It will become mandatory to re-evaluate farm-waste disposal practices resulting from large, highly concentrated animal populations. Feedlots and large dairy and poultry plants are industries in the real sense. Operators of such facilities will have to collect, treat, and dispose of their waste by-products as required by other industries. Site-selection criteria may even need to be adopted for these industries to minimize or eliminate ground-water pollution.

In other areas, the best that can be hoped for is that farm wells are properly designed and constructed to minimize pollution, and that rural and subrural water companies are developed to provide safe drinking water where pollution already is extensive.

Limestone Mining. High-purity limestone is mined from only a few thin beds within the entire 7,200-foot section of carbonate rocks. At least four environmental problems associated with such mining have been identified.

1. Dust from crushing and excavation operations and from lime processing operations creates nuisance problems through fallout on homes, cars, and buildings.
2. Soils of adjacent farmland in time may become excessively alkaline from such fallout.
3. Workmen are subjected to hazards related to unstable mine roof conditions and flooding where ground-water conduits are encountered. At one small mine alone, nearly 7 billion gallons of water are pumped each year. The inflow of water is most pronounced during periods of high ground-water recharge and is sufficient to halt mining operations for 3 to 6 months out of each year. This single mine operation pumps more ground water per year than the combined industrial, municipal, agricultural, and domestic use for the entire watershed where the population approaches 65,000.
4. Abrupt fluctuations in water levels within weathered bedrock and cavity-fill materials above mines also give rise to seepage pressures that create hazardous mining conditions and may endanger land uses above the mine areas.

The commercial value of limestone as raw material or as building stone encourages extraction operations and produces employment. On the other hand, strains on the local environment may require that mining be restricted or outlawed. Coexistence is possible where stresses related to mining are evaluated and compensated for in the design of mining and lime-processing operations.

Storm–Water Disposal. In addition to the usual storm-water disposal problems, urban sprawl may produce several problems unique to areas of carbonate rocks. New or developing sink holes may receive storm waters at points of discharge. The entire flow, approaching millions of gallons a day, may be recharged immediately to the ground-water reservoir through sink holes. Various petroleum products and chemicals, bacteria, trash, sediment, heavy organic loads, salt, and related objectionable substances are contained in storm waters. Where recharge is to open conduits within the carbonate rocks, little if any physical-chemical filtration or biologic renovation can be achieved and ground-water pollution is inevitable. Only dilution by ground water can be relied upon for renovation.

Where storm-water treatment plants are not feasible, discharge of storm waters should be to basins or plots high in the drainage basin that contain soils capable of providing filtration and renovation. Typically, storm waters are discharged to permanent streams below urban centers and ground-water recharge bypasses areas where water is in maximum demand.

Storm-water discharge with excessive sediment load in local areas may disrupt previously existing ground-water flow regimes by clogging conduits and openings with debris. Water levels may rise and cause local flooding or erosion of residual soils from other openings. In contrast, increased volumes of low-sediment water as sudden surges facilitate erosion within conduits. Subsurface erosion may proceed until land settlement or sink-hole development takes place. Settlement problems are common adjacent to large parking lots and buildings (figure 4), near major highways, within subdivisions where storm waters were not controlled during or after construction or downslope from any major storm-water recharge area.

Ground-water recharge by storm waters, where desirable or inevitable, should be achieved by carefully designing the facilities to minimize pollution and erosion. One method may be through recharge wells, which should be cased and cemented to avoid erosion damage and should feed directly to deep conduits known to be capable of accepting high rates of recharge. Natural filtration and reuse of storm waters are possible with ground-water development where a sufficient thickness of silt or clay is present beneath the stream channels or basins receiving the storm waters.

FIGURE 4. Tractor trailer trapped in a sink hole. Loss of ground was caused by the weight of the truck and runoff from a nearby shopping center which eroded residual soil at the bedrock contact.

Water-Supply Development. While supply and water-quality problems are common to the development of water supplies everywhere, the solutions to these problems vary considerably. Carbonate rocks are among both the most and the least productive aquifers. In carbonate terranes, ground-water development has centered around the use of surface reservoirs, springs, and wells. Such development must take into account possible damage brought about by three related stresses—physical, biological, and chemical. Examples of these stresses and the resulting strains are reviewed below.

Construction and maintenance of surface-water reservoirs in carbonate terranes are subject to several problems that must be resolved by careful selection, exploration, design, and treatment of sites. These include (1) failure of dams or embankments, (2) location within perched rather than true ground-water levels, (3) location on permeable soils through which leakage to subsurface conduits may occur, and (4) deepening of natural depressions which may remove the water-retaining seal. For example, the severe foundation problem at the lock abutment of Kentucky Dam would have been entirely predictable had fracture traces been mapped in advance (Parizek and Voight, 1968).

Of related importance are the hundreds of small ponds and reservoirs built annually which also fail, but go largely unnoticed except by owners and contractors. The aggregate cost of these failures is unknown but must be considerable. Some ponds are developed at sites believed to have a shallow water table when, in fact, soils with low permeabilities create a perched water table. Because the true water table lies at depth in the underlying carbonate rock, water levels within the ponds fluctuate greatly and the ponds may go dry all or part of the year.

Ponds may be excavated into residual and transported soils on side hills and water levels raised above original water-table level. Surface water then flows through the subsoils and into fractured and cavernous bedrock. Although flow rates may appear insignificant at first, seepage forces promoted by downward-moving water can produce piping failures (Parizek, 1970), and loss of ground, which is the downward erosion of soil, grain by grain, into underlying voids (figure 5). In time (a few hours to years), the piping hole may break through the reservoir floor, and the pond will drain in a matter of hours. Piping failures of this type may develop anywhere around the reservoir walls, beneath the floor, or around the dam. These failures, which result from improper lagoon location and sealing, are widespread.

Some reservoirs have been developed in upland areas where both perched ground water and surface water are present in natural depressions. These depressions develop in response to settlement of residual soils into irregularly dissolved depressions and solution openings in the bedrock surface. Where the resulting surface depressions have a sizable watershed, suspended sediment and organic colloids help clog the soil openings and may create perched surface-water ponds and pools. Deepening these ponds by dredging or flooding nearby drained depressions has met with failure, either because the impermeable seal was breached by the excavation or because the natural seal is missing in adjacent low areas.

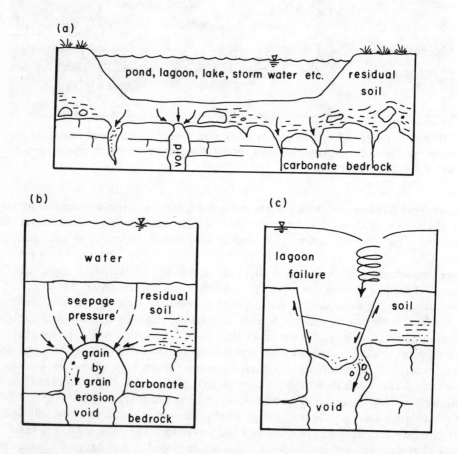

FIGURE 5. Pond and lagoon failure due to piping. In (a) a basin is excavated in residual soils and water percolates through the soils to openings in the underlying bedrock. Seepage forces cause grain-by-grain erosion into cavities (b) until the lagoon floor fails (c).

Where natural pond and reservoir seals are lacking, artificial ones must be applied. Chemical dispersants, bentonite, asphalt, and concrete liners have been known to fail where residual soils are relatively thin (less than 20 feet), or where soil thickness is irregular and differential settlement of the lagoon or pond floor occurs. Minor leaks develop along cracks in the floor, and in time piping failures may develop. Impermeable flexible liners or reinforced liners are the best solutions to these problems.

Where lagoons are used to store sewage sludge, sewage effluent, cannery wastes, or a variety of other chemical and organic wastes, similar failures may occur. Such failures cause serious ground-water pollution in nearby water sources that may extend for miles.

Although springs have traditionally been used for water supplies in carbonate terranes (figure 6), they can be rendered insecure by sudden pollution, decreased flows during periods of drought, and urbanization. In some instances, springs are still used for community supplies without chlorination, despite the fact that faulty septic tanks, sewage wells, and the like are in use in the watershed immediately adjacent to the springs. Garbage dumps are common in open sink holes that lead to conduits supplying water to the springs. Even in rural areas, runoff from barnyards, fields and septic tanks carry polluted water to these open conduits.

Springs may be risky sources of water supply. Although variations in spring flow are normally less pronounced and display greater lag times than in stream flow, they are subject to significant seasonal peaks and lows in discharge. Frequently, only spot checks on discharge are available before water-supply facilities are designed. Spring flows are also highly dependent upon changes in land-use

FIGURE 6. Benner Spring above Bellefonte, Pennsylvania. This spring has a reported discharge of more than 6 million gallons a day.

patterns. As urbanization progresses, storm-water runoff increases, ground-water recharge decreases, and spring flows are reduced. Further, carbonate aquifers in the Ridge and Valley Province have limited storage capacities—2 to 5 percent of the total rock volume. Thus extensive ground-water development by wells during periods of little or no recharge diverts water from storage and springs even where discharge areas appear to be quite remote. Although springs may be regarded as wasters of ground water, their use as sources of water is insecure, especially in growing urban centers where recharge water becomes limited or polluted.

Potential high-capacity wells and well-field sites are an asset to a region and should be regarded as a resouce worthy of recognition and protection (Parizek and Drew, 1967). Unfortunately, consulting engineering firms have usually ignored ground water as a possible source of municipal and industrial water supplies in carbonate terranes for the following reasons: (1) locating and developing a reliable and economical source of water is uncertain, (2) surface-water sources are obvious and appear more attractive, (3) greater profits are associated with surface-water supplies, and (4) ground water may easily become polluted.

High-capacity well sites may be located fairly consistently by using aerial photographs (Lattman and Parizek, 1964; Siddiqui and Parizek, 1969; and Parizek, 1969), while random drilling in carbonate rocks has been shown to be a dismal failure by comparison (Parizek and Drew, 1967). However, surface evidence of lineations used to delineate zones of fracture concentration, which are conducive to the development of conduit ground-water systems, is quickly obscured or eliminated with even slight modification in the landscape (figure 7). Once these features have been erased by urban sprawl,

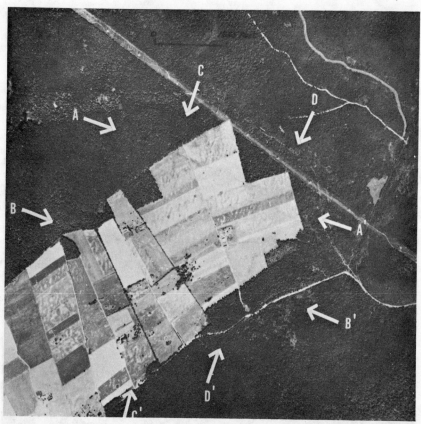

FIGURE 7. Surface lineations are faintly visible in the cultivated fields between A-A′, B-B′, C-C′, and D-D′. These reflect zones of fracture concentration in bedrock and are readily obscured by the effects of urbanization.

favorable ground-water sources can be located only by costly exploration techniques or by random drilling.

It is still not common knowledge that, under favorable conditions, a greater percentage of total available ground water can be obtained from carbonate aquifers with fewer wells than in almost any other terrane. There also is little awareness of the pollution in dominantly conduit flow carbonate aquifers which permit little if any renovation of contaminants. Consequently, ground-water development in carbonate aquifers must go hand-in-hand with intelligent waste-disposal practices.

Settlement is another problem related to ground-water development in carbonate terranes, particularly where the water table is within unconsolidated residual and transported soils. Characteristically, exploration wells that encounter major sources of water near the surface (10 to 400 feet) also yield large volumes of sediment which must be removed from cavities by surging operations. Unfortunately, however, surging action can quickly carry away soil support where the overburden is in contact with water-yielding openings. Sink holes, land subsidence, and subsurface soil erosion or loss of ground can result. This differential settlement constitutes a hazard to drilling equipment and crews and to nearby structures. Once the continuity of the soil filtration media is disrupted by sink development, potential for pollution of ground water is increased, particularly within flood plains.

Extensive ground-water development in valleys may create additional problems. Induced stream-bed infiltration, to provide for rapid ground-water recharge, may develop sinks within stream and river channels, greatly reducing or eliminating stream flow below the well field.

Geologically Controlled Airsheds. Land-use decisions have a critical effect upon air pollution in topographic settings such as the Ridge and Valley Province where long, narrow valleys are confined by 1,000- to 2,000-foot-high ridges. A single misplaced industry within this setting can lead to the development of severe radiation fog (figure 8), as dramatized by Myers (1968). This fog is produced by a combination of natural conditions and the industrial wastes contributed from a single paper and pulp industry located more than 30 miles away (Charles Hostler, 1969, personal communications).

FIGURE 8. Radiation fog spilling out of Bald Eagle Valley into Nittany Valley, at Bellefonte, Pa. Industrial wastes contribute to the fog-forming process in Bald Eagle Valley.

Differential Settlement. Differential subsidence of structures built on carbonate rocks and overlying soils is widespread. Characteristically the top of the bedrock is highly irregular, and isolated boulders of carbonate and more resistant rock are common in residual soils which vary considerably in texture, mineralogy, and thickness. Soils may be highly compact to partly cemented with iron and magnesium oxides, or bound together by clay. Elsewhere soils may be loose where they have been let down into sink holes and along crevasses. Damage to buildings, foundations, tanks, stacks, pipe lines, lagoon liners, and so forth is common where good exploration and design practices have been ignored or violated.

Subsidence due to improper backfilling and compaction during construction (figure 9a) is a common problem in all terranes. It is compounded in carbonate terranes, however, because loosely compacted backfill and even undisturbed permeable soils allow surface water to infiltrate and move soil particles into cavities and ground-water conduits. This problem can be all but eliminated by careful supervision of backfilling operations, by controlling storm waters (figure 9b), and by preventing pipeline leaks (figure 9c).

Differential subsidence due to compaction by loads on soils of unequal thickness (figure 9d) is universal in carbonate terranes and should no longer plague foundation designers. A program of test boring augmented by geophysical surveys can establish soil thickness variations.

"Act-of-God failures" occur where roofs of cavities fail under loading (figure 9e). This may happen under natural conditions after persistent chemical weathering, or it may occur in response to external loads unless proper exploration, design, and construction techniques are used. Cows, farm tractors, and buildings have all been trapped by these failures. Large voids with potentially unstable roofs can be located by geophysical surveys (Watkins and others, 1967) and sometimes by careful and detailed borings.

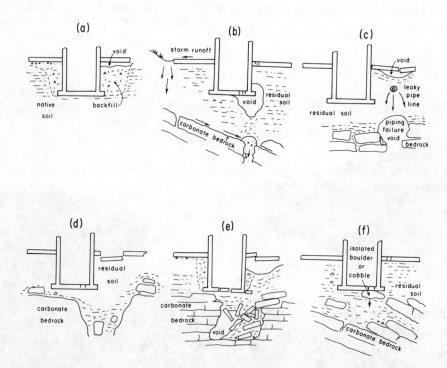

FIGURE 9. Foundation damage due to settlement of ground from improper backfilling and compaction (a), subsurface erosion by uncontrolled storm waters (b), leaky utility lines (c), differential settlement of soils of uneven thickness (d), cave roof collapse (e), and where footings were placed on "floating boulders" (f).

Structural failures and damage have resulted where exploration was based on "depth to refusal" information obtained from split-spoon sampling procedures, auger, or air-hammer drilling. All too frequently, the "depth to refusal" is fixed by a discontinuous "floating boulder" which itself is underlain by soil or decomposed bedrock (figure 9f). Some of these failures are difficult to distinguish from loss of ground caused by erosion of residual soils within a zone in which the ground-water table fluctuates (figure 10).

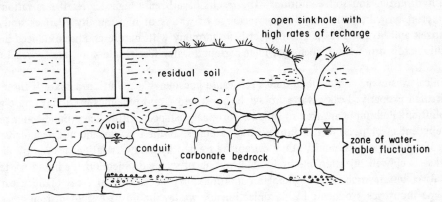

FIGURE 10. Land subsidence due to subsurface soil erosion by storm and ground water.

Highway Construction. Modern highways are built with minimum grades and gentle turns; frequently, thick fills and deep excavations within soil and bedrock are required. The cuts disrupt the soil-water and ground-water regime from that which existed before construction. Runoff during and after construction can erode and transport loose surface soils to adjacent sink holes and cause increased turbidity in the ground-water reservoir. These problems are usually most severe during construction, but many years may be required to re-establish stable equilibrium conditions within the soil and bedrock. Highway planning and construction in areas adjacent to public water supplies should take into account possible effects of changes in runoff.

Excavations below the water table may lower it or behead aquifers supplying water to existing collection facilities. Springs are particularly apt to be damaged. In the absence of a filtrating soil cover above voids, chemicals used to control snow, ice, and roadside vegetation may migrate freely into the ground water with little or no alteration. This problem is largely unrecognized in rural areas where there is limited ground-water development, but becomes important in urban areas where water sources are adjacent to highways.

Liquid Waste Disposal. Septic tanks, surface discharges, and dry wells are widely used in rural towns and on farms to handle domestic wastes. In major urban subdivisions, both septic tanks and regional collection and treatment facilities are commonplace. In soils with low permeability or in places where soils are thin or absent beneath tile fields, septic tanks are inadequate. Discharge of contaminated water locally is common in stratified residual soils that have been overloaded by tile fields (figure 11), where tile fields are in thick colluvium or alluvium, on steep slopes, or where perched or seasonally high ground-water tables exist. Leaky sewage and other pipelines may cause subsurface erosion or piping failures that, in turn, may end in pipeline breaks and ground-water pollution.

Disposal of sewage effluent into rivers draining carbonate terranes may pose pollution problems even greater than those in other areas. Extensive recreational use is generally made of streams in carbonate terranes because they have persistent flows and will support game fish. Consequently, the public is more aware of pollution in such streams. Also, in areas where flood-plain sediments are thin or absent, sewage effluent may flow through the streambed to adjacent water wells with little or no improvement in water quality. The location and design of sewage treatment plants is especially critical in the prevention of leakage and piping failures in carbonate areas. In one of several contact-stabilization tanks that failed costly repairs and delays in construction were involved, in addition to the fact that nearly 2 million gallons of raw sewage was recharged to the local ground-water reservoir.

Alternate methods of effluent treatment to reduce phosphate and nitrate concentrations have been attempted at Penn State. Sewage effluent has been used to irrigate lands containing favorable geologic, hydrologic, and soil conditions. The results have been a high degree of renovation, an increase in crop growth, and ground-water recharge of waters of high quality (Parizek and others, 1967; Parizek and Myers, 1959). The project is in harmony with nature and has produced increased soil fertility, crop production, recharge, higher ground-water levels, and food and cover for small game.

Chemical wastes in carbonate terranes can cause considerable pollution damage if these wastes are not treated properly. Leaky waste-storage lagoons, tanks, and pipelines inevitably cause ground-water pollution. Pollutants are free to migrate for great distances within the ground-water reservoir and thereby endanger present and future water supplies. If these wastes are not degradable in the presence of a biologic community, they cannot be treated by spray irrigation or even by discharge into creeks. Deep-well injection methods of disposing of selected objectionable liquid wastes offer an alternative, but favorable hydrogeologic conditions may be lacking in areas of thick carbonate rocks. Some industries producing highly objectionable wastes should be excluded from areas where the damages they create are not preventable. Selective planning or zoning policies can be adopted to assure that industrial activity is in reasonable harmony with the natural physical, chemical, and biologic system of an area and that future growth will not be depressed because of poor water quality.

Wherever possible, facilities such as storage tanks, lagoons, and sewage treatment plants should be located on stable noncarbonate rocks, and special precautions should be taken in the design of

FIGURE 11. One of many discharges of incompletely treated sewage effluent (weed area between house and sidewalk) within a subdivision located on stratified soils. Although these residual soils are relatively permeable, septic tanks fail because of the housing density, steep slopes, and soil stratification.

foundations to prevent leaks. Ground-water pollution can thereby be kept to a minimum in the event that leaks develop. One of the many examples of chemical spills that could be cited occurred during the past year. At that time, more than 200,000 gallons of refined gasoline were pumped from carbonate aquifers adjacent to three tank farms containing refined petroleum products near Mechanicsburg, Pennsylvania (A. A. Socolow, 1970, personal communication). In addition to the immediate fire and explosion hazards to nearby homes, it is reasonable to conclude that the local carbonate aquifer will remain contaminated for generations.

Solid Wastes. Solid wastes derived from communities and industries place a major chemical and biological stress on the carbonate environment. In many rural and semirural areas, such places as open sink holes, abandoned quarries, mines, and swampland are still being used as solid-waste disposal sites. Surface runoff into such sites, where little or no soil is present and filtration is impossible, almost always causes water pollution. Numerous examples can be cited in which hair, paper, cloth, and other objects were pumped from water wells in carbonate aquifers.

In recent years, sanitary landfills have been used to dispose of solid wastes in many areas. This procedure represents a vast improvement over the open dumping and burning practices previously used. Contrary to popular opinion, however, "sanitary landfills" may not be sanitary from a ground-water pollution standpoint unless runoff is filtered or the fill is sealed from the water table. Many chemical constituents in the leaching water far exceed concentrations considered acceptable in drinking water. Pollution from solid–waste disposal sites may have regional consequences on the development of ground water. The soils and the geologic and hydrologic conditions must be carefully investigated at each site before it is used for a sanitary landfill or as a site for ash disposal. Suitable sites for present and future waste disposal are a valuable resource and should be set aside for future use.

Conclusions

A stress-strain viewpoint is helpful when studying man's interaction with his environment. Stresses are common to many geologic terranes, but the nature and magnitude of resulting strains are dependent upon variations in the geologic setting. The carbonate terranes are particularly sensitive to man-induced stresses. An environmental approach to land-use activities is desirable and mandatory in such a region if costly damages are to be avoided or minimized and if maximum mineral resource and land-use benefits are to be derived now and in the future.

Strains become more numerous as the population density increases and as land-use practices intensify and diversify. Potential damage from unregulated urban and industrial sprawl in the folded and faulted carbonate terrane of the Ridge and Valley Province will be extensive, judging from that already incurred by semirural land use. Damage includes mechanical failures of foundations, pipelines, lagoons and ponds, sink-hole development, mine-roof collapse, mine flooding, and increased ground-water pollution by sediments, chemical, and organic matter. Damages may be brought about abruptly or slowly, but in either case financial losses are inevitable.

It is clear that environmental maps must be made available to planners, land developers, engineers, and others faced with land-use decisions. These maps must be prepared at a useful scale (at least 1:24,000) and must be comprehensive to the general user. Such maps should show both desirable and undesirable aspects of the terrane. It is as important to be aware of the resource potential of a given area as it is the hazards. It becomes immediately clear that maps must be prepared by men from different disciplines, including ground-water geologists, engineering and mineral-resource geologists, and soil scientists.

Soil maps or geologic maps alone are not adequate. A number of maps are required to display the desirable and undesirable aspects of the region adequately, particularly if diverse stresses are likely to be present and local conditions are complex. At least 25 such maps have been suggested for the author's local study area. These maps include: soils, surficial and bedrock geology, thickness and structure of all important soil and rock layers, mineral resources (metallic and nonmetallic), ground-water potential, ground-water chemistry, aquifer storage and transmission characteristics, thickness and distribution of all aquifer and nonaquifer units, vertical permeability variations, piezometric surface, depth to water table to define potential construction and pollution problems, ground-water recharge potential, flood hazards, dam-site locations, strength characteristics of soil and rock materials, areas of potential landslide and soil creep, sites suitable for solid and liquid waste disposal, slope characteristics, soil resources, distribution and type of potential sources of pollution such as tank farms, septic tanks, dumps, sanitary landfills, and others. Because color aids the user in interpretation, and because color in publications is expensive, the cost of environmental studies should be borne by local users who have the most to gain.

To develop grass-roots support for this work and to minimize environmental damage, the public must be educated about local problems and their causes and must become the watchdog for correction and enforcement. In addition to the need for local interest, regional, state and federal policies of land-use conservation also must be defined. Residual soils in carbonate terranes are among this nation's most productive agricultural soils, but urban growth threatens to engulf them, leaving less-desirable farmlands untouched. Incentives must be provided for the maintenance of open space in these productive lands, as food production ultimately will become a major constraint in the nation's growth. It is clear that both local and national land-use policies must be adopted.

REFERENCES CITED

Lattman, L. H., and Parizek, R. R., 1964, Relationship between fracture traces and the occurrence of ground water in carbonate rocks: Jour. of Hydrol., v. II, no. 2, pp 73–91.

Myers, J. N., 1968, Fog: Scientific American, v. 219, no. 6, pp 74–82.

O'Neill, B. J., 1964, Atlas of Pennsylvania's mineral resources: Pennsylvania Geol. Survey, Mineral Resources Report M 50, 40 pp.

Parizek, R. R., 1969, Permeability development in folded and faulted carbonates, Pennsylvania: Trans. Am. Geoph. Union, v. 50, no. 4, p. 155.

——, 1970, Land-use problems in Pennsylvania's ground-water discharge areas: Pa. Geol. Survey (in press).

Parizek, R. R., and Drew, L. H., 1967, Random drilling for water in carbonate rocks, *in* Proceedings of a symposium and short course on computers and operations research in mineral industries: Min. Ind. Experiment Sta., v. 3, Special Pub. 2–65, The Penn. State Univ., University Park, Penn., pp. PP1–PP22.

Parizek, R. R., Kardos, L. T., Sopper, W. E., Myers, E. A., Davis, D. E., Farrell, M. A., and Nesbitt, J. B., 1967, Waste water renovation and conservation: The Penn. State Univ., University Park, Penn., Penn. State Studies no. 23, 71 pp.

Parizek, R. R., and Myers, E. A., 1969, Recharge of ground water from renovated sewage effluent by spray irrigation: Proc. of the 4th Ann. Water Resources Conference, New York, pp. 426–43.

Parizek, R. R., and Voight, B., 1968, Fracture-zone analysis in geotechnical exploration: Int. Geol. Congress, Academic Press, Prague, Czech., p. 331.

Siddiqui, S. H., and Parizek, R. R., 1969, Hydrogeologic factors influencing well yields in folded and faulted carbonate rocks, Central Pennsylvania: Trans. Am. Geoph. Union, v. 50, no. 4, p. 154.

Watkins, J. S., Godson, R. H., and Watson, K., 1967, Seismic detection of near-surface cavities: U.S. Geol. Survey Prof. Paper 599-A, 12 pp.

29

Earth Science Data in Urban and Regional Information Systems— A Review

Victor W. Adams

Introduction

The San Francisco Bay Region Environment and Resources Planning Study (SFBRS) is a cooperative effort that began in January 1970 between the U.S. Geological Survey of the Department of Interior and the Office of Policy Development and Research of the Department of Housing and Urban Development. It is a study of physical environmental factors, particularly geologic hazards, and their relation to urban and regional planning. The area of study is the nine-county San Francisco Bay region. The need for such a study grew from the recognized need for incorporating physical environmental data in the regional planning effort. The products of the study are maps and reports divided into three series: basic data contributions, the technical series (derived from the data for a technical audience), and the interpretive report series (a final derivation for a nontechnical audience such as planners and government officials). The program elements are grouped into four categories: topographic, geologic and geophysical, hydrologic, and planning program elements. The U.S. Geological Survey and Department of Housing and Urban Development (1971) have published a detailed description of the program elements and products of the bay region study. This report is one of the planning program elements.

Environmental factors are becoming increasingly important to planners in the bay region. Hazards associated with these factors, such as earthquake fault zones and slopes that are potentially unstable, should be recognized and dealt with in the planning phase. The consideration of environmental factors also entails the need to estimate the impact on the environment of various land-use alternatives associated with rapid urbanization. Many environmental factors in the area under study are regional in nature. Earthquake fault patterns are very extensive. Depletion of an underground aquifer has caused land subsidence in adjacent areas as well as in the immediate area. Thus, the amount of data to be considered by planners in studying land-use alternatives can become very great, and use of this data in the traditional form of maps and reports can be very time consuming. Increasingly, this has led to the use of modern electronic computers and to the development of information systems to handle environmental and land-use type data.

The management of data has become a problem in modern society. Almost everyone is familiar with the vast amount of data involved in processing credit card information and in the processing of

Extracted with permission of the author from *U.S. Geological Survey Circular 712*, 1975, 29 pp.

hundreds of millions of federal and state income tax returns. Government agencies and private companies concerned with the land-use planning process are also deeply involved in this problem. The amount of data handled has grown, but more important has been the growth in requirements for managing and manipulating this data. Now environmental data must become a part of the pool of data used by the computer as a part of a land-use information system.

This study is concerned with problems associated with the inclusion of earth science data in computer-based urban and regional information systems. How, for example, is earthquake data on a map read into a computer? How are map areas with potentially unstable slopes to be stored in a computer data base? This report is a summary of the work of others since the SFBRS is not directly involved in the development of such an operational computer system but rather is interested in the proper and timely use of earth science data by regional planners. The characteristics of urban and regional information systems are determined mainly from a study of two systems in the San Francisco Bay region, that of the Metropolitan Transportation Commission (MTC) and that of Santa Clara County, which are taken to be typical of regional computer-based information systems. These systems were used to examine the problems involved in making earth science data compatible with existing urban and regional information systems.

This report is primarily for planners, especially those with a limited knowledge of computer technology. It may also be valuable to scientists and others working with planners in this application of earth science technology. In view of the intended audience of this report, a brief section on computer-based information systems provides background information and defines terms for an understanding of the sections that follow.

Computer Information Systems

This section presents a brief, nontechnical description of certain computer information systems to provide a frame of reference for later sections. First, digital computer systems in general are discussed to define terms and give a summary of the rapid development of computer technology and what may reasonably be expected in the near future. Next, two special computer systems are defined: management information systems and geographic information systems.

Computer Systems

A digital computer system can perform the following operations: (1) "read" data or instructions with such devices as card readers or keyboards, (2) perform arithmetic operations on data, (3) determine which operations to perform on the basis of instructions or the result of some previous operations, and (4) "output" the results in a form such as hard copy by a printer or by graphic display on a device similar to a television screen, hereafter referred to as a display tube. The sequence of operations is given by a set of instructions called a program. Within the computer the data and the instructions are in the form of a binary code because the circuit elements operate at two voltage levels that can be called "on" and "off" or "zero" and "one." Each on or off stage represents one binary digit (one bit of information).

A typical system consists of a central processing unit (CPU), various input and output (I/O) devices, and auxiliary storage such as disk storage units and magnetic tapes. The CPU is the heart of the computer system comprising main storage, which holds programs and data, an arithmetic unit, and associated circuitry. The way in which the physical units are put together is called hardware architecture.

Programs are of two types, systems or application, and together constitute what is called software architecture. Systems programs are a semipermanent part of the computer system since they are infrequently replaced. They include support programs for system and program control, programs for hardware testing, and standard mathematical subroutines, for example, and can be thought of as residing in the machine. As such, their instructions are in binary code in what is called machine language. System software relieves the user from the necessity of writing common segments of instructions for each program. Applications programs, as the name implies, depend upon specific user requirements, may be changed frequently, and can be thought of as being read into the machine for each use. Most applications programs are written in a higher level language such as fortran (an acronym for formula translation) in which the statements are quite similar to English. The advantages of a higher level language are that it is independent of the machine and easy to learn and use compared with machine language.

When an application program with all the data it requires is read into the machine at one time and results are outputted after the program has been completed, the computer system is operating in batch mode. If the user reads in a few instructions at a time at a keyboard terminal and waits for results to be outputted (as on a display tube) before reading in more instructions, the computer system is operating in conversational or interactive mode. This is usually done when more than one user shares the computer in a multiple access or timesharing system. Switching from one terminal (user) to another is so rapid that any one user has the impression that only he is using the system. Special higher level languages are used for the conversational mode.

Table 1 summarizes some information on four generations of computers and generally indicates the improvement in computer technology over the last 20 years. While the magnitude of any particular figure will be meaningful only to specialists, the trend over the 20-year period can be appreciated by all.

Management Information Systems

The first business application of the computer was recordkeeping in which the computer replaced clerks. This use was followed by simple control systems such as for inventory or production. For these applications the main function of the computer was to handle a large amount of data. These data, stored in the computer system in auxiliary storage devices, are called the data base of the system. The technical problems involved are those of information storage and retrieval, the computer system requiring a large I/O capability rather than a large capacity for computation.

Within the last several years computer systems have been developed with the goal of providing management with the information it requires for decisionmaking; these systems are called management information systems and incorporate many of the tools and techniques of the mathematical sciences such as statistical analysis of data, simulation and modeling of various parts of the business operation or segments of the economy, and utilization of various methods of optimization. The computing ability of the system has been enlarged without sacrifice of the I/O capability.

Geographical Information Systems

A geographical information system is a computer information system with the capability of handling spatially related data, specifically map-related data such as tract boundaries and stream networks. The spatial characteristics should be preserved in the system so that (1) the data can be indexed by geographical location, (2) the data can be manipulated with relation to these spatial characteristics, and (3) one form of output can be a map. The methods by which these are achieved are discussed in a following section.

TABLE 1. CHARACTERISTICS OF FOUR GENERATIONS OF COMPUTERS

Computer generation	1	2	3	4
Period	1952–58	1958–63	1963–69	1969–?
Basic electronic component	Vacuum tube	Transistors, solid-state diodes.	Integrated circuits.	Large-scale integrated arrays.
Component density/ft^3	10^4	10^6	10^7	10^8 up
Cost, $/bit: Core	2	.75	.1	.005
Memory	.5	.05	.005	10^{-5}–10^{-6}
Cost ($ to execute 10^6)	10	1	.05	.001
Relative failure rate	1	.01	.001	.0001

Earth Science Data and the San Francisco Bay Region

The earth science data involved in this study are restricted to the data generated by the San Francisco Bay Region Study Program. The San Francisco Bay region was chosen for study for the following reasons:

1. There is a wide variety of environmental factors in the area, such as the natural hazards of earthquakes, landslides, and flooding, as well as the environmental effect of the bay. These factors constitute the main reason why the bay region was originally selected for the study program.
2. Many of the land-use problems are regional in nature, such as waste disposal and industrial pollution, water supply and land subsidence, landfill and its effects on the bay, and those problems associated with industrial locations, residential development, and transportation.
3. The bay region is an area of rapid urban growth, and its land-use problems need to be solved soon.

The following statistics (U.S. Geological Survey and Department of Housing and Urban Development, 1971) of the San Francisco Bay region are included for those who may not appreciate its size:

Population (1970)	5,083,549
Dwelling units (1965)	1,404,146
Area (land)	6,952 mi^2
San Francisco Bay, original area (1835)	680 mi^2
Filled or diked area	280 mi^2
Remaining area	400 mi^2
Linear shoreline	276 mi
Shoreline, public access	5 mi

Comparisons (1970)	*Area*	*Population*
San Francisco Bay region	7,416 mi^2	5,083,549
Israel	7,993	2,910,000
Connecticut	5,009	3,082,217

The various interpretive studies, or program elements, underway on the San Francisco Bay region planning were reviewed. These studies, subject to change before completion of the SFBRS, are listed below:

Program Element	*Published Products*
Slope stability study	Landslide susceptibility maps, four to seven zones, depending on the area.
Bay mud	Maps of land-use categories, three to fifteen zones.
Coastal erosion (San Mateo County)	Coastal strip maps of erosion hazards, three to four zones.
Unconsolidated deposits	Map of land-use categories, five zones.
Active faults	Map of active fault zones.
Engineering behavior	Map with matrix of descriptive information and inferred engineering behavior for 30 to 50 map units (bedrock).
Water-quality studies	Report of water quality at various locations in streams, lakes, and reservoirs.
Erosion and sediment	Map of erosion provinces, six to seven zones (plus cross sections).
Flood inundation maps	Map of flood-prone areas (boundary of 100-year flood zone).
Urban drainage system	Peak discharge for design storms of 2, 5, 10, 25, 50, and 100 years.
Land pollution susceptibility study	Map of evaluation of site locations for four types of disposal systems.

Program Element (continued)   *Published Products (continued)*

Coastal Flooding . . . . Map of areas of potential inundation by tsunamis.

Mineral commodity study . . . . Commodity location maps, 30 commodities.

Seismicity and ground studies . . . . . Seismic susceptibility map, eight zones.

Earthquakes and their locations . . . . Computer data bank of recent earthquakes in the San Francisco area.

Ground water studies . . . . Map of aquifer yield, four zones. Map of certain chemical constituents of ground water, four zones. Ground water hazards map. Water storage tables for main alluvial valleys.

Most of the products are derived from basic information such as topography, location of active fault zones, and knowledge of bedrock formations, through the application of scientific and engineering principles. Basic data for the purpose of this report are considered to include:

1. Geologic map
   a. Bedrock (including depth, where available, and strike and dip)
   b. Fault lines (or zones)
   c. Unconsolidated deposits
   d. Landslides
   e. Mineral deposits, sand and gravel
2. Slope map (or slopes derived from topographic map)
3. Topographic map
4. Rainfall map (two types, annual average and maximum 48 hours)
5. Vegetation map
6. Land-use map
7. Land-subsidence map
8. Tabular information
   a. Engineering properties of soil, unconsolidated deposits, bedrock
   b. Stream-quality information and rating tables (spot locations)
   c. Temperature and other variables in lake and reservoirs
   d. Suspended sediment (spot stream locations)
   e. Accumulated sediment (various lakes and reservoirs)
   f. Depth to ground water (spot locations)
9. Earthquake data
10. Soil map
11. Historic flood data

For a geographical information system, this information can be classified as follows:

1. Areal or zonal information, such as land-use zones or bedrock zones, represented on map by boundary lines.
2. Line information such as stream networks or streets.
3. Point information such as well locations.
4. Tabular information such as engineering properties of soil.

Examples of these information categories are given on figure 1. Areal information is illustrated by surficial deposits and rock formations, for example, the bay mud. Line information is illustrated by the San Andreas fault line and also by the bedrock contour lines. An example of point information is the location of small landslide deposits denoted by the small triangles.

Methods of Earth Science Data Entry

This section examines the methods by which earth science data are entered into the computer data bank and the various kinds of equipment used in the process.

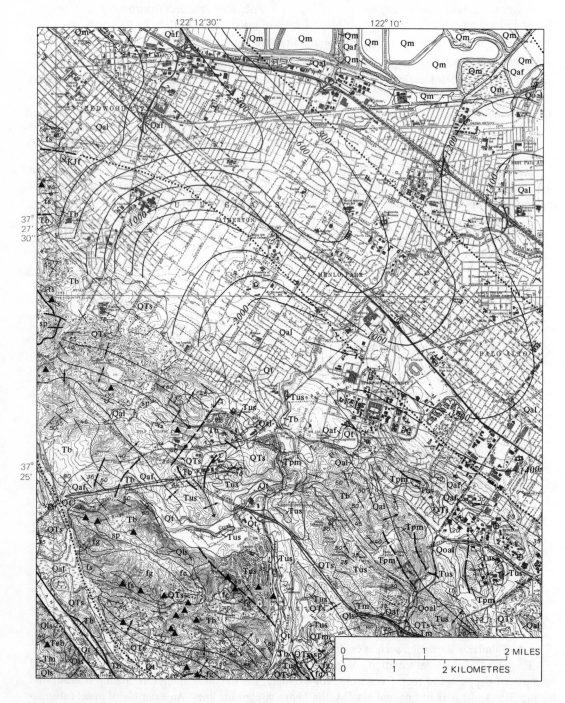

FIGURE 1. Preliminary geologic map of part of the San Francisco Bay region showing types of land-use information. San Andreas fault zone (heavy lines) is shown in lower left corner. Contacts between rock units shown by thin lines; letter symbols are keyed to brief descriptions of the rock units in the map explanation (for example, Qls = large landslide deposits, Qm = bay mud). Triangles denote landslides too small to show at the scale of this map. Depth to bedrock shown by contours in upper half of map (after Brabb, 1970).

Map Digitization and Image Digitizers

Earth science data was classified in the last section as tabular, point, line, and areal data. The entry of tabular information into the computer data bank presents no special problem. By properly labeling the table and organizing its contents, there is no difficulty in providing software that can locate the table and extract information from it. The same is true for point information because it can be referenced by its coordinates, for example, latitude and longitude. Areal and line information must be handled differently.

Because an area is represented on a map by its boundary line, the problem of entering areal or line information into a computer is the same—to convert a line into a set of discrete values that can then be read in. The process is called map digitization. One way this can be accomplished is by approximating a curved line by a series of straight line segments (figure 2). A straight line segment can be represented by its end points, so that a line can be represented by a series of points, each given by its coordinates. The closer together the points, the better the approximation to the original line.

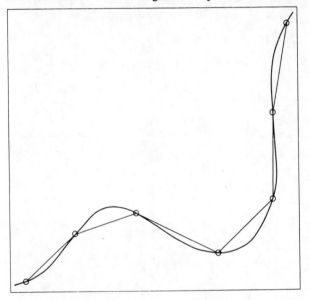

FIGURE 2. Approximation of a curved line by a series of straight line segments.

An image digitizer is a device with a reading head free to move in two dimensions over a flat surface on which the map to be digitized is placed. An operator follows the line with the reading head whose position is always digitally known. Coordinates of its position can be read in automatically (a "read in" for a preset time interval or a "read in" when displacement in the X or Y direction exceeds a preset amount) or at operator command. Coordinates are measured from some zero position set at start of digitization.

Optical Scanners

A map can be digitized by an optical scanning device that records coordinates (explicitly or implicitly as described below) of any information differing from the map background as the map is scanned in a regular way. On a map with line information of only one kind, the device will see background (white) or part of a line (black). It looks at a small square (for example, 0.001 X 0.001 inch) at a time and sees either predominant white or predominant black since line thickness is much greater than 0.001 inch (if the square is half black and half white, the scanner probably will see black). If white is seen, a zero is recorded, if black is seen a one is recorded. Thus output of the device is a series of zeros and ones with a coordinate implicit for each since the device scans in a regular way. One way is to scan from left to right in a horizontal line (0.001 inch wide), then move down 0.001 inch and scan the next line. Software processing then removes the zeros and attaches explicit coordinates to each "one." On the computer printout of a line from a small map section, an "x" is printed for each position where a "one" has been recorded (figure 3*A*). The scale is greatly enlarged because each print position represents the small square the device sees each time it looks at the map—the 0.001 X 0.001 inch square. It is also possible to record not the zeros but instead the explicit position (*x*, *y* coordinates) of each "one" as the scanner sees it. In either method, the next step in software processing is to identify lines from the series of "ones" by obtaining the center line of each band of "ones" (figure 3*B*).

Finally, a program replaces the series of "ones" with a set of straight line segments, each identified by endpoint coordinates and a direction. This produces a file of line segments as if the map had been digitized using an image digitizer (figure 3*C*).

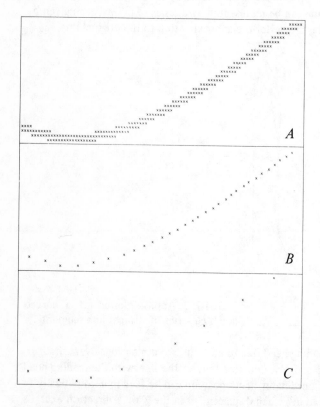

FIGURE 3. *A*, Computer printout of scanned line. *B*, Center line of the scanned line. *C*, Scanned line represented by end points of straight line segments.

Urban and Regional Information Systems

Data Base Organization for Geographical Information Systems

The fact that a system is a geographical information system is reflected in its data base because the information regarding the geographical distribution of data resides there. The data base of such a system can be organized in several ways. In the following discussion, a record is defined as a collection of related items of data treated as a unit. A data file is a collection of related records. A data item is an individual item of information in a record. Data structures refers to the arrangements and interrelation of records in a file.

Areal Type Data

Polygon or Area Boundary. Consider a land-use map (figure 4) in which the boundaries of the various land-use zones have been digitized as described in the previous section on earth science data

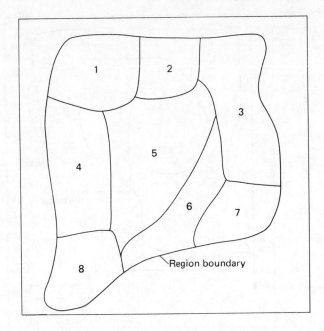

FIGURE 4. Sample map of study region containing eight digitized land-use zones.

entry. The set of line segments enclosing a zone constitutes a record of the area boundary enclosing that particular zone. Each enclosed land-use zone on the map has a separate record. All the land-use records from this map (and other maps, if more than one is needed to cover the region) constitute a file, the land-use file for the region. The set of line segments in a record is ordered so that a zone is always defined by going around it in the same direction, clockwise or counterclockwise. Each record contains other information regarding the zone—at least, a symbol representing its land-use category. For example, the zones numbered 1 and 6 might both be agricultural. For such a map, there would be other polygon files, one for each class of areal data (for example, soils or bedrock geology).

Two data files can be combined in the computer by an overlay process, which is analogous to overlaying two maps, both drawn on transparent material, so that the polygon boundaries on both maps may be seen and some particular combination of results studied. For example, a land-use map with four categories, L1, L2, L3, and L4 and a soil map of four types of soil S1, S2, S3, and S4 (figure 5) can be overlaid to show areas of soil type S1 and land-use category L1 (figure 6A). All area within either S1 or L1 forms the boundary of their union (figure 6B). All area common to both S1 and L1 is called their intersection (figure 6C). This overlay process, determining the boundaries of a new set of polygons on the basis of unions or intersections, can be done in the computer. Any number of files can be combined by cascading the results, the third file being overlaid with the set resulting from overlaying the first and second files, and so on.

Grid Structure. A map of areal data having four categories A through D can be overlaid with a grid of north-south and east-west lines, forming a uniform cell structure (figure 7). Each cell has a record, and the attribute of the predominant zone within the cell is assigned to the record for that cell. For example, the cell in row four, column one is B; the one in row two, column two is C. The cell structure need not be uniform. Quarter-quarter sections could be used, which are nonuniform in some places because of surveying inaccuracies.

If the cell size is large relative to the region, the areal maps could be hand encoded. If, however, the cell size is small relative to the region, hand encoding may be impractical. The grid file can then be created by first creating a polygon file and then, in the computer using suitable software, overlaying the grid structure and recording the data in each cell. When a map digitization of areal data is done, it is possible to write software to assign the data directly to cells without first digitizing the area boundary.

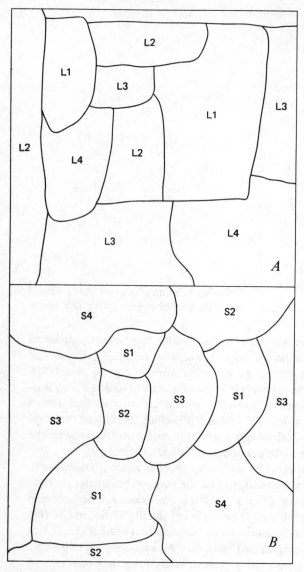

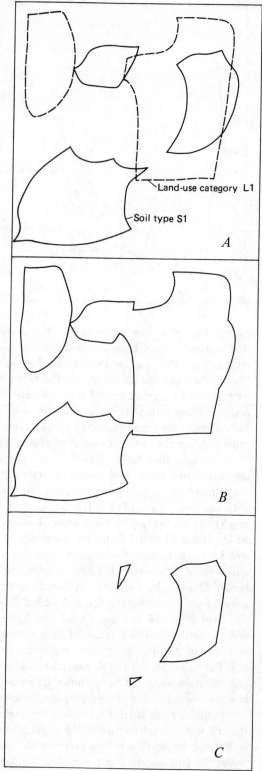

FIGURE 5 (above). A, Map of land-use zones. B, Map of soil types.

FIGURE 6. (right). Overlay of soil type S1 and land-use category L1. A, The overlay. B, The union. C, The intersection.

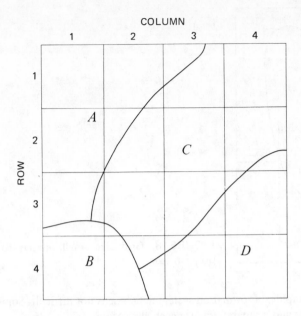

FIGURE 7. Map with grid overlay.

If an areal unit is large relative to the cell size, many contiguous cells will have the same information, thus wasting file space if they are all stored (figure 8). In such a situation a type of data compression can be used. Not all the cells overlaying the large polygon would be used. Only the first cell in each row wholly within the polygon could be recorded, with a notation as to the number of cells in that row within the polygon. Amidon and Akin (1971) discussed more sophisticated techniques of data compression.

Thus far, each class of areal data has been considered as constituting a separate file. For the polygon area boundary file, there is one record for each polygon, one set of polygons for each file. For the grid structure, there is one record per cell, one set of cells (covering the region) for each file. However, with the grid structure, files of areal data can be combined by assigning all the data to a single file of cells, one record for each cell with each record containing data on all classes of areal data for that cell location. It is obvious that the more numerous the classes of data, the less frequent the opportunity for data compression, since it will be increasingly rare that all classes of data will have polygons of large area in the same geographical location.

Incorporating Line and Point Data

There are two kinds of line data, isopleths and networks. Isopleths are equal-value lines, such as elevation contour lines. In one sense isopleths are area boundary lines since they separate areas of higher from areas of lower value. To the extent that they are used as such they can be handled as described in the preceding paragraph. However, an isopleth has a definite value associated with it (for example, a 2,000-ft elevation contour line), whereas area boundary lines, in general, have none.

Networks are lines representing areas, such as streets or streams, that are too narrow to be represented as areas on a map. In a polygon type file, networks can be stored as area boundaries are, but the definitions of a file and a record are much more arbitrary. The storage of network information in a grid basis is much more difficult. The simplest method would be a code indicating the presence or absence of a particular class of data in a cell. For example, the cell record could have a field for stream data in which a "1" would indicate the presence and a "2" the absence of a stream in that particular cell. If this information were inadequate, the cell record could be enlarged to include more detailed information. A separate file for that particular network could also be maintained, organized as it would be in a polygon file, thus creating a hybrid data base.

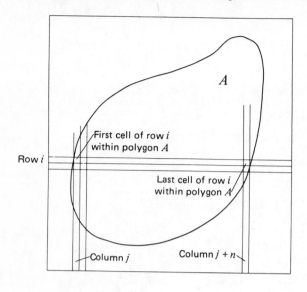

Row i

First cell of row i
within polygon A

Last cell of row i
within polygon A

A

Column j   Column j + n

FIGURE 8. Grid size small relative to polygon size.

The inclusion of point data in a geographical information system data base is not difficult. Some information can be added to a cell record, and a separate file for each class of point data, referenced by coordinates, is easy to create, use, and maintain.

Utilization of Earth Science Data

Natural Resource Information Systems. A few geographic information systems include only natural resource and land-use data. One of the oldest is the Canadian Geographic Information System, a very ambitious system for all of Canada, which was started in 1963 and implemented 1965–71. The data base, organized on the area boundary or polygon system, has files on present land use, capacity of the land for four categories (agriculture, forestry, recreation and wildlife), and watersheds, and has data manipulation capabilities to calculate areas and perform overlay operation. It operates on the batch mode, and experienced programmers are required (Boyle, 1972; Tomlinson, 1968).

GRIDS (Guided Resource Inventory Data System) was developed by the Department of Natural Resources of the State of Washington. The objective of the system is to maintain a current land inventory for use in making operational plans for land managed by the department. The data base is organized as a regular grid structure with a cell 660 feet square (10 acres, ¼ of a ¼ X ¼ section; 4.05 ha). There is one record per cell with the following information: land cover, slope, aspect, elevation, soil, watershed, road access, land use, forest cover (tree type) and nonforest type (R. A. Harding, written communication, 1972).

NARIS (Natural Resources Information System) was developed by the Center for Advanced Computation, University of Illinois at Urbana-Champaign; it covers parts of eight counties in northeast Illinois. Its data base is an irregular grid structure, each cell being a ¼ X ¼ mile section (40 acres, 16 ha). To date, each tract (cell) contains 15 classes of information under five major headings:
Geology:
1. Interpretation of waste disposal
2. Interpretation of construction
3. Water resources
4. Sand and gravel resources
5. Surficial deposits
Land Use:
6. U.S. Department of Housing and Urban Development codes
7. Northeastern Illinois Planning Commission codes

Forestry:
    8. Native woody vegetation
    9. Planted woody vegetation
Soil:
    10. U.S. Department of Agriculture Soil Conservation Service soil characteristics
Water:
    11. Watershed
    12. Wells
    13. Present impoundments
    14. Future impoundments
    15. Streams

Each of these 15 classes is, in turn, made up of data elements. The values of these data elements are the attributes of each tract. For example, soil information is collected by plots of various size within each tract. Each plot is described by the following data elements:

NUMBER—the type of soil in the plot;
SLOPE—the slope of the soil in the plot;
EROSION—the current erosion of the soil in the plot;
ACRES—area of the plot in acres;
OVERLAP—denotes whether or not the plot extends into an adjacent tract.

The objective of the system is to provide natural resources information to public agencies and to the private sector. It can be user operated in a conversational mode with its own language (Center for Advanced Computation, 1972b).

The Raytheon Company (1973) is currently developing a natural resources information system for the Department of the Interior (Bureau of Indian Affairs and Bureau of Land Management). It is to include natural resources and land-use information and will be used as an aid in the management of public lands. System specifications call for the ability to store and retrieve map data and for the capability of data manipulation such as overlaying maps to obtain unions or intersections of specified types of data and making area and perimeter calculations. The data base currently being developed is a variation of the area boundary structure. However, instead of storing complete polygons, the system stores only arcs, which are parts of an area boundary between two branch points. For example, polygon I consists of arcs ab, bc, cd, de, and ea, and polygon II consists of dc, cf, fg, and gd (figure 9). An index table in the data base gives (for each file) the arcs making up each polygon. When maps (files) are overlaid, new arcs are created whenever an arc from one file crosses an arc of another file. Also new polygons are created, and a new table of polygon arcs is written. It remains to be seen how effective this data base organization is.

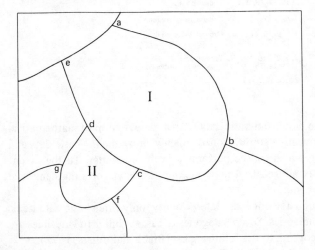

FIGURE 9. Polygons made up of arcs.

Program Inventory and Geologic Modeling. Earth science information in its most commonly available form consists of maps and tables of physical, chemical and engineering properties, which are the basic data. They are developed from raw data (field observations and actual measurements of various physical and chemical properties) with the benefit of scientific interpretation. These basic data are still very technical and generally require further interpretation by scientists or engineers to be useful to the planner. This interpretation of basic data has been one of the main features of the San Francisco Bay Region Study Program. The inventory of these studies listed previously is now presented in a slightly different form (table 2). The left-hand column contains basic data. Most of these data are generated routinely by the U.S. Geological Survey, although not uniformly for all areas of the country. The right-hand column lists results of the interpretive studies. The center column lists the basic data that would, ideally, be used in the interpretive study on the same row to the right. In some instances all of the basic data so listed is used. In others, only part of it is used, depending on the area being considered, the availability of the basic data for that area, and the current methods involved in the particular study. Most of the items in the right-hand column are generally not developed routinely by the survey but are the outgrowth of special requirements developed on the San Francisco Bay Region Study Program. The data in the right-hand column plus some items in the left-hand column can be used for the evaluation of land-use plans, especially to avoid hazards.

TABLE 2. PROGRAM INVENTORY

Basic data	Data used in interpretive studies	Interpretive studies
1. Bedrock	1, 3, 4, 6, 15, 17, 18, 19	A. Landslide susceptibility.
2. Unconsolidated deposits	1, 2, 4, 5, 7, 8, 12, 19, I	B. Land use implications— region of bay mud.
3. Landslides		
4. Active faults	1-6, 9, 11-15, 17-20, I	C. Coastal geologic processes.
5. Topographic map		
6. Slope map	2, 4, 5, 7-10, 12, 14, 17, 18, 19, I	D. Physical properties of unconsolidated deposits and land-use implications.
7. Bay mud		
8. Land subsidence	1-4, 6, 11, 12, 17	E. Hillside materials—inferred engineering behavior and land-use implications.
9. Ground-water		
10. (a) Stream networks (b) rating tables.	5, 10, 14, 15, 19	F. Flood-prone areas and land-use implications (boundary of 100-year flood).
11. Water bodies		
12. Earthquake locations	5, 10, 14, 15	G. Urban drainage system (technical report).
13. Mineral commodities		
14. Historic flood data	1, 6, 9, 11, 15, 16, 17, 19, A, F	H. Land pollution susceptibility.
15. Rainfall (isohyetal map)		
16. Evaporation data map	1-4, 7, 12	I. Seismic response map.
17. Soils		
18. Vegetation	1-5, 9, 10, 11, 15, 16, 18, 19	J. Ground water studies.
19. Land use		
20. Water quality and suspended sediment.	1, 2, 3, 5, 6, 10, 11, 14, 15 17-20	K. Erosion and sediment studies.

The development of most interpretive data from basic data is, in a sense, a form of mathematical modeling or simulation. Some of the interpretive studies consist mainly of overlaying basic data and interpreting the overlays (McHarg, 1969), which can be performed in the computer. To the extent that interpretation of the overlays can be reduced to a table look-up procedure or a mathematical formula, this can also be performed in the computer.

On the landslide susceptibility map prepared for San Mateo County, only three basic data items are used: bedrock, landslides, and slope categories. Seven categories of susceptibility to landslides are defined ranging from lowest to highest, according to the following list (Brabb and others, 1972):

I. Areas least susceptible to landsliding. Very few small landslides have formed in these areas. Formation of large landslides is possible but unlikely, except during earthquakes. Slopes generally less than 15 percent but may include small areas of steep slopes that could have higher susceptibility. Includes some areas with 30 percent to more than 70 percent slopes that seem to be underlain by stable rock units.

II. Low susceptibility to landsliding. Several small landslides have formed in these areas, and some of these have caused extensive damage to homes and roads. A few large landslides may occur. Slopes vary from 5 to 5½ percent for unstable rock units, to more than 70 percent for rock units that seem to be stable.

III. Moderate susceptibility to landsliding. Many small landslides have formed in these areas, and several of these have caused extensive damage to homes and roads. Some large landslides likely. Slopes generally greater than 30 percent but includes some 15–30 percent slopes in areas underlain by unstable rock units.

IV. Moderately high susceptibility to landsliding. Slopes all greater than 30 percent. Several large landslides likely. These areas are mostly in undeveloped parts of the county.

V. High susceptibility to landsliding. Slopes all greater than 30 percent. Many large and small landslides may form. These are mostly in undeveloped parts of the county.

VI. Very high susceptibility to landsliding. Slopes all greater than 30 percent. Development of many large and small landslides is likely. These areas are mainly in undeveloped parts of the county.

L. Highest susceptibility to landsliding. Consists of landslide and possible landslide deposits. No small deposits are shown. Some of these areas may be relatively stable and suitable for development, whereas others are active and causing damage to roads, houses, and other cultural features.

In developing the susceptibility map, the map of landslide deposits is first overlaid on the map of bedrock geology. Those areas with landslide deposits are zones in category "L." Next, the result is overlaid with a slope map of six slope categories. Those areas not categorized as zone "L" are categorized according to table 3 (from Brabb and others, 1972).

If it were possible to generate the results of all the interpretive studies by simulation or modeling, it would be feasible to have the computer data bank consist mainly of basic data. Interpretations could be generated as required. This approach has several advantages. Owing to the pressure of urbanization and its impact on the environments, interest in the type of data generated by the interpretive studies will grow, fostering the development of better geologic models so that a data base of interpretive data will probably have to be updated frequently. However, the basic data are relatively stable, requiring much less updating. As areas of application grow, the amount of data generated by models will probably result in a greatly enlarged data base if it consists of interpretive data. Finally, there is a great advantage if, instead of a digitized slope map, the data bank contains elevations at grid intersections of suitable size so that slopes can be computed as needed. Then models requiring slope information as an input are not locked into preselected slope categories.

Earth Science Data for Information and Predictive Land Use. Large-scale regional land-use models are developing a need for earth science data owing to the growing requirements to study the environmental impact of various land-use alternatives. The Oak Ridge National Laboratory, in developing the models for their environmental program, are providing for this need for including the necessary data, mostly assigned to the level of the 30 X 30 second cell. The data include geology (bedrock and surficial, mineral deposits, aquifers), surface water information, and soil types. Tables of physical and chemical properties are included in the data base (C. R. Meyers, Jr., oral communication, 1972). The Center for Advanced Computation of the University of Illinois included the following data in the data base of the recommended Illinois Resources Information Center for Advanced Computation, 1972a):

Geology

Surface deposits	Digitized area.
Oil, gas, and water wells	Point.
Oil and gas fields and storage	Section.
Oil and gas statistics	Township.
Coal statistics	Point.

Soil

Soil associations and interpretations	Section.
Soil types	County.
Soil productivity	County.
Soil and water	County.
Conservation needs	Watershed.

Land Use

Aerial photography	1:24,000.
Land-use interpretation	¼ X ¼ section.

Water

Stream network digitization	Network.
Water quality standards	Network.
Pollutant emissions	Point.
Surface water quality	Point.
Ground water quality	Point.
Public water-supply quality	Point.
Flood plains	Digitized area.
Flow duration and low flow frequencies	Point.
Time of travel	Network.
Public water-supply adequacy	County, municipality.

Evaluation and Recommendations

The need for user participation in the design of a computer information system is well recognized. In the design of an urban and regional land-use information system, participation of users must be preceded by identification of the using community, which may include not only various government bodies but also the private sector. The larger the region, the more varied the potential users of the system. Totschek, Almendinger, Kevany, and Needham (1970) discussed the need for a common information center for the nine-county bay region, its relation to the various components of the user community, and a recognition of the differing data requirements of the user. However, the report is concerned only with socioeconomic information and does not consider earth science data. The Center for Advanced Computation of the University of Illinois (1972a) recommends a statewide information system. A survey of user needs indicated five potential user groups: (1) social service agencies, (2) the economic and industrial sector, (3) the physical services sector (for example, transportation), (4) the natural resources sector, and (5) agricultural agencies.

Few land-use decisionmakers have much knowledge of earth science or the role it should play in land-use planning; many have little knowledge of computer technology. Therefore, in the design of a specific system, after the user community has been identified, considerable interchange of knowledge may be necessary between users, computer scientists, and specialists in the field of earth science technology, primarily geologists and civil engineers. Any design effort that bypasses or weakens this step may waste much time and money.

An urban and regional land-use information system with a large and diverse user community will require a wide range of capabilities. The main characteristics of such a system are:

1. Interactive and batch mode capability.
2. Large data manipulation and computational capabilities.

3. Multiple-type input and output devices.
4. Support of many terminals.
5. Support of multiple data bases.

Data Base Organization

One of the major problems in the design of a geographical information system or an urban and regional information system is the design of the data base, especially with regard to area type data. The two main types are the polygon and the cell, both previously described. The polygon type has the advantage of storing the boundaries of an area to within system tolerance. This may be useful where boundaries are precisely known, such as political or land ownership boundaries. It may be unnecessary where the boundaries are not precisely known, such as in many bedrock formations. If overlaying polygons must be done in the computer, it can be very expensive. The polygon type, therefore, is not conducive to mathematical modeling where a large amount of overlaying is required. The properties of the cell structure are just the reverse. The overlaying has already been accomplished in establishing the data base. The main drawback of the cell type is its imprecise representation of areal boundaries.

TABLE 3. LANDSLIDE FAILURE RECORD FOR ROCK UNITS IN SAN MATEO COUNTY
[Modified from Brabb and others, 1972]

Rock unit on geologic map in order of increasing proportion of surface having failed by landsliding	Map symbol	Approx. area in county (mi²)	Approx. area that has failed (mi²)	Relative susceptibility numbers	Susceptibility numbers in each slope interval					
					0–5°	5–15°	15–30°	30–50°	50–70°	>70°
No data for surficial deposits, undivided, Qu; alluvium, Qal; San Francisco Bay mud, Qm; windblown sand, Qd; beach deposits, Qb; artificial fill, Qaf; terrace deposits, Qt; Page Mill Basalt, Tpm; unnamed volcanic rocks, KJv; marble, m; shale near Palo Alto, Ksh; conglomerate, fcg; or metamorphic rocks, fm, but extent of landsliding probably small)				I						
imestone	fl	.30	.00		I	I	I	I	I	I
olma Formation	Qc	11.11	.01		I	I	I	I	I	I
andstone at San Bruno Mountain	KJs	4.77	.10		I	I	I	I	I	II
utano(?) Sandstone	Tb?	10.56	.19		I	I	II	II	II	II
nnamed sandstone	Tus	1.81	.04		I	I	I	I	I	II
ranitic rocks	Kgr	24.61	.90		I	I	I	I	I	II
erpentine	sp	4.76	.09	II	I	I	I	II	II	II
andstone of Franciscan assemblage	fs	22.19	.74		I	I	I	II	II	II
lope wash and ravine fill	Qsr	4.51	.18		I	I	I	II	II	II
reenstone of Franciscan assemblage	fg	11.70	.61		I	I	I	II	II	II
hert of Franciscan assemblage	fc	1.43	.10		I	I	I	II	II	II
ompico Sandstone	Tlo	.40	.03		I	I	I	I	I	II
heared rocks of Franciscan assemblage	fsr	9.99	.83		I	I	II	III	III	III
igeon Point Formation	Kpp	7.77	.84		I	I	II	II	II	III
an Lorenzo Formation, undivided	Tsl	1.00	.11		I	I	II	II	II	III
lerced Formation	QTm	7.91	1.01	III	I	I	II	II	III	III
andstone, shale and conglomerate	Tss	3.34	.51		I	I	I	I	II	III
utano Sandstone, Sky Londa area	Tb	22.55	4.33		I	I	II	III	III	III
anta Clara Formation	QTs	6.67	1.85		I	I	III	IV	IV	IV
ices Mudstone Member of San Lorenzo Formation	Tsr	1.37	.43		I	I	II	III	IV	IV
aqueros Sandstone	Tvq	7.60	2.41		I	I	II	III	III	IV
onterey Shale	Tm	5.11	1.76		I	I	II	IV	IV	IV
urisima Formation, undivided	Tp	23.06	7.81	IV	I	II	III	IV	IV	IV
ambert Shale	Tla	19.95	7.25		I	I	II	III	III	IV
indego Basalt and other volcanic rocks	Tmb	10.80	4.01		I	I	II	III	III	IV
utano Sandstone along Butano Ridge	Tb	20.18	7.66		I	I	II	III	IV	IV
anta Cruz Mudstone	Tsc	19.25	7.98		I	I	I	III	IV	IV
an Gregorio Sandstone Member of Purisima Formation	Tpsg	2.41	1.06		I	I	IV	V	V	V
unitas Sandstone Member of Purisima Formation	Tptu	2.76	1.24		I	I	III	V	V	V
ahana Member of Purisima Formation	Tpt	33.46	16.08	V	I	II	III	V	V	V
omponio Member of Purisima Formation	Tpp	11.97	5.76		I	II	III	V	V	V
wobar Shale Member of San Lorenzo Formation	Tst	.80	.42		I	I	II	III	IV	V
anta Margarita Sandstone	Tsm	.65	.41		I	I	I	III	III	VI
an Lorenzo Formation and Lambert Shale, undivided	Tls	6.83	4.56	VI	I	I	III	V	VI	VI
obitos Mudstone Member of Purisima	Tpl	3.71	2.57		I	II	II	VI	VI	VI
andslide deposits	Qls	83.88	83.88	L	L	L	L	L	L	L

At present, a cell structure is recommended for earth science areal type data for a region such as the San Francisco Bay region, especially if a large amount of simulation and mathematical modeling is to be done. Imprecise representation of the boundary is not a serious problem for these purposes. A cell size of about 150 X 150 m (or its equivalent in geodetic cell size) is required for some geologic areal data; for the remainder, a 300 X 300 m cell is satisfactory. Although it may be advisable to include line and point information with the cell record, it probably will be necessary to have separate network files of some line information for modeling purposes.

The handling of slope information depends on its use and on the terrain of the region. In relatively flat country, a slope map of about five zones may be amenable to digitization, since it is no more complex than many land-use maps. However, a similar slope map for mountainous terrain can be so complex as to be virtually impossible to digitize with an image digitizer or a line follower.

The compatibility of earth science data with other geographically distributed data depends on use of the data. An example is census data, generally organized on the ACG-DIME system (U.S. Bureau of the Census, 1970) or assigned to census tracts. Some systems include or provide for a limited amount of land-use information and transportation networks. The census tracts are small in urban areas and large in rural areas. However, much of the planning—hence much of the modeling—will be concerned with areas not presently urbanized. Census information should be assigned to cells in rural areas, cells much smaller than the census tracts and whose boundaries coincide with boundaries of square groups of earth science data cells as in the ORNL organization.

If there is much demand for the use of an interactive system, for example, using a storage display tube and not requiring much computation in the computer, it may be cheaper to maintain a separate set of polygon files, in addition to the cell file, for just such applications. Depending on the method of digitization, these files may be archival files derived from digitization of maps and used in the generation of the cell file.

Finally, the data should be organized on the basis of geodetic coordinates, and the metric system should be used for linear measure, since national adoption of the metric system is near. The difficulty of mathematical modeling across zones of a projective system, such as the Universal Transverse Mercator (UTM) is largely removed by the use of geodetic coordinates. Although cell size becomes smaller toward the north, the variation is small from one row to the next and is easily handled in a mathematical model. Finally, maps can be plotted in any of the commonly used projections with existing software routines.

Summary

The focus of this study is urban and regional information systems that must handle relatively large (multicounty) areas including urbanized parts that are expanding. The main concern has been with the incorporation of earth science data, whose main attribute, from the point of view of a computer system designer, is its spatial quality. This attribute must be preserved in the computer system.

The design of such an information system should recognize the following factors.

1. System specification should be developed considering the requirements of the user community. The users will need the aid of geologists, hydrologists, and engineers regarding the use of earth science data for their particular region.
2. A system can have a wide range of capabilities. Some of the more important ones are:
    a. Interactive and batch mode capability.
    b. Large data manipulation and computational capability.
    c. Multiple type input and output devices.
    d. Multiterminal support.
    e. Support of multiple data bases.

The extent to which a particular system incorporates these will depend on regional needs.

3. The initial cost of the data base will be high.

The greater the accuracy, the higher the cost, in a rapidly increasing, nonlinear fashion.

When considering specifically an information system for the San Francisco Bay region, it may not be necessary to build from scratch but only to modify the system of the MTC to make it truly regional. It must be decided whether to incorporate earth science data as interpretive data or as basic data plus the necessary software to develop interpretations as required.

Decisions must be made on two additional items. The data base may be organized on a cell basis or as an area boundary file. At present a cell-organized data base seems best if there will be much modeling and simulation. The area boundary file is best for a simple storage and retrieval system. If overlaying of files is required, it may prove very costly with an area boundary file, unless the Raytheon arc approach is a significant improvement.

Second, the operation of map digitization should consider the hardware used, map standards, and editing procedures together as a whole. Use of an image digitizer is probably most economical at present. Scanning devices may be better for very simple maps. However, for scanning, the production of overlays from complex maps may not be much different than digitizing with an image digitizer. For the San Francisco Bay region in particular, (1) a cell-type data base is recommended for the earth science data, (2) the slope maps for the area should not be digitized, and (3) the cost to digitize the earth science data can be only roughly estimated.

REFERENCES

Amidon, E. L., and Akin, E. S., 1971, Algorithm selection of the best method for compressing map data strings: Assoc. Computing Machinery Commun., v. 14, pp. 769–74.

Bay Area Transportation Study Commission, 1969, Bay area transportation report, 85 pp.

Boyle, A. R., 1972, Geographic information systems: Geographical Data Handling, Internat. Geog. Union, v. 2, pp. 1151–1200.

Brabb, E. E., compiler, 1970, Preliminary geologic map of the central Santa Cruz Mountains, California: U.S. Geol. Survey open-file map, scale 1:62,500.

Brabb, E. E., Pampeyan, E. H., and Bonilla, M. G., 1972, Landslide susceptibility in San Mateo County, California: U.S. Geol. Survey Misc. Field Studies Map MF-360, scale 1:62,500.

Center for Advanced Computation, 1972a, IRIS—Illinois resource information system feasibility study, final report: Urbana, Univ. Illinois, 204 pp. 1972b, NARIS—A natural resource information system: Urbana, Univ. Illinois, Doc. No. 35, 15 pp.

McHarg, I. L., 1969, Design with nature: Garden City, N.Y., Natural History Press, 197 pp.

Raytheon Company, 1973, Program summary report: The development of a natural resource information system, v. 1, 25 pp.

Tomlinson, R. F., 1968, A geographic information system for regional planning: CSLRO Symposium, Canberra, Australia, pp 200–10.

Totschek, R., Almendinger, V., Kevany, M., and Needham, K., 1970, Work program for a bay region information support center: System Development Corp., 117 pp.

U.S. Bureau of the Census, 1970, The DIME geocoding system: Census Use Study Rept. no. 4, 46 pp.

U.S. Department of Housing and Urban Development, 1968, Urban and regional information systems: Washington, D.C., 333 pp.

U.S. Geological Survey and Department of Housing and Urban Development, 1971, Program design, 1971: San Francisco Bay Region Environment and Resources Planning Study, 123 pp.

PART SEVEN

Utilization of Geologic Information in Regional Planning

Philosophers have suggested for centuries that it is primarily our ability to think at higher levels that distinguishes the human colony from the other inhabitants of the earth. In earlier parts of this book, examples have been chosen to illustrate how our thoughts have led us to both tragedies and well-founded plans in our interactions with the geological environment. The same thinking that leads us to urbanize a particular piece of land might, with more detailed information and better education, lead us to see the hazards of that land.

This information and analyzation step, sometimes known as planning, is covered in the last part of this book. Planning has been defined by Flawn (1970:xviii) as

> . . . an intellectual process wherein (1) data are analyzed and (2) a program is formulated to bring about a desired result. It is a process by which change is initiated, promoted, and controlled in an orderly manner. . . .

In previous parts of this book, articles have concentrated on specific aspects of geology in the urban environment. Readings in this section concentrate on the synthesis of geologic information and its application to the planning process.

The first article in this section discusses many aspects of the relation of earth science information to the entire planning process. Plans result from gathering, interpreting, and evaluating a great deal of information of which geology is only one part. Whether to preserve, conserve, or use a natural resource, whether development should be short- or long-term, whether local or national needs should be dominant, and how the often opposing ideas of public and private interests should be resolved—these are all questions which require geological information if intelligent decisions are to be made. The multidisciplinary world of the planner, which has seldom included geological information, and the narrow realm of most geologists, who are unfamiliar with planning processes, have not been closely related; therefore, plans have often been incomplete. Fortunately, interdisciplinary cooperation is increasing, as illustrated by many studies cited in previous parts of this book.

In the second article in this section, an attempt is made to estimate potential dollar-value losses due to geologic hazards in California. Such losses are difficult to estimate, but the authors feel it worthwhile to make the estimates because political decisionmakers are often more influenced by economic, rather than scientific, reasoning. Programs are suggested that should be undertaken, by planning and other agencies, at local, state, and federal levels, which would enable us to cope with geologic hazards.

REFERENCE

Flawn, P. T. 1970. *Environmental geology*. New York: Harper & Row.

Earth-Science Information in Land-Use Planning— Guidelines for Earth Scientists and Planners

William Spangle and Associates; F. Beach Leighton and Associates; and Baxter, McDonald and Company

30

Introduction

The principal question facing those responsible for land-use decisions is clearly expressed in the recently published report of the Task Force on Land Use and Urban Growth created by the President's Citizen's Advisory Committee on Environmental Quality (1973, p. 14) and funded by the Rockefeller Brothers Fund:

How shall we organize, control, and coordinate the process of urban development so as to protect what we most value in the environmental, cultural, and aesthetic characteristics of the land while meeting the essential needs of the changing U.S. population for new housing, roads, power plants, shopping centers, parks, businesses, and industrial facilities?

The land itself is a resource that must be used with wisdom. The needs of our growing population require that we conscientiously plan for the use of land, not only to protect its resources and esthetic values but also to reduce the exposure of urban development to natural hazards by giving explicit consideration to natural conditions and processes in land-use decisions. In this task, the work of the planner and the earth scientist can be mutually reinforcing.

From the earliest times the natural environment has influenced the location and form of human settlement. The land and its features present, in varying degrees, opportunities and constraints for various human activities. As expressed by Legget (1973, pp. 70–71),

When planning starts, for an urban community or region, the area to be developed is not the equivalent . . . of a piece of blank paper ready for the free materialization of the ideas of the designer, but it is rather an environment that has been exposed for a very long period to the effects of many natural modifying factors. . . . Development of new communities and the charting of regional development must, therefore, take account of this fundamental organic and dynamic character of Nature so that the works of man may fit as harmoniously as possible into the environment. . . .

To achieve harmonious blending of man's works and nature requires knowledge of resources to be developed and conserved and awareness of hazards to be avoided or mitigated. Information from the earth sciences is thus essential. Earth-science information (ESI) pertains to the natural materials, features, and processes of the land. It includes basic information from geology, soils, hydrology, and a large number of related scientific and engineering fields, together with interpretation of that basic in-

Extracted with permission of the authors from *U.S. Geological Survey Circular 721*, 1976, 28 pp.

formation. ESI thus encompasses much of the information concerning the physical nature and inter-actions of land and water. Because of the focus of the study, and these guidelines, information from chemical and biological sciences, meteorology, and climatology is not considered, although it, too, is highly relevant to land-use planning.

This circular presents and discusses a set of general guidelines for utilizing ESI in land-use planning. The guidelines concern subject areas of interest to both planners and earth scientists. Planners should find the report useful as a brief introduction to the kinds and sources of ESI available and to techniques for applying ESI to planning. For earth scientists, the report defines in broad terms the needs of planners and how ESI can be made more useful to planners. The report is intended to stimulate the development of effective communication between planners and earth scientists.

The main purpose of this report, however, is to introduce decisionmakers and interested citizens to the potential uses of ESI in a planning program. The desires of the community as perceived by decisionmakers are frequently reflected in land-use decisions. Both planners and earth scientists can be expected to respond to public pressures for land-use planning that recognizes natural opportunities and constraints. The reader is referred to the full technical report by Spangle and others (1973), for more detailed discussion of the material presented in this summary.

Guidelines for Utilizing Earth-Science Information in Land-Use Planning

ESI in the Planning Process

Land-use planning is an integral part of a broader planning process variously termed comprehensive, general, or master planning. Whereas comprehensive planning treats the future development of an area in terms of all major determinants of growth and change—economic, political, social, and physical—land-use planning highlights the physical expression of the plan on the land. As such, it is primarily concerned with the arrangement and types of land uses, their impact on the landscape, and relation to transportation and community facilities and utilities.

The land-use planning process consists of five conceptually distinct phases: (1) identification of problems and definition of goals and objectives; (2) data collection and interpretation; (3) plan formulation; (4) review and adoption of plans; and (5) plan implementation. Figure 1 depicts the land-use planning process and lists typical studies and documents associated with three phases. As shown by the arrows, each phase is interrelated with all others, and the sequence, while logical, is often varied especially in response to crises, political opportunities, or legal requirements. Interaction among the phases, however, should be virtually continuous. Plan formulation often indicates the need for additional information, and additional information may alter the concept of the objectives and problems; moreover, plan implementation may reveal the need for additional information or modification of the plan.

Public initiative and response is a key part of every phase of land-use planning. "Public" may refer to elective political bodies, special-interest groups, or interested individuals. Elected public officials have final responsibility for most key policy decisions, although persons in nonelective positions actually make many important day-to-day decisions. Decisions occur throughout the process, ranging from the decision to engage in a planning effort to the final approval of a plan and adoption of implementing regulations, programs, and procedures.

ESI is necessary in each phase of the land-use planning process. The following outline lists the basic steps for integrating ESI in each phase of land-use planning; planners and earth scientists should work together in carrying out each step:

1. Identify problems and define goals and objectives.
   a. Obtain readily available ESI for preliminary identification of natural hazards and resources.
   b. Review this ESI in relation to existing land-use plans and policies, projected growth trends, and anticipated changes to develop a tentative set of objectives and priorities, giving special consideration to hazards and resources.

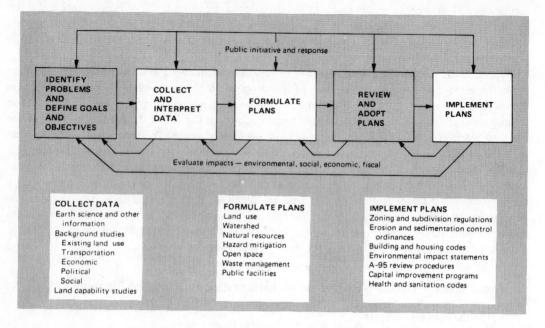

COLLECT DATA
Earth science and other
 information
Background studies
  Existing land use
  Transportation
  Economic
  Political
  Social
Land capability studies

FORMULATE PLANS
Land use
Watershed
Natural resources
Hazard mitigation
Open space
Waste management
Public facilities

IMPLEMENT PLANS
Zoning and subdivision regulations
Erosion and sedimentation control
  ordinances
Building and housing codes
Environmental impact statements
A-95 review procedures
Capital improvement programs
Health and sanitation codes

FIGURE 1. Diagram of the land-use planning process.

2. Collect and interpret data.
    a. Develop a program for utilizing available ESI and compiling new data.
    b. Arrange with earth scientists to prepare basic and interpretive maps and texts. Map informa-
       tion should relate in scale and detail to other basic planning information.
    c. Estimate the probable future demand for land considering projections of population growth
       and distribution, economic activity, social and cultural needs, and transportation require-
       ments.
    d. Prepare land-capability maps showing the natural capability of each land unit to accommo-
       date each potential use.
3. Formulate plans.
    a. On the basis of land-capability maps, appropriate projections, and economic, social, and
       political analyses, consider feasible alternative arrangements of land uses.
    b. Evaluate alternative land-use possibilities, selecting the most desirable.
    c. Prepare a land-use plan incorporating as much detail as necessary to serve as a basis for de-
       cisionmaking.
    d. Evaluate land-use proposals for environmental, economic, and social impacts. Make any in-
       dicated revisions in the plan.
4. Review and adopt a plan. Obtain official approval of plan from public decisionmaking bodies.
5. Implement the plan.
    a. Prepare and seek adoption of land-use regulations and any land-acquisition and capital-
       improvement programs needed to carry out the plan.
    b. Establish guidelines and a procedure for conducting the earth-science investigations needed
       to evaluate each development proposal.
    c. Develop procedures and staff capability for reviewing soils and geology reports, environ-
       mental impact assessments, and project proposals.
    d. Arrange for modification of previous steps as new or more detailed ESI becomes avail-
       able.

Sources, Types, and Interpretation of ESI for Planning

Sources of ESI. A variety of agencies at all jurisdictional levels in the United States produce ESI (table 1). Two Federal agencies—the United States Geological Survey (USGS), Department of the Interior, and the Soil Conservation Service (SCS), Department of Agriculture—are prime sources of information, and their publications are widely available throughout the country.

The USGS has a broad research base in the earth sciences covering work in topography, geology, and mineral and water resources. Major offices in Reston, Va., Denver, Colo., and Menlo Park, Calif., have professional staffs and extensive facilities for basic earth-science research. The USGS is specifically charged with the preparation of topographic and geologic quadrangle maps of the United States. The Water Resources Division of USGS (with district offices throughout the United States) produces

TABLE 1. SOME SOURCES OF EARTH-SCIENCE INFORMATION

Federal agencies
    U.S. Department of the Interior
        Geological Survey
        Bureau of Mines
        Bureau of Reclamation
        Bureau of Land Management
    U.S. Department of Agriculture
        Extension Service
        Soil Conservation Service
        Forest Service
    U.S. Department of Commerce
        National Oceanic and Atmospheric Administration
    U.S. Department of Army
        Army Corps of Engineers
    Energy Research and Development Administration
    Environmental Protection Agency
    National Aeronautics and Space Administration
    Tennessee Valley Authority
State divisions or departments
    Agriculture
    Conservation
    Forestry
    Geological Surveys
    Oil and Gas
    Soil Conservation
    Fish and Game
    Water Resources
    Water Quality
    Mineral Resources
    Colleges and universities
County or city departments or special districts
    Planning
    Water
    Flood Control
    Agriculture
    Parks and Recreation
    Engineering
    Building and Safety
    Public Works
Private producers
    Consulting firms
    Private colleges and universities
    Professional societies
    Industries with in-house capabilities

basic hydrologic data, inventories the nation's water supply, monitors its quality, and engages in other hydrologic research.

The USGS recently has placed an increased emphasis on production of ESI specifically applicable to planning and decisionmaking. Through a series of pilot projects, studies have been undertaken to interpret basic ESI in terms of its implications for various land uses. These products are particularly useful to planners.

The SCS is responsible for many soil and water conservation programs throughout the United States. Over 3,000 soil conservation districts established under enabling legislation in all 50 states are served by SCS field offices, each headed by a "district conservationist." District boundaries in most cases conform to county lines.

The SCS field offices are staffed largely by soil scientists involved primarily in classifying soils and evaluating their suitability for agricultural purposes. Because soil classifications have some engineering significance and because much agricultural land has been converted to urban and suburban uses, SCS products are often used in land-use planning. For this reason, and as agricultural applications of SCS products have been satisfied, SCS soil scientists are increasingly orienting their work to the needs of urban and regional planners.

The decentralization of work by the SCS brings its soil conservationists into close personal contact with local persons and agencies requiring technical assistance. Each SCS district responds to local needs and circumsta..ces, leading to considerable innovation and flexibility in presenting and interpreting soil data. Such data are of particular value in assessing foundation conditions and supporting systems near the surface for light structures such as single-family residences, utilities, and streets. Where foundation conditions at greater depths are of concern and natural processes such as landslides may be active, soil data can be a helpful supplement to the geologic and hydrologic information needed to characterize problem areas.

State geological surveys can be important sources of ESI for planners. These agencies may undertake geological surveys, publish statewide earth-science maps, and serve as information bureaus for the people of the state. All states, except Rhode Island, have geological surveys, but staff size, facilities, organizational structure, and areas of emphasis vary considerably from state to state.

Many state governments also have departments or divisions that are responsible for soil and water conservation. Such a department or division may work largely through the state SCS office or may act independently in developing a separate program of its own. It may be an excellent source of ESI related to soil and water resources.

Earth-science departments at public and private universities and private consultants are other sources of ESI. If the need is for fairly detailed data related to a specialized problem or particular site, a special study will ordinarily be required.

Scale, Accuracy, and Detail of ESI. A major consideration in building a data base of ESI for land-use planning is the relationship of scale, detail, and accuracy to an agency's planning responsibilities and requirements. There is often misunderstanding over the fact that scale, accuracy, and detail do not refer to the same thing and may not even be related to each other in a consistent manner.

Map scale is the relationship between corresponding distances on a map and on the earth. A scale of 1:24,000 means that 1 map-inch is equivalent to 24,000 inches on the ground. Planners would normally translate this to 1 map-inch is equivalent to 2,000 feet. A map's scale is considered "small" if the second figure of this ratio is "large"; a scale of 1:62,500 is thus smaller than a scale of 1:24,000. A small-scale map does not usually show as much detail as a large-scale map.

Accuracy has two distinct meanings. First, it refers to whether the information is right or wrong. Accurate information is correct, free from error. Second, accuracy in a relative sense refers to the degree of precision with which the information was obtained, measured, and recorded.

Although scale and accuracy are important in planning, obtaining data of an appropriate level of detail for the task at hand is usually the most significant informational concern of the planner. Confusion occurs when the common but sometimes unwarranted assumption is made that a large-scale map (say of scale 1:24,000) shows more detail and is more accurate than a small-scale map (say of scale 1:125,000). The planner who indicates a need for "larger scale" may really mean that he needs more detailed or more accurate maps. A map may easily be enlarged to a larger scale, but the enlargement process will result in a map no more detailed or accurate than the original. Enlarging a map may, however, render detail already present in the original more legible and hence make it more useful. Data plotted on the enlarged map cannot be located any more accurately than on the small-scale map. In fact, the enlarged map does not have the accuracy of a map prepared specifically at the enlarged scale.

The term "map detail" refers to the amount of information presented in a given map area—the more information per map unit, the more detailed the map. Map production techniques and legibility requirements impose physical limits on the level of detail that can be shown on a map of a given scale. Within these limits, however, two maps of identical scale may present data with different levels of detail.

Successful application of ESI to land-use planning requires that ESI be available in sufficient detail to meet the planning needs of an agency. The level of detail required varies in a general way with the jurisdictional level and phase of the planning process. The need for detailed data in plan formulation is generally hierarchical with respect to governmental level; that is, more detailed data are needed at the local level than at the state or national level. More detailed data are ordinarily required for plan implementation regardless of jurisdictional level. Administration of land-use regulations ultimately depends on decisions made at the site level where the need for detail is greatest.

The level of detail of ESI needed also depends on the environmental diversity of the planning area. It is generally true that the more varied the natural environment of a planning area, the more detailed its ESI requirements. Generalized data on geology, soils, and hydrology may be sufficient for land-use planning in relatively flat agricultural areas of the Midwest where similar natural conditions may prevail throughout the planning area. In parts of California, on the other hand, many single planning jurisdictions include mountains, coastsides, deserts, and valleys with a great variety of geologic conditions. The very diversity of terrain poses planning constraints and opportunities that can be identified only with detailed information.

The present and anticipated rate of development within a jurisdiction also determines its ESI requirements. Generalized ESI is usually sufficient for areas that are relatively unchanging, clearly inaccessible, or otherwise undesirable for urban development. Detailed ESI is needed in rapidly growing areas for effective, almost daily, evaluation of project proposals. In areas where growth pressures are especially strong, development may be guided primarily by the economic judgments of private landowners without regard for the natural features of the land. When an area is under growth pressure, the planner needs great persistence and accurate and detailed ESI to insure consideration of earth-science factors in land-use decisions.

Limitations and Qualifications on ESI. Planners should always read the notes on an ESI document before use. They may discover, for instance, that there is considerable variation in the precision or completeness of data for different parts of the same map. Inaccessible areas may be less thoroughly mapped than accessible ones; important assumptions may have been made about the relationship of certain features; or the data may have been derived from different sources. Such information should always be included with a map or report, and a planner should always heed it. The disclaimer in figure 2 is part of the legend provided by the California Division of Mines and Geology for a recently issued map on special studies zones for the State of California. The disclaimer makes it clear that for most planning purposes, supplementary information will be necessary.

The planner must also note the scale and detail of a map. For instance, a highly generalized landslide map at a regional level may show an entire mountainside as being in a high landslide-susceptibility category, whereas additional, more detailed information may reveal a range of conditions including stable areas within the more generalized hazardous areas.

The degree of specificity of a planning decision should be no greater than warranted by the data upon which it is based. Planners, in seeking firm data on which to base decisions, may risk placing

WOODSIDE QUADRANGLE

IMPORTANT — PLEASE NOTE

1) *This map may not show all potentially active faults, either within the special studies zones or outside their boundaries.*

2) Faults shown are the basis for establishing the boundaries of the special studies zones.

3) The identification of these potentially active faults and the location of such fault traces are based on the best available data. Traces have been drawn as accurately as possible at this map scale, however, the quality of data used is highly varied. The faults shown have not been field checked during this map compilation.

4) Fault information on this map is not sufficient to serve as a substitute for information developed by the special studies that may be required under Chapter 7.5, Division 2, Section 2623 of the California Public Resources Code.

FIGURE 2. Example of a qualifying note on a geologic hazard map (State of California, 1974).

undue reliance on ESI that is too generalized for their purpose. The planner is well advised to write plans or regulations to accommodate more specific data as they become available.

Types of ESI for Planners. The standard Geological Survey topographic map in the quadrangle series is one of the most basic and valuable sources of ESI and is of great use as a planning tool. It not only shows terrain features, such as the shape and elevation of the land, and cultural features, such as transportation networks and areas of urbanization, but also serves as a good base map on which to record both earth-science and planning information. Topographic maps are readily available for most areas of the United States at very modest prices. With these maps, the knowledgeable planner can, among other things, calculate slope, inventory surface water resources, identify some obviously hazardous areas, and make a good preliminary assessment of where land-use conflicts may occur.

In addition to standard topographic maps, the Geological Survey is now producing orthophotoquads and hopes to have within the next few years complete coverage of all conterminous areas of the United States that are not already mapped at 1:24,000 scale. An orthophotoquad is a vertical aerial photograph in quadrangle format, corrected for position distortion related to differences in elevation and camera angle. A planimetrically accurate and detailed photoprint is produced, providing planners with geographic and topographic information (with the exception of contours and elevations) more quickly than is possible with a standard topographic map. The Survey also has orthophotoquads overprinted with contours and elevations for some areas.

Geologic maps show the kinds, distribution, and some physical characteristics of geologic units at or near the earth's surface and can be especially useful to planners when supplemented by engineering and planning interpretation. Areas susceptible to such geologic hazards as faults, landslides, and subsidence can be identified from these maps. The most commonly used basic geologic maps are 1:24,000-scale geologic quadrangle maps published by the federal and state geological surveys. These may be supplemented by more detailed information available from local sources.

Soil classification maps show the distribution of different types of surface soils (figure 3). The Soil Conservation Service soils surveys, which provide information pertaining to the upper 5–6 feet of earth materials, are widely used by planners. SCS publications may also include tabulations of basic data and interpretation of the data. Recent soil surveys provide soil ratings (limitations and capabilities) for a variety of agricultural, urban, and engineering uses. Soils information is frequently more

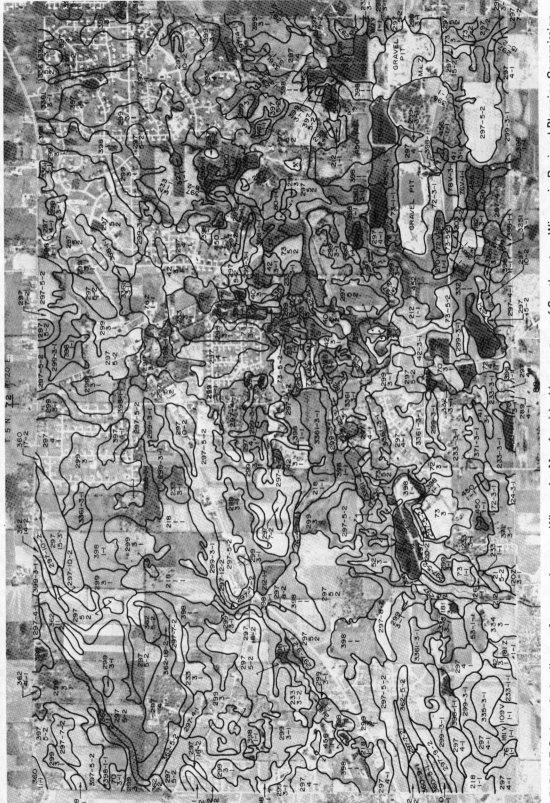

FIGURE 3. A typical soils map from southeastern Wisconsin. Map furnished by courtesy of Southeastern Wisconsin Regional Planning Commission.

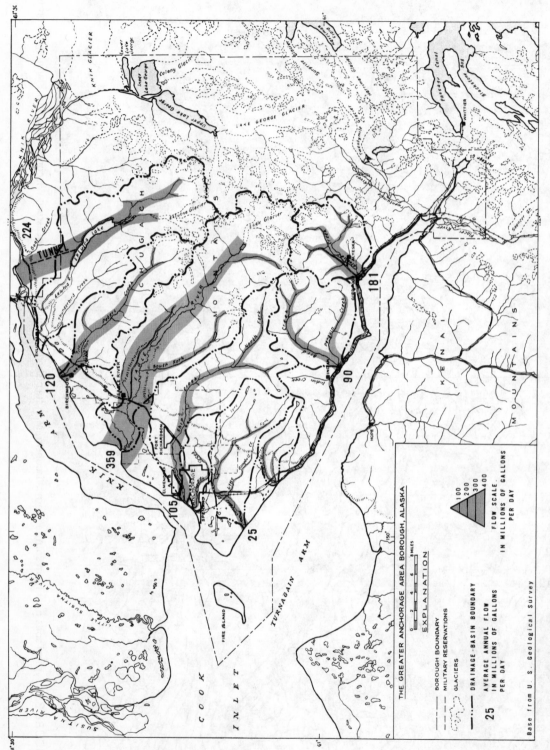

FIGURE 4. A typical hydrologic map from Greater Anchorage Area Borough, Alaska (Barnwell and others, 1972, p. 25)

readily available to planners than many other categories of ESI. When used in conjunction with geologic, hydrologic, and engineering data, it provides the basis for many studies on the natural limitations and potentials of the land for particular uses.

Data describing the hydrologic system of an area are always needed for land-use planning. Available from the Geological Survey, state and local water resources agencies or local flood-control and water districts, hydrologic maps depict the character of, and interrelationships between, surface and ground-water resources (figure 4). They are useful for delineating and evaluating water supply, flood-prone areas, water quality, areas of potential subsidence, seepage areas, and areas where erosion or sedimentation is a potential problem.

ESI in a Form Usable by Planners. Earth-science data applicable to land-use planning are often presented in map form. These maps may contain only basic data, or they may provide interpretive material as well. Actually, no sharp break separates basic and interpretive data. There is, instead, a continuum of information ranging from the very basic, such as bedrock material, to the highly interpretive, such as relative slope stability. When a planner says interpretive data are needed, he means, in a general sense, that a description of a natural feature or process is not very helpful to him unless accompanied by information concerning its probable behavior under certain natural and manmade conditions or by the implications regarding capability of land to accommodate particular uses.

Maps combining data on several natural conditions to provide interpretations related to complex natural processes can be particularly useful to the planner. One such example is a landslide-susceptibility map of another part of the Santa Cruz Mountains (figure 5) that synthesizes information from geology, slope, and landslide inventory maps (Brabb and others, 1972). Such a map is a very important planning tool, useful both in developing land-use policy and plans and in identifying areas that require detailed site investigation.

Planning for Natural Resources

Need for National Policies. Natural resources include earth materials such as minerals, soil, and water that are either consumed or altered by man. The combination of growing population and rising per capita consumption is leading to the real possibility of serious shortages of essential nonrenewable natural resources in the not-too-distant future. As a nation, we have not developed a systematic, comprehensive approach to resource planning. Planning and regulatory authority are dispersed; costs and benefits—both environmental and economic—fall unevenly on different jurisdictions and communities; and mechanisms for resolving basic conflicts over whether or not to develop a particular resource are lacking.

There is a need for broad, national policies to guide state and local jurisdictions in making land-use decisions related to resources. Except for the most widespread resources, the questions of adequacy and quality of resource supply are national, even global, concerns, while the direct environmental impacts from extraction are often localized. For instance, a decision to strip mine for coal may be a logical response to the growing national demand for energy, but the attending destruction of the land and loss of air quality may have a devastating local impact. Resource planning must address both the broad question of need and the more localized question of environmental impact.

The adequacy of known resources to meet present and projected needs is difficult to determine. There may be significant undiscovered sources for some materials, and moreover, technological advances may render the need for certain resources obsolete or make possible the utilization of presently inaccessible or unstable resources. Also, the location of a resource with respect to national or even regional boundaries influences the judgment of its adequacy.

National and state policy is needed to prevent the loss of resources through local decisions that, while individually rather insignificant, have a great combined impact. For example, one community's decision to permit the subdivision of agricultural land may yield local benefits and have little negative impact on the nation's food supply. If, however, many communities make this same decision, the impact on food supply may become critical. Such choices regarding alternative uses of land need to be

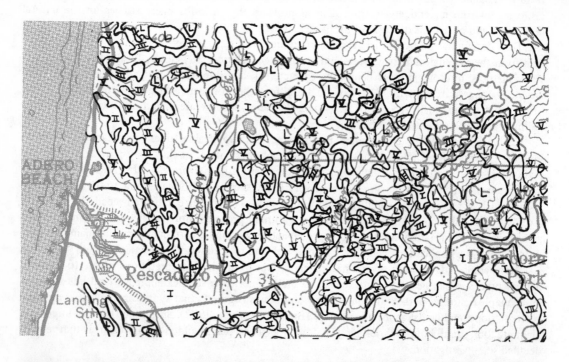

FIGURE 5. Landslide susceptibility in San Mateo County, California. *A*, Map specifically prepared for application in land-use planning studies. It was derived from a basic geologic map, an inventory of land-slides, and a slope map (Brabb and others, 1972). [Explanations on page 312.] *B,* Aerial photograph showing the area outlined in the landslide-susceptibility map.

Explanation of Map Units for Figure 5*A*[1]

I	Areas least susceptible to landsliding.
II	Low susceptibility to landsliding.
III	Moderate susceptibility to landsliding.
IV	Moderately high susceptibility to landsliding.
V	High susceptibility to landsliding.
VI	Very high susceptibility to landsliding.
L	Highest susceptibility to landsliding.

[1]See Article 29, p. 295 for detailed explanation of each unit.

FIGURE 5.–Continued

made on the basis of established national, state, and regional priorities that consider the long-term as well as short-term consequences.

Natural-Resource Plans. Decisions regarding the use of land are decisions concerning the allocation of a very important resource. This statement is true whether or not explicit policies and priorities regarding natural-resource conservation or development are adopted and adhered to. Obviously, however, it is desirable for decisions to be made in the context of full information and clearly stated policies.

Natural-resource planning is presently carried out to some degree by all levels of government. Federal and state agencies become most directly involved in resource planning in the management of government-owned land. For example, the U.S. Forest Service and Bureau of Land Management each plan for use of significant parts of the nation's important natural resources. At the regional and local level, resource planning is more likely to be an integral part of general land-use planning. However, the nature of the planning process and requirements for ESI differ less with jurisdictional level than with the particular resource involved.

Natural-resource planning is a prerequisite to development and administration of a resource management program. A natural-resource plan provides policies covering the basic question of whether or not particular resources should be developed or utilized. Such plans usually have three broad objectives: (1) Conservation of natural resources such as timber, water, agricultural land, and sand and gravel to provide a sustained yield for man's use, (2) preservation of areas with special scenic, scientific, ecological, and historical value, and (3) utilization of resources for the benefit of man.

Natural-resource management programs deal more specifically with the rate of resource utilization, the impacts of resource development or extraction, and the means of conserving or preserving certain natural resources. Management programs provide the basis for review of specific proposals for resource extraction and for administration of regulations pertaining to resource utilization.

Natural-resource planning requires an inventory of the resources of a planning area. Typically, resource areas are described, mapped, and classified according to resource potential. Special attention is given to areas with extractive resource potential or areas of special scenic, scientific, or cultural value. Policy recommendations are then developed to resolve possible conflicts between resource conservation and development.

The Natural Resources Plan produced by Bucks County, Pa., is an example of natural-resources planning appropriate to regional and local planning agencies. Phase I (1971) presented an inventory of natural resources, including prime agricultural soils, forests, wetlands, steep slopes, lakes and ponds, flood plains, extractive resources, scenic areas, and aquifers. In this phase, each natural feature was defined, weighted, and computer mapped on a grid. Phase II (1972) of the plan set forth specific policies for the protection of each natural resource in terms of the percentage of each grid cell containing a particular natural resource that should remain in open-space use. The land-use consequences of carrying out the policies are depicted on the Natural Resource Protection Map, which shows prime agricultural lands, existing parks, scenic areas, and open space required for resource protection.

The Bucks County planning effort was an integral part of a comprehensive land-use planning program. It is a particularly relevant example because the natural resources considered are those that occur to some extent in most local areas. The study and resulting plan respond primarily to concerns regarding resource preservation. As such, the Natural Resources Plan is an important contribution to open-space planning in Bucks County.

Usually the economics of resource development is calculated on a fairly short-term basis. This tends to militate against the conservation of resources for the use of future generations and, in addition, creates conflicts when resource potentials overlap. For example, fine agricultural land in some areas overlies rich coal deposits. In the short term, the gain from development of the coal may exceed that from the productive use of the agricultural land. It is possible that the reverse would be true in the long term. Each use of land has its economic effects. Careful assessment of both long- and short-term economic costs and benefits are needed to develop sound resource policy. In addition, any effort to balance economic costs and benefits must consider both costs and benefits as they relate to different economic and social groups and jurisdictions. Only recently have operators been required to assume the external costs of extracting and processing natural resources. In the past, it was legally and politically acceptable, for the costs of air, water, and noise pollution to be passed on to the owners and occupants of adjoining lands and downstream, downwind areas.

Planning for the conservation and utilization of commonly occurring natural resources such as agricultural land, sand and gravel, timber, water resources, and scenic areas has been left primarily to regional and local agencies. Regional agencies can be particularly effective in carrying out regionwide inventories of natural resources, for areas of significant resource potential often transcend local political boundaries. In addition, the production of resource inventories is often beyond the financial and technical capabilities of local government. The inventories form a foundation for preparation of regional policies concerning resource conservation and development that provide a useful context for local planning efforts. The implementation of natural-resources plans, whether formulated by regional or local agencies, depends primarily on local government under the present allocation of governmental powers. The key implementation mechanisms are land use, land division, land-development regulations, and land acquisition.

To assure that natural resources are utilized in a way that minimizes environmental damage requires a detailed resource management program. The National Environmental Policy Act of 1969 and various state requirements provide a framework for regional and local consideration of the environmental impacts accompanying resource development and use. The regulation of the utilization process is a part of the administrative process of project review. It is possible, for example, to plan for sequential multiple use of an excavation site. Issuance of a permit to extract the resource can be conditioned on the developer's commitment to leave the site usable for another purpose once the resource has been exhausted. For example, some exhausted sand and gravel pits can be used for sanitary landfills and later converted to open space and recreational uses with adequate planning and controls at the outset. Many states have passed legislation requiring the mine operator, after mining, to restore the land to a semblance of its original state. However, the responsibility to prevent environmental degradation historically has rested primarily with local government. The effort frequently requires extensive and detailed ESI and agency capacity to review earth-science reports that may be highly technical.

Environmental and Economic Impact. Most decisions to develop natural resources are based on economic judgments made by private and, in some cases, public entities. This fact affects the degree and sequence of development. Those resources that can be obtained with the least cost, closest to the user, are usually developed first. For example, a community usually looks first to the most immediately available water source of adequate quality—ground or surface. If the initial source proves to be inadequate, cost considerations will be dominant in choosing among alternative means of assuring a firm supply—to impound, import, increase the level of treatment of the local source, or recycle.

Judgments concerning the economics of resource development cannot be adequately made without thorough and accurate earth-science information. The cost of utilizing a given resource directly reflects natural conditions that must be understood. For example, information concerning geologic structure, ground-water level, and soil depth is needed to estimate the cost of extracting coal from a given location.

Adverse environmental effects often accompany the extraction and utilization of resources. The withdrawal of ground water may result in the subsidence of land; the overcultivation of soil may destroy its fertility or contribute to its loss through erosion; strip mining sharply alters the surface of the land; leaks from offshore oil wells may destroy beaches, pollute the water, and kill marine life. There is some environmental cost to be borne with almost any resource use. Assessment of the environmental impacts associated with the utilization of a resource should be made prior to its extraction and balanced against the net economic gains. Where utilization is clearly desirable, a thorough assessment of environmental impacts can lead to proper actions to reduce environmental degradation to an acceptable level.

Planning for Reduction of Natural Hazards

Identification of Hazardous Areas. The natural features of the earth are created by, and constantly altered by, natural processes. Some of these processes are potentially hazardous to man and his works. Man himself is an important hazard-creating agent. In fact, almost every natural hazard is aggravated by man's actions. Disturbance of the ground may increase storm runoff and erosion and decrease slope stability. Subsidence of land is often directly attributable to acts of man. There is even evidence that the injection of waste materials below the earth's surface near Denver, Colo., increased seismic activity in that area (Raleigh and others, 1972). Thus, not only is man acted upon by natural processes, he is also a prime agent in determining the course, speed, and nature of some processes. In this complex relationship, man and his activities must be viewed as part of the natural environment.

Table 2 lists widespread natural processes that are hazardous to man and his works. In areas where these processes occur, the identification of the hazards and evaluation of the potential for risk from natural hazards is an important part of land-use planning. Once an area has been identified as hazardous, appropriate land-use designations can be made. Intensive land uses; high-rise buildings, hospitals, schools, or other institutions with involuntary occupancy; critical public facilities such as dams or highway overpasses; and major utility installations should be prohibited or located and designed so as to withstand the hazard in areas determined to have high risk. Such areas should be considered for open-space uses, such as agriculture or recreation.

Impacts of Hazard-Mitigation Methods. There are four basic ways to reduce the risks associated with natural hazards. First, land use may be regulated to restrict man's use and occupancy of potentially hazardous areas. Flood plains and unstable slopes, for example, can be recommended for open space or very low intensity uses. Second, efforts can be made to control the hazardous processes. For example, channel improvements or holding ponds may be constructed to control floodwaters. And, since man is an agent in aggravating natural occurrences, regulation of how he treats the land can reduce risks. Third, measures can be taken not toward controlling the processes, but toward reducing their impact. Such measures include special foundation requirements and construction techniques for landslide-prone slopes, artificial recharge of ground water to prevent subsidence, or special structural safety standards for seismically active areas. Fourth, monitoring of natural processes may permit the

TABLE 2. NATURAL PROCESSES IMPORTANT TO LAND-USE PLANNING

Process	*Description of Hazard*
Flooding	Overtopping of river and stream banks by water produced by sudden cloudbursts, prolonged rains, tropical storms or seasonal thaws; breakage or overtopping of dams; ponding or backing up of water because of inadequate drainage.
Erosion and sedimentation	Removal of soil and rock materials by surface water and depositing of these materials on flood plains and deltas.
Landsliding	Perceptible downslope movement of earth masses.
Faulting	Relative displacement of adjacent rock masses along a major fracture in the earth's crust.
Ground motion	Shaking of the ground caused by an earthquake.
Subsidence	Sinking of the ground surface caused by compression or collapse of earth materials; common in areas with poorly compacted, organic, or collapsible soils and commonly caused by withdrawal of ground water, oil, or gas; or collapse over underground openings, such as mine workings or natural caverns.
Expansive soils	Soils that swell when they absorb water and shrink when they dry out.
High water table	Upper level of underground water close to ground surface causing submergence of underground structures, such as septic tank systems, foundations, utility lines, and storage tanks.
Seacliff retreat	Recession of seacliffs by erosion and landsliding.
Beach destruction	Loss of beaches owing to erosion and (or) loss of sand supply.
Migration of sand dunes	Wind-induced inland movement of sand accelerated by the disturbance of vegetative cover.
Salt-water intrusion	Subsurface migration of seawater inland into areas from which freshwater has been withdrawn, contaminating freshwater supplies.
Liquefaction	Temporary change of certain soils to a fluid state, commonly from earthquake-induced ground motion causing the ground to flow or lose its strength.

development of warning systems to allow evacuation of hazardous areas when disaster appears imminent. This method is especially effective in reducing loss of life and property damage from flooding.

There is often a fortuitous overlapping of hazardous areas and areas suitable for open-space uses. For example, areas subject to flooding are often ideal for water-related recreational uses, hiking trails, wildlife refuges, parking areas, or outdoor storage. Land-use planners can often achieve dual objectives of hazard mitigation and open-space preservation by recommending nonintensive uses for such areas.

Losses from some natural hazards can be reduced more readily than from others, but in most cases, the dollar savings from efforts to reduce losses are significant.

Man's ability to predict hazardous events varies considerably. For example, earth scientists can predict quite reliably where fault activity will occur but are less able to predict frequency or severity. Flooding, on the other hand, can be more exactly predicted with respect to location, severity, and statistical frequency, but the time of a flood cannot be determined very far in advance.

The selection of approach or combination of approaches appropriate to each situation should be based on a careful weighing of environmental, social, and economic costs and benefits. Costs of controlling natural processes may be very high. All four ways of reducing risks have social, environmental, and economic effects that need to be balanced against the nature of the risk and the degree to which it can in fact be mitigated.

Mitigation Methods and Acceptable Risks. The development of public policy to deal with natural hazards and the appropriate allocation of public resources to mitigate them require an answer to the question "How safe is safe enough?" Each individual may be able to answer this question for himself in any given circumstance, but planners and earth scientists share responsibility for providing a framework on which to base a communitywide response to the question.

Several steps appear to be essential to the public process of judging acceptable levels of risk. First of all, the presence of a hazard must be recognized. Development frequently has proceeded without explicit recognition of the natural forces at play. Towns have been built on flood plains, on unstable hillsides, astride faults, and on subsiding ground. The results are well documented in accounts of many of our nation's worst natural disasters. Second, considerable effort may be required to characterize the hazard. It is important to know its likely severity and the frequency of its occurrence, as well as the physical and cultural characteristics of the area that may be affected. Third, the degree of risk must then be evaluated. This step should take into account what can be done to reduce the hazards and balance these possibilities against public costs and benefits.

The accumulation and interpretation of detailed information as to the nature, severity, and frequency of the risk and as to the alternative responses to the hazard are necessary. Public decision-makers can then balance risk against the economic and environmental costs of mitigating risk to decide the level of risk acceptable to the community.

Integration of ESI in the Planning Process

Land-Capability Studies Basic to Land-Use Planning. In any area the existing natural features and processes present a range of advantages and disadvantages for different uses of land. It is well recognized that the natural characteristics of different parcels of land vary. Different uses of the land also have different physical requirements. For example, farmers seek fertile soils; manufacturers in heavy industry want level sites with good foundation conditions; golf course developers look for rolling terrain with adequate surface and subsurface soil conditions. An important part of land-use planning is matching land uses with the appropriate physical characteristics of the land.

Evaluating the physical features of an area with regard to different types of land use is termed a "land-capability study." The natural features and processes considered usually include topography, hydrology, geology, soils, vegetation, climate, and ecology. Although this report emphasizes the earth-science factors (mainly geology, hydrology, and soils), the concepts and methods discussed are applicable to land-capability studies involving a full range of natural factors.

Land-capability studies are a means of determining the relative physical merits of lands for a specified land use. However, such determination usually provides only a part of the information needed to make land-use decisions. Economic, social, and political considerations are also essential. A parcel of land may have a low physical capability for supporting intensive use, but other factors, such as location and accessibility, land cost, absence of alternative lands, and overriding public need, may well indicate that it should be intensively developed. In this report, a study that considers economic, social, and political factors in addition to land-capability factors is called a "land suitability study."[1] Thus, land-capability studies may be undertaken as part of a broader land-suitability study.

Many different methods are employed in making land-capability studies. A study may be largely descriptive, stating in narrative form information concerning the natural features and processes relevant to a particular land use. Such descriptive analyses are often used when the capability of a given site or alternative sites for a specific use are being considered. A land-capability study may also involve a fairly sophisticated effort to quantify, weight, and aggregate the earth science information relevant to specific uses for all lands within a planning area. Regional land-use planning agen-

---

1. The terms "capability" and "suitability" are often used without precise definition and are sometimes used interchangeably.

cies and those with computers for data processing are most likely to undertake such studies.

An example of a land-capability study integrated within a land-suitability study is contained in the report prepared by the consulting firm Livingston and Blayney (1971) for Palo Alto, Calif. Although the study is properly termed a land-suitability study, it provides a good example of the general methods employed in land-capability studies. Material adapted from the report is used below to illustrate each of the following five basic steps usually involved in a land-capability study:

1. *Identify the types of land use for which land capability is to be determined.*—In the Palo Alto study, land uses range from low-density residential to industrial. In formulating a land-use plan, the capability of the lands within the planning area for the reasonable alternative types of land use would need to be evaluated.

2. *Determine the natural factors having a significant effect on the capability of the land to accommodate each use.*—The choice of factors depends on the physical requirements of the land use under consideration. In the Palo Alto suitability study, 23 factors were selected and categorized[2] as geologic and soils factors (10 factors), ecologic factors (4 factors), visual and recreation factors (4 factors), and planning and market factors (5 factors). Most of the capability factors involving earth-science information were included in the first category, geologic and soils factors. These 10 factors were average slope, San Andreas fault zone, other fault zones, landslides, natural slope stability, cut slope stability, excavation difficulty, soil suitability as fill, soil erosion, and soil expansion.

3. *Develop a scale of values for rating each natural factor in relation to its effect on land capability.*—Two operations are involved in this step. First, the relevant range of conditions of each factor is determined. The expression of this range may be quite precise, as for average slope (table 3), or very general, as in the poor, fair, and good ratings shown for several factors on the table. The degree of precision depends on the degree of refinement needed (or possible, given the level of detail of data available) to make judgments regarding land capability for the selected use.

Second, a scale of values is established to quantify the different conditions within each factor. In the example from the Palo Alto study, the significant differences within each factor were rated on a scale of 1–5 (column 2 of table 3).

4. *Assign a weight to each natural factor indicating its importance relative to the other factors as a determinant of land capability.*—In the Palo Alto example, each factor was given a weight ranging from 1 to a possible 10 (column 3 of table 3). The weight represents a judgment of the relative importance of each factor for "development."

5. *Establish land units, rate each land unit for each factor, calculate the weighted ratings for each factor, and aggregate the weighted ratings for each land unit.*—This step involves the application of the rating system developed in the previous steps to the land under consideration. The study area is divided into land units for evaluation. The size and configuration of the land units depends on the diversity of physical conditions within the study area, the physical requirements for the land use under consideration, and the kind of land-use policy needed. The Palo Alto study area was divided by a grid into 330 cells each of 20 acres. Each cell was evaluated and rated for each factor (that is, was assigned a number from column 2 on table 3). The rating for each factor was multiplied by the weight assigned to the factor column 3 of table 3 to yield the weighted rating as shown in column 4. The weighted ratings for all factors were then added for each cell. The total is a score reflecting the capability of the cell for the selected land use.

In the Palo Alto study, the weighted ratings for the other suitability factors were added to those for capability factors shown on the table to produce the total score for each cell. The range of pos-

2. For purposes of illustration, the factor "average slope" was moved from the "planning and market" category in the original study to the "geologic and soils" category, since slope is a major determinant of land capability.

TABLE 3. RATING SYSTEM FOR LAND-CAPABILITY FACTORS

[Source: Adapted from Livingston and Blayney and others, 1971, p. 59–65]

1 Geologic and soils factors	2 Rating	3 Weight	4 Weighted rating
Average slope:			
Over 50 percent	1		10
31–50 percent	2	10	20
16–30 percent	4		40
0–15 percent	5		50
San Andreas fault zone:			
Within zone	1	7	7
Not within zone	5		35
Landslides:			
Within slide area	1	6	6
Not within slide area	5		30
Natural slope stability:			
Poor	1		5
Fair	3	5	15
Good	5		25
Cut-slope stability:			
Poor	1		4
Fair	3	4	12
Good	5		20
Soil suitability as fill:			
Poor	1		2
Fair	3	2	6
Good	5		10
Soil erosion:			
Severe	1	6	6
Moderate	5		30
Soil expansion:			
High	1		3
Moderate	3	3	9
Low	5		15

sible total scores for each category of factors was planning and market factors, 19–95; ecological factors, 18–90; visual and recreational factors, 11–55; and geologic and soils factors, 48–240. It is clear that the capability factors related to earth science are very important in the determination of land suitability. The total scores for all factors ranged from 96 to 480. These scores were divided into six groups and mapped as shown in figure 6.

Land-capability studies such as the one described above are increasingly important to land-use planning at all governmental levels. They assure that physical characteristics of the land will be given systematic consideration in the development of plans and policies. The earth-science information requirements for such studies vary with the total land area and the specific use to be studied. At the regional level, for example, fairly generalized data may be appropriate for an analysis of land capability for open space. On the other hand, a study undertaken, at any governmental level, to locate a specific site with a high capability for use as a sanitary landfill will require detailed information.

In most cases, the land-capability analysis provides only part of the information needed for land-use decisions, but on occasion capability factors are, or should be, determining. The studies can be useful in eliminating areas with very low capability for a particular use from further consideration and allow the planner to focus attention on more realistic options.

Interdisciplinary Relationships. Integrating man's works and activities with his natural environment is an objective generally shared by planners and earth scientists. To effectively attain this objective requires the contributions of both professions, and since it is unreasonable to expect either planner or earth scientist to become proficient in the other's area of expertise, the establishment of a cooperative working relationship is a prerequisite for a successful program.

There are, however, several obstacles to the establishment of such relationships arising from three factors, the education, working environment, and terminology of each profession. First, planners are generalists by education and are taught to draw information from a wide variety of subjects including architecture, engineering, landscape design, economics, sociology, public administration, and political science. Yet planning curriculums frequently offer little or no exposure to the earth sciences. Earth scientists, although conversant with related scientific fields, typically are not required to draw on the extensive range of subject matter normally dealt with by planners.

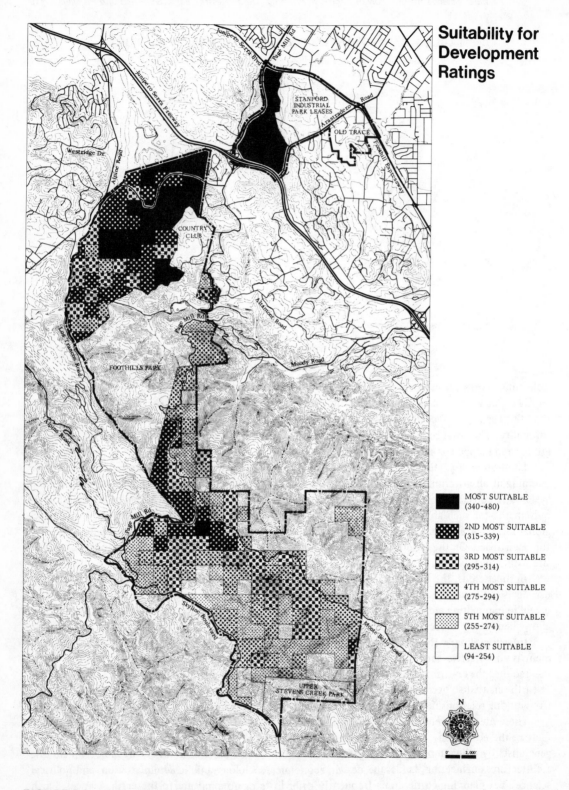

Suitability for Development Ratings

MOST SUITABLE
(340-480)

2ND MOST SUITABLE
(315-339)

3RD MOST SUITABLE
(295-314)

4TH MOST SUITABLE
(275-294)

5TH MOST SUITABLE
(255-274)

LEAST SUITABLE
(94-254)

N

0'   2,000'

FIGURE 6. Land-suitability map of part of Palo Alto, Calif., prepared by Livingston and Blayney and others (1971).

Second, a professional career is normally pursued within an institutional framework that limits opportunities for interdisciplinary effort. In addition, professional advancement in both fields usually requires an ever-increasing degree of specialization. Since specialists may be reluctant to tread on each other's professional territory, interdisciplinary contact is even further inhibited. Perhaps more important is the fact that, until recently, the earth scientist has not regarded the planner as a "customer" for his product. In turn, the planner has not recognized the need for ESI in land-use planning. Until fairly recently, natural resources were considered inexhaustible, the effects of natural hazards were viewed as "acts of God," and governmental bodies tended to place the rights of the private property owner above those of the public at large. Under these circumstances, economic and political considerations easily become the primary determinants of land use. Only with acceptance by public agencies of some responsibility for resource conservation and mitigation of dangers and damages from natural hazards has the planner needed ESI. The need for interdisciplinary efforts is being recognized by both professions.

Another working-environment problem arises from the fact that planning is a public undertaking usually culminating in decisions made by political bodies. The planner's role in the political process requires the ability and willingness to respond to the needs of conflicting interests of different segments of a community. The earth scientist's work is usually evaluated by fellow earth scientists according to scientific standards of truth. He is often uncomfortable when faced with the reality of political compromise and dismayed when a recommendation supported by exacting earth-science analysis is rejected by decisionmakers on political, social, or economic grounds.

The third obstacle to establishing interdisciplinary relationships is that each profession has its own jargon, which, though it may facilitate exchange of ideas within the profession, tends to inhibit communication with outsiders. Earth scientists employ a technical vocabulary that includes many words not in common usage. Even with a glossary, it is difficult for a person who is not an earth scientist to read and understand a report prepared for a professional audience of earth scientists. Planners, on the other hand, lack precision and consistency in their use of terms. They frequently use everyday words in specialized senses or borrow terms from other disciplines, altering their definitions.

Planners and earth scientists will find, however, that many of these problems will diminish rapidly once they are working together. With a little effort on both sides, they will find that their effectiveness in solving common problems and achieving common objectives greatly increases. The planner who joins the earth scientist in the field gains a new perspective not only of the natural characteristics of his planning area but also the application of the earth scientist's work. The earth scientist, similarly, gains insight into the nature and perspectives of planning. The result can be a creative synthesis in which innovative interpretations and applications of ESI are much more likely to occur.

A variety of arrangements permit the earth scientist and planner to work together directly. For the most part, the responsibility for establishing such arrangements rests with the land-use planning agency. With the growing awareness of environmental problems, all land-use planning agencies have some need for earth-science expertise. Some may require a full-time staff person; others may find that part-time or consultant services will suffice. However, for large agencies involved with varied and complex environmental problems, the addition of an earth scientist to the planning staff may prove valuable.

The presence of an earth scientist on the planning staff encourages the consideration of earth science in all phases of the planning process. The staff earth scientist would typically perform the following functions: Help develop and carry out a realistic data-acquisition and interpretation program, including advising on costs and priorities; assist in the determination and evaluation of land capabilities; help formulate plans and policy regarding such topics as geologic hazards and mineral and water resources; undertake detailed studies of particular development issues, such as the impact of urbanization on water pollution or the geologic stability of hillside areas; assist in the formulation and administration of land-use regulations, such as subdivision, zoning, grading, and erosion-sediment control ordinances; make field checks in connection with particular projects and prepare and (or) review soils reports, geologic reports, and environmental impact assessments prior to development approval; assist in presenting technical information directly to decisionmakers to facilitate evaluation of alternatives, prepare slides, models, or other graphic materials for these purposes, and respond directly to questions arising from the presentation; advise when additional earth-science expertise is needed and know where and how to obtain it.

While a few planning agencies interviewed during the course of this study employed a permanent earth scientist on the staff, considerable benefits were derived in those cases where planners established a close working relationship with earth scientists outside the agency. For example, in many areas, earth scientists are in frequent contact with planning agencies and perform a number of the functions discussed above. In many areas, private consultants and university scientists, on a contractual or informal basis, provide similar services.

Public Participation

As a governmental function, planning is inextricably bound to the political process. Land-use decisions have a strong influence on the quality of life. Whether or not a freeway is constructed, a new shopping center approved, or land zoned for open space is of concern to the whole community as well as to the property owners and residents whose land is directly involved. Land-use decisions affect different segments of the community in different ways and are commonly the subject of much controversy, for it is through the political process that conflicting interests and differences of opinion are resolved. Effective resolution requires the informed participation of all segments of the community at all stages in the planning process.

The professional planner may serve solely as a technical advisor to the decisionmakers or may be a more active advocate with respect to planning proposals or particular issues. The planner, however, rarely makes the decisions; this is the function of elected public officials. Even though the planner's information may be complete and accurate and his logic impeccable, there is no guarantee that his advice will be taken.

Both the earth scientist and the planner need to be aware that providing accurate and well-interpreted ESI for use in the planning process is only a first step. To assure that ESI will influence actual decisions requires public understanding of the issues. It is encouraging that in recent years much of the impetus for the use of ESI in planning has come from citizen groups concerned about environmental quality.

Conclusion

It is a human tendency to assume that the land upon which we live, work, and play is one permanent aspect of an otherwise constantly changing world. Yet the land itself undergoes continuous alteration as a result of natural processes and the actions of man. This report points to the importance of reconciling man's use of the land with its natural characteristics. Implementation of land-use plans formulated with full awareness of natural features and processes is the key to achieving such reconciliation.

The state-of-the-art in applying earth-science information to land-use planning and decisionmaking is currently undergoing rapid evolution. In the last few years, agencies producing ESI have dramatically increased efforts to provide data specifically for land-use planning. The new information is just now becoming widely available to planners, and it is too early to evaluate in detail its impact on land-use plans and decisions. Certainly the impact will be great. In most metropolitan areas the need to preserve open space, protect natural resources, and maintain high standards of environmental quality often conflicts with the need to expand employment opportunities, the housing stock, and the tax base. Land-use planners are faced with resolving basic land-use conflicts with what is now recognized as a finite supply of land. The decisions are becoming increasingly important and subject to controversy. In this context, the planner will seek out and use all relevant information, including ESI.

Studies of land capability are becoming much more common and serve to formalize the consideration of natural factors in land-use planning. ESI is increasingly translated into quantitative terms allowing aggregation of data relevant to a particular site or area. Quantification and weighting of physical factors is becoming an important feature of capability studies, especially in agencies with computer data-processing capacity.

Although the guidelines presented here are very general, they provide a framework for the effective utilization of ESI in land-use planning. However, no single set of guidelines can possibly include the wide range of conditions and problems encompassed by the fields of planning and the earth sciences. The essential point, however, is the need to foster an institutional, legal, and political climate favorable to full and effective interplay between planners and earth scientists on the one hand and professionals and public decisionmakers on the other. Ultimately, it is the public, through its representatives, who must assume the responsibility for considering long-term as well as short-term social, economic, and political impacts from the land-use decisions made today.

REFERENCES CITED

Barnwell, W. W., George, R. S., Dearborn, L. L., and others, 1972, Water for Anchorage: Anchorage, Alaska, U.S. Geological Survey, in cooperation with the City of Anchorage, 77 pp.

Brabb, E. E., Pampeyan, E. H., and Bonilla, M. G., 1972, Landslide susceptibility in San Mateo County, California: U.S. Geol. Survey Misc. Field Studies Map MF-350, scale 1:62,500.

Citizen's Advisory Committee on Environmental Quality, Task Force on Land Use and Urban Growth, 1973, The use of lands—a citizen's policy guide to urban growth: New York, Thomas Y. Crowell, 304 pp.

Dibblee, T. W., 1966, Geologic map and sections of the Palo Alto 15-minute quadrangle, California: Calif. Div. Mines and Geology, map sheet 8, scale 1:62,500.

Jennings, C. W., and Burnett, J. L., 1961, Geologic map of California, Olaf P. Jenkins edition, San Francisco sheet: Calif. Div. Mines and Geology, scale 1:250,000.

Legget, R. F., 1973, Cities and geology: New York, McGraw-Hill, 552 pp.

Livingston and Blayney and others, 1971, Environmental design study—open space vs. development, final report to the City of Palo Alto: Palo Alto, Calif., 190 pp.

Pampeyan, E. H., 1970, Geologic map of the Palo Alto 7½-minute quadrangle, San Mateo and Santa Clara Counties, Calif.: U.S. Geol. Survey open-file map, scale 1:24,000.

Planning Policy Committee of Santa Clara County, 1972, A policy plan for the baylands of Santa Clara Co.: County of Santa Clara Planning Dept., San Jose, Calif., 76 pp.

Raleigh, C. B., Healy, J. H., and Bredehoeft, J. D., 1972, Faulting and crustal stress at Rangely, Colo.: Geophys. Mon. Ser., v. 16, pp 275–84.

Rogers, T. H., and Armstrong, C. F., 1973, Relative geologic stability map, Montebello Ridge study area: Calif. Div. Mines and Geology.

Spangle, William, and Associates, Leighton, F. B., and Associates, and Baxter, McDonald and Company, 1973, Application of earth-science information in land-use planning—preliminary technical report: U.S. Dept. Housing and Urban Development and U.S. Dept. Interior, 330 pp.; available from the Natl. Tech. Inf. Service, U.S. Dept. Commerce, Springfield, Va., NTIS PB–238–801/AS.

State of California, 1973, Urban geology master plan for California: Calif. Div. Mines and Geology Bull. 198, 112 pp.

——, 1974, Special Studies Zones delineated in compliance with Ch. 7.5, Div. 2, Calif. Pub. Resources Code, Woodside quadrangle, official map: scale 1:24,000.

Woodward-Clyde and Associates, and McClure and Messinger, 1970, Geology and structural engineering: Prepared for the Baylands Subcommittee of the Planning Policy Committee of Santa Clara County, Part 1, 48 pp.; Part II, 74 pp.

31

Urban Geology Master Plan
for California—A Summary

John T. Alfors, John L. Burnett, and Thomas E. Gay, Jr.

Introduction

Purpose and History of the Project

The Urban Geology Master Plan project was conceived by the Department of Conservation in 1969 as a vehicle for state and local government to respond to the needs of California for safe and orderly growth relative to geologic hazards and conservation of mineral resources. The project was conducted by the Division of Mines and Geology of the Department of Conservation with the assistance of private consultants and in cooperation with the Office of Planning and Research of the Governor's Office. It was carried out in three phases over the three-year period from July 1, 1970, to June 30, 1973. Partial funding for the project was provided through comprehensive planning grants from the Department of Housing and Urban Development under provisions of Section 701 of the Housing Act of 1968, as amended.

The project was designed to include the regional identification of present and potential urban development-geologic environment conflicts; a critique of government and private sector responsibilities; recommendations; program priorities; and legislative and organizational needs. The final project report is to serve as a basis for policy making by state and local government, and by the private sector. In effect, the report is to be used as a guide for dealing with geologic hazards and the conservation of mineral resources in areas of urban development. The prime goal was to define and elucidate the measures necessary to avoid or minimize life loss and property damage in urban areas due to dynamic geologic processes and to reduce the loss of mineral resources to urbanization. Loss-reduction measures having the most significant benefit: cost ratios were determined.

Statewide Loss Projections

In order to estimate the magnitude of the total loss due to geologic hazards in California, the estimated dollar and life losses for each of the 10 geologic problems are projected for the 30-year period 1970–2000, and totaled. Total projected figures also are presented for possible amount of loss reduction, possible cost of loss-reduction measures, and benefit: cost ratios of those measures.

Extracted with permission of the authors from *Urban Geology Master Plan for California,* Bulletin 198, 1973, pp. 3–16. California Division of Mines and Geology, Sacramento.

The 10 geologic problems are estimated to cause projected losses totaling on the order of $55 billion to the urban and urbanizing areas of California by the year 2000 if current land-use planning, development siting, building design, and construction practices are continued unchanged.

General Summary

With the vigorous and widespread application of loss-reduction measures, most of which are economically attractive, the majority of the geologic losses projected below can be avoided or prevented. Otherwise, given a continuation of present practices, it is estimated that property damage and dollar equivalent of life loss directly attributable to geologic processes and conditions and the loss of mineral resources due to urbanization will amount to more than $55 billion in California between 1970 and the year 2000 (table 1, column 2). This loss compares closely with the estimated total loss of $50 billion[1] due to urban and wildland fires in the state during the same period. The relative losses attributable to the 10 geologic problems considered in this report, in order of decreasing percentage of the total $55 billion projected loss, are:

Geologic Problems	Percent of Total Loss
Earthquake shaking	38
Loss of mineral resources	30
Landsliding	18
Flooding	12
Erosion activity	1
Expansive soils	0.3
Fault displacement	0.15
Volcanic hazards	0.1
Tsunami hazards	0.1
Subsidence	0.05

The relative percentage losses are shown graphically in figure 1 and the dollar values are given in table 1, column 2.

The recommendations for reducing losses from geologic problems fall into two major categories: (1) those that propose to improve the state of the art by developing new capabilities, and (2) those that propose to extend the application of present state-of-the-art procedures. In general, a sequence of steps is required for any effective action program to reduce losses due to geologic problems. First, the nature, extent, and severity of the problem must be recognized. Second, solutions for the problem need to be devised where possible. Third, contingency plans and preparations need to be made for responding to those problems that cannot be solved adequately. Fourth, long-range recovery actions should be planned for the catastrophic problems. Often the key to whether loss-reduction measures are adequately implemented is the degree of enforcement provided by local government. Some of the problems, such as expansive soils, tsunami hazards, landsliding, and loss of mineral resources, can be solved to a large extent by the application of current state-of-the-art procedures. All that is needed is the requirement that appropriate known loss-reduction measures be applied and that the requirement be effectively enforced. Effective mitigation of the other problems requires various degrees of improvement in the state of the art.

If current practices were upgraded to the current state of the art and all presently feasible loss-reduction measures were applied throughout California, an estimated $38 billion reduction in projected losses could be realized. The total cost of applying the loss-reduction measures is estimated to be $6 billion, and the overall benefit: cost ratio 6.2:1. The estimated benefits, costs, and benefit: cost ratios for each of the 10 geological problems are given in table 1; figure 2 presents similar data graphically.

---

1. The fire loss figure has been extrapolated based on a value of $16 billion per year national loss from major structural fires and $7.5 million per year average fire loss to state responsibility wildlands in California.

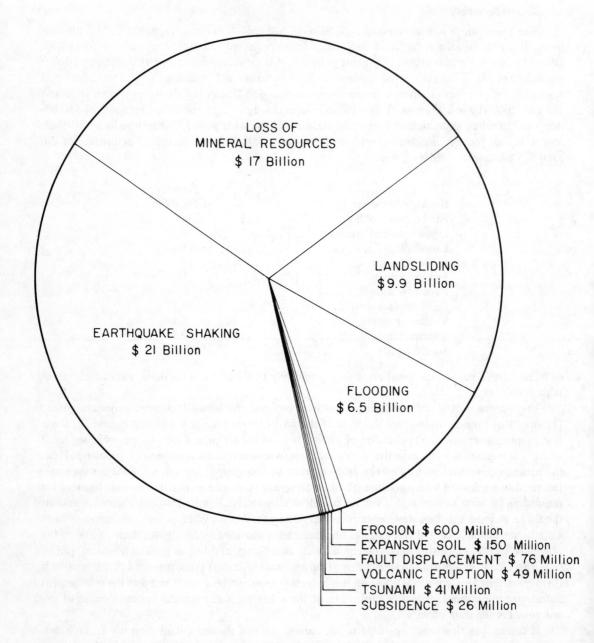

GEOLOGIC HAZARDS IN CALIFORNIA
TO THE YEAR 2000:
A $55 BILLION PROBLEM

LOSS OF
MINERAL RESOURCES
$ 17 Billion

LANDSLIDING
$9.9 Billion

EARTHQUAKE SHAKING
$ 21 Billion

FLOODING
$ 6.5 Billion

 EROSION $ 600 Million
EXPANSIVE SOIL $ 150 Million
FAULT DISPLACEMENT $ 76 Million
VOLCANIC ERUPTION $ 49 Million
TSUNAMI $ 41 Million
SUBSIDENCE $ 26 Million

FIGURE 1. Geologic hazards in California to the year 2000: a $55 billion problem. Estimated magnitude of losses due to 10 geologic problems in California projected from 1970 to the year 2000, if current loss-reduction practices continue unchanged.

TABLE 1. PROJECTED LOSSES DUE TO GEOLOGIC PROBLEMS IN CALIFORNIA, 1970–2000 (ESTIMATED)

(Column 1)	(Column 2)	(Column 3)		(Column 4)		(Column 5)
Geologic problem	Projected total losses, 1970–2000, without improvement of existing policies and practices	Possible total loss reduction 1970–2000, applying all feasible measures		Estimated total cost of applying all feasible measures, at current state of the art, 1970–2000		Benefit:Cost ratio if all feasible measures were applied and all possible loss reductions were achieved, 1970–2000
		Percent of total loss	Dollar amount	Percent of total loss	Dollar amount	
Earthquake shaking	$21,035,000,000	50*	$10,517,500,000	10	$2,103,500,000	5
Loss of mineral resources	17,000,000,000	90	15,000,000,000	0.53	90,000,000	167
Landsliding	9,850,000,000	90	8,865,000,000	10.3	1,018,000,000	8.7
Flooding	6,532,000,000	52.5	3,432,000,000	41.4	2,703,000,000	1.3
Erosion activity	565,000,000	66	377,000,000	45.7	250,000,000	1.5
Expansive soils	150,000,000	99	148,500,000	5	7,500,000	20
Fault displacement	76,000,000	17	12,600,000	10	7,500,000	1.7
Volcanic hazards	49,380,000	16.5	8,135,000	3.5	1,655,000	4.9
Tsunami hazards	40,800,000	95	37,760,000	63	25,700,000	1.5
Subsidence	26,400,000	50	13,200,000	65.1	8,790,000	1.5
TOTALS	$55,324,580,000	69	$38,411,695,000	11.2	$6,215,645,000	6.2

*90 percent reduction of life loss.

Column 2: Estimated total dollar loss, 1970 to 2000 for all of California; about 95 percent of the loss would be in urban areas. These values are based on the assumptions that the number and severity of each type of event occurs as estimated, and that no change is made in the 1970 type, effectiveness, or level of application of preventive and remedial measures.

Column 3: Estimated total loss-reduction in dollars and in percent of projected loss, for all of California, assuming an aggressive but reasonable degree of improvement in the 1970 type and level of preventive and remedial measures. Conservative improvements in the state of the art, application over wider area, and more effective application and follow-up of all known types of loss-reduc-

tion measures over the next 30 years are assumed.

Column 4: Estimated total cost of applying loss-reduction measures of the type, effectiveness, and extent visualized in column 3, for all of California, for the period 1970–2000 in dollars and in percent of projected total loss (column 4 : column 2).

Column 5: Estimated benefit : cost ratio (column 3 : column 4) based on the estimated cost (column 4) of applying the estimated loss-reduction measures to obtain the estimated reductions (column 3) of the estimated total losses (column 2).

Data in table 1 were collected from the analyses of losses and loss-reduction costs for individual problems in Section 7, Appendix A, "Costs of Losses and Loss-Reduction Measures". All figures are 1970 dollars.

In order to effect greater loss reduction, remedies other than those currently known and being applied would have to be devised and used. For example, breakthroughs in earthquake prediction and earthquake control could result in large reductions of projected losses due to earthquake shaking. Increased research by universities, governmental agencies, and private-firms, therefore, is indicated. The benefit: cost ratios for loss reduction by new or additional types of research are difficult to predict, but the potential for loss reductions is enormous, and the possibilities, therefore, for large benefit: cost ratios are equally great.

Losses can be reduced even further by vigorous enforcement of improved building codes that result in greater earthquake-resistant design of structures. The application of improved building codes, if begun in the design stage, generally adds only a few percent (typically 1 to 2 percent) to the total cost of the structures. Benefit: cost ratios relative to the enforcement of improved building codes are difficult to assess because of the many variables involved. However, the benefit: cost ratios that apply to the reduction of structural damage are likely to be relatively low because, although the increased costs would apply to every new structure, relatively few buildings would be subject to extensive damage during their useful life.

For existing hazardous structures, the cost of remedial work generally will amount to a relatively large percentage of the total value of a structure, and the benefit: cost ratio, therefore, may be relatively small when considering property damage alone. However, the improvement work would result

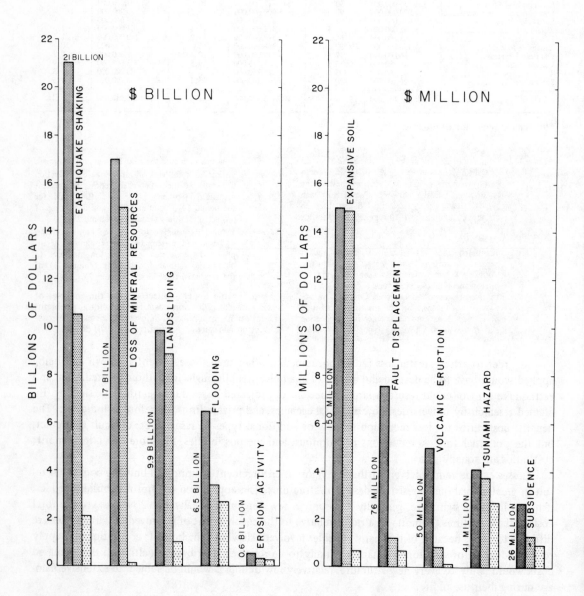

FIGURE 2. Estimated total losses due to each of 10 geologic problems in California for the period 1970–2000, under current practices; amount of loss-reduction possible, if state-of-the-art practices were used; and cost of applying state-of-the-art loss-reduction practices.

in substantial reduction to the threat of life loss and the social value alone should warrant carrying out such measures. The demolition of some hazardous buildings may be justified economically as well as socially, depending on the value placed on human life. Similarly, the strengthening or removal of hazardous parapets and appendages is almost always justifiable. An additional incentive is to reduce the possibility of lawsuits leveled against local governments in the event of subsequent damage. The courts are beginning to consider the liability of those responsible for the planning, design, construction, and permit approval where disasters have occurred rather than treating such catastrophes as "acts of God" (Hughes, 1971, p. 72).

Land-use zoning can be a particularly effective loss-reduction measure, yet is not fully used at present, partly because of concern for possible inverse condemnation lawsuits. Nonetheless, if any doubt exists as to the safety of a proposed development, construction permits should not be issued or issued only after such doubts have been investigated and removed. Public safety should be the primary concern.

The addition of geologists to the staffs of planning, engineering, building and safety, and/or public works departments of counties and the larger cities for plan review and on-site inspection of geologic conditions is recommended as an effective loss-reduction measure.

As demonstrated by many jurisdictions in California, the single most effective action that can be taken to reduce losses due to geologic problems is for cities and counties to adopt and diligently enforce modern grading ordinances and building codes.

Foreseeable advances in the state of the art of loss-reduction measures potentially could result in near-zero life loss due to geologic hazards. Property damage could ultimately be reduced by as much as 90 percent.

The magnitude of the geologic hazards problem in California and the degree to which it is being resolved should be subject to periodic review. It is recommended that an annual status report be prepared by an appropriate state agency, or agencies. The Governor's Earthquake Council, the Legislature's Joint Committee on Seismic Safety, or successor groups would be appropriate bodies to evaluate such reviews.

Although not strictly a loss-reduction measure, insurance programs can provide an element of protection to property owners. Consideration should be given to the establishment of a broad-coverage, natural-disaster insurance program to include geologic hazards. Such a program could parallel that already initiated by the Federal Department of Housing and Urban Development with respect to flood and mudslide insurance.

Earthquake Shaking

A. Findings. Given a continuation of present conditions, it is estimated that losses due to earthquake shaking will total $21 billion in California between 1970 and the year 2000. Most of the damage and loss of life will occur in zones of known high seismic activity; structures that do not comply with the provisions of the Field and Riley Acts, passed in 1933, will be especially vulnerable.

Losses from earthquake shaking will be greater than those from any other geologic problem. As many as 10,360 deaths and 40,360 hospitalized injuries have been projected to result from an 8.3 magnitude earthquake on the San Andreas fault near San Francisco (Algermissen *et al.*, 1972, p. 121). An estimated 30,000 probable deaths would result from earthquake-induced dam failures in the San Francisco Bay Area (Algermissen *et al.*, p. 132). A hypothetical, but expectable, large earthquake in the Los Angeles area has been projected to result in 10,000 deaths (Duke, 1971). If present-day techniques for reducing losses from earthquake shaking were applied to the fullest degree, life loss could be reduced by at least 90 percent, and the total dollar value of losses could be reduced by as much as 50 percent. Total costs for performing the loss-reduction work would be about 10 percent of the total projected loss, which with 50 percent effectiveness provides a benefit: cost ratio of 5:1.

The greatest threat to life and property is posed by those structures that do not conform to the current Uniform Building Code relative to earthquake loading. Applying loss-reduction measures to these structures is a major challenge because of the political, social, and economic problems involved. Great benefit would be achieved in preventing life loss, but the benefit: cost ratio to prevent property damage would be relatively low. Partial reduction of the structural hazards such as strengthening or removing parapets and cornices and reducing occupancy exposure by a lesser intensity of use will have higher benefit: cost ratios.

A generally higher benefit: cost ratio can be achieved by applying loss-reduction efforts to areas undergoing rapid urbanization rather than to areas already developed. The urbanizing areas are largely on the margins of the Los Angeles metropolitan area and to lesser extents the southern San Francisco Bay Area near San Jose and the vicinity of San Diego.

An effective earthquake prediction or warning system could save numerous lives both in existing urban areas and in rapidly urbanizing areas. With current and projected levels of funding, it is possible that an effective prediction system may be devised in 5 to 10 years. An effective earthquake control mechanism would result in tremendous reduction in property damage as well as life loss, but such a system does not appear feasible in the foreseeable future.

B. Conclusions. Losses, especially life loss, due to shaking from future earthquakes can and should be reduced through a combination of measures involving geologic and seismologic research, engineering practice, building codes, urban planning and zoning, fiscal and taxation policy, and preparedness planning. Close coordination is needed between local, state, and federal agencies, universities, and the private sector, to accomplish the goal without duplication of effort.

Priority efforts, such as strengthening, demolishing, or reducing to a lesser use, need to be applied to reducing life loss due to collapse of hazardous old buildings.

Priority for geologic and seismologic efforts should be given to areas which are undergoing redevelopment or rapid urbanization or which are anticipated to become urbanized between the present and the year 2000.

Enactment of controls and parapet ordinances must be implemented by providing funds and personnel for vigorous enforcement. Although the Uniform Building Code is designed to be a model for minimum acceptable standards, some designers and builders use it as a maximum. The Uniform Building Code, 1970 edition, should be upgraded relative to earthquake shaking forces.

C. Recommendations. Recommendations for earthquake loss-reduction measures are presented in detail in the *First Report of the Governor's Earthquake Council,* November 1972, available through the California Division of Mines and Geology at cost; further recommendations will develop as a result of continuing work by the Council pursuant to the implementation sections of those recommendations.

In addition, the forthcoming final report of the Joint Committee on Seismic Safety of the California Legislature will also contain recommendations, both complementary and supplementary to those of the Governor's Earthquake Council.

Loss of Mineral Resources

A. Findings. Loss of mineral resources due to urbanization between 1970 and the year 2000 is estimated to total $17 billion if current practices are continued. The mineral resources under greatest urbanization pressure are the construction materials, especially sand and gravel and crushed stone. The estimated losses are based largely on the added cost to the public due to increased transportation costs, the cost of relocating mining operations farther from markets, and the use of lower grade deposits that require more processing. Some mineral deposits being threatened by urbanization are unique and cannot be replaced. The environmental costs of mining deposits farther from markets, such as more vehicles required, more fuel used, and resultant increased air pollution, and increased road maintenance, are not included in the cost figures herein.

The per capita demand for construction materials has increased in the past and is expected to continue to increase in the future. Therefore, even more construction materials than are currently used per year will be required in the future despite lowered population growth expectations.

B. Conclusions. Mining operations required to supply urban needs should be located as close to markets as suitable deposits permit, and appropriate land use designations should be provided. Unique mineral deposits, especially, should be protected from urbanization.

C. Recommendations. The California Division of Mines and Geology, the U.S. Geological Survey, and the U.S. Bureau of Mines should intensify their efforts to catalog those mineral resources of critical importance to the future economy of California that are within and adjacent to urban areas.

Mineral deposits of economic size and quality constitute only a small fraction of one percent of the earth's crust, making them one of the rarest (and most valuable) environments of all. Therefore, local governments should protect the critical mineral resources, access thereto, and the mining thereof within their jurisdictions by special zoning, with buffer zones around them as necessary. In turn, mine operators should be required to conduct operations as compatibly as practicable with their surroundings and should be expected to rehabilitate depleted mined-lands for subsequent beneficial use such as parks, open space, or urban development.

Demand projections should be made for the critical mineral commodities used in California. Local governments should be aware of their future mineral resource requirements to plan better for the use of the deposits available to them.

Landsliding

A. Findings. Under present conditions, it is estimated that losses due to landsliding will total almost $10 billion in California between 1970 and the year 2000. Loss of life is not expected to be great. Most of the damage will occur in the hillside areas of western California that are underlain by Cenozoic and Mesozoic sedimentary rocks. The severity of the problem depends upon the local bedrock and soil conditions, including moisture content, vegetation, slope, and other factors.

Although landslides and landslide-prone areas can be identified with about 90 percent accuracy by geologic studies, only a small portion of the area subject to landslide damage has been mapped in sufficient detail for local government land-use planning. Many local governments thus are not fully aware of the potential landslide hazards within their jurisdictions.

Grading ordinances have been adopted by most local governments; many are based on Chapter 70 of the Uniform Building Code, 1970 edition. Although the grading ordinances may be adequate, often they are not adequately implemented for lack of trained personnel and thus are less effective than they should be. The benefit: cost ratio for an effectively enforced grading ordinance is estimated to be about 9:1.

B. Conclusions. Losses due to landsliding can be reduced by 90 percent or more by a combination of measures involving geologic investigations, engineering practice, and effective enforcement of grading ordinances. The Los Angeles City grading ordinance and enforcement procedures have resulted in effective control of almost 99 percent of the potential landslides in their jurisdiction. A less elaborate system could reduce 90 percent of the losses in California at a relatively low cost.

C. Recommendations. Geologic mapping, at scales ranging from 1:12,000 to 1:48,000, should be carried out in all areas subject to urban development, on a priority basis, to identify landslides and landslide-prone areas. Cities and counties should be responsible to see that this is done within their jurisdictions prior to approval of general development patterns. The geologic mapping can be done by private consultants, by local government staff, or in cooperation with the California Division of Mines and Geology.

Detailed engineering geology site studies should be required for proposed developments within landslide and landslide-prone areas, prior to designing each development. These studies should be carried out by private consultants hired by the developers.

Proposed developments within landslide and landslide-prone areas should be engineered to avoid or correct all slope stability problems found by the detailed engineering geology studies.

Geologic and engineering reports should be reviewed for adequacy by qualified professionals, and qualified local government grading inspectors should inspect various stages of the development to insure that all work necessary to prevent future landslide problems is being done.

Local government should enforce adequate grading ordinances (Chapter 70, Uniform Building Code) by on-site inspection of developments in landslide and landslide-prone areas by qualifying grading inspectors. Certification should be required by design civil engineers, soils engineers, and engineering geologists.

Flooding

A. Findings. It is estimated that losses due to flooding will total more than $6.5 billion between 1970 and the year 2000 if the present level of flood-control measures is maintained. More than half of the estimated losses could be prevented by the prompt application of all economically feasible control measures. The cost of the control measures would be slightly less than the estimated cost of the flood damage. Flood control measures can be taken to include:

1. construction and adequate maintenance of engineering works, such as dams, levees, unobstructed by-pass and overflow systems, and flood control basins,
2. implementation of flood warning systems,
3. preparation of adequate evacuation plans for all areas subject to flooding by 100-year floods or by dam failure, and
4. adoption of flood–plain zoning ordinances and regulations to control the type of structures permitted in high-risk areas, and requiring that structures permitted in high-risk areas are built in such a way as to minimize flood losses.

B. Conclusions. Most of the flood damage to urban areas takes place because flood plains provide much of the habitable area of the state. Development in these areas is often not regulated adequately to cope with runoff from infrequent intense storms in California. Natural drainage channels are filled, narrowed, or allowed to become obstructed to the extent that they no longer accommodate even minor floods. The past federal and state policy of providing disaster relief to cover flood damage without any limitations on rebuilding has not discouraged the practice of building on flood-prone areas. The recent National Flood Insurance Program of the Federal Department of Housing and Urban Development is a step in the right direction, in that flood insurance payments will be made only once, and structures are not to be rebuilt in recognized flood-prone areas.

C. Recommendations. Flood control projects such as those constructed by the Army Corps of Engineers in cooperation with local flood control districts should be encouraged where substantial benefit accrues to the public. Costs of the projects should be borne in proportion to benefits to the beneficiaries.

All cities and counties in California should regulate construction in flood-prone areas through the adoption and diligent enforcement of realistic flood-plain zoning ordinances and building codes. Cities and counties should take the measures necessary to qualify for the National Flood Insurance Program of the Federal Department of Housing and Urban Development.

The Department of Water Resources and the National Weather Service should evaluate the need to expand the flood warning service in California in areas which are not adequately covered.

The California Department of Water Resources should coordinate studies by federal and state agencies in detailed delineation of flood-prone areas in California and development of flood-plain information for local agencies.

Erosion Activity

A. Findings. It is estimated that losses due to erosion activity will total $565 million between 1970 and the year 2000 if current practices are continued unchanged. The losses due to erosion activity are difficult to separate from those due to flooding and landsliding. Within urban areas, the major costs of erosion activity are in removing sediment from public and private drainage systems.

Coastal erosion is a special problem involving wave action and is most severe during storms. Engineering works such as those constructed by the Army Corps of Engineers can reduce coastal erosion problems locally, but too often, as in the past, the problems may just be transferred to another site. Coastal erosion studies can provide a basis for avoiding development in areas subject to this problem.

B. Conclusions. About two-thirds of the projected losses due to erosion, siltation, and sedimentation in urban areas could be reduced by proper engineering design and construction practices. State codes and local regulations, such as grading ordinances, generally are adequate, but the main deficiency is lack of uniformly effective implementation. Losses due to coastal erosion can be reduced most economically by simply avoiding construction in areas subject to severe erosion.

C. Recommendations. All cities and counties should fully implement existing codes, ordinances, and regulations relative to grading (Chapter 70, Uniform Building Code), landscaping, and drainage by on-site inspection conducted by qualified engineers and geologists. This will reduce damage to property and protect cities and counties from lawsuits by citizens whose property otherwise might have been damaged.

Cities and counties in coastal areas should inventory areas subject to coastal erosion, determine erosion rates for each such area, and govern land use therein accordingly. These studies could be carried out in cooperation with the Army Corps of Engineers.

All construction projects designed to control coastal erosion should be carefully evaluated so that the correction of a problem in one area will not cause a problem in another. Similarly, prior to the construction of flood control facilities, the effect they have on coastal erosion by trapping sand and gravel that would otherwise be transported to beaches should be determined.

Expansive Soils

A. Findings. It is estimated that losses in California due to expansive (shrink-swell) soils will total $150 million between 1970 and the year 2000 if present practices are continued. Expansive soils occur locally throughout California wherever relatively large percentages of clay minerals are present in the soil. The general distribution of expansive soils is well known in about one-third of the state through recent soil mapping by the Soil Conservation Service. Losses due to expansive soils can be eliminated completely if the condition is recognized before construction and foundations are properly engineered. Adequate controls exist for preventing damage due to expansive soils, both in state codes and local government regulations. Costs for corrective action before construction are small, but remedial action after construction may amount to 10 percent or more of the value of the structure.

B. Conclusions. The principal reason that newly built structures sustain damage attributable to expansive soils is that not all local governments apply existing codes and regulations effectively.

C. Recommendations. All cities and counties should insure effective enforcement of existing codes and regulations through inspection of site soil conditions and foundation designs by qualified soils and foundation engineers. This will reduce property damage and protect cities and counties from lawsuits by citizens whose property otherwise might have been damaged. Losses can be greatly reduced by full implementation of Chapter 70, Uniform Building Code, or more stringent grading ordinances.

Fault Displacement

A. Findings. Losses from fault displacement are expected to be low compared to losses from earthquake shaking. It is estimated that between 1970 and the year 2000, under present conditions, fault displacement losses will reach a total of $76 million.

These losses will occur primarily along well-recognized faults in urban areas and at the margins of urban centers. However, past experience indicates that some active faults have not or cannot be recognized at the surface. Losses will result not only from displacement accompanying earthquakes, but also from fault creep, which displaces the ground along faults without violent earthquake shaking.

Very little can be done to provide protection for structures presently in place across active faults, short of moving the structures. Reduction of future losses can be accomplished best by careful selection of sites for construction. Careful investigation and selection of sites will result in re-siting, prior to construction, of an estimated 85 percent of the structures that otherwise would be built across active faults. When the cost of site evaluation is compared to the value of future structures saved by re-siting, a benefit to cost ratio of about 9.7:1 results.

B. Conclusions. The benefits from safeguarding future construction against fault displacement justify requiring detailed site investigations in and near seismically active zones. Zoning and inspection can assist in providing protection to the public against future losses by prohibiting the building of structures across active faults. Where structures, such as pipelines, aqueducts, and highways, must be built across active faults, they should be designed to accommodate the anticipated fault displacements and creep.

Insurance programs can provide an element of protection for owners of existing structures unknowingly built across active faults.

C. Recommendations. The identification and delineation of known and potentially active faults as called for under the Alquist-Priolo Geologic Hazard Zones Act (Chapter 7.5, Division 2 of the California Public Resources Code), should continue to be carried out rapidly by the California Division of Mines and Geology.

Geologic site investigations should be required prior to consideration of approval for development in all seismically active areas, and construction setback requirements should be required by local governments along all identified active and potentially active faults.

Cities and counties should inventory existing structures across active faults. These structures should be removed or downgraded in level of use or occupancy, in accordance with some reasonable timetable.

Consideration should be given to legislation that will require lending institutions to require fault displacement insurance on residential properties as a condition to the granting of a loan on such properties. The fault displacement insurance could be included within a broad-coverage natural disaster insurance program. Insurance organizations should assure themselves that proposed structures are relatively free from potential fault displacement damage before insuring properties against such damages.

Volcanic Hazards

A. Findings. Under present conditions, it is estimated that losses due to future volcanic eruptions could amount to $50 million between 1970 and the year 2000. Loss of life is not expected to be a large factor. Damage is most likely to occur in the vicinity of Mt. Shasta and Mt. Lassen and less likely at other Quaternary volcanic centers in California. General areas of potential hazard are known to geologists, but local government officials in the areas of concern may not be fully aware of the potential hazards.

Nothing can now be done to prevent and little to control volcanic eruptions. The most effective loss-reduction measure is to avoid vulnerable areas such as the natural drainage courses down slope from recently active volcanic areas. Major volcanic eruptions are generally preceded by smaller events that can be detected instrumentally and can serve as warnings of coming eruptions.

B. Conclusions. The major urban areas of California are relatively safe from the threat of volcanic eruptions. Warning systems can greatly reduce the threat of life loss from volcanic eruptions and land-use zoning can, to a limited extent, be used to prevent potential property damage.

C. Recommendations. The known recent volcanic centers in California should be instrumented or otherwise monitored to assure adequate warning prior to a volcanic eruption. This program should be conducted by the federal government, either through the U.S. Geological Survey or the National Oceanic and Atmospheric Administration; major potential volcanic threats are on federal lands.

Cities and counties in the areas of recent volcanism should evaluate the potential for damage to their jurisdictions and zone or regulate the development in these areas in accordance with the relative risks involved. There jurisdictions should also consider the development of evacuation and other contingency plans.

Some of the younger volcanic cones and the nearby surrounding areas could be obtained for county or state parkland. This would serve the geologic feature and provide protection to the public.

Tsunami Hazards

A. Findings. It is estimated that losses due to tsunami damage will amount to about $40 million between 1970 and the year 2000. Most of the losses will occur in the coastal areas below the 20-foot elevation above mean low water level. The greatest damage can be expected in Crescent City, Del Norte County, but other sections of the California coast and offshore islands such as Santa Catalina are also subject to damage. Tsunamis cannot be prevented, but an effective warning system may give many hours of warning. If the warnings are heeded and proper action taken, life loss can be eliminated and property damage reduced. The National Oceanic and Atmospheric Administration currently administers a reasonably effective seismic sea-wave warning system.

B. Conclusions. An estimated 95 percent of all projected losses due to tsunamis can be prevented by a combination of coastal land-use zoning and an effective tsunami warning system.

C. Recommendations. The National Oceanic and Atmospheric Administration should be requested to prepare information on the expected tsunami runup along the California coast for 20-, 50-, and 100-year recurrence levels.

Local governments should establish use zones along the coastline that:

1. no permanently inhabited structures other than those absolutely required be permitted within the 20-year recurrence runup zone,
2. low intensity uses only be permitted within the 50-year recurrence runup zone,
3. schools, hospitals, other critical facilities, and public buildings be located above the 100-year recurrence runup zone.

Subsidence

A. Findings. It is estimated that losses due to subsidence will total over $26 million between 1970 and the year 2000 if current practices are continued. Most of the losses will be due to ground-water withdrawal and hydrocompaction. Subsidence due to oil and gas withdrawal can be and has been effectively controlled by water injection where monitoring and regulation are in effect. Areas subject to subsidence by ground-water withdrawal are well known and subsidence can be avoided by restricting ground-water withdrawal to the amount of recharge. Hydrocompaction occurs mainly in the more arid parts of California when man first applies large amounts of water. Control of hydrocompaction is expensive, but losses can be reduced if the condition is recognized and corrective action taken.

B. Conclusions. Subsidence due to oil and gas withdrawal is being controlled satisfactorily as regulated by the State Division of Oil and Gas. Subsidence due to ground-water withdrawal is being moderated by state and federal water projects by providing surface water supplies to areas which are experiencing lowering ground-water tables. Subsidence due to hydrocompaction has been studied by the State Department of Water Resources and the U.S. Geological Survey, but not all the areas subject to hydrocompaction have been identified.

C. Recommendations. The State Division of Oil and Gas should continue their subsidence monitoring and regulating program with respect to oil and gas withdrawals and repressuring and extend this program as needed to prevent damage to urban development. The program should be coordinated with local county or city engineers to assure that no adverse effects are occurring.

Ground-water withdrawal should be regulated where necessary to reduce subsidence, particularly in urban areas.

Cities and counties should make evaluations of the potential areas of damaging subsidence due to hydrocompaction within their jurisdictions and require corrrective or preventive measures before approving permits for development of these lands. Geologic studies can determine if the potential for hydrocompaction exists. Detailed analyses of suspect areas should be made by a soils engineer.

REFERENCES CITED

Algermissen, S. T., Rinehart, W. A., and Dewey, James (1972) A study of earthquake losses in the San Francisco Bay area: Data and analysis. U.S. Dept. of Commerce, National Oceanic and Atmospheric Administration, Environmental Research Laboratories. A report prepared for the Office of Emergency Preparedness, 220 pp.

Duke, C. Martin (1971) The great Los Angeles earthquake. Keynote talk for conference on earthquakes and their problems for a concerned citizenry. Continuing education in Engineering and Science, University of California Extension Los Angeles.

Governor's Earthquake Council (1972) First Report of the Governor's Earthquake Council, November 21, 1972. Available from the California Division of Mines and Geology, P.O. Box 2980, Sacramento, California 95812, for $1.50.

Hughes, Thomas H. (1971) Risks of earth movement and liability that result therefrom. *in* Joint Committee on Seismic Safety, pp. 71–75.

APPENDIX I

Geologic Time Chart

Era	Period	Epoch	Duration (millions of years)	Millions of years before present
CENOZOIC	Quaternary	Holocene Pleistocene	2	2
	Tertiary	Pliocene Miocene Oligocene Eocene Paleocene	63	
MESOZOIC	Cretaceous		70	65 — 135—
	Jurassic		55	190 —
	Triassic		35	225 —
PALEOZOIC	Permian		55	280 —
	Pennsylvanian		40	320 —
	Mississippian		25	345—
	Devonian		55	400 —
	Silurian		40	440—
	Ordovician		60	500—
	Cambrian		70	570 —
PRECAMBRIAN ERAS	No widely recognized period names		4130	4700

APPENDIX II

Mathematical Information

Multiples and Submultiples			Prefixes	Symbols
1,000,000,000,000	=	10^{12}	tera	T
1,000,000,000	=	10^9	giga	G
1,000,000	=	10^6	mega	M
1,000	=	10^3	kilo	k
100	=	10^2	hecto	h
10	=	10	deka	da
0.1	=	10^{-1}	deci	d
0.01	=	10^{-2}	centi	c
0.001	=	10^{-3}	milli	m
0.000001	=	10^{-6}	micro	μ
0.000000001	=	10^{-9}	nano	n
0.000000000001	=	10^{-12}	pico	p

UNITS OF MEASURE

Linear Measure

1 mile (mi)	=	5280 feet (ft)
1 chain (ch)	=	66 ft
1 rod (rd)	=	16.5 ft
1 fathom (fm)	=	6 ft
1 nautical mile	=	6076.115 ft
1 kilometer (km)	=	1000 meters (m) = 10^3 m
1 centimeter (cm)	=	0.01 m = 10^{-2} m
1 millimeter (mm)	=	0.001 m = 10^{-3} m
1 angstrom (Å)	=	0.0000000001 m = 10^{-10} m
1 micron (μ)	=	0.001 mm

Area Measure

1 square mile	=	640 acres
1 acre	=	43,560 square feet
1 acre	=	4840 square yards
1 acre	=	160 square rods
1 mile square	=	1 section
6 miles square	=	1 township = 36 square miles
1 square meter	=	10,000 square centimeters (cm)
100 square meters	=	1 are (a)
100 ares	=	1 hectare (ha)
100 hectares	=	1 square kilometer

Volume and Cubic Measure

1 quart	= 2 pints = 57.75 cubic inches
4 quarts	= 1 gallon = 231 cubic inches
1 cubic foot	= 1728 cubic inches
1 cubic yard	= 27 cubic feet
1 barrel (oil)	= 42 gallons
1 barrel (proof spirits)	= 40 gallons
1 cubic foot	= 7.48 gallons
1 cubic inch	= 0.554 fluid ounce
1 gallon (U.S.)	= 128 U.S. fluid ounces = 0.833 British gallon
1 liter	= 0.001 cubic meter = 1 cubic decimeter
1 liter	= 1000 milliliters
10 milliliters	= 100 milliliters
1 milliliter	= approximately 1 cubic centimeter (cc)
1 cubic meter (m^3)	= 1,000,000 cubic centimeters

Weights and Masses

1 short ton	= 2000 pounds
1 long ton	= 2240 pounds
1 pound (avoirdupois)	= 7000 grains
1 ounce (avoirdupois)	= 437.5 grains
1 gram	= 15.432 grains
1000 grams	= 1 kilogram
1000 kilograms	= 1 metric ton

Force

1 dyne (d) = the force that will produce an acceleration of 1 centimeter / second^2 when applied to a 1-gram mass.

1 newton (nt) = the force that will produce an acceleration of 1 meter / second^2 when applied to a 1-kilogram mass.

1 nt = 100,000 d = 1 X 10^5 d

Energy and Power

1 erg = the work done by a force of 1 dyne when its point of application moves through a distance of 1 centimeter in the direction of the force.

1 erg = 9.48 X 10^{-11} British thermal unit (BTU)

1 erg = 7.367 X 10^{-8} foot-pounds

1 erg = 2.778 X 10^{-14} kilowatt-hours

1 kilowatt-hour = 3413 BTU = 3.6 X 10^{13} ergs = 860,421 calories (cal)

1 BTU = 2.930 X 10^{-4} kilowatt-hours = 1.0548 X 10^{10} ergs = 252 calories (cal)

1 watt* = 3.413 BTU/hour

1 watt = 1.341 X 10^{-3} horsepower

1 watt = 1 joule per second

1 watt = 14.34 calories per minute

1 joule* = 1 X 10^7 ergs

1 joule = 1 newton-meter

*The watt and the joule are the internationally acceptable units for power and energy, respectively.

Heat

1 calorie (cal) = the amount of heat that will raise the temperature of
    1 gram of water 1 degree Celsius with the water at 4 degrees Celsius.

1 calorie (gram) = 3.9685×10^{-3} BTU = 4.186×10^7 ergs

Pressure

1 millibar (mb) = 1000 dynes per cm^2
1 atmosphere (atm) = 76 cm mercury = 14.70 lb/in^2 = 1013 millibars (mb)

Additional Conversions

1 gallon of water = 8.3453 pounds of water
1 gallon per minute = 8.0208 cubic feet per minute
1 acre-foot = 1233.46 m^3

Temperature

To change from Fahrenheit (F) to Celsius (C)

$$°C = \frac{(°F - 32°)}{1.8}$$

To change from Celsius (C) to Fahrenheit (F)

$$°F = (°C \times 1.8) + 32°$$

English-Metric Conversions

1 inch	=	25.4 millimeters
1 foot	=	0.3048 meter
1 yard	=	0.9144 meter
1 mile	=	1.609 kilometers
1 sq inch	=	6.4516 sq centimeters
1 sq foot	=	0.0929 sq meter
1 sq yard	=	0.836 sq meter
1 sq mile	=	259 hectares
1 acre	=	0.4047 hectare
1 cubic inch	=	16.39 cubic centimeters
1 cubic foot	=	0.0283 cubic meter
1 cubic yard	=	0.7646 cubic meter
1 quart (liq)	=	0.946 liter
1 gallon (U.S.)	=	0.003785 cubic meter
1 ounce (avdp)	=	28.35 grams
1 pound (avdp)	=	0.4536 kilogram
1 short ton	=	907.2 kilograms
1 horsepower	=	0.7457 kilowatt

Metric-English Conversions

1 millimeter	=	0.0394 inch
1 meter	=	3.281 feet
1 meter	=	1.094 yards
1 kilometer	=	0.6214 mile
1 sq centimeter	=	0.155 sq inch
1 sq meter	=	10.764 sq feet
1 sq meter	=	1.196 sq yards
1 hectare	=	2.471 acres
1 hectare	=	0.003861 sq mile
1 cu centimeter	=	0.061 cu inch
1 cu meter	=	35.3 cu feet
1 cu meter	=	1.308 cu yards
1 liter	=	1.057 quarts
1 cu meter	=	264.2 gallons (U.S.)
1 gram	=	0.0353 ounce (avdp)
1 kilogram	=	2.205 pounds (avdp)
1 metric ton	=	2205 pounds (avdp)
1 kilowatt	=	1.341 horsepower

APPENDIX III

Surface Water Criteria
for Public Water Supplies

Constituent or characteristic	Permissible criteria	Desirable criteria
Physical:		
Color (color units)	75	<10
Odor	Narrative	Virtually absent
Temperature[*]	do	Narrative
Turbidity	do	Virtually absent
Microbiological:		
Coliform organisms	10,000/100 ml[1]	<100/100 ml[1]
Fecal coliforms	2000/100 ml[1]	<20/100 ml[1]
Inorganic chemicals:	(mg/l)	(mg/l)
Alkalinity	Narrative	Narrative
Ammonia	0.5 (as N)	<0.01
Arsenic[*]	0.05	Absent
Barium[*]	1.0	do
Boron[*]	1.0	do
Cadmium[*]	0.01	do
Chloride[*]	250	<25
Chromium,[*] hexavalent	0.05	Absent
Copper[*]	1.0	Virtually absent
Dissolved oxygen	$\geq$4 (monthly mean) $\geq$3 (individual sample)	Near saturation
Fluoride[*]	Narrative	Narrative
Hardness[*]	do	do
Iron (filterable)	0.3	Virtually absent
Lead[*]	0.05	Absent
Manganese[*] (filterable)	0.05	do
Nitrates plus nitrites[*]	10 (as N)	Virtually absent
pH (range)	6.0–8.5	Narrative
Phosphorus[*]	Narrative	do
Selenium[*]	0.01	Absent
Silver[*]	0.05	do
Sulfate[*]	250	<50
Total dissolved solids[*] (filterable residue)	500	<200

SOURCE: *Report of the Committee on Water Quality Criteria,*
Federal Water Pollution Control Administration, 1968.

[*]The defined treatment process has little effect on this constituent.
[1]Microbiological limits are monthly arithmetic averages based upon an adequate number of samples. Total coliform limit may be relaxed if fecal coliform concentration does not exceed the specified limit.
[2]As parathion in cholinesterase inhibition, it may be necessary to resort to even lower concentrations for some compounds or mixtures.
Note: The presence of the word "narrative" in the table indicates that the committee compiling the table could not arrive at a single numerical value which would be applicable throughout the country for all conditions.

Constituent or characteristic	Permissible criteria	Desirable criteria
Uranyl ion*	5	Absent
Zinc*	5	Virtually absent
Organic chemicals:		
Carbon chloroform extract* (CCE)	0.15	<0.04
Cyanide*	0.20	Absent
Methylene blue active substances*	0.5	Virtually absent
Oil and grease*	Virtually absent	Absent
Pesticides:		
Aldrin*	0.017	do
Chlordane*	0.003	do
DDT*	0.042	do
Dieldrin*	0.017	do
Endrin*	0.001	do
Heptachlor*	0.018	do
Heptachlorepoxide*	0.018	do
Lindane*	0.056	do
Methoxychlor*	0.035	do
Organic phosphates plus carbamates*	0.1^2	do
Toxaphene	0.005	do
Herbicides:		
2,4-D plus 2,4,5-T, plus 2,4,5-TP*	0.1	do
Phenols*	0.001	do
Radioactivity:	(pc/l)	(pc/l)
Gross beta*	1000	<100
Radium-226*	3	<1
Strontium-90*	10	<2

APPENDIX IV

Sources of Geological Information

1. United States: Federal Government

Branch of Distribution
U.S. Geological Survey
1200 South Eads Street
Arlington, VA 22202
(For books and for maps of areas east of the
Mississippi River)

Branch of Distribution
U.S. Geological Survey
Box 25286, Federal Center
Denver, CO 80225
(For maps of areas west of the Mississippi River)

2. United States: State Surveys

ALABAMA
Geological Survey of Alabama
P.O. Drawer O
University, AL 35486

ALASKA
Alaska Department of Natural Resources
Div. of Geological and Geophysical Surveys
Box 80007
College, AK 99701

ARIZONA
Arizona Bureau of Mines
University of Arizona
Tucson, AZ 85721

ARKANSAS
Arkansas Geological Commission
Vardelle Parham Geological Center
Little Rock, AR 72204

CALIFORNIA
California Division of Mines and Geology
1416 Ninth Street
Sacramento, CA 95814

COLORADO
Colorado Geological Survey
Department of Natural Resources
1845 Sherman Street
Denver, CO 80203

CONNECTICUT
Geological and Natural History Survey
State Office Building, Room 561
Hartford, CT 06115

DELAWARE
Delaware Geological Survey
University of Delaware
Newark, DE 19711

FLORIDA
Bureau of Geology
P.O. Box 631
Tallahassee, FL 32303

GEORGIA
Department of Natural Resources
Earth and Water Division
19 Hunter Street, SW, Room 400
Atlanta, GA 30334

HAWAII
Division of Water and Land Development
Department of Land and Natural Resources
P.O. Box 373
Honolulu, HI 96809

IDAHO
Bureau of Mines and Geology
Moscow, ID 83843

ILLINOIS
Illinois State Geological Survey
Natural Resources Building
Urbana, IL 61801

INDIANA
Publications Section
Indiana Geological Survey
611 North Walnut Grove
Bloomington, IN 47401

IOWA
Iowa Geological Survey
16 West Jefferson Street
Iowa City, IA 52240

KANSAS
Kansas Geological Survey
1930 Avenue "A," Campus West
The University of Kansas
Lawrence, KS 66044

KENTUCKY
Kentucky Geological Survey
307 Mineral Industries Building
120 Graham Avenue
Lexington, KY 40506

LOUISIANA
Louisiana Geological Survey
Box G, University Station
Baton Rouge, LA 70803

MAINE
Maine Geological Survey
State Office Building
Augusta, ME 04330

MARYLAND
Maryland Geological Survey
214 Latrobe Hall
Johns Hopkins University
Baltimore, MD 21218

MASSACHUSETTS
Massachusetts Geological Survey
Department of Public Works
100 Nashua Street, Room 805
Boston, MA 02114

MICHIGAN
Geological Survey Division
Department of Natural Resources
Stevens T. Mason Building
Lansing, MI 48926

MINNESOTA
Minnesota Geological Survey
1633 Eustis Street
St. Paul, MN 55414

MISSISSIPPI
Mississippi Geological, Economic and
    Topographic Survey
P.O. Box 4915
Jackson, MS 39216

MISSOURI
Division of Geological Survey and Water
    Resources
Box 250, Buehler Park
Rolla, MO 65401

MONTANA
Bureau of Mines and Geology
Montana College of Mineral Science and
    Technology
Room 203-A, Main Hall
Butte, MT 59701

NEBRASKA
Conservation and Survey Division
113 Nebraska Hall
Lincoln, NE 68508

NEVADA
Nevada Bureau of Mines and Geology
University of Nevada
Reno, NV 89507

NEW HAMPSHIRE
Department of Resources and Economic
    Development
State House Annex
Concord, NH 03301

NEW JERSEY
New Jersey Bureau of Geology and Topography
P.O. Box 1889
Trenton, NJ 08625

NEW MEXICO
Bureau of Mines and Mineral Resources
Campus Station
Socorro, NM 87801

NEW YORK
New York State Geological Survey
Room 973
N.Y. State Education Building
Albany, NY 12224

NORTH CAROLINA
Department of Natural and Economic Resources
P.O. Box 27687
Raleigh, NC 27611

NORTH DAKOTA
North Dakota Geological Survey
University Station
Grand Forks, ND 58201

OHIO
Division of Geological Survey
Ohio Department of Natural Resources
Fountain Square
Columbus, OH 43224

OKLAHOMA
Oklahoma Geological Survey
University of Oklahoma
830 Van Vleet Oval
Norman, OK 73019

OREGON
Oregon Department of Geology and Mineral
    Industries
1069 State Office Building
Portland, OR 97201

PENNSYLVANIA
Pennsylvania Geologic Survey
Department of Environmental Resources
Harrisburg, PA 17120

RHODE ISLAND
Rhode Island Development Council
Roger Williams Building
Hayes Street
Providence, RI 02908

SOUTH CAROLINA
State Development Board
Division of Geology
P.O. Box 927
Columbia, SC 29202

SOUTH DAKOTA
South Dakota Geological Survey
Science Center
University of South Dakota
Vermillion, SD 57069

TENNESSEE
Division of Geology
G-5 State Office Building
Nashville, TN 37219

TEXAS
Bureau of Economic Geology
University of Texas
Box X, University Station
Austin, TX 78712

UTAH
Geological and Mineralogical Survey
606 Black Hawk Way,
Research Park
Salt Lake City, UT 84108

VIRGINIA
Virginia Division of Mineral Resources
P.O. Box 3667
Charlottesville, VA 22903

VERMONT
Vermont Geological Survey
University of Vermont
Burlington, VT 05401

WASHINGTON
Department of Natural Resources
Division of Geology and Earth Resources
Olympia, WA 98504

WEST VIRGINIA
Geological and Economic Survey
P.O. Box 879
Morgantown, WV 26505

WISCONSIN
Wisconsin Geological and Natural
    History Survey
University of Wisconsin—Extension
1815 University Avenue
Madison, WI 53706

WYOMING
Geological Survey of Wyoming
Box 3008, University Station
Laramie, WY 82071

3. Canada: Federal Government

Geological Survey of Canada
Department of Energy, Mines and Resources
601 Booth Street
Ottawa, Ontario K1A OE8

Canada Map Office
615 Booth Street
Ottawa, Ontario K1A OE9

Environment Canada
Ottawa, Ontario K1A OE9

4. Canada: Provincial Surveys

ALBERTA
Department of the Environment
10040 104 Street
Edmonton, Alberta T5J OZ6

Department of Energy and Natural Resources
9915 108 Street
Edmonton, Alberta T5K 2C9

BRITISH COLUMBIA
Department of Lands, Forests, and
    Water Resources
Parliament Buildings
Victoria, B.C. V8V 1X5

Department of Mines and Petroleum
    Resources
Parliament Buildings
Victoria, B.C. V8V 1X4

MANITOBA
Department of Mines, Resources and
    Environmental Management
989 Century Street, Box 9
Winnipeg, Man. R3H OW4

NEW BRUNSWICK
Department of the Environment
Box 6000
Fredericton, N.B. E3B 5H1

Department of Natural Resources
Box 6000
Fredericton, N.B. E3B 5H1

NEWFOUNDLAND
Department of Provincial Affairs
    and Environment
Confederation Building
St. John's Nfld. A1C 5T7

Department of Mines and Energy
95 Bonaventure Avenue
St. John's, Nfld. A1C 5T7

NOVA SCOTIA
Department of the Environment
Box 2017
Halifax, N.S. B3J 3B7

Department of Mines
1649 Hollis Street
Box 1087
Halifax, N.S. B3J 2X1

ONTARIO
Ministry of the Environment
135 St. Clair Avenue, W.
Toronto, Ont. M4V 1P5

Ministry of Natural Resources
Whitney Block
99 Wellesley St. W.
Toronto, Ont. M7A 1W3

PRINCE EDWARD ISLAND
Department of the Environment
Box 2000
Charlottetown, P.E.I. C1A 7N8

QUEBEC
Department of Natural Resources
1620 boul. de l'Entente
Quebec City, P.Q. G1S 4N6

SASKATCHEWAN
Department of the Environment
11th Floor
Saskatechewan Power Building
Regina, Sask. S4P OR9

Department of Mineral Resources
Administration Building
Albert Street
Regina, Sask. S4S OB1

Glossary of Selected Environmental and Geologic Terms[1]

ABSORPTION. To take up and incorporate within the body.

ACID MINE DRAINAGE. Drainage with a low pH (<4.5) from mines. Pyrite (FeS_2) in mines is oxidized by oxygen or ferric iron to produce ferrous sulfate and sulfuric acid. At low pH, heavy metals such as iron, magnesium, manganese, copper, zinc, and calcium are more soluble and further pollute the water.

ACTIVATED SLUDGE. A process that removes organic matter from sewage by saturating it with air and biologically active sludge.

ACTIVITY RATIO. The ratio of the plasticity index to the percentage of clay (particles less than 0.002 mm in diameter) in a soil sample.

ADSORPTION. To take up and hold by adhesion to the surface.

AERATE. To charge or treat with air or other gases, usually with oxygen.

AEROBIC. Having oxygen.

AFTERSHOCK. An earthquake which follows a larger earthquake. A series of aftershocks, which originate at or near the focus of the larger earthquake, generally follow a major earthquake and decrease in frequency with time.

AGGREGATE. Uncrushed or crushed gravel, crushed stone or rock, sand, or artificially produced inorganic materials, which form the major part of concrete.

ALGA, ALGAE. A group of simple primitive plants that live in wet or damp places, are generally microscopic in size, contain chlorophyll, and lack roots, stems, and leaves.

ALGAL BLOOM. A high concentration of a particular algal species, amounting to more than one-half million cells per litre of water.

ALKALI. An accumulation of soluble chloride and sulfate salts, such as sodium chloride (table salt), calcium sulfate (gypsum), or sodium sulfate (white alkali), on or near the surface of the soil in arid regions due to upward movement of soil moisture during drying periods.

ALLUVIUM. A general term for all sediment deposited (in land environments) by streams.

AMPLIFICATION. The increase in earthquake ground motion that may occur to the principal components of seismic waves as they enter and pass through different earth materials.

ANAEROBIC. Devoid of oxygen.

AQUICLUDE. A rock formation which, although porous and capable of absorbing water slowly, will not transmit it rapidly enough to furnish an appreciable supply of water for a well or spring.

AQUIFER. Permeable rock strata below the surface through which ground water moves; generally capable of producing water for a well.

ARTESIAN. Refers to ground water which is under sufficient pressure to rise above the aquifer containing it.

ASBESTOS. (1) Fibrous materials used for their resistance to heat and chemical attack. (2) Fibrous variety of amphibole, usually tremolite or actinolite, or of chrysotile, the fibrous variety of serpentine.

ATOMIC ENERGY (NUCLEAR ENERGY). The energy liberated by a nuclear reaction (fission or fusion) or by radioactive decay.

ATTERBERG LIMITS. Certain properties of clay soils that are dependent upon water content. The three most common limits are: The liquid limit, the plastic limit, and the shrinkage limit. These represent the water content as a percent of dry soil weight at transitions from liquid to plastic behavior and from plastic to solid, and the water content below which further loss of water by evaporation does not result in a reduction in volume of the soil. These soil parameters are determined by standard laboratory tests.

1. Sources include the Glossary of Geology published by the American Geological Institute and glossaries in the originals of Articles 10, 12, 14, 23, and 24 of this book. The content of this glossary remains the responsibility of the authors. Words are defined only as they are used in this volume; many have other connotations which are not included.

AUTUMN OVERTURN. The mixing of the entire water mass of a lake in the autumn.

BACTERIUM, BACTERIA. Microscopic unicellular organisms. Some bacteria cause disease while others perform an essential role in the recycling of materials.

BEDDING. Strata or laminae in rocks which are generally of sedimentary origin.

BENCH MARK. A permanent marker which designates a point of known elevation.

BENTHOS, BENTHIC ZONE. Organisms living in or on the bottom of an aquatic environment. The bottom of a lake or stream.

BENTONITE. A clay consisting mainly of the mineral montmorillonite and formed from the decomposition of volcanic ash. Bentonite commonly has great ability to absorb water and to swell. It is usually white to light green in color, but is light blue when fresh.

BIOCHEMICAL OXYGEN DEMAND (BOD). The quantity of dissolved oxygen, in milligrams per litre, used for the decomposition of organic material by microorganisms such as bacteria.

BIOMASS. The amount of living matter present in a unit area or volume at any given time.

BIOTA. All the plants and animals in a particular area.

BLUE-GREEN ALGAE. A group of algae with a blue pigment in addition to the green chlorophyll. The blue-green algae group usually causes nuisance conditions in water.

BRINE. Water which is saturated or nearly saturated with salt.

CALIFORNIA BEARING RATIO (CBR) TEST. The ratio of the pressure required to penetrate a soil mass with a 2-in. diameter, circular piston at the rate of 0.05 in. per minute to the pressure required for corresponding penetration of a standard material.

CAPACITY. The ability of water or wind to transport material as measured by the quantity that can be carried at any given time.

CARBONATE. A mineral formed by the combination of the complex ion $(CO_3)^{2-}$ with a positive ion. For example, $CaCO_3$ (Calcite).

CHANNELIZATION. Straightening of a stream or construction of a new channel to which a stream is diverted.

CLAY. The term clay carries three implications: (1) Particles of very fine size, less than 1/256 mm (sometimes .002 mm). (2) A natural material with plastic properties. (3) A composition of minerals that are essentially hydrous aluminum silicates.

CLEAVAGE. The capacity of a mineral to break along plane surfaces as determined by the crystal structure.

COLIFORM BACTERIA. A type of bacteria whose presence in water is evidence of contamination by human or animal waste. High coliform levels indicate relatively recent pollution since their survival is short termed.

COLLUVIUM. Any loose, poorly sorted mass of soil or rock material deposited by rapid, water-deficient processes such as landslides, rockfalls, and mudflows; usually formed at the base of a steep slope; the soil or rock may range in size from clay to boulders.

COMPENSATION LEVEL OR DEPTH. The depth of water at which oxygen production by photosynthesis balances oxygen uptake by respiration of plants and animals.

COMPOST. A mixing of organic waste materials such as garbage, grass clippings, and leaves with soil in a pile to allow soil bacteria to cause decomposition and thereby return desirable organic material to the soil.

CONSOLIDATION-SWELL. A test in which a thin cylindrical soil sample, confined by a brass ring but with free access to water, is loaded axially to determine percentage consolidation or swell under load.

CORROSION. The disintegration of concrete in foundations, basement floors, porches, sidewalks, and driveways due to the chemical action of sulfate salts.

CREEP. The imperceptibly slow, more or less continuous downslope movement of regolith.

CRYSTALLINE ROCKS. Usually refers to igneous and metamorphic rocks as opposed to sedimentary rocks, but it may also refer to any rock consisting of minerals in an obvious crystalline state.

DAMPING. A resistance to vibration that causes a progressive reduction of motion with time or distance.

DARCY'S LAW. The equation for the velocity of flow of ground water which states that in material of given permeability, velocity of flow increases as the slope of the ground water table increases.

DDT. A widely used colorless contact insecticide, discovered in 1939 and first used commercially in 1945. DDT remains active in the environment for years, passing from the air and water to plants, animals, and humans.

DEBRIS FLOW. The rapid downslope plastic flow of a mass of debris.

DECOMPOSITION. The breakdown of dead plant and animal tissue by bacteria to the elemental state.

DEMOGRAPHY. The science of population and the factors affecting its dynamics (that is, growth, decline, distribution, and changes).

DESIGN FLOOD. The flood against which a given area is to be protected.

DETRITUS. Fragmented material of inorganic or organic origin.

DIP. The angle by which the plane of rock layering (or other planar element, such as joint) is inclined from the horizontal. Commonly expressed in degrees or in feet per mile.

DISCHARGE. The amount of water passing a given point in a given unit of time.

DISSOLVED OXYGEN (DO). The extent to which oxygen occurs dissolved in water or wastewater, usually expressed in parts per million or percent of saturation.

DISSOLVED SOLIDS. Solids which are present in solution.

DRY UNIT WEIGHT. The ratio of the oven-dried weight of a soil sample to its original wet volume; also called "dry density."

EARTHQUAKE. (1) A local trembling, shaking, undulating, or sudden shock of the surface of the earth, sometimes accompanied by fissuring or by permanent change of level. (2) Groups of elastic waves propagating in the earth, set up by a transient disturbance of the elastic equilibrium of a portion of the earth.

ECOLOGY. Science of the relationship between organisms and their environment.

ECOSYSTEM. The community of plants and animals interacting together with the physical and chemical environment.

EFFLUENT. The discharge from a relatively self-contained source, such as from a sewage treatment plant, an industrial smokestack, or a nuclear power plant thermal discharge; generally carrying pollutants.

ELASTIC STRAIN. Deformation per unit of length produced by load on a material, which vanishes with removal of the load.

ENVIRONMENT. The sum of all the external physical, chemical, and biological conditions and influences that affect the life and development of an organism.

EPICENTER. That point on the earth's surface directly above the point of origin of an earthquake.

EPILIMNION. The upper, relatively warm, circulating zone of water in a thermally stratified lake.

EROSION. The general process or group of processes whereby the materials of the earth's crust are loosened, dissolved, or worn away and moved from one place to another by weathering, solution, corrasion, and transportation.

EUPHOTIC ZONE. That part of the aquatic environment where light penetration is sufficient for photosynthesis.

EUTROPHICATION. The natural process of enrichment and aging of a body of water that may be accelerated by the activities of man. Pertains to water bodies in which primary production is high because of a large supply of available nutrients.

EXCHANGE CAPACITY. The capacity to exchange ions as measured by the quantity of exchangeable ions in a soil.

FAULT. A fracture or fracture zone in the earth along which the opposite sides have been relatively displaced.

FAUNA. A collective term for all the types of animals in an area.

FLOOD PLAIN. That portion of a stream valley which is adjacent to the stream and is built of stream-deposited sediments and which is covered with water when the stream overflows its banks at flood stage.

FOCUS. The true center of an earthquake; the point from which the energy of an earthquake is released.

FORMATION. The basic rock-stratigraphic unit in the local classification of rocks, commonly of considerable thickness and lateral extent.

FUNDAMENTAL PERIOD. The longest period (duration in time of one full cycle of oscillatory motion) for which a structure or soil column shows a response peak—commonly the period of maximum response.

FUNGUS, FUNGI. Plants lacking chlorophyll, including molds, yeasts, mildews, rusts, and mushrooms.

GABION. A bottomless wicker cylinder or basket from 20 to 70 inches in diameter and from 33 to 72 inches high; used in engineering, when filled with stones, to form the foundation of a jetty.

GAGING STATION. Section in a stream channel equipped with a gage and facilities for measuring the flow of water.

GEODETIC MEASUREMENTS. Controls on location (vertical or horizontal) of positions on the earth's surface of a high order of accuracy, usually extended over large areas for surveying and mapping operations.

GEOLOGIC HAZARDS. Geologic features or processes that are dangerous or objectionable to the human colony; they may be natural or induced phenomena.

GEOLOGIC MAP. Map showing distribution of formations, folds, faults, and mineral deposits by appropriate symbols.

GEOLOGY. Science dealing with the origin, history, materials, and structure of the earth, together with the forces and processes now operating to produce changes on the earth's surface and within it.

GEOMORPHOLOGY. The branch of geology which deals with the form and the general configuration of the earth's surface, and the changes that take place in the evolution of landforms.

GLACIAL DRIFT. Sediment in transport or deposited by glaciers.

GLACIER BURST. A sudden release of a reservoir of water that has been impounded within or by a glacier.

GRADIENT. (1) Applied to a stream, it is the slope measured along the course of the stream. (2) Change in value of one variable with respect to another variable, that is, geothermal gradient, change in temperature with depth.

GRAVEL. (1) Small stones and pebbles or a mixture of sand and small stones. (2) Loose, rounded fragments of rock or mineral pieces larger than 2 mm in diameter.

GREEN ALGAE. Algae that have pigments similar in color to those of higher green plants. Some forms produce algal mats or floating "moss" in lakes.

GROUND WATER. Water beneath the surface of the ground in a saturated zone.

GROUND WATER RECHARGE. Addition of surface water to ground water by injection through wells or by infiltration from pits or streams.

GROUT. A pumpable slurry of cement or a mixture of cement and fine sand that is commonly forced into a borehole to seal crevices in a rock.

HARDNESS. (1) The resistance of a mineral to scratching. (2) A relative term that describes the reaction between soap and water. Carbonate hardness refers to the hardness caused by calcium and magnesium bicarbonate; noncarbonate hardness is hardness caused by calcium sulfate, calcium chloride, magnesium sulfate, and magnesium chloride in water. Hardness is usually reported as mg/l of $CaCO_3$: 0 to 60 mg/l is soft, 61 to 120 mg/l is moderately hard, 121 to 180 mg/l is hard, and 180 mg/l is very hard water.

HYDROCOMPACTION. Spontaneous consolidation, settling, and cracking of some dry, unconsolidated deposits after wetting. Hydrocompaction commonly occurs in areas which are normally dry, but which are subjected to abnormal wetting resulting from activities such as sewage disposal systems, irrigation systems, or water carrier breakage.

HYDRODYNAMICS. (1) The branch of science that deals with the cause and effect of regional subsurface fluid migration. (2) The branch of hydraulics that relates to flow of liquids through pipes and openings.

HYDROGRAPH. A graph to show the level, flow, or velocity of water in a river at all seasons of the year.

HYDROLOGIC CYCLE. The complete cycle of phenomena through which water passes from the atmosphere to the earth and back to the atmosphere.

HYDROLOGY. The science dealing with water standing or flowing on or beneath the surface of the earth.

HYDROSTATIC PRESSURE. The pressure of, or corresponding to, the weight of a column of water at rest.

HYPOLIMNION. The lower, relatively cold, noncirculating water zone in a thermally stratified lake.

ICEWEDGE. A form of clear ice in perennially frozen regolith in the continuous zone of permafrost. Size ranges from 1-mm wide dikelets to wedges more than 10 m wide and 10 m deep.

IMPERMEABLE. Having a texture that does not permit water to move through it perceptibly under the pressure differences ordinarily found in subsurface water.

INTENSITY. A subjective measure of the force of an earthquake at a particular place as determined by its effects on persons, structures, and earth materials. The principal scale used in the United States today is the Modified Mercalli, 1956 version, as defined below:

I. Not felt.

II. Felt by persons at rest, on upper floors, or favorably placed.

III. Felt indoors. Hanging objects swing. Vibration like passing of light trucks. Duration estimated. May not be recognized as an earthquake.

IV. Hanging objects swing. Vibration like passing of heavy trucks; or sensation of a jolt like a heavy ball striking the walls. Standing automobiles rock. Windows, dishes, doors rattle. Wooden walls and frame may creak.

V. Felt outdoors; direction estimated. Sleepers wakened. Liquids disturbed, some spilled. Small unstable objects displaced or upset. Doors swing. Shutters, pictures move. Pendulum clocks stop, start, change rate.

VI. Felt by all. Many frightened and run outdoors. Persons walk unsteadily. Windows, dishes, glassware broken. Knickknacks, books knocked off shelves. Pictures off walls. Furniture moved or overturned. Weak plaster and masonry D^2 cracked.

VII. Difficult to stand. Noticed by drivers of automobiles. Hanging objects quiver. Furniture broken. Weak chimneys broken at roof line. Damage to masonry D, including cracks; fall of plaster, loose bricks, stones, tiles, and unbraced parapets. Small slides and caving in along sand or gravel banks. Large bells ring.

VIII. Steering of automobiles affected. Damage to masonry C; partial collapse. Some damage to masonry B; none to masonry A. Fall of stucco and some masonry walls. Twisting, fall of chimneys, factory stacks, monuments, towers, elevated tanks. Frame houses moved on foundations if not bolted down; loose panel walls thrown out. Decayed piling broken off. Branches broken from trees. Changes in flow or temperature of springs and wells. Cracks in wet ground and on steep slopes.

IX. General panic. Masonry D destroyed; masonry C heavily damaged, sometimes with complete collapse; masonry B seriously damaged. General damage to foundations. Frame structures, if not bolted, shifted off foundations. Frames racked. Serious damage to reservoirs. Underground pipes broken. Conspicuous cracks in ground and liquefaction.

X. Most masonry and frame structures destroyed with their foundations. Some well-built wooden structures and bridges destroyed. Serious damage to dams, dikes, embankments. Large landslides. Water thrown on banks of canals, rivers, lakes. Sand and mud shifted horizontally on beaches and flat land. Rails bent slightly.

XI. Rails bent greatly. Underground pipelines completely out of service.

XII. Damage nearly total. Large rock masses displaced. Lines of sight and level distorted. Objects thrown in the air.

ION. An electrically charged particle of matter dissolved in water. For example, in water, salt forms sodium ions (Na^+) with positive charges, and chloride ions (Cl^-) with negative charges.

2. See Uniform Building Code for specifications on quality of masonry construction.

JOINT. A fracture in rock along which there has been no visible movement.

KAOLINITE. A common clay mineral. A two-layer hydrous aluminum silicate, $Al_4(Si_4O_{10})(OH)_8$.

LANDFILL. A place where solid waste or earth is dumped, usually to dispose of garbage or to create new land for development.

LANDSLIDE. The downward sliding or falling of a mass or mixture of soil, regolith, and rock.

LEACH. To wash or to drain by percolation. To dissolve minerals by percolating solutions.

LEACHATE. A solution obtained by leaching; leachate from a sanitary landfill is a mineralized liquid with a high content of organic substances.

LEFT-LATERAL MOVEMENT. A generally horizontal movement along a fault in which the ground across the fault from the observer has moved to the left.

LEVEE. An embankment beside a river to prevent overflow.

LIMNETIC ZONE. The open-water zone of a water body above the compensation level.

LIMNOLOGY. The science or study of inland waters.

LITHOLOGY. The character of a rock described in terms of its structure, color, mineral composition, grain size, and arrangement of its component parts.

LITTORAL ZONE. The shallow zone of a body of water where light penetrates to the bottom.

LOAM. A mixture of sand, silt, or clay, or a combination of any of these, with organic matter.

LOESS. A windblown silt or silty clay having little or no stratification.

MAGNITUDE. The rating of a given earthquake is defined as the logarithm of the maximum amplitude on a seismogram written by an instrument of specified standard type calculated to be at a distance of 62 miles (100 km) from the epicenter. The zero of the scale is fixed arbitrarily. The scale (Richter) is open ended but the largest known earthquake magnitudes are near 8-3/4. Because the scale is logarithmic, every upward step of 1 magnitude unit increases the recorded amplitude by 10.

MASS MOVEMENT. Unit movement of a portion of the land surface as in creep, landslide, or slip.

MASS-WASTING. A variety of processes by which large masses of earth materials are moved by gravity either slowly or quickly from one place to another. Often used synonymously with landslide.

MATRIX. (1) The rock containing a mineral or metallic ore. (2) The principal phase or aggregate in which another constituent is embedded.

MEANDERS. A series of regular and looplike bends in the course of a stream.

MESOTROPHIC. Intermediate stage in lake classification between the oligotrophic and eutrophic stages, in which primary production occurs at a greater rate than in oligotrophic lakes but at a lesser rate than in eutrophic lakes. This is due to a moderate supply of nutrients.

METABOLISM. The sum of the chemical reactions in living cells in which energy is provided for vital processes and materials are assimilated for growth and tissue repair.

METALIMNION. The middle layer of water in a thermally stratified lake, in which temperature decreases rapidly with depth (also known as thermocline).

MICROEARTHQUAKE. An earthquake having a magnitude of 2 or less on the Richter scale.

MICROSEISMIC EVENT. Natural or induced earthquake vibrations observable only with instruments.

MINERAL. An inorganic substance occurring in nature, which has a definite or characteristic chemical composition and molecular structure and distinctive physical properties.

MODIFIED MERCALLI. See INTENSITY.

MONTMORILLONITE. Clay minerals that have a theoretical composition which is essentially $Al_4Si_8O_{20}(OH)_4 \cdot nH_2O$; the most highly swelling of the clay minerals.

MUDFLOW. A rapidly moving stream of mixed soil or rock and water having the consistency and composition of mud.

NORMAL FAULT. A vertical to steeply inclined fault along which the block above the fault has moved downward relative to the block below.

NUTRIENT. Any chemical element, ion, or compound that is required by an organism for the continuation of growth, reproduction, and other life processes.

OLIGOTROPHIC. Pertaining to waters in which primary production is low as a consequence of a small supply of available nutrients.

ORE. A mineral or aggregate of minerals from which a valuable component can be profitably extracted.

ORGANIC. Pertaining or relating to a compound containing carbon.

OXIDATION. The process in which oxygen chemically combines with a substance, or in which an element loses electrons.

PERIPHERAL DRAIN. Also called a "footing drain"; open-jointed clay tile or perforated plastic pipe laid in a trench beside the foundation of a structure and covered with coarse gravel backfill; aids in preventing swell or settlement by collecting water near the foundation and draining the water away through "French drains" (gravel fill) or by "daylighted drains" (tile or pipe discharging onto a slope below the level of the peripheral drain).

PERMAFROST. Permanently frozen ground.

PERMEABILITY. The capacity of rock or unconsolidated material to transmit a fluid.

PETROLEUM. Gaseous, liquid, or solid substances, occurring naturally and consisting chiefly of chemical compounds of carbon and hydrogen.

pH. A measure of acidity or alkalinity. It is the negative logarithm of the hydrogen ion activity. pH7 indicates an H^+ concentration (activity) of 10^{-7} mole/litre.

PHOTOGRAMMETRY. The art and science of obtaining reliable measurements from photographs.

PHOTOSYNTHESIS. The process whereby green plants use light as an energy source and convert chemical compounds to carbohydrates. In the process, carbon dioxide is consumed and oxygen is released.

PHYTOPLANKTON. The plant part of the plankton.

PIEZOMETRIC. Refers to the surface to which the water from a given aquifer will rise under its full pressure.

PLANKTON. The community of floating organisms which drift passively with water currents.

PLASTIC DEFORMATION. A permanent change, excluding rupture, in the shape of a solid.

PLASTICITY INDEX. The difference in water content between the liquid limit and the plastic limit. (See Atterberg limits.)

POLLUTION. The process of contaminating air, water, and land with impurities to a level that is undesirable and results in a decrease in usefulness of environment for beneficial purposes; adverse effects on the environment that are definitely man-produced.

POROSITY. The proportion, usually stated as a percentage, of the total volume of a rock material or regolith that consists of pore space or voids.

POROUS. Containing pores, voids, or other openings which may or may not be interconnected.

POTABLE. Refers to water which is drinkable.

PRIMARY PRODUCTION. The synthesis of organic compounds by green plants in the presence of elements and light energy.

PYRITE. A mineral, FeS_2, commonly called fool's gold because of its brassy yellow color. The iron sulfide minerals, mainly pyrite and marcasite, are the minerals which break down chemically to form mine acids.

RECLAMATION. (1) The act or process of restoring to cultivation or other use land that has been mined. (2) The recovery of coal or ore from a mine, or part of a mine, that has been abandoned because of fire, water, or other cause.

REDUCTION. The process in which a substance loses oxygen, or in which an element gains electrons.

REGOLITH. The layer or mantle of loose, incoherent rock material, of whatever origin, that nearly everywhere forms the surface of the land and rests on the bedrock.

REMOTE SENSING. The acquisition of information or measurement of some property of an object by a recording device that is not in physical or intimate contact with the object under study. The technique employs such devices as the camera, lasers, infrared and ultraviolet detectors, microwave and radio frequency receivers, and radar systems.

RESPIRATION. A life process in which carbon compounds are oxidized to carbon dioxide and water. The liberated energy is used in the metabolic processes of living organisms.

REVERSE FAULT. A steeply to slightly inclined fault in which the block above the fault has moved relatively upward or over the block below the fault.

RICHTER SCALE. A scale of earthquake magnitude based on the logarithm of the amplitudes of the deflections created by earthquake waves and recorded by a seismograph. (See Magnitude.)

RIGHT-LATERAL MOVEMENT. Generally horizontal movement along a fault in which the ground across the fault from an observer has moved to the right.

ROCK. Any naturally formed, consolidated or unconsolidated (loose) material generally composed of two or more minerals (occasionally of one mineral).

RUNOFF. Water that flows over the land surface.

SAG POND. Enclosed depression, generally occupied by water, formed when movement along a fault has disturbed the surface or subsurface continuity of drainage.

SALINE. Salty. Possessing a high degree of dissolved mineral matter, that is, common salts, in water.

SAND. (1) Particles of sediment having a size range of 1/16 mm to 2 mm. (2) Commonly refers to siliceous detrital material composed mainly of quartz particles of sand size.

SANITARY LANDFILL. A disposal area for solid wastes where the wastes are compacted and covered daily by a layer of impermeable material, such as clay.

SATURATED ZONE. That part of a water-bearing material in which all voids, large and small, are filled with water.

SCARP. A cliff or steep slope formed by a fault. Also a steep slope along the margin of a plateau, mesa, or terrace.

SECONDARY WASTE TREATMENT. A step in waste treatment in which most of the organic matter of sewage is removed.

SEDIMENT. Solid material, both mineral and organic, that is in suspension, is being transported, or has been moved from its place of origin and deposited by air, water, or ice.

SEDIMENTARY ROCKS. Rocks formed by the accumulation of sediment in water (aqueous deposits) or from air (eolian deposits). A characteristic feature of sedimentary deposits is a layered structure known as stratification or bedding.

SEISMIC. Pertaining to an earthquake or earth vibration, including those that are artificially induced.

SEISMOGRAPH. An instrument that scribes a permanent continuous record of earth vibrations. The record made by a seismograph is called a seismogram.

SEISMOLOGY. The science concerned with the study of earthquakes and measurement of the elastic properties of the earth.

SEISMOMETER. A device that detects vibrations of the earth, and whose physical constants are known sufficiently for calibration to permit calculation of actual ground motion from the seismograph.

SEPTIC TANK. A sewage settling tank in which sludge is in immediate contact with wastewater flowing through the tank. The organic solids in the settled sludge on the bottom of the tank are decomposed by anaerobic bacterial action. The overflowing wastewater is dispersed into the soil through a lateral, subsurface drainage field.

SHEAR WAVE. A distortional, secondary, or transverse wave.

SILICATE. A compound whose crystal lattice contains SiO_4 tetrahedra, either isolated or joined through one or more of the oxygen atoms to form groups, chains, or sheets.

SILT. A fine-grained sediment having a particle size intermediate between that of fine sand and clay (between 1/16 and 1/256 mm in diameter).

SLAB FOUNDATION. A type of foundation without a basement or crawl space in which the weight of the building is supported by a concrete slab poured directly on the soil; not recommended in areas of swelling, settlement, hydrocompaction, or high water table.

SLUMP. The downward slipping of a mass of rock or unconsolidated material, moving as a unit or as several subsidiary units, usually with backward rotation; or the material that has slid downslope.

SOIL. (1) The unconsolidated material above the bedrock that forms as a result of weathering by organic and inorganic processes. (2) In pedology, the weathered material that will support rooted plants. (3) In engineering geology, soil is equivalent to regolith.

SORPTION. To take up and hold by either adhesion or incorporation. A collective term for absorption and adsorption.

STAGNATION PERIOD. The period when warming or cooling of the surface water in lakes forms a thermal-density stratification, preventing the mixing of the entire water mass.

STRAIN. The amount of any change in dimensions or shape of a body when it is subjected to deformation.

STRATIGRAPHY. The definition and description of major and minor natural divisions in layered rocks, such as groups, formations, and members.

STRESS. In a solid, the force per unit area, acting on any designated plane within the solid.

STRIKE-SLIP FAULT. Fault in which movement is principally horizontal. (See Right-lateral and Left-lateral.)

STRIP MINING. The mining of coal by surface mining methods as distinguished from the mining of metalliferous ores by surface mining methods, known as open-pit mining.

STRONG MOTION. Ground motion produced by a "strong" earthquake or one capable of producing damage to structures. The magnitude of such an earthquake may vary considerably according to the character of the earthquake.

SUBSIDENCE. Sinking or lowering of a part of the earth's crust.

TALUS. An accumulation of coarse rock waste at the foot of a cliff.

TECTONIC. Pertaining to rock structures and topographic features resulting from deformation of the earth's crust.

TERTIARY WASTE TREATMENT. An advanced step in waste treatment, in which excess nutrients, suspended matter, color, odor, and most of the organic matter is removed.

TEXTURE. The physical appearance of a rock, as shown by size, shape, and arrangement of the particles in the rock.

THERMAL STRATIFICATION. A temperature distribution in which the lake water is distinctly layered because of thermal-density differences.

TILTMETER. A device for observing surface disturbances using a bowl of mercury; employed in an attempt to predict earthquakes and volcanic eruptions.

TOXIN. A poisonous substance.

TSUNAMI. A wave caused by a submarine earthquake or volcanic eruption, mistakenly used as a synonym for tidal wave.

TURBIDITY. The ability of materials suspended in water to disturb or reduce the penetration of light.

URBAN GEOLOGY. The application of geology to problems in the urban environment.

UNCONSOLIDATED STRATA. Rocks consisting of loosely coherent or uncemented particles.

UNIFORMITARIANISM. The concept that the present is the key to the past.

WASTEWATER-SPRAY IRRIGATION. A system for disposing of organic wastewater by spraying on land, usually from pipes equipped with spray nozzles. Part of the wastewater is used by crops or indigenous vegetation. The remainder may percolate through the soil column or to a subsurface drainage-collection system or run off into a surface drainage-collection system.

WATER TABLE. The upper limit or surface of the zone of saturation of ground water.

WEATHERING. Response of materials that were once in equilibrium within the earth's crust to new conditions at or near contact with water, air, and living matter. With time the materials change in character and decay to form soil.